introductory
sociology

fourth edition

Introductory Sociology

Tony Bilton, Kevin Bonnett, Pip Jones

Tony Lawson, David Skinner,

Michelle Stanworth and Andrew Webster

with Liz Bradbury, James Stanyer and Paul Stephens

First edition 1981
Reprinted eight times
Second edition 1987
Reprinted nine times
Third edition 1996
Reprinted three times
Fourth edition 2002

Published by
PALGRAVE MACMILLAN
Houndmills, Basingstoke, Hampshire RG21 6XS and
175 Fifth Avenue, New York, N.Y. 10010
Companies and representatives throughout the world

PALGRAVE MACMILLAN is the global academic imprint of the Palgrave
Macmillan division of St. Martin's Press, LLC and of Palgrave Macmillan Ltd.
Macmillan® is a registered trademark in the United States, United Kingdom
and other countries. Palgrave is a registered trademark in the European
Union and other countries

ISBN-13: 978-0-333-94572-8 hardback
ISBN-10: 0-333-94572-7 hardback
ISBN-13: 978-0-333-94571-1 paperback
ISBN-10: 0-333-94571-9 paperback

This book is printed on paper suitable for recycling and made from fully
managed and sustained forest sources. Logging, pulping and manufacturing
processes are expected to conform to the environmental regulations of
the country of origin.

A catalogue record for this book is available
from the British Library.

A catalogue record for this book is available
from the Library of Congress.

10   9   8   7   6   5
11   10   09   08   07

Printed and bound in China

brief contents

part 1   Introduction: Studying Modern Society   1

part 2   Social Divisions and Power   67

part 3   Dimensions of Modern Social Life   227

detailed contents

part 1 Introduction: Studying Modern Society   1

part 2 Social Divisions and Power 67

list of boxes

list of tables

list of charts

list of figures

preface

> “Ours is essentially a tragic age, so we refuse to take it tragically. The cataclysm has happened, we are among the ruins, we start to build up little habitats, to have little hopes. It is rather hard work: there is no smooth road to the future: but we go round, or scramble over the obstacles. We've got to live, no matter how many skies have fallen.”
>
> **D. H. Lawrence**
>
> (cited in F. L. Schuman, *International Politics,* 3rd edn, McGraw-Hill, 1941)

Following the events of 11 September 2001, the world seems to be a dark and troubled place. We are completing this new edition of our textbook at a time when the quest for understanding in society is more urgent than ever. We desperately need to understand competing ideals and profoundly divided ways of life – and more than that, we need to learn how to distance ourselves from our own taken-for-granted beliefs and assumptions. We also need to understand how ordinary people in society have the strength to piece together lives that, if not shattered, have been threatened and destabilised. They are doing this through interacting with others in everyday settings and rebuilding routines that express mutual trust and support. D. H. Lawrence wrote the words above in the wake of the First World War, reminding us that, although the skies have fallen, and the cataclysm has happened, 'we've got to live' and we achieve this through the everyday skills of social life: 'we start to build up little habitats, to have little hopes'.

Fear has less hold if we can counter it with knowledge and understanding. By understanding the forces that drive globalisation, spreading the power of capitalism and Western capitalism, we can also understand why some groups and cultures oppose it so bitterly. We need sociology to help us understand changing social structures. At the same time, if we can understand the complex processes of everyday social life, we can see how people can cope with their lives in the face of these great social forces and sometimes find alternative ways of living and shaping their lives.

As sociologists, we must understand the structures of power and domination in the world while staying sensitive to the way people build their lives creatively through interaction with others. Social organisations are never seamless and all-powerful; people always find spaces in these structures to live a life and find an identity that is not wholly shaped from above. What is more, big social systems hardly ever work smoothly, and in the problems or crises that result, people find opportunities to change things.

In this fourth edition, we have built on our previous approach and broadened it. We still highlight the importance of understanding the power and problems of

modernity along with the transforming impact of **globalisation**. As before, we see personal and social **identity** as a fast-changing and hotly debated area. Preparing this new edition has given us the opportunity to broaden and deepen our approach to these issues. For example, we have now been able to offer more detailed discussion of areas such as mass media, feminist social theory, and critical debates around postmodernism. We have also been able to update our treatment of policy-related areas such as education and crime. Less obviously, we have moved further than ever from listing a stock set of 'standard' sociological studies and theories. The work of sociologists is more wide-ranging and diversified than ever, and so we have avoided any temptation to set out a 'canon' of received sociological wisdom.

Instead, we try to convey the richness and fascination of sociology as a quest for understanding in a confusing, and sometimes frightening, world. Sociologists are incurably curious, and we all celebrate the distinctiveness (or 'relativity') of differing beliefs and ways of life. But sociologists also want to make sense of this world, and in this book we try to convey a sense of sociology as a rigorous craft where standards of logic and evidence prevail. For us, this craft must never dissolve into a trivial sort of 'relativism' where any argument or assertion is as good as any other.

This textbook has always had one aim: to offer students a path into sociological understanding that is stimulating and challenging, through being up to date with recent research and current debates in the subject. Underpinning that aim is our hope that by promoting sociological reasoning, we are equipping our students to understand their social world and hence to change it creatively.

using this book

In preparing this new edition, we have looked to develop those features that our readers found most useful in the last edition, while also finding new ways to present what we recognise is a considerable amount of material memorably and clearly.

First of all, as with the last edition, we have grouped our chapters into parts, in order to provide a clear pathway through, to highlight the themes that link distinct topics together, and to help you to structure your studies. We explain the thinking behind our part structure in each of the part introductions, which you will find on pages 1, 67, 227 and 439. But it might be helpful to say a word or two about these here too:

- **Part 1** sets up the framework and foundations for the rest of the book, focusing first on what it means to adopt a sociological perspective and then exploring some of the broad themes that will inform the rest of the text.

- **Part 2** looks in detail at the debates surrounding a range of social divisions, from the 'classic' social divisions of class, gender and race to forms of difference and inequality that have more recently become a source of research and debate. This section also looks at theories of power and politics.

- **Part 3** focuses on social institutions – that is, social practices that are recurrent or continuous and come to be seen as established aspects of society. These range from the family to the mass media to crime. In the awareness that different courses can be structured quite differently, we have designed the chapters to be used in order of preference rather than necessarily in the given sequence.

- **Part 4** concentrates on questions of theory and method, on the basis that you will find these topics easier to grasp having built up a familiarity with how they apply to specific aspects of social life in the course of earlier chapters.

Sociology is an immensely wide-ranging subject, as you will see, and it is important to be able to divide up topics into digestible chunks in order to understand and internalise them. It is important too, however, to think laterally and read widely around each subject you study. The best sociological thinking is imaginative and critical. To help you, therefore, we have introduced a 'Connections' feature in the text, which points you to related sections of other chapters that are relevant to the specific topic under discussion. Chapter by chapter, we list other publications, also written in an accessible style, which will deepen and extend what we have covered in this text. At the back of the book, you will find a full bibliography and, on our website at www.palgrave.com/sociology/bilton, there are still further suggestions for reading and research, including a range of internet links to interesting websites you could usefully explore.

As experienced teachers, we are all too aware that the terminology sociology uses can sometimes seem bewildering to newcomers. On the other hand, we firmly believe in the importance of developing and building a conceptual vocabulary, as this will help you to formulate and communicate your arguments precisely and with confidence, as well as demonstrate your understanding of others' ideas. Our on-page glossary offers at-a-glance support, allowing you to avoid the bother of having to flip to the back of the book (where you can also find a full version of the glossary, alphabetically ordered) if you are uncertain of the meaning of a particular term. We highlight major concepts at the start of each chapter in the boxed Chapter Aims, so that you can use this as a checklist to make sure that you have gained a good grasp of the most significant theoretical ideas introduced in each chapter in turn. Also, on our website, we list the concepts we think you would find it most useful to read up about before you embark on a particular chapter of the text, or attend a lecture or first seminar on the same topic.

We have interspersed questions to think about throughout the text, both in the course of chapters and at the end of each one. We are sure you – and, indeed, your lecturers – will want to use these as the basis for seminar discussion, further writing or research. They also offer opportunities, of course, for pausing for thought and recapping briefly on what you have read from a slightly different angle. As a further aid to revision and consolidation, you will find banks of questions, organised by chapter topic, on our website, which you can work your way through as a self-test exercise.

We have also suggested some guidelines regarding how to make the most of your studies, which you will again find on our website, along with some 'writing frames' which we hope will assist you in taking notes, either during lectures or in the course of your reading of the text.

Finally, we have tried wherever possible to communicate ideas in the most vivid and lucid ways and to offer you opportunities to consolidate your learning, whether through chapter summaries or picture captions! As we hope we have conveyed here, there is a wealth of further resources on our website – at www.palgrave.com/sociology/bilton – so do log on and check it out. Above all, enjoy your reading and your course…

acknowledgements

This fourth edition of **Introductory Sociology** would not have been completed without the invaluable contributions of Rob Moore at Homerton College, Cambridge, James Stanyer at the University of Leicester, Paul Stephens at University College, Stavanger, and Liz Bradbury and Ian Pinchen at Anglia Polytechnic University. We are extremely grateful to them for both their willingness to help and for the high quality of their scholarship.

When the first edition of the book was published in 1981, all the then authors were members of the Department of Sociology at the Cambridgeshire College of Arts and Technology in Cambridge. Much has changed since then. The Department is now part of the Cambridge Campus of Anglia Polytechnic University (APU) and, of the original authors still involved in this edition, four are no longer at APU. Tony Bilton, formerly Head of Sociology at APU, left in 1999; Kevin Bonnett is now Director of the School of Social Science and Law at Sheffield Hallam University; Michelle Stanworth, formerly Professor of Sociology and Women`s Studies at APU, is now, as Michelle Spring, a full-time crime novelist; and Andrew Webster is Professor of Sociology of Science and Technology at the University of York. In addition, Tony Lawson, Senior Lecturer in the School of Education at the University of Leicester, has joined the main authors for this edition.

Coordinating the production of a book of this size and complexity with the authors so widely dispersed was inevitably going to be a mammoth task. Catherine Gray, our editor at Palgrave, was more than equal to it, however. Demonstrating a level of tact and diplomacy beyond the call of duty as well as an impressive grasp of sociology, she made our task much less onerous than it would otherwise have been, and we are delighted to take this opportunity to thank her sincerely for all her efforts. Similar thanks also go to Keith Povey, who led and orchestrated the process of copy-editing and proof-reading with his usual blend of precision, thoroughness, common sense and good humour.

Tony Bilton
Kevin Bonnett
Pip Jones
Tony Lawson
David Skinner
Michelle Stanworth
Andrew Webster

part 1

Introduction: Studying Modern Society

In Part 1 of this book, we set up some of the broad themes which will frame more specific topics in the chapters that follow. In Chapter 1, we consider what it means to think sociologically. What questions does sociology ask? What kinds of answers does it provide that other disciplines (such as biology and psychology) overlook? In particular, we consider why it is that, even though people can behave in sometimes unpredictable or surprising ways, they do not experience or perceive social life as completely random or chaotic. There are interesting questions to be asked about why and how social life is patterned, and we begin to engage with these here.

In Chapter 2, we look backwards in time to gain a better sense of the broad historical changes that have helped to form and develop the complex world we live in today. In this chapter, we single out some of the themes of particular concern to sociologists investigating social change in the last two centuries. Chapter 3 is its contemporary counterpart. It focuses on recent interest in the way the world is 'shrinking'. Here we look at debates about globalisation both because of the subject's importance to the discipline generally and because of its significance for several of the chapters that follow.

1

Studying society today

CHAPTER CONTENTS

Aims of the chapter

In this chapter, we introduce you to some of the puzzles of society that engage the attention of sociologists. We draw attention to the fact that we all have to live in society and, as active participants, seek to understand and explain it as best we can. We illustrate the usefulness of the sociological approach to understanding what happens in society by looking at the events surrounding the spread of Bovine Spongiform Encephalitis (BSE). Finally, we suggest that sociology cannot and should not seek to solve the problems of the world, but that it does play an important part in assisting individuals to shape their own and their society's destiny. By the end of this chapter, you will have been introduced to the following concepts:

- Social institutions
- Social action
- Social solidarity
- Norm

- Risk
- Reflexivity
- Capitalism
- Rationalisation

The puzzle of social life

Social life is a puzzle, and sociologists spend their professional lives trying to make sense of it. As you open this book, you are joining sociologists in a journey of exploration – a journey that does not have a fixed destination. You will find that sociology can open your eyes and your minds, and stimulate all sorts of questions and ideas. Sometimes it will be unsettling, and you may find yourself questioning things that most people take for granted about living in society. Along the way you will discover facts and even explanations that sociologists have established. But more importantly, you will find that sociology is a moving project, an unending quest to understand the puzzle of social life.

Why is it such a puzzle? At one level, just about all of us manage to live in society and relate to other people pretty successfully. We can talk to and respond to others, and they respond to us in ways that we can (more or less) understand. This social interaction often goes wrong or brings misunderstandings, but we all know how to do it. We all know, too, that there are established frameworks for social interaction – we know that there are laws and rules laid down by authorities and that we will be in trouble if we do not abide by them. We even know that our social system has some large-scale features that shape our lives – we all know that it makes a difference whether we live in a democratic society or under a dictatorship.

So, if we know all this, why do we need to have a special academic discipline of sociology that tries to understand society? If we get along just fine using our common sense, why ask a load of difficult questions and make things complicated? One answer is that some people are insatiably curious and are not satisfied with common sense. They want to think more systematically and rigorously, they want better facts and more reliable explanations; in other words, they want to be social scientists. Another answer is that, actually, a lot of the time we do not get along just fine using our common sense. We have conflicts, even wars, and we have social problems that cause suffering and insecurity. We are bombarded by rapid social change that can seem bewildering, or even threatening. Our actions have all sorts of consequences that we do not expect. Even at the day-to-day level, we often just do not know the right way to act for the best. It would be nice to think that sociologists could stop all this grief and provide everyone with the basis for a peaceful, happy life, but sadly they cannot. But if sociology can give us better information and a fuller understanding, we will be in a stronger position to shape our own lives.

QUESTION Think of the last time you were in a dilemma, when you genuinely did not know what to do for the best. Where did you go for advice, and did that advice help you to resolve your problem?

Sociology has not just been about producing knowledge, though. When sociologists have looked at society, they have often started from a key idea: 'if things do not have to be as they are, then surely they could be better?' Sociological knowledge shows us that societies can be structured in different ways, and it shows us that change and transformation are part of human living. So if social change is not only possible but also inevitable, can sociology help us to make sense of it, and can it help to build a better society?

The trouble is that people often disagree violently about what is 'better' – and sociologists have no special authority to tell people the correct values to live by. Sociologists now understand this and no longer try to dictate remedies for the social ills they diagnose (unlike Émile Durkheim, one of the first and greatest sociologists, who tried to do just that – see Box 1.1). Instead, they try to ask interesting questions about why people behave in the ways they do, and what the possibilities and consequences of their actions might be. Learning from such analyses can put people in a stronger position to shape their own future.

BOX 1.1 Durkheim

When sociologists investigate the puzzles of society they often refer to previous sociologists' attempts to make sense of it. Indeed there is a long and honourable tradition of sociology that constitutes a resource for today's sociologists as they seek to unravel contemporary puzzles. In particular, they often refer back to the classical sociologists – Durkheim, Marx and Weber – because of the insights they can offer into contemporary issues as a result of their investigations of their own and other societies.

These early sociologists (and many others since) have provided their successors with a basic tool kit of sociological concepts that can be deployed in most investigations of social phenomena. Of course, it is not only the classical sociologists who have something to offer those seeking to understand their own time and society. Societies are constantly changing, and new concepts have been devised to explain developments unthought of in previous times.

Durkheim was one of the earliest social scientists and he

devised a number of important concepts that could be used to explore the nature of societies. For example, writing during a time of great upheaval and change, he used the concept of 'social solidarity' to explore the differing ways in which societies might be integrated, so that individual or group desires would not tear apart the social fabric.

- He identified *mechanical solidarity* as typical of traditional, or pre-modern, societies, in which individuals identified with each other primarily because they lived fairly similar lives. So tribes, clans, small peasant communities and so on held together because everyone in them lived and worked in virtually the same way.
- In modern societies, a new form of solidarity emerged that he called *organic solidarity*. This was identification with others through difference, in that individuals had very different roles and economic functions and needed

each other to fulfil all their needs. For Durkheim, therefore, modern societies were typified by 'the interrelationship of interdependent parts'. No individual or section of society could function effectively without engaging in interaction with others. All the component parts of society contributed in their different ways to the effective functioning of the complete system, and the very survival of the society depended on their close interrelationship.

- Durkheim used the concept of *anomie* to describe the situation in a society where the sense of collective identity and shared interests and values were in decline and individuals acted independently of commonly recognised norms of behaviour or social standards. He believed that modern societies, with their highly developed and specialised divisions of labour and more loosely regulated economies, were at greater risk of such social disintegration,

because of the growing sense of uniqueness of every person (leading to greater individualism) and the increasing divergence of experiences and values.

- Lastly, Durkheim argued that sociologists should 'treat social facts as things', that is, they should accept that society had an existence that was independent of the individuals who comprised it. He showed that this was the case by pointing out the existence of patterned regularities in social behaviour that persisted over time, regardless of the birth and death of individuals. His most famous work, *Suicide* (1897), took a subject widely perceived to be pre-eminently personal (unique to the individual and rooted in psychological factors) and analysed it in terms of social causes. In similar fashion, we could now ask: why are young men, more than any other social group, at risk of taking their own lives?

Living in society

As Durkheim recognised, one of the first real puzzles about social life is how it continues at all. Individuals die, others are born, and society carries on. It is rather like a football club whose team seems to maintain its characteristic style of play over time, even though individual players and managers come and go. On the other hand, sometimes individual managers or special players can make a real difference and change the style and fortunes of the club, sending things in a new direction.

In the same way, there is much more to society than the particular individuals who make it up. Many things persist over time, such as language and writing, legal frameworks, churches with their traditions, families with their property and histories, cultures of art and architecture, the sense of history and identity that particular communities (whether ethnic, national or religious) develop. With just a moment's thought, you could easily add many other things to this list. For most individuals, this established social context is solid and real, part of the furniture of everyday life. Because

Social institutions
Social practices that are regularly and continuously repeated, legitimised and maintained by social norms.

Social movement
A broad alliance of people with common interests or goals acting collectively to promote or prevent some form of social change.

of this, it would be a mistake to view these **social institutions** simply as constraints on individual action. They also make social life possible – providing a framework of language so that we can communicate, or a culture so that we have something in common with others, or laws and rules so that we are not harmed by the selfish actions of others. Taking away society would not in itself make us free, because we need society in order to exist as human beings. Because of this, not many sociologists believe in anarchy – but we often do wish to support movements for change and the reform of social institutions.

Whether or not there are collective **social movements** working for change, there always will be change as a result of social action. Social action can consist of small choices made by individuals, or large decisions backed by the resources of huge companies. Different actions have different power and consequences, but there is always action, and therefore society is always changing to some extent. Often our choices are made within tight constraints, but sometimes they are more open, or we make them so by breaking through constraints.

CONNECTIONS There is a strong tradition of looking at social action as a shaping influence on society. We shall look in more depth at theoretical work on this topic in Chapter 18, pages 499–509.

Making sense of society

Sociologists use a range of concepts to further the understanding of social life (that is, particular words and categories that express ideas about aspects of society). You will find brief explanations of many concepts in the margin through the course of the book, and these should be of help to you. However, the best way to learn is to see sociological words used in context, applied to particular topics and examples. You will gradually gain confidence as you see sociological ideas used in practice – this is much better than memorising fixed definitions, and it is the approach adopted in this book.

Example: parents and children

The relationship between parents and children is the fundamental building block of society. You may not be a parent, but you are definitely a daughter or a son. Who tells you how to behave in that role? Do you know what makes a good son or daughter as opposed to a bad one? (Perhaps you should pause to make a mental list.) If you compare your ideas with those of others, you will probably find that there is a lot of agreement, but considerable variation too.

The official or formal obligations involved in being a daughter or son are not that clear. If our parents fall ill and need care or financial support, are we obliged to provide it? There may be pressure from social service staff to give support, but if we cannot or will not do so, then the welfare state will (at least in rich industrialised countries, though the state may raid our parents' savings to do so). We may feel a more informal social obligation to help our parents, but this may not be backed up by any real social pressure from others. The situation is very different in societies without a welfare state, where the family's well-being depends on very strong social expectations. These are reinforced by sanctions – condemnation and social shame, or even direct punishment – if we do not conform.

Within these limits, there is always some choice and uncertainty about how to perform our roles – even roles as fundamental as those within the family. This inevitably means that social expectations are fluid and changing over time. Such changes can be very rapid: for example, the huge expansion of female paid employment outside the home has meant that mothers, mothers-in-law and grandmothers have had to adapt their ideas about how children should be looked after. In this case, values and ideas have had to change to accommodate practical changes in behaviour. Once women have made practical choices in response to employment opportunities, then further actions and adaptations are needed from families and employers. In these complex and shifting ways, economic changes are interwoven with personal actions and wider patterns of values and expectations.

However, this fluidity and room for choice in social life should not be taken for granted. Changing things can threaten powerful interests, and then we are in danger of losing our freedom to act. Strong measures can be imposed to re-assert particular values and prevent the changes that result from personal choices. One vivid example of this at the end of the twentieth century was provided by the Taliban regime in Afghanistan, which imposed extreme measures of control over women to create a patriarchal power structure in fundamental opposition to prevalent Western ideas about individual choice and personal freedom.

From this we can see that issues of power and control affect the whole of society, including the most fundamental dimensions such as family and gender. Sometimes things can work the other way. A large-scale issue or event may seem beyond our control, an 'act of God'; but when we look closer, we find that it is not a natural or uncontrollable event at all. Instead it is a socially created problem linked to economic, political and cultural factors in our society. The 1990s 'mad cow disease' crisis was just this kind of event.

Rationality, trust and mad cows

Cases of a rare and devastating neurological illness began to emerge during the late 1990s in Northern Europe. A few, mainly young, people began to suffer from a range of worrying and rapidly worsening symptoms – including loss of coordination and personality changes – that tragically led to their death. It gradually emerged that the disease was rooted in recent changes in social and economic life. Changes in the ingredients of animal feed had caused a terrifying disease in cattle: bovine spongiform encephalitis (BSE or 'mad cow disease'). This was capable of transmission across species to humans as new variant CJD (Creutzfeld-Jakob disease). It seems that new variant CJD has caused the death of around 100 people since 1996, including a cluster of five in one village in the UK. Some have suspected that the effects of BSE may have been overlooked among elderly people, having been seen as symptoms of dementia, though this claim has so far gained little support (www.mad-cow.ord). After a ban on and the boycott of certain beef products in the UK, where the disease was concentrated, a drastic culling programme and changes to practices in slaughtering and meat processing put British beef back on the menu.

This tragic tale demands answers. Some of these answers will come from medical science, which will find out who is susceptible and seek a cure for CJD. But other answers must come from social scientists, because the BSE crisis was not in any sense 'natural'. Rather, it involved a series of changes to the social organisation of food production, and a range of economic and political interests were deeply implicated. In particular, the case raised vital social issues concerning power, trust, risk, styles and patterns of consumption, and political **ideology** and policy. Sociologists have important things to say about all these things.

Ideology
A set of ideas and beliefs about reality and society which underpin social and political action. Ideologies are often used to justify and sustain the position and interests of powerful social groups.

For example, as Durkheim argued (see Box 1.1), living in modern society requires us to put our trust in others. We cannot be aware of or understand all the complex processes that lie behind the simple act of buying a beefburger and eating it. We have to rely on farmers, manufacturers, retailers, food scientists and government agencies to ensure that our food is safe and nutritious. In other words, we are dependent on experts and those with the responsibility for protecting us – and we trust them until a crisis such as mad cow disease forces us to question their knowledge, integrity and motives.

Many consumers were, for example, disturbed to discover that the relaxations of meat-processing requirements had led to animal by-products being processed to make feed for naturally herbivorous animals. They were further disturbed by the obvious disagreement among scientists about the origins of new variant CJD. Most of all, they were disturbed when government agencies seemed to be much more concerned about protecting the interests of the food industry than those of the individual consumer.

Many sociologists argue that we are witnessing the widespread breakdown of trust in politicians, scientists and other figures of authority. As we shall see in later chapters, the modern era has been marked by secularisation, or a decline in religious authority, exemplified by the marked fall-off in participation in religious rituals. Furthermore, there has been a growing erosion of trust in other traditional bases of authority in society – whether the institutions of the state, science or the professions. This has been accompanied by growing interest in alternative medicines and therapies (from homeopathy to acupuncture and counselling) and an expanding consumer market for organic foods and natural remedies. It has also led to violent popular protests at

Figure 1.1   Organisations like Greenpeace have spearheaded popular campaigns to address social problems that traditional political institutions seem unwilling or unable to deal with. This photo shows protesters obstructing nuclear tests in the South Pacific.

international trade and financial conferences, and to collective social action against initiatives that are seen as damaging to the environment.

Sociologists argue that our social world is being experienced as increasingly uncertain and precarious. The German sociologist Ulrich Beck calls this the 'risk society'. As we shall see in the chapters that follow, sociology has much to say about these important changes.

If risk and trust lie at the heart of the problem of BSE and new variant CJD, so does the issue of rationality. Food processors thought they were acting in accordance with economic rationality when they started to put animal by-products into animal feed; in the 1980s, the British government thought that the relaxation of regulations would help the food industry to generate more wealth; individuals did not doubt the safety of food on sale in the shops, so they bought what they saw as offering the best value, and the least well off were most likely to opt for the cheapest (and most risky) beef products. Each of these seems in itself to have been a rational choice. But as the great sociologist Max Weber argued, modern society's commitment to narrowly

BOX 1.2 Marx

The second classical sociologist to remain hugely influential in contemporary sociology is Karl Marx. He gave primacy to the economy when developing his ambitious and compelling theories of social relations and social change.

- Marx coined the term 'mode of production' to describe the ways in which the production of goods needed for individuals to survive and prosper was organized in society. In the case of capitalist society,

Marx argued that the primary motivation for productive activities was the pursuit of profit. He would therefore have had a great deal to say about the BSE crisis in terms of the production of cheaper feed in order to maximise profits.

- Marx also used class analysis as a central aspect of his sociology. He saw power as unequally distributed across societies, and economic power as the basis for other forms of power. In his model, society is a system dominated by market relations and exchange values. The cash nexus is intrinsic to class relations, and this offers a useful starting point for analysing the differential effects of BSE on the different social classes.

- Another important concept developed by Marx is 'alienation'. This has a very strict definition in Marxism and describes the ways in which

individual workers become separated from the products of their labour, from each other and from other classes through the organisation of production in specifically capitalist ways. However, other sociologists have used the concept in a broader way and suggest that alienation has more than just an economic dimension. This broader concept could be applied to the BSE crisis to describe the alienation of consumers from the producers of beef. The importance of this is that this alienation has real effects in terms of meat consumption patterns, the income of livestock farmers and the general levels of trust between the farming industry and society at large.

rational calculations often results in considerable irrationality, as revealed when the unintended consequences begin to emerge (Box 1.3). Much greater rational goals – such as good health and improved quality of life – may be ignored for the sake of narrow cost savings or quick profits. Another great sociologist, Karl Marx (Box 1.2), taught us how economic systems (especially capitalism) can generate deep conflicts of interest even though all the individuals within them think they are behaving in a perfectly rational way.

CONNECTIONS Marx's work has been extremely influential in sociology. For a fuller account of his work and the important contributions he has made, see Chapter 17, pages 476–82.

It is very difficult to make rational choices when you have imperfect information, or when powerful interests play down inconvenient evidence. Families may be aware of warnings against eating too much red meat, but they are also exposed to other pressures, such as advertisements to back the fast-food culture and other high-fat convenience foods, lack of time due to the need to juggle working life and family commitments, and so on. It is also very difficult for individuals to judge degrees of risk when there is so much conflicting information. Should we join in the panic whenever there is a food scare? Or should we shrug our shoulders, light another cigarette and tell ourselves 'we've all gotta die some day'? Without independent, unbiased knowledge, rational choices are very difficult.

Although economics and politics played their part, the BSE and new variant CJD crises were not the result of a conspiracy to do harm. No parents wanted to harm their children by buying cheap food. The farming and food industries learnt the hard way that their markets (especially exports) depended on consumers' trust in safety and quality. In the process, they suffered grave damage and heavy costs. Even politicians, with their ideological support for the de-regulation of the meat processing industry, did not anticipate the consequences of their actions.

But although harm was not intended, great harm was done. Because the modern world is complex and interdependent, we have to use systematic knowledge to understand it, and we must try to produce that knowledge in the most rigorous and open-minded way. This is obvious in the case of medical research on the transmission of CJD, but it is just as important to have sociological understanding. We need to understand the place of food and consumption in our culture, and how this has changed in a world of industrialised food processing and mass advertising. We need to understand how people make choices and how this relates to knowledge and trends in the wider culture. We need socio-economic analysis to explain how decisions and policies come to be made. Above all, we need to understand how the different dimensions of society mesh together and influence each other, so that we can comprehend the complex consequences of actions and decisions. Things hardly ever turn out as we intend. The early sociologists considered that sociology would enable them to predict social outcomes. This proved hugely overambitious, but the discipline can help us to understand why things turn out the way they do, and it can help us to think more creatively about alternatives.

QUESTION Think of a long-running current news event. Using one or two of the concepts you have read about in this chapter, describe how sociologists might begin to explain it. What questions might they start by asking?

BOX 1.3 Weber

The third classical sociologist is Max Weber. He has remained highly influential and continues to have an impact on sociological theorising in many ways. He developed many of the central themes of sociology, and these still have a powerful resonance in contemporary sociology, despite the many social changes that have occurred.

- One of Weber's most important contributions to our understanding of modernity was his idea that, as societies moved from the pre-modern to the modern state, they were increasingly characterised by rational modes of thought and organisation. In Weber's view, capitalist development depended on the systematic application of impersonal rules and regulations – through rational administration, rational accounting, science, the law and so on – in the pursuit of specific practical goals.

- Weber was also concerned to explore social action in all its facets, including the intentions of social actors and the consequences of their actions, which are not always anticipated or intended. He insisted that a full theory of society needed to be 'adequate at the level of meaning'. By drawing attention to the need for sociologists to examine the motivations of social actors, he identified an important subjective dimension of social action. In a complex scenario such as the development of CJD amongst the population, it is important to be aware of the many viewpoints and decisions that are brought to bear by the different participants in the events. Thus, the meanings and intentions of farmers, government officials, consumers, the media and others need to be taken into account for a full sociological rendering of the story.

- Finally, Weber was concerned with the concept of authority, and in particular the rational-legal authority that for him characterised modern societies. This form of authority is based not on tradition or charismatic individuals, but on impersonal rules that have been rationally worked out and formalised. Scientific knowledge, as an aspect of rationalism, is an important component of this authority. If rational-legal authority is undermined, as happened in the BSE crisis, this has fundamental implications for the legitimacy of society's power structure and the way in which individuals choose to act within society.

 ## Reflexive sociology

All this is why sociologists want sociology to be a reflexive discipline. They try to understand society, and to feed the knowledge they gain back into social life. Social change is informed by our understanding of how society works and what the consequences of various actions might be. Anthony Giddens summed up this idea in his book *The Consequences of Modernity* (1990a, p21):

> The practical impact of social sciences is both profound and inescapable. Modern societies together with the organisations that compose and straddle them, are like learning machines, imbibing information in order to regularise their mastery of themselves. . . . Only societies reflexively capable of modifying their institutions in the face of accelerated social change will be able to confront the future with any confidence. Sociology is the prime medium of such reflexivity '.

This concept of a reflexive sociology is nothing new, but it can help us to grasp the place of sociological understanding today. We need to note what Giddens is *not* saying in this passage. He is not suggesting that social scientists know best, and this means they cannot plan social development from above. The people who take action to change society are not social scientists, but members of society with varying amounts of power. Social science knowledge is a resource that people can draw upon when creating social change. Human beings constantly act upon their society and change it to some extent. It is not just programmes of reform or revolution that use social science knowledge. All of us need frameworks to interpret our world and act upon it; social science is one important source (amongst others) of frameworks to guide action. This means that sociology does not provide a critique of society on behalf of people, dictating their future for them.

Even so, there is inevitably a critical dimension if sociology is offering people an understanding of their social position. Alvin Gouldner emphasised this in 1971 in *The Coming Crisis of Western Sociology*. The solution he offered then – a liberating, reflexive sociology – is extremely relevant today. Gouldner was one of the first modern sociologists to reject the 1950s focus on social order and continuity in favour of studying change, conflict and social renewal through action. His work expressed the mood of radicalism in sociology in the 1960s and 1970s.

Since that time, most sociologists have become more cautious about the idea of a leading role for sociology in radical change. Instead, there is a widespread sense of what Giddens (1984) calls the 'recursiveness' of social knowledge. That is, sociologists' knowledge can never be wholly neutral and detached because, in whatever form, it is used by people to interpret and reshape their society – and this is the society that sociologists have studied. So the study needs to be renewed, and the new knowledge must feed back into social life, and so on. This endless, looping interaction between sociology and social life has important consequences. For one thing, sociologists need never be out of work, for our knowledge of a particular society can only be provisional and temporary. As Bauman (1992, p. 213) put it during an interview:

> I am rather inclined to see Sociology today as an eddy on a fast-moving river, an eddy which retains its shape but which changes its content all the time. . . . Sociology is a constant interpretation of, or commentary on, experience . . . and this commentary is sent back into the society itself.

As we have seen, sociologists do not write the script for the future. They cannot tell people what values they should believe in, nor what their dreams and goals should be. Making the future is up to the members of society. However, as we have also seen, we are not free to do exactly as we will. Life in society is influenced by many factors, some of which we can control and some we cannot. It is to this central problem of 'living in society' that we now turn. What are the influences that shape human behaviour?

Society and the subject: individuals in social contexts

Biological, psychological and ecological influences

Sociology stresses the importance of questioning what is 'obvious', 'common sense' or 'natural' in order to get underneath the surface of things and shed fresh light on ideas and social practices that are otherwise very easy to take for granted. But our biological make-up and physical environment also affect what we do and who we are in striking ways. Hunger, thirst, physical fatigue and the gradual and seemingly inexorable degeneration of the human body all affect patterns of behaviour and human experience in vivid and compelling ways. For instance, however much they may wish it were otherwise, vigorous physical exercise is beyond the capacity of most 80 year olds. Likewise, although we may be able to deploy increasingly sophisticated technologies to try to control our environment, elemental phenomena such as hurricanes, droughts, earthquakes and erupting volcanoes continue to exert their force on communities, which then have to adapt their living arrangements in order to survive (through temporary or permanent migration, the reform of building regulations and so on).

While there may be disagreement about the exact contributions made by our genetic inheritance and our social experiences, it is widely acknowledged that individuals have particular psychological characteristics or traits that influence their behaviour and capacities, in the form of specific skills and aptitudes and/or psychological disposition and temperament. For instance, few of us possess the mental agility and disposition required to become a world chess champion, but a warm personality may well win us the friendship or respect of others.

However, while biological, physical, environmental and psychological influences on human life are clearly important, and often offer highly persuasive explanations of human behaviour for lay persons, sociologists believe they do not provide the sole or even necessarily the most significant basis for understanding human lives.

Take falling in love, for example. This is usually described as a uniquely personal experience: unpredictable, surprising, based on personal chemistry and striking apparently at random, often 'across a crowded room'. Sociologically, nothing could be further from the truth. In Western societies, a very significant proportion of people tend to form permanent relationships in their twenties, having completed their education and obtained secure employment. Partners are likely to come from similar educational, ethnic and religious backgrounds, and women tend to fall in love with men of their own age or a few years older. If there is an increasingly high failure rate for these relationships, with a growing number ending in divorce and single-parent families, these – again intensely personal – experiences also conform to clearly perceptible patterns when examined at the societal level. Why is this? Clearly, even our emotional relationships are developed and sustained according to our social circumstances. For example, who we fall in love with is likely to be more or less prescribed by the circles in which we socialise, which might in turn be affected by the community in which we live and/or the institutions in which we spend our time (workplaces, sites of religious workshop, places of leisure such as bars, gyms, clubs or associations, and so on).

QUESTION What reasons can you come up with for the regular pattern of falling in love in your society? Asterisk the reasons that could be said to be sociological.

Social influences on human life

The above example makes it clear that distinct and complex elements are involved in shaping human experience and behaviour. In the same way that we do not exist in an unbounded physical world, so we do not live in a shapeless social world in which we are free to act purely according to our wishes and desires. To return to the example of BSE, the farmers who unwittingly fed their cattle contaminated foodstuffs operated in an economic system in which they had to make a profit or lose their farms and thus their livelihoods. Societies are, in other words, characterised by distinctive social, economic and political patterns and processes. There are multiple social frameworks and social locations – structured social environments characterised by regularities – in which individuals develop from childhood into adulthood and through to old age.

Stressing the powerful impact of social influences on individuals does not commit us to a simple **deterministic** position: that is, we do not need to see these social influences as being independent of humans and affecting individuals and their identities in a regular and predictable way. This would be very simplistic. Social forces do, however, form distinct frameworks and **structures** that shape individuals' identities and socially regulate their behaviour, and they are clearly not manipulable at will. Many of the things we experience as individuals are beyond our control and are the products of society as a whole, its historical development and its current patterns of organisation. For instance, capitalism is an economic system characterised by production for profit and private ownership of the means of production. In order to enhance their profits, capitalist employers seek to minimise their costs of production, including the cost of materials, equipment and labour. Employees, on the other hand, seek to maximise the rewards they receive for their labour, and to negotiate the best possible employment conditions in terms of hours of work, lunch and tea breaks, paid holidays, job security and so on. These motivations cannot be explained by characterising all employers as miserly, cold-hearted individuals and all workers as work-shy. The behaviour of and relationships between employers and workers in capitalist societies are substantially shaped by their structural position within the system of production and are not reducible to their individual characteristics, personalities or desires.

Determinism
A simple, causal, reductionist explanation (see *biological determinism*).

Structures
Refers generally to constructed frameworks and patterns of organisation that serve to constrain or direct human behaviour.

CONNECTIONS Workers orientation towards work (that is, the attitude they take with them into their workplace) is important in shaping the relationship between them and their employers. For a fuller account of this, see Chapter 11, pages 310–11.

One basic fact is important here: our own society and its social institutions, arrangements and conventions *pre-date* us. They were there before we were born, and our arrival sets us off on associations with both the living and the dead in a **socially constructed** world developed in part by previous and present generations. Thus, our identities are formed within more or less clearly defined social contexts, and are significantly shaped by complex interplay between the influences exerted by intimate and anonymous predecessors and contemporaries – from our loved ones, family and kin, our friends and peers at school and at work, our employers, through to the bureaucratic state and the giant transnational corporations.

Social construction
The process whereby natural, instinctive forms of behaviour come to be mediated by social processes. Sociologists would argue that most forms of human behaviour are socially constructed.

Playing by the rules: norms, values and social constraints

Living in a social world, then, is an action-constraining experience: we experience the social world around us as limiting and constraining, even if we do not all do so to the same extent. Those constraints can range from the physical coercion of, say, forced or slave labour to the much more subtle mechanisms to generate compliance that operate in society and the social groups within it. The point is that social living places both external and internal constraints on individuals as they take on board an awareness of the social world around them.

This is because the behaviour of human beings is underpinned by beliefs, values, ideas, purposes and goals. Societies are characterised by complex, more or less definite (although, of course, not unchanging) networks of relationships, institutions, organisations, groups and practices, but there are also important shared cultural **norms** and **values** and symbols interwoven into these social arrangements and into the consciousness of individual members. Thus, people work out their lives individually and collectively by drawing on shared ideas about what is desirable or undesirable, appropriate or inappropriate, good or bad, right or wrong.

The most obvious illustrations of this are laws – systematically codified legal rules with formal social sanctions attached to them in the form of graded punishments and retributions, with designated agencies responsible for their construction, interpretation and enforcement. There is, then, a 'reality' to laws and the legal system – lawbreaking and the subsequent apprehension of lawbreakers by the authorities produce definite consequences. But, as any casual reading of newspaper crime reports confirms, laws do not have a completely binding capacity. Of course, most of the social rules that we follow in our lives are not legally enforced and do not have laws to back them up, but they do have persuasive power. Customs, conventions, fashions and so on constrain individuals, even though their violation is subject to no formal sanctions and few informal ones. For example, there is no law requiring us to use cutlery in a restaurant, yet few if any of us would risk eating with our fingers and thus incur the sanction of our fellow diners' disapproving glances, whispers or mocking laughter. Hence, norms and values, too, are 'real' even if they are not straightforwardly visible. They may not be a part of the material world, but their existence influences individuals and their actions just as the physical world does – there is constraint from a world of *ideas*.

Norms
Socially accepted 'correct' or 'proper' forms of behaviour. Norms either prescribe given types of behaviour or forbid them.

Values
Ideals and beliefs regarded as important by a society or social group.

The subject and society: creative social action

'We think, therefore we are': conscious actors, creativity and agency

Human behaviour is distinctive in that it is informed by what Max Weber (1930) called 'an orientation to values' – that is, it is guided by ideas, beliefs, principles and so on, and not simply by automatic, programmed responses. This is due to human beings' special ability to reason, to reflect upon themselves, their behaviour, their experiences and their environments – in short, their capacity for conscious and self-conscious thinking and creativity. Human beings are characterised by **agency**, the capacity to influence events and to behave independently of the defining constraints of society. They are what Giddens (1984) has called 'knowledgeable agents' – they construct perceptions of the social world in which they are located, know a great deal about the circumstances and consequences of what they do in their day-to-day lives, and can articulate what

Agency
Purposeful action. This term implies that actors have the freedom to create, change and influence events.

| BOX 1.4 | Global hip hop culture: humans as knowledgeable agents |

In his book *Popular Music and Youth Culture* (2000), Andy Bennett describes how an African-American musical form (rap) originating on the streets of New York in the early 1970s was being used as a stylistic resource for young people in quite different social settings around the world to articulate local dissatis-factions and forge distinctive, collective, cultural identities.

He found that some rappers in the city of Frankfurt in Germany, many of whom were of North African, South-East Asian or Southern European origin, felt that their songs had only begun to work as an authentic form of communication with their audi-ence when they had begun to rap ▶

▶ in their adopted tongue, German, rather than in rap's language of origin, English. The rap group Advanced Chemistry, made up of three rappers, each holding German citizenship but originating from Haiti, Ghana and Italy respectively, explained: 'We rap in German in order to reach our own public in order that they understand our problem . . .' Despite their commitment to exposing through their music the racial exclusion suffered by Germany's ethnic minority groups, they were subjected to strong criticism by certain members of Frankfurt's ethnic minority communities. Their shift from English to German-language rapping, far from being seen as embodying increased authenticity, was perceived as a betrayal of their own cultural heritage. As one young Turkish woman put it, 'I think that they should be proud of their roots. When people say to me, 'Are you German?' I say, 'No, I'm not,' and I'm not ashamed to say that.'

they do and their reasons for doing it. Because they are aware of their circumstances and the influences upon them, they can entertain the possibility of exercising choice (Box 1.4).

Humans, then, are reflexive, meaning-creating beings who actively develop their self-image and social identity and negotiate their way through the social arrangements and relationship in which they find themselves. They do not act in isolation from each other but draw on common cultural, social and political resources. While these to a certain degree structure or shape their behaviour, what they do is never merely an act of conformism. It is also coloured by and oriented towards their own meanings and understandings.

'Others think like us, too': identity, the self and interaction

To sum up, we have seen that everyday behaviour is not simply a matter of following predetermined, clear-cut social scripts but also, both potentially and actually, of creating, improvising, adjusting and negotiating. Social actors work out their lives with what have variously been called 'shared meanings', 'shared understandings', 'mental knowledge' and so on, and in doing so, they make sense of what they and others are doing in their social lives. They produce, reproduce and amend these meanings, understandings and knowledge by applying them and/or subtly refining them in practical circumstances and context: norms and values, rather than being absolute, substantial things from which social order is unambiguously constructed, can be better regarded as negotiable ideas.

But the reference to 'shared meanings' and 'negotiation' should signal that these conscious, creative, knowledgeable human agents do not do this in isolation but in processes of interaction with others. Thus, identity formation and individuals' perceptions of themselves are not totally unbounded – the views, opinions and reactions of others significantly influence their conceptions of themselves. But as conscious agents, they endeavour to deal with varied and frequently conflicting responses from others in order to develop a coherent sense of self or identity. Hence, these responses are not simply absorbed or imposed – they are filtered, evaluated, accommodated, cunningly manipulated or even ignored. For instance, people do not simply or invariably take on board the evaluations of all the other social actors with whom they interact. Rather, they are, often consciously, selective in according importance to some while granting little or none to others. Hence, for generations of teenagers, it did not matter if their teachers did not appreciate the Rolling Stones in the 1960s, the Clash in the 1970s, Madonna in the 1980s or Oasis in the 1990s if their contemporaries – their **significant others** – shared their admiration of these musicians.

Significant others
Those particular individuals whose views, opinions and reactions contribute to and influence the conception we have of ourselves.

Humans as creations and creators: the duality of structure and agency

So far we have explored the external or objective influences on humans' lives and identities and their subjective and creative capacity to shape their social world. Clearly, it is much too simple to separate or dichotomise societies or 'systems of social institutions' on the one hand and individuals on the other. Structure and agency, constraint and creativity are not contrasting and independent polar opposites: rather, there is a complex interplay between the constraints of structures and agents' autonomy – a double involvement or interdependence in which human beings create society and are at the same time created by it. This is sometimes referred to by sociologists as a 'dialectical' relationship, where two apparently contrasting elements work upon each other to produce a synthesis.

QUESTION When was the last time you felt constrained to do or not to do something? Was the source of this constraint physical, psychological, social or moral? Did you have any element of choice in the situation?

BOX 1.5 Social structure and human creativity

Tourism offers a fertile example of the complex interplay between structure and agency. There has been considerable debate on whether tourism has accelerated the demise of authentic local traditions or whether it has instead revived the fortunes of communities and regions that were struggling on the economic periphery.

In structural terms, the exponential growth of the tourism industry started with the de-regulation of the global economy (in favour of private enterprise over national interests), the growth of big multinational corporations, the falling cost of transport, the spread of information technology, and the relatively low investment costs required to develop 'tourist spaces' in comparison with 'industries with chimneys'.

The impact of tourism has been felt at the local level in terms of commodification under what Urry (1990) calls 'the tourist gaze'. Indigenous peoples have sought to meet tourists' demands by bowdlerising traditional dances and other performances for tourist consumption and making once individually handcrafted artifacts on an assembly-line basis. Local dress, food and so on have also changed with increased exposure to Western influences, further eroding the distinctiveness of traditional ways of life.

While it would be easy to draw pessimistic conclusions from all this, a number of sociological arguments demonstrate that tourism does not have a stifling market effect and that local communities creatively shape tourism to their own ends. One example of this is the way in which local communities use heritage sites as a space to present political or religious claims to sightseers. This may involve the recovery of aspects of local history that have previously been ignored, such as the US-based travel itinerary themed on the 1960s civil rights movement, or post-apartheid policies in South Africa designed to foster a new sense of nationhood by encouraging internal and external tourism based on the heritage of the anti-apartheid struggle. Likewise, tourism has contributed to the largest street festival in Europe, the annual Notting Hill carnival in London, which offers a public celebration of identity for British people of Caribbean origin or descent. In such ways, tourism both transforms and is transformed by people's individual and collective actions and ideas.

Source: Meethan (2001)

In this view, social structure and human creativity interact with each other and change each other in a simultaneous and mutually influencing process. As the American sociologist C. Wright Mills observed in *The Sociological Imagination* (1970, p. 12):

" Every individual lives, from one generation to the next, in some society . . . he [*sic*] lives out a biography, and . . . he lives it out within some historical sequence. By the fact of his living he contributes, however minutely, to the shaping of his society and to the course of its history, even as he is made by society and by its historical push and shove. "

Opportunities and limits: social life as enabling and constraining

One major implication of the above is that it is possible to conceive of social structures and the patterns and features of our social lives as at once enabling and constraining. That is, society and systems of interaction do not simply and inevitably limit individuals, they also provide opportunities for the growth of individuals and their identities. Many (valued) personal experiences and emotions depend on and are made significant by collective activity – religious celebration and watching sport, for instance, are made more meaningful for the individual by being conducted in collective association with others.

This can be illustrated by another example. Although not all schools of sociological thought would agree, it is possible to argue that language is both enabling and constraining. It is enabling in that its acquisition enriches our understanding of the world. It expands our cognitive and practical capacities, and as a symbolic system shared by a community, it provides us with the means to communicate with others and to articulate our own perceptions, experiences, emotions and so on. It is also the vehicle for the transmission of historically constructed cultural values, meanings and practices.

CONNECTIONS Language became an area of immense interest to sociologists during the last quarter of the twentieth century. We shall look at language in more detail in Chapter 18, pages 509–11 and Chapter 19, pages 520–25.

That language can both enable and constrain can be further demonstrated by the case of children. While children's language acquisition and the sharing of a common communication system with adults means that the latter can (attempt to) control and regulate them via linguistic messages, children themselves can also use language for their own purposes to resist or negotiate with adults. Generations of parents have often come to see their children's growing linguistic ability as a mixed blessing, as the gleam in their offspring's eyes grows ever brighter with the realisation that merely being able to ask the questions 'Why should I?' and 'Why can't I?' is a vital weapon in the family battle for a negotiated order.

 ## Conclusion

We hope that by now you will have gained an initial understanding of what sociology can offer as a discipline. While it is sometimes popularly seen as little more than common sense, we have tried to demonstrate that it provides a much more systematic, sophisticated and disciplined analysis of society than common sense can ever provide, and that it is informed by and itself informs the common stock of knowledge we draw on in the process of living. Sociology offers a valuable tool for questioning assumptions about why things are the way they are and why people act in the ways they do. Moreover, it raises questions and issues that other scientific and social scientific perspectives often overlook.

While sociologists cannot offer prescriptive answers to the social problems that face us all, they do offer a way of thinking that helps us to clarify certain questions and move towards better understandings. In the next chapter, we shall consider the backdrop of social change that has helped to form our contemporary social world, and we shall delve more deeply into the vocabulary and knowledge base of sociology.

Chapter summary

- Social life can be understood in terms of patterned regularities as well as individual actions.
- Social meaning and social identities are embedded in wider social environments and processes.
- The social world constrains us through norms and values shared and reproduced in our relations with others.
- Social actors are creative agents who construct their own sense of social identity and are able to challenge the prevailing social constraints and social structures.
- Social structure and social agency are interdependent, mutually influencing processes.

Questions to think about

- What are the limits of a sociological explanation of such events as the BSE crisis, and what other disciplines might have something useful to say about them?
- To what extent do you agree with the proposition that we make our own histories, but not in times and circumstances of our own choosing?
- What is the importance of language as a form of action, rather than just as a description of the social world?

Investigating further

Albrow, Martin (1999) *Sociology: the basics*, Routledge.

Billington, Rosamund, Jenny Hockey and Sheelagh Strawbridge (1998) *Exploring Self and Society*, Palgrave.

> A number of chapters in this book would be useful to supplement your reading (for example on the life course, work, health and illness). Chapter 1 provides a good overview and starting point.

Bruce, Steve (2000) *Sociology: a very short introduction*, Oxford University Press.

> These are short and cheap introductions to sociology as a discipline – good books to get you started.

Mills, C. W. (1970) *The Sociological Imagination*, Penguin.

Still one of the best introductions to sociology, this book has stood the test of time. It is readable and filled with the excitement of doing sociology. If you read none of the other books, you should read this one.

CHAPTER CONTENTS

Aims of the chapter

This chapter introduces the concept of modernity in order to explore the distinctiveness of life in modern (as opposed to traditional or pre-modern) societies. It highlights the ways in which historical structural changes, often of global proportion, have altered our everyday experiences and continue to do so. In particular, it considers the impact of four key processes of modernity: the development of industrial capitalism; the growth of rational forms of thought and organisation; the rise of the nation-state; and the separation of social life into public and private realms. It then briefly touches on whether society has now changed to such an extent that we can be said to be living in a postmodern era.

By the end of this chapter, you should have an understanding of the following important terms:

- Modernity
- Industrialisation
- Urbanisation
- Fordism

- Consumption
- Bureaucracy
- Nation-state
- Postmodernity

Modernity
A term coined to encapsulate the distinctiveness and dynamism of the social processes unleashed during the eighteenth and nineteenth centuries, which marked a distinct break from traditional ways of life.

 ## Introduction

Project of modernity
A belief in the possibilities opened up by modernity, involving a commitment to social progress.

Sociology emerged and flourished in the late nineteenth and early twentieth centuries – the era of **modernity**. As a **modernist project**, it was committed to the idea that it was possible to produce reliable knowledge about society that human beings could use to shape their futures for the better. In everyday language, 'modern' often means up-to-date or contemporary. Sociologists use it in a different sense – for them, modern societies have a long history! Modern societies and sociology emerged from a period that is sometimes referred to as **the Great Transformation** (Polanyi, 1973), a term that reflects the magnitude of the changes that took place during this time. The Great Transformation involved complex social, economic, political and cultural processes that together resulted in the development of strikingly new forms of social life. It is these changes that are the subject of this chapter.

The all-encompassing nature of these changes makes them hard to date exactly or explain fully. What we can say is that, although they were to exert a world-wide influence, they initially centred on Western Europe. Also, while their origin can be traced back hundreds of years, it was only in the nineteenth century that recognisably modern societies appeared.

The origins of modernity

The birth of modernity involved a number of interrelated processes, contemporary aspects of which are examined in more detail in the succeeding chapters of this book. Here we shall identify some of the main features.

- Rapid, continuous growth of productive capacities was made possible by new kinds of economic activity and new ways of working. Crucial factors in the emergence of modern societies were the application of more efficient forms of food production, and then the replacement of agriculture by industrial manufacture as the dominant form of productive activity. Manufacturing had been taking place for many hundreds of years – what was new was the scale of the undertaking and how it took place. In the seventeenth and eighteenth centuries, the Industrial Revolution was primarily about new ways of organising and controlling production: the factory system, for example, established greater control over workers and allowed the segmentation of tasks into sophisticated divisions of labour.

- A precursor of industrialisation was the development of a new, dynamic form of economic activity – capitalism – which was initially applied to agriculture and trade but in the nineteenth century became the driving force behind the growth of industrial manufacturing. Capitalism involved new attitudes and institutions: entrepreneurs engaged in the sustained, systematic pursuit of profit; the market acted as the key mechanism of productive life; and goods, services and labour became commodities whose use was determined by rational calculation.

- There were significant changes in population growth and movement. As birth rates rose and death rates fell, the estimated number of people in Europe grew rapidly from 120 million in 1750 to 468 million in 1913 (Kumar, 1978). This period witnessed mass movements from the countryside to the city in a process of urbanisation. Also significant was the extent of forced and voluntary migration around the world: a striking example of this was the way in which North and South America were rapidly populated by European migrants and African slaves.

- Modernity saw the development of new forms of government. The nation-state, claiming absolute control over a bounded territory, became the key unit of power. Modernity involved the establishment of highly developed political apparatuses: bureaucratic organisation allowed the state to play a greater role in the lives of ordinary people. This was accompanied by the development of new political ideas such as nationalism, citizenship, democracy, liberalism, socialism and conservatism. The development of new philosophies of government was part of a wider change in the intellectual and cultural landscape. In the eighteenth century, **The Enlightenment** brought new ways of understanding the natural and social worlds. It heralded an era of great medical, scientific and technological innovation. Religious institutions and doctrines declined in influence – a process called secularisation – and for the emerging **secular** intelligentsia, science, truth and progress were the new faith.

- Finally, Western expansion around the world was a crucial factor in the formation of modern societies. As early as the fifteenth century, Europeans began to travel the globe. In the years that followed, contacts between the West and the rest (Hall, 1992a) meant trade, plunder and eventually colonisation. This expansion provided the wealth, raw materials and then markets that drove European economic development. In other regions, it led to the destruction of societies and cultures in the face of Western power.

It is no coincidence that sociology emerged as an academic discipline during the nineteenth century. It was a response to a prolonged period of unprecedented social change when the old order, the old ways of life and old certainties were disappearing. The social changes investigated by the early sociologists were so rapid and far-reaching that they were convinced they were witnessing the birth of a different kind of society.

The Great Transformation
The name given by Karl Polanyi to the historical moment – characterised by massive social, political, technological, economic and intellectual change – that marked the onset of modernity.

The Enlightenment
An eighteenth-century philosophical movement based on notions of progress through the application of reason and rationality. Enlightenment philosophers foresaw a world free from religious dogma, under human control and leading ultimately to emancipation for all humankind.

Secular
Not concerned with religion.

Figure 2.1 In the nineteenth and early twentieth centuries, photography played a significant part in defining the 'Otherness' of the indigenous peoples of Africa, Asia, Australia and America, its documentary status concealing an exercise in symbolic control.

Social theorists of the nineteenth and early twentieth centuries saw their task as making sense of the Great Transformation and understanding the new societies that were being created.

It is perhaps not surprising that early theorists assumed that the dynamics of modernity would shape and structure all societies in a similar – positive – way. Societies were understood in terms of national boundaries or particular forms of society (for example, capitalism), and individual societies were seen as more or less conforming to the form and content of a modern society. Modernity provided a sort of template for social development.

Now the dynamics of modernity are no longer seen in terms of a template or model of a single modern society that all nation-states are destined to become. It is true that a significant number of societies in the world are industrialised, urbanised nation-states, yet, as we shall see in Chapter 3, their industries, cities and governments are shaped by global processes that cut across states and societies. The result is that 'It is increasingly difficult to understand local and national destinies without reference to global forces' (McGrew, 1992, p. 63), but at the same time a growing division and divergence means that modernity does not have the same pay-off all over the world. This is an issue to which we shall return later, particularly in the next chapter. First, however, let us look in more depth at the experience, character and meaning of modernity.

> **CONNECTIONS** The question of whether we live in a late modern or a postmodern society has engaged sociologists for a number of years. Although no agreement has been reached on the matter, an account of the dimensions of postmodernity are provided in Chapter 19, pages 514–20.

 ## The process of becoming modern: transformations of time and space

Major changes in the sense and use of time and space were central to the formation of modernity (Berman, 1983; Harvey, 1990; Giddens, 1990a). From the late fifteenth century onwards, European exploration led to the forging of new trading links between Eastern and Western civilisations and subsequently to European colonial expansion. In one of the largest population movements in history, an estimated 24 million Africans were enslaved, some eleven million of whom survived the terrible journey across the Atlantic to the Americas, where they were exploited on rural plantations in the production of American tobacco, Caribbean sugar and other products that became part of the staple diet of white populations in Europe and North America. The slave trade, eventually abolished in the British Empire in 1833 and in the US in 1865, provides a graphic example of how people were caught up in the development of modernity in profoundly unequal ways, as well as illustrating one aspect of the long and sometimes troubled history of what Robertson (1992) calls 'the compression of the world'.

Scientific and technological advances, from the discovery that the earth was round to the invention of the mechanical clock and the harnessing of steam power (greatly reducing the time taken to cross sea and land), obviously contributed significantly towards a changed understanding of space and time – a change that Giddens and others highlight in order to demonstrate the uniqueness of the institutions that emerged during the great transformation to modernity. Giddens (1990a, pp.19–20), for example, argues that the modest railway timetable can be seen as epitomising the modern era, terming it 'a time-space ordering device' that 'permits the complex co-ordination of trains and their passengers over time and space'.

We shall now consider four key aspects of change in the rise of modernity:

- Industrialisation.
- Increasing rationalisation.
- The rise of the nation-state.
- The differentiation of public and private spheres.

 ## Living with industrial capitalism

The origins of the Industrial Revolution can be traced back to about 1780 in England. Its impact on both the social and natural world was profound. The development of steam power and the spectacular transformation of the coal, iron and textile industries in the late eighteenth and nineteenth centuries irreversibly changed the landscape, the economy and relations between the social classes. The following (quoted in Jennings, 1985 p. 165) describes England's Black Country in the 1830s:

> "The earth seems to have been turned inside out. . . . The coal . . . is blazing on the surface . . . by day and by night the country is flowing with fire, and the smoke of the ironworks hangs over it. There is a rumbling and clanking of iron forges and rolling mills. Workmen covered in smut, and with fierce white eyes, are seen moving amongst the glowing iron and dull thud of the forge-hammers. "

Living as a worker

The development of capitalism and industrial production had major consequences for the mass of ordinary people. The invention of power-driven machinery led to the concentration of production in bigger workplaces. Initially, large-scale workshops replaced the domestic unit, but by the mid nineteenth century, the factory system was fully in place. Labour became synchronised – beginning punctually and proceeding at a steady pace for a set number of hours on particular days of the week. Hierarchies of skill, training and wages developed around the specialised tasks of a more systematised division of labour. Workers responded by forming unions to fight collectively for better wages, working conditions and working hours, as well as to resist the dilution of their skills through further technological advancement. In pre-modern societies, financial remuneration had been only one of a number of strategies for achieving the means to live: much production was for subsistence or to fulfil non-monetary obligations. Under the new conditions of industrial capitalism, a regular wage became crucial to the survival of the mass of the population. The wage de-personalised relations between employer and employee, turning the worker into abstract labour to be used as efficiently as possible in the pursuit of profit.

By the twentieth century, a conventional view of work was established that was very different from that of a hundred years before: it was waged, it took place outside the home, it was governed by the clock and it was performed predominantly by men. The household had lost much of the status it had enjoyed in pre-modern times as an arena of economic activity. This development contributed to the marginalisation of women from production. While pre-modern societies had also been characterised by significant social differences and inequalities, the economic conditions of industrial capitalism generated new kinds of social division. The separation of home and work helped to sharpen gender differences inside and outside the home: many (particularly wealthier) women were squeezed out of economic activity and left with a more clearly defined domestic role. Age divisions were heightened as children and the elderly were excluded from production and segregated socially. The fluid, impersonal relationships of capitalism also generated the modern class structure.

Capitalism proved to be organisationally and technologically dynamic, generating new experiences of work and encouraging the development of ever more sophisticated techniques for the management and control of labour. Employers increasingly engaged in the observation and regulation of their workers to maximise productivity and eliminate inefficiency. In the twentieth century, this was epitomised by the development of large-scale mass production pioneered by motor manufacturer Henry Ford, who used a moving assembly line to manufacture low-cost products for a mass market.

The new conditions of work increased output (Ford could make a car for a tenth of the cost of old-style craft production) but they also prompted considerable dissatisfaction and conflict. A recurring theme of nineteenth- and twentieth-century thought was that a contradiction existed between the development of mechanical and human potential under industrial capitalism. A wide range of critics, from Karl Marx onwards, argued that modern work conditions were dehumanising (Meakin, 1976). The **alienation** and exploitation of industrial labour were not accepted passively, however: workers reacted both informally via sabotage, absenteeism, pilfering and day-dreaming, and, as we have seen, in a more organised fashion through trade unionism and other forms of political activity. This resistance in turn contributed to changing conditions of work.

Alienation
Originally utilised by Marx to describe the feeling of estrangement experienced by workers under industrial capitalism. Now more generally employed to describe people's feelings of isolation, powerlessness and self-estrangement.

BOX 2.1 Working for Ford

What is it like to work on an assembly line? In a classic study, Huw Beynon (1973) researched the lives of shopfloor workers at the Ford plant at Halewood on Merseyside in the late 1960s. The following quotes from his interviews give an indication of the monotony and estrangement experienced.

'You don't achieve anything here. A robot could do it. The line here is made for morons. It doesn't need any thought. They tell you that. 'We don't pay you for thinking', they say. Everyone comes to realise that they are not doing a worthwhile job. They're just on the line. For the money. Nobody likes to think that they're a failure. It's bad when you know that you're just a little cog. You just look at your pay packet – you look at what it does for your wife and kids. That's the only answer.' (p.114)

'It's different for them in the office. They're *part* of Fords. We're not, we're just working here, we're numbers.' (p.121)

'They decide on *their* measured day how fast *we* will work. They seem to forget that we're not machines. ... The standards they work to are excessive ▶

▶ anyway. They expect you to work the 480 minutes of the eight hours you're on the clock. | They've agreed to have a built-in allowance of *six minutes* for going to the toilet, blowing your | nose and that. It takes you six minutes to get your trousers down.' (p.135)

QUESTION   Drawing on any of your own work experiences, to what extent were your working conditions similar to or different from those recounted by Beynon? What might account for the differences you have identified?

Living as a consumer

Capitalism generated a consumer revolution as well as an industrial one. With industrialisation, the world of work was effectively split from the sphere of leisure in both spatial and temporal terms. With the advent of rail travel, day trips to the seaside became possible for the urban working classes as well as for the fashionable rich, and when holidays were made statutory, and later still were paid for by employers, annual holidays became part of an established pattern of conspicuous consumption of leisure (Meethan, 2001). In the cities, department stores became key sites for the display as well as the purchase of a diverse range of commodities, and music halls, bars and pubs, and later cinemas, all contributed to the development of a new, more glamorous and thoroughly commercial urban leisure culture. Mail order catalogues, billboards and public exhibitions combined with increases in the real value of the wage and the use of large-scale production to fuel consumer demand. The early twentieth century saw the birth of occupations such as design, marketing and advertising, all devoted to selling an increasing range and diversity of consumer goods.

The emergence of **consumerism** was not only about institutional change; it also involved shifts in attitudes and behaviour (Ewen and Ewen, 1982). One example of this was the way in which the practice of following new fashions in clothing, previously confined to elite groups, become commonplace. Increasingly, the choice of clothing, hairstyle and even body shape came to be seen as an expression of self. A crucial change in outlook was a growing interest in novelty – a willingness to reject existing goods and practices in favour of new ones (Campbell, 1992).

Consumerism
A culture based on the promotion, sale and acquisition of consumer goods.

Some have argued that these developments amounted to the invention of the consumer. Certainly during the twentieth century, powerful forces sought to influence and shape consumer needs and desires. At the beginning of the twentieth century, producers consciously set out to create markets and audiences for their products, socialising consumers into new values and giving them the knowledge and competence to distinguish between goods. By its end, producers and retailers had developed advanced techniques such as market research for observing consumer behaviour and utilised the new science of psychology to sell goods more effectively (Bowlby, 1993).

In retrospect, the 1950s and 1960s were a golden era of mass consumption in the industrialised countries of the West. Across the developed world, sustained rises in real income contributed to the growth of leisure industries and to the spread of consumer goods such as cars, televisions and washing machines. The emergence of a consumer society was seen, however, as a disturbing development by some critics, because they felt it involved the manipulation and exploitation of the mass of ordinary people. Writers such as Theodor Adorno (1903–69), Max Horkheimer (1895–1973) and Herbert

Marcuse (1898–1979) from the Frankfurt School of critical theory drew on Marxist theories of alienation and ideology to argue that the rise of the culture industries and preoccupation with the acquisition of consumer goods posed a threat to individuality and independent, critical thought, producing what Marcuse (1964, p. 9) called 'One Dimensional Man': 'People recognise themselves in their commodities; they find their soul in their automobile, hi-fi set, split level home, kitchen equipment'.

By portraying consumers merely as dupes or hedonists, such writers tended both to exaggerate the coherence and power of the messages of advertisers and marketers and to downplay the actual role and experience of consumer goods in modern social life. Items such as cars, washing machines and refrigerators were, for example, part of a major change in the running of households (Gershuny, 1983). Consumer goods also represented cultural as well as material resources, mediating relationships and embodying meaning. Conventions about clothing, for example, added up to a system of classification that involved differences in gender, age and class, recognised times of the day, week and year, and marked spaces and occasions. Clothes and other goods established and reflected distinctions between social groups (Bourdieu, 1984).

As this discussion implies, consumer goods became implicated in a whole range of social activities and cultural meanings in the modern era. While viewing consumption simply as a form of manipulation is simplistic, the growing involvement of industrial capitalism in these everyday practices is highly significant.

BOX 2.2 Consumption as opposition?

As we have seen, the term consumption is often associated with passivity. This can, however, blind us to the creativity of consumers. The varied ways in which we utilise goods often challenges the intentions of producers. In some cases, far from demonstrating conformity, they can express resistance to dominant structures and values. For example, youth subcultures have appropriated everything from the motor scooter of the Mods to the safety pin of the Punks to establish oppositional identities. Such is the dynamism of capitalism, however, that it has been able to reappropriate and sell this rebellion back as commodities, in profitable form.

The story of Napster offers a nice illustration of this. This apparently revolutionary website for the free trading of music amongst fans on the world wide web was the brainchild of a North American college student, Shaun Fanning, and two friends. Launched in June 1999, it was an instant and quite unprecedented success, allowing users to share digital music files and to follow up mutual musical interests in a quick, easy and dynamic way. Despite the fact that Napster actually had very little effect on record sales during its lifetime, the record industry was outraged at the potential loss of revenue from their traditional commercial channels and counter-attacked with legal action to stop what they saw as copyright violation on a massive scale. After a string of last-minute legal reprieves, Napster was shut down. In its wake, a number of subscription sources were launched by major record labels, none as comprehensive, and all effectively under the record industry's control.

Source: Guardian, 4 August 2001.

Living with rationality

With hindsight, the intellectual revolution of the eighteenth-century Enlightenment was a crucial element of the Great Transformation. It instigated what has been called 'the project of modernity' (Habermas, 1987) by challenging religion, myth and tradition and trumpeting a new belief in progress through knowledge and reason. How this change in the world of ideas altered the outlook and behaviour of ordinary people is open to question. Chapter 15 will describe how religious beliefs and institutions – albeit in distinctly modern forms – continue in the contemporary world. Nonetheless, in contrast to those which preceded them, modern societies are secular societies characterised by a belief in the power of rational thought.

For proponents of the modernist project, reason, particularly as manifested in science and technology, promised control of nature and society. Thinkers of the early modern era were convinced that progress in knowledge held the solution to all social ills: 'The Golden Age of the human race is not behind us but before us; it lies in the perfection of the social order' (Henri Saint-Simon, quoted in Kumar, 1978, p. 13).

This approach to social and political problems indicates a shift in outlook that is referred to as the growth of **rationality**. As we saw in the previous chapter, rationality involves the systematic pursuit of goals – finding the optimum means to a specified end. It is impersonal and preoccupied with technique, calculation, logic and control. In the early years of the twentieth century, sociologist Max Weber broke new ground when he argued that the key developments of the Great Transformation were, at heart, all manifestations of the growth of rationality. These were:

Rationality
A preoccupation with calculating the most efficient means to achieve one's goals.

- The rise of science and academia, signalling the dominance of rational thought.
- Industrial manufacture involving the rationalisation of production.
- Capitalism, geared towards the calculated, systematic pursuit of profit.
- Codified law representing the rational organisation of justice.

Living in modernity therefore meant being subject to these rational forms of thought and rational social organisation. This is best illustrated by referring to the example of rationality that particularly preoccupied Weber – bureaucracy.

Bureaucracies are the essence of a modern form of organisation – think of the complex hierarchies of government civil services, transnational corporations or even educational establishments. They are large impersonal organisations in which power lies with the institutional structure rather than with the individuals who people it. Bureaucracies involve the specialisation of tasks with clear demarcations of authority and formal rules and regulations. In the modern world, we are subject to the discipline of bureaucracies as employees with clear sets of duties and responsibilities, and we are expected to subsume our own feelings and interests to those of the organisation. We also have to deal with impersonal bureaucratic structures as citizens and consumers. These systems of rational thought and organisation can be inhuman or dehumanising, and, ironically, in some circumstances they can be irrational and inefficient – as anyone who has been tangled in red tape will testify.

BOX 2.3 The McDonaldisation of society?

Max Weber viewed bureaucracy as the ultimate manifestation of rationality in social organisation. American sociologist George Ritzer (1993) argues that in the contemporary world the fast-food restaurant is a more appro-priate model for the influence of rationalisation. In 1991, it was estimated that the leading one hundred restaurant chains oper-ated 110 000 outlets in the US alone – that is, one per 2250 Americans. According to Ritzer, the success of these chains is based on the four key elements of 'McDonaldisation':

- Efficiency: economies of scale, assembly-line pro-duction of food and limited ▶

menus cut costs and facilitate the rapid processing of customers.

- Calculability: every aspect of the food production and consumption process is measured and evaluated on the basis of rational calculation.
- Predictability: according to Ritzer, 'in a rational society people prefer to know what to expect in all settings at all times' (1993, p83). McDonald's epitomises the drive towards 'a world that offers no surprises' (1993, p83). Enter a McDonald's anywhere in the world and not only will the menu be the same but you can guarantee that the french fries will be 9/32s of an inch thick and the hamburgers 3¾ inches in diameter.
- Control: McDonald's exercises rigid control over its employees, taking skills and autonomy away from individual workers and investing

it in the organisation of production, so that, instead of a chef, there is a food production line. Technology plays an important part in this: people serving drinks, for example, have no discretion over how much they pour – this is determined by automatic dispensers. Control is exercised over the customers as well as the employees: hard seats, bright lights and, in some cases, security guards ensure that they do not linger too long when consuming their food.

Ritzer argues that McDonald's success also illustrates the irrationality of supposedly rational systems. Rational organisation has succeeded in producing and promoting food of poor quality and devaluing the experience of having a meal:

'the fast food restaurant is often a dehumanising setting in which to eat or work. People lining up

for a burger, or waiting in the drive-through line, often feel as if they are dining on an assembly line, and those who prepare the burgers often appear to be working on a burger assembly line. Assembly lines are hardly human settings in which to eat, and they have been shown to be inhuman settings in which to work . . . dehumanisation is only one of the many ways in which the highly rationalised fast-food restaurant is extremely irrational (Ritzer, 1993, p12).'

Critics of Ritzer, however, consider that he lays too much emphasis on production and fails to account sufficiently for human agency (the diverse practices and experiences of consumption). Also Parker (1998) argues that Ritzer's analysis is essentially elitist, presupposing a high or unspoilt culture that is under threat from mass society.

A new faith? Living with science and technology

Rational forms of thought and organisation may be defining features of modernity but our relationships with them are far from straightforward, as we have seen. This is particularly apparent when we consider people's experiences of two areas of modern life that are often said to epitomise the triumph of reason and rationality: science and technology.

During the twentieth century, science became a huge undertaking, and technologies grew rapidly in pervasiveness, scale and power. Scientific knowledge and technological systems have played a pivotal role in transforming the natural world into a created environment subject to human coordination and control. The size and complexity of these systems means, however, that our ability as individuals to shape or even understand them is compromised. It is an inevitable consequence of modern life that people use technologies such as electricity, medicines and computers without really understanding how they work. As we saw in the previous chapter, we have to trust the claims of scientific knowledge and take the advice of technical experts. A striking illustration of this is the way we hand our bodies over to doctors.

In pre-modern societies, people could only be unwell if they felt unwell, and many sources of danger to health – such as the Black Death, which wiped out around a third of the English population in the fourteenth century – were seen as beyond human control – as 'Acts of God'. Although, over the centuries, people who were in a position to call a doctor did so, they did not have high expectations of what could be achieved. Medicine typically achieved little and carried little prestige or power (Porter, 1999).

However, with the rise of scientific understanding (Louis Pasteur's theory of the relationship between bacteria and infectious diseases being one major milestone), medicine became more effective and was the focus of rising expectations. It also assumed the mantle of professional expertise. Thus, the invention and popularisation of as simple an instrument as the stethoscope (invented by a Frenchman called Laennec in 1816) made it possible for doctors to 'see' beyond the patient's story into the patient's body. No longer was the patient the main authority on his or her own state of wellbeing: it had become possible to be diagnosed as seriously ill and yet feel fine (Duffin, 1999).

CONNECTIONS An example of how the medical profession has intervened to regulate a previously unregulated aspect of social life is in the area of fertility and childbirth. You will find a discussion of this in Chapters 6 and 9, on pages 148–9 and 237–9 respectively. Chapter 13 discusses the professionalisation of medicine in more depth (see pages 356–73 and especially 367–9).

Conventional accounts of modernity portray the pre-eminence of science and technology as evidence of the triumph of reason over religion and superstition. Science was seen as expert, non-political and above all progressive. But the belief that society's ills could be stamped out by scientific advances proved hugely over-optimistic. Medicine and improved sanitation did control infectious diseases such as smallpox, scarlet fever and tuberculosis for a time in the West. But some are resurgent – tuberculosis notifications rose by 20 per cent in England between 1988 and 1998, for example (Baggott 2000); others, such as influenza and malaria, have developed more resistant strains; and new infectious diseases have also broken out. HIV/AIDS is one such: it is estimated that some 32 million adults and 1.2 million children have been infected world-wide, of whom 23 million live in Sub-Saharan Africa and have very limited or no access to the therapeutic drugs now available on the market.

Add to these concerns other major threats to modern life resulting from scientific and technological developments – nuclear, chemical and biological warfare, global warming and large-scale pollution – and it is no wonder that we feel a new anxiety about science and technology. Here lies a paradox of contemporary life: we are at once more dependent on science and technology than ever before and are, at the same time, more aware than ever of their limitations.

BOX 2.4 Technological futures: fact and fiction

One illustration of our ambivalent relationship with technology is the way in which the Internet, the latest in a long line of developments to prompt utopian and anti-utopian visions of a world transformed by tech-nology, has engendered powerful hopes and fears for the future. Technological advances have often been portrayed as routes to heaven or hell – a source of deliverance or damnation.

The popularity of science fiction is another indicator of the power that technology holds in the modern world. The links between science fiction and science fact are interesting. For example, before he was employed by the US space ▶

programme, German scientist Werner Von Braun designed fictional rockets for the film industry. Walt Disney's *Man in Space* – featuring a Braun-designed rocket – promoted among the American public and politicians the concept of sending humans into space. Later, a million people petitioned NASA to name the first space shuttle after *Star Trek*'s 'Enterprise'. The blurring of the lines between fantasy and reality suggest that hopes and fears for the future are an important driving force behind technological and scientific innovation.

Living under state government

During the Great Transformation, people in the West became subject to a new form of authority: the nation-state. National government was not only a product but also a carrier of modernisation. The nation-state took a variety of forms – totalitarian and democratic – but in every case it claimed ultimate control over a bounded geographical territory. In doing so, it established an unprecedented position of power and influence over its population.

During the nineteenth and twentieth centuries, the state played an increasingly important part in ordinary people's lives. For example:

- Through codified systems of civil and criminal law, it claimed the ultimate right to judge and punish wrongdoing and to mediate disputes between individuals. The state disciplined people through incarceration in new prisons and asylums, and, in some cases, it was prepared to kill those who transgressed its laws. It sought to regulate not only public conduct but also private behaviour by, for example, policing sexual activity and childrearing.

- The government also established a key role in economic life, either by taking control of production out of the hands of capitalists or by establishing a close relationship with them. One consequence of this was that the state became the largest employer in modern societies.

- The state also claimed the right to regulate what its citizens should have access to in the case of media outlets. Forms of regulation ranged from outright censorship to more subtle means of denying individuals the right to view, read or listen to what they wanted.

- National systems of education and welfare meant, for example, that all children were required to attend school and that people in poverty could expect some aid from the state.

As this list suggests, the nation-state has developed a role that is at once coercive and supportive of its people. Sometimes both elements coexist within the same function. For example, welfare systems, by starting from the assumption that everyone in a nation's population has the right to a minimum standard of living, enshrine the idea of social citizenship, but they have another side that is about maintaining the work ethic and disciplining 'the underserving poor' (Morris, 1994).

The development of the modern state was an element of the rationalisation story: the reach and power of modern government rested on new, impersonal, bureaucratic forms of organisation. The state's authority was maintained through a mixture of force and consent. It exercised a monopoly of coercive power within its borders, engaging in the surveillance of and, if necessary, violence against its people. Through control of both material resources and information, it sought influence over their thoughts and actions. Highly significant was the way in which subjects of the state were reconstituted as 'citizens' who shared a common destiny. Nationalism – loyalty to the nation-state – became a potent source of identity and a justification for behaving with great brutality. One aspect of this was summed up by George Orwell, writing in Britain during the Second World War and quoted in Bauman (1989, p.ii):

> " As I write, highly civilised beings are flying overhead, trying to kill me. They do not feel any enmity to me as an individual, nor I against them. They are only 'doing their duty', as the saying goes. Most of them, I have no doubt, are kind-hearted law-abiding men who would never dream of committing murder in private life. On the other hand, if one of them succeeds in blowing me to pieces with a well-placed bomb, he will never sleep the worse for it. He is serving his country, which has the power to absolve him for evil. "

As this example suggests, a striking illustration of the authority of the state is the way it has mobilised its citizens for war. Thanks chiefly to the developments in industrial production, rational organisation and science and technology, warfare in the modern era has been of a scale and ferocity previously unknown. It is estimated that as many as 187 million people – civilians as well as soldiers – were killed in wars during the twentieth century (Hobsbawm, 1994). Even in times of peace, nation-states have demonstrated a huge commitment to armies and arms. At times of war they have organised all human and economic resources at their disposal in order to fight other states.

BOX 2.5 | Modernity and the Holocaust

There is no greater testimony to the potential power and destructiveness of the modern state than the millions who died at the hands of totalitarian governments during the twentieth century. The Holocaust – the attempt during the Second World War by the Nazi-controlled German state to eradicate the Jewish population of Europe – is an horrific example of this. Between five and six million Jews were killed by the Nazis as part of a wider programme of genocide against Slavs, Gypsies, the mentally ill, the disabled, homosexuals and political opponents.

The Holocaust was rooted in anti-Semitism, which had a history stretching back to the Middle Ages. 'The Final Solution' (the Nazi euphemism for the genocide of the Jews) was, however, a phenomenon of modernity, according to a number of sociologists. It was made possible by the scientific, technological and political developments discussed above. A historian of the death camps writes:

'[Auschwitz] was ... a mundane extension of the modern factory system. Rather than producing goods, the raw material was human beings and the end-product was death, so many units per day marked carefully on the manager's production charts. The chimneys, the very symbol of the modern factory system, poured forth acrid smoke produced by burning human flesh. The brilliantly organized railroad grid of modern Europe carried a new kind of raw material to the factories. It did so in the same manner as with other cargo. In the gas chambers the victims inhaled noxious gas generated by prussic acid pellets, which were produced by the advanced chemical industry of Germany. Engineers designed the crematoria; managers designed the system of bureaucracy that worked with zest and efficiency more backward nations would envy. Even the overall plan itself was a reflection of the modern scientific spirit gone awry. What we witnessed was nothing less than a massive scheme of social engineering' (Feingold, quoted in Bauman, 1989, p. 8).

As this quotation vividly suggests, the Holocaust was rationally planned and carried out by a bureaucratic apparatus that was sponsored by a powerful centralised state. Initially, the killing ▶

▶ was carried out by death squads, who shot their victims by the thousand and buried them in mass graves. Within a few years, a far more sophisticated technique – the use of gas chambers – was applied in extermination camps. These camps processed large numbers of people quickly and cheaply: the Final Solution was financed by selling the labour of some camp inmates, seizing the inmates' possessions and recycling the by-products of extermination, such as victims' hair.

Of all the experiences of modernity, it is hard to imagine any more terrible than those suffered by the children, women and men who were the 'raw material' of genocide. The Holocaust, in the words of sociologist Zygmunt Bauman (1989), was a 'test of the hidden possibilities of modern society'. Bauman sees the Final Solution as a telling illustration of the way in which the institutions of modernity distance people from moral responsibility for their actions. He argues that, far from being a product of barbaric uncivilised forces, the Holocaust was made possible by a meticulous functional division of labour that separated distinct tasks from their consequences and substituted technical for moral responsibility. Thus, employees could focus simply on following orders and doing their small task 'well', and the whole operation could be discussed in a technical, rational language that helped to depersonalise the killing. (A notable more recent example of this is the term 'ethnic cleansing', coined to describe the genocide that took place during the Bosnian civil war, which erupted in Europe in 1992.)

Living in public and private

If some developments of modernity grouped people into anonymous masses, then others contributed to a heightened feeling of individuality and self-consciousness. The complexity and flux of the modern social environment presented people with new problems and opportunities as they attempted to do two fundamental things – interact with others and maintain an identity. Relationships in pre-modern times took place in comparatively small-scale and stable contexts and rested on clear notions of social position, grounded, for example, in kinship or feudal hierarchies. The following trends have all contributed to a transformation in the ways in which people are sociable:

- The dynamic character of modernity has undermined custom and tradition as a grounding of social relationships, forcing us to reflect on and re-evaluate our contacts with others. One element of this is that there is now less emphasis on ascribed or inherited status when defining who people are and more emphasis on actively selected or achieved social positions.

- Many social practices in pre-modern societies rested on the relative similarity of background and outlook of all participants. Modern societies are far more diverse, and our individual experiences are unlike those with whom we come into daily contact. Living in modernity therefore requires us to deal with people who are different from ourselves.

- In comparison with earlier social forms, there is a greater level of complexity and specialisation in modern societies. The range of social roles has grown rapidly.

- In pre-modern societies, 'others' could be clearly categorised either as familiar or as strangers. Living in modernity requires a more subtle range of stances towards the many people we come across. For example, even when we choose not to engage with those we meet in passing on the street, in a bar or at college, we must manage that non-contact by maintaining a stance of 'civil indifference' (Goffman, 1969).

- Modern life is characterised by a great number of impersonal relationships, particularly those governed by formal rules where contact is not really with an individual but with their bureaucratic rank or professional status. A vast array of social interactions come into this category, such as those between welfare officer and claimant, bus driver and passenger, doctor and patient, and so on.

CONNECTIONS For a fuller account of the idea of life-worlds, see the section on phenomenology in Chapter 18, pages 504–5.

Living in public

Urbanisation was also a crucial dimension of the making of modern societies. Industrialisation fuelled the growth of urban centres as large numbers of people migrated from the countryside to the city in search of work. For example, in 1810, 20 per cent of the British population lived in towns and cities; a hundred years later, the figure had risen to 80 per cent (Kumar, 1978). Cities changed qualitatively as well as quantitatively. Their unprecedented scale and complexity required new levels of planning and organisation. In contrast with the irregular, twisting street of medieval cities, shaped by the contours of the land, industrial cities were increasingly characterised by broader, straighter streets that were more suitable for the growing

Figure 2.2 With a population of about 18 million, Sao Paulo is the fourth largest city in the world. Originally founded in 1554 as a colonial settlement, it began to grow around 1850, gaining wealth from surrounding coffee plantations. Its population first exceeded one million in 1928, and large-scale redevelopment of the centre took place in the 1930s to address the pressure of rapid growth.

volume of commercial traffic, and more regular plots of land that, as Mumford (1961) has pointed out, were shaped by the interests of developers looking to make a profit from their purchase and sale.

Many commentators in the nineteenth and early twentieth centuries suggested that urbanisation produced a new kind of social as well as a physical environment. Ferdinand Tonnies (1855–1936), for example, argued that urbanisation transformed the basis and character of social contacts. He charted a shift from *Gemeinschaft* or community, characterised by close-knit, personal and stable relationships between friends and neighbours and based on a clear understanding of social position, to *Gesellschaft* or association, based on transitory, instrumental relationships that were specific to a particular setting and purpose and, in this sense, did not involve the whole person. Similar themes are evident in the writings of Georg Simmel (1858–1918), who described the emergence of a district urban personality. He argued that the pace, complexity and segmentation of modern life increased the number of non-intimate, standard relationships, such as those based on legal rules or the exchange of money. It also fostered a more calculating and self-conscious state of mind, with city dwellers often adopting a blasé attitude towards the multiplicity of sights and people they encountered. In other words, city life produced both a greater sense of individuality and a sharper sense of detachment.

The fluid, large-scale and often impersonal character of modern societies renders impression management – how we present ourselves to others – a highly significant but problematic endeavour. Difficulties arise out of 'the pluralisation of lifeworlds' – a diversification of both the contexts of social interaction and the types of encounter that can take place (Berger, 1974). This puts a strain on our skills of what Erving Goffman (1969) calls 'self-presentation'. Goffman argues that acting is an appropriate metaphor for the conduct of modern life, since it requires us to play a variety of roles, each with a different stage and script. He highlights some of the problems of identity we face in the modern world. In the kind of social environment described above, people are forced to reflect constantly on who they are and how they fit into the world around them.

QUESTIONS	How many people have you made contact with in the last 24 hours? What was the nature of those contacts? What proportion could be described as intimate? What do your answers to these questions suggest about the nature of living in modernity?

BOX 2.6 Public and private worlds: the impact of mass media

The development of mass media, notably books, newspapers, cinema and broadcasting, offered a new kind of public sphere. For example, it was a major factor in establishing nations as 'imagined communities' (Anderson, 1983). Mass media allowed people to participate in events and communities over long distances. One has only to think of modern democratic elections, World Cup soccer, national lotteries or royal weddings to realise the intensity with which we can share in these electronically mediated events, as 'one people'.

Interestingly, the most powerful contemporary media span the public and the private. Television, radio and newspapers bring the outside world into our homes. The times of programmes also help to set the routine of life within the home, and their content provides us with something to talk about around the dinner table – that is if we are not eating in front of the TV! The Internet has the opposite effect, allowing the individual (usually) to gain access to a wealth of information, entertainment and pleasure from anywhere in the world at any time of day or night.

Being private

Early analysts of the Great Transformation viewed developments such as urbanisation, industralisation and the growth of bureaucracy as giving rise to a society of impersonal relationships. This, however, was only part of the story: intimacy and familiarity did not disappear but instead became compartmentalised in a new private sphere. In fact, an important element of modernity was a sharper distinction between the public and private worlds. Nowhere was this more apparent than in attitudes towards home, family and marriage.

In some respects, modernity limited the role of the household. Industrial capitalism robbed it of much of its productive function, separating resting-place and workplace. Other changes, such as the establishment of formal education systems, took away some

BOX 2.7 Private rituals, public pressures

The modern home may have been screened from the outside world by ideas of privacy but this does not mean that it has been unaffected by public pressures. Housing design in the nineteenth and early twentieth centuries reflected the distinction between public and private, and between masculine and feminine space, with the front of the house being kept for 'best' even in small, working-class terraced houses where space was at a premium. The parlour, for example, was kept for formal entertaining and displayed the socio-economic status of the household, while everyday domestic activities took place in the female sphere at the back of the house, where the children were also confined (Madigan and Munro, 1991).

New domestic technologies – time-saving devices such as the vacuum cleaner – also created new pressures for women, who bore responsibility for domestic labour and presenting a 'respectable face' to other members of the local community. Carolyn Steedman (1986, p.36) recalls how, at a young age in a working-class household, 'I liked the new vacuum cleaner at first, because it meant no longer having to do the stairs with a stiff brush. But in fact it added to my Saturday work because I was expected to clean more with the new machine'.

Figure 2.3 The increasing range and popularity of domestic gadgets in the 1950s did little to change perceptions about who was responsible for housework.

of the household's responsibility for socialising the young. Far from withering away, however, the household was given a new significance as 'home', thanks largely to a domestic ideal that portrayed the family as a crucial site of intimacy (Crow and Allen, 1990). In the words of one of its supporters, the modern family came to be viewed as 'a haven in a heartless world' – a source of support and security in an often impersonal and threatening social environment (Lasch, 1979). However, some critics argue that the modern preoccupation with the intimate family is itself 'anti-social', sucking life out of the world that lies beyond the boundaries of home: 'As a bastion against a bleak society it has made that society bleak' (Barrett and McIntosh, 1982, p. 80).

Home life often fails to live up to the aspirations of the domestic ideal. Feminists have shown how notions of privacy have masked violence, abuse and exploitation. They also point out that the modern household depends on the unending labour of women, which, thanks to ideologies of domesticity and motherhood, has not been fully acknowledged or rewarded.

CONNECTIONS The issue of gender and domesticity has been high on the feminist agenda in the study of the family. For an account of this, see Chapter 9, pages 248–53, and Chapter 6, pages 141–3.

Living in postmodernity?

So far we have focused on the development of modern social forms and their impact on everyday experience over an extensive time period. We have seen how the global processes of modernity have reworked all aspects of social life, transforming patterns of social behaviour and people's perception of themselves and their relationships with others. The defining characteristics of the modern experience have been diversity and dynamism.

Since the 1970s, however, new social trends have prompted some commentators to suggest that another Great Transformation is under way – heralding an era of **postmodernity** (Lyotard, 1984; Bauman, 1989). We shall discuss this much contested claim in later chapters of this book, and particularly in Chapter 19, but it is worth considering here a number of recent changes that have provoked debate on the nature and future of modernity:

Postmodernity
For its supporters, the transformation of social, cultural economic and political arrangements that has taken society beyond modernity.

- Intellectual life is now dominated by a crisis of faith in the major modern ideas of science, progress and reason; individuals have lost their trust in the ability of science to give them answers.
- The world-wide development of capitalism has undermined the power of national governments and corporations to regulate economic life. The new international division of labour means that manufacturing now takes place on a global scale, with much industrial production being conducted outside the West. In Europe and the US, service-sector employment has become the mainstay of the post-industrial economy. Individual workers are now subject to global forces way beyond their and their managers' control.
- The size of productive units has shrunk, and mass production has been replaced by more flexible systems that allow a greater range and faster turnover of goods. Mass marketing has similarly been replaced by niche marketing, and consumerism has stimulated a proliferation and multiplicity of identities and lifestyles.
- Rapid population growth and urbanisation is taking place in the Third World, while, in the First World, cities are in decline.

- Transnational economic, cultural and political activities are undermining the influence of the nation-state. Political ideas that once attracted the support of millions (such as conservatism, socialism) are being replaced by political opportunism and pragmatism, and by new social movements centred on social issues and identity politics.
- A more diverse range of family forms has emerged, with new values of intimacy and more individualistic notions of selfhood.

What does this mean at the everyday level? At its most extreme, it means that post-modern individuals are no longer 'unified subjects', they no longer possess fixed, stable, permanent and coherent identities but are increasingly composed of fragmented, multiple and sometimes contradictory identities. The challenge that postmodernism presents to sociology is that postmodern social actors may either not wish to or are denied the opportunity to develop a coherent sense of self.

What is clear is that the interplay between modernity and its global dynamics, and postmodernity and identity have become of central interest to sociologists. Talk of the onset of postmodernity is further evidence that life in the contemporary world is as rapidly changing, exciting, threatening and disorientating as it has ever been. Many of the old certainties are going, forcing us to (re)evaluate social developments and our own place in them. This means that we require the skills and insights of sociology even more than ever, and in both the substantive and the more theoretical chapters of this book, we show how contemporary sociologists are developing new ways of exploring and making sense of society.

 Chapter summary

- The onset of modernity unleashed processes of global proportion – notably the development of industrial capitalism, the dominance of rational forms of thought and organisation, the extended reach of the nation-state, and major changes in social relationships and in people's sense of self – that had and continue to have a profound impact on the conduct of everyday life.
- A defining characteristic of modernity has been the continuing pace and scope of social change.
- The global processes of modernity have generated diverse local experiences.
- Some sociologists argue that we are now experiencing a second 'great transformation' as we move into the era of postmodernity.

 Questions to think about

- The division of history into pre-modern and modern suggests a sharp contrast between then and now. To what extent do you think that pre-modern forms survive in the modern world? Give specific examples to support your answer.
- To what extent do you agree with Bauman's suggestion that the Holocaust represented an advanced form of modernity? Give reasons for your response.
- In what ways could you be said to be living in a postmodern world? Provide examples from your own life to support your case.

Investigating further

Berman, Marshall (1983) *All That is Solid Melts into Air*, Verso.
    A classic account of the experience of modernity. Well worth dipping into.
Hall, Stuart and Bram Gieben (eds) (1992) *The Formations of Modernity*, Polity Press.
    A particularly useful starting point for thinking about modernity, with an
    emphasis on how modern societies have developed, and clear and accessible
    chapters on the Enlightenment, the modern state, class and gender, culture and
    imperialism.
Jervis, John (1998) *Exploring the Modern*, Blackwell.
    Like Berman, Jervis takes quite a cultural approach to modernity. You will find
    interesting chapters on imperialism, women, the urban experience,
    consumption, dress and so on.
Ritzer, George (2000) *The McDonaldisation of Society*, revised edition, Sage.
    Ritzer draws on Weber's theories of rationalisation and bureaucracy to produce
    an insightful analysis of contemporary forms of doing business, based on the
    fast-food chain.

3

Globalisation and modernity

CHAPTER CONTENTS

Aims of the chapter

This chapter introduces you to the concept of globalisation and discusses its roots in modernity. Globalisation has raised new issues for sociologists in a number of areas. This chapter shows how different sociologists have responded to this phenomenon in varying ways. It explores the tensions between the global and the local as they relate to economic, cultural and political processes.

By the end of the chapter, you should have an understanding of the following concepts and debates:

- Globalisation
- International division of labour
- Transnational corporations
- Post-Fordism

- Development
- Network society
- Cultural imperialism

Introduction

Capitalism
An economic system in which the means of production are privately owned and organised to accumulate profits within a market framework where labour is provided by waged workers.

Transnational corporations (TNCs)
Large companies with economic activities in more than one country and with the flexibility to shift resources and operations between locations globally to increase their competitive advantage.

As discussed in Chapter 2, sociology has been especially concerned with understanding the development of modern society and the impact of modernity. This has created a core set of interests that has informed the conceptual and applied work of sociologists for over a century. Modernity has been associated with the onset of industrialisation, the growth of **capitalism** (its inequalities and forms of conflict), and the appearance of an increasingly complex and differentiated institutional culture. The classical contributions of Marx, Weber and Durkheim (whose work will be discussed in more detail in Chapter 17) were, in their differing ways, devoted to improving our understanding of all these aspects of modernity. Engaged with its time, sociology could do no other than this. The great body of material that now makes up the sociological discipline has grown rich by addressing the issues set by the agenda of modernity.

However, an additional item emerged onto the sociological agenda at the turn of the twenty-first century that has posed new challenges for sociology. This too is tied to aspects of modernity, but it reflects changes to the contemporary temporal and spatial dimensions of the social world, of the boundaries of society. If sociology were to be created anew today, it is unlikely it would begin with the same set of issues that have dominated it since its birth in the nineteenth century. While it would undoubtedly explore industrialisation, gender and family relations, the emergence and maintenance of a legitimate nation-state, the cultural dimensions of class, ethnicity, community and so on, most if not all of these would have to be located in a new context – a global context.

The dimensions of modernity can only be mapped out properly today in global terms. The conventional assumption that these features can be understood within the spatial and socio-cultural boundaries of countries such as the UK, Australia or Japan, will no longer do. The dynamics of modernity have made the world grow smaller, and countries have become increasingly interlinked. Time and space – and hence our sense of the local and the distant, the traditional and the strange – have taken on new meaning in the context of electronic and satellite communication, **transnational corporations** and international, even global, political authorities (such as the European Union and the United Nations). The key term for this is the **globalisation** of modernity.

> **Globalisation**
> The process whereby political, social, economic and cultural relations increasingly take on a global scale, and which has profound consequences for individuals' local experiences and everyday lives.

This contrast between the conventional and the newly emergent global sociological agenda is summarised in Box 3.1. The first list of concerns highlights some – though not all – of the issues that have been central to sociological debate. Note the key themes of industrialism, capitalism, class and nation-state. Note too that each of these (and other) features has often been equated with and understood in terms of the social boundaries defined by nations: 'society' was British society, Swedish society or whatever. The second list presupposes a global context for industrialisation, capitalism and culture, and patterns of linkage that are not contained by, and so perhaps threaten, the conventional national boundaries of society. Note too the attention to new, non-class forms of social protest and change (such as radical ecology), indicative of new socio-political dynamics at work in society today.

Of course, the second of the two lists has not fallen from the sky: the agenda it sets out and the concerns this creates arise from our interrogation of the traditional sociological agenda and an awareness that it needs to be modified. For example, it is only because so much importance has been given to the role of the nation-state in the past that we can understand the challenge that the globalisation of modernity poses to the legitimacy and autonomy of the state today.

BOX 3.1 | Changing sociological agendas

Some key concerns of classical sociology:

- The growth and impact of industrialisation.
- The development of capitalism and class conflict.
- The emergence and legitimation of the nation-state.
- The growing complexity and differentiation of social institutions.
- The congruence between 'society' and 'nation'.
- The importance of class-based sources of protest and change.

Some key concerns of contemporary sociology:

- The emergence of global industrialisation.
- Capitalism as a world economy.
- The growth of transnational economic and political structures.
- The compression of time and space.
- The legitimacy and role of nation-bound political institutions.
- The origins and impact of (non-class) social movements.

This chapter provides a summary of the sociological debates on the global dynamics of modernity. The latter may seem to be about abstract and remote processes that have little bearing on our lives at the local level, but nothing could be further from the truth, since the very dynamics of globalisation mean that its dimensions operate at both the global level and the local level at the same time. People who work for large transnational corporations may find that, despite achieving high levels of productivity, they are to be made redundant as part of a world-wide restructuring of the firm. Our TV programmes are sponsored by foreign companies whose products are available in the high street. The Bush administration's refusal in 2001 to endorse the Kyoto agreement on global warming could have major consequences for local climates everywhere, as the US is continuing to pump out greenhouse gases. Wars in other parts of the world provoke mass migrations of people who create new pressures and dynamics in the communities in which they choose to settle. Our homes cost more when interest rates rise because of international currency speculation via electronic financial exchanges. These are just some illustrations of the effect of global dynamics at the local level: they shape a society's labour market and its pattern of inequality, its consumption, its health, its political stability and legitimacy, and the life chances of its households and families.

CONNECTIONS Consideration of the media at the global level is central to the contemporary study of communications. See Chapter 12, pages 333–43, for a discussion of the relationship between new communications technologies and globalisation.

Sociology is exploring such global/local processes and developing new concepts and new research questions to bring them to life. Why has modernity led to the globalisation of social life? In what sense is this process unique to the modern era? Is it caused by one or many factors? How do people in different nations respond to global processes? Is globalisation uniform or uneven in its effect? How can nation-states sustain their power as socio-political systems when supranational and transnational organisations and agencies threaten to undermine them? Are people at the local level threatened by globalisation? What can individuals do to influence developments at the global level? Does this explain the growing attractiveness of regionalism, ethnicity, the community and tradition as protection against a culturally homeless global society? Finally, and most importantly, in what sense are these global processes not just international but truly global? The term international implies a pattern or set of relationships between discrete nations or countries. 'Global' implies a system of relations that cannot be reduced to or explained in terms of the interests or activities of particular nations. To say that there are global structures and processes is to imply that there are new global phenomena that supersede and shape international and national levels of social behaviour.

QUESTION Look at the last item of clothing/footwear you bought and identify where it came from. What are the global processes that brought this item to you?

Globalisation and modernity

In the previous chapter, we saw that modernity was, and for many still is, equated with progress. Moreover, such progress has often been identified with Western ideas and political culture. That is, when we think of modernity, we tend to think of Western modernity. The collapse of the Soviet Union in 1991, its subsequent dissolution and the apparent demise of socialism throughout Europe were seen by some as the inevitable result of the historical triumph of free-market capitalism and liberal democracy on a world scale. One commentator even spoke of this as heralding 'the end of history' (Fukuyama, 1989b), in the sense that history thus far had been some sort of trial of strength between liberal capitalism and everything else. However, despite the sustained growth of the world economy in the 1990s and early 2000s, the trials and tribulations of world capitalism since late 1989 – growing protectionism, currency crises, the decline of once strong economies, the threat of recession – make triumphalist declarations of history's end look a little premature.

Sociologists have, however, recognised that modernity does have certain global characteristics, even if these do not necessarily add up to some liberal-capitalist new world age. Giddens (1990a) has developed one of the more detailed discussions of the dynamics of modernity that together produce a globalised modernity. That is, from this point of view, the globalisation of social life is both unique to modernity and an expression of it. Chapter 2 discussed some of the ways in which people experience modernity and sociologists theorise about it. Giddens has shown that the spread of the features of modernity on a global scale has been made possible by the play of three processes unique to modernity:

- The separation of time and space.
- The disembedding of social systems.
- The reflexive ordering of social relations.

Each of these processes involves, in different ways, a going beyond of the here-and-now, beyond the physical and temporal constraints of immediate social relations. Each encourages a spreading, an opening, a diffusion of relationships. In this way, modernity carries within itself the basis for its own diffusion and installation at the global level. Let us look briefly at each of these three features in turn.

The separation of time and space

As we saw in the previous chapter, in pre-modern society, the time of day or season of the year was directly related to a particular space or locale within which time could be marked out. This was often based on the rhythm of agricultural life, where the time of day was marked by the tasks that had to be completed. There was neither the need nor the technology – the mechanical clock – to refer to time in any other way. Standard clock time and its universal application, based on Greenwich Mean Time, allowed time to be separated from any specific locale. This was followed by the universal standardisation of calendar years and dates. Birthday cards, international newspapers, currency deals, and international travel timetables all presuppose this global time frame. Global space has its own framework in world maps whose grid of lines of longitude and latitude privilege no particular locale. As a result of these developments, time and space are no longer jointly tied to place, to tradition, to face-to-face interaction. Global communications via computer networks are devoid of both face-to-face interaction and locale: some foresee the emergence of 'electronic tribes' operating in cyberspace and requiring the development of a whole new type of social anthropology that can understand the electronic virtual community.

The disembedding of social systems

This second dimension of modernity, which encourages its globalisation, follows directly from the first. Giddens (1990a, p.21) describes this as the 'lifting out of social relations from local contexts of interaction'. In advanced modern society, the social relations that allow us, for example, to exchange money are not tied to any particular instance of exchange or transaction: it is the disembedded invisible institutional relations that lie behind money – whatever particular form it takes – that make it acceptable. It is the liquidity of the banks, the assumption that credit cards are credit-worthy, that cheques will be cleared and so on that sustain the billions of face-to-face and remote transactions conducted every day. Another important form of social relation that is routine in our daily lives is expertise – that of a doctor, mechanic, or plumber, for example. Despite crises such as the BSE crisis discussed in Chapter 1, we still call on experts to assist in specific situations and we trust their judgement, not because we know them personally but because of the distant, disembedded nature of their authoritative knowledge. Money and expertise are two examples of the social relations found only in modern social systems.

The reflexive ordering of social relations

Finally – again as we saw in Chapter 1 – modern social actors are reflexive individuals, monitoring and questioning their own behaviour and that of others, recognising both social constraint and the possibilities of social change open to them. Individuals engage in risk analysis when they choose to act, rather than bank on the certainties of the past. This **reflexivity** is enhanced by and in turn helps to reinforce the two dimensions of modernity sketched out above. The security and parochialism of traditional life are replaced by the options and uncertainties of a modern culture whose reference point is both global and local. One can see how these three dynamics of modernity facilitate and help create the globalised context within which and through which we experience the world. Reflexive tourists sitting on beaches in Montego Bay, Provence, Vancouver or Sydney worry about contracting skin cancer because of the hole in the ozone layer; calculate the price of the hotel bill yet again as international currency rates change; sit by the pool and devour the latest blockbuster, whose mass readership depends on globally recognised themes, detail and storyline; and with a sense of foreboding read about the latest tour company collapse and wonder whether they will ever make it home.

Giddens' account of the globalising processes of modernity suggests that four broad components make up the world system and give it its basic institutional shape. Thus the global system:

- Is made up of nation-states.
- Operates in a world capitalist economy.
- Creates an international division of labour.
- Is dominated by a world military order.

While Giddens has given a clear picture of the dynamics and dimensions of globalisation in broad terms, there are those who argue for a more historically based explanation of how globalisation has appeared. For example, Robertson (1992) sets out the various phases that have marked its development, ranging from the situation in the fifteenth century, when there was a very low degree of global density, to that in the present, where globalisation is both extensive and complex. He describes the phases as follows:

- *The germinal phase* (1400–1750): characterised by the growth of new national communities, the widespread influence of Catholicism, new conceptions of the individual, and the birth of modern geography and the calendar.
- *The incipient phase* (1750–1802): characterised (especially in Europe) by the emergent nation-states, international trade, regulation and legislation, and the dominance of the West.
- *The take-off phase* (1870s–1920s): characterised by a strong notion of the modern ideal towards which all societies should aspire, the emergence of global communication, the establishment of standard international time zones and almost global acceptance of the Gregorian calendar, the organisation of international events (such as the Olympic Games), and the onset of global warfare (the First World War).
- *The struggle-for-**hegemony** phase* (1920–1960s): characterised by conflict between states for power and leadership in the world, attempts to control conflict through the development of the United Nations, the emergence of two superpower blocs and the Cold War, the nuclear age and the growing poverty of the Third World.
- *The uncertainty phase* (1960s–1990): characterised by a new awareness of threats to the global environment and a challenge to materialist values, the end of the Cold War and

Reflexivity
The process of examining, questioning and monitoring the behaviour of the self and others, promoted by the social conditions and experiences of late modernity.

Hegemony
Refers to consent or acceptance of an ideology, regime or whole social system. Full hegemony exists when a social order is accepted as natural and normal.

of the superpower blocs, and the strengthening of local nationalism correlated with increasing global cultural patterns and communication processes, post-socialism and the resurgence of traditional beliefs, such as Islam.

Although Robertson and Giddens approach globalisation in different ways, they share, as do most sociologists, the view that the dynamics of contemporary globalisation are not reducible to what goes on at the level of the nation-state. In other words, the global whole is greater than the sum of its parts, and it has a dynamic that will continue to create social, economic and political problems as well as opportunities for individual countries. There exist, then, social actors, such as transnational corporations (for example, Ford, Siemens, Exxon and Hoffman La Roche) that are only found at the global level. As Harvey (1990) notes, the massive corporations that operate globally are not indifferent to where they locate their research, development and production activities. In fact, it is precisely because they have the technical capacity to orchestrate their affairs globally (through electronic and related communication systems) that they are able to

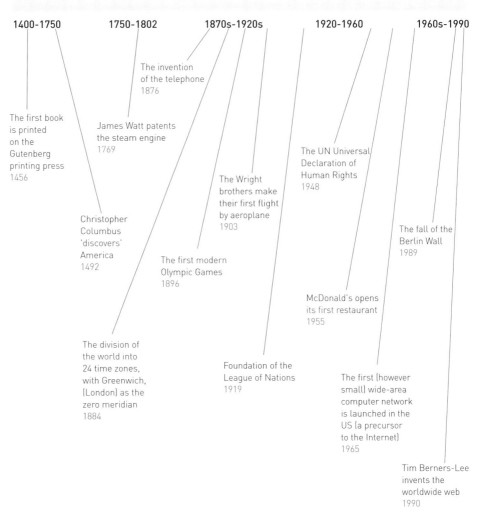

Figure 3.1   Selected milestones in the globalisation of the world

choose where in the global space to set up plants in order to take advantage of local factors such as cheap labour.

In the rest of this chapter, we shall examine three aspects of the global system – the economic, the cultural and the political – from a sociological perspective. This system, as we stressed above, is unequal and uneven in its effects. The effort to understand the nature of globalisation has, not surprisingly, led to debates and disagreements among social scientists. We shall discuss these briefly to see whether any clear conclusions can be drawn about the power and significance of globalising processes.

> **QUESTION**   Next time you surf the Internet, take note of the location of the web sites you visit and find out the time in each place. In what sense do you think you are experiencing 8a shrinking of time and space, and does it seem real to you? Give reasons for your answer.

Debating globalisation

A comprehensive account of the differing interpretations of globalisation can be found in Held *et al.* (1999), who identify three broad approaches to understanding global-isation – those adopted by the 'hyperglobalists', the 'sceptics' and the 'trans-formationalists'.

The hyperglobalists

According to authors such as Ohmae (1990), the tide of globalization is overwhelming and cannot be resisted by policies that attempt to protect a country's economy or preserve its local culture. Instead, nations should welcome the economic gains offered by free trade and open competition. If a nation wishes to prosper and not to be impoverished by competition, then people and their governments must be prepared to price their labour accordingly and be flexible in terms of skills and working practices. More creatively, they must seek some or other comparative advantage – some area of production or services where they can offer something better or cheaper than the rest of the world. Those who fail do any of this, or try to protect their current way of life, will lose out in the new borderless world.

Furthermore, there is a unifying dimension to globalisation as we are all drawn together into a common global culture (symbolised by McDonald's food or Madonna's music). The fact that this culture is commercially defined and driven makes it part of the restless expansion of global competitive capitalism that is the driving force behind globalisation. Nothing can stop this process, so we should all participate and try to profit from it – and as we do, we shall help to homogenise the world, leading to increasingly similar ways of life.

For those who celebrate this vision of the future, it is an optimistic scenario of material prosperity and peace, where nation-state rivalries give way to the dynamics of the free market. In some ways, it is a return to the mid-nineteenth-century idea that military rivalry belonged to an old outdated world where wealth and power came from the land, leading to territorial disputes and wars. Free capitalist trade would bring prosperity through peaceful exchange and a stable rule of law, so contracts would be honoured. In other words, wars were a hangover from prehistory, and capitalism and liberal democracy would bring peace. Fukuyama's vision of the 'end of history' (1989) is a classic example. The intimate relationship between war and capitalism throughout the twentieth century never seems to trouble such theorists.

Just as importantly, these hyperglobalist assumptions can justify fatalism or inaction by national governments (Ohmae, 1995). If global competition is so strong, and global commercial culture is irresistible, then the only thing to do is to ensure that the nation's workforce is sufficiently skilled and flexible to adapt and survive in a competitive world. Education becomes a high priority so that individuals can make themselves adaptable. This stance of acceptance and adaptation replaces any attempt to change the decisions of global corporations for the sake of national interest. In 2000–1, this was a key concern in the UK, as major car plants were closed (despite their being modernised and productive) in response to global overcapacity in the car industry. The national government appeared to feel powerless to resist in any way.

The sceptics

Sceptics generally feel that this sort of weak response to globalisation is profoundly mistaken (see, for example, Hirst and Thompson, 1996). They argue that there is nothing new about international links and interdependence –indeed, the colonial empires of the nineteenth century imposed much stronger links that were political as well as economic. These writers strongly reject the idea that there is a unified global market for trade and investment, with the uniform prices that competition should bring. Instead they argue that the world is increasingly divided into large trading blocs (Europe, Asia–Pacific, and North America), within which there are powerful national economies and important cultural divides. They strongly reject the notion that there is a process of unification going on, creating political and cultural similarity on a global scale. The end of the Cold War brought fragmentation through nationalism, or splits into rival trading blocs (such as the European Union, whose policies have damaged poorer food-producing nations). In such an unequal and fragmented world, there are still important choices to be made by governments in respect of economic policy and welfare. Free markets need not rule supreme.

The transformationalists

Transformationalists such as David Held *et al.* (1999) and Castells (1996) reject both the sceptics' attempt to play down the significance of globalisation and the hyperglobalist vision of free-market capitalism in a shared global culture. For these theorists the unprecedented scale, speed and intensity of global connections has greatly broadened the scope for global links and interactions. Global links are spreading wider, and are faster, more frequent and more intense in their impact than those of previous political and military empires, leading to the transformation of social, economic and political institutions as well as knowledge and culture. There is a big change going on, and it should not be played down.

This does not mean it is easy to forecast the nature of changes and their consequences. Social scientists have used new imagery to portray the new world (such as Castells' 'network society', which draws inspiration from the Internet). But there is no sense that a single new social structure is emerging, or a single sociological model that can portray the results. Instead, globalisation is producing division and difference as much as similarity and integration. Powerfully integrative elements are emerging, such as global forms of governance in the United Nations and elsewhere. At the same time, fragmentation and conflict are occurring, as states split apart into new nation-states and separatist movements flourish.

Links and interactions bind all the people of the world into a single global system, but this is not a one-world society or culture. Furthermore, this linked system is highly inegalitarian in terms of wealth, power and information. As the sceptics note, new forms of stratification are emergng between nations and within them. What is more, the boundaries around different kinds of power (legal, military, economic and so on) do not coincide – national sovereignty need not coincide with economic power or cultural influence (Bull, 1977). This is an important break with the nation-state system of modernity.

Politics now has various layers, from global and transnational measures to localised links (with local regions in Europe obtaining money directly from the EU). It is often argued that the power of nation-states has been hollowed out as a result, with shifts of power to multiple layers of government, and new kinds of public and private organisation gaining great power at the transnational level (such as business corporations, regulatory agencies, charities and many others).

If the tranformationalists are correct, then we are moving rapidly beyond the social structures that characterised nineteenth- and twentieth-century modernity. Whatever label we give to this – postmodernity, globalised modernity, or the network society – we can be sure that globalisation matters. We shall now look at some aspects of its impact in more detail.

The globalisation of production: transnational corporations

A central feature of the contemporary world is the globalisation of industrial production, a process that grew at an astonishing pace in the last decade of the twentieth century and continues in the first decade of the twenty-first. A simple indicator of this is the growth of foreign direct investment by First World transnational corporations (TNCs), which in the period of 1980–90 was four times faster than the growth of the gross national product of these corporations' home countries. TNCs from the three strongest regions in the world, the US, Japan and Europe, now operate on a global stage. The greater the globalisation of their activities, the more TNCs have to be recognised as placeless, associated with no one country. Governments in these three areas now find it difficult to rely on TNCs to act in the national interest and invest locally. In the 1980s in the UK, a disproportionate amount of manufacturing investment came from Japanese rather than UK, companies, while UK companies in turn invested overseas.

We should not underestimate the power and scale of TNCs today: they form what Sklair (1991) calls a new 'transnational capitalist class' operating within the world capitalist economy. They have three priorities:

- To keep production costs as low as possible.
- To target production at rapidly changing markets.
- To stay innovative through the latest scientific and technological developments.

This last point means that TNCs' new products are increasingly science-based and related to new areas of research in bio-technology, materials science and electronics. Acting globally requires TNCs to give their subsidiaries more freedom to respond quickly and flexibly to changing conditions and markets. The goal is to achieve what has

Figure 3.2 TNCs in the information industry not only stimulate the global economy through their own productivity but also help to remove constraints on the business activities of other multinationals.

been called 'lean production', a flexible global capacity that relies on rapid computer-based communication and management information systems.

One result of this, of course, is that work and the way it is experienced by workers has become very different. The workforce has been more or less divided into members of the primary labour market – those in relatively highly skilled, secure, well-paid, typically male-dominated jobs with good career prospects – and those who make up the secondary labour market, involving lower-paid, insecure, low-skilled and low-mobility jobs, often occupied by women, working-class youths or ethnic minorities. The traditional relationship between the firm people work for and the local community in which they live has become increasingly meaningless, as TNCs' investment and employment policies operate according to global rather than local agendas.

Sociologists have explored the impact of this new globalised system of production in various ways. Some – especially those working in political economy (for example, Froebel *et al.*, 1980; Sanderson, 1985) – have focused on the way in which labour has been reorganised globally, such that there is now a new international division of labour, in which TNCs take advantage of low-wage labour in less developed countries by establishing 'world market factories' free from union involvement, often employing cheap female labour. A second approach has focused on the way in which the Fordist system of production has been superseded by a post-Fordist one in the globalised modern world. As we saw in Chapter 2, **Fordism** refers to the system of mass production inspired by the Ford car company's assembly-line process, producing identical cars for a mass market. Adopted by a wide range of industrial sectors, Fordism was commonplace during the postwar period in First World economies.

Fordism
A form of industrial economy based on mass production and mass marketing that was prevalent in the postwar period. The techniques and processes were pioneered by Henry Ford in the manufacture and sale of Ford motor cars.

BOX 3.2 From Fordism to global post-Fordism

Fordism:

- Mass production of standardised products.
- Strong, centralised control over labour.
- Assembly-line system.
- Mass production for mass consumption.
- Oriented to First World markets.

Post-Fordism:

- Rapid modification of products for new markets.
- Identification of specific target groups for products.
- Specialisation in specific product areas.
- More flexible assembly-type production systems.
- Global orientation.

Post-Fordism
The use of sophisticated computer-controlled production systems, with an emphasis on flexibility and the production of specialised goods tailored to meet the demands of a competitive world economy.

Post-Fordism emerged during the 1970s in response to growing competitiveness in the world economy. This was especially associated with Japanese and South-East Asian enterprises. The more traditional, longer established TNCs found it necessary to restructure themselves in order to face the competition from these new centres of capitalism. The era of 'flexible specialisation' arrived, whereby companies turned over new products more quickly, shed large numbers of long-serving blue-collar workers and moved into smart, high-tech production for a global market with highly diverse consumers. Automated, computer-controlled and networked manufacturing systems – fed with a continual flow of information from research and development departments, market intelligence staff and sales personnel – can fine-tune manufacturing to meet orders as they arrive, the so-called **just-in-time production** system, developed in Japan.

CONNECTIONS For a description of the just-in-time production system, see Chapter 11, pages 309–10. Chapter 12 offers a more in-depth discussion of transnational media corporations.

Just-in-time production
A finely balanced and controlled manufacturing production system designed to produce goods to meet demand as and when required.

Implications

These developments have at least three implications. The power, global orientation and exploitative ability and practices of TNCs means that they have a strong effect on national and international employment patterns and the development of new technologies. Moreover, their 'placelessness' can create serious problems for national governments, which can find it extremely difficult to rein-in and control firms for the sake of the national interest. When controls are imposed – by declining First World or disadvantaged Third World countries – TNCs can simply avoid them by moving part or all of their activities to another area in their global arena.

Finally, and this last point is of particular relevance when one considers controls of the environmental impact of TNC production: companies that are thought of as 'green' in Germany, the US, the UK and elsewhere can be very polluting overseas, or simply relocating prohibited activities to less stringently regulated areas, often poorer countries. Yet at the 1992 Rio Earth Summit in Brazil and during the Kyoto discussions in 2000, the role of and control over TNCs in respect of pollution was almost completely neglected by politicians. Indeed, the refusal by the US to ratify the Kyoto agreement followed the election victory of President Bush in 2000, who is seen as very sympathetic to the interests of TNCs.

In what ways could national governments attempt to control the activities of TNCs? Do you think it is possible to do so? Do you think it is desirable to do so?

 ## The globalisation of culture

The global spread of capitalism entails the spread of commodities that, while finely tuned to local markets, carry messages and advertising slogans that deliberately reach out to as wide a market as possible. One only has to think of the global familiarity of Lara Croft, Nike, Microsoft and Gap to realise how successful global marketing has become. Does this spread of global commodities imply a globalisation of culture – especially a Western, US-dominated one?

BOX 3.3 The world's top ten brands

1. McDonald's
2. Coca-Cola
3. Disney
4. Kodak
5. Sony
6. Gillette
7. Mercedes-Benz
8. Levis
9. Microsoft
10. Marlboro

Numbered among the key ingredients for creating a successful brand are:

- Brand exposure: visibility in the public eye at the global level.
- Brand experience: successful brands are seen as a means to an experience, not merely to an end.

- Brand essence: the ability to cross cultures, appealing to consumers at the universal level.
- Brand lexicon: creating a symbol that expresses a value or idea.

Source: PR Mania.

Cultural imperialism

One answer to the latter question is provided by neo-Marxist sociologists such as Tunstall (1977) and Becker *et al.* (1987), who argue that the strength of world capitalism is directly related to its ability to sell not merely goods but also ideas, and more generally ideologies that sustain our levels of consumption. **Consumerism** and the consumer culture it reflects has a powerful grip on societies throughout the world, including the less developed and post-socialist countries of Eastern and Central Europe. One of the first Western-type stores to open in post-socialist states was a boutique selling Nike and Reebok sport/fashion shoes: highly profitable, easy to import and making a very obvious statement about 'being modern'.

Consumerism
A culture centred on the promotion, sale and acquisition of consumer goods.

The growth of consumerism has been heavily reliant on the growth of transnational mass media, dominated by firms such as Sony, Sky TV, CBS and so on. These try to reproduce at the global level what they have succeeded in establishing at the national: a large, hungry market for goods, especially in leisure and service sector goods. The mass media have hugely expanded in terms of both the scope of the audiences they reach and the range of media available to those audiences.

Exposure to and consumption of media products has become an integral part of the everyday lives of most members of contemporary society, and for those in the West the media occupy a considerable proportion of their leisure time, providing them to a considerable extent with their picture of the wider world. Television, for example, is today the largest and most pervasive medium, providing a vehicle for the delivery of a range of satellite and terrestrial media products. Television is the principal leisure activity of most adults and children, the 'organiser' of their entertainment and social life, missed when unavailable, and a source of information and ideas that are widely regarded – as in TV news – as authoritative and trustworthy.

Given their vast audience, the media are important agencies of **socialisation**. They constitute an institutionalised channel for the distribution of social knowledge and hence are a potentially powerful instrument of social control (as well as social critique), sustaining or challenging the status quo. Much of our knowledge of the world is gained from the media, especially in respect of people, places, events and how to make sense of the world more generally – how to interpret the current state of the economy, why the police should or should not be armed, what is happening in Africa and so on. At school, work, university or in the pub, last night's TV programmes make for lively but easy conversation, a conversation in which, usually, a broad consensus forms about what went on and its meaning. The globalised media allow us to travel without moving from our chairs, and – when we actually travel abroad – to receive our home programmes on satellite TV or the Internet. Although media products are no doubt entertaining, they also help to construct and reproduce a broad range of social norms and values.

Socialisation
The ongoing process whereby individuals learn to conform to society's prevailing norms and values (see *norms* and *values*).

CONNECTIONS For further discussions of the media, turn to Chapter 11, pages 323–6, and Chapter 12, pages 328–53.

A key aspect of the globalisation of the media is that it requires the existence of globalised media corporations. Indeed, there has been a concentration of media ownership, in major corporations such as Time Warner, News Corporation and Reuters. While these TNCs might make us more informed about the world, they also structure and package the world they present to us in certain ways, and most obviously in such a way that we are likely to go out and buy something – be this merchandise attached to a programme, or other consumption goods more generally.

These massive firms depend on new information systems and communication technologies (such as fibre-optic cable) to condense, pack, transmit and unpack information around the world. While the infrastructural cost of building these media technologies is so great that it can only be borne by the most powerful firms, growing public access to communication technologies such as the Internet means that ordinary users will be able to set their own agenda and build up their own audiences and constituencies through 'virtual communities'. Indeed, this is already happening and it is something that the major corporations are keen to control, typically by ratcheting up the cost of use. More generally, attempts by developing countries to develop their own media agencies have made little headway, as the renewal in 1994–95 of the General Agreement on Tariffs and Trade (GATT) has allowed media giants to flood local markets. The strength of globalised media firms is central to any argument about **cultural imperialism**, since these firms can swamp local media forms and messages, and thereby impose a set of values governing what should be regarded as good, stylish, right or wrong, just as they have long done in the West. In the process, local cultures are undermined. A key aspect of this is that global firms tend to use English as the 'world language' (Table 3.1).

Cultural imperialism
The aggressive promotion of Western culture based on the assumption that its value system is superior and preferable to those of non-Western cultures.

In historical terms, the ubiquity of English is relatively recent. It has much to do with the spread of the British Empire – upon whose land 'the sun never set'. But more important has been the massive post-1945 influence of the United States: the country with the largest commercial market in the world is responsible for the widespread

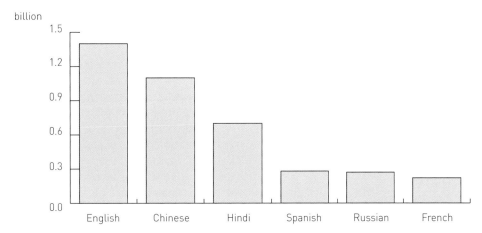

Figure 3.3 World use of the English language compared with the other main languages

diffusion of (American) English as well as burgers. In addition, the communications technology upon which global interconnectedness so heavily relies uses English for the bulk of its data information storage and exchange. The leisure industry is similarly tied to English, especially via the predominantly English-language music industry.

In short, many theorists believe that the dominance of Western cultural products will ensure the long-term survival of capitalist world markets for TNCs and their penetration of countries such as the **post-socialist states**.

While critics of cultural imperialism have highlighted the power of TNCs and the ideological baggage they impose on others, they have been criticised for failing to recognise that countries subject to TNC influence do not necessarily act as cultural sponges. Sklair (1991) argues that local cultures not only reinterpret or mediate transnational messages to modify their meaning, but may also counteract these messages with messages of their own. Sreberny-Mohammadi (1991), for example, shows how local culture mixes with and redefines global culture. She shows how local culture can prevail in the face of overseas ideologies, partly because the two are kept distinct by people at the local level: 'the trans-cultural mix of symbols is apparent when one young [Egyptian] girl organises a traditional religious feast yet defiantly wearing a denim skirt and earrings' (ibid., pp. 132–3).

Smith (1992), from a slightly different perspective, challenges the idea that cultural imperialism can lead to a homogeneous 'global culture'. The notion of global culture is a contradiction in terms, he suggests, since any culture must be rooted in a sense of community, history and heritage. He accepts that while the dynamics of transnational consumerism may prevail, sustaining a world capitalist economy, the suggestion that it could engender a common Western-centric culture is untenable. A global culture would, by definition, be universal and therefore would lack specific roots; it would be timeless since it would have no shared history; and it would be merely 'technical', having no capacity to inspire a sense of emotional commitment or loyalty to it from anyone. He, like many other sociologists, argues that globalisation has instead led people in many countries to renew their loyalty to the local, to tradition, ethnicity and national culture. For example, the Islamic culture of the Middle East has been presented as an alternative to both capitalism and **socialism**.

These criticisms of the cultural imperialism thesis suggest that we should expect a reawakening of local culture and local politics at the national and regional levels in

Post-socialist states
The former Soviet states of Central and Eastern European countries that since the 1980s have abandoned or adapted socialist practices and principles in favour of capitalist ones.

Socialism
An economic theory or system in which the means of production, distribution and exchange are owned collectively, usually mediated by the state.

response to the globalising pressures we all experience in our own immediate context. As Robins (1994, p. 197) says, 'It is the escalating logic of globalisation – paradoxically it seems – that is the force behind the resurgence and revaluation of local economic and cultural activity. What seems to be emerging is . . . a new global–local nexus.' This is being expressed in a variety of ways. For example, Robertson (1992, p. 171) points to the 'strong move across the world towards indigenous, communal medicine', but notes that 'much of it [is] encouraged by the World Health Organisation', a well-known international agency. Thus, 'in various parts of the world – Africa, Latin America, Asia and in many Islamic countries – while the drive towards the indigenisation of health care has taken the form of demands for local autonomy, there also appears to be a desire for local medicine to make a definite contribution to "world health" '.

Hence, the globalisation of modernity must not be taken to mean the globalisation of sameness or uniformity. On the contrary, the dynamics of globalisation, especially in its cultural dimensions, create greater pressure for local variety while at the same time incorporating communities into an uneven and unequal world economic system. That this system is first and foremost a capitalist one seems to have been reinforced by the collapse of socialism in Central and Eastern Europe. It is to this question of a changing global politics that we now turn.

Globalisation and political change

> " The seismic changes which have transformed Europe as a whole (from 1989 onwards) cannot be understood purely in terms of development within Europe. The fact that political union is even on the European agenda reflects deep-seated global economic and political trends as well as internal factors. At the heart of these changes has been the decline of the bi-polar system dominated by the two super-powers – the United States and the former Soviet Union. "

Palmer (1992, p.143) draws attention here to the key socio-political shifts that have occurred in the world since the 1980s, and especially since 1989, when the fall of the Berlin Wall led to the abandonment of Central and Eastern European socialism and eventually to the end of the Soviet Union itself. The Soviet leader, Gorbachev, had opened up the moribund socialist state to new internal debate and self-critique via *glasnost*, but he had failed to bring about the restructuring of the polity and economy, via *perestroika*, that could have secured a renewed socialist future. The changes that took place were rapid and in many ways revolutionary, in that fundamental social change and the removal of the incumbent political elites went hand in hand. Yet the models that have since been adopted by most post-socialist states are very close to those of Western liberal-democratic capitalist countries, rather than providing an alternative to either capitalism or over-centralised state socialism.

The most important strategic consequences of these dramatic changes were the end of the Cold War and the confirmation of the US as the sole superpower. This led to US president, George Bush Sr, to herald the arrival of a 'New World Order' founded on peace and prosperity for all. The first test of this New Order came quickly, as the Gulf War of 1990–1 inflamed the Middle East, with America leading a very wide range of allies, with the backing of the United Nations, in reversing Iraq's invasion of Kuwait by extreme force. However, the Gulf conflict raised no new principle of international relations: Iraq had violated the territory of a sovereign state and self-defence was Kuwait's right (albeit massively helped by the world's powers). Much more complex forms of world disorder, and new modes of intervention, began to emerge after 1991. Civil wars and 'ethnic cleansing' led to interventions in the former Yugoslavia that were partly concerned with regional security and partly linked to humanitarian concerns. In Africa, 'humanitarian' interventions in Somalia, along the lack of intervention as genocide took place in Rwanda, showed how far the New World Order was highly disorderly, and how unclear it was about who had the responsibility for international order, or on what grounds intervention was justified. The former Yugoslavia exposed the weakness of European security organisations, and of the United Nations. The exercise of real power was the issue – and this could only come from the USA or from US-led NATO.

These uncertainties and instabilities crystallised into crisis in the wake of the terrorist atrocities in New York on 11 September 2001. The lack of stability was cruelly demonstrated, as the world's sole superpower was exposed as vulnerable. International engagement in the 'war against terrorism' that followed was founded on US power and NATO – not on the authority of international law or of global institutions like the UN. Indeed, the new US president George W. Bush had previously disengaged from global cooperation on matters such as the environment.

Globalisation creates global interdependence, and international terrorism exposes this without pity. The necessity for global political responses is made obvious, even when the world's superpower tries to resist them.

It is now impossible to avoid the impact of globalisation on the nature of power and government. Most importantly, the globalisation of capitalism, the growth of international agencies and the strengthening of new political and economic unions, such as the European Union, have posed a major challenge to the sovereignty and autonomy of all nation-states.

All nation-states wish to have control over the social, economic and political activities within their borders, although this is not always secured. From a modernist perspective, control must – to be effective in the long term – be legitimated via some form of democratic accountability to the people. Although mature liberal democracies such as the Netherlands, the UK and France remain sovereign states led by representative governments, they have found it increasingly difficult to control the movement of capital, whether finance capital (as in currency speculation) or productive capital such as factory investment. As we saw earlier, TNCs' investment strategies often disregard the national interests of their home country and ship investment to overseas countries where labour is cheap. Moreover, national governments are required to abide by international laws, such as those regulating pollution at sea and in the air. This growing loss of control by the nation-state over its economic and political direction can pose severe legitimation problems for government, feeding as many calls for reactionary nationalism to reinstate cherished values as for demands for new democratic mechanisms through which people's voices can be heard at the local and international levels (Held, 1991). Power is leaking upwards and outwards from the nation-state or larger transnational political authorities as it is leaking downwards to regional, even local and ethnic, communities. Ironically, then, the political dynamics of modernity at the global level are challenging the institutional roots and structures of the nation-state that modernity helped to foster in the first place.

To summarise, there are two different but related processes at work in the world: on the one hand, the growing economic incorporation of countries into an unequal and unevenly successful capitalism; on the other, a tendency for political break-up at the local and regional levels, often fuelled by nationalist rivalry. This of course confirms the two dynamics of the global–local nexus mentioned above.

A new world order?

As we have just seen, the end of the Cold War in 1989 did not bring a new era of stability, but instead its collapse left a legacy of international disorder that is taking new and more dangerous forms as the twenty-first century unfolds. New forms of genocide, civil and ethnic conflict, nationalism and terrorism now haunt the world. We cannot see these as mere throwbacks to more primitive forms of rivalry and hatred. This is not a 'failure of civilisation' that allows barbarity to reassert itself. Instead we see a situation where no group in the world is willing to lie back while others have more power, wealth or autonomy. Political and military leaders claim to speak for their nation or people and demand the right to self-determination and sovereignty, even if this is at the expense of other ethnic groups or minority values and rights.

All this occurs in a world where competing political and religious value-systems are not subordinated to overarching authority. That authority was imposed in the past by imperialist nations (for example, Britain in the nineteenth and early twentieth century), or by rival superpowers (as during the late twentieth-century Cold War).

The dream since the United Nations was founded (in 1945) has been to replace this imposed order with an international consensus order, based on agreed values and laws. Even though nation-states would remain sovereign, they would bind themselves to common humanitarian values and rules, and enforce these collectively. Each decade since 1989 has shown how far we are from this dream. The United Nations has no independent military power to enforce its rulings. The nations that compose the UN differ vastly in power and are far from united in their core values, despite subscribing to the UN's declarations. When it is expedient to get legitimacy from UN resolutions (as in the Gulf War), powerful states will do so. Otherwise the UN is left watching NATO action in Afghanistan or Russia's in Chechnya.

If the Cold War brought stability through nuclear fear, the world since 1989 is constantly destabilised by global integration and local fragmentation. Policies that give free rein to market-based economic globalisation give no basis for any new stabilisation at the level of global politics, and leave the way open for localised conflicts. As we noted above, international terrorism has then been able to expose our globalised interdependence and our localised suffering.

Clearly, these developments in world politics have major links to other transformations: in technology, in trade, manufacturing and finance, and in culture. Social scientists are currently grappling with the task of comprehending the scale of these changes and making sense of them.

Figure 3.3 September 11, 2001: the beginning of a new world order?

Industrial and technological implications

In most advanced capitalist countries, the defence industry long relied on a steady demand for the research, development and production of new weapons systems, particularly in the UK and US, where almost half of total government expenditure on research was allocated to defence. From the early 1990s, however, this industry was affected by major structural and organisational problems, including the following:

- Dramatic growth in the cost of weapons systems.
- A need to shift from mechanical to electronic-based technology.
- A cut in state expenditure on defence.
- The opening of all defence contracts to civil competition.
- The collapse of the old certainties about 'the enemy' and thus the equipment needed to fight wars.

Hence, defence organisations found themseves on the defensive! There were calls for the end to open-ended contracts for massively expensive, overly sophisticated equipment, such as the US Stealth Fighter and, in late 1992, European fighter aircraft. State funding was predicted to decline rapidly, so much so that a discrete defence sector might cease to exist (Gummett, 1991). However, 'Star Wars' technology was revived at the start of the twenty-first century to provide a boost to the beleaguered defence industry.

Nevertheless, weapons companies tried to secure new markets overseas, or moved into non-defence activities, shedding substantial numbers of workers. Hence, the new world order meant growth in long-term **structural unemployment**. Similar problems could be found in East and Central Europe (Kaldor, 1991). In many ways, the Soviet bloc countries were even more geared towards military expenditure than the NATO countries. For example, over one third of the USSR's manufacturing capacity was devoted to armament production. Reorienting production to civilian consumer goods associated with the nurturing of a new capitalist market economy might be regarded as a victory for modernity, but it came at the same price we have long paid in the West: growing unemployment. As the ranks of the poor have grown, so they have become susceptible to the charms of the extreme right, whose racist scapegoating of other disadvantaged groups (in eastern Germany and former Yugoslavia, for example) echoes the 1930s.

> **Structural unemployment**
> Chronic, long-term unemployment due to changes in the structure of the economy.

Strategic implications

The end of the Cold War reduced the importance of the Third World countries that the two superpowers had fought over for strategic reasons. Today, powerful states view poorer Third World countries less as strategic assets in the geo-political chess game and more as burdensome commitments to be rid of as quickly as possible. This withdrawal of superpower support has in fact helped to quicken the end of local conflicts in some countries – especially in Africa – while allowing other countries to begin to shape their own political direction free of overseas agendas.

At the same time, the US has not ceased to intervene where it sees fit to assert the broader interests of the West (or 'the free world'), as, for example, in Afghanistan following the events of 11 September, 2001. Geo-politically, the US (and other core countries) is concerned about the spread of nuclear weapons and the legal and illegal arms trade, especially since most conventional weapons have a nuclear version. But as Kaldor (1991) notes, private arms trade with Third World countries is growing, as it provides employment and foreign earnings for First World states: the 'militarisation of the periphery' continues.

Ideological implications

The most important ideological outcome of the 1989 revolutions and the end of the Cold War has been the demise of socialism as a powerful and credible alternative to capitalism. Some commentators believe that European socialism is dead and buried. Even the diluted form of parliamentary social democracy that is called socialism is viewed as out of date, discredited and unelectoral poison. Communist parties in West and East have given themselves new names and distanced themselves from the heavy handed state communism of the past.

However, we must remember that socialism emerged in response to and to challenge the inequalities of capitalism: since capitalism – now globalised – prevails, there is always a possibility that this challenge will re-emerge, but perhaps via a different sort of language and organisation, perhaps based on ecological considerations, gender, anti-consumerism and so on. Certainly for many in the newly expanded capitalist world, life in the free market has not brought any improvement in quality of life.

Possible futures

This chapter has sketched out profound social, economic and political changes that have been associated with globalisation. As we have seen, transnational corporations operate an increasingly sophisticated global market that is turning us into consumers of global products. As a result, traditional customs and patterns of consumption and distribution are being undermined, be these the traditional family farms of East Africa or socialist collectives elsewhere. International agencies such as the United Nations, the EU and the World Bank are constructing broader political and economic agendas for regional or international security. The global media are able to compress time and space into the briefcase that carries the portable satellite dish.

Those who view these changes as the inevitable result of the march of modernity and liberal capitalism fail to see the uneven and unequal impact that globalised modernity is having. Moreover, as we have stressed, the global dynamics are simultaneously generating a countervailing localisation of culture: hence the weakness of the cultural imperialism thesis.

How, then, to chart the future? Change, whether locally, nationally or globally, reflects the different interests and capacities of individuals, groups and national and international agencies. McGrew (1992) offers five possible futures for the world:

- 'The world transformed': a newly integrated global society and polity.
- 'The primacy of continuity': a competitive, conflict-ridden world will prevail.
- 'The world in crisis': impending population, ecological and economic crises could lead to the eventual collapse of any potential global security.
- 'The bifurcated world': a world split between competing nation-states on the one hand and transnational agencies on the other.
- 'Global politics in transition': dramatic global change means we are moving towards a new global context whose nature remains uncertain.

QUESTION Which of these five futures would you most like to materialise, and why?

If one or other of these futures emerges during the twenty first century, sociology will have to rise to the challenge and provide new concepts and new models to help to understand the unfolding changes.

Chapter summary

- Globalisation is rooted in the dynamics of modernity, but has opened up new questions for sociology to address.

- Globalisation is encouraging the integration and convergence of social and economic relations, but at the local level, diversity and inequality remain.

- Giddens' three key dimensions of modernity and his fourfold characterisation of the world system help to explain the momentum behind the globalisation process.

- The key agents of globalisation are transnational corporations and cultural and media agencies, new political institutions that go beyond the nation-state.

- Globalisation does not mean that the future of the world is predictable: there are many possible futures.

 Questions to think about

- What contribution can sociologists make to the debate on global warming?
- Which of the three positions on the impact of globalisation (hyperglobalist, sceptic or transformationalist) seems most convincing to you, and why?
- To what extent do you agree with the proposition that now we all live in a global culture? Give reasons for your answer.

 Investigating further

Cohen, Robin and Paul Kennedy (2000) *Global Sociology*, Palgrave.

Held, David (ed.) (2000) *A Globalising World?*, Routledge.

> These are all useful general texts, pitched at the introductory level and covering a range of topics. *Global Transformations* is more political in orientation. *A Globalising World?* is written primarily from a British perspective, but in a very clear way. You might find the chapters on nation-states, transnational corporations and uneven development in *Global Sociology* a particularly useful starting point.

Held, David, Anthony McGrew, David Goldblatt and Jonathan Perraton (1999): *Global Transformations*, Polity.

part 2

Social divisions and power

A common feature of all societies is that they are stratified: people in those societies are often categorised according to social differences that carry particular social meanings and implications. Whether we are male or female; what our ethnic background is; what social class we identify with; all affect both how we see ourselves and are seen by others. These differences also affect the possibilities that are open to us in terms of the material and cultural resources at our disposal.

In this section of the book, we look at a range of social divisions and ask what are the social consequences of being black, for example, or female, or working-class. What sociological debates have taken place around issues of social inequality, social identity and power? How do social differences of these kinds cut across each other to create more complex and subtle forms of social interaction?

The chapters in this section are designed to build a further layer of understanding in how we think about the puzzle of social life.

Social divisions

CHAPTER CONTENTS

Aims of the chapter

In this chapter, we begin our exploration of social divisions, a theme that runs through the following four chapters. After explaining the broad meaning of the term social divisions, the chapter explores how these are constructed and expressed through inequality associated with social stratification and social exclusion. It is particularly concerned with topics such as wealth, poverty, and age- and disability-related divisions in the life course. Subsequent chapters take this analysis further by considering topics such as class, gender and ethnicity.

By the end of the chapter, you should have an understanding of the following concepts:

- Social division
- Stratification
- Social exclusion
- Wealth

- Poverty
- Life-course
- Age
- Disability

Introduction

In this chapter, we consider some of the most important social divisions found in all societies, but especially in contemporary industrial societies. Social divisions mark the broad patterns and processes that produce forms of social inequality and disadvantage. These are in turn associated with economic, **life-course** or health-related social processes. We shall look at the broad indicators and measures of a number of core social divisions – those relating to wealth and poverty, youth, age and disability. In subsequent chapters, we shall explore the more theoretical and detailed empirical aspects of the most important drivers of social inequality related to class, gender, ethnicity and political power.

Two related but distinct dimensions of social division will be examined here: social stratification related to structured patterns of wealth and poverty, and social exclusion, related to more contingent processes whereby vulnerable groups in society – such as the aged – are denied access to what others regard as normal rights and resources. These two dimensions are of course often linked, but they need not be: the advantages that accrue from wealth and high income may not always ensure that the elderly rich can fend off ageist discrimination or related forms of exclusion. Social divisions can, then, be both complex and pull in different directions. As Payne (2000, p.4) says, 'In any one situation, a particular social division may assume greater importance, but people do not exist in a social world where only class, or only gender, or only ethnicity matters. ... All of us have multiple-membership in a number of such groups, so that depending on one's standpoint, people may be different in one context, but similar in another.'

The general meaning of 'social divisions'

In broad terms, the concept of social divisions refers to the ways in which, either as individuals or more commonly as members of social groupings, we construct social differences among ourselves – as white or black, young or old, attractive or unattractive,

Life-course
This term encompasses the diversity of experiences and differences that people encounter during the course of their lives. It came into being because contemporary experience is considered to be more diverse and less predictable than the traditional concept of the life-cycle suggests.

skilled or unskilled, 'cool' or a 'geek', and so on. It should be clear from this list that social divisions are about material differences between people as well as cultural differences between them. Many of these differences can be seen as forms of social categorisation that are reproduced through everyday interactions, but they are also routinised in more abstract and formalised ways; for example, the social divisions imposed by customs and immigration officers when granting right of entry to some but not to others.

It is also normally the case that social divisions are made up of or presume their opposite categories – the customs official will use criteria of admission into a country based on the definition of what a citizen of that country is, so by implication determining what a non-citizen is too. These divisions are not determined randomly, though some – for example, those associated with more status-based factors, such as perceptions of beauty or what is fashionable – are likely to change more quickly over time. Social divisions are not random, because they are normally rooted in positions of power and advantage, where those blessed with both of these define themselves as 'above' those who do not share their particular advantages or the attributes associated with them, such as ways of speaking, mode of dress and other symbols of personal and group identity. Norbert Elias's (1984) work on the historical development of social manners provides a very good example of this. He shows how social divisions based on class advantage have long been expressed through the continual refinement of table manners, dress code, public hygiene norms and so on. This has ensured that the social elites from the sixteenth century onwards have been able to sustain their social position relative to the emerging middle classes.

The more important social divisions are those which help to reproduce social hierarchies – differences in power, economic advantage, status and so on – over time. Some societies' social divisions have been sufficiently strong to continue broadly unchanged for generations: this was true of most societies before the impact of modernity and the growth of more complex social orders and patterns of social differentiation. In modern social systems, the pattern of social division and how it is expressed is more complex, dynamic and changes more rapidly, as we shall see in Chapter 5. Nevertheless, significant continuities in the broad structure of advantage and disadvantage in late-modern societies show that the underlying social divisions have remained intact.

CONNECTIONS To review the debate on the relative importance of social class and the social divisions of gender and race, see Chapter 7, pages 184–9.

Social stratification
The division of a population into unequal layers or strata based on income, wealth, gender, ethnicity, power, status, age religion or some other characteristic.

These patterns of inequality structure society into different levels or social strata. This process is known as **social stratification,** which refers to all forms of inequality based on class, gender, ethnicity, age and political power. The analysis of social and economic inequality was a central concern of sociology from its inception. One reason for this was that modernity was creating new patterns of social inequality that needed to be understood. At the same time, these inequalities between social groups threw up new problems for social order as well as new possibilities for social change, both of which needed to be addressed by the early sociologists.

Most of the time, we do not experience the world as members of a particular gender, class, ethnic group or any other category of social stratification. We tend to see ourselves as individuals with particular jobs, as members of families, as students, and so on. And even though we might experience our gender in a more immediate, everyday sense through our interactions as men and women, we may not see those interactions as having any sort of patterned inequality. We may think that it is only natural for men and women to behave in certain ways and want different things.

Our individual lives inevitably lead to the construction of personal life histories that tell us why we are where we are in society. These stories tend to speak of inequality and our position in highly individualistic terms: we write CVs listing our biographical details, achievements and current position; we know we are strong at some things but not at others, and that only by our efforts will we make anything of ourselves. In other words, people often think that inequality is not something to be explained or experienced collectively, for it seems to exist, if at all, because of the advantages or disadvantages that individuals have created for themselves.

Occasionally, a very different story of inequality is told, one that has not an individual but a collective narrator – a trade union defending its members' pay, a civil rights march demanding votes for blacks, a women's caucus asserting equal rights for their sisters around the world, a gay and lesbian rally against discrimination on the basis of sexuality. At times like these, people regard themselves as holding a shared position, and they construct a powerful sense of collective identity as members of a single economic class, ethnic group, gender or sexual minority. When we witness such events, we should ask ourselves two things: what sort of response do those involved receive from the authorities and why; and could people generate such powerful collectivities on the strength of a persuasive but nevertheless constructed sense of inequality? Perhaps collective stories are based on more fundamental, half-glimpsed inequalities that are masked by the concerns of everyday life.

Sociologists are interested in exploring both the experience and the realities of social inequality. Does it exist, and if so, on what basis? If it exists, how do people respond to it? Are the patterns of inequality related to each other? Are some inequalities more important than others in some situations? How are inequalities mediated by everyday life? Are there major forms of inequality that can be linked to different types of society? These questions have been asked by sociologists for more than a century.

QUESTION How has inequality affected your life so far? Identify five events in your life that may have turned out differently if you had been born into a different social position.

Key socio-economic divisions: wealth and poverty

Class
A term widely used in sociology to differentiate between sections of the population. It is based on economic considerations such as wealth or income.

All industrialised societies have structures of inequality that reflect unequal economic positions. Crompton (1998) argues that economic **class** is a defining feature of modern society, in contrast to the ascribed status differences – such as those to do with kinship (see Chapter 9) – that typically characterise non-modern traditional social orders. The class structures of today are a manifestation of modernity, where complex social, economic and political institutions regulate and secure the interests of different social classes. The conflict between classes has been a key factor in social change. As Crompton notes, 'in the modern world, class-based organisations – that is, organisations claiming to represent classes and class interests – have been the dynamic source of many of the changes and transformations which have characterised the modern era' (ibid., p. 4).

Social classes existed before industrial society, but the economic hierarchies they reflected were more to do with political, religious or hereditary forms of domination than with individuals' relationship to the system of production – the sort of job they had, the resources under their control, the reward they received for work, and so on. Today it is the second set of relationships that are most likely to shape the pattern of social inequality: class-based social divisions are closely associated with the ownership of property as wealth, and with the material and cultural advantages and disadvantages of different occupational positions. Those denied both will be among the poor and socially excluded.

The UK has often been tagged as a class-ridden society in which the inequalities of social class are pronounced, from the established upper class – the landed gentry and the new super-rich – down to the traditional working class. However, this image and the different lifestyles it evokes – often recreated through film and TV costume dramas – is said by some to be out of date. Thatcher's social revolution during the 1980s was in part an attempt to dismantle the established class hierarchy, while the Major government of the mid 1990s proclaimed its intention to create a classless society. The Labour government elected in 1997 also sought to distance itself from policies that addressed class-related divisions and inequalities.

CONNECTIONS Read Box 5.6 for a view on whether the US and the UK are still class-based societies, or whether they are open, classless societies.

However, this (politically) popular notion of a shift towards a classless society fails to capture the reality of the underlying changes to the system of social stratification that marked the last decades of the twentieth century, not only in the UK but also in Europe, the US and other core capitalist regions of the world economy. Rather than bringing an end to class, successive developments have weakened the traditional social and economic bases on which the conventional model of social class has stood. A number of changes illustrate this point:

- There has been increasing polarisation of the living standards of the wealthy and the growing ranks of the poor.
- A culture of individualism has become prevalent and has been given added weight by government initiatives to encourage the private purchase of benefits that until now have been provided by the state, such as personal health insurance and pension plans (see Chapter 13).
- The labour market has become more strongly segregated as the nature of the available work has changed, and so movement between occupational classes has declined.
- The character of occupational positions has changed in terms of degree of autonomy, conditions of work and the flattening of occupational hierarchies within organisations.

Indeed, these changes have led to the first major reworking of the UK-based classification of class position (ONS, 1999), which we shall review in Chapter 5. (And it is there that we ask whether these changes herald an overall decline in the importance of class as a determinant of social position and reward, or a restructuring of the terms on which a person's class is based). While patterns of social stratification associated with occupational position are changing, we should not lose sight of some of the more persistent social divisions that have been created by and help recreate the dynamics of inequality. Two of the most notable of these are wealth inequalities and poverty, to which we now turn.

Wealth

Massive inequality in the distribution of wealth is one of the most important and perhaps most obvious forms of social division. Wealth is often taken to mean the same as property, a word that is commonly used to refer to anything from Arundel Castle to the clothes one wears. But this general notion of property conceals a crucial distinction between different forms of property. We should distinguish between consumption property and productive property. Property for personal consumption includes consumer durables (for example, CD players, clothes, cars) and family homes that are owner-occupied. Productive property is significantly different and includes factories, farms and building land, as well as stocks and shares. This kind of property is called capital and it yields income through profits on its productive use. Privately owned property of this sort provides massive unearned income through:

- Rent on buildings and land.
- Dividends paid from the profits of firms to shareholders.
- Interest on monetary investments, such as deposit accounts and government bonds.

Moreover, the purchase and sale of property provides capital gains, the basis of the property speculation that fuelled much of the boom in the UK and Western Europe during the 1980s.

Such unearned income generates wealth, and wealth holding tends to produce more wealth through the reinvestment of unearned income. International property speculation produced rapid rises in the market value of commercial and residential properties in London during the mid 1980s, much of this fuelled by Middle-Eastern, American and other foreign wealth holders. For example, as King (1991) reports, 'The Dorchester Hotel, sold in 1976 for £9 million by its British owners, McAlpines, was bought and sold four times over before being purchased by the Sultan of Brunei for £43 million in 1985. Shortly after, it was bought by the American group, Regent International Hotels, for £45 million.' To find multimillionaires in more residential London settings, one has only to visit Bishop's Avenue in Hampstead, Avenue Road in St John's Wood, and Kensington Palace Gardens. Table 4.1 summarises the distribution of personal marketable wealth between 1976 and 1999 in the UK.

The table shows that the distribution of wealth has in fact become more unequal, as the holding of the top 5–10 per cent has increased. This reflects not only massive rises in property-based unearned income but also a reduction in real terms of the burden of tax falling on the wealthy. Many of the 'new wealthy' are those with high salaries but lighter tax burdens who can afford to save and invest, and hence accumulate wealth and join an upper class of corporate stock holders, financiers, landowners or inheritors of wealth.

TABLE 4.1 Distribution of wealth in the UK, 1976–99 (per cent)[1]

	1976	1981	1986	1991	1996	1999[2]
Percentage of wealth owned by:						
Most wealthy 1%	29	26	25	28	20	23
Most wealthy 5%	47	45	46	50	40	43
Most wealthy 10%	57	56	58	63	52	54
Most wealthy 25%	73	74	75	79	74	74
Most wealthy 50%	88	87	89	92	93	94

1. Percentage of population aged 18 and over.
2. Provisional figures only.

Source: Inland Revenue.

BOX 4.1 Increasing levels of global wealth and global poverty

The United Nations Development Programme (UNDP, 1999) reported that in 1998:

- The world's 225 richest people had a combined wealth of $1 trillion, equivalent to the total annual income of the world's 2.5 billion poorest people.

- The wealth of the three most affluent individuals had come

to exceed the combined GDP of the 48 least developed countries.

- In 1996, 100 countries were worse off than 15 years previously.

- Three decades previously, the people in affluent countries were 30 times better off than those in countries where the

poorest 20 per cent of the world's people lived. By 1998, this gap had widened to 82 times (up from 61 times since 1996).

Similar trends can be found in other industrial societies, and the contrast between the rich and poor globally can be very dramatic, as shown by the United Nations report summarised in Box 4.1.

CONNECTIONS Chapter 3, pages 54–6, has an account of the implications of the globalisation of production. You could usefully link that up to the material here on global wealth.

Massive disparities in wealth persist within and between countries, and changes to the pattern of wealth reflect changes at the national and global levels. National changes can be said to have occurred during the last half of the twentieth century, while global changes are the result of more recent processes. With regard to the first, a propertied upper class is still apparent in all mature capitalist countries, but there have been two key changes.

First, at the national level, the wealth holding of the rich has been, to a limited extent, redistributed downwards to the next 5–10 per cent of wealth holders, while the management of private capital – be this of landed property or corporations – is in the hands of powerful managers or the service class. This means that there has been a separation of the ownership of capital from its control, though this does not necessarily mean that the managers of capital are working against the interests of owners and dominant shareholders: indeed, most senior managers are major shareholders in the companies they manage.

Second, at the global level, the stability and reproduction of a specifically national upper class – in the US, the UK, Canada, France, Italy and elsewhere – is being eclipsed by the emergence of a transnational capitalist class (some of whom figure amongst the world's 225 richest people, as described in Box 4.1), based on the control of transnational corporations (TNCs). These are particularly associated with the ownership and management of finance capital – the wealth associated with international banks, major currency dealers, insurance conglomerates and the like. It is important to remember that this wealth is held in three different forms: landed property, productive manufacturing firms, and finance. Today, it is finance that is the most important form of global wealth and is shaping the fortunes of both rich and poor in all capitalist countries. Andreff (1984) highlights the importance of what he calls 'transnational finance capital', and Carrol and Lewis (1991, p. 507) point out that international capitalists 'operate within … transnational circuits of [capital, and they therefore] can be expected to manifest less and less of a connection to "national" priorities'. This means that many of the new recruits to senior management are working for banking and insurance companies operating at the global level.

Taken together, these two processes have led to what Scott (1986, 1991) calls the 'depersonalisation' of capital – the gradual dissociation of the holding of major wealth from specific individuals and their families. The rich are still with us, of course, as Box 4.2 indicates. But increasingly, the basis on which they enjoy and increase their fortunes depends on the dynamics of global capital investment and the profitability of money markets. As Lee (1991, p. 410) notes, 'Today, impersonal capitalisation and ownership means huge international movements of money funds made at the behest of multinational corporations and wealthy governments, as they respond speculatively to the ebb and flow of money markets'. Thus, we can see that social divisions based on economic advantage are increasingly likely to be of a globalised form (a point noted in Chapter 3).

We can see the effects of the global dynamics of capital investment on wealth holding in the UK by looking at King's (1991) study of London as the financial centre of the world. His account reveals the dramatic changes that have taken place in terms of wealth holding, the impact on this of finance capital, and the way the latter has shaped London's social and economic structure. King outlines some of the key changes in London's international role between the early part of the twentieth century, when it was closely tied to the interests of empire, and the present day – it now acts as a 'global control centre' or a world city for international finance capital. This will remain true even if the UK joins the single European currency.

BOX 4.2 Wealth and work in London: the changing context

In the first half of the twentieth century, London's role in the old international division of labour was still largely that of imperial city. It was the control centre of a colonial mode of production and, as such, its largely indigenous population was characterised by a social and class composition principally influenced by this role. This social composition also included a significant working-class element based on a substantial amount of manufacturing: it was also both spatially as well as physically expressed in the built environment.

With the disintegration of the colonial mode of production and old international division of labour from the 1950s, the transition from the role of imperial to world city was well under way. ... Since the 1960s, the increasing specialisation of London as world city, with its specific functions in the world-economy ... has had various important effects on the social, ethnic, and spatial composition of its population. At the lower end of the social hierarchy, the collapse of industry has left the country- and culture-specific Black and Asian migrant labour, drawn from the poorest countries in the world, largely trapped in the run-down parts of the inner city...

At the top end of the social hierarchy, however, London's enhanced role in the international division of labour as world banking, financial trading, as well as 'global control' centre, has had an equally important impact on its social composition.

The first effect is the concentration of a highly paid elite principally (though not entirely) indigenous. The second effect results from the banking, finan- cial, and trading function. As London is a principal financial centre in the capitalist world-economy, it requires the presence of representatives of the world's richest nations, most specifically, Japan and the United States. The effect of the world city, therefore, is to bring representatives of the richest and poorest countries in the world into the ambit of each other. It is ambit, rather than contact, because the historical economic, class, spatial and built-environment divisions, between the West End and the East End, which divide rich and poor in the Imperial City, continue to keep both groups apart. ... [T]he world city becomes ... an international enclave whose space, social relations, and politics increasingly depend on decisions made outside national boundaries.

Source: King (1991), pp. 142–5.

QUESTION In what ways do you think the growth of transnational corporations will affect industry and commerce in any single country? Will this stabilise or jeopardise economic prosperity in that country?

 ## The poor and the underclass

CONNECTIONS For further discussion of the underclass, and some of the problems with this term, see Chapter 5, page 120, and Chapter 7, page 185.

The above discussion of wealth throws into relief the scale of the disadvantage experienced by those who are poor in society. As noted earlier, social divisions will always be expressed as a series of opposites, and wealth and poverty are clearly very strong material opposites. Many social theorists would argue that poverty is not simply the absence of at least some form of wealth, but is also a direct result of the economic system that produces the wealthy. Hence, poverty continues to prevail in affluent societies that enjoy high levels of consumption. Despite the fact that the absolute level of poverty – a rather crude and oversimplified term for the non-fulfilment of basic needs – may not apply to most people, in relative terms, poverty has remained fairly constant in Europe and the US, despite measures of unemployment that show an increasingly tight **labour market** and growing average income. If we consider the income of people in households with less than half the average income as a measure of those in poverty, it is possible to see how patterns change over time. Until 1998, the UK government did not base the official definition of those in poverty on this measure.

Labour market
The supply of people who are willing and able to work.

We can see from Table 4.2 that, based on this measure, the number of persons in poor households increased between 1979 and 2000. However, these figures should be treated with caution, since the average income level rose over the period. Nevertheless, it is true that from 1979 the share of total income fell for all lower-income groups.

Figures released in 2000 by the UK government provide further details on income-related inequality, including the following:

- Ten per cent of households have an income of £132 or less per week.
- About two thirds of those with less than half the average income (about nine million) are not in paid work.
- The number on very low incomes (defined as less than 40 per cent of the average income) rose by one million between 1995 and 1998.
- Forty per cent of lone parents are on very low incomes.
- Over two million children live in households where there is no adult in paid work.

The proportion of the population earning much less than the average income is a valuable measure of the overall income-distribution patterns in society, and it allows us to compare changes over time. But in itself it says nothing about other aspects of everyday life that worsen the plight of those in poverty, such as unequal income distribution within a household, gender inequalities, insecure (often seasonal) work, relative access to low-cost (or free) healthcare, public goods and services, dependency on or support given to wider family networks, and so on. Understanding the key role these play enables a more sophisticated analysis of the relative vulnerability of not only

Figure 4.1   Research shows that the developed countries with the longest life expectancy are not the richest (such as the US) but the most egalitarian (such as Sweden and Japan). Put simply, inequality kills.

poor individuals but also poor households. In this sense, poverty has to be understood as multi-dimensional.

Who is most likely to suffer from poverty? While one might at first think it would be those out of work – and indeed, the unemployed are among the more vulnerable – it is people in low-paid, insecure work who constitute the bulk of those below the income poverty line. The second group consists of the elderly. Because life expectancy has increased, earlier retirement has become more common and state pensions have reduced in real terms, the elderly comprise an ever-larger section of the poor. Unequal life chances continue through to old age. Dilnot and Johnson (1992) show that those who were able to contribute to a private pension scheme during their working life enjoy a pension income that is almost five times higher than that received by those on state benefit alone.

TABLE 4.2 Persons in households with less than half of the average income

	Number	Per cent
1979	5.0 million	9
1981	6.2 million	11
1987	10.5 million	19
1989	12.0 million	22
2000	14.0 million	24

Source: DSS (1993); SEU, Cabinet Office (1999); Joseph Rowntree Foundation (2000).

Also likely to experience poverty are lone-parent families. Irrespective of whether lone parenthood is the result of choice, death, desertion or divorce, such families make up a growing percentage of the poor. Large families too, though less common today, are vulnerable to poverty. Finally, those who are sick or disabled often experience chronic deprivation and isolation.

According to Millar (1993), the growth in the number in poverty is the result of three related factors:

- A significant level of unemployment.
- The increase in low-paid work.
- The growth of 'precarious' or 'flexible' employment.

Millar (ibid., p.15) describes the most vulnerable as follows:

> " It is women who make up the vast majority of part-time and low-paid workers. It is men in unskilled and low-paid jobs who are most vulnerable to unemployment. Young people cannot get a secure hold on the labour market and instead move between unemployment, low-paid work, and low-paid training schemes, while older workers cannot get back into paid work if they lose their jobs. Black people are more vulnerable on all counts: more prone to unemployment, more likely to be low-paid, more likely to be in insecure employment. "

Other writers argue that women have come to figure particularly prominently among the new poor – the so-called **feminisation of poverty** (Dey, 1996). While the absolute figures do suggest an increase, it is evident from earlier data that women have always been most susceptible to poverty because of their weakness in the labour market, their domestic burden, the distribution of resources within households, and so on. Whatever the relative change in the proportion of women among the poor, the general point is that social divisions can stack up in particular ways – in this case, gender and economic disadvantage are at play.

Feminisation of poverty
The increasing concentration of poverty among the female population.

In relation to the wider social hierarchy, some argue that the poor can be regarded as an 'underclass'. This notion, which has its roots in UK and US sociology of the 1970s, suggests that those who are most poor suffer growing exclusion from normal society and social intercourse, and constitute an increasingly similar group locked into a cycle of socio-economic and cultural deprivation. They are likely to be living in appalling conditions on inner-city estates, without work and often in receipt of state benefits, unable to escape the poverty in which they (often as single-parent households) are trapped.

According to this argument, these poor are not simply at the bottom of the social hierarchy – in a sense, they are outside it, outside the boundaries and the dynamics of that hierarchy. They are 'under' the class structure. Although formed by the hierarchy, they are excluded from it. Ethnic minorities and immigrant workers are especially likely to be found here. For these groups, participating as members of a competitive labour market is far removed from their daily experience. Crompton (1998) argues that the underclass has always been a feature of capitalist socities throughout the world, and she dismisses the view that the existence of an underclass is peculiar to late capitalism. Whether recent or long-standing, there are a large number of people who are distinct from those who lapse into poverty during certain crucial periods of their life (for example, the elderly, families with young children). Those who consistently experience what Townsend (1979) calls **relative deprivation** are unable to participate in 'the activities, living conditions, and amenities which are customary' to society (ibid., p. 31). Scott (1994) believes that in such circumstances, the fundamental deprivation is the loss of a genuine sense of social citizenship. In this respect, economic deprivation produces

Relative deprivation
Developed by Townsend in the late 1970s to conceptualise the deprived living standards of some people compared with the vast majority of the population.

additional forms of social division that are related to a disadvantageous social and political status.

While the notion of the poor as an underclass captures the sense of social marginalisation that poverty brings, it has been criticised for encouraging the view that poverty is transmitted from one generation to the next by reproducing a culture of dependency in which socio-economic failure is the norm. Yet despite governmental demonisation of this culture, sociological research has found little evidence of its existence. Rather, studies have shown that the poor have the same hopes and ambitions as those outside poverty, but lack the resources to realise them.

In the UK, the state's response to the continuation of high levels of poverty and social deprivation has been to develop a national strategy on poverty, as enshrined in the Labour government's Poverty and Social Exclusion Act of 1999, which has the ambitious objective of not only reducing but even eradicating poverty. Getting rid of poverty would require a major redistribution of resources and a degree of state intervention that New Labour would not support (though it did implement the European Commission's minimum wage directive in 1999). In fact, as in many other areas of government, the national strategy is based on a mixture of empowering the poor by means of programmes (in education and social services) aimed at increasing the choice and opportunities open to individuals, while at the same time monitoring their preparedness to respond to the new policy regime. As the extract in Box 4.3 suggests, this approach was introduced in gradual steps in the last two decades of the twentieth century and, despite the dramatic electoral victory of Labour over the Conservative Party in 1997, still shapes the government's approach to the socially disadvantaged in UK schools.

BOX 4.3 Educational policy and social disadvantage

From the outset schooling has been about more than the three Rs. Educational policy has always had underlying social objectives, even though the focus of this social dimension has shifted. At the start the concern was to get children from poor families into the classroom; later school meals and school based health services were to help children 'take full advantage of the education provided for them'. The second stage focused on equality of educational opportunity: comprehensive secondary reorganisation in the late 1960s set out to ensure equal access to educational opportunities for all children. But equality of access did not necessarily lead to greater equality of result. The third stage focused on raising educational quality and performance in the poorest areas. In the fourth stage in the 1980s and 1990s, this 'social dimension' to educational policy has been explicitly rejected as 'social engineering'. In its place the emphasis is now on individual choice and opportunity in the educational market place, with the national curriculum providing the common framework; and pupil assessment, league tables and school inspection reports the 'market intelligence' on relative quality. The onus for success is now placed firmly on individual pupils (or their parents), or on individual schools.

Source: Smith and Noble (1995), pp. 132–3.

This approach to alleviating poverty by providing better opportunities and choices may address some of the sources of social disadvantage, but it is unlikely to counter all the multi-dimensional aspects of poverty. Moreover, as we shall see in Chapter 11, the features of the labour market that Millar (1993) describes as generating low, unstable incomes will be made more prominent by the extensive globalisation of production. By definition, this problem is faced by all countries, so we can expect to see a growing similarity between the patterns of disadvantage at the global level. Just as wealth has been shaped by the impact of globalised corporate capital, so too has poverty. Therefore, it is not sensible to depict poverty as the result of a particular cultural failing or orientation on the part of a particular section of the population, since people worldwide experience poverty yet live in quite different cultural environments.

Recognition of the common experience of the poor has encouraged a move to contstruct an international framework for the measurement of poverty. For example, at the World Summit in Copenhagen in 1995, indicators of both absolute and overall levels of poverty were agreed by 117 countries. Hence, to some extent, the globalisation of some of the key engines of chronic poverty are paralleled by the globalisation of policies designed to reduce it.

Social exclusion
The ways in which people are marginalised from society by having limited or no access to public services, and little participation in education and the political process.

A similar process has led, particularly in Europe, to the adoption of a discourse of **social exclusion** among policymakers, and this has been taken up by all the member states of the European Union. Rather than simply seeing poverty as a problem for the poor, the discourse of social exclusion – based on social-democratic assumptions – argues that poverty also impoverishes society at large. This discourse is clearly far removed from that of cycles of cultural deprivation, which puts the blame for poverty squarely on the shoulders of the poor themselves. Exclusion assumes that some members of society are actively being deprived of economic, cultural and political rights. This takes us to a consideration of patterns of social exclusion that result from the ways in which societies construct status hierarchies based on social differentiation, especially those to do with the life course.

Patterns of social exclusion

Analysing social divisions by concentrating on patterns of social exclusion is especially useful, in that it draws attention to the complex, multidimensional aspects of inequality. Social exclusion refers to the way in which people are marginalised from society by having limited or no access to public services, education or the political process. It also refers to inequalities in other key areas of social life, such as access to sources of communication and information. This has led to studies of the 'digital divide' (Loader, 1998), which explore patterns of social exclusion in the information society, which requires hardware, software and the skills to use them that the information poor do not have.

Social exclusion therefore refers to processes that intentionally or unintentionally serve to exclude individuals, social groups or whole communities from the benefits and rights that are considered normal. The UK government has defined social exclusion as a process that can 'happen when individuals or areas suffer from a combination of linked problems such as unemployment, poor skills, low incomes, poor housing, high crime environments, bad health and family breakdown' (DETR, 1999, p. 2). As a DEMOS report notes, 'Social exclusion is more than just income poverty – it is a lack of access to the networks of support and information that help people into education, homes, jobs, services and appropriate benefits' (Perri 6, 1998, p. 1). The report goes on to say that 'network poverty is the real challenge facing policy makers'. Sociological interest in social networks has grown in recent years (see Granovetter, 1992) because of the greater significance attached to the role of informal and formal networks in facilitating geographical and labour mobility, economic development and political participation. Networks have become important social resources, and those outside them experience 'network poverty'. One obvious sense in which mobility via networks is important is access to transport, whether public or private: again, lack of access can lead to what has been called 'transport poverty'.

Patterns of social exclusion therefore relate to processes that disadvantage or discriminate against social groups. Sometimes these are associated with a specific issue (such as transport poverty), at other times with a more chronic problem (such as network poverty). More extensive forms of social exclusion can be found in all societies and affect large sections of the population. Racism is a clear example of this (as we shall see in Chapter 7) and creates numerous forms of social exclusion: black and Asian immigrants and their descendants have experienced exclusion in the form of discriminatory practices in employment, access to housing and education. In many cases – in the US and UK especially – this has led to excluded minority groups gradually adopting a 'politics of identity', affirming their distinctiveness in order to improve their position in society, either through self-help groups or direct political action.

Ethnic identity plays a part in social divisions in many societies, but there are a number of other forms of social differentiation that also lead to lower status and therefore social exclusion. We shall first consider those associated with the socially constructed statuses that figure in an individual's life course, particularly when young or old, and then the experience of social exclusion suffered by those defined as disabled. In all cases, the socially constructed status of being 'young' (immature), 'aged', or 'disabled' becomes a (stereotypical) label or social category by which the person – and his or her identity – is defined. The growing interest in these topics by sociologists partly reflects the phenomenon of postmodernity, since they point to new forms of social identity, status and agency that culturally, economically and politically cannot be understood in terms of the traditional, class-based relations that are central to modernist social orders.

The life-course

The term life-course refers to the social processes that shape the social career of an individual during his or her life. To a large extent, it has displaced the term life-cycle, which suggests that the passage of life is made up of clearly defined stages from birth, adolescence, marriage and so on through to death. This model conflates social, psychological and biological development and remains firmly at the level of the individual. In contrast, 'life-course' is not only able to address chronological changes in an individual's life but also to locate them in the wider societal dynamics, where the individual's social career is shaped by his or her relationship with wider social groups. In one sense, the term has resonances with the Weberian concept of life-chances: Weberians use this term to point to the social divisions – social, cultural, material and political – that characterise differing social statuses.

CONNECTIONS For a further discussion of the life-course, see Chapter 9, pages 255–6.

Age-related life-chances are central to any understanding of the life-course. Let us examine what this means for the youth of society.

Youth

First we need to acknowledge that being young, or youthful, is only in part determined by one's chronological age. As many sociological studies of childhood and adolescence have shown, there is no precise relationship between chronological age and the boundaries between childhood, youth and adulthood. According to James *et al.* (1998,

p. 146), childhood should be understood as a social or cultural construction ... it cannot be straightforwardly "read off" from the biological differences between adults and children such as physical size or sexual maturity'. Moreover, the experiences of children and youth vary dramatically in different countries. Children in rural Africa, downtown New York, the prosperous farmsteads of Australia, poor shanty towns of Brazil and across Europe (see Liebau and Chisholm, 1993) will have dramatically different life chances, social statuses, and cultural and material resources upon which to draw. Their respective life courses will involve different routes to adulthood, some more precarious than others. There is considerable variety in the transitions to adulthood that young people must negotiate, with different political and sexual rights and conventions about maturity and social competence (such as those related to the organisation and management of time in the home and school), different degrees of dependency on the family and the extended family, and different times for, forms of and opportunities for work. In short, while there may be a biological basis to being young, its meaning and identity is socially mediated, varying culturally and historically. It follows that the ways in which young people experience the transition to adulthood will also vary, because the notion of being an adult is itself so variable across cultures. As the Australian sociologists Wyn and White (1997, p.9) observe, 'The period of youth is significant because it is the threshold to adulthood, and it is problematic largely because *adult status itself is problematic*' (emphasis in original).

There is a considerable body of work that maps out the process of youths' transition to adulthood by focusing on the experience of young people in schools, work and the family. However, we need to be careful about generalising this work at the global level, for there are many societies in which the idea of a prolonged period through which youths eventually manage to secure adult status is irrelevant. In the poorer agricultural societies of the South, many youngsters are in full-time work by the time they are 12 years old – in 2001, the International Labour Office (ILO) estimated that at least 50 million are in this position. The tendency in the West to regard this as harmful reflects our more recent cultural subscription to and economic resourcing of both childhood and adolescence as a prolonged period spent preparing for adulthood. In other words, the social division marking off childhood from adulthood is socially constructed and not biologically determined.

Subculture
The set of values, behaviour and attitudes of a particular group of people who are distinct from but related to the dominant culture in society.

Marginalisation
The process whereby specific population groups are excluded from mainstream activities because of lack of income, cultural bias and so on.

Secondly, most sociological studies of youth have tended to focus either on the cultural (or **subcultural**) aspects of youth and the strong sense of identity that can be shared through music, fashion, sport and other forms of leisure, or on the more structural aspects of being young in a capitalist (global) economy whose institutional and political structures can marginalise young people, especially those from disadvantaged backgrounds. There has been a move to bring these cultural and structural analyses together (for example Gayle, 1998) to show how young people, though often constrained by social structure, can nevertheless use their identity as youths as a resource to redefine (and perhaps improve) their social position. There is considerable disadvantage that young people can experience as their life chances are affected by unequal access to housing, education and the labour market. Young people in general, but especially those from deprived social backgrounds, may feel **marginalised** from the mainstream economic and cultural life that surrounds them. Or, as Wyn and White (1997, p. 124) put it, they feel a 'disconnection from institutions revolving around production, consumption and community life'. The form of this disconnection is likely to be highly class-dependent, with those from middle-class backgrounds enjoying much better life chances than those from more deprived households, especially those, as we saw earlier, from lone-parent or larger families. A key determinant of the degree to which younger people are able to avoid exclusion and poverty is the transition from school to work.

CONNECTIONS For a fuller account of the importance of education to young people, see Chapter 5, pages 118–19, and Chapter 10, pages 273–93.

This transition – described more fully in Box 4.4 – is affected by a number of factors, including:

- The class position of the family, and the resources it can use to secure better employment for its young members.
- The gender of the new jobseeker.
- The locality in which work is sought.
- The educational skills the young person possesses and brings to the labour market.
- The state's policies on youth training and employment.

Much depends on the first job that the young worker secures after leaving school, for in a segmented labour market, this can initiate an employment pattern of either secure or insecure work in the future. A labour market is 'segmented' when it is made up of occupational groups that share similar conditions of work but are relatively closed off from each other, with some enjoying greater security than others. Young people working in shops, cafes or call centres have little prospect of upward social mobility. They are more likely to experience merely horizontal movement between similar jobs in this particular segment of the labour market. Coupled with this segmentation is the decline of appreticed-based work in manufacturing industries, which has closed off many of the employment opportunities once enjoyed by the young. Partly in response to this, in 1999 the UK government announced that it was to invest in a modern apprenticeship scheme to provide new opportunities in the labour market.

BOX 4.4 First jobs and future life chances

The transition from school represents a crucial point of intersection between major life domains, namely the educational system and the labour market. It is at this point that most young people are at considerable risk in their attempts (and frequently those of their parents) to ensure continuity in their life course. Apart from those people for whom the first job is a temporary expedient or fill-in job, such as students or young people waiting to enter jobs such as nursing, with age requirements for entry, the level at which they enter the labour force is crucial in influencing their future life chances. It plays a large part in influencing the amount of income they will receive, their chances of obtaining occupational security and their chances of increasing their income and status in later life.

Source: Layder *et al.*, (1991), p. 453.

The problems for the young job seeker have been further exacerbated by the global changes in employment, with many jobs being exported to cheaper labour markets overseas (much of this in the form of sweatshop labour).

Some sociologists (for example, Raffe, 1987) believe that youth employment is not strongly structured or segmented in this way but is cyclical, reflecting the general state of the economy. Thus, during recession – which all industrialised countries experienced during the 1980s and early 1990s to a greater or lesser degree – the young are the first to suffer, either because those with a job are easier to dispose of than other employees, or because no one wants to take on new labour. However, when the economy improves, the young are the first to benefit from the availability of new jobs, especially in urban areas where the provision of service sector jobs, such as retailing, can expand quickly.

Perhaps, as Lee (1991) suggests, both arguments have some value. That is, the restructuring of labour has produced a two-tier labour market that, as an economy comes out of recession, provides many new jobs, but the longevity of the latter is uncertain. According to Lee, in many countries 'large firms cut back their training places and labour overheads during the recession of the early eighties. Insecure, low skill work simultaneously became more widespread, because hiring young workers and "trainees" on low wages offered a means by which more marginal (mostly smaller) firms might survive' (ibid., p. 89).

What is apparent from the segmented labour market perspective is that throughout the European Union there are a number of industries where a disproportionately large number of young people are employed, and where wage rates are low and the chance of intragenerational mobility is slim. However, it is important to recognise that various other factors, such as household resources and so on, influence the chances of young jobseekers. For example, locality is an important factor in the sort of work they can pursue, since they are likely to be less geographically mobile than other job seekers. Some studies (for example, MacDonald, 1997) have shown that in certain rural areas, middle-class youths take up jobs that offer worse life chances than those available to working-class youths in urban regions, where the range of jobs is better.

State policies on youth training are also important (see Chapter 12). Germany has institutionalised stronger training programmes and cultivated stronger links between vocational and academic study, apprenticeships, and firms than has been the case in the UK. In the UK, there has been a switch in policy in schools and colleges towards vocationalism, but this has typically been underfunded, poorly managed and, most importantly, regarded as being of lower status than the traditional academic training that most undertake. In reality, therefore, the UK has tended to create a 'cheap, "surrogate" labour force of trainees', which has made it even 'more attractive to profit-making firms to work young people hard rather than to train them' (Lee, 1991, p. 102).

There are, therefore, important regional and national differences in the life chances of working and middle-class youths seeking to move into the labour market. At the same time, the broad dynamics shaping the labour market as a whole – segmentation, polarisation and globalisation – mean that the changes being experienced by adult workers – growing vulnerability, higher pay accompanied by ever greater job pressures, casualised insecure work and so on – will have to be confronted by new workers too.

Finally, another theme explored by sociologists is young people's response to marginalisation. Rather than this being a condition that some have the misfortune to experience through no fault of their own, there is evidence that some young people may actively marginalise themselves from wider society. This is linked to the notion that some sections of youth act as an anti-social underclass, linked to a subculture of crime or an alternative dropout culture. However, it is debatable whether such a status is deliberately pursued or is a choice that a restrictive and disadvantaged social environment forces on some young people.

Despite this, governments appear to regard the marginalisation of young people – for example, from the labour market – as self-inflicted, since in the US, many European countries and Australasia, it is defined as unwillingness to work. MacDonald (1997, p. 19) noted that government policies have penalised the young through 'the withdrawal of unemployment benefits for under 18 year-olds, punitive policies on young offenders, authoritarian restrictions on young people's cultures and social lives ... and the growing clamour for citizenship or workfare programmes for the young unemployed'. Good examples of this are the New Deal programmes introduced by the UK and US governments.

Hence, there are a variety of ways in which young people may, during this part of their life course, experience social exclusion – and react against government policies to tackle it. We should not tie these problems to the state of being young, nor regard this stage of the life course as necessarily linked to social exclusion. The same applies to older people: we should not regard those who are older as more likely to be subject to social exclusion. The danger here, as with the conventional notion of youth, is that we will treat the aged as a homogeneous group who experience disadvantage and inequality because of their advancing years.

QUESTION Were there experiences in your own youth that you think excluded you from mainstream society? Write a paragraph on those experiences and why you see them as exclusion.

Older people

The physical process of growing older may not in itself lead people to view themselves and their personal identity as growing older too. Many people comment that their advancing years have no effect on how they see themselves, but they do change the way in which other people – bolstered by social institutions such as the official retirement age – relate to them. There are, of course, especially in a population whose average life expectancy is about 80 years, increasing numbers of older people who experience physical and mental deterioration as a result of the gradual slow-down of physiological processes. There are also increasing numbers of older people who, thanks to better health care, nutrition, exercise regimes and so on, do not conform to the cultural stereotype of the aged. Yet it is likely that these too will experience some form of social exclusion and marginalisation, simply because of the stigma of being old.

Retirement from work is one form of age-related segregation that sets off those who still have a future in work from those for whom work, with its cultural and material benefits, is at an end. While many older people do not feel any different, they find that – as Biggs (1997) argues – a gap has opened up between their sense of self and the restrictive, dependency-generating social environment. Because of this, despite having different physical and social circumstances, many older people have a shared sense of generational identity that sets them off from the younger generations. This process haas been given added momentum by the growth of products designed specifically for the elderly – such as specialist holiday packages, furniture, gardening devices, fashion and so on.

The sociology of ageing is sometimes referred to as social gerontology. This focuses on important issues related to a person's physical age – such as the official retirement age, or whole-society phenomena, such as the increase in the number of people aged 65 and over (Box 4.5). But it does not treat the process of social ageing as tied in any simple, linear way to the chronological passing of the years. Age is not only socially constructed, but is also continually being redefined as a result of overall improvements in health, changes in welfare provision, new forms of leisure, and changing social norms in respect of sexuality, marriage, reproduction and so on. State provision for older people is also changing in response to these dynamics, especially with regard to the State redefining its obligation to older people in light of the increasing number who are dependent on government support.

BOX 4.5 The demographic shift

By 2025 [the world population] is likely to have reached over eight billion, 10 times what it was in 1750. By the end of the first quarter of the twenty-first century ... there are likely to be 800 million people over 65, well over three times the number in the mid-1980s. They will constitute nearly 10% of the world population.... The proportion of the European population in 2025 who will be over 65 will be more than 18%, nearly twice the world aver- age. What cannot be gainsaid is the massive worldwide increase in older people; by the year 2000 there will be as many older people on earth as there were people of all ages 300 years ago in 1700.

Source: Midwinter (1997), pp. 5–6.

Much of the sociological analysis of social ageing has focused on the patterns of social exclusion and marginalisation that older people experience. For example, a considerable amount of research has been conducted on the material deprivation experienced by the elderly and the growing number who fall into poverty. We have seen that for young people the experiences of marginalisation and social exclusion are often associated with the difficulty of moving into the labour market. But for older people, it is their exit from work through retirement that is the main source of social exclusion. Retirement is likely to be particularly hard for those for whom work was an important source of social status, identity and, most importantly, independence (see Turner, 1993). Nevertheless, it is also true that once retirement was institutionalised in Europe and elsewhere as a socially acceptable period in which state and/or private pension provision would be made, it offered those who left the labour market a legitimate role as ex-worker. As long as this provision is sustained and sustainable, retirement need not necessarily mean sudden social isolation or a significant drop in living standards. However, this is most likely to be true of white-collar, middle-class professionals who continue some aspect of their working life during retirement. For less advantaged social classes, retirement may well be accompanied by a sense of social redundancy and exclusion.

CONNECTIONS For an exploration of the potential link between marginalisation and crime, see Chapter 14, pages 386–9 and 394–8.

The differing experiences of the impact of retirement tend to reflect differences between the incomes that older people take with them to retirement. Until relatively recently, a significant minority (44 per cent) of over 65s were counted among the poorest 10 per cent of the population. Today, in the UK and elsewhere across Europe, their relative position has marginally improved, though this reflects a worsening of the situation for the lowest-paid workers in employment rather than a real increase in the disposable income of older people. At the same time, the pensions upon which the retired depend have become more unequal than in the past, in that many new pensioners enjoy higher levels of support via private or employment-related pensions. This means that income inequalities among pensioners are likely to continue to increase, pointing to the need for us to differentiate among older people themselves as much as between them and the younger generations.

Moreover, as in the past, older women are most likely to experience higher levels of deprivation and marginalisation than men, reflecting the historically poorer pension rights and provision that women had been accorded, as well as the fact that the majority of women have had to withdraw from work or take part-time positions in order to look after their children. In other words, child-rearing responsibilities play an important role in later life. As Irwin (1999, p. 707) observes, this “demonstrates the 'coherence' of relations across generations: the claims of children to care are met through the obligations of parents which are in turn embedded in a structure of distributional arrangements which place most women at a 'remove' from economic independence. These processes are very important in shaping patterns of poverty and inequality in later life. ”

As well as social class and gender differences among older people becoming increasingly significant, many sociologists argue that an intergenerational conflict is likely to emerge as the resource demands made by older people will place a growing burden on the actively employed and economically productive – and therefore taxable – younger generation. Growing resentment among those in work will, it is argued, be directed against the elderly as government policy will ensure that those in work will also have to take increased responsibility for their own retirement provision. The social contract between the generations and the moral consensus associated with the welfare state will be more difficult to honour and sustain as the tension between the generations grows.

This tension will be accentuated by the already present tendency to regard older people as out of step with the youth-oriented consumer society. Ageism distances the elderly from mainstream culture and can be found not only in everyday family life – where the elderly are given lower social worth and suffer what has been called 'elder abuse' – but also in institutional settings (such as hospitals and residential homes) where professional care is provided and where, in theory, ageism and abuse should not be found. Within families, elder abuse is typically a result of the pressure on family members, usually middle-aged women, not simply to care *about* but to care *for* elderly relatives. Carers within families have to perform tedious and often physically and mentally demanding tasks to meet the needs of highly dependent relatives. As Hugman (1994, p. 81) observes, 'in such circumstances the carer may experience the role as a burden, and transfer this to the older person psychologically (through the emotional and other interpersonal aspects of the relationship) or physically (by withholding care or by direct ill-treatment)'.

As stated above, similar patterns of behaviour have been found in professional settings. For example, Biggs (1999) argues that professional staff have the same negative stereotypes of the elderly as those found in the wider culture. They may also give priority to the organisational demands of the institution in which they work, rather than to the individual needs of its residents, resulting in ill-treatment or neglect.

The increasing proportion of older people in society has led to growth in the number of professional medical services and staff to service them. In the past, geriatrics was regarded as a low-status medical field, since it was geared to serving the needs of patients who were close to the end of their lives and for whom curative treatments were few and far between. However, demographic changes and the greater affluence of many in the older population have led to an increased professional and commercial interest in this new 'medical market', with the result that there has been a 'bio-medicalisation' of ageing, where preventing the decline and decay of the body has opened up a profitable drugs market (see Estes and Binney, 1989; Phillipson, 1998).

Governments' response to the dependency of the old has been to reduce welfare provision and benefits and to expect more people to make provision for their own care, framed in terms of 'empowerment' and 'user involvement'. For Phillipson (1998, pp. 3–4), this withdrawal of services is creating a social crisis of ageing linked to new forms of social exclusion:

“For a period, retirement and the welfare state ensured a focus for the social construction of old age. Both were seen to contribute to the emerging identity associated with later life. …

However, with the foundations of both now removed, the location and meaning of old age has become uncertain. "

Phillipson argues that sociology needs to develop a 'sociology of exclusion', especially one that focuses on later life (Box 4.6). He also argues that governments should focus less on older people and more on the ageing society as a whole, a point also made by Bernard and Phillips (2000), who call for policies that will foster better links between the generations and construct a new social contract between them.

BOX 4.6 Towards a sociology of exclusion

The argument ... is for developing a 'sociology of exclusion' ... that focuses on the way in which identities in later life are controlled and managed within dominant social institutions. In the early twenty-first century, these are likely to focus around four types of exclusion: firstly ideological, with the continuing alarmism and scapegoating associated with population ageing; second, economic, with the construction of regular crises and threats to the funding of state pensions and other types of support; third political, with the curtailment of civil rights in areas or zones (for example, retirement communities) where older people congregate; fourth, affective, with the failure to recognise the emotional needs associated with the various changes running through the life course.

Source: Phillipson (1998), p. 138.

The above discussion of the patterns of social exclusion experienced by those at both ends of the life course, has not considered the way in which their marginalisation is complicated by discrimination associated with gender and ethnicity. This oversight is partly because these issues are explored in Chapters 6 and 7, but it also reflects the relative absence of research on the relationship between gender, ethnicity and old age. As Hugman (1994, p. 141) comments in respect of ethnicity, 'this is an issue which is only just beginning to be addressed. The relatively small proportion of older people within ethnic minority communities makes them even less visible to white European policy-makers and professionals, so that they are further marginalised: a minority within minorities.' A similar story can be told about those in society who, because of disability, have suffered from various forms of economic and cultural marginalisation. They have only recently become the focus of sustained sociological research and analysis, primarily through a subfield of the discipline called disability studies, which originated in the late 1980s. It is to this issue that we now turn in order to complete our examination of patterns of social exclusion. In the following discussion, we move away from patterns of inequality and social division that can be explicitly linked to the life course, as for many disabled people, disability lies at the heart of inequality throughout their life.

Disability

Sociological analysis of disability has been limited, as disability has tended to be regarded as the concern of social psychology, public health or the clinical sciences. However, this marginalisation of the disabled from the sociological perspective has been challenged by US and European sociologists – some of whom are themselves disabled – who have recognised the need to open up disability to both theoretical and empirical research. In the past few years, we have seen the development of a number of areas of work that have been usefully summarised by Barton (1996), as shown in Box 4.7.

BOX 4.7 Areas of work in the sociology of disability

The following are the main areas of interest in the sociology of disability, or 'disability studies':

- Generation of a social theory of disability.
- The social construction of categories of disability.
- Professional ideologies and practices.
- The construction of policy.

- Accounts of the lived experience of disabled people.
- The development of enabling forms of methodology and research practice.
- Examination of the disability movement as a social movement for change.

Source: Adapted from Barton (1996), p. 6.

Much of this work has been geared to developing a strong social and political critique of the conventional social stigma of the disabled as incapable, impaired people – as 'in-valid' – and redefining disability as a condition and a process that is exacerbated and reproduced by social structures and institutions designed to meet able-bodied needs. As Hahn (1989, p. 128) says, 'disability stems from the failure of a structured social environment to adjust to the needs and aspirations of citizens with disabilities *rather than* from the inability of a disabled individual to meet the demands of society' (emphasis in original).

In Chapter 13, we examine the sociology of health, illness and medicine and discuss the 'sick role' that people play as patients subject to medical examination and intervention. Disabled people find playing a sick role much more problematic because of the chronic difficulties they face, such that getting better and ending the sick role

Figure 4.2 Disability theorists differentiate between physical 'impairment' and 'disability', locating the latter in the social arrangements that effectively exclude physically impaired people from participating fully in society.

BOX 4.8 The medical model of disability

The medical model of disability

- sees disability as a specialised medical condition requiring the intervention of suitably skilled and qualified professionals;
- fosters the fallacy that our needs are special or some-how different from everyone else's;
- sees disabled persons and their families as passive recipients of care, patients who have no informed opinion and therefore need not be consulted about matters that directly concern them;
- highlights inabilities and ignores less manifest abilities;
- strives after cures, no matter how time-consuming, expensive or futile these may be.

Source: Adapted from Camilleri (1999), p. 849.

performance is often impossible. The absence of an alternative role through which to define their disability means that their life and their identity, as seen by others, are often defined entirely in terms of their disability, rather than the latter being something that is peripheral or temporary, as in the case of acute but remedial illnesses. This point is made strongly by Camilleri (1999, p. 848), who observes that 'The common assumptions about disability focus on our lack of abilities. The negative terms most frequently used to describe us: crippled, handicapped, less fortunate, all accentuate our post-lapsarian imperfections compared with our (presumably) more "blessed" brethren'. Camilleri also argues that – as we saw with the elderly – disability is primarily framed by the medical model, as summarised in Box 4.8.

When challenging the medical model, some writers have adopted a neo-Marxist perspective and argue that a **materialist** reading of disability is needed, in that, historically, the disabled were marginalised from society by being excluded from the labour market when capitalist factories began to base employment on individual waged labour. As Oliver (1996, p.28) notes, when the capitalist mode of production was established during the industrial revolution, 'so many [disabled people] were unable to keep or retain jobs that they became a social problem for the capitalist state whose initial response to all social problems was harsh deterrence and institutionalisation'. Even today, 70 per cent of disabled people of working age do not have jobs, and disabled people are three times more likely to be unemployed than others. The promise of modernity to create modern institutions that would foster secure and meritocratic employment has been highly selective in the way it has been delivered. Indeed, these same institutions have in effect constructed an environment that is itself disabling for some people, and it is this that disability theory draws to our attention and challenges.

The marginalisation of the disabled has led to calls for their 'normalisation' as socially valued members of society, and government programmes in the US, Europe and elsewhere have been developed to pursue this apparently enlightened goal, particularly for those with learning difficulties. Such programmes have, however, been criticised by those who are disabled, since they tend to foster the view that normalisation requires incorporation into the dominant social norms and values under the direction and control of professional services. This merely reconfirms the social division that enforces their deviant status and identity and fails to accord value to their own competences.

Materialism
In its Marxist usage, an emphasis on economic and political relations.

CONNECTIONS For a fuller account of the position of the disabled with regard to work, see Chapter 11, pages 317–18.

One response to this has been the development of a disabled people's movement to assert the disabled identity as empowering, and to challenge the dependency role and the subordination of the disabled by professionals and those around them. However, mobilising such a movement has been particularly problematic, not only because of the wide variety of disabilities, but also because such a movement could serve to confirm, rather than weaken, the view that disabled people's identities are defined through their disability. This movement, then, has both positive and negative aspects. It has sought links with other groups experiencing discrimination, such as gay, ethnic, labour and women's movements, but these links have not always proved successful. For example, there is evidence of disablism among trade unions, who have shown reluctance to change their working practices or revise job specifications to accommodate the needs of disabled people. Even so, these links with other minorities have highlighted both the cross-cutting discrimination experienced by, for example, disabled women, and the extra burdens of disadvantage and marginalisation that such people confront. Disabled women's sexuality and femininity is conventionally marginalised or regarded as deviant. Tom Shakespeare (1996, p.200) reports the words of one respondent in his study on disabled people:

> "I heard there were these two people in the supermarket, and they were both wheelchair users, and they had a kiss, I don't know why they wanted to kiss in a supermarket, but they did, and somebody came up to them and said 'Do you mind, it's bad enough that there are two of you'."

The disabled, like older people, are stereotypically defined as sexually inactive, and activities that go against this label are seen as deviant. Disability identities are therefore especially difficult to construct as 'normal' in a society where normality is defined primarily in terms of being white, heterosexual and physically able-bodied.

Likewise, the cross-cutting relationship between disability, ethnicity, gender and class means that being, for example, gay and disabled can lead to even greater social marginalisation, although as Vernon (1999, p. 395) notes, 'one plus one does not equal two oppressions'. Vernon comments that 'the stigma of being impaired and black and/or female and/or gay interacts in varied and complex ways in shaping daily experience' (ibid.) It is likely, however, that, at the individual level, this daily experience will be one of discrimination and complex forms of social exclusion.

QUESTION Do you think that disability is more about a disabling environment than physical impairment? Support your argument with appropriate sociological material.

 ## Conclusion

This chapter has examined the concept of social division and shown how divisions based on economic resources, the life course and the body have been socially constructed and institutionally reproduced in late modern societies. We have seen how these divisions are typically patterned along clear lines of social stratification, which in turn can be closely related to various forms of social exclusion and marginalisation. The cross-cutting dynamics of all three processes can create very complex social orders and hierarchies, and complex patterns of social identity. Modernity has not simplified the processes of social division and differentiation. On the contrary, it has accentuated them. It has also encouraged a feeling of fragmentation and dislocation among those who respond by attempting to redefine their position in the social divide, as illustrated by the disability movement, 'grey power' and some youth movements.

We have also seen that social divisions can be particularly resilient, especially when tied to wider social structures, such as those associated with the major class divisions in society. In the next chapter, we shall consider whether class is still important in shaping social inequality.

 Chapter summary

- The term social divisions refers to the ways in which we construct social barriers between ourselves, based on economic, cultural or political considerations. Core social divisions reproduce ongoing inequalities in society.

- Structures of inequality lead to hierarchical social divisions known as social stratification, expressed in terms of gender, age, class, ethnicity and so on.

- Wealth and poverty are economic forms of social division shaped by national and global processes that determine patterns of advantage and disadvantage.

- Social exclusion refers to the ways in which individuals or social groups experience social marginalisation and discrimination: youth, disability and the ageing process are closely associated with social exclusion.

- Social divisions in modernity both fragment identity and create new forms of identity, sparking new social movements, such as those associated with youth or the disabled.

 Questions to think about

- What are the principal forms of wealth, and how is wealth holding changing at the national and international levels?
- What evidence is there that the poor constitute an underclass?
- To what extent are new forms of social exclusion creating new forms of social identity in late modern society?

 Investigating further

Alcock, Pete (1997) *Understanding Poverty*, 2nd edition, Palgrave.
> This clear introductory text has useful chapters on what poverty is and its causes and dynamics. It links the understanding of poverty to detailed examinations of gender, racism, ageing and disability.

Bradley, Harriet (1995) *Fractured Identities: Changing Patterns of Inequality*, Polity Press.
> This book examines the view that societies are becoming more fragmented and social identities more fluid. It argues that polarisation between the 'haves' and 'have nots' is still very much in evidence. It explores how class, gender, race and age interact with each other, locating the analysis in current debates on modernity and postmodernity.

Oliver, Michael (1996) *Understanding Disability*, Palgrave.
> This book, published as a collection of discrete essays, analyses the relationship between disability, its bio-medical definition and its construction in contemporary capitalist society. It explores the emergence of the disability movement and develops a powerful account of the connection between the personal and the political.

Payne, Geoff (ed.) (2000) *Social Divisions*, Palgrave.
> A comprehensive text with chapters on a range of social divisions, including class, race, gender, childhood, old age, disability and sexuality. A useful introductory chapter explains the broad meaning of social divisions and suggests how these might change over time.

Pilcher, Jane (1995) *Age and Generation in Modern Britain*, Oxford University Press.
> As the title suggests, the empirical material in this text is British, but it offers a very concise and accessible introduction to the subject.

Social class

CHAPTER CONTENTS

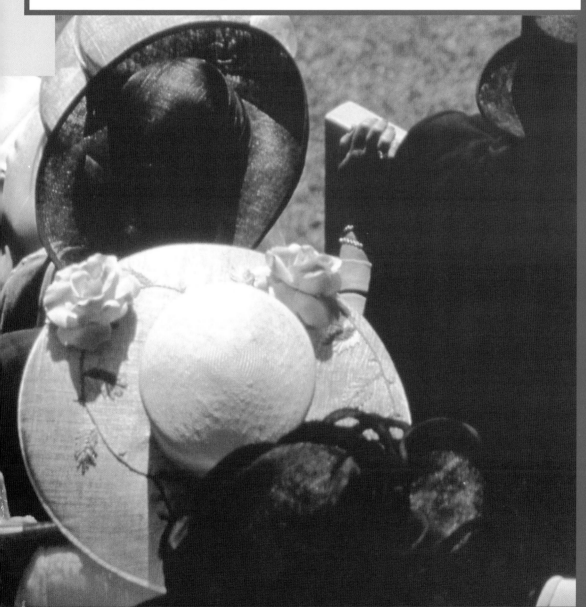

Aims of the chapter

In this chapter, we focus on one of the most historically important forms of social division, namely social class. We shall examine debates about the continuing significance of class in contemporary society. In order to do this, we have to understand the various ways in which class is defined. The chapter concentrates on the processes by which occupational classes (the middle and working classes) have been reproduced over generations, and the ways in which the class identity that this has encouraged has depended on a stable, nationally determined labour market. It goes on to suggest that this reproduction is being weakened by the impact of global processes. It then looks at the implications of these changes for established jobs and social mobility, and ends with a discussion of the contemporary significance of class and class identities.

By the end of the chapter, you should have an understanding of the following concepts:

- Capitalism and social class
- Social status
- Class reproduction
- Embourgeoisement
- Labour market segmentation
- Social mobility
- Class decomposition

 Introduction

In Chapter 4, we described the principal forms of social division found throughout contemporary societies. We noted that class is one of a number of forms of social stratification along with gender, ethnicity and so on. We saw how these are not only interrelated but are also shaped by the impact of globalisation, a process that has (as we saw in Chapter 3) both economic and cultural dimensions. Globalisation is creating important changes in the way in which class culture, identity and positions are reproduced at the national level.

We begin with a discussion of the two main theories which have informed much of the sociological understanding of class – the Marxist and the Weberian. Each of these perspectives locates the fundamental basis for and boundaries of class in different social and economic processes; Marxism in property relations and Weberianism in occupational labour-market relations. We then consider an approach to defining class boundaries developed in the UK for the purpose of statistical classification and examine its assumptions. The bulk of the chapter explores the reproduction of the middle and working classes, who constitute the majority of people in late modern capitalist societies.

In early 2000, the working class (skilled manual, partly skilled and unskilled manual) and the middle class (professional, intermediate and skilled non-manual) comprised approximately 35.4 per cent and 51.6 per cent of the UK population respectively; 12.9 per cent of the population were described as 'other' (including members of the armed forces, those who did not state their current or last occupation and those who had not worked in the past eight years). If the group described as skilled non-manual are defined as working class rather than middle class, the approximate percentages are as follows: middle class, 30.8 per cent; working class, 56.2 per cent; other, 12.9 per cent (Office for National Statistics, 2001a, 2001b).

The upper class, though small (perhaps 1 per cent or so of the UK population), wields a degree of power that is disproportionate to its size, largely through property relations. It therefore warrants (and receives) some discussion. That said, our main focus is on the processes that appear to be destabilising the traditional means by which the middle and working classes have been reproduced, and we argue that these groupings – as stable occupational groups – are being fragmented both culturally and economically. We conclude by asking whether the declining significance of occupational membership and the growth of a consumption culture is decomposing class and thus reducing its significance.

These processes have major implications for anyone competing for work in the US, Europe and Australasia, especially newcomers to the labour market – the younger generation looking for their first job. The traditional routes by which careers have been secured are less likely to be available. Occupational communities in towns and cities are being broken up, new, more flexible work patterns are appearing, and greater individual mobility across a more volatile labour market is required.

In these circumstances, many may have little or no sense of class position or class identity, and think that survival depends more on personal enterprise and being entrepreneurial. Indeed, the 1980s and 1990s saw the emergence of an **enterprise culture** in which supposedly anyone, given sufficient drive, initiative and training, could get on. The UK Labour government, it is argued, kept faith with this culture when we entered the twenty-first century.

Is this true? What has happened to the traditional forms of class identity and class-based jobs? In what ways did occupational groups reproduce themselves in the past? Are similar patterns in evidence today? Before we answer these questions, we need to define the boundaries of class, for unless we do that, we cannot know whether substantial changes have taken place.

Enterprise culture
An environment that acclaims and rewards those who show initiative by setting up businesses and creating wealth.

Understanding social class

As noted in Chapter 4, social classes are one of the defining features of modern industrial society. Social classes did exist prior to the Industrial Revolution: in the feudal period, for example, classes were by and large determined by birth and were closely related to access to and ownership of land. The move from pre-industrial to industrial society was marked more than anything else by a shift in the nature and experience of work, and how it was controlled, rewarded and mobilised geographically. These dramatic changes led not only to massive growth in economic productivity, but also to new patterns of social inequality and social conflict. Two classical sociologists who have contributed to our understanding of the dynamics of class are Marx and Weber.

Marx's theory of property relations

For many sociologists, modern society is distinguished from earlier society by its essentially industrial character. Marx recognised the importance of industrialisation as a moderning process, but for him this process could only be properly understood as a capitalist one. Thus, although industry produced wealth, it did so in a highly unequal way, with one class, the bourgeoisie, monopolising the profits of industrial production, while the mass of the people who worked in the new factories were made poorer, not richer, by the social and technical advances of industrial development. In the unfinished Volume 3 of *Capital*, Marx identified three social classes (cited in Coser and Rosenberg, 1969, p. 379):

> "The owners of mere labor-power, the owners of capital, and the landlords, whose respective sources of income are wages, profit and ground-rent, in other words, wage laborers, capitalists and landlords, form the three great classes of modern society resting upon the capitalist mode of production "

As the Industrial Revolution gathered pace, the owners of capital and the landlords gradually fused into a new ruling class. The members of this class came from a variety of social backgrounds, but all had a distinctly capitalist outlook. Once the economic and social dust had settled, English society was characterised by two main classes; a ruling bourgeois class of property-owning employers and a working proletariat class of employee wage earners. These classes, claim Marxist sociologists, were in conflict with each other as exploiter and exploited. The bourgeoisie derived their class position from the fact that they owned productive wealth: it was not their high income that made them capitalists but the fact that they owned the means of production (that is, the inputs necessary for industrial manufacture – factories, machines and so on).

There was a general tendency, Marx claimed, for wages to stick at an exploitative level except when some skills were temporarily scarce. In addition, the capitalist owned the product and pocketed the difference between the value of the labour and the value of the product – 'surplus value', as Marx called it. Property rights also gave capitalists control – through their managers – over the process of production. Workers had to sell their labour power in order to survive, and so their labour became a commodity on the labour market. Thus, the crucial division between the two main classes lay in their different relationship to the ownership of the means of production.

In *The Critique of the Gotha Programme*, Marx explored the emergent strains and tensions that arise between the two main classes. He argued that class conflict was not only inherent but also inevitable within capitalism: the logic of capitalism was to exploit workers to realise profit, while workers' exploitation would lead them eventually to challenge the system. The working class would then become a revolutionary class, ushering in first a socialist regime and then the communist utopia, 'where society inscribes on its banners: "From each according to his ability, to each according to his needs!"' (cited in McLellan, 1977, p. 569).

It is clear that there are serious problems with Marx's account. When socialist revolution has occurred, it has mainly been in societies on the threshold of entering capitalism, such as Russia in 1917, or via a nationalist populism, such as China in 1949, rather than in mature capitalist states ripe for change. Secondly, in Western states, the working class has enjoyed an increase in wages in real terms, while the development of the welfare state has ameliorated some of the worse effects of unemployment. Thirdly, state socialism in Europe collapsed like a house of cards between 1989 and 1992, and the ensuing charge towards capitalism in former communist states in Central and Eastern Europe took, among other things, BMWs, McDonald's and Marlboro cigarettes to the streets of Bucharest, Budapest and Moscow.

Marx's ideas seem to have been disproved by these late-twentieth-century events. This has led to a gradual distancing from Marxist analysis in sociology as the newer theories of consumption, postmodernism and post-socialism take root (see Chapter 19). Yet there is much to be said for Marx's basic assumption that class should be defined not merely in terms of categories such as occupation, but in terms of a deeper under-

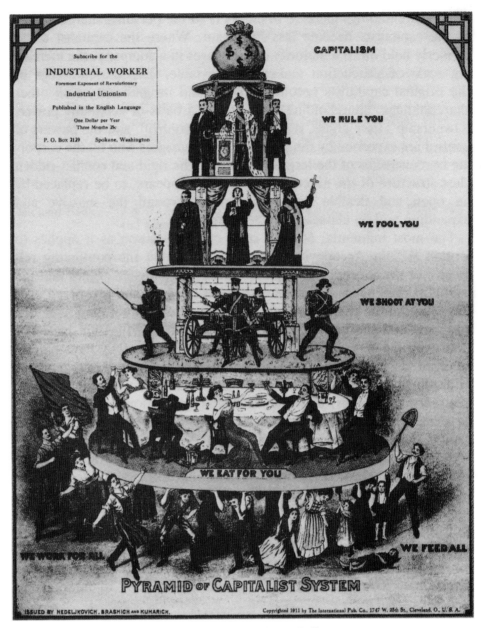

Figure 5.1 A Marxist view of the class system under capitalism.

standing of property relations, control and ownership. In property relations lies much of the source of economic and social power, even if this does not adequately account for all forms of power and inequality. In addition, Marx envisaged the expansion of capitalism on a global scale as capital sought to exploit markets and labour overseas: to this extent, his analysis anticipated the global concentration of capital discussed in Chapter 3.

What we can say in criticism is that Marx's emphasis on the ownership of productive wealth and the structure of power associated with it is unable to explain all the differences in rewards and political consciousness within society. Indeed, this has led many sociologists to look elsewhere for insight into the complexity of social inequality. It is to the ideas of Max Weber (1864–1920) that some turn for a more nuanced analysis of patterns of inequality. Yet the Marxist insight should not be lost. Indeed, there is ongoing debate between those who define class in revised, neo-Marxian, terms and those who define it in neo-Weberian terms.

Weber's theory of market relations

Status
Prestige of social standing in the eyes of others. A term particularly associated with Weber.

Weber argued that social inequality needed to be understood in terms of a number of distinct categories that were not just reducible to economic property relations. While the ownership of land, factories and so on was an important determinant of social position, it was only one factor shaping social stratification. Weber proposed that inequality should be understood through the threefold categories of 'class', '**status**' and 'power'. Some social positions were more to do with one of these than the others: for example, caste in India is based more on status differences associated with a religious ranking of ritual purity than on anything else. Weber argued that those who were advantaged in any one of these categories could use that as a basis for amassing privileges and rewards more commonly associated with the other two. For example, someone who enjoys high status may use this as a form of leverage to secure an improved economic or political position. Alternatively, powerful politicians can use their position to mobilise their party for economic gain. This may sometimes be pursued in such a way as to end in mass corruption and clientelism, as was the case in Serbia during the 1990s, when political office at all levels of society was used in an illegitimate way to secure economic benefit.

For Weber, therefore, these different forms of inequality – class, status and (political) power – were to some extent independent of each other. Unlike Marx, he would not have argued that social class was the principal determinant of inequality. Nevertheless, Weber did agree with Marx that in capitalist industrial society, economic relations played a crucial role in shaping inequalities between individuals and groups. However, Weber more than Marx recognised that occupation differentiated the fault line between employers and employees.

In that respect, Weber wanted to stress inequalities associated with the occupational *market* rather than just with the ownership of property. Inequalities in market capacity determined the position people occupied in the occupational hierarchy. The capacities people had in terms of the skills they brought to the labour market as employees explained the rewards they received. Those with good market capacities – such as accountants and doctors – would have good life chances. These chances included income perks and pensions, together with benefits such as job security, pleasant working conditions and considerable autonomy at work. Different groups with different occupational market capacities, and therefore unequal life chances, could be regarded as different social classes. Inevitably, this definition led to a larger number of social classes than Marx's basic division between the owners and non-owners of the means of production.

Weber's work has been supported by many contemporary sociologists, such as Marshall *et al.* (1988) and Goldthorpe and Marshall (1992). They see it explaining both the broad differences in occupational reward and position of manual and non-manual workers, and gradations of social position within each class grouping – for example, between senior managerial staff and routine clerical workers in the non-manual sector. Similarly, manual classes' market capacities vary as one moves down the social hierarchy from skilled, to semi-skilled and to unskilled manual jobs.

It is possible to acknowledge the merits of both the Marxist and the Weberian account of social stratification, since they provide valuable insights into different aspects of the contemporary capitalist system. A combination of these two traditions would produce a threefold distinction between a propertied upper class, a large white-collar middle or service class, and a working class of manual workers. Beneath these are 'the poor' – a fourth group whose members have the worst life chances because they are excluded from or marginalised in the labour market. These are the infirm, the disabled, the aged, lone-parent families and so on. Figure 5.2 depicts a combined Marxian/Weberian model of stratification.

CONNECTIONS For a fuller account of the work of Weber, see Chapter 17, pages 482–7.

Before considering recent (government-formulated) models of class, which place more emphasis on occupational differentiation than on property relations, it is pertinent to consider the small but powerful group at the top of the pyramid: the upper class. Here we find big property owners with huge capital assets and share incomes. The richest 1000 of these people are identified each year in *The Sunday Times'* 'Rich List'. Upper-class people are tribalistic, moving and marrying within relatively closed social circles, marked by lavish homes and life styles, attendance at public school and Oxbridge and participation in the 'social calendar'. Upper-class people are disproportionately over-represented – aided by elite self-recruitment – in some of the key strategic command posts of British society: politics, the civil service, business, the military and the judiciary.

QUESTION Which of the two approaches – Marxist or Weberian – do you think is most useful for explaining class divisions in late modern societies? Give reasons for your answer.

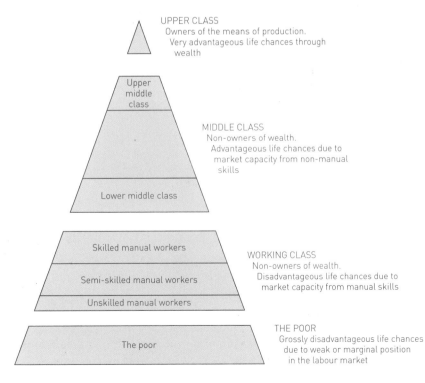

Figure 5.2
Social class stratification by income and wealth.

UPPER CLASS
Owners of the means of production.
Very advantageous life chances through wealth

Upper middle class

MIDDLE CLASS
Non-owners of wealth.
Advantageous life chances due to market capacity from non-manual skills

Lower middle class

Skilled manual workers

WORKING CLASS
Non-owners of wealth.
Disadvantageous life chances due to market capacity from manual skills

Semi-skilled manual workers

Unskilled manual workers

The poor

THE POOR
Grossly disadvantageous life chances due to weak or marginal position in the labour market

Classifying social class

It should be clear that the social class hierarchy shown in Figure 5.2 makes assumptions about the relative importance of the ownership of wealth, compared with the advantages derived from the labour market. The life chances that wealth and skill-based occupational positions bring are uneven and create the ordering, and therefore the classification, of social class presented in the figure.

The divisions of social class this produces have for many years been used as the basis for governmental classifications of the class hierarchy to distinguish between occupational groups. Traditionally, the labour market hierarchy has been based on differential skill levels and the rewards they bring (such as the differentiation between **blue-collar** and **white-collar** work). However, as with any classification, social changes have produced new models to represent class stratification. In the UK, a social classification system called the National Statistics Socio-Economic Classification (NS-SEC) was produced for the government in the 1990s. This replaced the Registrar General's 'Social Class Based on Occupation' scheme. Although the new approach (not unlike a Weberian model) still focused on the rewards associated with different occupations, social classes were differentiated not on the basis of skill but on employment conditions and relations.

The NS-SEC is now based on the Standard Occupational Classification (SOC) 2000 (see National Statistics, 2001b). The first division is into three broad groups: employers, own-account self-employed, and employees. Employees are further divided in terms of their employment conditions: ranging from higher managerial and professional salaried occupations with good promotion prospects, sick pay and discretion over the planning of work, to routine occupations with hourly pay or piecework, no prospects of promotion and limited fringe benefits. Other categories fall between these two extremes.

The SOC 2000 NS-SEC has seven main classes, the first of which is split into two subdivisions:

1. Higher managerial and professional occupations:
    1.1 employers and managers in large organisations;
    1.2 higher professionals.
2. Lower managerial and professional occupations.
3. Intermediate occupations.
4. Small employers and own-account workers.
5. Lower supervisory, craft and related occupations.
6. Semi-routine occupations.
7. Routine occupations.

An additional grouping, Class 8, defined as 'Never worked and long-term unemployed', is added when applicable. Class 8 also includes full-time students, occupations not stated or inadequately described, or not classifiable for other reasons.

In some respects, the SOC 2000 NS-SEC combines the Marxist (employers and employees) and Weberian (occupations) perspectives. It can also be used to provide a general map of the relative position of social classes to each other, defined largely in terms of different occupational groups. It does not, however, tell us much about the ways in which social classes are sustained as discrete social groups, maintaining specific identities over time. To understand this, we need to look more closely at the processes by which classes are reproduced from generation to generation, and it is to this that we turn next.

Blue-collar worker
A manual worker.

White-collar worker
A non-manual employee, for example an office or junior administrative worker.

> **QUESTION** Which social groups do not appear in occupational classifications of class? Does it matter if there are some groups missing from these models? Justify your response.

 ## The reproduction of social class

Social closure
Employed by Weber to describe the efforts made by social groups to deny entry to those outside the group and thereby maximise their own advantage.

Social classes survive from one generation to the next: they do this through **social closure** and **social reproduction**. Social closure refers to the extent to which a social class closes itself off from others. A class 'acts' in this way to secure its interests against other social classes, for example, by making upward social movement into its ranks difficult for members of subordinate social groups. In practice, of course, we do see the members of social classes acting together to build boundaries between themselves and others. What we do see are occupational groups who enjoy certain class-related advantages – such as high incomes, educational advantage and so on – using their class resources to sustain their relatively privileged position and exclude others from it. For example, an occupational group with a scarce skill may use its rarity as a bargaining chip to secure higher wages than other groups. The greater the ability of occupational and propertied classes to close themselves off, the more likely it is that the broad positions they occupy will be socially and culturally cohesive.

Social/class reproduction
The process by which, over time, groups of people, notably social classes, reproduce their social structures and patterns.

Social reproduction is about how social classes reproduce themselves from generation to generation. So while closure is a measure of the boundaries between classes, reproduction involves the economic and cultural resources that classes use to pass their privileges on to their children. As we shall see, these can include educational privileges and advantages – for example, the ability to pay for a private education.

In general, closure and reproduction can be used to understand the class differences and broad class boundaries that characterise a society. They tell us about the dynamics by which class structures are experienced and sustained as lived realities and not merely as abstract conceptions.

> **CONNECTIONS** For a further discussion of social closure, see Chapter 10, pages 270–1.

However, global processes have altered the context in which **class reproduction** occurs. One of the principal factors in this has been the decline of the manufacturing industry and the appearance of subsidiary factories owned by overseas capital investors. We saw in Chapter 3 how national economies have to be understood in terms of the dynamic of international, globalised processes, notably the actions of the large transnational corporations (TNCs) that act on behalf of what Sklair (1991) calls the emergent transnational capitalist class.

So, local class structures within a nation and their relative advantages and disadvantages are increasingly being shaped by external forces operating at the transnational level. The tension between domestic and global interests is most evident in countries where TNCs are particularly powerful, notably in the **Poor World** (still sometimes referred to as the Third World). As Sklair (ibid., p. 68) says:

The Poor World
(sometimes referred to as the Third World)
Poor countries not aligned politically with the large power blocs.

> "The transnational capitalist class, fractions of the labour force, and other support strata that the TNCs have created, will all increasingly identify their own interests with those of the capitalist global system and, if necessary, against the interests of their 'own' societies as the transnational practices of the system penetrate ever deeper into the areas that most heavily impact on their daily lives."

Before the emergence of a transnational class, however, there is likely to be a prolonged period of 'casino capitalism', as financial speculators move money around the world to cash in on differential rates of currency, interest and profitability (Strange, 1990).

Given that these factors are at work at the global level, we should recognise that the dynamics of class reproduction might be changing at the local level too. Before we explore this, we shall look at how social closure and reproduction have characterised the occupational groups of all middle and working classes until relatively recently. We shall not look at the upper class because the focus is on inequalities associated with occupational groups – groups or classes whose material resources derive primarily from the work they do rather than the wealth they own or inherit.

The middle class

Material advantages
Money and other material goods that offer people a greater chance of success in life than they would otherwise have.

The occupational positions of the middle class are diverse, and talking about a singular middle class tends to hide this. The SOC classification described on page 104 gives a rough approximation of the 'middle' in the first four groups listed, but covering a heterogeneous set of occupational contexts. Such is the diversity – in terms of income levels, occupational authority, employment status and so on – of those belonging to the middle class that some sociologists prefer to talk of the middle class*es*. While this is understandable, it is perhaps better to establish the broad boundaries of the middle class to identify its distinguishing features (Box 5.1).

BOX 5.1 The old and new middle class

The new and the old middle classes were separated by their respective relationships to property. Whereas the old middle class was a largely entrepreneurial, property-holding bourgeoisie ... the new middle class ... was essentially propertyless. ... The new middle class was also gaining influence in the United States outside business. Fields such as medicine, education, administration and social work were rationalised and professionalised as they expanded in response to the demands of an increasingly complex, urbanising, corporate society. ... The new middle class as a whole was therefore defined, and defined itself, not by the possession of material capital but rather by cultural capital – skill, expertise and educational attainment. Of course, these things cannot automatically be transmitted to one's descendants in the same way that wealth and property can; they have to be renewed by each generation through individual effort.

Source: Heffernan (2000), p. 32.

Cultural advantages
Life styles, religious beliefs, values and other practices that give people a greater chance of obtaining economic success and/or social status.

Broadly speaking, two key features characterise the middle-class position and provide a boundary between the middle and working classes. First, middle-class occupations provide significantly more **material advantages** than working-class jobs: not only are they better paid, they are more secure and enable the middle class to cover medical, schooling and housing costs. Such jobs are typically less health-threatening and involve more autonomy and responsibility than blue-collar work. In contrast, the working life of the working class normally lacks career prospects and is often disjointed, reflecting their vulnerability in the labour market.

Second, the middle class enjoys **cultural advantages** that derive from significantly higher levels of education and training, especially among professional, administrative and managerial groups. Although the expansion of educational provision has benefited all social classes since the Second World War, the sons and daughters of the middle class have secured much higher levels of achievement and advancement than other social groups (see Chapter 10).

The middle class can be divided into two broad groupings – the 'established' and the 'new'. The former refers to those with white-collar occupations associated with the emergence, from the late eighteenth century onwards, of the established professions – law, accountancy and medicine, for example – and with the civil service needed to cater for the growing administrative demands of the nation-states of Western Europe and North America. From the late nineteenth century, the ranks of the established middle class were swollen by newcomers following the growth of new managerial positions in private industry and the public sector.

There were not enough children from the older middle class to fill these new positions. One reason for this was the demographic impact of the First World War: the war decimated a whole generation of middle-class offspring serving as officers at the front. Hence, there emerged an expanding new middle class, that is, professional, salaried employees working in administration, banking and business, recruited in part from an increasingly educated and mobile working class. The post-1945 growth in private and public sector white-collar work gave further impetus to the growth of the new middle class. There was also an increase in the more junior ranks of white-collar office workers – a lower middle class, often also drawn from the working class.

But what about today? Given the different pay and terms of employment that exist between employees, it would be wrong to conclude that we are all middle class now. Indeed, some Marxists would probably argue that all employees are, in an important sense, working class because they all work for a living. If, however, we accept that some jobs are distinctly middle class, then we can reasonably expect that the middle class will expand as more people enter higher education and thereafter middle-class occupations.

CONNECTIONS The relationship between class, education and the labour market is explored in Chapter 10, pages 292–4, where the changing value of educational qualifications is discussed.

Reproduction of the middle class

Cultural capital
The cultural resources, skills and qualities which individuals possess, such as linguistic ability, social style and manners. Associated with Pierre Bourdieu, who claims that the more cultural capital individuals possess, the more successful they will be in the educational and occupational system.

While the older and newer branches of the middle class still enjoy considerable advantages over many working-class groups, their reproduction and closure is never fully secure. Why?

Though the growth of education and the expansion of non-manual jobs have favoured middle-class offspring, the fact is that non-manual job opportunities have grown at a much faster rate than the middle-class birth rate and hence the supply of employees from the established middle class. While the traditional professions such as medicine have continued to draw new members from solid middle-class backgrounds, elsewhere the story is rather different. The growth in managerial and office jobs has required recruitment from a much wider pool, including people from working-class backgrounds. Many of these recruits do not have the **cultural capital** – for example, that obtained from an Oxbridge, Harvard or Sorbonne education – of their more established peers.

These processes are affecting the cohesion of the middle class in two ways. First, since educational success is an important (though never sufficient) means of securing middle-class jobs, middle-class children who do not succeed in education are in danger of losing their middle-class status when they join the labour market. Indeed, they may

Social mobility
The movement of
individuals in a
stratified society
from one position
in the social
hierarchy to
another. Usually
relates to
occupational
position or social
class.

undergo downward **social mobility** and find themselves working in low-paid white-collar work or blue-collar working-class jobs. Such children are among what the French sociologist Pierre Bourdieu (1999, p. 508) calls the 'long-term sufferers from the gap between their accomplishments and the parental expectations they can neither satisfy nor repudiate'. Second, educational success can result in upward social mobility for children from traditional working-class backgrounds, sometimes as the proxy accomplishment of an ambition not quite accomplished by the parents (see Bourdieu, 1999). When this happens, the social mix of those occupying positions in the middle class increases, blurring the cultural boundary that marks off the middle class. (The broad relationship between educational opportunities and social position is explored much more fully in Chapter 10.)

Life for older-generation middle-class people has generally been good – higher pay and perks have enabled the trappings of middle-class respectability, such as a well-appointed suburban home, a cleaner, a child minder, two cars and so on. However, concern about their children's future has been growing among middle-class parents. They can see that the labour market is changing and that some of the older, well-trodden paths to respectability – well-paid public sector jobs in education, health and even the military – are becoming more difficult to negotiate. This is because cutbacks in state expenditure that favour the relatively well-to-do, **privatisation** and a decline in the number of career-long jobs in industry and elsewhere are undermining middle-class occupational positions. The loss of career-long jobs is especially threatening, since it means that the effort spent on securing good educational credentials might be wasted. Without the prospect of a steady career, training seems less worthwhile. As Grey (1994, p. 494) observes in connection with accountancy, 'Career provides a meaning and rationale for the otherwise disillusioning grind of accountancy training'.

Privatisation
The process of
transferring state
assets from public
to private
ownership.

Moreover, as the capacity for social closure declines, a growing number of people are occupying an intermediate position between the two broad middle- and working-class occupational groups. These intermediate positions have some of the features of middle-class status – white-collar, office or technical work reliant on educational qualifications – yet in terms of material reward – wages, pension rights, job security and so on – they are closer to typical working-class positions. Sociologists debate whether this once-respectable, secure and relatively well-paid clerical work has been down-graded: have routine non-manual workers such as clerks and secretarial staff become **proletarianised**? This change is partly due to the wider availability of clerical skills in the labour market. For example, in the UK in 1851, there were about 60 000 clerks, all of them male and working in small-scale professional settings such as banks. The subsequent growth of this tertiary sector means that there are now more than 14 million people working in office, administrative, retail and service sector jobs that do not offer high pay, are much less secure than in the past, and are often so tedious and routine that they are little different from jobs on an assembly line in a factory. Thus, according to some sociologists, the work is similar to that undertaken by the traditional (proletarian) working class, such that routine white-collar tasks are done by what might be called the non-manual section of the working class.

Proletarianisation
The process
whereby some
parts of the middle
class become
absorbed into the
working class.

Others, such as Goldthorpe (1987), argue that despite their low pay, office (and related) staff have (1) high job security, (2) enjoy staff status and (3) are functionally associated with the established middle (or service) class. According to Goldthorpe, office workers form an important part of a new intermediate class, a 'white collar labour force'. They do not have a strong sense of collective identity because there is considerable horizontal movement of workers between jobs of similar status, and therefore there is less possibility of a strong work-based culture developing. Also, many office workers,

Figure 5.3 Class schemes do not adequately reflect the pattern of women's employment, which is largely concentrated in the lower professions and in clerical, sales, cleaning and catering work.

especially women, take up part-time jobs, which limits the sense of a shared class culture.

Much depends, however, on the importance given to the material conditions and rewards of routine office work. If we believe that low levels of pay, job insecurity and poor working conditions are significant in determining the class position of a particular occupational group, we should agree with Heath and Britten (1984) that many women workers in routine non-manual jobs – for example, in offices, hotels and catering – cannot be differentiated from women in manual work. They have to be seen as occupying a 'fundamentally proletarian **market position**' (ibid., p.481). Indeed, gender subordination within the workplace applies across the full range of occupational classes. For example, women in higher-status non-manual jobs such as hotel management find that **patriarchal** discrimination works to exclude them from more senior, better paid jobs. Instead, they tend to be restricted to jobs such as housekeeping management (Bagguley, 1990). Determining the relationship between occupational class and gender is therefore of great importance to the study of social stratification.

Overall, the key factors in the ability of the middle class to reproduce itself are its capacity to mobilise its economic resources (as Goldthorpe, 1996, has stressed) and its continuing enjoyment of wider forms of cultural and social capital, such as access to private schools and the subsequent privileges and status this bestows on middle class children (Devine, 1998).

Market position/situation
Relates to the skills one has to sell in the labour market relative to others.

Patriarchal
Used to describe a system that perpetuates the dominance of senior men over all women and junior men.

QUESTION We contend that it is inappropriate to claim that we are all middle class now. Write a paragraph defending the idea that we are all middle class and a paragraph attacking it.

The working class

The working class has perhaps the most strongly developed class culture and has been at the centre of European and US sociological research on stratification for many years. One reason for this is that traditional workers in mining, steel-making, ship-building and so on both live and work together, which makes working-class communities relatively easy to study. A strong sense of community encourages a strong sense of identity. Insiders can be clearly distinguished from outsiders, especially those who represent officialdom, employers, authorities or the better off. Working class people are brought together by their common experience of adversity and subordination, yet their disadvantage limits their chance of improving their position.

Thus, the reproduction of the working class has two dimensions. First, the class is located in the labour market, so its disadvantage within capitalism is structural and therefore difficult to overcome. Second, precisely because of this, their continuing subordination produces a range of cultural frameworks for interpreting and drawing on the experiences of working-class life in order to get by or adjust to the situation. This might be expressed in working-class pride and respectability, in the masculinity and toughness of the shop floor, or in radical trade unionism.

Many studies of this traditional working class focus on the mutual support – often kin-based – found among members of mining (Dennis *et al.*, 1956), textile (Wild, 1979) and steel (Beynon *et al.*, 1991) communities. These studies, which are often rich in observational detail, add to the epic story of the working class, a narrative that at best is insightful and credible but at worst is overly romanticised. There is a tendency to extrapolate these community studies to the working class as a whole, to assume that the story holds true for all manual workers. However, this notion of a homogeneous traditional working class has been challenged, not least by Penn (1985), who has shown in his studies of the skilled working class that skilled workers constitute a distinct group between the middle class and the less skilled working class. Indeed, it is the division between occupational strata among the working class that explains why some occupational groups use their social resources to close off their occupation from others. Coal mining communities have, for example, exercised this form of social closure to construct strong boundaries between the mineworkers and the subcontracted, non-unionised workers that have been brought into the industry, as has happened in the US, the UK and Germany.

During the 1960s, some US and European social scientists claimed that the skilled stratum of the working class, found in the new automotive and electronic industries, were experiencing a wholesale shift in their class culture and broad social position in the social hierarchy. Their better pay and conditions, their specialist skills, their **individualistic** (rather than collective trade-union) orientation towards other workers and employers suggested a new stratum of affluent workers experiencing a process of **embourgeoisement**, whereby they took on middle-class status. Indeed, in the US, this view was accompanied by a wider claim about the disappearance of the unequal class structure itself, as more and more traditional jobs with low pay and poor working conditions were being replaced by well-rewarded, skills-based work.

However, evidence of this, even in the UK, was patchy, and UK studies that looked in detail at more affluent workers (Goldthorpe *et al.*, 1968) cast doubt on the idea that better pay and new forms of work were changing the real position of these workers. Rather than there being collective upward mobility into the ranks of the middle class, Goldthorpe *et al.* showed that the most significant change among affluent workers was that they led more privatised, home-centred lives, rather than contact with kin, neigh-

Individualism
A doctrine or way of thinking that focuses on the autonomous individual rather than on the attributes of the group.

Embourgeoisement thesis
An explanation of the decline of working-class solidarity. It claims that, because of increasing affluence, working-class people tend to adopt middle-class values and thus become absorbed into the middle class.

Instrumentalism
An approach to work in which workers derive satisfaction not so much from the job itself, but from benefits it brings, such as good pay or secure employment.

bours and friends being part of the daily routine. New homes in new towns meant that mortgages had to be paid. Workers were more **instrumental** in their work, earning as much as they could, even if this meant putting in long hours of overtime in tedious and noisy assembly-line work. These two factors, privatisation and instrumentalism, encouraged a more individualistic outlook among manual workers, with a consequent weakening of communal and kin orientations. But this did not lead to any strong desire to attain and identify with the middle-class lifestyle and values typical of white-collar work. Manual workers' reactions to changes in the workplace were more complex than that (Box 5.2).

BOX 5.2 | **Manual workers and changes in the workplace**

The debate on new developments in the workplace (and their effect on manual workers) is confused, but some broad positions can be identified. First, there are those who argue that new managerial techniques have undermined traditional differences between management and worker. The implication in terms of class is that differences have been dissolved, and replaced perhaps with an 'enterprise con-sciousness' in which managers and workers in one firm share the same goals, namely to compete against other firms. A second position would agree with the first that overt opposition to management has been eroded, but explains this in terms of *force majeure* rather than willing consent. Here, class struggle is repressed rather than dissolved. Third are writers who argue that resistance remains in evidence, though they would differ in how far they see this as having any class basis. The tendency is to focus on small-scale adjustments in the labour process which may be important in their own right but which may have little apparent class relevance. Others in this third group argue that traditional forms of workplace conflict in fact remain.

Source: Edwards (2000), p.157.

Reproduction of the working class

Our schematic model of the class structure (Figure 5.2) shows relatively poor life chances for those occupying working-class positions. These relate in Weberian terms to their poor market situation, itself a direct result of the low esteem accorded to the cultural capital of the working class. (However, see Box 5.3 for an account of other forms of capital available to the young working class). The symbolic violence issuing from the cultural judgement of the school (anti-working class; pro-middle class) is well documented (see, for example, Bernstein, 1973; Bourdieu and Passeron, 1977).

Educational disadvantage and poor job prospects are closely linked, and it is this link that is crucial to the reproduction of the working class. It results from both the under-resourcing of schools in inner-city areas as well as the favouring of middle-class children in schools. For the latter, as Chapter 10 describes, schooling is often an extension of pre-school family experience, culture and tuition. While it is possible for working-class children to overcome these constraints (Halsey *et al.*, 1980), the experience of disadvantage and discouragement at school – especially among working-class ethnic minorities – can push children into leaving school at the first (statutorily permitted) opportunity – at 16 in the UK and 15 in the US. The traditional pull of the local labour market and its adult status can and does draw some young boys and girls into jobs that offer little or no prospect of security or good pay (Ashton *et al.*, 1990). Escaping the constraint of school as soon as possible, young working-class people run into the constraints inherent in their subordinate position in the labour market (Willis, 1977).

BOX 5.3 Different forms of capital

Sarah Thornton (1997) uses Bourdieu's analysis in her study of 'club cultures' to show how different forms of capital (cultural, such as haircuts, style, being gendered, knowledge of particular music) and social capital (who you know, the groups you associate with) are forged to make a form of 'sub-cultural capital', which has a currency outside of the 'legitimate' circuits of capital. So, knowing about white label pre-release dance records does not have much value outside of the arena of the sub-culture and is unlikely to improve your chances of social movement (unless you are lucky enough to work for a specialist music company). What ultimately defines cultural capital as capital is the ability to convert it into economic capital. For Thornton, sub-cultural capital is not as class-bound as cultural capital.... However, her research shows how even the distinctions between different sorts of music and music use have strong class signs: 'Handbag House', 'Sharon and Tracey music', 'Cheesy House' and different sorts of music are associated with different social groups.

Source: Skeggs (2000), p. 14.

Underclass
Describes those at the bottom of the social hierarchy who are economically, politically and socially marginalised from the rest of society.

De-industrialisation
Decline of industrial manufacturing and concurrent increase in output and employment in the service sector.

There is, however, a crucial condition that must hold for any reproduction and closure of the working class to occur: there must be a reasonably stable labour market for them. Thus, any wider changes in the structure of capitalism that undermine local labour markets threaten the availability of paid jobs and therefore working-class cultural identity. If these jobs decline in significant numbers, an increase in the absolute number of those in poverty and those tumbling out of the working class into the so-called **underclass** is likely.

So far, we have examined the basic meaning of social class, suggesting that both Marx's and Weber's ideas have value in understanding class. We have also discussed the ways in which the two main occupational social classes have been reproduced from generation to generation. We now move on to ask whether there have been changes in the labour market that make this reproduction much less likely, so eroding the economic and cultural basis of class.

Changes in the labour market

De-skilling
A term describing what Braverman (1974) believed to be a strategy by employers to reduce the skills of their labour force. This often occurs alongside the introduction of new technological processes into the workplace.

Two important trends during the 1970s and 1980s characterised the labour markets of all industrialised states: **de-industrialisation** and **de-skilling**. Both were closely associated with traditional industrial sectors (such as raw materials and manufacturing) and therefore held the greatest significance for the traditional working class. De-industrialisation typically refers to the process by which the number of jobs in these sectors declined in both absolute terms and, compared with the volume of service-sector work in the economy, in relative terms. During this period, many jobs were lost because of cuts in or the privatisation of state-run industries, as well as competition from cheaper labour markets abroad. De-skilling is the process whereby firms respond to the threat of de-industrialisation and competition by introducing more machine-based technologies to replace the skills and tacit knowledge of human labour – for example, the use of robots on car assembly work. In the process, human labour is reduced to the smallest possible tasks. As Chapter 11 describes in more detail, the de-skilling thesis has been most strongly argued by Braverman (1974) and a number of European sociologists (for example, Wood, 1982; Gorz, 1982). During the 1970s and early 1980s, the UK car industry underwent both de-industrialisation and de-skilling, with the result that the number of individuals experiencing structural unemployment – the permanent loss of certain types of work – and long-term unemployment in general grew steadily. This

decline in traditional working-class jobs created major problems for the cultural and economic reproduction of the working class, because substantial sectors of the old working class were no longer working.

Yet the story of the relationship between classes, specific occupations and the labour market is even more complex. In some of the older industrial states of Europe, such as France and the UK, the process of de-industrialisation and de-skilling had started long before the 1970s. Andrew Gamble (1985) argues that UK industrial decline can be traced back to the much earlier failure – from the 1920s onwards – of UK capitalists to invest in new infrastructural technologies as they became available. In many ways, the UK was living on borrowed time, financed by the wealth derived from the old colonial empire.

It is not surprising that the OPEC-initiated oil crisis of the 1970s, which hit the UK and France particularly hard, triggered a rapid rise in unemployment, especially among the working class, when the **economic growth rate** fell below zero. However, during the last decade of the twentieth century, unemployment continued to rise in most industrialised countries – throughout the EU, for example – even though the average growth rates were positive. In other words, the traditional connection between economic growth and job creation seemed to come unstuck.

Economic growth rate
Level of economic expansion.

According to data from the Commission of the European Communities (CEC), the economic growth rate needs to be above 2 per cent to create any jobs – any lower than this, and jobs are actually destroyed. Extrapolating from these data, Hingel (1993, p. 7) notes that EU economies would have to 'increase by 68% in order to absorb the present 10.6% [rate] of unemployment'. This average would in fact vary by country. Thus, 'the equivalent domestic figures are situated between 198% of necessary economic growth in the case of Britain and 49% in the case of Germany' (ibid.) These differences reflect the different technological and institutional capacities (such as science and education, the regional development agencies) of the two countries. But even allowing for this, the economic growth required to soak up unemployment in what economists regard as one of the stronger European economies – Germany – is still high at nearly 50 per cent. This is unlikely to be achieved, not least because of the additional economic costs incurred by German reunification.

What is going on here? Why has the simple relation between the growth of the economy as a whole and an expanding job market been altered? Three main reasons have been advanced. These relate to:

- The restructuring of the economy.
- The polarisation of the labour market.
- The globalisation of production.

CONNECTIONS The issue of globalisation provides a backdrop for most contemporary sociological and political discussion. You will find a fuller account of the process of globalisation, especially its effect on production, in Chapter 3, pages 44–65.

As we shall see, the three processes listed above have altered the nature of the labour market, in that the traditional patterns of the occupational structure, recruitment to jobs, mobility within the labour market and, more generally, the reproduction of social classes have changed significantly. This is true for all occupational groups, both middle and working class. In many ways, the traditional labour market has failed to keep pace with the wider changes associated with these three processes.

We shall examine the three processes in turn, exploring the impact they have had on both the middle and the working class.

The restructuring of the economy

During the late 1970s and throughout the 1980s, the industrialised economies of Western Europe experienced a rapid drop in the relative contribution made to the economy by manufacturing and related industrial sectors. In technological terms, much of the older postwar infrastructure was insufficiently competitive, while manufacturing lacked the flexibility and skills needed to move into the new markets being captured by countries such as Japan and South Korea. There was a large restructuring of the labour market, with greater emphasis on service sector work. Domestic consumer markets were depressed because of the prolonged recession in the earlier part of the period. This was eventually resolved by a massive expansion of credit and an accompanying property boom, but these events did little to secure new investment in the basic industrial infrastructure. Instead, imports flooded into countries such as the UK, the Netherlands and France. The slump of the late 1980s and early 1990s – when the credit bubble burst – was therefore inevitable.

During the latter part of the 1980s, however, larger corporations at last restructured their production to make it more flexible, adopting **lean production** techniques to enable them to compete more effectively with the countries of the Far East and the **Pacific Rim**. For some commentators, this was confirmation of a final shift away from the Fordist mass production approach, which had dominated industrial strategy from the 1950s onwards, to a post-Fordist approach, manufacturing products for more specialised markets and producing these products on a 'just-in-time' basis, rather than keeping large stockpiles of goods and commodities (see Chapter 11).

These changes in the nature of production inevitably had a massive impact on the labour market. According to some commentators (for example, Atkinson and Gregory, 1986; Leadbeater, 1987), they led to the segmentation of the labour market into:

- A core of securely employed workers (many in knowledge-based work with above average pay).
- A periphery of casual workers – low-income self-employed, part-time staff and so on – with few if any occupational rights or benefits (such as guaranteed sick pay).
- A growing number of structurally unemployed people who might remain out of work for good, people who formed what Scambler and Higgs (1999, p. 285) call a displaced segment of the working class, 'who have only their labour power to sell but who find themselves, as a by-product of new – post-industrial, post-Fordist or "flexible" – forms of work organisation in globalising markets, unable to secure a wage in the present and for the foreseeable future'.

Lean production
A highly competitive, streamlined, flexible manufacturing process that operates with a minimum of excess or waste (see *just-in-time production*).

Pacific Rim
The rapidly developing South-East Asian economies that border the Pacific Ocean, such as Singapore, Taiwan, Hong Kong, Malaysia and South Korea.

According to this view, this restructuring of work means that the older manufacturing jobs have largely vanished and that new knowledge-based, specialist skills are needed to enter the post-industrial labour market – skills that can be adapted to new needs and opportunities (Grint, 1998). Restructuring has therefore opened up a skills-gap in a whole generation of workers aged 45–50 plus who are unlikely to find secure work again. While this is a depressing thesis, some commentators (notably in the US) believe that, given proper training and education, a new generation of skilled and flexible working- and middle-class employees will emerge who will be more attuned to the restructured labour market. The long-term structural unemployment that has brought poverty and deprivation to many over the age of 40 will be relieved once a supply of newly skilled workers is available. The new jobs, however, will be very different from the old, reflecting the shift in the occupational structure from manual to non-manual work, and especially knowledge-based jobs, requiring ever more sophisticated and flexible skills. In fact, according to the Canadian sociologist Stehr (1994), contemporary society can be characterised as a 'knowledge society'.

QUESTION What evidence can you produce to support the idea that we now live in a 'knowledge society'?

The Conservative governments of the 1980s made significant changes to the provision of state social security and health and welfare benefits. There were reductions in the real level of benefits, creeping privatisation of health care and insurance cover, and an erosion of occupational rights and union power. All this meant that the capacity to survive came to depend on one's position in the labour market, since unemployment became increasingly difficult to cope with as the holes in the security net widened. Despite the election of a Labour government in the late 1990s and its re-election in 2001, there has been no let up in the drive to reduce welfare expenditure. Indeed, the present government believes that work is the best form of welfare. But those in vulnerable positions in the restructured labour market often find it hard to get work and are threatened by poverty and poor life chances. This has led many commentators to point out that the restructuring of the labour market has not merely changed the sort of jobs on offer, but has also resulted in the increasing **polarisation** of those in secure, non-manual work and the growing army of low-paid, often casual workers. This takes us to the second trend.

Polarisation of the labour market
The deepening division of the labour market into jobs that are well paid and secure and those that are not.

The polarisation of the labour market

Those who believe that the labour market has become polarised (for example, Sassen, 1988; Pahl, 1991; Morris *et al.*, 1994) claim that the restructuring of the economy has tended to split the job market into two: well-paid, secure jobs for the middle and upper-middle classes, and insecure, low-paid work for the sons and daughters of the older working classes or those experiencing downward social mobility from the middle class. Those in insecure jobs are not always able to improve their life chances through education and training because an insufficient number of skilled jobs is being generated. Instead, there has been considerable growth in the number of low-skill, low-wage jobs, and there is a danger that this might become a permanent rather than a transitional feature of the labour market. Nor should we overlook the fragile position of people on the fringes of the labour market, those who are not officially unemployed but are seeking work. Their number actually rose during the 1990s even though recorded unemployment went down (Joseph Rowntree Foundation, 1998).

The polarisation of the labour market, by definition, has divided work into secure, better-paid jobs and insecure, poorly paid jobs. There are also gender and ethnicity factors at play in the way this polarisation is experienced. As Morris *et al.* (1994) show in their study of the US labour market, while some groups initially gravitate towards the better-paid jobs, they subsequently suffer a gradual drop towards insecure work. This has been particularly true of black men and white women. Again, ethnicity and gender mediate class in important ways.

CONNECTIONS For a discussion of the complexities of the meshing of gender, ethnicity and class, see Chapter 7, pages 184–9.

One of the better developed sociological analyses of the polarisation of the labour market is that by Castells (1989). He argues that, in the late twentieth century, the most important feature of capitalist corporations was their increasing reliance on science and technology and more general forms of knowledge and information as the basis of their competitiveness. Knowledge and information are the principal factors in production today. For example, access to and control over information technology (IT) is crucial if corporations – even those outside the knowledge sector – are to orchestrate effectively their research, development, production and distribution of new products. Moreover, new science-based technologies such as biotechnology have had a major impact not only in bioscience areas such as pharmaceuticals, but also in energy, food and other sectors. Production is therefore dependent on information in its broadest sense.

This transformation of industry has had a major impact on the labour market. Knowledge-based occupations for professionals and highly educated middle-class people are richly rewarded but require constant effort on the part of those who occupy them if they are to stay in the race. Long hours of stressful work that requires the constant monitoring and filtering of information puts considerable pressure on individuals. For those without knowledge-based skills, work can be insecure, low-paid and at risk of being replaced by new technology. The 'informational mode of development', as Castells describes this situation, adds to the fragmentation of traditional class structures and undermines their reproduction.

So the middle classes are under increasing pressure to deliver professional expertise quickly and correctly if their employers are to remain in business, and, while they are often well-rewarded for this, they are exposed to much greater competitive pressure than in the past. In part, this also reflects companies' concern to reduce their core of professional expertise to the minimum while subcontracting out less central tasks to other agencies: hence the massive growth of consultancy firms surviving on short-term contracts from larger firms. Twenty years ago, many of those working for such consultancies would have been secure members of the established middle class.

Jobless growth
Economic growth that is not accompanied by rising employment.

The working class has been increasingly squeezed by these developments, not only because of automation, which has created **jobless growth**, but also by the professionalisation and fragmentation of the labour market. As a result, the working class has become increasingly casualised and disorganised, both structurally and politically. The fragmentation of the once large working-class occupational structure and the parallel decline of unionism have undermined the social and cultural basis upon which working-class identity has relied. The cultural reproduction of the working class today is very different from that of the past. An interesting illustration of this can be obtained by comparing Warwick and Littlejohn's (1992) study of four mining communities in the UK, *Coal, Capital and Culture*, with the much earlier study by Dennis *et al.* (1956), *Coal is Our Life*. The Dennis *et al.* study described the strong community ties that existed in a traditional (male-dominated) Yorkshire mining town, while Warwick and Littlejohn (1992) show how such 'occupational communities' changed dramatically in the 1980s and 1990s as the core of their community – their mines and the support structures upon which they depended – were closed or privatised. In such circumstances, the cultural reproduction of the working class is threatened, and occupational closure is less possible.

The globalisation of production

As well as the restructuring of the economy bringing major changes to the sort of work available and the polarisation of this work producing a highly segmented labour market,

Figure 5.4 There is a slow decline in manual jobs, but skilled manual jobs in manufacturing and extractive industries are in much steeper decline than unskilled jobs, despite increased governmental emphasis on the importance of educational qualifications.

the globalisation of production means that significant sections of the labour market are being shaped by transnational organisations – notably multinational corporations – whose location, investment and relocation strategies are determined globally, not locally. Sadler (1992) discusses the arrival of Japanese car assembly plants in the North-East of England, which was once famous for coal and steel production, but by the 1980s was in decline. Attracted by regional development aid and other incentives provided by the state, the car firms were able to impose their own version of workplace flexibility and labour market needs simply by dangling the threat of relocation over the workers' – and the government's – heads.

As we saw in Chapter 3, transnational corporations – such as the global car corporations of Nissan, Honda and Ford – are establishing globalised systems for research design and production to cover all their plants and research centres. This requires the development of computer-based management control systems to integrate, monitor and control the manufacturing process. Moreover, these same corporations, which have considerable control over the productive sector, **outsource** some of their work to 'preferred suppliers' who must meet their detailed design and component specifications.

These changes in the organisational structure of workplaces as a result of globalisation are strongly affecting the nature of local labour markets, and therefore the formation of occupational classes and class identity. During the Fordist period of mass production, primarily for the large domestic markets in the **Rich World** (sometimes referred to as the First World), substantial numbers of manufacturing and service-based jobs were generated. These were also generators of local communities and identities. With the segmentation of work and the globalisation of the production process, the existing labour market is being destabilised and broken up. This means that in countries such as the US and UK, there is now room for regional pockets of well-paid work

Outsourcing
The subcontracting of work, that is, passing on certain research and development tasks to external contractors that were previously undertaken inside the firm.

The Rich World
(sometimes inappropriately referred to as the First World) These days, post-industrial capitalist societies, such as those of Europe, North America and Japan.

Segmentation
The restructuring of social class boundaries, associated with the polarisation and fragmentation of occupational groups.

Gendering
The process of differentiation and division according to gender.

Entrepreneurial
Used to describe activity in business or economic development based on the promotion of innovative ideas and decision-making.

associated with globalised production, as well as low-paid, casual, low-skilled work that serves global interests but through subcontracting firms or agencies.

Class reproduction?

The restructuring of the economy, polarisation and globalisation have therefore had a profound effect on the structure and stability of the traditional manual and non-manual labour markets in industrialised countries. One result of this is that the boundaries between the classes, while still marked, are being redefined by processes such as **segmentation** and the **gendering** of occupational structures. Global corporations' desire for a flexible labour force and the outsourcing of some of their production to cheaper subcontracted labour have resulted in greater numbers of women entering (but less often progressing within) the labour market.

For the middle class, secure white-collar work is still available, and an elite of knowledge-based (predominantly male) executive professionals and managers can be found in the financial, manufacturing, service and other sectors, and they still enjoy considerable command over other (subordinate) occupational groups within and between organisations (Clement and Myles, 1997). Yet many of the cultural and material resources upon which the middle class once relied – schooling, contacts, good pay – no longer guarantee life-long security. Life-long careers are in decline. In the UK, for example, fewer than one third of jobs are full-time, tenured career posts. The middle class have found that they must be prepared for a sudden reduction in their job security, perhaps as a result of global firms making strategic changes in their investment and market policies. Consequently, according to Scase (1992), the middle classes have had to become more **entrepreneurial** in order to maintain their well-paid but less secure perch in the labour market. This is especially so for managerial staff who have found their organisational position (firms or large public sector agencies) more vulnerable to contracting-out, to global investment switches and to mergers or privatisation. In these circumstances, many have fallen back on their property assets and sought to maintain their middle-class position through self-employment, often in consultancy-type work. Being entrepreneurial in this way is one way of surviving in the more volatile labour market, but clearly the terms on which middle-class reproduction is sustained are also rather different from those in the past.

 ## Implications for social mobility

Intragenerational mobility
The movement of individuals of the same generation from one position in the social hierarchy to another.

Intergenerational mobility
The movement of individuals from their parents' position in the social hierarchy to another.

These changes in the occupational labour market and in the boundaries of broad occupational class have important implications for social mobility – the movement of people up or down the social hierarchy, either within a generation (**intragenerational mobility**) or between the generations (**intergenerational mobility**). Typically, sociologists identify three main factors that affect social mobility in modern industrial societies:

- The changing number of positions (types of occupation) to be filled.
- The methods of access and entry to these positions.
- The number of suitable offspring available to fill the positions.

With regard to the first of these, since the early 1980s, there has been a marked decline in the number of manufacturing jobs and a shift towards service-sector work, especially of the intermediate non-manual type. Women have been the most likely recruits to this work.

In relation to the second point, entry to the labour market has increasingly depended on qualifications and skills. Thus, education and good credentials have grown in importance. When working-class children secure good qualifications, they are in a better position to secure upward social mobility relative to others in their class. However, analyses of statistical data (Goldthorpe, 1980; Heath, 1981; Gallie, 1988) indicate that the chances of entering secure, well-paid, middle-class jobs is much higher for the sons (and, to a lesser extent, the daughters) of middle-class parents than for young people of working-class origin, even when qualifications are held constant. A greater degree of overall mobility, therefore, does not necessarily mean increased equality of opportunity for young people of all social classes. And for the disabled and those from disadvantaged ethnic backgrounds, there are even higher barriers to social mobility both within and between generations.

With regard to the third factor, the expansion of middle-class, white-collar jobs at both the intermediate and the solid middle-class levels has not been matched by an increase in the number of middle-class young people to fill these new posts. As a result, young working-class people with the necessary qualifications have been able to move upwards into new professional posts. In 1991, for example, almost 25 per cent of professional and managerial staff in the UK were drawn from the working class.

Data on female mobility (Heath, 1981) show that women from all social classes have been (and still are) systematically excluded from top managerial and professional jobs, as well as from skilled manual work. As a result, women are concentrated in routine, non-manual work, in lower professions such as nursing and teaching, and in low-paid manual jobs. Thus, while over 50 per cent of the daughters of professional and managerial households enter non-manual jobs, these are at the routine, inter-mediate level and offer little or no chance of upward mobility. There is, in other words, strong evidence that the so-called **glass ceiling** exists for many non-manual women workers.

Traditionally, the mobility rate has been lowest for the sons and daughters of the working class. Put another way, they tend to fill jobs similar to those of their parents. The stronger this pattern, the stronger the sense of a stable class identity and the stronger the social closure. Conversely, greater social mobility into the lower ranks of the middle class blurs the class boundary at the intermediate level and weakens class identity.

Glass ceiling
A metaphorical concept used to explain how women are prevented from reaching the top managerial, political or professional jobs.

Changes in mobility patterns

Given the impact on the occupational labour market of restructuring, polarisation and globalisation, do they in any way affect the patterns of social mobility? If, for example, the labour market is segmented into two broad polarised sectors – a core of secure work and a periphery of casual, low-paid jobs – we might expect that entry into core work has become increasingly difficult. It will be even more difficult for the sons and daughters of working-class parents, for whom securing the credentials needed for such work is especially problematic. It might also be the case, as Savage *et al.* (1992) argue, that staying in middle-class jobs and avoiding downward intragenerational mobility has become difficult for professional white-collar workers. As we shall see in Chapter 11, Charles Handy (1991) argues that the future of the middle-class worker is very different from in the past. For many, the new circumstances might lead to downward mobility into less prestigious class positions.

BOX 5.4 The future of professional work

The next generation of full-time core workers, be they professionals, managers, technicians or skilled workers, can expect to start their full-time careers later – and to leave them earlier. This is the crucial point. The core worker will have a harder but shorter job, with more people leaving full-time employment in their later forties or early fifties, partly because they no longer want the pressure that such jobs will increasingly entail, but mainly because there will be younger, more qualified and more energetic people available for these core jobs. ... Work will not stop for people after 50 but it will not be the same sort of work; it will not be a job as they have known it.

Source: Handy (1991), pp. 36–7.

The growth of a large, part-time, casual job sector has meant a large increase in the number of women – especially married women – entering the labour market. The decline in traditional blue-collar work, on the other hand, has meant that many men have been ejected from the labour market into long-term unemployment or early retirement rather than securing new jobs in the intermediate or more senior white-collar service sector. The scale of this downward mobility into the ranks of the poor or, as some would argue, underclass (but see Box 5.5 for a discussion of the complexity of the concept of an underclass), has varied between regions and, within regions, by gender. As reported in a study by Bagguley (1990) on socioeconomic change in the North-West of the UK, the rate of downward mobility as a result of the restructuring of the economy has been twice the national average for men of all social classes, while women in the area have had a better chance of surviving in the service class or entering the intermediate white-collar stratum. This reflects the expansion of jobs in the health service, hotels and catering, and of casual clerical work. Nevertheless, relative to male workers, such women are still disadvantaged in terms of pay and conditions.

For the secure middle classes, the erosion – but not removal – of their secure, life-long position in well-paid white-collar work means that the possibility of downward

BOX 5.5 Problems with the idea of an underclass

We would argue that such underclass theories are mistaken. Even in such promising territory for 'underclass hunting', it was very difficult to locate evidence for the existence of a distinct deviant underclass culture. Nor was it easy to locate individuals who had become wholly cut off from the labour market. Even in desperate economic circumstances ... these most marginal workers (young people with very little in the way of cultural capital) seemed able to resist falling into complete economic inactivity and permanent worklessness, as underclass theses suggest would be the case. Young people remained attached to work: they retained personal values which stressed its moral and social worth and they were able to maintain, sporadically, the practice of working (albeit in jobs and informal economic activities which were usually precarious and unrewarding).

It would seem that in poor areas of Britain there is not a class of people beneath the lowest class of the gainfully employed population almost permanently kept there by separate cultural outlooks and activities or by the structures of the labour market, but a restructuring of the lower levels of the labour market typified by cyclical movements around peripheral work and unemployment. Unemployment, job insecurity and underemployment have become common working-class experiences rather than the preserve of an underclass separated from and beneath them.

Source: MacDonald and Marsh (2000), p.132.

mobility during their working life has increased, though a large-scale survey of this phenomenon has yet to be conducted. There has been, however, as Scase's (1992) notion of entrepreneurialism suggests, growth in the number of self-employed consultants among the ranks of the middle class. Technically, this denotes a small degree of upward mobility. While the rewards for work of this kind can be very great, they can also be intermittent and more immediately dependent on the state of the economy than are professional jobs in large organisations, where job losses may take longer to work their way through. Thus, middle-class self-employment is never very secure, and households where the main breadwinner is self-employed are likely to rely on the earnings of other members to buffer short-term reductions in or loss of income. However, these professionals are, more than any other class group, likely to avoid downward mobility by being able and willing to travel considerable distances for work, either as long-distance commuters to their regular place of work, or as mobile consultants prepared to travel extensively to service client markets.

In short, both inter- and intragenerational social mobility patterns are being affected by the changing structure of the labour market.

The continuing significance of social class

We saw earlier in this chapter how the social reproduction and social closure of the middle and working classes depends on a number of conditions: differential access to cultural credentials, differential access to work and a broad structure of occupational roles that provide for long-term non-manual and manual employment, albeit unequally. The social reproduction of class is central to a shared sense of social identity. So, occupationally based cultures have been very important for all classes, particularly when they have been related to residential communities, as in the case of mining.

The changes associated with globalisation suggest that the capacity for social reproduction among both classes has reduced, as uncertainties about life chances for those in work and those new to the labour market increase. The promises offered by modernity as we move into the globalised world of **late modernity** look less certain. Economic growth without job increases – as we saw with the EU studies – has become the norm. The payoffs from industrialisation in terms of gradual improvement in living standards, life chances and personal security seem to be disappearing for many people today. Gorz (1989) argues that the polarisation process will produce extreme divisions between a privileged, relatively small professional class and a massive new 'servile' class.

Whatever vision of the (not-so-distant) future is offered, it may well be that these changes will result in class identities becoming more difficult to reproduce over generations. As Brown and Scase (1991, pp. 21–2) suggest:

> **"** The restructuring of class relationships has increased material inequalities but reduced the subjective awareness of them. Inequalities, privileges and disadvantages are now more likely to be viewed as the outcome of *individual* actions rather than of structurally-determined economic and political forces. A strongly nurtured dominant ideology of individualism has reinforced a prevailing culture of *indifference* which serves to sustain both the privileges and deprivations experienced by different groups in society. **"**

This perhaps points to the arrival of the postmodern era, in which class identity will be less central to people's lives because identity will derive more from what they consume than from the type of work they do (or do not do). Identities in the postmodern world will be less stable, more subject to changing consumption styles and desires (Featherstone, 1991b; Bauman, 1992).

Late modernity
A term that implies a change in the nature of modernity, characterised by increased reflexivity and globalisation, but without a qualitative shift to postmodernity. Similar terms are 'high modernity' and 'radicalised modernity'.

CONNECTIONS For a fuller discussion of what is meant by postmodernism, see Chapter 19, pages 515–20.

What we need to ask, then, is whether these changes herald a decline in the import-ance of class as a determinant of social position and reward, or a restructuring of the terms on which a person's class position is based.

There are a number of views on this. Some sociologists, such as Abercrombie and Urry (1983), argue that there has been a decline in the traditional sense of social class in all industrial societies, as working-class trades unionism has lost its importance (reflected in declining numbers), a range of new middle classes have appeared, and as the property-owning industrial capitalist class had been replaced by a highly qualified managerial class acting as part of a new 'service class' for contemporary business. Certainly there is still a hierarchy, and there are still social actors who occupy powerful positions in society, but it is argued that inequality is now better measured in terms of the credentials one holds, the political influence one wields and the type of consumption one engages in. Saunders (1990) argues that consumption is the defining feature of all contemporary capitalist societies. It is not so much individuals' class position in the production process that determines their location in the social hierarchy, but more their status as consumers and the style and range of consumption in which they engage. Where there is a dividing line, it is between those who rely on state benefit for their consumption needs and those who have sufficiently well-paid jobs to satisfy the bulk of their material requirements. We shall explore Saunders's argument more fully a little later.

In related fashion, Offe (1985) argues that work itself no longer has as important a meaning for a large number of people, both individually and collectively, either because they are effectively excluded from the workforce by chronic unemployment (for example, in 1994 one in four adult males was unemployed), or because the welfare state will provide benefits to meet their basic needs, or because a collective work ethic can no longer be sustained by the growing ranks of casual, part-time workers. Offe argues that 'not only has work been objectively displaced from its status as a central and self-evident fact of life . . . [it] is also forfeiting its subjective role as the central motivating force in the activity of workers' (ibid., p. 148).

Other argue that possession of a class (and work-based) identity has lost its meaning for most people, and that new social movements – such as the environmental movement, advocates of alternative medicine and technologies, peace movements and feminism – now command the allegiance and respect that the labour movement once enjoyed. For example, the relationship in the UK between the (new) Labour Party, trade unions and the working class has been deliberately downplayed by the party leadership in order to appeal to this wider and changing constituency (see Chapter 8). The shift from national collective to local plant bargaining and subsequently, for many white-collar workers, to individual contracts has further weakened trade unionism.

Two arguments can be levelled against this view of the decomposition or demise of class. First, the degree to which traditional class distinctions and inequalities have been eroded has been exaggerated – the basic class structure, in terms of widespread economic inequality, is still alive and well. A stark illustration of this is provided by a national survey highlighting the extent of poverty and social exclusion among the UK population at the close of the twentieth century (Joseph Rowntree Foundation, 2000). Second, where there have been significant changes, they have primarily resulted from global economic processes that are forcing a restructuring of class at the national level

BOX 5.6 The reality of class in the US and UK

The following is an account by Kirby (1999) of Fiona Devine's (1997) conclusions on class structure in the US and the UK:

'[She] considers the reality of social class inequalities in the United States and Britain. She argues that there have long been stereotypical assumptions about both those societies, namely that Britain is a class-bound society and that the United States is a classless society. She believes that both these stereotypes are false and that the class structures of the two societies are remarkably similar, with considerable upward mobility in both societies, which means that people can and do escape their class of origin. However, in both societies social class remains an important influence on people's life-chances. She concludes that Britain and the United States are neither entirely open nor entirely closed societies, and while they share a similar class structure due to a similarity of industrial and occupational change in the twentieth century (for instance the decline of manufacturing, the growth of low-level service sector jobs), these changes have occurred faster in the United States than in Britain.'

Source: Kirby (1999), p. 87.

throughout the capitalist industrialised world (see Chapter 3 and Box 5.6 for discussions of the uneven effects of globalisation on class structure in the US and the UK).

The argument that class is still important receives compelling support from a study undertaken by researchers at the Universities of Bristol, Loughborough, York and Heriot-Watt, with fieldwork conducted by the Office for National Statistics (Joseph Rowntree Foundation, 2000). The survey, based on government low-income data, confirms that the poverty rate has risen sharply, with 26 per cent of the UK population living in poverty (measured by low income and multiple deprivation of necessities) by the end of 1999. Such data reveal that economic disadvantage (a crucial indicator of low class ranking) is a stark feature of the UK socioeconomic landscape.

The view that class is still prominent in society has been advanced by sociologists such as Bottomore and Brym (1989) and Crompton (1993). Crompton (1993, p. 206) maintains that:

" capitalist industrial societies are still stratified, and theories of social class still provide us with essential insights into the manner in which established inequalities in wealth and power associated with production and markets, access to educational and organisational resources and so on have systematically served to perpetuate these inequalities over time. "

Bottomore and Brym (1989) found in their comparative study of capitalist classes in various countries that capitalists still enjoy privileged access to the networks of power (in governmental, administrative and judicial circles) that have defended the wealth upon which the reproduction of capitalist class power depends. They note that until the mid 1960s there was a 'gradual diminution of inequality' in most countries, but from the late 1970s, there was 'an increasing inequality of income and almost certainly of wealth', so that in most countries the capitalist class had been 'remarkably successful in defending its wealth' (ibid., p. 13). In the case of Germany and Japan, for example, they highlight the very strong ties forged between the state, the major banks and principal firms to secure and sustain the profitability of local capitalism and the wealth upon which it relies.

At the same time, the maintenance of private capitalist wealth at the national level is increasingly subject to the transnational interests of private capital. Like capital at the national level, global capital has its own agencies and institutions – such as the World Bank, international commodity and currency exchanges, international banks and the

International Monetary Fund (IMF) – acting broadly on its behalf. It is crucial to remember that the transnational interests of the global capitalist system may at times challenge the national interests of local capitalism. The World Bank, the IMF and the exchanges act to police and regulate the wider global system, which may mean pressure on national capital, currency holders and workers across a range of occupations. So, factories in the UK, the US and elsewhere may close, even when they are making a profit locally. New jobs appear because labour costs are comparatively cheaper than elsewhere. An interest rate rise in one country may force others to defend their currencies by pushing up their own base rates, thus hitting their own national private capital holders.

A well-developed critique of class analysis is provided by Saunders (1990), who is critical of what he calls the 'socialist-feminist orthodoxy' rooted in the Marxist approach to class. He argues that class analysis has been too long wedded to the old notion of structured social inequalities generated by the property relations of capitalism, as though (1) the benefits of private ownership under capitalism do not 'trickle down' to all eventually; (2) the individual can do little to improve his or her position in the social hierarchy by means of upward social mobility; and (3) there is still a dominant capitalist class today. He argues that stratification is better understood by applying the Weberian model of class, which stresses differential occupational market capacities and embodies the neo-liberal idea that individuals can overcome the disadvantages that confront them. Moreover, the neo-Weberian model offers a better account of the increasingly complex and fragmented social structure, in particular the rise of the new middle classes.

According to Saunders, because of the widespread diffusion of share ownership (especially via the wholesale privatisation of state enterprises in the Thatcher years) 'the capitalist class ... has fragmented into millions of tiny pieces' – the millions of share-holders, including many workers, who buy into private enterprises. Consequently 'the capitalist class has all but disappeared as a distinct stratum' (ibid., p.202).

Saunders claims that he offers a more objective analysis of class, in that it is based on an open-minded approach to the empirical evidence. That said, he overlooks a considerable body of empirical evidence – for example, Scott's (1991, 1996, 1997) highly detailed and up-to-date studies on the upper class, and equivalent work by Zeitlin (1989) on the US situation. More importantly, it is naive to say that data 'speak for themselves', for the significance of evidence is invariably linked to the assumptions one makes when reading them in the first place.

Thus, rather than seeing the growth of share ownership as signalling the demise of the capitalist class, we need to locate the capitalist class in two arenas, the national and the transnational. It is clear that a dominant class representing the interests of trans-national finance capital shapes the fortunes of all the small shareholders who Saunders (1990) is keen to point to. Moreover, Saunders' claim that it is increasingly hard to find a distinct group of private capitalists sharing a tight social network need not mean that the specific interests of private capital have dissipated. Indeed, Scott (1991, p.152) acknowledges the depersonalisation and institutionalisation of the ownership of capital, and thereby 'a change in the structure of the capitalist class'. 'Instead of being organised around an upper circle of status superiors, the capitalist class became organised around an inner circle of finance capitalists.' These finance capitalists have both national – in the City of London and the equivalent financial centres in New York, Tokyo and Paris – and transnational networks whose members play a crucial role in shaping national and international (such as EU) state and business policies.

We argued earlier in this chapter that it is best to combine the insights of both the Marxist (property) and the Weberian (occupational market) approach to the study of stratification, as both have their strengths and weaknesses. One strength of Weber is his additional focus on status and power as forms of social stratification and social differentiation that are analytically quite separate from, but in practice often tied to, class inequalities. We commented on these dimensions when describing Weber's basic approach to inequality. Marx's focus on the abiding inequalities associated with the unequal distribution of productive (and not merely consumption) property and the globalising dynamics of capitalism provides us with important insights. In Chapters 6 and 7, we explore the dynamics of ethnic and gender subordination in contemporary society, and these are obviously two important forms of social differentiation and inequality, along with class. The relationship between them and social class is, however, problematic, as these chapters suggest. We can give a sense of this here by discussing some of the feminist criticisms of class theory in general, for feminism has posed a serious challenge to conventional approaches to class inequality.

Three main feminist criticisms have been made of the research on social class, and all three have been most strongly directed against the work of John Goldthorpe and David Lockwood (see, for example, Abbott and Sapsford, 1987).

- Conventional approaches classify households' class position according to the occupation of the male breadwinner. This clearly ignores the class position of women in households. Women in paid work may be – and in poorer families often are – the principal or sole breadwinner.

- Conventional research tends to assume that the female partner shares the same class position as the male and enjoys equal access to the resources that the family breadwinner brings in. But there is considerable evidence to the contrary. Women do not share the household resources on equal terms with men, they have less power in the home, and some suffer violent physical abuse from their male partners (Dobash and Dobash, 1980).

- There is an assumption that class rather than gender is the more important determinant of social inequality.

There have been a number of responses to these attacks on class theory. Maynard (1990) has usefully described these responses as coming from 'detractors', 'revisionists' and 'radicals'. The detractors – Goldthorpe, Lockwood and others who have developed the conventional approach – defend the practice of allocating married women to their husband's class position. They believe that the evidence still favours this strategy and that, methodologically, treating women separately from men could require the development of separate stratificatory schemes for each gender, which would be practically problematic.

Revisionists have responded more sympathetically to the feminist critique and have tried to revise the classification of women and men in households by examining more fully the jobs that women do and the resources they bring to the family unit. This has led to the notion of 'cross-class' families in which the partners have different class positions. In such cases, the household as a unit is allocated a different class position from one in which both partners are regarded as sharing the same class position.

The radical response has come from a number of other feminists (for example, Delphy, 1984), who argue that we need to reconsider the whole basis on which we view social class. We need to move away from seeing class in terms of an economic category primarily associated with occupation, and to see it instead as expressing a more fundamental gender division in society. That is, class conflict has essentially been and remains a conflict between women and men. It is in the home where this conflict is rooted and reproduced, a place where the man exploits the woman as she provides both sexual and domestic services for him.

Maynard offers a number of observations on these feminist critiques, particularly the radical perspective, noting, for example, how there would be severe methodological difficulties in operationalising the notion of gendered classes in empirical research on the contemporary class structure. Nevertheless, the challenge to the conventional approach to class provided by the feminist critique does raise important questions for debate.

Conclusion

The approach to social class we have adopted here has sought to combine the Marxian and Weberian accounts in a coherent fashion. Contemporary analyses of social class, we have argued, need to broaden their focus to include the impact of transnational aspects of global capitalism on national capitalist interests and the experience and cohesion of social classes within a country. While much of our empirical material relates to the UK, our arguments can be applied to all mature post-industrial capitalist societies. We have also noted at various points how the traditional dynamics of social class are being increasingly shaped by wider global forces. The thesis of this chapter is that while there have been some fundamental changes in the composition and reproduction of social classes as a result of national and global processes, the continuing significance of social class as an important form of social division should not be denied. It may be that the older forms of class identity associated with community, job, accent, schooling and so on are no longer as relevant as they were. Indeed, as Scott (2000, p. 53) observes, 'social divisions do not always lead systematically to a sense of distinctive group identities, or to action with others on the basis of such shared personal social identities'. But Scott also observes that it would be a mistake to assume that – as some postmodern writers do, as well as those who share Saunders' position – our apparent ability 'to manipulate the cultural trappings of identity' means that class is no longer significant. As Scott puts it, 'No amount of personal choice to "mix and match" consumption behaviour or symbolic life goals will remove the underlying constraints of class situations' (ibid.)

Chapter summary

- This chapter has mainly focused on classes as occupational groups divided in broad terms into the middle and working classes.

- Occupational groups are sustained over time via the processes of social reproduction and social closure.

- The stability of both classes is being threatened by marked changes in the occupational labour market at the national level, changes that often, though not always, reflect global processes in the world economy.

- Class identities are being weakened as a result of these changes, but this is not necessarily undermining the importance of class in the social structure.

Questions to think about

- Which principal factors have been associated with the reproduction of social classes in modern industrial society?
- To what extent has the globalisation of the world economy changed the nature of social class at the national level?
- To what extent might consumer culture erode the cultural significance of social class?

Investigating further

Crompton, Rosemary (1998) *Class and Stratification: An Introduction to Current Debates*, 2nd edition, Polity Press.

> Although it is called an introduction, this is a more difficult book, but it is worth persevering with. Crompton takes a different position from Roberts and gives a useful overview of different theories of class.

Metzgar, Jack (2000) *Striking Steel: Solidarity Remembered*, Temple University Press.

> This book offers a very powerful account of the US steel industry strike of 1959, much of it autobiographically based. Its importance for class is that it investigates why the strength of class and union identity among the steel workers is so diluted today. Metzgar provides a rich ethnographic commentary on this compared with the more abstract debates on class decomposition.

Roberts, Ken (2001) *Class in Modern Britain*, Palgrave.

> As the title suggests, this book is mainly British in focus, but it offers a very clear and readable overview, both of the way in which the class structure has changed over the last hundred years and of what it is like today. It also offers very helpful insights from some of the major sociological studies of class.

Saunders, Peter (1990) *Social Class and Stratification*, Routledge.

> Short and inexpensive, this very clear book covers some issues not tackled by mainstream sociological approaches and offers a nice contrast to the theoretical perspectives of Crompton and Roberts above.

Walkerdine, Valerie, Helen Lucey and June Melody (2001) *Growing up Girl*, Palgrave.

> Based on original research and packed with insightful quotes from the working-class girls interviewed, this book looks at the relationship between gender and class and adopts an innovative approach to class analysis. It is immensely readable.

Gender relations

CHAPTER CONTENTS

Aims of the chapter

While class has been one of the main interests of sociologists when exploring social divisions, other social characteristics have increasingly become a focus of concern. As a result of feminism, issues of gender now occupy a central position for many sociologists. In this chapter, we provide you with an overview of some of the social processes that shape gender relations in contemporary societies. We emphasise that there are many masculinities and many femininities. We describe and assess two major accounts of the process of becoming gendered people and argue in favour of viewing gender as a property of social institutions and culture as much as of individuals. We examine in some detail the way in which key institutional areas – divisions of labour, the social organisation of childbirth and childcare, sexuality, popular culture and the media – have been permeated by gender, and consider some of the implications of this for gender inequalities and contemporary gender relations.

We recognise that when thinking about gender, people frequently resort to explanations couched in terms of 'naturalness', and so our discussions of child-birth and childcare, sexuality and gender difference itself begin by contrasting biological explanations with social ones. But we also question whether biological and social phenomena can be so neatly separated. Even male and female bodies, it is suggested, are constituted partly by social processes.

By the end of this chapter, you should have an understanding of the following concepts:

- Gender
- Feminism
- Patriarchy
- Socialisation
- Sexual scripts

- Essentialism
- Occupational segregation, both horizontal and vertical
- Femininities
- Masculinities

Introduction

In late August 1995, some 25 000 women from all over the world gathered in China. Their intention was to press their agendas upon the government delegations from 185 nations that had been invited by the United Nations to debate a programme of action for women for the coming decade. There was anything but consensus in the early days: marching with their mouths bandaged, Tibetan women bore silent witness to the Chinese occupation of their country – and were harassed by Chinese police; a 'conservative' nine-delegation alliance (including the Vatican, Iran and Sudan) vigorously opposed proposals for sexual and reproductive freedom; all delegates applauded the recognition by the UN that women's rights are human rights, and yet many argued that the emphasis on rights detracted from the fact that, especially in poorer countries, lack of resources spelled disaster for women.

CONNECTIONS The growth of a global women's movement is one of the consequences of globalisation. For a wider view of global politics, see Chapter 3, pages 60–4.

The reporting of the conference by the media often focused on disagreements among delegates, highlighting the fact that a common identity as women does not generate a uniform consciousness or a uniform set of priorities and interests; other circumstances and other identities – national, ethnic, religious, class – may be crucial. But the conference also illustrated the widespread recognition of and challenge to patterns of inequality that generate **gender** disadvantage. There was a remarkable commitment by diverse groups to seek measures to improve the health, educational standing and economic power of women across the world. The extent to which these measures have succeeded is explored in Box 6.1.

Gender
Refers to the socially constructed categories of masculine and feminine that are differently defined in various cultures and the socially imposed attributes and behaviours that are assigned to them.

BOX 6.1 | Gender inequality on a global scale

In the press release accompanying the publication of *The World's Women 2000* (UNIFEM, 2000), the United Nations Under-Secretary-General for Economic and Social Affairs attempted to answer the urgent but complex question of what real progress the world's women are making with their lives. The basepoint for comparison was 1995, the year of the Beijing Conference. Nitin Desai said:

'Available data show that women are making gains, but persistent disparities exist between women and men. We can see that the gender gap in enrolment in primary and secondary levels of schooling is closing, but it is unlikely that this gap will be closed by the target date of 2005. While the gender gap in rates of economic activity is narrowing, women still must reconcile their family responsibilities with employment outside the home. Recent declines in early marriage and early child-bearing in most regions show real improvement in the quality of women's lives, but in three of five countries in southern Asia and in 11 of 30 countries in

sub-Saharan Africa, at least 30 per cent of young women aged 15 to 19 have been married.'

The World's Women 2000 offers ample evidence of gains made by women since 1995, of continuing disparities between women and men, and of marked variation in the circumstances of women in different regions. For example, the report shows that:

- Women now comprise an increasing share of the world's labour force – at least one third in all regions except in northern Africa and western Asia (see Box 6.4).

- Life expectancy continues to rise for women and men in most developing countries, but has decreased dramatic-ally in southern Africa as a result of AIDS.

- Two thirds of the world's 876 million illiterates are women.

- In Africa, a woman's risk of dying from pregnancy-related causes is 1 in 16; in Asia it is 1 in 6; in Europe, 1 in 1400.

Source: United Nations press release DEV/2245, WOM/1197 (31 May 2000).

 ## Men, women and gender difference

What is gender difference, and where does it come from? Why, for example, in Western societies, are men more sparing with their smiles? Why are they less likely to coo over other people's babies, or to abandon their careers to care for their own babies?

The answers to such questions can be placed along a continuum, according to the importance they attach to biology in explaining gender difference. At one end of the continuum, **biological determinists** highlight similarities in male behaviour across different environments. They argue that male traits (whether a preference for competitive sport, or a lack of 'maternal' feeling) have their roots in chromosomal differences (XY rather than XX chromosomes), hormonal differences (for example, testosterone) or some other natural characteristic that distinguishes men from women.

At the other end of the continuum, social constructionists contend that gender differences derive from social and cultural processes. These processes create systems of ideas and practices about gender that vary across time and space. They also create gender divisions of labour, allocating women and men to different activities and responsibilities. Individuals raised within such a framework will come to have appropriately gendered identities and desires. For example, Bob Connell (1987) argues that every society has a gender order that generates a variety of **masculinities** (some dominant, some not) and **femininities**. The gender order acts as a framework within which gender differences emerge and are reproduced or challenged.

Assembling evidence on the origins of gender difference is more difficult than is sometimes suggested. To support a biological determinist case, we would need, first, to establish that a substantial and universal difference exists: that men across societies are characterised by more or less identical behaviours (and that the same is true of women). Second, we would need to show that this difference is caused by biology and not, for example, by similarities in the upbringing of boys or in the responsibilities they have as adults. The more segregated the worlds that women and men inhabit, the harder it is to demonstrate that nature, rather than nurture, accounts for gender difference.

CONNECTIONS To explore a similar dispute about the biological basis of ethnic difference, read pages 162–5 in Chapter 7.

Sociological, historical and anthropological research shows that femininities and masculinities vary dramatically across cultures. The emphasised femininity among bourgeois women in Victorian Britain, for example, involved physical delicacy, exclusion from paid work and lack of sexual feeling; womanhood in many rural parts of Africa today is synonymous with physical robustness, breadwinning and sexual confidence. In the face of such diversity, it is difficult to sustain the claim that there is a necessary connection between female bodies (or male bodies) and particular gender traits.

Femininities and masculinities are subject to change not only across cultures but also over time. In the US, the dominant masculinity of the 1940s and 1950s had breadwinning at its core; it was portrayed in popular culture by the sober-suited, domestically incompetent, hard-working family man, as played in films by actors such as James Stewart. Ehrenreich (1983) argues that this form of masculinity became less prominent over time. The publication of *Playboy* magazine (promoting an exploitative bachelor style), the writings of the beat poets (who scoffed at conventional morality), the trumpeting of the dangers of workaholism – these and other cultural influences helped to articulate new masculinities and contributed to the erosion of the breadwinner ethic.

If masculinities change over time, then men – even at a single point in time – are likely to be diverse. Men are no more homogeneous than are human beings, Germans or the young. Even in a single society, different social and cultural contexts – linked to race or ethnicity, age or physical capacities, sexual orientation or social class – alter the meaning of male or female bodies and of gender difference, often in quite dramatic ways. The delicate bourgeois lady of Victorian England coexisted with the sturdy, hard-working

Biological determinism A simple causal approach that explains human behaviour in terms of biological or genetic characteristics.

Masculinities Various socially constructed sets of assumptions, expectations and ways of behaving that are associated with and assigned to men in a particular culture.

Femininities Various socially constructed sets of assumptions, expectations and ways of behaving that are associated with and assigned to women in a particular culture.

QUESTION Select a particular time and place (say, England during the second world war; or Pakistan today) and describe what 'femininities' would apply for each of two women who have different class positions or marital statuses in that society, or who belong to different religious or ethnic groups. Repeat the exercise referring to masculinities for men who are differently placed.

housemaid. Indeed, without the robust housemaid, the fragility of the lady would have been unthinkable.

This recognition of diversity puts paid to **essentialist** views of gender – to the claim that some natural feature (or essence) is shared by all women (or all men). As Brown and Jordanova (1982, p. 390) conclude: 'there is no such thing as woman or man in asocial terms; women and men, or rather femininity and masculinity, are constituted in specific cultural settings according to class, age, marital status and so on'.

Essentialism
An approach that assumes some universal feature that identifies the phenomenon under study. Essentialist approaches to gender assume that all women share traits in common, as do all men.

Gender and the body

If gender difference is socially constructed, what about the relationship between gender and the body? Does the fact that males and females are anatomically different have nothing to do with gender?

BOX 6.2 Ain't I a woman?

Because gender varies so dramatically across time and space, sociologists have to be careful to challenge the universal validity of models developed in particular contexts. Often descriptions of femininity (or masculinity) are presented as standard when they really only fit Western, white, middle-class heterosexuals. Such models of femininity (or masculinity) render the experience of other groups of women (or men) invisible – or make them 'deviant'. They make diversity invisible.

In nineteenth-century America, for example, the emphasised femininity stressed women's delicacy and their need for male protection. This description may have seemed real to some people, but of course it did not correspond to the experience of a great many women. The definition was challenged forcefully by Sojourner Truth, a feminist activist. Truth was a former slave who campaigned vigorously for the extension of suffrage to black men and to women. At a convention in Ohio in 1852, women's rights campaigners were jeered by hostile men who insisted that women needed protection, not the vote. Sojourner Truth strode to the platform to repudiate these claims. She declared:

'That man over there says women need to be helped into carriages, and lifted over ditches, and to have the best place everywhere. Nobody ever helps me into carriages, or over mud-puddles, or gives me any best place! And ain't I a woman? Look at me! Look at my arm! I have ploughed, and planted and gathered into barns, and no man could head me! And ain't I a woman? I could work as much and eat as much as a man – when I could get it – and bear the lash as well! And ain't I a woman? I have borne thirteen children, and seen most all sold off to slavery, and when I cried out with my mother's grief, none but Jesus heard me! And ain't I a woman?' (quoted in hooks, 1982, p. 160).

Collins (1990, pp. 14–15) comments that although Truth had never learned to read, she demonstrated in her speech that the idea of 'woman' that appeared to reflect bodily reality was in fact a cultural construct, and relevant only to certain sections of the female population.

Sex/gender distinction
Early feminist sociologists, made a distinction between sex (the universal biological division between male and female) and gender (the social and cultural meanings that are attached to this distinction). Later theorists questioned whether there is anything outside the cultural constructions of gender

Berdache
A practice among the native peoples of North America to allocate male gender roles on the basis of cultural preference rather than on anatomical maleness (see *gender*).

One answer, influential in the 1970s and 1980s, is the **sex/gender distinction**. Gender is the cultural gloss put on a natural foundation of sex. Sex refers in this formulation to universal differences between male and female bodies – between chromosomes, genitals and reproductive capacities. Sex is said to be rooted in nature; it distinguishes males from females. Gender, on the other hand, refers to the socially constructed and infinitely variable categories of masculine and feminine. As Anne Oakley explained in her influential book *Sex, Gender and Society* (1972), bodies are the trigger for the assignment of gender difference; femininity of some sort will be elaborated for anatomical females, and masculinity of some sort for males. 'The chief importance of biological sex', argues Oakley, 'is in providing a universal and obvious division around which other distinctions can be organised' (ibid., p. 156).

Examination of other cultures throws doubt on the claim that 'male' and 'female' are universal categories based on natural anatomical differences. Before the twentieth century, among many of the native peoples of North America – for example, the Cheyenne, the Ojibwa, the Navajo and the Iroquois – anatomy was not the only criterion for deciding whether a person ranked as a man or a woman. Following a practice called **berdache**, anatomical males who strongly preferred basket weaving or burden carrying – women's work – to hunting with the bow or going to battle could move in female circles, dress as women did and even take husbands. Although they retained their male genitals, they ceased to be males. Activities were as significant as anatomy in determining sex.

In the developed world, the conventional approach is rather different. We assume that men can readily be distinguished from women by reference to genitals. We also assume that there are only two sexes, that every individual is either male or female, that a person's sex remains the same throughout life, and that a natural dichotomy between male and female exists independently of any social practices based on gender. These assumptions are part of what Garfinkel (1967) describes as the 'natural attitude' of modern Western societies towards sex. Kessler and McKenna (1985) argue that although we may perceive the Western view of sex to be objectively correct, it is as much a constructed reality as that of the societies that practised berdache. When we come across a 'man' who wears stilettos and speaks of giving birth, instead of accepting the evidence of our senses – that not everyone fits neatly into male or female – we search for further evidence (facial hair, name, jewellery). We conduct ourselves in everyday life so as to confirm the view that sex is clear-cut, and in so doing we shore up the belief that the male/female dichotomy is universal and obvious.

Moreover, professionals play a large part in sustaining the natural attitude. Where the anatomical sex of a baby is ambiguous, consultants authorise treatment to reconstruct it as either male or female. Adult transsexuals are people whose anatomical sex is out of synch with their gender identity. When an anatomical man claims he is a woman, he may be referred for psychiatric and medical treatment, including surgery, to remove the penis and create a vagina and breasts. What is interesting is that in Western societies it is perceived as less problematic to want surgical reconstruction of the genitals than it is to be a woman with a penis. Transsexualism, Kessler and McKenna (ibid., p. 120) claim, 'is a category constructed to alleviate ambiguity – to avoid the kinds of combinations (e.g., male genitals–female gender identity) that make people uncomfortable because they violate the basic rules about gender'.

CONNECTIONS Many contemporary sociologists adhere to the idea that postmodern societies are concerned with the control of the body in general and not just women's bodies. For an explanation of this view as it affects society, see Chapter 13, page 365.

This type of evidence suggests that the simple division into male and female sex – regarded as an obvious and universal distinction based upon bodies – is itself a social construction. In Western societies, it is our gender ideas (not bodies themselves) that make us insist that people are unambiguously male or female. The process of gender attribution – whereby we classify people as male or female – is a social process that varies from one social setting to another.

Ideas about masculinity and femininity mould male and female bodies in other concrete ways. There are a range of social practices – from bodybuilding to cosmetic surgery, from hormonal treatment to nutrition, from styles of dress to forms of work – that contribute to bodily sexual difference. In Western societies, women are on average smaller than men, and slimness is a strong element in emphasised femininity. If a high proportion of girls are dieting in their teenage years in order to lose weight, is this not a powerful example of the way in which gender produces sexual difference?

In Box 6.3, following Michel Foucault's idea that the emergence of modern society is marked by a new and unprecedented discipline against the body, Sandra Bartky (1990) documents the range of disciplinary practices that women must master in pursuit of an acceptably feminine appearance.

Our male and female bodies are, in short, the product of the interaction between nature and social processes – including those of gender. Recognising this challenges the

---

BOX 6.3 | Gendering the body

A woman's skin must be soft, supple, hairless and smooth; ideally, it should betray no sign of wear, experience, age, or deep thought. Hair must be removed not only from the face but from large surfaces of the body as well, from legs and thighs, an operation accomplished by shaving, buffing with fine sandpaper, or foul-smelling depilatories. With bathing suits and leotards, a substantial amount of pubic hair must be removed too. The removal of facial hair is more specialized. Eyebrows are plucked out by the roots with a tweezer. Hot wax is some-times poured onto the moustache and cheeks and then ripped away when it cools. The woman who wants a more permanent result may try electrolysis.... The procedure is painful and expensive.

The development of what one 'beauty expert' calls 'good skin-care habits' requires not only attention to health, the avoidance of strong facial expressions, and the performance of facial exercises, but the regular use of skincare preparations, many to be applied oftener than once a day: cleansing lotions (ordinary soap and water 'upsets the skin's acid and alkaline balance'), wash-off cleansers ('milder than cleansing lotions'), astringents, toners, make-up removers, night creams, nourishing creams, eye creams, moisturisers, skin balancers, body lotions, hand creams, lip balms, suntan lotions, sunscreens, facial masks.... Black women may wish to use 'fade creams' to 'even skin tone'. Skin-care preparations are never just sloshed onto the skin, but applied according to precise rules: eye cream is dabbed on gently with movements towards, never away from, the nose; cleansing cream is applied in outward directions only...

Are we dealing in all this merely with *sexual difference?* Scarcely. The disciplinary practices I have described are part of the process by which the ideal body of femininity ... is constructed; in doing this, they have produced a 'practised and subjected' body, i.e., a body on which an inferior status has been inscribed. A woman's face must be made up, that is to say, made over, and so must her body: she is ten pounds overweight; her lips must be made more kissable; her complexion dewier; her eyes more mysterious. The 'art' of make-up is the art of disguise, but this presupposes that a woman's face, unpainted, is defective. Soap and water, a shave and routine attention to hygiene may be enough for *him*; for *her* they are not.

Source: Bartky (1990), pp. 69–71.

opposition between biological determinism and social construction with which we began; the search for biological differences between the sexes, unadulterated by culture – or, for that matter, for cultural differences that have not had an impact on our bodies – may in fact be misguided.

| QUESTION | Other than the ones Bartky documents, how many 'disciplinary practices' and forms of specialised knowledge that help to produce gendered bodies — male as well as female — can you describe? |

Becoming gendered people

By the time children in Western societies reach their second birthday, many will have acquired a firm sense of themselves as male or female, a gender identity that remains throughout life. In addition, many pre-schoolers have a firm awareness of gender stereotypes, insisting that certain activities or items of clothing are not for girls and others not for boys. Yet – as a consideration of transsexuals makes clear – gender identity does not automatically follow from biological sex. Money and Ehrhardt (1972, cited in Oakley, 1981, p. 53) report a case in which a seven-month-old boy lost his penis in an accident. A few months later, the boy's genitals were surgically reconstructed as female. He was assigned a girlish name, girlish clothing, a girlish hairdo. According to the researchers, he developed 'normally' as a very feminine girl.

Socialisation theory offers a straightforward account of the acquisition of gendered identities. Infants are seen as blank slates, waiting to be written on by their environment. Through their interactions with people close to them and exposure to the values of their society, infants learn what sex has been attributed to them and what is expected of them as little girls or boys. Reinforcement (praise and other rewards for gender-appropriate behaviour, punishment for deviation) brings the message home. A process of modelling (imitating parents, older siblings or teachers of the same sex) may also occur, until eventually children internalise (incorporate as part of their sense of self) the gender prescriptions of their society. And the more polarised the culture in respect of gender, the greater the gender difference in the identities of girls and boys.

In spite of public interest in gender equality in the second half of the twentieth century in Europe and the US, it is undeniably the case that children receive frequent reminders of the difference between the sexes. The division of labour in most families points to different responsibilities for women and men. Boys' clothing differs from girls' clothing in crucial details (*Star Trek* pyjamas versus *Forever Friends* nightgowns, or joggers versus leggings), and on the occasions when children dress up, the differences are even sharper. Even bedrooms are gendered: floral designs and ruffles or pleats for girls, military or animal designs for boys.

Parents, whatever their intentions, tend to treat girls and boys differently in ways that influence their development. Parents are far more likely to engage their infant sons in rough physical play – tossing them up in the air or wrestling with them – than they are their daughters (McDonald and Parke, 1986), and it has been argued that long-term consequences may follow (in this case, a head start for little boys in the development of physical confidence, aggressiveness and motor skills). Adults respond differently to the communicative efforts of girls and boys. In a study by Fagot *et al.* (1985) of infants aged 13 months, when boys demanded attention – by behaving aggressively, or crying, whining or screaming – they tended to get it. By contrast, adults tended to respond to girls only when they used language, gestures or gentle touches; girls who used attention-grabbing techniques were likely to be ignored. There was little difference in the communicative patterns of girls and boys at the start of the study, but by the age of two, the girls had become more talkative and the boys more assertive in their communicative styles. There is a possibility that, through patterns of reinforcement, adults helped to create these gender differences, as socialisation theory predicts.

But although socialisation theory may explain certain aspects of gendered behaviour, it cannot stand as a complete explanation for gendered identity and gendered desires. For one thing, socialisation theory makes children the passive receivers of gendered messages from their environment. But this assumption is incompatible with research that shows that even very young children often make gender-stereotyped choices for themselves. A study of pre-school children in North Carolina (Robinson and Morris, 1986) found that their Christmas presents tended to be heavily gender stereo-typed (for example, military toys for boys, dolls and domestic items for girls). But these gifts, it turned out, had been purchased largely at the insistence of the children them-selves. The toys that had been selected for them by grown-ups tended to be sex-neutral (for example, art supplies, games, musical instruments). Children's early, spontaneous gender commitments cannot readily be explained by socialisation theory.

Moreover, socialisation theory may be insufficiently subtle to account for the com-plexity of gender identity and gendered desires. The attachment of adult men and women to elements of masculinity or femininity that they would like to slough off (something experienced by many women in the women's movements and men in men's movements), the depths of emotion accompanying gendered desires (excitement, passion or shame), and the conflicts that continue to trouble fully socialised women and men – all these suggest that socialisation theory operates too much at the level of conscious processes and pays too little attention to the underlying psychic processes by which gender may be embedded.

One of the most influential of the psychoanalytic theories of gender identity – those that take account of unconscious processes – is the perspective developed in Chodorow's (1978) book *The Reproduction of Mothering*. Nancy Chodorow traces the implications for emotional development of the fact that mothers generally care for infants in their early years, while fathers are more emotionally distant. The formation of the self involves separating from the mother, with whom the infant is initially psychically merged. But this process operates differently for girls and boys. Girls can separate gradually, maintaining a continuous sense of relationship with the mother, who is, after all, experienced as like. For boys, on the other hand, separating from the mother, who is experienced as different, involves repressing the feminine aspects of themselves and rejecting much of the tenderness that was central to that early relationship. Boys' sense of maleness is, Chodorow suggests, achieved at great emotional cost.

As a result of these processes, adult men are likely to have a more autonomous sense of self, and to be more independent, more instrumental and more competitive in their dealings with others. They are also likely to have difficulty expressing emotions and to be anxious about intimacy. Women, on the other hand, have more need and more ability to sustain relationships with others; they have greater empathy with others. They have difficulty, however, in maintaining the boundaries of an independent and autonomous self.

Thus, asymmetrical mothering helps to explain, in Chodorow's view, the reproduction of divisions of labour based on childcare. 'Because women are themselves mothered by women, they grow up with the relational capacities and needs, and psychological definition of self-in-relationship, which commits them to mothering. Men, because they are mothered by women, do not' (ibid., p. 209).

Figure 6.1 Chodorow's theory of mothering explains why women enjoy mothering and why gender is rooted so deeply in our psyche.

In Chodorow's view, however, these patterns are not inevitable. Changes in the social arrangements for care of children – changes such as dual parenting, which would involve fathers in emotional intimacy with their children and in close physical care – could break the cycle, developing in both women and men the parts of their psyches that are currently stunted and raising a generation of children who might be very different.

Chodorow's theory of the reproduction of mothering has been influential in sociology. In particular, many writers on masculinity have found her analysis helpful in understanding the problems some men experience in relating to others.

We can, however, question the scope of the theory, the range of situations to which it might apply. We might ask, on the one hand, how many societies are characterised by full-time mothers and emotionally distant fathers? Can the idea that women are psychologically driven to mother be squared with the evidence of variations in mothering at different times and in different places – with, for example, communal patterns of mothering in some African communities, or with the strong tendency of wealthy mothers in eighteenth-century France to send their babies away to be wet-nursed? We can also challenge the idea of a single femininity (a self attuned to relationship, lacking autonomy) and a single masculinity (instrumental and uncomfortable with emotion). It is not clear whether Chodorow's account would apply, for instance, to the black London schoolgirls in Riley's (1988) study, who expected to be economically independent and to enter emotional relationships on their own terms.

Moreover, the proposed solution of dual parenting has been rejected by some critics, who point out that it rests upon a particular model of family life – not all children have a reliable father who could be more closely involved in their care – and upon a faulty logic. If men are as lacking in the capacity (and not simply the will) to mother as Chodorow suggests, if they are unable to empathise with or relate to others, then how could they possibly be entrusted with the intimate care of children?

More important than the specific limitations of Chodorow's theory, or of socialisation theory, is the need to recognise that all theories that focus on how the individual becomes gendered, however well-crafted, are limited in what they can explain. These theories tend to be deterministic, underestimating the fluidity of gendered behaviour and the capacity of women and men to change. In her retrospective study of a sample of white American women, Gerson (1985) found that their orientations in adolescence towards domesticity or careers provided a poor guide to their later behaviour; changes in circumstance (for example, divorce) or opportunity (for example, promotion) marked for many women the first stage in constructing completely new identities. In short, identity may be more malleable than accounts of the acquisition of gender identity often imply. A little girl can wear frilly pyjamas and still grow up to be a tough union negotiator; and a little boy who plays at warfare can become a gentle and caring father.

CONNECTIONS For further discussion of sociological views on the family in relation to these issues, see Chapter 9, pages 242–3.

Theories of gender identity may also contribute to an unhelpful view of gender as a watertight compartment of identity that coexists with but evolves independently from other aspects of identity. Such theories may give the impression that while women are differentiated by race, ethnicity, sexuality and class, the meanings that womanhood holds for them will be common to all. But earlier we emphasised that femininities (or masculinities) often differ dramatically for people in different social positions, even within the same society. As one anthropologist puts it, 'class, race, sexuality and religion completely alter the experience of a "lived anatomy", of what it is that sex, gender and sexual difference signify' (Moore, 1994, p. 25). Or in the snappier words of a poet: 'The juice from tomatoes is not called merely *juice*. It is always called TOMATO juice' (Gwendolyn Brooks, cited in Spelman, 1990, p. 186). There may be no such thing as gender identities that are not also constituted as identities of race, ethnicity, sexuality and class. This issue is examined in Chapter 7.

QUESTION How might particular structures outside the family influence the involvement of women and men in parenting?

Moreover, gender is not primarily a property of individuals, but a property of societies, social institutions and culture. Theories about how people become gendered may help us to understand why individuals accept their position in a gendered world, or even why individuals sometimes feel compelled to resist. But such theories cannot explain how the social world came to be gendered in the first place. To account for inequalities in earnings; to explain why, in parts of the US, childcare workers earn less than parking attendants; to account for the concentration of power among men rather than women in the state, banking and finance; to understand why rape in marriage was legal in Britain until 1991 – in short, to understand gender relations, gender inequality and their links to the distribution of power – we have to look beyond psychological processes to social patterns and societal arrangements. Indeed, thinking of Chodorow's analysis, we might wonder whether a gendered society – a society, for example, in which women's average pay is only three quarters that of men – has any part to play in ensuring that it is women rather than men who mother.

Creating a gendered society

The persistence of gender inequalities across a range of different societies has intrigued sociologists. One of the most sophisticated theories that attempts to account for the persistence of gender inequalities is Sylvia Walby's (1989) theory of **patriarchy**. Another is Bob Connell's attempt to develop a social theory of gender that focuses on the gender order.

The theory elaborated by Sylvia Walby grew out of earlier dual-systems theories that attempted to explain the subordination of women in modern societies by proposing a complex relationship between capitalism on the one hand and patriarchy on the other. Walby identified six discrete structures:

1 Household production and the relations between men and women that it sustains.

2 The organisation of paid work.

Patriarchy
A term used by feminists to refer to an overarching system of male dominance, often involving the dominance of senior men over junior men as well as over women.

3   The patriarchal state.

4   Male violence.

5   Heterosexuality and the sexual double standard.

6   Cultural institutions and cultural practices that help to shape women's identities.

Together, she argues, these comprise the system of patriarchy, which is 'a system of social structures, and practices, in which men dominate, oppress and exploit women' (ibid., p. 214). Not all systems of patriarchy are identical; on the contrary, there are different degrees of patriarchy, and the six structures can interact in very different ways.

Walby describes two distinct types of patriarchy in modern Western history. The first is private patriarchy, in which household production is the crucial structure. Women are excluded from public arenas (for example, by being barred from influential occupations or denied the vote), and they are controlled, directly and individually, by their husbands or fathers. It is husbands and fathers who benefit most directly from patriarchal relations. The model of private patriarchy can be used to describe mid-nineteenth-century Britain, when women's lives were constricted by domestic confinement. But over the past 150 years, the shape of patriarchy has altered. Walby argues that the re-entry of women to paid employment, the increase in divorce and autonomous motherhood, and greater sexual freedom for women combined with male-centred accounts of sexuality have together created a shift from private to public patriarchy. The demand of advanced capitalism for a freeing up of female labour, and feminist campaigns for women's liberation have both played a part in this shift. In public patriarchy, women have access to public arenas but are disadvantaged within them. Husbands and fathers have far less control, but women are controlled collectively through, for example, employment patterns, unequal pay structures or pornography. Men benefit from public patriarchy not as husbands or fathers of particular women, but collectively, for example, through systematically higher wages. Public patriarchy, rather than confining women to certain sites, subordinates them in all. Walby (1990, p. 201) concludes: 'The form of patriarchy in contemporary Britain is public rather than private. Women are no longer restricted to the domestic hearth, but have the whole society in which to roam and be exploited.'

CONNECTIONS For a feminist view of the impact of patriarchy on the world of work, see Chapter 11, pages 302–3 and 311–13.

Walby's theory of patriarchy says little about the proliferation of femininities and masculinities in contemporary society. However, this proliferation is a central feature of Bob Connell's social theory of gender. Connell (1987, p. 287) defines gender as 'the linking of fields of social practice to the reproductive division', and, in turn, to bodies. In other words, human beings make interpretations of the sexual and reproductive capacities of human bodies, and in so doing they produce a variety of masculinities and femininities, and embed them in social institutions. Through their social practices, people support these interpretations or challenge them. In the contemporary Western gender order, hegemonic masculinity (involving an emphasis on heterosexuality, strength and toughness, paid work, authority and control) is the culturally dominant form, though it is increasingly under challenge from a variety of fronts. Below hegemonic masculinity in the gender hierarchy are complicit masculinities (in which men benefit from the ideal – for example, through higher wages – while not embodying it), subordinated masculinities (homosexual masculinities and other forms that are far from the macho ideal), and, at the bottom, subordinated to all masculinities, are a variety of femininities.

For Connell (1987, 2000), the gender order refers to a historically constructed pattern of power relations between men and women that incorporates the definitions of masculinities and femininities that are current in society. It has four important elements:

- Labour – the organisation of housework, childcare and paid work.
- Power – expressed in the association of masculinity with authority, and manifest in the power structures of state and business, the institutions of violence and interpersonal violence, the mechanisms for regulating sexuality and struggles over domestic authority.
- **Cathexis** – the pattern of emotional relations.
- Symbolism – the symbolic structures that are used in communication and that are often important sites of gender practice.

Cathexis
Originally employed by Freud to describe a psychic charge or an emotional attraction towards another person. More generally associated with the social and psychological patterning of desire and the construction of emotionally charged relationships.

Each of these elements may vary from one society to another, and the way in which the four interconnect may also vary. Connell suggests that a 'structural inventory' or structural analysis of the current gender order of affluent Western societies would include:

- The gendered separation of domestic life from the moneyed economy and the political world.
- Core institutions (for example, the military, the state and government) that are heavily masculinised and a more open-textured periphery.
- Institutionalised heterosexuality and the repression of homosexuality and lesbianism.
- Overall subordination of women by men, which is sustained by the other three.

The gender order exerts a powerful influence over men and women in society, but it is by no means fixed or immutable. The structures of the gender order are maintained by practice, by the things people do, and at any moment social practice can either reaffirm the gender order or push in the direction of change. Change may occur through the constitution of social interests. In the second half of the twentieth century, for example, many gender interests were articulated through collective projects – for example, women's liberation movements, which made feminist ideas and practices credible to a mass audience; men's movements, which defended and promoted particular masculinities; and the campaigns mounted by homosexuals and lesbians to assert gay rights. The gender order represents the current state of play in this political to and fro.

The theories developed by Walby and Connell highlight different things and differ in their assessments of the prospects for change, but both offer a sociological way of looking at the way in which gender is embedded in society. We now turn to the key aspects of the social processes that construct our gendered world, including some that have been identified as significant in the theories of Walby and Connell – divisions of labour, the social organisation of childbirth and childcare, popular culture and the media, and sexuality.

Divisions of labour

In pre-industrial Britain, prior to 1780, economic activity – agricultural production, craft work and so on – was organised by households. Household members, whether male or female, young or old, contributed to the family's livelihood. Although women might do some types of work and men others, depending on region and class, the distinction between men as breadwinners and women as housewives did not characterise pre-industrial divisions of labour.

Industrialisation shifted much productive activity to factories, shops and offices. This separation of work from home signalled a profound change in gender relations and gender discourse. The home came to be understood not as the site of a family enterprise, but as a refuge from the world of work. Women were defined as the keepers of the home, as it was seen as their nature to create harmony and virtue rather than services and goods.

This **ideology** of domesticity, and the associated notion of separate spheres for women and men, originated in the middle classes but affected all women in different ways. For the wives of wealthy men, it spelled a life of enforced idleness. For the daughters of the lower middle class, it meant a desperate search for a husband; debarred from higher education and many forms of employment, an unmarried 'lady' risked impoverishment and degradation. For working-class women, the ideology of domesticity brought not relief from labour, but exclusion from skilled occupations, even lower earnings and sharper segregation from men in daily life. The notion that masculinity meant having a wife who did not have to work inspired the trade union movement to set its sights on securing for male workers a family wage. As a result, much of the work (paid or unpaid) that working-class women did to sustain their families became invisible, while single, separated or widowed working-class women could expect to live and die in poverty. Although the ideology of domesticity has been dealt a severe blow by changing patterns of employment, its legacy survives in four important ways.

First, the ideology of domesticity lives on in contemporary divisions of labour – in the association of (dominant forms of) masculinity with rational calculation, productive work and the exercise of authority, and of femininity with emotionality, domestic work and the provision of care. It is no accident that, of the six million adults in the UK who are carers of the sick, elderly and disabled, 60 per cent are women; moreover, women are more likely than men to be the only carer or sole main carer (Office for National Statistics, 1998). Nor is it an accident that although both sexes tend to value family and intimate relationships, men in Western societies express this commitment primarily in terms of financial maintenance, while women tend to shoulder responsibility for day-to-day physical and emotional care and the running of the home, as well as earning wages. The gender division of labour, in its broadest sense, encapsulates these differences.

Second, the ideology of domesticity renders important forms of work invisible, with consequences that are practical as well as theoretical. For much of the past century, only paid employment (preferably that done by men in large-scale enterprises and on full-time 'permanent' contracts) has been given full recognition as work. This narrow definition obscures those forms of work (for example, labour sharing between households) that are characteristic of the **informal economy** but may become more important in the future. It also excludes unpaid domestic work (done mainly by women), which is a crucial factor in maintaining quality of life, and the important subsistence work (again done mainly by women) that provides the basic necessities for much of the rural population of countries in the South. The failure of economic statistics to take account of subsistence work has often underpinned development policies that increase the gross national product but endanger lives.

Third, the ideology of domesticity contributes to the continuing tendency to see the work women do as a natural by-product of femininity – of pliability or caring – rather than skill. The skills involved in housework, for example, often go unnoticed, except perhaps by housewives themselves, struggling to measure up for curtains or to stretch the grocery money from one week to the next. In the UK, jobs undertaken by part-time women workers in the social services, often involving complex competences, tend to be classified and paid as 'unskilled caring work'. Further afield, multinational companies, when shifting some of their production of computer parts, toys, clothing and pharma-

---

Ideology
A set of ideas and beliefs about reality and society which underpin social and political action. Ideologies are often used to justify and sustain the position and interests of powerful social groups.

Informal economy
Includes unwaged work such as housework or labour-sharing between households.

ceuticals to new factories in countries in the South, often justify their recruitment policies by reference to the naturally nimble fingers of young women; it has been pointed out that the 'natural' dexterity of these women in fact reflects their earlier training in sewing and darning techniques that parallel the assembly process. Thus, in global as well as national divisions of labour, the definition of skill is underpinned by discourses of gender. Phillips and Taylor's (1980, p.79) assertion remains valid: 'Far from being an objective economic fact, skill is often an ideological category imposed on certain types of work by virtue of the sex and power of the workers who perform it.'

Fourth, the ideology of domesticity has contributed to practices that have produced and reproduced gender segregation within employment. Over the past 150 years, for example, ideas about the protection of women have often been deployed to secure their exclusion from certain types of work – from night work in factories or from heavy work in the printing trade. Although such arguments have often been hypocritical – the restriction on night work for women factory workers has seldom been extended to hospitals or to cleaning jobs – they have nevertheless been effective.

Feminisation of the labour force

While gender segregation in employment has deep roots in the nineteenth century, events in the second half of the twentieth century posed a challenge. In the 1950s and 1960s, economic growth created expansion in employment, an expansion met in the UK first by seeking Commonwealth workers and then by recruiting indigenous women. From 1960 onwards, the service sector began to overtake manufacturing. During the 1970s and 1980s, de-industrialisation and de-skilling radically altered the nature of employment (see Chapters 5 and 11).

A consequence of these changes has been a massive influx of women into the paid labour force, and an increasing tendency for them to stay longer in employment and to take shorter career breaks when their children are young. In the UK, almost 90 per cent of the new jobs that have been created since 1970 have gone to women (Cohen and Borrill, 1993). During recent decades, feminisation has characterised the labour force of many industrialised nations, although the percentage of women in the non-agricultural labour force (that is, in industry and services) varies enormously by country and region (Table 6.1).

The extent of change in the UK has been documented by McDowell (1992), who shows that between 1971 and 1988 the number of women of working age who were in (or seeking) employment rose by 1.7 million, while the number of males in employment fell by a similar amount. Women constituted 38 per cent of the labour force in 1971 but almost half in 1988. The flexibility for which women workers were notorious in the earlier part of the twentieth century appears now, in the post-Fordist era (see Chapters 3 and 11), to be part of their appeal to employers.

However, feminisation does not mean that gender segregation has been eradicated, nor that women have come out on top in employment terms. On the contrary, restructuring has been accompanied by the reproduction of gender segregation and the creation of new forms of inequality between and among women and men.

Horizontal gender segregation is less marked now than in the past. In 1900, over 70 per cent of the labour force were men; jobs such as clerical work were over-whelmingly done by males, and members of professionals such as barristers and solicitors were exclusively male. By the start of the last decade of the twentieth century, men made up only 54 per cent of the labour force, and 28 per cent of barristers, solicitors and advocates were women; many of the barricades that had previously separated men's work from women's work had been breached. However, horizontal segregation

---

Horizontal gender segregation
The separation of men and women into qualitatively different types of job.

TABLE 6.1 Global divisions of labour: women in the non-agricultural labour force, 2000

Region	Country with highest and lowest proportion of women in the non-agricultural labour force, by region	
	Highest	Lowest
sub-Saharan Africa	38%, Botswana	5%, Chad
central and western Asia	47%, Israel	10%, Bahrain
Asia and the Pacific	45%, Thailand	39%, Republic of Korea
Latin America and the Caribbean	50%, Jamaica	32%, El Salvador
Eastern Europe	54%, Ukraine	40%, Macedonia
Western Europe and the developed countries	52%, Iceland	29%, Malta
other developed countries	47%, Australia	
	48% New Zealand	
	48% United States	
	50% United Kingdom	

Source: UNIFEM, Progress of the World's Women (2000), UN Development Fund for Women Table 3.2.

continues to persist, though in a more muted form. Many occupations continue to be gender-skewed; for instance, in 1991, 92 per cent of nurses and midwives and 85 per cent of housekeepers and cleaners were women, while 89 per cent of police officers and 93 per cent of the members of the armed forces were men (Office of Population Censuses and Surveys, 1991; Office for National Statistics, 2000b).

Vertical gender segregation
The separation of men and women into higher or lower grades within the same occupation.

There is also some evidence of a decline in **vertical gender segregation** in the UK in the last few decades; the concentration of women in the lower grades of occupations has become rather less marked in, for example, the civil service, school teaching and in sales work. However, the conclusion reached in 1990 by the Hansard Society Commission on Women at the Top – that 'in any given occupation, and in any given public office, the higher the rank, prestige or influence, the smaller the proportion of women' – still holds good (Hansard Society for Parliamentary Government, 1990, p. 2).

In spite of the popular image of women storming the citadels of male employment, the feminisation of the labour force has not eradicated demarcations or divisions of reward between men's and women's work. Bakker (1988, p. 31) refers to 'the paradox of, on the one hand, an enormous growth in female labour force activity and, on the other hand, an intensified segregation of women into secondary, low-wage jobs'. This paradox can be partly accounted for by the nature of restructuring itself. 'Women as a group have more work', Bakker explains, 'but it is often poorly-paid, unprotected and part-time, because restructuring has brought fewer good jobs in its wake' (ibid.) The expansion of work that is casual and part-time, of contract labour that is temporary and insecure, and generally of employment in the growing deregulated fringe, has depended heavily on women's labour (Pascall, 1995).

Another explanation of gender segregation in employment invokes wider divisions of labour, arguing that childcare responsibilities force women into part-time work and

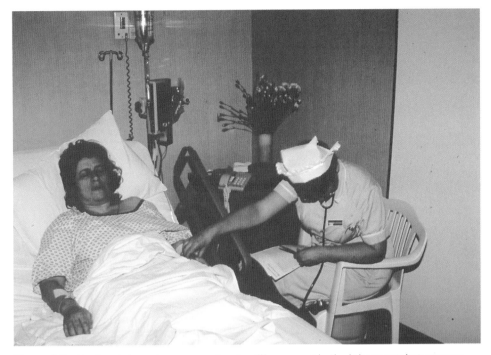

Figure 6.2 Horizontal gender segregation is still apparent in the labour market: women continue to outnumber men in the caring professions.

jobs at the bottom of the hierarchy. But while part-time work may disadvantage some women, it cannot explain the employment position of all. In the UK, Afro-Caribbean women are likely to work full-time regardless of their childcare responsibilities, but they are nevertheless concentrated in less well-rewarded jobs (Bruegel, 1994).

Moreover, comparative data offer a serious challenge to explanations that focus on women's responsibilities for child care. In the UK, 43 per cent of women workers are part-time, and the move into part-time work often follows a career break for the care of children. In France, by contrast – where women tend to leave the labour market only if they have three or more children, or are made redundant – only one woman worker in five is part-time. If women's disadvantaged employment position were due to the relationship between family responsibilities, interrupted work histories and part-time work, Beechey (1992) argues, we would expect job equality for French women, whose work profile resembles that of men. But in fact, though French women have had more success than British women in moving into lower-level managerial positions, the degree of horizontal and vertical segregation in the two countries is not dissimilar.

What this analysis points to is the importance of understanding how women, and especially mothers, become constructed as 'inferior' workers. One factor is **discourses** that blame working mothers for social problems; in the UK, for a long time 'being a mother and being a paid worker have been constructed as contradictory' (Beechey, 1992, p. 163). Another is the role of the state in structuring the labour market, for example, by drafting employment laws that create temporary contracts without maternity and other protections, and hence encourage the development of a two-tier labour force.

Finally, any explanation has to consider how gender has been embedded in organisational processes – that is, the ways in which the organisational culture of the workplace may perpetuate horizontal and vertical segregation and offer deterrents to

Discourse
A body of ideas, concepts and beliefs that have become established as knowledge or as an accepted world-view. These ideas provide a powerful framework for understanding and action in social life.

women's promotion. Several studies of organisations have shown, for example, how male managers frequently mobilise masculinity in work settings to valorise or affirm men and to exclude women (Martin and Collinson, 1999).

CONNECTIONS If you are interested in the sociology of organisations, a good starting point is Weber's account of rationality and bureaucracy in Chapter 17, pages 482–7.

Consequences of gender-segregated employment

The first consequence of gender segregation in employment is marked gender differences in earnings, as demonstrated in Table 6.2. Among full-time non-manual employees in the UK in April 1999, women on average earned £179 less per week than men. For manual workers, the male advantage was £113; on average, male manual workers were paid only marginally less than women in non-manual jobs. A male earnings advantage is clearly visible in many countries around the world (Table 6.3).

Men boost their take-home pay by working overtime to a greater extent than women do. This does not, however, account for the male earnings advantage; in 1999, women in non-manual work earned £179 per week less than their male colleagues, even though their working week was only two hours shorter. Even with the effects of overtime excluded, there was a male earnings advantage of £1.88 per hour for manual workers, and £4.16 for those in non-manual jobs.

These data are for full-time workers only. Part-time workers – predominantly women – have poorer prospects, greater insecurity and lower hourly rates, than their full-time colleagues. In 1998, women who worked part-time received only 73 per cent

TABLE 6.2 Earnings and hours worked by women and men, April 1999: adults in full time work whose pay was not affected by absence

	All women	All men	Manual women	men	Non-Manual women	men
Average gross weekly earnings (before tax or other deductions) (£)	327	442	222	335	347	526
Proportion whose gross weekly earnings were:						
less than £250 (%)	39	19	71	27	33	13
less than £350 (%)	67	45	93	62	62	31
Average hours worked per week (hours), of which overtime	37.5	41.4	39.9	44.4	37.0	39.0
hours are:	0.8	2.7	1.9	4.9	0.6	1.1
Average gross hourly earnings (excluding overtime pay and overtime hours) (pence)	870	1075	548	736	936	1352

Source: Department of Employment (1999), Part A.

TABLE 6.3 The male earnings advantage around the world, selected countries, 1997[1]

Republic of Korea	62	New Zealand	81
Switzerland [2]	67	Panama	83
Mexico [2]	72	Paraguay	83
Chile [2]	73	Costa Rica	85
Brazil	74	Argentina	87
Singapore	74	Jordan	87
Netherlands [2]	77	Australia	90
Belgium	80	Sri Lanka	90
United Kingdom	80	Colombia	95
France [2]	81	Egypt	97

1. Female wages as percentage of male wages, non-agricultural labour force, industry and services
2. The nations in which women's wages have declined relative to those of men since 1980. Elsewhere the male–female wage gap has narrowed.

Source: UNIFEM (2000), Progress of the World's Women UN Development Fund Chart 4.4.

of the hourly pay of full-time women workers, and only 59 per cent as much as full-time men (Equal Opportunities Commission Pay and Income website, p. 3).

Secondly, gender segregation in employment makes women particularly vulnerable to poverty. In 1999, 71 per cent of full-time women manual workers (but only 27 per cent of their male counterparts), earned less than £250 per week, placing women disproportionately among the low-paid. The earnings advantage enjoyed by men in employment is likely to be carried over into old age, since women's occupational pension entitlements are generally less than those of men. The gendered concentration of poverty is not a new phenomenon; now, as at the end of the nineteenth century, women make up the majority of the poor.

The third consequence of employment patterns relates to the impact of economic recession and restructuring. Although women in general lag behind men in earnings, the last two decades have seen a widening of inequalities within each of the two groups. While full-time women workers have closed some of the earnings gap between themselves and their male counterparts; (during the 1980s, on average, their hourly earnings rose from 72 per cent of men's to 76 per cent), within each of the two groups there has been a widening of differentials – the rich got richer and the poor got poorer. Bruegel's (1994) analysis of London living standards confirmed that the distance between winners and losers among women has been greater than that among men. Direct racial discrimination and the vulnerability to unemployment that comes from their concentration in manual work, she finds, have combined to place a disproportionate number of black women firmly among the losers.

Figures also show a considerable variation in earnings across ethnic and gender groups in the UK. As Table 6.4 indicates, women of Pakistani/Bangladeshi and Indian origin earned well below the female average earnings; men of Pakistani/Bangladeshi origin also earned less than the average male earnings, but Indian men were the top

TABLE 6.4 Average hourly earnings (£) of full-time employees, UK, 1998/99

	Women	Men
White	7.50	9.29
Black	7.78	8.32
Indian	6.84	9.34
Pakistani/Bangladeshi	6.33	6.87
All groups	7.51	9.27

Source: Office for National Statistics (1998, 1999) for Spring 1998 to Winter 1998/99.

earning group. In spite of this variation, within every ethnic group, the average hourly earnings of women working full-time are less than those of men (Equal Opportunities Commission, 2000, p. 3).

 ## Childbirth and childcare

The conception, bearing and raising of children is an area of human activity that may appear to be driven by biology: humans, like other animals, reproduce; and women, like other mammals, bear the growing infant. But in the case of human beings, all behaviour surrounding reproduction – the decision to have intercourse, contraceptive knowledge, the taboos and obligations surrounding pregnancy, the manner and place of birth – is meaningful in social (rather than biological) terms.

In all societies, it is women who give birth to children, but the implications can and do vary dramatically. During the eighteenth and nineteenth centuries in Europe, as changes in the economy and society reshaped the lives of women and men, the identity of 'woman' and 'mother' came substantially to overlap. By contrast, in some tribal societies – where fertility is the responsibility of everyone, and where men are thought to play an important part in life creation – the notion of motherhood is a more peripheral part of women's identity (Moore, 1994).

The social conditions surrounding childbirth and childcare have changed dramatically in Western societies in the past century in ways that are important for gender relations. Among the most significant changes are, first, the availability of more effective means of preventing or terminating unwanted pregnancies. Better fertility control, combined with a shrinking ideal family size, mean that the proportion of women's lives typically devoted to pregnancy and early infant care has been dramatically reduced.

Second, while women today spend less time on breastfeeding, the care of children has come to be defined in a far more rigorous way; mothering involves responsibility not only for the physical maintenance of children, but for detailed attention to their psychological, social and intellectual development. One illustration of this is the concern that has emerged for what is called 'preconceptual care'; young women are urged to behave, eat, exercise and cultivate their minds and their bodies as if they were already mothers months or even years before they conceive. While fatherhood is high on the public agenda in Western societies, and while the prevailing view of the 1950s that fathers should hold themselves at a distance from the messy world of childhood has less appeal, it is still mothers who take the greatest responsibility for childcare. Motherhood is seen, in a way that it was not in the past, as a full-time occupation as well as a lifelong identity;

BOX 6.4 Making babies

In modern societies, medical science provides the dominant cultural categories by which pregnancy and childbirth are understood. Emily Martin (1989) argues that the terms used in obstetrical discourse are reminiscent of Fordist production. Indeed, she suggests that childbirth, like factory labour, is subjected to time-and-motion strictures – so many minutes for this stage of labour, so many minutes for that. One consequence is that mothers' active involvement in childbirth tends to be devalued and that of the obstetrician is glorified. Barbara Katz Rothman (1987, p. 161) contends that in spite of campaigns and movements to reclaim some control for women over birth-giving, 'the pattern in hospitals remains the same. Doctors deliver babies from the bodies of women. The women may be more or less awake, more or less aware, more or less prepared, and more or less humanely or kindly treated, but within the medical model the baby is the product of the doctor's services.'

---

and mothers can be expected to lavish as much care on two children as they might have on six in pre-modern times.

Third, the most dramatic increases in the workload of mothers have occurred during the same period as women's paid workload has accelerated. A demanding form of motherhood sits uneasily with the feminisation of the labour force. Some Western countries have accommodated this, to an extent, by extensive nursery provision, after-school programmes and schemes for parental leave; but others have not. Between 1987 and 1997 in the UK, the provision of childcare places increased substantially; however, there is still only one registered childcare place for every 7.5 children under the age of eight, and the estimated cost of care for preschool children – between £50 and £180 per child per week – is beyond the means of many families. Four out of five mothers who are not currently employed say they would work if they had satisfactory childcare provision.

Fourth, in Western societies during the twentieth century, pregnancy and childbirth became increasingly **medicalised**. There was a dramatic increase in the proportion of babies born in hospital (from 15 per cent in 1927 to over 99 per cent in 2000), and a proliferation of reproductive technologies for monitoring pregnancy, intervening in childbirth and for caring for newborn infants. In some respects, medicalisation has made childbearing safer for women and their babies (though it has also brought new dangers in its wake – Oakley, in Stanworth, 1987). But it also provides a prime example of the ways in which women's lives and bodily processes have become more closely regulated by professionals, the majority of whom are men.

Fifth, and finally, although most children are born to married women in their twenties and thirties, in some developed countries there has been a marked increase in births to single women. In the UK in 1998, births outside marriage represented 38 per cent of all births and 89 per cent of births to women under 20 years of age. However, it is worth noting that births to women under 20 years of age, married or not, constitute fewer than 8 per cent of all births; this is many fewer than in 1971, when 10 per cent of all births were to mothers under 20 years of age.

Medicalisation
Increasing medical intervention in and control over areas that hitherto have been outside the medical domain.

Autonomous motherhood
The assumption of sole responsibility for childcare without the close involvement of a father. May be voluntary, as in the case of single mothers who choose not to involve the father, or involuntary.

CONNECTIONS For a further discussion of the medicalisation of motherhood, see Chapter 9, pages 238–9.

The trend towards **autonomous motherhood** reflects the increasing capacity of women (and men) to leave their partners when they are unhappy, to have a sex life outside marriage and to bring up their children on their own. On the other hand, in the context of lower earnings and lower occupational opportunities for women, and the meagreness of the support many receive from fathers, autonomous motherhood often also means poverty and hardship. Research by the Institute of Social and Economic Research (*Observer*, 22 October 2000) indicates that men's disposable income, in the years following divorce, increases by an average of 15 per cent, while that of women falls by 28 per cent. Women not only bear the children, they also shoulder a disproportionate share of the cost of bringing them up.

Popular culture and the mass media

Content analysis
Analysis of the content of communications; usually refers to documentary or visual material.

Ever since the women's movement triggered off a new interest in the analysis of gender in the 1970s, the mass media and popular culture have been a focus for research.

Content analyses measured the frequency of portrayals of women and men in particular roles or situations. They often produced alarming evidence of the cultural invisibility of girls and women, especially in the public sphere. One American study (Grauerholz and Pescosolido, 1989) examined all the titles for young readers in the catalogue of children's library books. Over the period 1900 to 1984, there were three male characters for every one female character; this gender imbalance was particularly marked in the 1940s, 1950s and 1960s. The bias toward males in children's literature was most pronounced among adult and animal characters; within these categories, male characters continued to be more prominent right into the 1980s.

CONNECTIONS For a further discussion of media representation, turn to Chapter 11, pages 323–6, where issues of gender, class and race are discussed in relation to television.

Studies of magazines have raised questions about the place of popular culture in shaping masculinities and femininities. Magazines aimed at women and girls – even those as different as *Woman's Own* and *Sugar* – display a strong concern with personal relationships (especially with men), and with the cultivation of beauty and style. This is apparent not only in feature articles but also in advertisements and advice columns. Men's magazines, on the other hand, tend to represent specialised interests. They tend to be concerned with sports and hobbies (computers, fishing, cars and the like), business and finance, or sex. Even general men's magazines such as *Esquire* have few articles on interpersonal relationships. In magazines, it seems, femininity is defined by personal appearance and relationships with men, masculinity by a single-minded pursuit of projects (including sex) and an indifference to relationships (Renzetti and Curran, 1989, pp. 114–17).

According to Ferguson (1983), who has studied women's magazines published in the UK between 1949 and 1980, such magazines promote a cult of femininity that locks women into subordination. Ferguson's argument is all the more interesting, in that women's magazines are one of the few areas of popular culture in which women are often in controlling positions (as editors and managers).

Postmodern feminist approaches to women's magazines focus on the difference that new female producers of magazines have made to the content of the 'glossies'. In particular, the emphasis on sex in magazines such as *More!* and *Marie Claire* is claimed to represent a new freedom for young women as they define their own attitudes towards femininity (McRobbie, 1996). The magazines of the 1990s are therefore said to be reflective of 'postmodern culture' in stressing irony and an independence of spirit, which throws off the traditional definitions of what it means to be a woman. However, the representations of women in their pages still retain an emphasis on the white, heterosexual woman, with other representations (black or gay) being marginalised or treated as somehow exotic.

Other approaches to popular culture, such as that of Janice Radway (1994), take issue with content analyses on the ground that they can obscure the complex processes by which meaning is produced. For example, they obscure the heterogeneity of the audience – the way in which different groups of readers and watchers find different meanings in the same magazine or television programme. They deny the range of pleasures available from popular culture. In opposition to Ferguson (1983), Winship (1987) points to the pleasure that women get from their magazines and insists that women (or men) may still produce oppositional readings of the forms of popular culture they enjoy.

Finally, research based on content analyses fails to recognise that meaning comes in part from the social context of its reception. For example, the television drama *The X-Files* deliberately presents special agent Dana Scully in an unglamorous way, but she is nevertheless cast as a sex object by the many fan clubs that circulate more titillating photos of her. Another example is the way in which the reading of romance novels provides a basis for community and conversation for women readers, rather as football does for many men. In short, the impact of popular culture and the media is now recognised to be more complex, more differentiated, and more ambiguous than simple content analyses might suggest. Gender may be part of virtually all media productions, but it is subject to a variety of readings or interpretations.

And often the meaning of these images is far from obvious. Do action films with macho heroes attempt to mould men into one narrow form of masculinity? Or do they help men to come to terms with male interpersonal violence? Or could the appeal of action films be that they allow a display of tenderness between men in an acceptable (heterosexual) form? Should we see 'slasher films' primarily in terms of their portrayal of women as the ultimate victims of violence – for the way they make terror 'sexy' – or

Figure 6.3 Sigourney Weaver as Ripley in *Alien*: spectacle of a beautiful and terrified woman in a film made by and for men, or a charismatic heroine in an ambiguous movie about gestation and birth?

should we see them, as Clover (1992) suggests, in terms of the emerging tendency for the hero (the person who vanquishes the monster, as do the film characters Ripley in the various *Alien* movies and Jamie Lee Curtis in *Halloween*) to be gendered female? Should we think of popular romances as books that sell women the illusion that their happiness lies in losing themselves in love, or should we see them as providing women with psychological relief from their fears of men and a fantasy of revenge for ill-treatment? These competing interpretations demonstrate that the analysis of popular culture raises as many questions as it answers.

However, as the example of prime-time television suggests, in the midst of flux and change there are certain continuities that are worthy of remark. On the one hand, new themes have appeared – including issues of gender equality. The prominence on UK television of journalists and news presenters such as Kate Adie and Kirsty Wark, the presence of Oprah Winfrey as the monarch of US chat shows, and the airtime given to comediennes such as Ruby Wax – all these indicate that, to a degree, television has responded to the challenge posed by the changes in gender relations.

On the other hand, an international study of the world's media demonstrates that, even at the start of the twenty-first century, women continue to be the second sex in the media (GMMP, 2000). One of the most striking features of the report is the discrepancy between women's increasing involvement as media workers, and the starkness of their continuing under-representation as interviewees or subjects. Women constitute 28 per cent of radio reporters, 26 per cent of newspaper reporters and 36 per cent of television reporters. Women form a majority (56 per cent) of television announcers, but their proportion declines dramatically over the age of 35, suggesting, the authors of the report say, that appearance remains a stronger occupational prerequisite for women than for men.

Yet, only 18 per cent of people interviewed in the world's media are women; in 1995, the figure was 17 per cent – an extremely slow pace of change. The few women who are interviewed, or made the subject of media stories, are twice as likely as men to be presented as victims and five times more likely to be identified in terms of marital or family status; moreover, as Table 6.5 shows, the visibility of women as interviewees or subjects is related to the topic under discussion in a gendered way. When it comes to the presence and representation of women in the mass media, the term '**symbolic annihilation**' (Tuchman *et al.*, 1978) still has currency today.

Symbolic annihilation
A term coined in 1978 to signify how, as a result of under-representation in the media, women have been dismissed and ignored in the public domain.

TABLE 6.5 Predominance of men in the world's media, 2000 (percentage of male interviewees/subjects)

Topic		Occupation of interviewees/subjects	
Arts and entertainment	65	Homemaker/parent	19
Health	71	No stated occupation	75
Education	71	Scientist	88
Economy and business	83	Politician	90
Sports	88	Athlete	91
Politics and government	88		
War	89		
International crises	89		

Source: GMMP (2000).

QUESTION Construct an appropriate table to analyse and compare two different types of non-fiction television programme (for example, an arts programme and a news broadcast or *Crimewatch*) in terms of the visibility of men and women as reporters or presenters, subjects or interviewees.

 ## Sexuality

From an essentialist perspective (and such a perspective colours much commonsense thinking), when a man and woman are attracted to one another and become sexually involved, they are 'doing what comes naturally'. Sexuality in this view is a universal phenomenon that reflects deep-seated sexual drives.

Sociologists instead insist that sexual beliefs, practices, relationships and identities reflect social patterns rather than natural ones. Sexuality is socially constructed, and as a consequence, it is almost infinitely variable. Even sexual pleasures and desires are as much a matter of culture and history as they are of bodily potential. The erotic delight that Trobriand Islanders experienced when biting off the eyelashes of their beloved (Malinowski, 1932) was related not to bodily but to cultural difference. Sexual response is at least in part a learned response.

The concept of 'sexual script' was developed by Gagnon and Simon (1973) as a way of understanding the social construction of sexuality. A sexual script provides a kind of blueprint for sexual desire and sexual practice. Through socialisation, individuals internalise the sexual script, learning not only how to behave towards sexual partners, but also to desire particular things in particular circumstances, and to pursue gratification in particular ways.

But for the concept of sexual scripts to be useful, the gendered nature of scripts needs to be acknowledged. Rose and Frieze (1989) invited undergraduates at a college in midwestern America to describe in detail actions on a hypothetical first date. The respondents produced a script for men that was much more detailed than the one for women. Both male and female daters, undergraduates agreed, would worry about their appearance, try to impress their partner, and laugh, joke and talk. But men were expected to take responsibility for deciding what to do, picking up the date, paying, initiating physical contact and promising to get in touch. Men, the authors conclude, were the planners, the economic providers and the sexual initiators. Women, on the other hand, were expected to be 'sexual objects and emotional facilitators'; they had to find ways to keep the conversation going, and it was their responsibility, above all, to set limits to sexual demands.

The belief that it is men's place to initiate sex, and women's responsibility to decide how far a sexual encounter should go, is one plank in what is commonly called the **double standard of sexual morality**.

Gagnon and Simon's (1973) concept of sexual script offers an insight into the ways in which sexual practices differ across time and place, and between women and men. However, the approach has been criticised for being ahistorical, for failing to consider where sexual scripts and sexual meanings come from, and for failing to consider how the sexual behaviour of women and men reflects not only the learning of cultural scripts but also the effects of differential social power.

The claim that commonsense thinking treats sexuality as universal and natural should, more accurately, be restricted to heterosexuality. There are many forms of

Double standard of sexual morality The assumption that promiscuous or sexually assertive behaviours are to be expected or admired in men, but that the same behaviours are deviant in women. For example, there is no male equivalent of the term 'slag'.

BOX 6.5 | Compulsory heterosexuality?

Although many heterosexuals insist that they have come by their preference 'naturally', it is noticeable that a great deal of effort is expended in reinforcing that sexual preference. The state plays a crucial part by, for example, denying citizenship to known homosexuals or lesbians, refusing to recognise the marriages of same-sex partners, discriminating against arts projects that show homosexual families in a positive light, and maintaining a higher age of consent for homosexual practice than for heterosexual sex. By these and other means, Western states help to ensure the dominance of heterosexual identities and the relative invisibility of alternative sexualities.

Sexual identities are constructed in routine settings. In many workplaces, for example, heterosexuality is alluded to in the way people look and dress, in the practice of sexual harassment, in 'secret' affairs and in jokes and gossip. The sexual 'normality' of daily life in the office is, as Pringle (1989, p. 94) points out, 'relentlessly heterosexual', creating difficulties for homosexual men or lesbian women who want to fit in. Rich (1984, p. 130) coined the term 'compulsory heterosexuality' to draw attention to the possibility that desire for the other sex is not merely a preference, but also something that has to be 'imposed, managed, organised, propagandised, and maintained by force'.

The suppression of alternatives to heterosexuality is of broad significance for the understanding of gender difference, gender relations and gender inequality. The culturally constructed fear of homosexuality and lesbianism – homophobia – functions to police the behaviour of all men and women, whatever their sexual preference. The question 'What are you, a fag?' is not reserved exclusively for erotic display between men: it may be directed at boys or men who allow themselves to enjoy 'womanly' things, who display tenderness, whose clothes, interests or occupations do not fit the macho mould. The social taboo against sex and love between men serves to keep all men in line, defining what proper masculinity is.

Hegemony
Refers to consent or acceptance of an ideology, regime or whole social system. Full hegemony exists when a social order is accepted as natural and normal.

sexuality, but in contemporary Western societies, heterosexuality is in a dominant or **hegemonic** position. If heterosexuality as an institution shapes the behaviour of all individuals, as Box 6.5 suggests, its impact differs between women and men. In Western societies, heterosexuality incorporates a double standard of sexual morality. Sexual activity, even promiscuity, is seen as tolerable or admirable in boys, while – except in the context of love and domesticity – an active sexual life brings girls into disrepute. As Willis (1977, p. 146) has said of the behaviour of a group of working-class lads, 'Girls are pursued, sometimes roughly, for their sexual favours, often dropped and labelled "loose" when they are given'. Lads expect to be promiscuous, but promiscuous girls are despised.

Since Willis wrote his account, girls have gone further in asserting their right to sexuality. But the double standard has by no means evaporated. Sexual reputation is still significant in the experience of adolescent girls. To be branded as a 'slag' may have severe consequences, and girls try to avoid behaving, dressing or speaking in a manner that might attract this dangerous label. But the way that the term slag is used suggests that it is more about the nature of a girl's relationship with men than about sexual activity *per se*; a young woman who is unattached (sexually active or not) is more likely to be called a slag than one who sleeps with a regular boyfriend. The term slag functions, Lees (1986) suggests, to steer girls into the 'safety' of steady heterosexual relationships.

CONNECTIONS For more on the criminal justice system and the way in which it treats women differently from men, see Chapter 14, pages 401–5.

BOX 6.6 Sex and violence in the courtroom: the impact of the sexual double standard

Fictional accounts of rape and sensational reports in the media often give disproportionate attention to that small minority of rapists who attract the label 'psychopath'. The image of rape they produce is at odds with analyses of actual rape cases in Western societies, which indicate that few rapists are seriously disturbed, that many plan their crimes carefully, and that many are friends, relatives, acquaintances or workmates of the victim.

If rape is analysed in terms of its relationship to the social construction of sexuality and to the power relations between women and men – rather than being viewed as an idiosyncratic act by disturbed individuals – then we can begin to understand its incidence and its social implications.

The incidence of rape is related to the sexual double standard through cultural expectations about male initiative-taking in sexual encounters and female compliance. Pressure on men to 'prove themselves' by establishing sexual dominance may be reinforced by the representation of women not as complex human beings, but as objects to be admired and 'consumed'.

But the double standard has its most serious impact in courtrooms. If a victim of rape has been sexually active, this is often introduced in court by the defendant's lawyers to discredit her – the implication being that women who are sexually active in one circumstance have no right to refuse in another; they are seen to have placed themselves, in some sense, beyond the protection of the law.

As Matoesian's (1993) analysis of courtroom cross-examination demonstrates, qualities that serve a woman well in everyday life are likely to be deployed against her in a rape trial,. Evidence that a rape victim is independent and clear-headed, that she is friendly and open in her dealings with men – for example, she 'calmly enters a man's car' – tends to discredit her testimony. Matoesian (ibid., p. 223) concludes that 'Patriarchal ideology functions as a dominational resource for interpreting the sexual reality of the incident: a resource powering and concealing the sense of what happened. If a woman dates a man, if she goes off with him to an apartment, if she kisses him and so on ... then, according to the legal system, she has consented to sexual intercourse.'

The double standard constitutes a crucial part of the explanation of why the proportion of convictions from arrest to judgement is lower for rape than for other serious crimes such as murder, burglary, other sexual offences and aggravated assault. The double standard – permitting promiscuous sexuality to men and forbidding it to women – has, as Connell (1987, p. 113) says, 'nothing to do with greater desire on the part of men; it has everything to do with greater power'.

The double standard of sexual morality, then, both reflects and reinforces gender inequality. Men are encouraged to show they are 'real men' by dominating and objectifying women. Women are encouraged to demonstrate their love and to enhance their attractiveness to men by curtailing their own independence. Women who do not dress primarily to please males, go their own way, do not defer to male authority, value the company of other women – and above all, women who publicly side with other women, whether they call themselves feminists or not – run the risk of being dismissed as 'dykes' or 'man haters'. The suppression of lesbianism functions to put a brake on female autonomy; through heterosexuality, Rich (1984) argues, women are persuaded to turn aside from other women and to place men at the centre of their lives.

Rich's analysis of compulsory heterosexuality sits oddly with commonsense thinking about the impact of sexual liberalisation in the last third of the twentieth century, when changes in legislation on divorce, homosexuality and abortion, and changes in sexual mores, ushered in a new, more permissive sexual climate. In many Western societies, the years since the 1960s have seen greater tolerance of premarital sex, widespread recognition of women's capacity for sexual pleasure and more explicit public discussion of sexuality.

Many feminist writers have pointed out, however, that sexual practice continues to be structured by sexism. Consider, for example, the continued importance (in spite of the promotion of 'safe sex') of definitions of the sexual act centring on the penis and on intercourse; sensuality and alternative forms of touching tend to be seen merely as foreplay, the prelude to 'the real thing'. Similarly, dominance and submission are often presented as sexy, so that inequality is eroticised and therefore reinforced. Furthermore – as the study of tourist operations in the UK by Adkins (1995) demonstrates – for women, getting and holding a good job often depends on being sexually pleasing to men; women's sexuality is often commodified, becoming something they provide for others, not something they do for themselves. The working-class wives studied by Rubin (1976) in San Francisco in the 1970s often complained that sexual liberation had created another set of demands; at the end of a long day, after doing an outside job, caring for the children and looking after the house, they were now expected to have orgasms too!

Some writers argue that the term 'sexual liberation' is relevant only to men. But in spite of the ways that sexism and the double standard – and the greater social power of men – continue to structure sexuality, a verdict of 'no change' for women will not do. On the contrary, although full sexual equality would certainly depend on equality in other spheres, sexual liberalisation has been important for women. As Segal (1994) points out, it was women who were penalised most severely in earlier decades for sexual activity – being, for example, the ones who were 'blamed' for pregnancy, and the ones who died from backstreet abortions. By reducing the dangers associated with sexuality, sexual liberalisation may arguably have had a greater positive impact on women's lives than on men's.

Moreover, research into sexuality has challenged the notion of male sexual confidence. Hall's (1991) study of advisory literature for men in the first half of the twentieth century vividly exposes male anxieties about sexuality. The tendency to define men as healthy and women as pathological worked against the sympathetic resolution of male sexual problems. Hall raises the possibility that insecurity about sexuality may be one of the motivations that drives some men to seek power over women in other respects (ibid., p. 173). Her work suggests that the popular image of men as sexually in control, and as insistent on their own gratification at the expense of their partner, may mistake a patriarchal discourse of masculine potency for the real thing.

The discussion of sexual liberalisation and debates on how to read the sexual history of the late twentieth century again illustrate that sexuality is historically constructed. Early in the twentieth century, in Western societies, legitimate sexual activity seemed to be firmly established within the family; one hundred years on, sexual relationships are pursued before marriage, alongside marriage, after marriage or without marriage, and fewer people blink an eye. Partly because the connection between family and acceptable sexuality has been effectively challenged, sexuality has become more open to commercial exploitation – as any glance at a magazine or film will testify – and less significant as a means of binding people together in long-term relationships. In addition, hegemonic heterosexuality, though defended by, among others, fundamentalist religious groups, has lost some of its taken-for-granted authority. All of these things suggest alterations in the social organisation of sexuality that might eventually lead to deeper changes in the gender order.

Chapter summary

● Answers to questions about the origin of gender difference range from those that emphasise biological sources to those that stress the social, cultural and historical construction of women and men.

● The diversity of masculinities and femininities in different times and places, and among different social groups, works against the idea that there is some fixed essence or nature that all women or men have in common. The simple division into male and female sex can itself be seen as a social process, varying from one social setting to another.

● Theories of patriarchy, and social theories of gender, such as Connell's, attempt to explain how different structures in a society interact to sustain or challenge gender processes and to produce gender inequality.

● The early period of industrialisation gave rise to an ideology of domesticity that lives on in contemporary divisions of labour, for example, by rendering invisible some important forms of work.

● Horizontal and vertical gender segregation in employment contributes to marked gender differences in income, and to the greater vulnerability of women to poverty.

● The impact of popular culture on gender relations is complex and differentiated, and the meaning of texts and visual images is often ambiguous. In spite of changes in the media that acknowledge the greater prominence of women and girls in public life today, men are still far more visible in the global media than are women.

● Sexual beliefs, practices, relationships and desires follow social patterns rather than natural ones. In contemporary Western societies, heterosexuality is a dominant or hegemonic form of sexuality, reinforced by the state and many routine practices. The restrictions on same-sex sexuality serve to enforce particular expressions of masculinity and femininity, albeit in a manner that is contested.

Questions to think about

● Outline two different theories that attempt to account for why male and female individuals often differ in their behaviour, personalities and appearance.

● How would you explain the fact that most men and women in the UK today would identify themselves as heterosexual?

● Why, in spite of the influence of equal opportunities legislation and the women's movement, and in spite of altered patterns of educational attainment, do women on average earn less than men? Is it true to say that all women earn less than all men? If not, why not?

Investigating further

Abbott, Pamela and Clare Wallace (1997) *An Introduction to Sociology: Feminist Perspectives*, 2nd edition, Routledge.

> A very useful text, as it looks at all the key areas of sociological study but through the lens of gender.

Bryson, Valerie (1999) *Feminist debates*, Palgrave.

> This looks at a range of important social issues – family, paid work, abortion, pornography and so on – from a feminist perspective.

Lovell, Terry, Carol Wolkowitz and Sonya Andemahr (eds) (1997) *A Concise Glossary of Feminist Theory*, Arnold.

> A useful reference and source book for key ideas in feminist theory.

7

Race and ethnicity

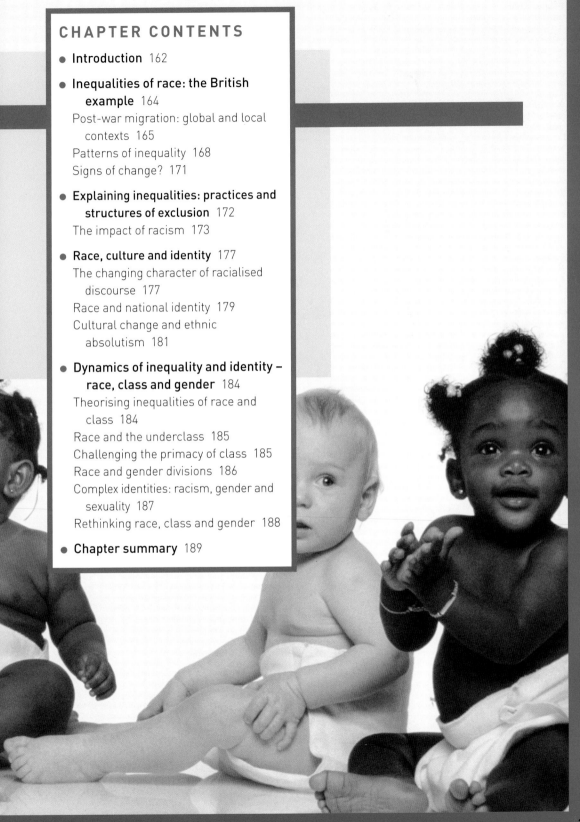

CHAPTER CONTENTS

Aims of the chapter

In this chapter, we introduce you to the sociological analysis of racial and ethnic differences and divisions. We explore their continued significance as bases for both social inequalities and social identities, looking particularly at the issue of national identity. The chapter concludes by linking the discussion of race and ethnicity to a consideration of the other dimensions of stratification (class and gender) addressed in Chapters 5 and 6. By the end of this chapter, you should be familiar with the following concepts:

- Race
- Ethnicity
- Scientific racism
- Racialisation
- Racial dualism
- Institutional racism
- Identity politics
- Diaspora
- Hybridity

Introduction

The meaning and significance of the term race has altered markedly during the modern era. The idea that the world's population could be divided into distinct groups developed during the early stages of European expansionism, when Europeans expanded their geographical influence and came into greater contact with people of other cultures. Chapter 3 has already described how the contacts between what Stuart Hall (1992a) calls 'the West and the Rest' were unequal and exploitative. Europeans enslaved others and colonised their lands. It was in this context that powerful notions developed about the superiority of the North European 'race' over all others (Sami – erroneously called Lapps – aside). The attitudes of the colonial era are summed up at the start of Rudyard Kipling's poem 'The White Man's Burden', written in 1899:

> Take up the White Man's burden –
> Send forth the best ye breed –
> Go bind your sons to exile
> To serve your captives' need;
> To wait in heavy harness
> On fluttered folk and wild –
> Your new-caught sullen peoples,
> Half devil and half child.

As this quote suggests, beliefs about the different capacities of distinct races offered an explanation of and justification for the sharp inequalities in colonial societies. The colonisers' racial characteristics were purported to equip them to rule over their 'child-like' subjects, and they believed it their duty to control and civilise the innate savagery of the 'half devil' natives.

In the nineteenth century, Western science played a key role in developing the concept of race. Peoples of the world – within and beyond Europe – were classified and ranked into superior and inferior races with allegedly inherent capacities and characteristics. Scientists often talked of these groups as separate species, at higher or lower points on the evolutionary scale (Box 7.1). There are clear parallels here with the way in which the science of this period justified the existence of gender and class inequalities by rooting them in innate biological differences (Gould, 1984). This classificatory process was part of the 'project of modernity' – an attempt to construct an understanding of differences on the basis of scientific inquiry. However, the resulting hierarchies of groups closely resembled the existing distributions of power, as this application of science turned out to be a justification for class, gender and ethnic inequalities rather than offering an explanation.

BOX 7.1 Race and science

Two examples, cited by geneticist Steve Jones in the 1991 Reith Lectures, illustrate how entrenched scientific racism was in the early modern era.

When Victorian John Langdon Down identified the chromosomal disorder in children we now know of as Down's Syndrome, he chose to call it Mongolism. Down believed that a superficial resemblance to people from central Asia (the Mongols) indicated that the children he studied were throwbacks to an earlier phase in human evolution. Thus, disability was equated with membership of a lower ranked race.

In 1906 the Bronx Zoo in New York opened a new exhibit – an African Pygmy called Ota Benga was placed in the same cage as a chimpanzee. The aim was to popularise theories of evolution by demonstrating that apes and humans were related. Ota Benga was eventually released, partly because of his habit of shooting arrows at the visitors to the zoo who mocked him, but killed himself a few years later (Jones, 1994).

Eugenics
A nineteenth- and early-twentieth-century pseudo-scientific movement concerned with the alleged 'genetic improvement' of the human species.

Although disputed, scientific ideas about racial difference continued to have a significant impact in the twentieth century. For example, in the 1920s, arguments by **eugenicists** led to the introduction of immigration restrictions in the US, designed to prevent members of the Nordic race being swamped by inferior genetic material from Eastern and Southern Europe. Most horrifically, in the 1940s, the idea of maintaining 'racial hygiene' had a direct influence on the Nazis' Final Solution, which set out systematically to destroy what were considered inferior races (see Chapter 2).

Using pseudo-science as a masquerade for anti-Semitism, the then German notion of *Volk* emphasised the blood as well as the cultural dimension of nationhood. Being a patriotic German Jew was not considered sufficient, because *Bildung* (cultural education) could never transform a blood Jew into a blood Aryan (see Burleigh, 2000).

QUESTION Why do you think that respected scientists espoused such racist practices as eugenics? Offer sociological explanations only.

In the aftermath of the Nazi Holocaust, many scientists were keen to debunk not only the idea of racial hierarchies but also racial classifications as they were conventionally understood (Kohn, 1995). In particular, advances in genetics undermined the notion of pure races and showed that variations within groups were as significant as the differences between them. More fundamentally, scientists challenged the links between biology and behaviour that had underpinned earlier beliefs. The impact of this sea-change in scientific opinion on everyday understandings has, however, varied. Beliefs do not have to be coherent to be powerful, and remnants of the old scientific account are still viewed as common sense by many – part of the unquestioned, often contradictory, assumptions by which people conduct their lives and understand the world. In particular, the belief that superficial variations in appearance between peoples are markers of more profound differences in abilities and outlook, and that these racial categories are natural and obvious, has proved remarkably resilient.

CONNECTIONS To explore the relationship between the Holocaust and modernity, see the section on Bauman's views in Chapter 2, pages 35–6.

Reify
To treat a social phenomenon as an independent thing, with its own qualities.

Introducing a collection of essays on race and racism, James Donald and Ali Rattansi (1992) highlight what they see as a paradox. While genetic or physical characteristics that might distinguish races are hard to define and appear trivial, socially constructed notions of racial difference continue to be highly influential. This chapter will examine this influence with reference to two broad topics:

- Race appears to have a major impact on life chances. There are numerous examples of inequalities of wealth, status and power along lines of race.

- Race remains a potent basis for identity – our sense of sameness and difference.

Ethnicity
While the term 'race' emphasises biological differences based on skin colour, ethnicity denotes the sense of belonging to a particular community whose members share common cultural traditions.

Donald and Rattansi's paradox presents sociologists with a problem: how can they explore the importance of the concept of race without **reifying** it? Some social scientists attempt to do this by dropping all talk of race in favour of **ethnicity**. Others indicate their unease with the term by placing inverted commas around it. Ethnic differences are deemed cultural rather than physical, based on shared traditions, experiences and ways of life. This approach has the merit of highlighting questions of identity, but some issues are left unresolved if race is ignored:

- In discussions of ethnicity, the emphasis is on the active choice of identity. In some circumstances, attribution by others is a more significant factor: for example, someone can be the victim of racism whatever his or her own sense of ethnicity.

- By focusing almost exclusively on cultural difference, some analysts of ethnicity have downplayed key issues of power and inequality. A crucial question is why some cultural differences come to be racialised (Miles, 1989) – that is, seen as markers of race divisions. This is important, since ethnic differences that are given a racial dimension usually have a clearer relationship to disadvantage.

- Accounts of ethnicity often utilise an understanding of cultures – adapted from anthropological studies of tribal societies – as stable, exclusive ways of life. As this chapter will argue, this is an inappropriate way to understand the complexities of identity and difference in contemporary life. Ironically, some sociologists wrongly ascribe similar qualities to ethnic groups that used to be applied to races, and in doing so, they perpetuate old discussions of fixed, obvious differences in a coded form.

Reflexive
Normally employed to describe a process of self-reflection that may modify beliefs and action (see *reflexivity*).

Rather than avoid all talk of race, in this chapter we shall utilise an alternative means of dealing with Donald and Rattansi's (1992) paradox, that is, we shall be **reflexive** in our use of the terms race and ethnicity. This means seeing racial inequalities and racial identities as essentially social rather than natural phenomena. It also involves asking questions about how social divisions come to be racialised – investigating how and why racial classifications are used to label, constitute and exclude social groups.

 ## Inequalities of race: The British example

Inequalities that have a racial or ethnic dimension can be found around the world. There are, however, great variations in the nature and significance of such inequalities. In

BOX 7.2 Problems with terminology

Everyday and academic racial classifications are full of ambiguities: at times, groups are defined by skin colour, country of origin, descent or even by religious affiliation. Labels can be contradictory—for example, the majority of those labelled as West Indians in the UK were actually born here. Another complication is that racial terms and classifications alter over time and are the subject of controversy and struggle. An example of this is the term black. Previously seen as pejorative, it was claimed as a source of pride by African American radicals in the 1960s who rejected the classification 'coloured', then in common usage. Today, some African Americans have reclaimed colour, as in the expression 'people of color'. In the UK, 'black' is at the centre of dispute, as Asian academics and political activists argue about its validity as a blanket term for all non-white groups (Modood, 1994).

Disputes about the meaning and usage of words can be confusing. It is important to ask, however, why they occur so frequently in discussions of race. That the language is uncertain, changing and, above all, political shows that, far from being natural and fixed, racial and ethnic divisions are socially constructed.

Without wishing to push conceptual crispness too far beyond personal sensitivities, one might be able to make some analytical progress by characterising race as the socially constructed perception of outward physical appearance (notably, skin colour) and ethnicity as all that and more (notably, common language, nationality and religion). Both of these social constructs can have real consequences, as, for example, when racial eugenics led to the slavery of Africans and the genocide of Jews, and when ethnic cleansing resulted in the forced expulsion of ethnic Albanians from Kosovo.

It is important to add that, in natural scientific terms, biology has little to say about race. Indeed, greater genetic variations exist within black and white populations than between them. That said, some small groups (for example, the Basques) do share similar gene frequencies.

Europe, racial divisions have emerged out of the colonial past and the recent history of inward labour migration. It would be simplistic to argue that these are in some way equivalent to the situation in South Africa, where, until the early 1990s, races were defined and segregated by law. Equally, patterns of racial and ethnic disadvantage have very different flavours in the melting-pot societies of the US and Australia. If these varied divisions are not the natural and inevitable product of something called race but instead are socially constructed, it follows that they can only be understood in their particular historical and political contexts. This argument will be developed through a discussion of race inequalities, paying particular attention to the situation in the UK.

Post-war migration: global and local contexts

Discussions of race in the UK have focused on the consequences of the mass immigration of people from the New Commonwealth (India, Pakistan and the West Indies) in the 1950s and 1960s. This migration was not a novel event. British history is full of inward and outward movements of people. Although it has been and continues to be a net exporter of people, the UK has experienced other sizeable influxes of migrants. During the 1800s, for example, large numbers of people from Ireland settled in the UK. Similarly, between 1870 and 1914, many Eastern European Jews crossed the Channel to escape religious persecution. Significantly, both these groups were initially treated as racially distinct from the British in a way that would appear incongruous today (Miles, 1989).

BOX 7.3 Global migration, 1945–73

New Commonwealth migration to the UK was part of a worldwide process. In the decades following the Second World War, around 30 million people entered Western Europe in one of the greatest migratory movements in history (Castles *et al.*, 1984). The economic boom this area enjoyed during the 1950s and 1960s was threatened by labour shortages in key sectors of the economy. Governments and businesses actively recruited foreign workers in an attempt to solve this problem. If this was the 'pull' for people to uproot themselves and move into Western Europe, then the 'push' was the underdevelopment that beset other parts of the world. In particular, newly decolonised countries suffered from overpopulation, economic crises and political instability. Thus the movement of people into Western Europe was an important aspect of the development of the global system, as outlined in Chapter 3: it was at once a story of nation-states, the world capitalist economy and the international division of labour.

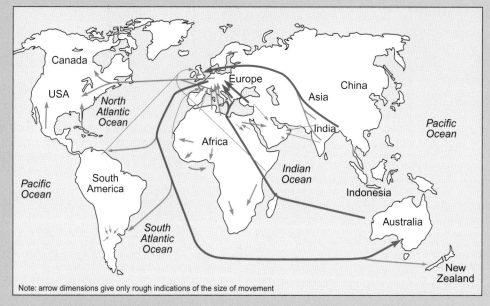

Note: arrow dimensions give only rough indications of the size of movement

Figure 7.1　Global migrations, 1945–73

CONNECTIONS For a fuller account of the impact of globalisation on the nation-state see Chapter 3, pages 60–5.

Mass migration may have been shaped by the economic and political inequalities of the world system, but there were important local factors specific to the UK. People of Caribbean, Indian and African origin had lived in the UK for hundreds of years (Fryer, 1984). One of the main reasons for this long and rich history was the UK's imperial past. Post-war migrants were drawn from former colonies, and citizenship of the Commonwealth gave migrants the right of permanent settlement. This was in marked contrast to European countries such as Germany and Switzerland, which operated a guest-worker system whereby migrants could be forced to return to their place of origin at the end of their employment contract.

People arriving from the West Indies, India and Pakistan in the 1950s and 1960s found the UK to be an inhospitable place in many ways. Open racial discrimination was lawful, and job or room advertisements would often state 'No Coloureds'. Although work was available, there was an acute housing shortage, and migrants ended up in areas and accommodation that whites did not wish to occupy. Whatever skills or ambitions migrants brought with them, most were slotted into the lower echelons of the labour market. This Afro-Caribbean woman's experience (quoted in Bryan *et al.*, 1985, pp. 22–3) is not untypical :

> " I remember getting up every morning to go to the Labour Exchange to see if there were any jobs. I was actually looking for nursing work but they wouldn't have me. Somebody told me that they would take me on as an auxiliary nurse and that later I could train. But when I got to the hospital, the woman there offered me a cleaning job. "

Migrant labour was seen as a way of filling the jobs that others did not want. In some cases, employers, white employees and their trade unions (see Miles and Phizacklea, 1992) channelled migrants into those jobs that were low paid, had poor conditions and involved shift work.

Almost from its inception, New Commonwealth immigration prompted rigorous public debate about its desirability. A range of analysts (see Saggar, 1992; Layton-Henry, 1992; Miles, 1993; Solomos, 1993) have described how race became an increasingly high-profile political issue during the 1950s and 1960s. Successive Immigration Acts, passed in 1962, 1968 and 1971 by both Conservative and Labour governments, restricted primary immigration from the New Commonwealth. Although the legislation did not mention race explicitly, examination of the intentions of its promoters and its subsequent impact leaves no doubt that it was designed to prevent black immigration. No equivalent concern was expressed about migration from Ireland or from the Old Commonwealth (Canada, Australia and New Zealand).

Hand-in-hand with the restriction of immigration, and in the face of mounting evidence of the disadvantages being faced by immigrants, came a series of Race Relations Acts (in 1962, 1966 and 1976) that attempted to outlaw discrimination on grounds of race. The thinking behind this dual strategy was summed up by Roy Hattersley, then a junior minister in the Labour government that introduced the first Act: 'Integration without control is impossible but control without integration is indefensible.' (cited in Miles and Phizacklea, 1984, p. 57). This reasoning has been challenged by some commentators: 'Hattersley's clever syllogism was really arguing that in order to eliminate racism within Britain, it is necessary to practise it at the point of entry into Britain' (Miles and Phizacklea, 1984, p. 57). Arguably, this remains a contradiction in government policy and highlights the difficult position that immigrants, their children and grandchildren have occupied within the British social formation. Whether or not more recent immigrants, such as asylum seekers and refugees from the Middle East, Somalia, Turkey, Vietnam and former Yugoslavia, will face the same kind of problems as black and Asian immigrants remains to be seen. But the early signs are not auspicious, with charges being levelled both in the press and in parliament that some of those desperate people who have left their countries in search of a better future are abusing the UK immigration system.

The last of the Acts referred to above, the 1976 Race Relations Act, was strengthened and extended (but not replaced) by the Race Relations (Amendment) Act 2000, which came into force on 2 April 2001. The new legislation makes it unlawful to discriminate against anyone on grounds of race, colour, nationality (including citizenship) or ethnic or national origin. The amended Act also imposes a positive duty on all major public bodies to promote equality of opportunity and good race relations. The aim of positive action is to ensure that people from ethnic minority groups can compete on equal terms with other applicants. The Race Relations Act does not, however, permit positive discrimination or affirmative action. Thus, for example, if an employer tried to change the balance of the workforce by favouring applicants from a particular ethnic group, this would be unlawful and treated as racial discrimination.

Patterns of inequality

With few exceptions, since the 1970s, only dependants of existing settlers from the New Commonwealth have been allowed to settle in the UK. However, the non-white population has continued to grow, primarily because of the higher than average birth rate of this population. Estimates of this population growth are presented in Table 7.1 By the turn of the twenty-first century, growth had stabilised at around 6 per cent. Today, the majority of black people in the UK were either born here or are residents of long standing.

Although a black presence in the UK is well established, it is striking how many continuities there are between the problems faced by minority groups today and those which confronted the migrants who arrived in the 1950s and 1960s. It can be assumed that the Race Relations Acts have done little to improve the position of the UK's ethnic minorities. It is hard to say whether the Race Relations (Amendment) Act 2000 will do better. According to Stuart Hall (2000, p. 14), the tale of racial tension is both banal and persistent:

> " From the early race riots of Nottingham and Notting Hill in 1958, through the 1970s campaigns against the 'sus' laws, the death of Blair Peach in 1979, the uproar following the death of Colin Roach in Stoke Newington police station in 1983, the Deptford Fire, the 1980s 'disorders' in Brixton and Broadwater Farm, to the murders of Stephen Lawrence in 1993 and Michael Menson in 1997, black and Asian people have been subjected to racialised attacks, had their grievances largely ignored by the police, and been subjected to racially-inflicted policing practices. "

Hall reports that each of these events was followed by campaigns, inquiries, recriminations from authorities and promises of reform, 'Yet, very little seems to have changed' (ibid., p. 14). Commenting on the report by Sir William Macpherson, which concluded the official inquiry into the death of the black teenager Stephen Lawrence, Hall concedes that the inquiry was a remarkable affair. (Stephen Lawrence was stabbed to death at a bus stop in south-east London in April 1993. Four white men were tried for his murder and acquitted, but the police investigation was subject to a barrage of criticism, focusing on the failure of the police to act swiftly and their refusal to accept that it had been a racial attack until well into the investigation.) The minute recording of evidence provided at the inquiry into the police investigation, contends Hall, 'has its own impact, since the slow motion unravelling in public of the justificatory narratives offered by the police constituted a drama of its own' (ibid., p. 15).

TABLE 7.1 Percentage of British population drawn from ethnic minorities

1951	0.4 per cent
1961	1 per cent
1971	2.3 per cent
1981	3.9 per cent
1991	5.5 per cent

Institutional racism
The unwitting reproduction of racism by institutions. Implicit, taken-for-granted racism.

One important issue that captured the public attention was **institutional racism**, which, was central to the report. Although some critics of the report are wary of its emphasis on 'unwitting' and 'unconscious' racism, Hall believes that the official use of the term institutional racism to characterise the conduct of the Metropolitan Police was an important advance, striking at the heart of a distinctively English racism that was and still is flourishing not against, but comfortably within, a supposedly traditionally liberal culture.

Progress has also been documented elsewhere. For example, the report on the Stephen Lawrence Inquiry and the Home Office action plan to implement its recommendations made it easier for the Commission for Racial Equality – according to the latter – to pursue its central policy work in 1999/2000 of mainstreaming racial equality throughout the public, private and voluntary sectors.

QUESTION To what extent do you agree that the forces of law and order (the police and judiciary) exhibit institutional racism in their dealings with ethnic minorities? Refer to Chapter 14 for assistance.

Noble policy aims aside (and this is not to belittle them), major studies conducted by an independent research organisation, Political and Economic Planning (later the Policy Studies Institute), in the 1960s, 1970s, 1980s and 1990s (Daniel, 1968; Smith, 1977; Brown, 1984; Policy Studies Institute 1997) revealed a continuing pattern of disadvantage. A striking illustration of this is that it was and remains possible to identify distinct black and Asian experiences of employment and unemployment. For example, a large survey conducted by the Policy Studies Institute (1997) in conjunction with survey specialists SPCR disclosed that:

- Bangladeshis and Pakistanis are the poorest people in the UK
- There is a marked under-representation of all minorities in the top 10 per cent of all jobs.
- Many black and Asian people have worse jobs than white people, despite having similar educational qualifications.
- Racial prejudice, discrimination and harassment affect all minority groups.
- Young black men and Bangladeshi and Pakistani men and women continue to be disproportionately without educational qualifications.
- Indians and Afro-Caribbeans are more at risk of being poor than white people and Chinese people.
- Fifty per cent of Afro-Caribbean families are headed by a lone parent, heightening the risk of poverty and social exclusion.

On a more upbeat note, the same study also noted some important areas of improvement for ethnic minority groups:

- In many respects, African Asians and Chinese people are doing as well as white people.
- African Asians and Chinese people are more likely than white people to earn more than £500 per week, and their unemployment rates are as low or lower than those of the general population
- Indian men are well represented in managerial and professional occupations, and, even though their average earnings have not caught up with white men's, the gap is narrowing.

From the 1950s to the 1970s, ethnic minority unemployment was 'hyper-cyclical' – that is, it expanded and contracted faster than that of the majority of the population. When mass unemployment took hold in the late 1970s, however, a different picture emerged, in that ethnic minorities were at greater risk of unemployment and, on average, remained unemployed for longer. This trend continued, and, figures from the national Labour Force Survey for the period 1989–91 showed that the black and Asian unemployment rates were approximately double those for whites (Jones, 1993). They also showed that qualifications did not afford minorities the same protection against joblessness that they afforded others.

At the end of the twentieth century, according to the International Labour Organisation (ILO), unemployment among white people had remained at the low point (6 per cent) it had reached in 1990. Yet over the same period, the ILO found that unemployment among black people increased by 2 percentage points, reaching 13 per cent (see Trades Union Congress, 1999). The TUC grimly concluded that 'Racism is rife in the jobs market and has got worse during the 1990s, despite growing employment opportunities' (ibid.)

Focusing on an ethnic group with an exceptionally high risk of unemployment – young Caribbean men – Richard Berhoud of the Institute for Social and Economic Research at the University of Essex (see Joseph Rowntree Foundation November, 1999) discovered that:

- Young Afro-Caribbean men were more than twice as likely to be out of work as young white men. They also earned less.

- Bangladeshi and Pakistani men were, on average, more likely to be unemployed than Afro-Caribbeans.

Berhoud also found that well educated African men faced severe disadvantages, with an African graduate being seven times more likely to be unemployed than a white graduate. His overall analysis disclosed three main groups:

- White people and Indians, with a fairly consistent but relatively low risk of being unemployed.

- Bangladeshis and Pakistanis, with a consistently high risk of being unemployed.

- Africans and Afro-Caribbeans, with a high average risk of being unemployed. However, there were strong variations within the group depending on individual characteristics.

CONNECTIONS   For further information on the disadvantages experienced in work by ethnic minorities, see Chapter 11, pages 313–15.

BOX 7.4   Dimensions of racial disadvantage

The labour market is only one of many spheres of social life where there is evidence of racial disadvantage, as the following findings indicate.

Amin and Oppenheim (1992) have highlighted the high levels of poverty among minorities.

Being poor often means spending all one has on essentials with no chance to save. In that context, more recent data make for grim reading. In 1998–99, 54 per cent of black households and 59 per cent of Bangladeshi and Pakistani households in the UK

had no savings. By contrast, white and Indian households were much more likely to have savings, and indeed had very similar savings patterns (Office for National Statistics, 2001a).

Although there have been improvements since the 1960s, ▶

▶ by the early 1990s, ethnic minority people were still, on average, living in lower-quality, lower-value housing. They were also more likely to suffer from overcrowding and lack of basic amenities (Office for National Statistics, 1993).

A contributory factor to inferior housing has been poor treatment by local state agencies. This is evident in other areas, such as social services, where research has found that black people 'are under-represented as clients receiving the preventative and supportive elements of social services provision, but over-represented in those aspects of social services activity which involve social control functions and/or institutionalisation' (Skellington with Morris, 1992, p. 87).

Black people are more likely to be compulsorily admitted to psychiatric hospitals, and, once there, they are more likely to receive treatments such as drugs and ECT. Disparities are most striking in the diagnosis and treatment of schizophrenia, perhaps the most stigmatising of all mental illnesses (Littlewood and Lipsedge, 1982). Another ethnic minority, the Irish, seem to do less well in the health stakes, with data suggesting that Irish people have higher rates of illness and mortality (Acheson, 1998).

In 1989 the Prison Reform Trust reported that if all groups had been imprisoned at the same rate as black people, the prison population would have been 300 000 instead of 50 000. A range of studies have pointed to the unequal treatment of black people by the police and courts (see Hood, 1992; Skellington with Morris, 1992). (This issue will be explored in more detail in Chapter 14.)

Although the relationship between ethnicity and educational achievement is complex (and is more fully examined in Chapter 10), Ofsted (1999) has identified underachievement among Romany and traveller pupils, Bangladeshi and Pakistani primary school pupils, and Afro-Caribbean pupils in secondary schools.

Signs of change?

While the story from the 1960s to the early 1980s was one of continuity in the patterns of disadvantage experienced by many minority groups, recent studies suggest that significant changes are under way. A Policy Studies Institute report examining the situation at the start of the 1990s (Jones, 1993) points to some shifts in the patterns of employment.

A key change from the 1980s was that ethnic minority men had started to enter professional and managerial jobs in larger numbers than before. Some groups, notably African Asians and Indians, had come to enjoy labour market positions that were different from but comparable to those of the majority of the population, while others, notably Pakistanis and Bangladeshis, continued to occupy much weaker positions. More recent findings by the Policy Studies Institute (1997) also reveal a nuanced picture of ethnic minorities' chances in the labour market.

Care must be taken when interpreting such developments, however. Rather than illustrating a straightforward march towards greater equality for all ethnic minority people, they sometimes indicate greater inequalities within and between minority groups . This must be understood in the context of the wider changes in the UK labour market that have taken place in recent years (discussed in more detail in Chapter 11). Like the rest of the population, ethnic minority workers have been caught up in the major economic restructuring taking place at the national and international levels. As with so many other aspects of this process, the outcome is greater polarisation. On the one hand, growth in the number of professional and managerial positions, combined with labour shortages in some occupations and regions, have created opportunities for highly qualified members of the minority groups. On the other hand, unemployment, the decline of manufacturing, the flight of jobs from inner cities (where ethnic minorities are mostly concentrated) and the restructuring of the public sector have worsened the prospects of those at the lower end of the socioeconomic scale. One major reason for the increased percentage of ethnic minority workers higher up the scale is that some of those who would previously have been counted as manual workers are now jobless and hence missing from the statistics.

Some commentators on the right (Honeyford, 1993) claim that labour market data indicate that racism is no longer having a serious impact on the life chances of ethnic minorities. As we have seen, however, disadvantages persist. It should also be noted that apparently positive patterns of employment have been influenced by actual or potential discrimination. For example, ethnic minority people categorised as 'professional and managerial' have entered self-employment in far larger numbers than they have joined the middle management of medium or large firms (Ram, 1992). Similarly, the professions may be attractive to members of minority groups because they hope that educational credentials will provide some protection against racism in recruitment.

BOX 7.5 | The limits of 'racial dualism'

The UK's ethnic minority population consists of many different regional and ethnic groups. These groups each have their own histories of migration and have brought with them distinct cultural traditions, expectations and skills (Hiro, 1991).

According to Tariq Modood (1992b), many analysts are guilty of 'racial dualism', seeing racism as the only factor shaping the life chances and expectations of non-white Britons and largely ignoring the significance of ethnic differences. Modood challenges these assumptions by examining the experiences and aspirations of various Asian groups. He identifies a major divide between, on the one hand, the many Hindus and Sikhs from India who are gaining entry to the professions, building successful businesses and achieving educational success, and, on the other hand, the Sunni Muslims from Pakistan and Bangladesh, who are suffering acute disadvantage. While Modood's account of Indian success is arguably simplistic, he raises important questions about the feasibility of discussing a single 'black' experience in the UK, and, about the links between discrimination and disadvantage.

Explaining inequalities: practices and structures of exclusion

How can the persistence of the disadvantages discussed above be explained?

Early discussions of race in postwar UK sociology focused on the social processes and consequences of immigration. The assumptions that informed this work were absorbed into the **immigrant–host model** (Richardson and Lambert, 1985). Immigrants were viewed as strangers whose different cultural traditions were an impediment to acceptance by the majority and to their own economic success. The racism of the hosts (that is, the indigenous population) was viewed as a product of ignorance and confusion in response to strangers. It was assumed that the normal consensus and stability of British society, which had been temporarily disrupted by the migrants' arrival, would be restored through their assimilation into mainstream culture. From the late 1970s onwards, however, these assumptions, and the sociology of race relations and ethnic difference they spawned, became increasingly beleaguered (Solomos and Back, 1994). In light of the experiences of immigrants' children, the predictions of gradual assimilation and decline in disadvantage rang hollow. Some radical critics (for example, CCCS, 1982) went as far as to argue that the immigrant–host

Immigrant–host model

An approach to racial inequality that saw assimilation as the solution to racial disadvantage, based on the view that the problems experienced by immigrants arose from their situation as new arrivals.

approach reflected and reinforced racist assumptions by defining immigrants and their cultures as social problems and largely ignoring the part played by structural inequality in shaping their experience. Today, some commentators believe that one way of tackling racism is to adopt a 'fruit salad' rather than a 'fruit compote' model of race relations, celebrating diversity instead of worrying about assimilation and cohesion (see Hylland Eriksen, 1997).

Critics of the race relations problematic have shifted the focus of sociological analysis to the ways in which social practices and structures generate and reproduce racial disadvantage, and, in particular, to the problem of racism and its role in generating inequality.

The impact of racism

Despite the legislation outlawing discrimination on grounds of race, racism continues to blight the lives of the UK's minorities. Most blatantly, this takes the form of violence and harassment from some members of the white majority – a Europe-wide phenomenon with a long and inglorious history (Holmes, 1991; Bjorgo and Witte, 1993).

The extent of the problem is not always easy to measure, but since 1999, racial violence in London and elsewhere has markedly increased. According to the Institute of Race Relations (IRR, 2001a), between 1994 and 1998, reported racist incidents in the Metropolitan Police area were around 5000 a year. But in 1998–99, the number of reported incidents rose to 11 050, an increase of 89 per cent. In 1999–2000, that figure more than doubled to 23 346, a rise of 111 per cent. Even allowing for the possibility that people are now more willing to report attacks than they were in the past, and for the undoubtedly greater willingness of the police to record these attacks, the IRR maintains that there has still been an increase in very serious attacks – often resulting in permanent disability or death. The IRR recorded 28 known or suspected racially motivated murders in England and Wales between January 1991 and December 1998, and 21 between January 1999 and August 2001 (IRR, 2001c).

The emergence (or re-emergence) of what has been termed xeno-racism (derived from xenophobia – hatred or fear of strangers) is another recent problem. This type of racism is meted out to asylum seekers and so-called economic migrants, many of whom have been displaced as a result of the collapse of the Soviet bloc. Those seeking a better life in richer countries such as the UK often encounter what the human rights organisation Migration Rights International describes as a reception where 'the dominant considerations regarding displacement of people have deteriorated from assistance and hospitality to rejection and hostility' (cited in IRR, 2001b).

Writing in the *Guardian* (22 June 2001), Herman Ouseley (former chair of the Commission for Racial Equality) highlighted 'the negative obsession with immigration and asylum seekers' and 'the fear of being over run by outsiders' – hence the dehumanising description of immigrants and refugees as a 'tide', a 'sea', an 'army', an 'influx', a 'swarm' and other derogatory terms. There are sinister echoes here of the Nazi depiction of Jews as 'vermin'. And, of course, the labels have consequences: marginalisation, victimisation and, in the Jew's case, extermination.

CONNECTIONS Chapter 14, pages 380–409, provides further material on ethnicity and violence.

Violence and ill-feeling may be the most blatant manifestations of racism in the UK, but other, less open practices also harm ethnic minority people. As mentioned earlier, the publication of the report on the Stephen Lawrence Inquiry on 24 February 1999 was a watershed for the highlighting of institutional racism. The report accepted the

Figure 7.2 'Muslims are terrorists': a spate of attacks on Muslims and presumed Muslims followed the terrorist attack on the World Trade Centre on 11 September 2001 despite Western leaders' concern not to blame Islam.

Commission for Racial Equality's submission that institutional racism was an issue not just for the police service, but also for all public and private institutions. In that wider context, a report published in 2001 by the King's Fund (an independent health think tank) has documented overt and covert forms of racism in the NHS, ranging from the daily harassment of black and Asian doctors to commonplace prejudices about their abilities and lifestyles.

The problem of institutional racism is difficult to tackle in organisations that ignore the evidence of tacit discrimination within their own structures. This raises a methodological problem for researchers attempting to explain racial inequalities: how does one measure the extent and impact of attitudes and practices that are rarely made explicit in public arenas?

BOX 7.6 Evidence of discrimination

The persistence of disadvantage in the labour market suggests that racial discrimination is continuing to limit employment opportunities. But how can we detect and measure this, since it is hard to prove in its subtler forms? A now dated but groundbreaking study (Smith, 1977) used interesting methods. As part of the research, actors furnished with similar bogus job histories applied for a series of manual jobs. White British applicants were significantly more likely to be interviewed and offered a job than ethnic minority applicants. Similarly, when letters of application were sent for a range of white-collar posts, those bearing a West Indian or Asian name were 30 per cent less likely to result in an invitation for interview than comparable applications bearing a British-sounding name. Interestingly, there was no comparable discrimination against the 'Greek' applicants, suggesting that discrimination was against racial difference rather than simply foreignness. Repeats of these exercises in the mid-1980s▶

generated the same kinds of result (Brown and Gay, 1983).

A later study using a similar approach found that racial discrimination was prevalent in the medical profession (Esmail and Everington, 1993). The researchers composed curriculum vitae for six fictional doctors of similar age and experience, three with Asian names and three with British. These were sent, in pairs, with completed applications for appropriate NHS hospital posts. The initial results suggested that the fictional British candidates were twice as likely to be short-listed for interview as the Asians, but Esmail and Everington's research was stopped before completion, and they were threatened with prosecution for making fraudulent applications. As doctors themselves, they were also sanctioned by the General Medical Council – clearly they had touched a raw nerve! It would be surprising if the problem of discrimination was confined to medicine – a sphere with a relatively large number of ethnic minority workers. Indeed, findings emerged from a study looking at speculative employment enquiries made to one hundred of the largest companies in the UK (Noon, 1993): 48 per cent of these companies responded more positively to letters from fictional MBA students signed 'Evans' than those signed 'Patel'.

These studies reveal something of the influence of everyday discrimination in employment. However, they only consider one phase of the recruitment process. They tell us nothing about what takes place during interviews or once people enter employment. They also reveal little about whether ethnic minority people limit their job applications in the expectation of rejection.

In addition to problems with methodology, analysts face a related dilemma – how to define and operationalise the concept of racism. In everyday discussions, it is common for people to see racist beliefs as the irrational prejudices of a few abnormal individuals, and racist practices narrowly as acts of open and intentional discrimination. Social scientists challenge both these assumptions on a number of grounds:

- Racist beliefs are shared cultural phenomena, not simply aberrations of deviant individuals – this theme is developed later in the chapter.
- By seeing racism as irrational, we may miss the ways in which it can be a rational or useful way of justifying and preserving inequalities in access to employment, housing and other areas of social life (Cashmore, 1987).
- As Braham *et al.* (1992) point out, in addition to direct discrimination, knowingly and deliberately applied, it is important to consider discrimination which is covert, indirect and unintentional. This broader approach to racism is highly significant, since attention is moved from motives to outcomes. Supporters of this shift would argue that it is possible to participate in racist practices without necessarily holding racist beliefs. Those employed to enforce UK immigration law, for example, could be said to be implementing racist rules whatever their personal beliefs.
- Policies or practices not directly constructed in relation to race may nonetheless have the effect of disadvantaging minorities. Elite schools whose entry requirements include evidence of regular church attendance, for example, automatically exclude the children of non-Christian minority groups.

In different ways, these points all beg one question: can social organisations and structures be dubbed racist in the way that individuals are? Some political activists and sociologists believe so, using the term institutional racism – originally applied to the US context – to refer to processes that generate or reproduce racial inequalities (Carmichael and Hamilton, 1968; Sivanandan, 1982). The concept of institutional racism has the great merit of highlighting the systemic processes that reproduce disadvantage, suggesting that racism can be rooted in society's organisational structures. The concept of institutional racism has, however, been the subject of controversy. For example, Robert Miles (1989) argues that it stretches the use of the word racism to breaking point, and he maintains that the term should only be applied to forms of belief. There is a danger here of getting bogged down in an abstract debate about the meaning of words. A more significant pitfall of the concept is a potential lack of rigour. Although it may be of polemical value as a call for fundamental change, a blanket description of institutions or even societies as racist may actually stand in the way of effective study and reform of the mechanisms of inequality. As the debate about definitions suggests, racism is a multi-faceted phenomenon with many causes and manifestations (Cohen, 1992). Analytically, therefore, distinctions between state, institutional and individual racism and between beliefs and behaviour are crucial.

QUESTION Have you ever experienced any discrimination yourself for whatever reason? Describe the experience, stating whether it was it state, institutional or individual.

BOX 7.7 Dimensions of racism: the example of housing

Any satisfactory analysis of the relationship between racism and disadvantage must consider a number of different levels. In a review of the factors that generate racial inequality in housing, Norman Ginsberg (1992) attempts to do this by identifies three distinct phenomena:

- Subjective (or individual) racism: This is manifest in overt prejudice and discrimination by individual house-sellers, landlords, estate agents and council officials against ethnic minorities. A related subjective issue is the way in which the fear or reality of harassment limits the housing choices of ethnic minorities.

- Institutional racism: Ginsberg cites a number of studies that suggest that, in both the private and the public sector, a range of institutional practices (some now reformed) have, intentionally or otherwise, disadvantaged minorities. An often-quoted example from the public sector is the operation of rules for housing allocation utilising criteria such as length of residency or family connections with the area. This is by no means the only practice that reproduces inequality. Studies show how council officials, under pressure to fill housing quickly, have offered poor accommodation to ethnic minority people in the expectation they will take it. Also significant is the way in which officers avoid conflict with white residents by not allocating certain accommodation to ethnic minorities. In the private sector, building societies, by refusing loans on properties in particular areas or below a particular value, have indirectly discriminated against ethnic minorities.

- Structural (or state) racism: Ginsberg argues that it is wrong to focus on local factors to the exclusion of wider structural influences, particularly the role of the state. For example, the government policy of selling off council housing stock heightened racial disadvantage because the better properties were creamed off by existing white tenants while black people were over-represented among the growing numbers of homeless on council waiting lists.

Thus, to explain or tackle disadvantage, in housing or any other area, we must be clear about the impact of quite different processes. However, Ginsberg argues that while it is important to distinguish between these factors (which may vary in importance from context to context), they usually operate together.

Many of the problems faced by analysts of racism and disadvantage have their roots in the ambiguity and power of the concept of race highlighted at the start of the chapter. The significance of racial inequalities is great, but these are social, not natural, phenomena. This means that the structured inequalities of race are capable of social intervention. However, this intervention must not exaggerate the obviousness or coherence of racial divisions. As Donald and Rattansi (1992) write: ' "Race" can produce simplified interpretations of complex social, economic and cultural relations for antiracists as well as racists.'

 ## Race, culture and identity

The introduction to this chapter argued that the significance of race in the contemporary world can be organised under two broad headings – inequalities and identities. So far, we have considered inequalities. We now move on to questions of cultural identity – how people understand and define themselves and others. Of course, inequality and identity are intimately related: cultural exchanges take place in an unequal setting. Beliefs about race are themselves powerful manifestations of or even ways of maintaining social divisions. This is illustrated by the Kipling poem quoted at the start of the chapter. Kipling's account of racial similarities and differences reflected and justified the inequalities and exploitation that characterised colonialism.

CONNECTIONS The issue of identity is an important component of postmodernist readings of society. See Chapter 19, pages 512–35, for an account of postmodernism.

To write in terms of identity is not to imply that understandings of race are simply a matter of personal choice or prejudice. Identities are shaped by wider societal influences. This is why many contemporary sociologists understand notions of race in terms of either ideology (Miles, 1989) or discourse (Goldberg, 1993). Discourses are ways of knowing and talking about the world that promote thought, action and representation, constitute identities and structure social relationships. Thinking in this way directs inquiry towards the ways in which systems of meaning are produced, how they work and in whose interest. All these issues are pertinent to the study of race.

The changing character of racialised discourse

Although race may have been an influential concept for hundreds of years, the form and object of racialised discourse has altered over time and varied from context to context. Discussions of racial differences today are very different from those which took place in colonial societies. Similarly, a century ago, groups such as the Irish and Southern Europeans were discussed in the UK as distinct races, which would be considered strange today.

Although the term race has a long history, the term racism only entered common usage after the Second World War as a way of describing the horrors of the Holocaust. Because of the pseudo-scientific justifications used by the Nazis, analysts such as Ruth Benedict (1983, first published in 1942) defined racism as bad science: unfounded beliefs about the superiority of one race over another based on inherited biological characteristics. Not only is knowledge tainted in bad science, so too are the methods used to produce such knowledge. For example, by packing gun shot pellets more firmly into the skulls of the remains of white people than into those of black people when measuring cranium capacity, pseudo-scientists arrived at the erroneous conclusion that white people had larger brains than black people. Even if this were true (it is not: the largest human brains in the world are those of the black Masai tribe of Kenya), objective scientific research shows that human brain size does not correlate with intelligence.

In the twenty-first century, this definition is largely irrelevant. Arguments that explicitly present races as biological categories or claim the superiority of one group over another are comparatively rare, confined to the political and intellectual margins.

The decline of old-style scientific racism has provoked a variety of responses in sociology. Michael Banton (1988), one of the key UK figures in the sociology of race relations, argues that the only legitimate application of the term racism is to describe biologically grounded claims of racial superiority. Exasperated by the changing and variable use of the term, Banton dropped it in his later work, preferring to write only of the use of 'racial typologies'.

In contrast to Banton, Martin Barker (1981) argues that racism has not disappeared but has taken different forms. He describes the emergence of a **new racism** that:

- Claims that the significance of racism in contemporary societies is exaggerated.
- Defines groups not as biological types but as cultural communities.
- Denies that hostility towards other groups is necessarily racist, talking instead of the incompatibility of cultures and arguing it is 'natural' for people to wish to be with their 'own'.
- Bases its arguments on notions of difference rather than superiority.

Barker's definition has some limitations. There is a danger of exaggerating the coherence of racist ideas: popular beliefs about race are neither coherent nor consistent but a ragbag of 'facts' and allusions. Remnants of older racisms relating to biology or colonial history are still evident, even if it is not always considered appropriate to voice them publicly. Nevertheless, Barker has highlighted two of the key characteristics of contemporary discussions of race: that the definition and extent of racism is contested; and that statements about race are often disguised as claims of cultural difference. The implication of his work is that, rather than operate with a definition of racism based on a fixed content or object, we should talk of racisms, manifested in plural forms.

More recently, Ian Law (2002) revealed that about a quarter of the broadsheet articles he studied conveyed a negative message about ethnic minorities in the UK. Half of these articles covered social problems connected with ethnic minorities. However, the

New racism
Racism based on ideas of cultural difference rather than on claims to biological superiority.

BOX 7.8 Making the headlines: racism and the press

One area of social life where there is a vigorous debate about the extent of racism is news coverage. A study by van Dijk (1991) supports those who claim that the UK press, in common with newspapers in other countries, portrays minorities in a negative and stereotypical fashion. His study involved a systematic analysis of the headlines of race-based stories in five papers – *The Times*, *Guardian*, *Daily Telegraph*, *Daily Mail* and *Sun* - over a six-month period in the mid 1980s, during which time there were a number of highly publicised episodes of urban unrest involving both white and black youths. Measuring headline content in this way brought the hostility of much of this press coverage into stark relief – incidents of inner-city unrest were defined as race riots, and, more generally, there was a strong association between race and violence, conflict, crime and social problems. Van Dijk points out that even the non-violent actions of ethnic minority people often attracted the use of aggressive metaphors by the press.

bulk of radio and television coverage – more than 80 per cent – was generally conveyed positive messages about ethnic minorities. Table 7.2 provides an overview of pro- and anti-immigrant messages in various media.

CONNECTIONS For an overview of the way in which media messages are influenced by social circumstances, including social difference and division, see Chapter 12, particularly pages 336–52.

TABLE 7.2 Pro-immigrant and anti-immigrant messages by type of medium (per cent)

Message	Tabloid	Broadsheet	Radio	Television
Immigration				
Pro-immigrant	2.8	7.4	22.4	14.9
Anti-immigrant	11.6	4.3	5.2	4.7
General election				
Pro-minorities	10.0	15.7	9.9	20.9
Anti-minorities	3.4	2.8	0.5	2.7
Racism				
Exposing	44.7	34.2	39.1	35.1
Denying	1.6	2.4	2.6	1.4
Social value				
Assets	3.8	6.5	2.1	0.7
Problems	14.1	12.3	7.8	4.1
Multiculturism				
For	1.9	3.9	2.1	1.4
Against	1.3	1.3	0.0	0.0
Opportunities				
Improve	3.1	5.7	5.2	10.8
Restrict	1.3	0.5	0.0	0.0
Other	0.6	3.2	3.2	3.4
Total	100.0	100.0	100.0	100.0
Total hostile anti-immigrant	33.3	23.6	16.1	12.9

Source: Law (2002).

Race and national identity

For supporters of the concept, a prime example of the new racism is the way in which the politics of race in the UK has come to be dominated by the debate about national identity and national belonging.

Nation-states are not only the primary administrative products of modernity, they are also 'imagined communities' (Anderson, 1983). The rhetoric on patriotism and national identity is one of the most emotive cultural manifestations of modernity. These concepts are very powerful, but they are also nebulous and contested. For example, while there is much talk of 'Britishness' or the 'English way of life', just what these are is open to question. How do they fit in with the claims of cultural distinctiveness for Scotland, Wales or the various English regions? Do all Britons share a single way of life despite differences of class or gender? Is Britishness a fixed quality or one that changes over time? Such ambiguities have not prevented the concept of national identity playing an important role in contemporary discussions of race.

One of the most effective strategies followed by those hostile to a black presence in the UK has been to argue that blackness and Britishness are mutually exclusive. Growing ethnic diversity is portrayed as a threat to the order and cohesiveness of the British way of life. Analysis of political debates about race reveals that this argument has taken a variety of forms (Solomos, 1993):

- In the 1960s and 1970s, black immigration was portrayed as a threat to national identity. For example, in 1978, prior to her election as prime minister, Margaret Thatcher talked of the British people's fear of being swamped by alien cultures. In stark contrast, a few years later, she described the Falkland Islanders, living 8000 miles away, as belonging to the nation: 'Their way of life is British; their allegiance is to the Crown' (quoted in Miles, 1993, p. 75).

- In the 1970s and 1980s, the emphasis shifted to the threat that ethnic minorities were deemed to pose to the order of British society. A striking example of this was the way in which black youths were constructed as a social control problem requiring special policing.

- In the 1990s, the argument that ethnic minorities were not part of the British nation was likely to focus less on black criminality than on the problems of the **multi-cultural society**. Calls for separate Muslim schools, campaigns to ban Salman Rushdie's novel *The Satanic Verses* (1988) and even attempts to develop anti-racist policies were portrayed as un-British and evidence of the incompatibility of cultures and the unwillingness or inability of immigrants to become British.

Multi-culturalism
An approach that acknowledges and accommodates a variety of cultural practices and traditions.

Diaspora
Originally used to describe the dispersion of the Jews from Palestine, it now more generally refers to any dispersed ethnic group, with a common culture or heritage.

Although notions of majority nationhood can be used to exclude minority groups, some minority groups invoke a sense of their own nationhood in order to make their history more visible. For example, Sami people in Norway (Box 7.9) have developed a sense of nationhood by establishing themselves as a political force at the national and international levels (Brantenberg, 1999). Their struggle for political mobilisation has important parallels with other indigenous peoples across the Arctic as well as in countries such as Australia, New Zealand and the US. Nor should we under-estimate the cultural and political significance of nationhood for **diaspora** Jews and Palestinians.

BOX 7.9 Building a sense of nationhood: the Sami people of Norway

In recent decades, ever more groups 'without history' have demanded to be taken seriously by historians and social scientists (Minde, 1992, p. 1).

In 1992, under the rallying call '500 years of resistance', the indigenous peoples of the world put their case to the international court of opinion. One year later, by United Nations decree, 1993 was declared the Year of the Indigenous Peoples.

A tiny but important thread in the story of indigenous identity building can be found at the University Museum in Tromsø, where an important cultural project was launched in 1998. The museum is located in a region of Northern Norway that is part of the homeland of the indigenous Sami people. This homeland extends across national borders into Sweden, Finland and Northern Russia. The Sami have

lived in Fenno-Scandinavia since before recorded time, existing as a sub-arctic hunting and fishing people until the seventeenth century, when they came into conflict with national expansion and agrarian and trading interests.

The history and culture of the Sami are still relatively unknown among the Norwegian public. To address this, anthropologists and curators at the Department ▶

of Sami Ethnography at Tromsø Museum have produced an exhibit that charts the story of how the Sami have developed from a scattered and politically unorganised people into a politically active nation. This epic narrative is presented in three rooms: the Norwegian Room, the Sami Room and the Indigenous Room. Each room presents different phases of the building of the Sami nation. The Norwegian Room addresses the construction of the welfare state and the quest for equity (1945–1960), the Sami Room the struggle for equal worth (1960–1980) and the Indigenous Room the making of a nation (1980–2000).

The idea of *making* is important in all aspects of race relations because it implies that things can be different and better.

Cultural change and ethnic absolutism

The vision of an ethnically pure nation sharing a common way of life has always been a myth, albeit a potent one. The great migrations of the post-war period have, however, openly challenged notions of unified, shared national cultures not only in the UK but also across the Western world (Hall, 1992b). There has been a growing multiplicity of religions, languages and ways of life within and across national borders. This is a striking illustration of the trends outlined in Chapter 3: globalising pressures are accompanied by the reawakening or reinvention of local identities.

The way of expressing the growing cultural diversity of Western societies is to talk the language of multi-culturalism – neatly dividing up societies into homogeneous traditions or communities. However, this approach has serious limitations, not least because it shares many of the assumptions of new racism about fixed, immutable differences between ethnicities. 'Culture is conceived along ethnically absolute lines, not as something intrinsically fluid, changing and unstable, and dynamic, but as a fixed property of social groups rather than a relational field in which they encounter one another and live out social, historical relationships' (Gilroy, 1993b, p. 24).

The realities of contemporary life are more interesting than proponents of **ethnic absolutism** contend. What is striking are the variety of subjectivities and the complex patterns of cultural change that emerge as ethnic groups are dispersed throughout the world.

Ethnic absolutism An understanding of ethnic divisions as fixed and absolute, resting on unchanging cultural traditions.

BOX 7.10 A dilemma of identity? Mixed descent

A visible challenge to ethnic absolutism is presented by the growing number of relationships taking place between members of different ethnic groups. In the US, there are an estimated one million children and adolescents of mixed descent. In the UK, this is the fastest growing of all population categories. The prevalence of mixed relationships calls into question the vision of societies divided into hermetically sealed communities. In addition, the experiences of people of mixed descent challenge the exclusivity of unilateral ethnic identities, adding hyphenated notions such as Black-British, Irish-American and Pakistani-Norwegian

Until recently, it was commonly considered that being of mixed descent presented children with problems of social integration and identity construction. For example, this belief has become orthodox among certain social workers involved in adoption and fostering, many of whom argue that the only way to deal with these difficulties is to place mixed race children with black parents. Barbara Tizard and Ann Phoenix (1993) challenge these assumptions. When interviewing a UK sample of mixed race teenagers, they found that the majority had a positive self-image. The young people implemented a variety of successful strategies of identity construction and did not necessarily have to feel black to feel good about themselves.

Figure 7.3 Born in the Moroccan suburbs of Brussels and brought up in the English town of Northampton, Natacha Atlas sings in French, Spanish, Arabic and English, fusing Arabic musical traditions with Western pop sounds.

The term diaspora was originally used to describe the dispersion of Jews from Palestine after the Babylonian and Roman conquests, but more recently, it has been applied to any dispersed group, such as people from India or Africa, with shared elements of experience and culture. It would be a mistake, however, to see the diaspora as the transporting of unchanged ways of life from location to location. In the UK, for example, studies of migrants and their children have charted the emergence of minority cultures that are distinct both from those of their homeland and from those of the majority population (Watson, 1977).

An important consequence of dispersion is that it has generated novel expressions of culture. A striking example of this is what Paul Gilroy (1993a) calls 'The Black Atlantic' – a cultural network spanning Africa, the Americas, the Caribbean and the UK that has provided a source of strength and continuity to people of African descent, wherever they are in the world. This is not, however, simply about the maintenance of cultural traditions. According to Gilroy, 'the transnational structures which brought the black Atlantic world into being have themselves developed and now articulate its myriad forms into a system of global communications constituted by flows' (ibid., p. 80). As Bennett (2000) puts it, black culture has thus become a global culture, initiating a plurality of responses as it crosses with local cultures. This process is most pronounced in inner-city areas with mixed populations, where black styles, music and language have had a profound influence. Roger Hewitt's (1986) study *White Talk, Black Talk*, for example, highlights the impact of Jamaican creole on the speech of young white Londoners. Similarly, Simon Jones (1988) describes how, in parts of Birmingham, the sensibilities of white, Afro-Caribbean and Asian youths have fused around their shared interest in reggae music, and Robins (1997) points to the progressive hybridisation of different ethnic groups' musical and artistic styles, such that 'Salma and Sabine are Pakistani sisters who sing Abba songs in Hindi'.

Examples of cultural change and hybridity are important because they illustrate that identities are actively constituted and negotiated. This is not to say, however, that ethnicity is declining in significance – far from it. As we argued in Chapter 3, a common response to the globalising character of late modernity has been the revival (or perhaps redefinition would be a better word) of local identities and ethnic differences.

In the UK context, 'ethnic revival' can in part be understood as a defensive response on the part of immigrants to discrimination and disadvantage. The history of Afro-Caribbean migrants is a case in point. Many people arriving from the Caribbean in the 1950s and 1960s saw the UK as the mother country and fully expected to participate in mainstream British life. The dashing of these hopes heightened their perception of cultural distinctiveness. In the face of hostility from the established churches, for example, many Afro-Caribbeans established their own congregations and took solace in

BOX 7.11 The limits of hybridity

The appeal of black forms of expression to young whites and the emergence of hybrid (that is to say, multi-dimensional) cultures have encouraged optimism about the decline of racism. However, care must be taken when interpreting these developments. An ethnographic study by Les Back (1993) of a racially mixed London council estate shows that it is possible for hybridity and racial violence to exist side-by-side. Back found that, in contrast to their parents, the young white and black people he studied lived in a colour-blind world of inter-racial friendships, bound together by a strong sense of shared neighbourhood. This was, however, only one of a number of factors that influ- enced the white youngsters' out- look on racial difference: family and the media had also played a formative part. Equally, while black and white youths lived in harmony, Vietnamese residents of the estate were perceived as outsiders and were frequently harassed and attacked.

Pentecostalism (Pryce, 1979; Hiro, 1991). In the 1970s, many of the younger-generation Afro-Caribbean victims of racism with limited opportunities were drawn to Rastafarianism – a religion with a black messiah (Ethiopian Emperor Haile Selassie) that prophesied the fall of Babylon (the West) and a return to Africa (Cashmore, 1983).

CHART 7.1 Religion still matters: of a nationally representative sample of people, the following percentages said religion was very important 'to their way of life'.

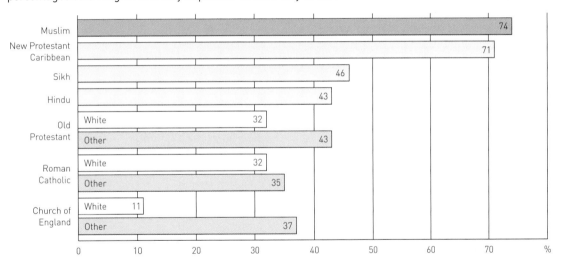

Muslim		74
New Protestant Caribbean		71
Sikh	46	
Hindu	43	
Old Protestant	White — 32	
	Other — 43	
Roman Catholic	White — 32	
	Other — 35	
Church of England	White — 11	
	Other — 37	

Source: PSI/SCPR Survey, 1994

Paradoxically therefore, ethnic revival is a symptom of the greater awareness of difference that springs from increased contact between ways of life and the growing pace of cultural change. These processes inevitably promote greater reflection (or reflexivity) on identity (Giddens, 1991), which is also seen as a hallmark of late modernity. Hybridity is one response to these developments, but just as significant is the way in which people attempt to deal with the problem of identity by proclaiming absolute, fixed ethnicities. The aggressive assertion of 'white Englishness' is an example of this phenomenon – a claim of ethnic absolutism in the face of cultural uncertainty. Similar processes can be seen at work within minority communities, particularly those with religious affiliations.

Islamic fundamentalism
A contentious, often pejorative term for strict adherence to the Koran and Islamic law.

Although it claims to be concerned with the maintenance of tradition, so-called **Islamic fundamentalism** is very much about the here and now. Fundamentalism is normally understood as a conservative reaction to the uncertainties of globalisation and other social changes associated with modern society that are perceived as a threat. Rather than a simple expression of an essential ethnic identity, militant Islam is a selectively created identity, part of a bid by religious leaders to construct and lead an imagined community. This becomes clearer when we consider why this identity has more appeal to some Muslims than to others: it is a more powerful idea for the young than for the old, for the working class than for the middle class, for Pakistanis than for Bangladeshis and so on (Samad, 1992). To remark on this is in no way to explain away the demands of the Islamists: it simply places their claims in the wider story of the diaspora. Few things better sum up the ironies and complexities of ethnicity at the end of the twentieth century than the emergence of Islamists in Western Europe – a group whose *raison d'être* appears to be the continuation of a traditional way of life and the protection of eternal truths. Even ethnic absolutists have been reflexive in their rejection of reflexivity.

Dynamics of inequality and identity – race, class and gender

As we have seen, race and ethnic differences are not the only bases of inequality and identity in late modernity – Chapters 4, 5 and 6 have described a range of other social divisions that structure modern and late-modern societies. Although social relationships of race, class and gender are often considered in isolation from each other, in practice they operate together to generate structures of power and inequality. Similarly, gender, class and race are all potential (and sometimes competing) sources of identity and collective action. The need to understand the interplay between these distinct but related forms of difference is made more pressing by the recent economic and cultural changes analysed in other chapters of this book. Chapter 11, for example, discusses the significance of the growing polarisation of the labour market; this is not just a class issue – the labour market is also gendered and racialised (Brah, 1993). Other chapters discuss the uncertainty and fragmentation of contemporary cultural life. An important aspect of this is the way in which identities of race, class and gender mix and clash, as modernity progresses into late modernity or even postmodernity.

Theorising inequalities of race and class

Although there is a strong link between racialised differences and disadvantage, ethnic minority people can be found at all levels of the class structure. For example, there is a small but growing black middle class in the UK (Cashmore, 1991; Jones, 1993). How, then, do we theorise race and class inequality?

At one time, discussions in this area were essentially a debate between the Marxist and Weberian positions. Put broadly, Marxists argued for the primacy of class relations, maintaining that racial divisions were illusory or ideological, reinforcing the interests of capital (Westergaard and Resler, 1976). Weberians' multi-dimensional model of stratification meant that they were prepared to assign greater explanatory power to race and racism. Races, in some circumstances, could be treated as analytical categories – status groupings competing for scarce resources and/or power (Rex and Moore, 1967). As Chapter 5 has already argued, however, analyses of class are now much harder to divide into these two clearly defined camps – Marxist and Weberian. That this is also true of discussions of race and class is illustrated by two important developments.

Race and the underclass

The term underclass originated in the US to describe groups permanently trapped in poverty, but now it regularly crops up in discussions of racial disadvantage. Despite its popularity in some circles, the term is an ambiguous and contested one, applied to issues of class and gender as well as race (Morris, 1994; see also Chapters 5 and 6 of this book). 'Underclass' can mean either a structurally distinct group or a culturally distinct one. Proponents of the structural account raise important questions about the position of ethnic minorities. They argue that, due to discrimination against native-born ethnic minorities and the marginal status of migrant workers, ethnic minorities are over-represented among the socially and economically disenfranchised and therefore constitute an underclass. This claim is often linked to a discussion of the special problems found in inner-city areas where ethnic minority populations are concentrated. Commentators who adopt a cultural stance claim that it is the behaviour of a racialised underclass in the context of an over-generous welfare state that is at the root of their disadvantage.

The notion of a racialised underclass has been expounded in a variety of forms. John Rex and Sally Tomlinson (1979) argue that the position of many black people in the UK can be understood in terms of an underclass occupying a systematically disadvantaged position in comparison with the bulk of the white working class in respect of employment, housing, education and political influence. Rex and Tomlinson write from a neo-Weberian perspective, but a similar argument has been put forward by those neo-Marxists who maintain that black people constitute a **sub-proletariat** (Sivanandan, 1982; Castles and Kosak, 1985).

Sub-proletariat
Used by some neo-Marxists to describe a socio-economic group in the lower echelons of the working class (see also *underclass*).

Challenging the primacy of class

A growing awareness of the significance of racism in the determination of life chances and the formation of identities has led to a vigorous debate among neo-Marxists about race and class. Most now recognise that it is not enough to portray race and racism as capitalist ideology masking the unitary interests of the working class. There is, however, serious disagreement about whether it is legitimate to treat racial groupings as analytical categories.

Some neo-Marxists, notably Robert Miles (1989), argue that, while racism is a significant social phenomenon, the class relations of capitalism are the fundamental organising principle of society. To discuss race rather than racism is to confuse the appearance of capitalist societies with their 'essential relations' of class. In other words, the social structure is capitalist and class-divided, but racism and the use of migrant labour play an important part in determining positions within that structure.

QUESTION   How convinced are you that class is more important than race in modern societies? In your answer, refer to theoretical positions that support or undermine your view.

Others claim that Miles' argument makes little sense, given the crisis that Marxism is facing as a political and intellectual project (Solomos and Back, 1994). Analyses of race (and indeed gender) in the contemporary world have pointed to new issues of inequality and power that are not adequately addressed by classical Marxism. The significance of racial divisions challenges the myth of a unified working class emerging out of objective economic conditions. Although this form of analysis has the stamp of Marxism in its discussion of capitalist development and its emphasis on struggle, Weberians might well argue that it is groping towards a multi-dimensional account of class, status and power divisions. Like the Weberian perspective, it sees danger in searching for **underlying structures** and dismissing the ways in which social divisions are defined in ethnic terms. Racial inequalities and identities are very real to those who live them. One crucial illustration of this is that, for both minority and majority populations, race can prove a more meaningful basis of political action than class.

Race and gender divisions

Black women often suffer both racism and sexism (Bryan *et al.*, 1985). Highlighting this **double burden** tells only part of the story, however, since race and gender divisions work together to produce quite diverse patterns of inequality. When we consider the UK context, we see that:

- The relationship between gender and race disadvantage varies between contexts and within ethnic minorities – for example, Afro-Caribbean girls perform better than Afro-Caribbean boys in the education system, while in other groups, notably Pakistani and Bangladeshi, boys do markedly better than girls (Jones, 1993).

- Although there are differences in earnings, employment conditions and status between ethnic minority and white majority women workers (Lewis, 1993), these are less pronounced than those experienced by men. Some commentators have drawn parallels between the employment position of women and that of ethnic minorities, arguing that they both form reserve armies of labour or operate in secondary labour markets.

There are major gaps in our knowledge about gender and racial disadvantage. Many studies have ignored ethnic minority women. This is a considerable oversight, since they have a distinct social position that cannot be understood simply by combining the experiences of black men and white women. Gender-blind research has also generated inadequate analyses of the significance of race. Both these points are made by Heidi Mirza (1992) in *Young, Female and Black*, a study of young Afro-Caribbean women. Mirza argues that discussions of race and education have focused almost exclusively on boys, and this has led to a distorted picture of race and educational performance, contributing to a spurious analysis of educational under-achievement. In particular, explanations of boys' low exam passes based on family structure or cultural deficits ring hollow once girls' relatively good performance is taken into account. The young black women Mirza interviewed had aspirations and experiences that were distinct from those of young black men and of young white women. Their prospects were limited by factors that had little to do with their background: the girls suffered from poor schooling and low teacher expectations, and when they left education, they had to operate in a racially and sexually segregated labour market.

As with class, discussions of race inequalities and differences raise difficult questions for analysts of gender. This is illustrated by the academic and political debate about race inequalities that has taken place among feminists. Second-wave feminism in the 1960s and 1970s was based on the notion of a common experience and common interests among all women. This fundamental tenet of sisterhood was challenged by black women in the women's movement (Davis, 1981). In the 1980s, black radicals in

---

Underlying structures Associated with realism, this concept refers to organisational features of society that, while not observable, affect human behaviour.

Double burden A term used to describe black women's experience of both sexism and racism.

BOX 7.12 Unpacking the fashion industry

Race, class and gender can combine to funnel people into different occupations or different levels of the employment hierarchy within occupations. One example of this is provided by Annie Phizacklea (1990) in her analysis of the gendered and racialised division of labour in the UK fashion industry. This sector of the economy has developed in a very specific way. Unlike their counterparts on mainland Europe who farm out production to other parts of the globe, large UK clothing suppliers and retailers utilise a **dual sector model** – subcontracting manufacturing to small firms that are forced to operate very tight profit margins. Often – in the face of redundancy from large manufacturing companies and few alternatives – ethnic minority men have become subcontractors. As small employers, they exploit family and cultural ties to recruit female workers with few other work options. The survival of these firms depends on the poor conditions and low pay suffered by such women.

Phizacklea's study is not intended as a general model of the labour market but as one example of how the dynamics of race, gender and class can be articulated.

Dual-sector model
A model of work that suggests there are both primary and secondary labour markets.

Cultural imperialism
The aggressive promotion of Western culture based on the assumption that it is superior and preferable to non-Western cultures.

---

the UK argued that the experiences of Asian, African and Afro-Caribbean women cast doubt on feminist orthodoxy (Carby, 1982; Amos and Parmar, 1984). They argued that women from different ethnic backgrounds had distinct traditions and concerns that were not reflected in the priorities of the women's movement. White feminists were accused of **cultural imperialism** in the judgements they made about minority lifestyles, and of failing to address racism both outside and within the women's movement.

What might appear at first sight to be a dispute amongst feminists actually highlights a fundamental debate about power and inequality (Ramazanoglu, 1989). Black critics asked difficult questions of gender theory. Can all women be said to share a common experience of oppression? What is the relative status of racism and sexism? Do black men hold the same patriarchal power as white men? These questions have not necessarily been answered adequately: a new wave of analysts have, for example, challenged black feminists' claim to speak for all minority women, pointing to the diversity of their traditions, experiences and social locations (Brah, 1992).

Complex identities: racism, gender and sexuality

Ethnic absolutism can be seen as an attempt to impose order on a changing and fragmented cultural landscape. It recognises the significance of ethnic divisions while denying the many ambiguities of identity evident in the contemporary world. These ambiguities relate not only to ethnicity itself but also to the ways in which race intersects with other sources of identity such as gender, sexuality and class. It is to this intersection which we now turn.

Historically, ideas about gender and sexuality have often been inseparable from racist beliefs and practices (Ware, 1992). Racial stereotypes are, for example, usually about gender and sexuality as well as race. Consider the portrayal of Afro-Caribbean men as possessing uncontrolled sexual potency and the potential for violence and criminality, or the image of Asian women as sexually exotic, passive and unambitious – the docile victims of a traditional culture. The power of such stereotypes highlights the part that notions of masculinity and femininity can play in maintaining racial and other cultural differences. These connections can be traced back to the era of slavery and colonialism, when the protection of white femininity against 'defilement' by blacks was used to justify acts of great brutality. In the post-slavery American south, for example, many black men accused of sexual interest in white women were lynched. The policing of white femininity went hand in hand with the sexual exploitation of black women by white men: rape was a routine aspect of plantation slavery, and prostitution was institutionalised in colonial societies. Perhaps it is the legacy of this era that, despite the number of cross-racial sexual relationships in contemporary societies, these are still considered transgressive and/or exotic by some.

Identity politics
A political agenda based on shared experiences and forms of self-expression (see *the personal is the political*).

Race, class, gender and sexuality can all be bases of community and action – the dilemmas this can cause are illustrated by the problems of **identity politics**. We have already discussed the difficulties racial difference has posed for the women's movement. Similarly, political movements that seek to mobilise people around a shared racial identity to struggle against racism and racial disadvantage and to fight for the free expression of ethnicity have found it difficult to deal with gender difference. It is worth citing two examples of this.

In the 1960s, the US saw the growth of black political consciousness, expressed through the civil rights movement and more militant forms of black nationalism. In the late 1960s and 1970s, some of the assumptions and practices of this black politics were questioned by women members of these movements. For example, Michele Wallace in *Black Macho and the Myth of Superwoman* (1990), argued that they had a male bias and marginalised black women. Wallace maintained that the militants understood liberation in masculine terms – emphasising sexuality, physical prowess and aggression. In this world view, black freedom meant asserting male power and establishing a subservient, feminine role for black women. This analysis was met with hostility from men and some women in the black community in the US. Concern with women's issues was seen as a distraction from the main issue of racial disadvantage, and feminism and gay rights were seen by some as white issues. Michele Wallace was attacked for breaking the taboo on criticising other blacks in front of whites. In a similar way, Alice Walker's novel *The Color Purple* (1998) was criticised for discussing physical and sexual abuse in black families. When the film of the book was nominated for an Oscar, some political groups picketed the ceremony.

In 1989, a major demonstration was held in London calling for the banning of Salman Rushdie's *The Satanic Verses* (1988). There was also a counter-demonstration by far right groups. Some of the marchers united with the fascists to attack a small third group – Asian women from the organisation Women Against Fundamentalism, who had come to proclaim their support for Rushdie. Once again, to understand this hostility, we have to consider the challenge that groups such as Women Against Fundamentalism pose to the formation of a united Islamic community in the UK (Yuval-Davis and Sehgal, 1992).

By revealing the variations in black experiences and aspirations, these examples highlight the contested, changing and sometimes contradictory character of identities of race, gender and sexuality (Hall, 1992b). These complexities of identity thrown up by analyses of race bring into stark relief a wider concern: the pace and global character of social change are forcing us to be more reflexive about who we are and how we fit into our social environment (Giddens, 1991; Bauman, 1992).

Rethinking race, class and gender

Taking race seriously involves challenging conventional approaches to understanding both class and gender. The debates about the underclass and the future of Marxism are, for example, far from resolved, but the fact that they are taking place suggests that it is

Essentialism
An approach that assumes some universal feature that identifies the phenomenon under study. Essentialist approaches to gender assume that all women share traits in common, as do all men.

not enough to integrate race into existing models of the class structure. Instead, race and racism must be an important part of renewed thought on the nature and significance of social class. Similarly, greater awareness of racial disadvantage has prompted challenges to **essentialism** in gender theory. Elizabeth Spelman in *Inessential Woman* (1990, p. 187) argues that feminist analysis has wrongly attempted to isolate gender from other sources of identity and to isolate sexism from other sources of oppression: 'Though all women are women, no woman is only a woman.'

Equally, no working-class person is only working class, and no black person is only black. Therefore, while it may sometimes be legitimate for sociologists to discuss race, class and gender separately, to understand fully the dynamic and complex nature of inequalities and identities in late modernity, we must consider how race, class and gender divisions combine to produce specific effects.

Chapter summary

- Racial and ethnic divisions are highly significant bases of inequality and identity in the contemporary world.

- Although racial and ethnic differences are often represented and understood as obvious, fixed and physically based, they are social constructions that change over time.

- The experience of racialised minorities in the UK must be understood in the context of the colonial legacy, patterns of post-war migration, the changing labour market, recent economic restructuring and the different histories and traditions of the various ethnic groupings.

- Racism has played a crucial part in limiting the life chances of minorities in the UK. To understand this fully, we must consider not only the impact of individual prejudice but also the extent to which racism is rooted in institutional structures and shared beliefs.

- The globalisation of late modernity is destabilising traditions and bringing people into greater contact with cultural differences. The meeting of ethnicities is generating hybrid cultural forms, but, paradoxically, it is also lending urgency to the reassertion of absolute, unchanging ethnic identities.

- Although race, class and gender divisions are often discussed in isolation from each other, in reality they operate together to generate complex patterns of inequality and identity.

Questions to think about

- How important was the experience of colonialism in fixing racist assumptions in the minds of imperial citizens?

- Assess the success of anti-discrimination legislation in removing disadvantages from minority populations. Refer to more than one society in your answer.

- Of class, ethnicity and gender, which do you think is the most important in terms of the likelihood of experiencing discrimination? Justify your answer.

Investigating further

Cohen, Robin (1997) *Global Diaspora*, Routledge

A very clear introduction to the idea of the diaspora, exploring the relationship between migration, identity and homeland for both older and newer diasporas.

Malik, Kenan (1996) *The Meaning of Race*, Palgrave

Malik examines the emergence of the concept of race and takes a critical stance on postmodern theory. For starters, read the last section of Chapter 6, 'Biological Hierarchy to Cultural Diversity', the section entitled 'The West and Its "Others"', and Chapter 8 on 'Universalism and the Discourse of Race'.

Pilkington, Andy (2001) 'Institutional Racism and Social Exclusion', *Developments in Sociology*, vol. 17.

This offers a very clear account of the position of ethnic minority groups in the labour market and a good critical exposition of the idea of the underclass.

8

Power, politics and the state

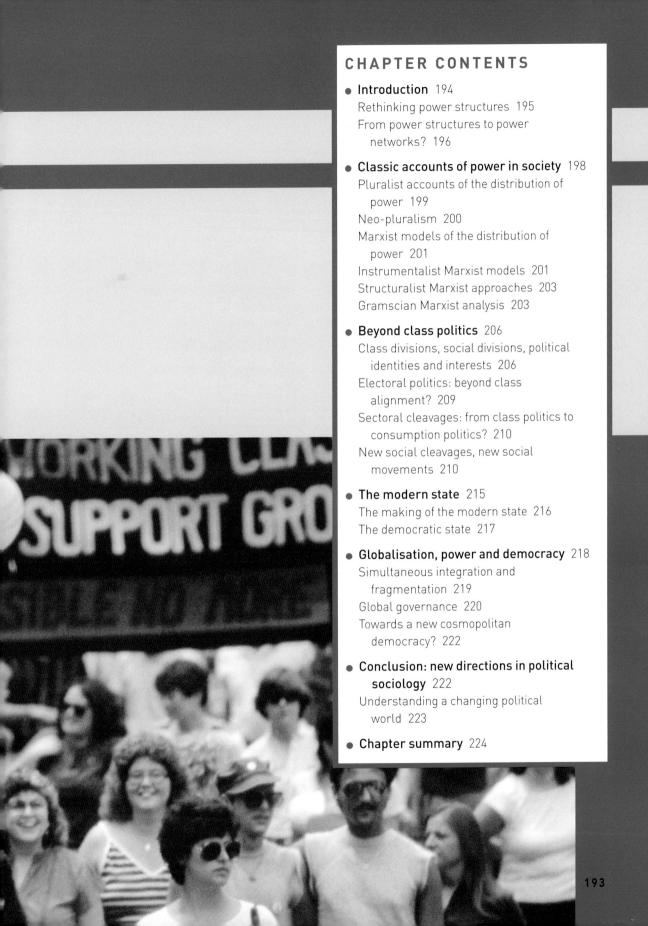

CHAPTER CONTENTS

Aims of the chapter

Important dimensions of social division are power and the political systems that act as a conduit for power. In this chapter, we show how political sociology focuses on power in society and the nature of the state. We examine models of the distribution of power and discuss whether class politics has come to an end. In so doing, we explore whether a new type of politics has emerged. We also analyse the origins and character of the modern state and the nature of democracy. Finally, we look at the impact of globalisation on power and governance, asking whether democracy is still a conceivable concept.

By the end of this chapter, you should have an understanding of the following concepts:

- Democracy
- Citizenship
- Pluralism
- Hegemony

- Partisan de-alignment
- Class de-alignment
- New social movement
- Global governance

Introduction

Power in the state and power in social life – this is the terrain of political sociology. In this chapter, we explore both of these issues. We start with a review of the debates on power in society and then discuss power, the modern state and globalisation. We shall not cover the process of policy making, as to do so would require analysis of the internal structures of the state and the methods of putting policies into practice, as well as social support for policies, all of which are outside the scope of this chapter.

Some sociologists, notably Max Weber, have paid close attention to the state. But rather than exploring the policy-making process in a 'state-centred' way, sociology has often adopted a society-centred approach to politics, focusing on the interests of social groups and the ways in which they mobilise power to defend or promote their interests. Increasingly, though, sociologists have returned to the state and its organisation, studying the pre-modern state and drawing lessons about the importance of nationalism, warfare and administrative organisation (Giddens, 1985; Mann, 1986). Sociologists are thus concerned to analyse the diverse nature of power and the complexities of the relationship between state and society.

Generally, the sociological analysis of politics has been seen as the study of political behaviour in a social context, exploring the relationship between politics and the social structure. Sociology has analysed power and domination in many different areas of society, from the workplace to the family. Political sociology does study behaviour that is directly political – such as voting and pressure group activity. However, sociologists recognise that the study of power ranges much wider than this: we acknowledge that politics is potentially present in all social relationships, because politics involves the exercise of power. As Worsley (1964, pp. 16–17) says: 'We can be said to act politically when we exercise constraint on others to behave as we want them to . . . the exercise of constraint in any relationship is political.'

According to this view, political behaviour is essentially power behaviour, and this is not confined to governmental institutions but can be present in any social situation. Political decisions are made – and hence power is exercised – not only when taxation laws are changed by parliaments or when prisoners are herded into concentration camps, but also when parents forbid their daughter to attend an all-night party or when an individual worker is sacked. In this sense, since all areas of social life involve elements of power, politics cannot simply be seen as 'what politicians do'. Instead any process involving the exercise of control, constraint and coercion in society is political. Any unequal relationship has political dimensions, and since unequal relationships exist throughout social life, any search for patterns in social life must look for patterns in the distribution of power. A sociological approach to politics always involves an analysis of the operation of power in social contexts and relationships, and an investigation of the consequences of power for social conflict and stability.

More recent theories of power have extended these ideas in both micro and macro directions. Michel Foucault (1979) regarded power as a net-like structure, diffused throughout social life, while others pay attention to power on a global scale, examining powerful institutions and forces that go beyond the boundaries of any one national society (Castells, 1997; Held *et al.*, 1999).

CONNECTIONS For an account of power at the micro level, consider the information in Chapter 9, pp. 234–44, on the workings of power both on and within the family.

Rethinking power structures

Marxism is one of the most far-reaching attempts to explain state power in terms of the wider social structure. For Marxism, the underlying economic structure of society consists of the social relations between classes (see Chapter 5). By nature, these class relations involve exploitation and domination, so politics and potential conflict are built into the heart of any class society. It follows that state power reflects these underlying class relations in society. Later we shall explain how modern Marxist theorists have extensively modified this basic theory (Jessop, 1982). Despite the work of the latter, the Marxist model is often taken for dead, now that the Eastern European communist regimes have been consigned to the dustbin of history.

This drive to go beyond the Marxist approach can be seen in the work of sociologists such as Michael Mann and Anthony Giddens. According to them, it is not possible to understand the nature of power or the roots of change in society unless we move away from the idea that economic power and economic class are the basis of politics. This is not just a critique of Marx: these theorists claim that there are many dimensions of power with different institutional bases.

Mann (1986, pp 2 and 3) emphasises 'four sources of social power: ideological, economic, military and political power'. Instead of there being a single power structure within each neatly bounded society, Mann emphasises that power involves overlapping, interlocking networks that may well be transnational. Also, we should not assume that any one of the four types of power will always predominate (as in simple Marxism). In Europe in the Middle Ages, for example, economic, political and military power was very fragmented, but the ideological power of Christianity was a strong connecting force that transcended boundaries. But these complex networks of power, says Mann, have to have a basis in organisations. Different ways of organising armies, churches, trade unions or whatever have a profound influence on the amount of effective power they can mobilise.

These approaches are grounded in historical evidence from non-capitalist societies, and they put the state and state power at the centre of analysis. This implies a partial move away from society-centred analysis towards greater emphasis on state power and the changing relationship between state and society at different times and in different places.

From power structures to power networks?

Writers such as Mann are sceptical of previous theories of power structures, but Mann nonetheless constructs a structural account of organisations and the exercise of power. Foucault was also sceptical about treating societies as bounded, separate structures, and he too rejected any generalised economic explanation of power. But Foucault went further than Mann by rejecting the notion of a large-scale macro structure. Foucault saw power in a micro way, finding it present in all social relationships and operating in specific ways in various institutional settings, including the prison and the clinic.

CONNECTIONS Foucault's work is discussed in detail elsewhere, especially Chapter 9, pages 234–40, and Chapter 19, pages 523–30.

According to Foucault, we must explore the intimate relationship between power and knowledge, as ideas become established and put into practice as powerful discourses. It follows that notions such as 'ruling class domination' simply obscure the micro realities of power (Smart, 1983), where power has a net-like structure interlinking all sorts of social positions.

Claims to knowledge are also claims to power (for example, in the field of medicine) and particular forms of knowledge have direct power as they are put into practice in institutions (such as the clinic or the asylum). However, discourses can be challenged, and Foucault saw both power and resistance as constant elements in the complex networks of social interaction. For example, an expectant mother may have a dependent relationship with medical staff but a dominant relationship with the child once born. But the actual nature of these power relationships changes as social discourses on parenting and patient–doctor relations change. Indeed, this becomes a site of political pressure when women form a movement (as they did with the National Childbirth Trust) to challenge the dominant philosophy of maternity provision.

Foucault's ideas reflect the shift away from economic conflicts in society towards diverse, non-economic political struggles. When feminists demonstrate that 'the personal is political', then sociologists must seriously examine power and domination in the family and the control of bodies through powerful discourses, whether in medicine or in advertising. These power relationships, and the struggles relating to them, do not fit into any neat hierarchical model of the power structure – hence Foucault's image of a net.

Figure 8.1 Foucault conceived power as a ubiquitous, inescapable feature of all human interactions.

This imagery of the net has a great deal of contemporary resonance with the Internet and our increasing familiarity with 'virtual' social connections that are not limited by space or time. These ideas are at the heart of Manuel Castells' radical new vision of power for a globalised era (Castells, 1996, 1997, 1999) – what he calls 'the information age'. It is a matter of debate among political sociologists whether these concepts of power as a network (both micro and macro) are compatible with longer-established approaches to power. This debate is one of the many disputes about modernity and postmodernity explored in this book.

This digital divide apart, it is clear that the open nature of the Internet makes life very difficult for commercial interests that wish to make it profitable and for governments that wish to control it. Once connected, the costs are very low, so it

BOX 8.1 Power and the Internet

The Internet is a remarkable phenomenon by any standards, having become so quickly established as a major means of communication and information transfer. The internet has not just dissolved the obstacles presented by time and space, its very nature is remarkable. Its openness, its vast scale and its almost infinite interconnectedness make it difficult to police and hard to commercialise successfully. If knowledge is power, then power structures are profoundly changed when exchanges of knowledge are open and uncontrolled. The endless cross-connections, leads and links of the Internet suggest that the relationship between power and resources has become fluid, interwoven and horizontal, rather than vertical, fixed and authoritative.

Of course, it is true that there are vast inequalities of access to the Internet between social groups, and between whole continents. As the United Nations Human Development Report (UNDP, 1999) shows, Africa has been largely excluded from the Internet revolution, partly because few people can afford it, but especially because of Africa's underdeveloped telephone network. Some African leaders see this as further excluding their continent from international economic developments. Africa has only 0.25 per cent of all Internet hosts, and its share is falling. The overwhelming majority of these Internet hosts are in South Africa.

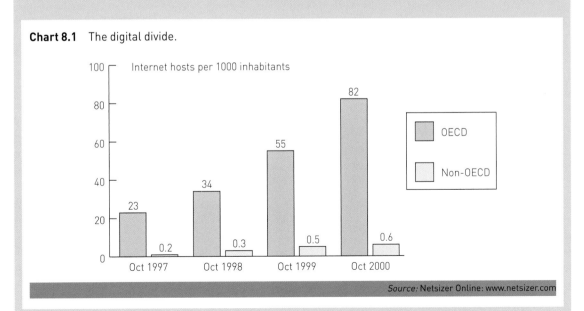

Chart 8.1   The digital divide.

Internet hosts per 1000 inhabitants

Source: Netsizer Online: www.netsizer.com

does not require exorbitant amounts of money and skill to compete with rich companies. It is impossible to buy up every competitor or to squeeze them all of out business. Even when governments do attempt to control content, there are jurisdictional problems, as the Internet is global, not national. The only possibility is to punish national firms that provide Internet connections, even though they have no responsibility for content.

Such pressures point to the need for a system of gatekeepers and mediators. Companies such as AOL make Internet access easier, but they also stand between the user and the Internet, filtering and commercialising content. At one level, this may add value, since most people need some signposts, trails and familiar websites to lead them through the vastness of the net to brands they feel they can trust.

But such a system would also give power over content to the mediating company, and provide a lever for government agencies seeking to control and censor. Although many people could be controlled or influenced by these means, it could prove impossible to prevent anarchical exploitation of the freedom of the web. The Internet still has the potential to disrupt and recast power in ways we have yet to determine.

 ## Classic accounts of power in society

Political sociology has its roots in modernity – specifically in Western capitalist societies. Consequently, sociology has been concerned with the potential tension between two distinct institutional systems – the liberal democratic constitutional state and the capitalist economy. Liberal democracy proclaims equal rights for citizens: each vote is worth the same, and each of us should be equal before the law. However, equal rights do not necessarily bring equal amounts of power. If the capitalist economic system produces systematic inequalities in economic power and benefit, will these produce great inequalities in political power? Liberal politics has been deeply divided from socialism over this question, as have different sociological theories.

For the liberal, economic advantage is not the key to political advantage. The political system gives rights and protection to all. The democratic process should reflect all the diverse political demands and interests in society. In the classic liberal account, the class most likely to win individual democratic rights was the bourgeoisie. This middle class wanted political and economic freedoms and rejected aristocratic rule. When political citizenship was extended (to women or poor people), this was the logical extension of the liberal principle of universal individual rights. In contrast, socialist critics of bourgeois rights (Marx, for example) argued that liberty for capitalists simply set them free to impose their economic and political power: 'freedom for the pike is death for the minnow'. The formal equality of rights hid and justified the practical reality of inequality. People could not exercise their political rights effectively if the economic system denied them power, resources and influence.

Thus, debates have revolved around questions about the distribution of power, especially the relationship between economic power and political power. This can clearly be seen in the competing models of the distribution of power provided by Pluralist and Marxist analyses. For Pluralists, liberal democratic institutions genuinely confer substantial political rights, opportunities and benefits on citizens, preventing any concentration of power in any one social group. Even if a small elite actively decides policy and governs, it is influenced by social pressure and answerable to all citizens. In the Marxist critique, liberal democratic political arrangements are largely spurious, cosmetic illusions hiding the reality that power is concentrated in the hands of a small, economically powerful class.

Pluralist accounts of the distribution of power

Pluralist accounts of the distribution of power reject the assertion that class interests are the key to politics. Instead, there are many social divisions, political needs and preferences among the citizens. Pluralists see multiple, overlapping social groups in society with varied and cross-cutting political interests. Rather than class conflict, Pluralists envisage a fluid and indeterminate power structure in which power and influence over decision making are dispersed among a variety of social groups. As long as politicians are open to multiple influences, and as long as people have the means to give voice to all their diverse demands, then it is possible to achieve a genuine pluralist democracy or **polyarchy** (Dahl, 1989).

People have gained this voice, according to Pluralists, through the extension of citizenship rights and the democratic right to organise collective representation via political parties (such as mass socialist parties) and via social and industrial organisations (such as consumer groups, trade unions and so on). Pluralism is thus not purely about individual rights, because the driving force behind liberal democratic politics is the political activity of organised groups. Modern twentieth-century politics was distinctive because of the variety of social groups and sectional interests to which individuals belonged, such as social classes, occupational groups, gender groups, ethnic groups, religious groups and so on. So a key element in the pattern of power is the increased complexity and social differentiation of modern industrial societies, which create very varied group interests. Society is an arena of diverse and contending interests, but it is not fundamentally split by social divisions. Instead, there is an underlying common interest in maintaining a framework in which different groups can compete and pursue their interests without destroying the basic foundations of society. This means that political actions that step outside the boundaries of liberal democracy are violating the commonly shared 'rules of the game'. Violent or radical politics are defined as threats that undermine mutual tolerance and moderate political competition. Neo-Nazis, black power movements, student radicals and striking workers have all been seen as 'enemies within', breaking the fundamental consensus that underpins democratic pluralism.

Polyarchy
A pluralistic view of the distribution of power that rejects the notion of class division. It sees power as emerging from the interplay of various social groups with multiple, cross-cutting political interests.

> **QUESTION** Which of your citizenship rights are enshrined in law? Look up any that you are unsure of.

For pluralism to work there have to be opportunities and mechanisms available for groups to articulate their interests effectively. Democratic politics involves competition among organised interest groups to win the ear of the government. Political decisions are the outcome of a complex process of accommodation, bargaining and compromise between the various groups attempting to exert influence over formal political decision makers in government.

Although the government is seen as playing a crucial role in resolving diverse group interests, Pluralism is essentially a society-centred, not state-centred, approach. This is because the government stands apart as a neutral broker, mediating and arbitrating between competing groups and interests. It is effectively autonomous from control by one group or from serving the interests of one group. All legitimate interests have some claim to be heard and to be taken into account in policy formation: no one group or major interest is systematically favoured or disregarded. No single group can consistently monopolise power, so the power structure is fluid and complex, not unitary and monolithic.

Specifically, Pluralists refuse to equate economic power with political power, or to accept that a dominant economic class holds the reins of power. The following changes in traditional capitalism and private ownership mean, they argue, that this ruling class can no longer exist:

- Capital has had to accommodate the countervailing power of organised labour in the workplace.
- The economy is increasingly politically regulated, as the state plays a more interventionist role, planning economic development and directly controlling some of its key sectors through nationalisation.
- Owners of capital have become fragmented with the rise of joint stock companies and large corporations, and with diversified shareholding rather than concentrated ownership.
- The increased scale and size of economic enterprises has required the expansion of managerial control of companies.
- Since the functions of controlling capitalism are no longer in the hands of a few, economic power can no longer be concentrated in a dominant class.

CONNECTIONS For a discussion of the effect that capitalist power has on work, see Chapter 11, pages 301–8.

Neo-pluralism

Many critics have pointed out the highly optimistic assumptions behind Pluralist models. Key criticisms focus on the actual distribution of influence and the boundaries of legitimate politics:

- Different groups have markedly different resources. The amount of influence they can bring to bear depends on the economic resources they can mobilise, or the negative consequences they can bring about by some action. For example, trade unions can mobilise collective resources and impose costs on employers through strikes, but individual workers in small firms cannot.
- The Pluralist focus on open political competition neglects other 'faces' of power. In the 1960s, Bachrach and Baratz (1963) showed how certain issues were deliberately kept off the political agenda, thereby denying some social groups a voice. One example of this 'second face of power' was the silence that reigned in British politics about political and social discrimination against Catholics in Northern Ireland. The civil rights protests of the 1960s eventually put this issue onto the agenda, but the failure to resolve the problem drove the conflict outside the boundaries of peaceful liberal-democratic politics.
- The 'third face of power' (Lukes, 1974) is when politics systematically serves the interests of one social group rather than others, even when no explicit political conflict or decision is evident. Here we have to ask the question 'who benefits?', bearing in mind that the power to retain privilege may be most potent when it is never questioned or challenged. One example here is the taken-for-granted maintenance of male dominance in social institutions.
- Political groups or movements that seek radical change in society are often seen as illegitimate. If their demands question the fairness of current political arrangements

and they break its rules, they can be marginalised and suppressed. Pluralist democracy only works if we all stay within liberal democratic rules and do not use force as a means to gain power. Violent protests, for example, by animal rights campaigners, illustrate the effect of this on those who feel powerless or without a voice. Pluralism assumes a degree of moderation and basic conformity to the system that is not really present.

In response to these criticisms, some Pluralist theorists have revised their position. They have conceded that formal political equality in liberal democracies does not square with the real socio-economic inequalities in these societies. These neo-Pluralists (Dahl and Lindblom, 1976) recognise that particular interest groups, such as big business, and institutions such as multinational corporations, occupy positions of great influence and are therefore able to exercise more political muscle than other interests (such as consumer groups) in order to influence government policy making.

Thus, while neo-Pluralists maintain that governments are genuinely controlled by electoral competition, lobbying and pressure by interest groups, they acknowledge that business interests do have a great influence on public policy – polyarchy exists, but it is a deformed polyarchy (Dahl, 1989). Diverse interest groups influence the political process, so the government cannot have a single purpose – such as serving the interests of capital.

Marxist models of the distribution of power

Society-centred models of power are based not only on class but also on other social divisions, such as region, gender and ethnicity. However, Marxism firmly bases its model of power on economic classes and has been enormously influential in doing so. The fundamental reason for this is the strength of Marxism's claims that:

- The most important structural feature of modernity is capitalism.
- Capitalism rests on economic class relations, and these necessarily involve exploitation and domination.
- There is thus a fundamental class conflict at the root of capitalist societies.
- Furthermore, these economic relations shape the other social relations in society, so that class is ultimately the most powerful and fundamental political division in society. Other divisions are conditioned by class and will not be so decisive in determining the society's political development (see Chapter 4).

Even though Marx and Engels acknowledged that politics and social change could not simply be 'read off' from the economic level, they did regard economic factors as ultimately decisive. Furthermore, while more recent Marxists have tried to make their analysis more subtle, finding more room for politics and ideology, the fundamental primacy of economic structures is usually affirmed. We shall now explore how these basic Marxist propositions have been developed and the directions they have taken.

CONNECTIONS For a good basic account of the work of Marx, see Chapter 17, pages 476–82.

Instrumentalist Marxist models

Marx and Engels sometimes used simple models of politics where the state was described as an instrument of the ruling class: that is, the economically dominant class either ruled directly or others ruled at its behest. For example, in the *Communist Manifesto*

(1848), the capitalist state is described as 'the executive committee of the whole bourgeoisie'. But elsewhere, as in Marx's analysis of French politics in *The Eighteenth Brumaire of Louis Bonaparte* and in Engels' *Letter to Bloch* (Marx and Engels, 1968), they offered more sophisticated accounts, acknowledging the importance of specific political and ideological influences. Even then, the analysis of ideas and political interests was related back to economic interests.

The instrumentalist Marxist position is deeply sceptical about democracy in capitalist states. Parliament and government are not seen as the major sources of power, because real power is a consequence of the ownership and control of capital. Democracy and popular participation will remain limited, or even illusory, as long as Western societies remain capitalist societies in which a dominant economic class holds sway.

The dominant economic class holds the preponderance of economic power because of its ownership and control of the means of production. It has close links with and penetrates important institutions such as the mass media, the military, religious institutions and so on and is closely associated with the key decision-making domains (the command positions) of the state. Thus, the dominant economic class is a ruling class. Even if they do not rule directly, capitalists – an exclusive, unified group sharing a common social background and common interests – consistently exercise considerable power and influence over political decision making.

Given their emphasis on economic power as the precondition for political power, Marxists have to demonstrate that the private ownership of capital still matters, and that the needs and goals of capital still do much to shape society. They point to the continuing existence of massive material inequalities, in which the distribution of wealth remains heavily skewed in favour of a small but economically powerful class, with the vast bulk of people possessing little real wealth.

Although the dominant class has changed in terms of social composition, it is still an exclusive group, socially distinct from other groups in the class structure and closed to them. This has been achieved by various strategies of class reproduction or social closure, such as:

- Intermarriage and kinship connections.
- Interconnected economic interests such as interlocking directorships, where individuals are directors of more than one company.
- Exclusive educational background, such as attendance at certain public schools and then Oxford or Cambridge University, or an Ivy-League college in the case of those in the US.

Quangos – Quasi-Autonomous Non-Governmental Organisations Nominally independent bodies whose members are funded and appointed by central government to supervise or develop activities in areas of public interest.

- Cross-sphere contacts and linkages, where individuals occupy and/or shuttle between elite positions in various spheres (such as MPs who also hold company positions, former civil servants or government ministers who join the boards of private companies, and high-profile business personnel who are appointed to **quangos**).

While it is acknowledged that some economic redistribution has occurred, according to this view, the social system has not really changed. The spread of share ownership and the advent of so-called people's capitalism have made only marginal dents in the pattern of wealth holding. Scott (1982) and others show that substantial private shareholdings, with the concomitant power to exert decisive control over economic enterprises, remain tightly concentrated in a few hands.

Marxists, then, maintain that in the UK and elsewhere, the capitalist class has not disappeared but rather has survived and prospered. This reflects a dominant value system that equates business interests with the national interest and defends the principles of private property and ownership, free enterprise, profit, the free market economy and all the inequalities that follow from this.

This instrumentalist position has a problem explaining how socialist or social democratic governments also serve to maintain capitalism. One response is to suggest that the state has to act on behalf of capital in order to promote reforms to reduce political resistance and adapt capitalism to solve some of its problems. Reform is necessary for the system, regardless of what capitalists might think they need. (Miliband, 1968). Thus, Marxists have argued that Labour governments in the UK have not significantly threatened capitalist class interests and have been concerned to run capitalism efficiently. They have neither wanted nor been able to make any substantial or qualitative changes to the capitalist economy and political system. Their reforms have not fundamentally changed the dynamics of capitalist investment and profit.

Structuralist Marxist approaches

Ideas about the power of capitalism as a system and the state's dependence on a profitable economy have been developed further by structuralist Marxists such as Althusser (1969) and Poulantzas (1973). They argue that the actions of individual groups or classes are fundamentally constrained by the structures in which they are located. These structures exert an independent influence on social and political processes.

According to this view, instrumentalist Marxism misunderstands the impersonal nature of power. Power is located not in particular people but in systems of domination. It does not matter what individuals do or who occupies which elite positions. What are important are the structural constraints that a capitalist system places on individuals and their lives. The social backgrounds, networks, values and motives of those in elite positions are irrelevant to understanding power relations. Individuals are merely 'bearers' of objective structural relations and can do little other than reflect the logic of the capitalist system in their actions.

For the structuralist, it is possible for large numbers of people from humble, non-capitalist backgrounds to administer the state and the economy, but it will still be a capitalist state and society run in the interests of the capitalist class. The actions of politicians and state officials are simply the surface manifestations of the underlying structural relations, and the structural constraints of the capitalist system mean that dominant class interests will almost inevitably win out. This position has serious problems, however. There is a danger that structuralist Marxism simply produces a new functionalism (see Chapter 17), where the reproduction of the system is inevitable and guaranteed. This leaves little room for real political processes. These weaknesses led Poulantzas to move away from structuralism towards a more Gramscian emphasis on political alliances and programmes, and to examine more fully how the state worked as an institution (Poulantzas, 1978).

Gramscian Marxist analysis

Marxists who draw on the ideas of the Italian writer and political activist Antonio Gramsci (1971) offer a more qualified, society-centred approach. This approach identifies a greater element of human autonomy in relation to struggles in the political arena over policies and strategies. Stuart Hall (1983), David Coates (1984) and others emphasise that many Marxist approaches are too quick to reduce politics to economic interests and class conflicts and to underplay the political divisions and struggles within classes.

Instead, they use the idea of power blocs to analyse the social basis of the exercise of power. A power bloc is 'an alignment of social groups, generally under the dominance of one of them, which is able to monopolise the levers of political power in a society over a sustained period' (Scott, 1991, p. 33). This coalition of social groups comprises classes, fractions of classes, status groups and so on. Their interests may be divergent and even conflicting, but they effectively hold the reins of power by forming an alliance around a political programme that unifies their interests to some degree. For example, post-war governments in Western Europe adopted policies that combined state economic management with an expanded welfare state. Numerous and varied groups were able to unite behind such a programme because it brought benefits to each of them.

A power bloc may exclude certain groups (for example, the Thatcher governments excluded trade unions), but it may try to co-opt other social groups when this is deemed necessary – for example, when such groups pose a greater threat outside the power bloc than in it. Power blocs are not constant in composition, but are reshaped as different groups are admitted over time. They may experience shifts in the balance of power among their constituent groups as different fractions take leading positions. Such changes may be associated, for example, with shifts in the relative strength of different fractions of capital. Thus, in the UK in the early nineteenth century, the landed and commercial classes were key elements in the power bloc. The second half of the nineteenth century saw the rise of powerful industrialists who became incorporated into a new power bloc of urban manufacturing, commercial and landed capital. The twentieth century saw the relative decline of the manufacturing sector and the rise in power of the **finance fraction** of the capitalist class (Coates, 1984, p. 117).

Ideological hegemony is the second key concept of Gramscian Marxism. Power blocs always face demands and challenges from below. These demands may force political concessions to accommodate them and create a need to foster acceptance among the wider populace. Thus, it is necessary for the power bloc to attempt to create and sustain hegemony, where subordinate groups accept the cultural domination of particular ideas. If people interpret politics through particular taken-for-granted frameworks ('of course everybody is selfish and self-interested') then the 'natural' dominance of the current political order is more secure.

Maintaining hegemony has to be worked at perpetually, using social and political institutions and strategies to mobilise and reproduce consent. This could include utilisation of the mass media, the manipulation of nationalist sentiments and the making of welfare concessions, for example. At the same time, it may be necessary to fight off competing hegemonic claims and resistance from groups not included in the power bloc.

The structuralist and Gramscian approaches come together in the idea of the **relative autonomy** of the state. This concept suggests that there is a necessary separation between economic power and the formation of political programmes through the state. The interests of capital are not self-evident, and not all capitalists have the same interests. There may be significant differences between the interests of manufacturers and financiers, for example. This necessitates a relative autonomy for politics. Furthermore, at times – for example, when political forces are balancing one another, or when policy programmes are in crisis – it may be possible for political leaders to enhance their autonomy. To do so, they may impose programmes 'for the good of the nation' that entail direct costs for sections of capital (Jessop et al., 1988).

Through these theoretical innovations, the Marxist tradition has renewed itself and tried to maintain its critical perspective on politics in capitalist society. Nonetheless, many social theorists (including former Marxists) are now asking themselves whether class and class politics really are the key to understanding power in society. Other sociologists still regard capitalism as the key institutional structure of modernity and the dynamics of capitalist profit-making as the most powerful force shaping our lives.

Finance fraction
That part of capital, for example, banking, concerned solely with financial activities rather than production.

Relative autonomy
The situation where a link exists between two institutions, for example, the state and the economy, but each institution has a degree of independence in deciding outcomes.

However when this capitalism operates on a global scale and infiltrates every aspect of our lives, it is difficult to link it directly to identifiable classes.

> **QUESTION** What forms of economic power exist in late modern societies? Do individuals have any economic power, and, if so, how do they exercise it?

BOX 8.2 The Third Way – a new hegemony?

Has 'Third Way' politics become the new commonsense in politics, backed by a stable and powerful coalition of interests? In other words, is the 'third way' the new hegemony, and can it form the basis of a new social and economic stabilisation or 'settlement'?

The idea of a 'third way' in politics has spread out from the UK and its New Labour governments to enjoy a wider resonance in other liberal democratic countries. Its origins lie most obviously in the 1990s with the move of the Labour Party away from socialism and class politics, and away from oppositional political campaigns with limited appeal (such as nuclear disarmament). As an idea that mixes many elements, the origins of its components go back much further, but it does claim to be a new approach for a changed world.

According to its main academic advocate, Anthony Giddens (1998, pp. 26–7), 'the "third way" ... seeks to adapt social democracy to a world which has changed fundamentally over the past two or three decades'. Giddens singles out five particular changes:

- Globalization has forced external restraints on governments.

- Individualism has weakened older forms of collective politics.

- There have been moves beyond left and right in political ideology, so that old policy battles have become outmoded (for example, state planning has been abandoned in favour of the market economy).

- Political action has moved away from older mechanism of democracy and towards new movements and forms of action (for example, Greenpeace).

- Ecological risks demand a new global politics.

Third way politicians tend to accept that the old political divisions and conflicts in industrial societies are outdated and discredited. For them, there is no fundamental opposition of interest between capital and workers as long as wealth is increased productively and everyone gets a share. No person or group need be socially excluded, as long as everyone who is capable takes part in productive employment. Each of us must be flexible and adaptable, ready to meet the needs of a dynamic global economy.

Third way politics does not encourage naked self-interest and individualism. Market-driven economic activity needs to be embedded in a wider environment of social rules and responsibility. Nobody can claim rights without responsibilities; selfish individualism is not compatible with a society where everyone is part of a safe and secure community. Collectivism is communal and all-embracing, not class-based. At the same time, diversity – be this is ethnic, religious or sexual – must be cherished, not just tolerated. Above all, politics should be a process of finding solutions that benefit everyone; cooperation and consensus should benefit us all and include us all.

If this really is an all-embracing politics where everyone can join in and there are no individual winners and losers, then it seems a good candidate for achieving hegemony. Hegemony would imply that third way politics had become the dominant 'common sense' and that a large and powerful base of support had been established behind this politics. However, if the third way is to offer a new social and economic settlement, it will need to provide a stable framework for policy, where opposing ideas and forces of resistance will be marginalised.

The resounding victory of Blair's New Labour in two ▶

successive UK elections might seem to point that way, and it certainly does seem that wide sections of the electorate support this programme. Opposition has been marginal, whether from the Conservatives, who have abandoned their centre-right politics, or from the trade unions, who have no obvious alternative political home. But the turnout for the 2001 UK general election was very low, and it was not obvious that New Labour policies on markets and public services were viewed as successful in ideological or practical terms.

It is also possible to identify policy tensions that may undermine third way politics, if economic circumstances become more difficult. The ethics of social inclusion and communal responsibility are potentially in tension with other policies. The UK version of the third way followed on from previous policies that favoured the market over social welfare provision. In response to global pressures, individuals are required to adapt flexibly to the demands of the labour market and accept redundancy, job change or re-skilling as the price of a fast-moving market

economy. The dominance of free markets has meant that prosperity has come with sharply increased income inequality, but if recession should return to bring major structural unemployment as well, it is hard to see how the values of social inclusion and gains for everyone could be sustained. Apparent hegemony and consensus would be replaced by sporadic, perhaps violent, expressions of discontent. Whether there is any scope for more organised opposition by the disadvantaged, or even for a more radical third way among politicians, remains to be seen.

CONNECTIONS For a discussion of the impact of the 'third way' on health care, see Chapter 13, pages 374–8.

Beyond class politics

Class divisions, social divisions, political identities and interests

There is an apparent paradox in many affluent societies today. Although there were dramatic improvements in the standard of living in the last decades of the twentieth century, these improvements were distributed unequally. The trend towards reduced inequality of income in societies such as the UK was reversed in the 1980s and 1990s, and relative poverty increased for a substantial minority. Some writers, by referring to the 'haves', the 'have lots' and the 'have nots', pointed out that a substantial minority of people were socially excluded from the prosperous mainstream. The paradox is that class became less significant in people's perceptions at a time when inequality had become greater.

This creates real problems for those who consider that politics in modern society is still inevitably dominated by issues of class. Clearly, we cannot make any simple assumptions about the relationship between class position, class interests, political values and political action. There is no direct link between structure, consciousness and action. It has always been true that class position, class identity and class consciousness are only three of many bases of social division on which interests and political identity are formed. People construct social identities and consciousness out of multiple social experiences, so there are numerous bases on which they can mobilise or be mobilised for political action. Class also remains a strong discourse in most industrial societies – the idea of class is a handy point of reference when attempting to understand our own position in society. But class does seem to be of diminishing importance in defining social identity or political interests. Therefore, it is not likely to have a direct effect on conscious political actions.

Social divisions and interests other than class position can predominate at any one time and reduce the salience of class division and class interests. For example, class divisions and class interests are frequently cross-cut by non-class variables such as religious affiliation, age, gender or ethnicity. Gender and ethnic divisions, for instance, have been common both within the workplace and outside it. Many of the traditional manual workplace cultures have been aggressively masculine, with open discrimination against and hostility towards women workers. White male trade unionists have often gained at the expense of unorganised workers such as women and ethnic minorities. Black people have experienced racism from whites both inside and outside the workplace. Hence, organisations that are most associated with class politics can sometimes be hostile to other identities and interests.

The importance of this can be seen if we consider how people come to define their own social position in class terms. Even though many people experience the impact of inequality in their daily lives, this experience still needs to be interpreted through a set of ideas or frameworks. We can identify two of these. The first is the set of values and ideas that are commonplace in daily interaction – the words that people routinely use in everyday life. The second is the range of organisations that provide ways of seeing the world – the media spring to mind, but schools, trade unions and political parties may be more significant. Seeing the world in class terms is most likely when class is a constant theme – in the school, the workplace trade union or the local community. Class then becomes both a lived reality and a framework for understanding the world.

If we think sociologically about how affluent societies have changed over the last few decades, it is clear that class has become less central, both in everyday interactions and in the world views put across by influential organisations (see Chapter 5). We can point to important social changes that have influenced the internal structure and composition of social classes. These have particularly affected working-class people, by opening lines of division among them and by changing their sense of class identity and their aspirations, and hence their political actions. At the level of everyday lived experience, there have been profound changes in the economy, the occupational structure and residential patterns, as well as in working-class culture and patterns of consumption. These, along with substantial social mobility, have undermined people's sense of living within the boundaries of a social class with its own culture, values, traditions and forms of consumption.

In most affluent societies, one of the most significant changes in the second half of the twentieth century was the emergence of a more complex occupational structure associated with the decline of some industries and the rise of others, largely as a consequence of sectoral shifts in the economy (see Chapters 5 and 11). Traditional heavy manufacturing and extractive industries such as shipbuilding, heavy engineering, mining and metal extraction and processing contracted as the first phase in the general decline in manufacturing employment. In turn, the mass-production industries lost their dominance in favour of service industries (such as banking and finance) and knowledge-based activities. With these changes came an increasing division between a body of core workers working in full-time, reasonably secure jobs with good wages, and an increasing number with insecure, often part-time jobs that were less well paid.

These changes resulted in shifts in the shape of the class structure and in the internal structure of classes – that is, a more complex hierarchy emerged between and within class boundaries. The decline of traditional manual occupations and an overall contraction of the size of the working class produced a smaller, more divided 'proletarian' group working in a diverse and uneven economy.

Alongside these occupational structural changes, shifts in working-class residential patterns affected class identity, solidarity and political loyalty. Increased geographical mobility and urban redevelopment programmes relocated many working-class people from traditional urban working-class communities to suburban housing estates, new towns and the like. Communities linked to industry once provided a base for class solidarity and political identity, but private home ownership and commuting by private car often served to destroy people's sense of shared communal interest.

At the same time, mass marketing transformed the home, leisure and entertainment, with an increasing array of consumer durable goods (such as electrical items and cars) and package holidays. Better standards of living, plus the opportunity to define oneself through consumption, became part of the working-class experience.

CONNECTIONS For an account of the way in which social divisions cut across class solidarities, return to Chapter 7, pages 184–9.

These changes influenced working-class people's sense of class, their aspirations, and their material and political interests and loyalties, creating more individualism, more home-centred lifestyles and a more calculating, economic approach to political choice. All this dislodged older communal solidarity and political loyalty. Early signs of this were found in the 'affluent worker' studies conducted by Goldthorpe et al. (1969). While rejecting the notion that 'we're all middle class now' (embourgeoisement was their grand name for this idea), they concluded that affluence was having important consequences. Workers were more privatised, home-centred and instrumental in their non-work lives and more instrumental and calculating (rather than principled) in their views of politics and trade unions.

Goldthorpe (1978, 1988) and others argued that the periods of inflation and economic recession during the 1970s and 1980s intensified rather than diminished the orientation towards privatisation and the instrumental (calculating) stance towards trade unions and social democratic parties. While the relative economic security, affluence and full employment of the 1960s were sufficient to sustain their loyalty to trade unionism and social democratic parties, the fact that this loyalty was conditional and fragile meant that it could easily change in new circumstances. During the 1970s and 1980s, with inflation and recession threatening, working-class voters turned to parties that promised direct personal gains – such as the right-wing parties that promised tax cuts and individual prosperity in the 1980s and 1990s.

QUESTION To what extent do you think that voters cast their ballots in accordance with their wallets and purses? Support your answer with appropriate evidence.

We must not neglect the important changes that also took place in the broader social institutions that influenced world views and interpretive frameworks. In the early 1990s, trade unions and left-of-centre political parties were not just dismayed by the success of right-wing politics, they were also losing core elements of their support. Appealing only to the manual worker trade unionist living in public-sector housing was a recipe for permanent minority status – the membership and power of trade unions were ebbing away, and the politically promoted shift from public to private housing was proceeding rapidly. As a result, organisations that had promoted a class-based view of politics abandoned this in favour of a more inclusive and generalised appeal to 'ordinary people'. Social democratic parties such as the UK Labour Party steadily abandoned their policy of economic intervention and accepted the sway of market forces and their inegalitarian effects. They also felt unable to challenge the politics of lower taxation for fear of alienating potential voters from all economic classes.

Thus, a process of mutual reinforcement took place: class culture and group identity became less of an immediate social reality in people's everyday interactions, and this was reflected in and strengthened by the abandonment of class-based frameworks for politics by organisations that had previously promoted them. With the triumph of ideas such as New Labour's third way, we could argue that, although inequality is alive and well, class politics has been buried by mutual agreement.

Electoral politics: beyond class alignment?

Pronouncements of the death of class politics are nothing new. In the late 1950s, some commentators claimed that class politics was on the way out, with consensus and the 'end of ideology' lying just around the corner. The expansion of the welfare state, higher standards of living and better working conditions were expected to end class politics even that long ago. However, the death notice proved premature, as there were high levels of industrial conflict in many countries in the 1960s.

Nonetheless, important shifts in electoral behaviour did become visible in the 1970s and 1980s (Table 8.1), with political support becoming more volatile, party loyalty becoming less predictable and the traditional links between class and party loyalty declining. In other words, partisan de-alignment (loss of party loyalty) and class de-alignment (loss of predictable class patterns in political support) took place.

The notion of partisan de-alignment suggests that there was a general decline in the strength of people's loyalty to and identification with political parties. Indeed, Crewe *et al.* (1977), Butler and Kavanagh (1984) and others argued that the number of people claiming strong identification with political parties declined during the 1970s and 1980s. In the UK, for example, the old pattern of two main classes linked to two dominant parties was eroded by a rise in Liberal (and later Liberal Democrat) support and the growing popularity of the nationalist parties in Scotland and Wales. In the general election of 1997, there was a massive swing against the ruling Conservatives across the social classes, with a higher swing (15 per cent) among middle-class voters (Saunders, 1997). This was a contest in which the out-going government had been badly discredited, and the New Labour opposition was explicitly attempting to appeal to voters across class divides. Labour's strategy was based on the presumption that class de-alignment and party de-alignment had made it possible to appeal to the interests and

TABLE 8.1 Occupational class and voting, 1964–2001 (per cent)

	Non-manual	Manual	Non-manual	Manual	Non-manual	Manual	Non-manual	Manual
	1964		**1966**		**1970**		**1974(1)**	
Conservative	62	28	60	25	64	33	53	24
Labour	22	64	26	69	25	58	22	57
	1974(2)		**1979**		**1983**		**1987**	
Conservative	51	24	60	35	55	35	54	35
Labour	25	57	23	50	17	42	20	45
	1992		**1997**		**2001**			
Conservative	56	36	38	29	38	28		
Labour	24	51	40	58	36	49		

Sources: Saunders (1997), *Observer*, 10 June 2001.

concerns of all social groups. However, if an electorate is encouraged to be both de-aligned and instrumentally calculating, this hardly provides a secure basis for continued support to any one party and its policies.

Sectoral cleavages: from class politics to consumption politics?

Despite periods of economic recession, advanced capitalist societies have experienced great improvements in material living standards, in which most sections of the working class have shared. These societies also have a materialist ethos, systematically promoted by media advertisements persuading people to acquire goods and services in order to find happiness and self-fulfilment. Encouraged by easier access to credit, people are under constant pressure to define themselves through consumption, and some social scientists see distinct political effects emerging from this.

In the 1980s, Dunleavy and Husbands (1985) and others suggested that a new and significant social division or cleavage had emerged that was cutting across class lines and affecting political attitudes and loyalties. This theory of **consumption sector cleavage** took as its central focus people's involvement in the public and private sectors as both employees and consumers. Dunleavy and Husbands also identified a growing social division between those who were dependent on state provision and those who had opted for private housing, health care, pension plans and education. They claimed that the former were more likely to be loyal to left-of-centre parties, while the latter were more likely to support the Conservatives.

Evidence from the UK General Elections in the 1980s seems to support the consumption cleavage idea, but this was less clear in the 1990s. Perhaps political agendas have more causal power than social structure – the public sector/private sector issue was heavily exploited by the Thatcher governments in the 1980s. They attributed much of the UK's national and economic decline to excessive state interference in the economy, and in people's lives generally. Many incentives for private consumption (especially in the case of housing) were put in place.

Consumption sector cleavage A social division based on people's consumption patterns and their location in the private or public sectors of production and consumption.

New social cleavages, new social movements

Another aspect of 'politics beyond class' concerns forms of political action that are explicitly issue-based rather than linked to the interests of a particular social class. These political movements may be concerned with defending the interests of some or other social category such as gay men and lesbians, but often they are linked to a particular issue or principle, such as promoting fair trade with poor countries. Characteristically, these forms of political expression arise within society as a whole rather than being promoted from the top down. In this sense, people may come to invent new political frameworks for themselves.

When experiences change because social structures change, social actors are faced with the problem of finding an alternative framework to make sense of their social position and construct a new political identity. The solution to this may come from above in the form of ideological mobilisation by politicians and political parties. Dictators may mobilise support around the banner of national interest and destiny, or by emphasising law and order. More modestly, social democratic parties such as New Labour have reconstructed their political programmes in order to shed their image as class- and trade-union-based parties, and thereby appeal to a wider social constituency.

New frameworks can also come from below, generated by social actors and social movements. These new social movements are viewed as distinct forms of political mobilisation, potentially providing new identities, both individual and collective. Those which sprang up in the latter part of the twentieth century were concerned with such matters as:

- Citizenship rights and personal autonomy and identity (for example, the American black civil rights movement, feminist movements, gay rights movements).
- The preservation of the environment (for example, Greenpeace, Friends of the Earth).
- Peace and military disarmament (for example, the anti-Vietnam War movement, the Campaign for Nuclear Disarmament).
- Animal rights (for example, antivivisection movements, the Animal Liberation Front).
- National identity and self-determination (for example, ETA – the Basque separatist movement).

Older social movements were more associated with the changes taking place under modernity – for example, organised labour movements. These movements were mainly concerned with fighting for the more equal distribution of material resources, opportunities and power between social classes.

According to many analysts, such as Kriesi *at al.* (1995), the latter half of the twentieth century saw the decline of old social movements and the emergence of new ones. This change was closely linked to the gradual but fundamental transformation of the conflict structure of contemporary societies, where older social divisions and cleavages were being marginalised. The new social movements thus reflected the transition to a new phase of modernity or even a qualitative shift beyond modernity. Green movements and peace movements, for instance, represented fundamental challenges to industrialism and militarism, two of what Giddens (1990a) calls the 'institutional dimensions of modernity'.

The distinctive feature of contemporary societies, it is argued, is that lines of social cleavage and conflict persist, but they are no longer those of the workplace and class. Social conflict has shifted away from workplace and class relations to civil society and non-economic, non-class forms of cleavage and identity. Society has become more fragmented, with a plurality of struggles and movements. Unlike socialism's view of class, no single issue is more fundamental than any other.

New social movements reflect that fragmentation. They are at the centre of a new politics of identity that is not generated by class position or experiences in the workplace. The target of their opposition is not capitalist society or capitalist social relations, and they appeal to bases of collective identity that either transcend class or are not reducible to it – gender identity, sexual identity, membership of the planet or whatever.

Some new social movements fuse the personal with the global – that is, they embrace a politics that combines a sense of personal identity with a stress on fundamental human and global concerns, beyond the nation-state. The concerns of feminist movements, for instance, in principle address all women irrespective of class or country, on the basis that all women confront problems that are specific to them as women. Similarly, gay and lesbian movements provide a basis for identity based on sexual preference, seeking to instil 'gay pride' and attempting to expose and confront homophobic attitudes and beliefs among heterosexuals. Others, such as green movements and peace movements, are even more explicitly concerned with the global forces of social transformation and the impact of globalisation processes.

As stated above, the social composition of these movements is linked to the fragmentation of the class structure and new class cleavages. Many of the new social movements have attracted a broader cross-section of the population, but they tend to find their strongest support among people with middle-class, service-oriented occupations, such as academics, teachers and social workers, and among socially peripheral groups such as students, the unemployed and the retired. These groups are sometimes regarded as either marginal or ambiguous in terms of class.

BOX 8.3 Future values

Ronald Inglehart further explores his ideas on post-materialist values in *Culture Shift* (1990). He claims that evidence on values demonstrates a generational shift since the mid twentieth century. After the 1950s, material needs were satisfied more fully as prosperity grew, and priority began to shift away from materialism and towards quality of life. With the rise of the New Right in many countries during the 1980s, individualistic materialism seemed to hold sway, along with hedonistic consumption by the new rich (in the popular image the con-

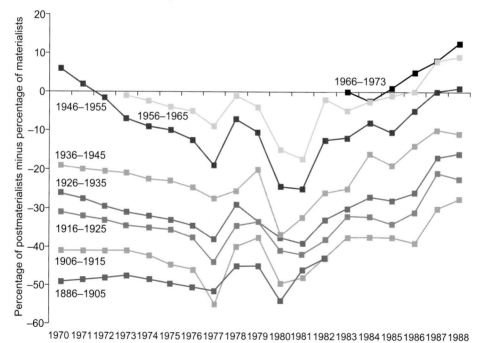

Chart 8.2 Value changes across the generations.

- The date labels on each line refer to the birth dates of different groups of respondents. So, its topline tracks the views of younger people, and the lowest lines track the views of the oldest.
- The dates on the horizontal axis show the time-period over which changing attitudes were measured.
- The vertical axis measures the strength of materialistic attitudes (minus scores) compared with non-materialistic attitudes (positive scores).

Source: Inglehart (1990) – based on data from six West European countries.

► **Chart 8.3** The fracturing of British values.

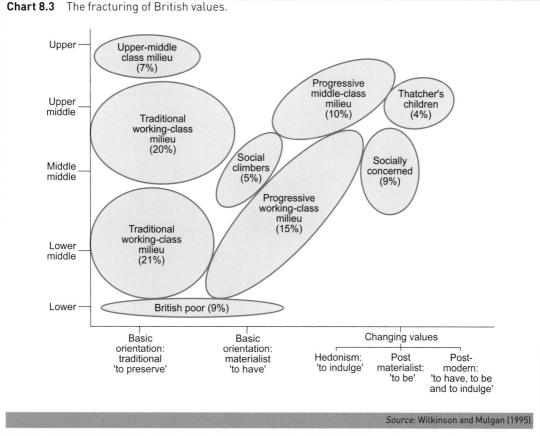

Source: Wilkinson and Mulgan (1995).

sumption of Porsche cars and cocaine). But new social movements such as Greenpeace and Friends of the Earth gained influence internationally, and the anti-nuclear movement gained strength following the increased deployment of nuclear weapons in Europe and later the disaster at the Chernobyl nuclear energy plant.

Chart 8.2 shows the trend in materialist values across the generations. Each line shows the way in which the views of different age-groups changed during the time period 1970–88. Not surprisingly, concern with economic issues increased during periods of slump or recession and receded during prosperous periods. But more importantly, although attitudes changed in a similar way in the short term, the younger groups were always less materialist – that is, basic economic issues were less important to them.

Chart 8.3 plots simplified social rankings (vertical axis) against changing values, as described along the base of the diagram, resulting in clusters of values among different social groups. (The data originated from the MORI polling company, working on the Socioconsult project for the London think-tank Demos.) Wilkinson and Mulgan emphasise the pattern of attitudes among younger (18–34 year old) respondents. The materialistic, individualistic ones (4%) are far outweighed by the 'progressives' (middle class 10%, working class 15%). This is seen as consistent with Inglehart's thesis.

Predictions of trends in political and consumer values are always fraught with difficulty – changing circumstances can wreck future-gazing – but there may be a real connection, as Demos argues, between changes in values and the new political agendas that go beyond left and right, or socialism versus markets. The 'third way' may have some basis in changing values.

Some commentators go further and suggest that the new social movements are displacing class-based movements as the principal agents of social transformation and a new social order. Touraine (1971), for instance, sees new social movements as key agents in the transition from industrial to post-industrial society, and Inglehart (1977) argues that Western industrial societies are undergoing a fundamental shift from a materialist to a post-materialist culture. According to Inglehart, when basic needs have been satisfied by material prosperity, people turn their attention to non-material goals, away from 'an overwhelming emphasis on material well-being and physical security towards a greater emphasis on the quality of life' (ibid., p. 3). Thus, priority shifts to personal freedom, self-realisation and identity fulfilment, as well as concern about the price of prosperity and its impact on the environment.

In the light of the above arguments, it is tempting to cry 'class politics is dead, long live the politics of new social movements'. However, we should be careful not to view the latter type of politics as the inevitable and universal shape of things to come. Firstly, while class-based political loyalties may have significantly loosened, we cannot assume that class no longer plays a part in shaping political identities and affiliations. As long as material inequality and disadvantage continue to grow in advanced economies, the potential for class politics remains. Secondly, the new social movements are not all the same: they are by no means a homogeneous, unified social and political phenomenon. There is considerable diversity in their ideologies, organisational styles and political strategies. Some employ conventional political channels (such as nationalist movements in mainland Britain), others use direct action (such as animal rights groups), while others use both parliamentary and extra parliamentary strategies. Moreover, there are frequently divisions within these movements – divisions between 'realist' and 'fundamentalist' green movements, divisions between the various branches of the feminist movement and so on.

Thirdly, a significant factor is the response of the state and established political parties to the new movements. While these responses vary from society to society and from movement to movement, the issue of incorporation and integration is faced by all new social movements. Like trade unions and socialist movements in the past, they have to decide how to respond when mainstream political parties take over their concerns (such as developing green policies or creating a minister for women). Should they accept being drawn into the conventional realms of politics and compromise on their goals?

Nonetheless, new social movements have made a significant impact by extending the boundaries of conventional politics. They have broadened political agendas by politicising untouched issues and thrusting them into the mainstream of politics. Social and cultural cleavages exist in societies, but these only become politically significant if and when they are actively politicised. This is what has happened with nuclear energy, pollution, gender inequality, sexual discrimination and so on. Green movements, for example, have made people more knowledgeable about the consequences of industrialism, about the dangers and threats posed to natural environments and other animal species, and about the need to protect them.

In conclusion, the political future will not be solely based on new social movements, but nor will they go away. For one thing, the actions taken by mainstream parties frequently fail to live up to the expectations and aspirations of the movements. For example, government actions on the environment have not satisfied the green movements. The political costs of implementing environmental policies can be considerable when they require the electorate to make sacrifices and lifestyle changes, so governments are bound to be cautious. In addition, when governments do take action, their initiatives frequently generate further conflict and resistance. This can include counter mobilisation by other movements: for example, in the US, women's successful demand for legalised abortion produced militant and violent responses from the pro-life movement.

The discussion in this section has highlighted issues of political identity and action, and we have looked at frameworks for the construction of political identities, as well as how they change over time. It remains to be seen whether the decline of class politics will prove terminal, and whether the new social movements will become central to the political agenda. It may well be that we are moving into an era characterised by an absence of any dominant framework of political identity.

 ## The modern state

Nation-state
A form of political authority that is unique to modernity. It comprises institutions such as the legislature, judiciary, police, armed forces, and central and local administration. It claims monopoly over power and legitimacy within a bounded territory.

The idea that the world should be entirely divided into autonomous sovereign **nation-states** is a peculiarly modern notion. In Europe, for example, Germany and Italy did not consolidate all their component regions and provinces into unified nation-states until late in the nineteenth century. In fact, such a world did not fully exist until the break-up of colonial empires in the second half of the twentieth century. As defined in the margin, the key point here is that the sovereign nation-state has sole legal jurisdiction and (as Weber emphasised) monopoly over legitimate violence in a specific, bounded territory. We tend to assume that every people that sees itself as a nation has the right to self-determination in a separate political nation-state; so when peoples or societies and states do not fit, there is a potential problem – consider the nationalist movements in three of the constituent countries of the UK: Ireland, Scotland and Wales.

Even this straightforward concept of sovereignty is problematic. The modern state claims legal authority, shared with no other, within its territory. For example, no religious organisation can override the state's laws, and no privileged group can claim to be above the law. Thus, a principle of legal equality for citizens underpins the modern state, and this legal citizenship is normally extended to political citizenship, in that the government claims to be accountable to citizens and to rule with their consent. The right to challenge policies and laws is fundamental to citizenship, but it is accompanied by the duty to accept the resulting decision and obey it. However, in reality, few modern states are fully autonomous and free from the influence of powerful outside bodies. Many states voluntarily relinquish some of their sovereignty to an international body in order to reap the benefits of acting in concert with other states, and they lose some of their autonomy in the process. The European Union is the most obvious example; others include NATO (the North Atlantic Treaty Organisation) and the International Monetary Fund, both of which are dominated by the US (see Chapter 3). Other powers beyond the state may have no formal status but still limit the state's capacity to act. The ability of the international money markets to force the pound sterling out of Europe's Exchange Rate Mechanism in 1993 is one example of this. In the face of global power, simple notions of sovereignty and citizenship are no longer sustainable. Nation states have to co-operate to resist global pressures. This raises the question of whether citizenship and accountability can have any meaning in globalised politics.

QUESTION In the light of your reading, in what ways do you think sociology can contribute to the debate on the UK's membership of the European Monetary Union?

Further sources of tension are claims to nationhood and national self-determination. The break-up of empires and protected territories has created a world of nominally autonomous sovereign states. Within any political unit, there may be different social groups who claim to be a separate people, often on the basis of language or ethnic distinctions. It is a new step, however, to suggest that every people should regard itself as a nation (for example, Bosnian Muslims) and that every nation should have its own nation-state. This principle may be bloodily pursued when small new states are established, as in former Yugoslavia. This is a powerful force for fragmentation in a world where other forces are demanding cooperation and the pooling of sovereignty.

The making of the modern state

The growth of capitalism in Western Europe was associated with the rise of centralised, specialised state institutions employing increasingly complex and sophisticated forms of administration and social control that contrasted sharply with those of the feudal past. The decline of **feudalism** was associated with the emergence of militarily successful monarchs and the growth of towns as trading centres, which increased the importance of merchants and manufacturers. The independence of the town from feudal control introduced an economic dynamism that undermined the rural base of feudalism and paved the way for the emergence of new, economically powerful classes and a landless class of wage labourers.

By the sixteenth century in England and the seventeenth century in Europe, a centralised form of absolutist monarchy had emerged. Monarchs imposed laws and taxes on their territory, and adherence to these measures was ensured by their monopoly over the use of force. The central administration needed functionaries to run it, and initially these were powerful men in their own right, trusted allies of the monarch. Gradually, they were replaced by administrators whose power depended on their official position and not on their personal military power or wealth. Professional lawyers became important as codifiers of a recorded body of law, replacing the arbitrary rules imposed by nobles and local customary laws.

With this centralisation of power and rationalisation of politics, the state came to be the only legitimate authority in its territory, and its administration increasingly operated according to a set of principles and procedures. The trend towards rational administration by officials culminated in bureaucracy and the constitutional nation-state. As Poggi (1978, p.93) defines it:

> " There is a unity of the State's territory, which comes to be grounded as much as possible by a continuous geographical frontier that is militarily defensible. There is a single currency and a unified fiscal system. Generally there is a single 'national' language. … Finally there is a unified legal system that allows alternative juridical traditions to maintain validity only in peripheral areas and for limited purposes. "

However, this constitutional nation-state was not necessarily democratic: European states became fully democratic – that is, with votes for all citizens and free political association – only after the late nineteenth century. This development followed earlier struggles for representation in these states by the new economic groups, above all the bourgeoisie; merchants, traders and manufacturers. Such struggles occurred at different times and with varying degrees of success, but in all cases, the constitutional nation-state aided the rise of capitalism because it maintained peace, protected property rights and contracts, promoted foreign trade and regulated money as a means of exchange, all of which aided trade and the development of markets.

Feudalism
A social and political power structure prevalent in parts of Europe during the twelfth and thirteenth centuries. Power was fragmented and enjoyed by a number of authorities including the Church, the monarchy and local lords.

At the same time, the bourgeoisie could be threatened by this centralised state if it had no representation in it, and if the monarch tried to tax or regulate trade for his or her own purposes. In much of Europe, this led to struggles by the bourgeoisie (in alliance with other dissatisfied social groups) to gain political representation and resist absolutism.

The contrast between the English and German roads to capitalism and liberal democracy is significant. In England, the principles of representative liberal democracy were established gradually, as first the commercial landowners, then the industrialists and finally the working class won a voice in state affairs. Individual citizenship and the right to free political expression were slowly established. This evolution may have been punctuated by struggle and conflict, but it nonetheless stood in marked contrast to the German experience, where the political failure of the bourgeoisie enabled bureaucratic absolutism to continue until the end of the First World War. The central state made concessions to the growing working class and organised the growth of industrial capitalism, but democratic institutions and principles were weak and had extremely shallow roots. Thus, in Germany and elsewhere in Europe, government and capitalist development in the twentieth century were authoritarian and undemocratic, gaining their ultimate expression in **fascism**. In Germany, full liberal democracy was stabilised only after the Second World War, and in Portugal and Spain it was not established until after the downfall of the fascist regimes in the 1970s. However, there was no natural and inevitable link between liberal democracy and capitalism, even though it is now the dominant state form in Western Europe. Elsewhere in the world, the development of capitalism occurred in very different types of state.

Fascism
An authoritarian and undemocratic system of government that emerged in the first half of the twentieth century. It was characterised by extreme nationalism, militarism, and restrictions on individual freedom. The will of the people was held to be embodied in the leader (for example, Mussolini in Italy).

The democratic state

Apparently, there is universal agreement about the desirability of democracy: nearly all regimes claim democratic justification for their rule. (Even Stalin's Soviet Union had a constitution proclaiming rights and freedoms.) Indeed, towards the end of the 1980s, Fukuyama (1989b, p. 3–4) heralded 'the universalisation of Western liberal democracy as the final form of human government'. We were witnessing 'the end of history', moving beyond ideological conflict. The dominance of liberal democracy, partly fashioned by the defeat of fascism, was completed by the collapse of communism in Europe. For Fukuyama, because the West had won the Cold War, Western liberal democracy and free-market capitalism had been confirmed as the only viable and desirable systems.

The notion that there was a natural and unstoppable historical tide towards democracy ignores the bitter struggles through which democracy was won, and neglects the political revolutions and the wars that were fought to secure it. Furthermore, we should be wary of any account that links the fight for democracy to only one class. It has often been claimed that the natural proponents of liberal democracy were individual capitalists seeking to benefit from political and economic freedom. But the economic freedoms of liberalism were often valued more highly than democracy itself. When the working class seemed to be posing a threat, bourgeois classes were only too happy to support authoritarian regimes (as with General Pinochet in Chile). There was a long history of struggle by poor people for a more equal or socialistic democracy. The extension of democracy in Western European countries derived from a mixed set of pressures: bourgeois liberalism and socialist struggles were combined with democratic concessions by conservatives to avoid worse alternatives, such as revolution (Rueschemeyer et al., 1992; Moore, 1967).

Even when democracy was extended in the nineteenth century, electoral participation was limited, excluding groups such as the propertyless, women, foreigners and

Figure 8.2 Marching for the vote. The campaign for female suffrage divided male progressives of the time. In Britain, they feared that if it was limited rather than universal (as proved the case from 1918 to 1928), it might effectively increase support for the political right. In the US, they feared that extending support to women might jeopardise the struggle for black male suffrage.

(in the case of the US) slaves, as these were deemed to be insufficiently reliable and responsible to be given voting rights. Comprehensive, universal democracy – the participation of all adult members of society in the political process – was not put into practice in its full form until well into the twentieth century (Therborn, 1976). Male industrial workers won the right to vote through their own organised efforts, often backed by enlightened middle-class support or by an upper class that felt it advisable to make concessions. It took longer for other groups to gain voting rights. For example, in the UK, women did not gain the right to vote, and in some US states, it took the civil rights movements of the 1960s to win black people real political citizenship.

This extension of democratic rights meant, at least formally, that political power could be enjoyed by ordinary people. In principle, elections could be used to gain power and bring about social reform or even radical change. In Western Europe (if not in the US), this process of inclusion resulted in a new division between those with property and those without, and alignment between political parties and organised groups defending the capitalist status quo against those attempting to change it. Today, political alignments and party programmes are changing further, with new regional parties (such as the Scottish Nationalists) and issue parties (such as the Greens) securing many votes, even in systems where class-based parties have hitherto been dominant.

Globalisation, power and democracy

Two simultaneous and apparently contradictory trends are at the heart of modern politics: globalisation, and the fragmentation of states into smaller states and regions. These two trends present dangers and challenges, as we saw earlier in this chapter. One danger is that militant nationalism will lead to war over territory and the unilateral declaration of new states – as occurred in former Yugoslavia. At worst, fragmentation can involve racism, ethnic cleansing and territorial warfare. In contrast, we are also confronted with powerful links between societies and economies that override national boundaries. Many of the economic, political, military and ideological forces that shape our lives work across nations – and they are increasingly operating on a global scale. The challenge is to build an effective politics with enough global reach to gain control over those forces, whilst establishing some degree of accountability and democracy at the global level.

Globalisation itself is nothing new. Far-reaching empires have a long history. What is new is the scale and intensity of the global links, and the shrinking of space and time by means of low-cost electronic communications and air travel. Space, time and cost considerations have ceased to present barriers to business, and instant communications make it feasible to run global economic enterprises and conduct worldwide financial transactions.

CONNECTIONS For an account of the impact of globalisation on politics, see Chapter 3, pages 60–5.

David Held is one of the foremost writers on the politics of globalisation. He is committed to promoting a new form of politics and democracy that transcends the nation-state, but sees globalisation as presenting threats as well as opportunities. He summarises the features of globalisation as follows (Held, 1993a, pp. 38–9):

- Political, economic and social activities are rapidly becoming global in scope.
- The links between states and societies have greatly intensified, facilitated by high-speed communication.
- People, ideas and cultural products are moving around, merging and influencing each other more than ever before.
- Military and intelligence organisations are able to operate on a truly global scale with the help of high technology.
- Economic activities now involve globally integrated production and marketing, extending global economic activities far beyond trade (which has been world-wide for centuries).
- Transnational political organisations such as the UN, the IMF, the EU and NATO have transcended the nation-state and its sovereignty.
- With the end of the Cold War and the collapse of European communism, the world is no longer divided into opposing superpower blocs. New alliances will be required.

Simultaneous integration and fragmentation

When considering these features of globalisation, we must remember that global linkages may not necessarily lead to greater unity and uniformity. On the contrary, they may lead to decentralised fragmentation and the absence of a discernible new structure. As Held (1993a, p. 38) puts it:

"Globalisation can generate forces of both fragmentation and unification. By creating new patterns of transformation and change, globalisation can weaken old political and economic structures without necessarily leading to the establishment of new systems of regulation. Further, the impact of global and regional processes is likely to vary under different international and national conditions – for instance, a nation's location in the international economy, its place in particular power blocs, its position with respect to awareness of political difference as much as an awareness of common identity; enhanced international communications can highlight conflicts of interest and ideology, and not merely remove obstacles to mutual understanding. *"*

The forces that are driving globalisation are not creating uniformity or homogeneity at the national level. Rather, they are causing uneven development, greater inequality and new divisions. At the same time as workers are being interconnected through employment by the same multinational firm, they are becoming less able to act collectively to defend their interests, as their employer can always shift the work elsewhere. The forces for change are distant and seemingly uncontrollable: are there any forms of resistance to globalised power?

While economic resistance has become harder, paradoxically localism or small-scale nationalism has been facilitated by globalisation. For example, it is no longer necessary for small countries to be self-supporting and capable of their own defence. In the past, small and weak states had to rely on powerful neighbours or accept absorption into stronger states – hence, the formation of the UK. Now that economic growth and military security depend on transnational, even global relationships, it is possible for countries such as Scotland and Ireland to use the EU to escape political and economic domination by England. In the EU, they have access to funds and other benefits (and an independent Scotland would have a voice as a member state).

Parts of the former USSR, such the Baltic states, have been able to proclaim independence by virtue of their links with wider economic and military networks. However, any small state that goes it alone on the assumption that globalisation will give it security is likely to be sorely disappointed. Fragmentation may simply leave it vulnerable to new pressures for economic and military alliance with stronger states. Such alliances can often become rivals to others. Much will depend on the capacity of transnational organisations such as the United Nations to transform themselves into effective providers of security.

Global governance

Albert Einstein saw world government as the only means of creating global security in the age of nuclear weapons. Although this may not seem such a preposterous idea as it did during the Cold War, we are still far away from the realisation of a world government with the power to enforce peace.

However, if we think about the process of governing on a global scale (which is what is meant by the term global governance), it is clear that a great deal of international governance is actually taking place through a highly complex set of overlapping and interlocking institutions. Some of these have formal legal status, backed by the national governments that have signed up as members. For example, the World Trade Organisation exists to promote and enforce trade agreements, with the ultimate aim of removing all barriers to trade. Sanctions are applied to member countries that break its binding rules and agreements. In that sense, national governments have accepted the sovereignty of the WTO in the field of trade regulation – they are bound by WTO measures. Almost as importantly, as with governments, the World Trade Organisation is subject to organised pressure from those who oppose its policies. For example, individuals and new social movements came together (linked via the World Wide Web) to demonstrate against the WTO during its meeting in Seattle in 2000. Also, poorer nations can use international forums, such as the United Nations Conference on Trade and Development, to put their

Figure 8.3 The UN Security Council has 15 members of which five are permanent: the US, China, Russia, France and the UK. Any decisions made by the council require nine out of 15 concurring votes, including from all five permanent members, who can otherwise veto any action with which they do not agree.

case on trade. In that sense, normal politics does exist at the global level, as do elements of law and governance.

There is no common form or structure to the various elements of global governance. Some are truly representative at the international level, such as the United Nations, though even here the most powerful states hold sway through the UN Security Council. Other institutions have a global impact but are dominated by one superpower – for example, the World Bank and the International Monetary Fund. Other elements are not even institutions at all (such as arms control negotiations and summit meetings) and yet they have a worldwide impact. Non-governmental organisations such as the International Red Cross and Amnesty International are other important global actors.

It is impossible here to give a full account of the current scale and range of global governance. But one important point should be noted: global governance exists primarily because it is a necessity. Although shared ideals about peace, security and social development do play a part (especially in the United Nations), the primary reason for global governance has to do with the power of global forces and risks that need to be governed. It is generally in the interests of states to come together on issues such as trade and nuclear weapons, and on matters concerning 'global common goods' such as the environment. For example, an international convention on the moon and other celestial bodies agreed that no one nation could lay claim to the moon – even if it had got there first!

Thus, by all manner of complex means, global governance is taking place. Therefore an important question follows: if we have global governance, is there any possibility of a global democracy?

Towards a new cosmopolitan democracy?

Globalisation is challenging the ways in which nation states and democratic processes work, as the nation-state is finding itself less able to resist external events and forces. New local, regional and nationalist movements are challenging the nation-state from within and questioning its sovereignty over them. We see here the dual dynamic of internationalism and localism, linkage and fragmentation.

David Held (1993b) argues that dramatic changes in political institutions are needed to give some element of democracy in this new context, where aspects of monetary management, environmental questions, elements of security and new forms of communication cannot be controlled adequately by national governments. Held argues that transnational organisations such as the EU should be strengthened but also made much more democratically accountable through institutions such as the European Parliament. In addition, other cross-national institutions of this kind might need to be created (for example, in Southern Africa and Latin America), and international organisations such as the World Bank need to be run more democratically. Held also advocates that enhanced rights for citizens – civil, political, economic and social – be written into national constitutions and enforced by a strengthened body of international law.

Thus, Held has a vision of a cosmopolitan global democratic order, which would require 'the formation of an authoritative assembly of all democratic states and agencies – a reformed General Assembly of the United Nations, or a complement to it' (ibid., p. 15). This 'world parliament' would be 'an authoritative international centre for the consideration and examination of pressing global issues, e.g. health and disease, food supply and distribution, the debt burden of the Third World, the instability of the hundreds of billions of dollars that circulate the globe daily, ozone depletion, and the reduction of the risks of nuclear war' (ibid.)

Held's vision is an inspiring one, but it highlights our lack of control, as so much of the power and politics that affect our lives are now operating at the global level. To achieve Held's new global democratic order, states and their citizens will have to accept that their local and national interests can only be served by acting collectively in larger groupings. The challenge will be to sustain local and national identities at the same time as participating in larger international groupings and institutions. The alternative will be to cease trying to have any real influence over the global forces that shape our lives, and to face the danger of increasingly bitter local conflicts.

CONNECTIONS For a discussion of the problem of structure and agency, which frames the debate on how influential individuals can be in the face of global forces, see Chapter 1, pages 13–19.

Conclusion: new directions in political sociology

We have seen in this chapter that political sociology is currently being pulled in many directions. This is a reflection of two things: the flux and diversity of opinion within sociology today, and the rapid change and disorder in the contemporary world of politics. For both these reasons, it is impossible for political sociology to cling to simple models of power in society, and it is certainly wrong to focus on politics in any one society without considering the wider power structures beyond the nation-state. If, as sociologists, we are to retain our commitment to a just and democratic society, then we must not only rethink our analysis of the present but also renew our ideas about possible futures. This renewal of political analysis and vision needs to operate simultaneously at two very different levels. At the macro level, we must rethink our models of power structures in the context of globalisation and transnational politics, while at the micro level, we must acknowledge the diversity of power relations and the constant renewal of political struggles in a multitude of forms. Vicious, nationalist civil war is as much a part of contemporary politics as protests over animal rights. That does not mean that every power struggle is as strong or consequential as any other – we do not have to descend into total relativism about power structures. But sociology has to be acutely aware that in the contemporary world, as in the past, political identities must be defined, constructed and mobilised before they can have any impact.

Understanding a changing political world

Sociologists today face the challenge of understanding a highly complex and apparently fragmented political world. It never was enough to focus on social groups and their interests within one nation-state, but now we have to look even more at forms of power that cut across societies and shape them from outside – whether this power comes from international capitalism, military blocs or global commercial culture (Chapter 3 explores these issues). Even when we do focus on a single society to consider social groups and their politics, we find that many of the numerous issues and interests at stake are actually global in scope: for example, environmentalism, concern about nuclear weapons and the alleviation of poverty.

What we clearly cannot do is construct a simple model of the social structure of a society and deduce the interests and politics of social groups from that. The social world is much more complex than that – which makes things interesting and unpredictable, but also complicates the formulation of sociological explanations. One assumption of political sociology is overdue for revision: we cannot focus solely on power within single societies, taking for granted that these societies have boundaries that coincide with the legal nation-state. As already stated, the sovereign nation-state is a recent phenomenon, and power relations certainly do not stop at national boundaries. Unforgivably, sociology has neglected war and international power relations when describing societies – a remarkable failing in the face of the twentieth century's history of technologically sophisticated bloodshed. At the present, we are witnessing remarkable transformations in world politics following the collapse of communism, and new nation-states are struggling to establish themselves in a very disorderly world.

Even as the great political blocs broke up, there were powerful moves towards greater global interdependence and dominance through economic expansion, aided by the lowering of barriers to travel and communication. As already discussed, the huge forces for global interdependence are accompanied by a strong tendency towards fragmentation – and both seem invulnerable to effective political control by national governments.

Thus, political sociologists face the challenge of making sense of a dramatically changed political world – both within societies with diverse interests and struggles, and across societies with the forces of globalisation and fragmentation:

- New forms of politics within societies have redefined issues and political interests on a non-class basis. Many of these issues are global in scope, such as environmental concerns and opposition to racist regimes.

- We have witnessed a revival of forms of politics which liberals and Marxists both expected to wither away – racism, expansionist nationalism and fundamentalist religious movements.

- The interdependence of nations world-wide is increasing; global economic structures (including commercialised culture) are transcending national boundaries and increasing the need for global politics.
- Globalisation is giving rise to forms of power – economic, political and cultural – that lie beyond the effective control of nation states, let alone individual citizens.
- Communist regimes have collapsed and state socialism has been discredited, to the advantage of capitalism. Socialist politics based on trade unions and economic concerns has been seriously weakened in most capitalist societies.
- Global governance is expanding, but the extent to which this will ensure that peace and prosperity are evenly spread across the globe remains open to question. No matter how much sociologists resist simplistic models of power in social life, we must recognise that power is spread very unequally in today's world.

Chapter summary

- Political sociology addresses power in society.
- Power is an element of all social relations, but political sociology focuses on social divisions that have evolved into political divisions – especially, but not only, in respect of economic classes.
- This focus on social power must also show how power in society relates to power in the state institutions through which politicians govern.
- There has been a long debate between those who see power as highly concentrated (for example, in the hands of a dominant class) and those who see power as distributed widely across many different groups and settings.
- Political interests and action are not static and given. Ideologies and structural changes play an important part in defining and redefining political identities.
- Policies pursued by governments may have an impact on society that changes the lives and experiences of people, altering the social and political divisions in society.
- Political sociologists have attempted to trace and account for changes in the relationship between social class and politics, and to evaluate the historical and current significance of class politics and class-based political identities.
- A distinctive feature of contemporary politics has been the emergence of new social movements that appeal to bases of identity other than class location.
- The pace of change in the contemporary world is so great that we can expect a degree of flux in politics, with new issues and interests emerging.
- Power is both local and global. We can expect to see more transnational political initiatives, but also more diverse local struggles. The future of democracy and political accountability in this new world seems fragile and uncertain.

Questions to think about

- Which of the competing explanations of power do you find most convincing in the context of late modern societies? Justify your choice.
- Does the power of the state inevitably have to grow? In what ways can citizens seek to limit the power of the state over their lives?
- Is there any future for democracy in a globalised society? Develop an argument both for and against the survival of democracy.

 Investigating further

Foucault, Michel (1991) *Discipline and Punish*, Penguin.

> This is the classic exposition of Foucault's theory and is of relevance to a number of chapters in this book. If you can bear the graphic descriptions, try the first section (about 15 pages) of the first chapter. You could also try one of the later chapters, such as the first part of the chapter entitled 'The Means of Correct training' (pp. 170–84) or the last section of the chapter on 'Panopticism' (pp. 209–28).

Marx, Karl and Friedrich Engels (1998) *The Communist Manifesto*, Oxford University Press.

> This book offers a very short, clear and bracing introduction to some of Marx's key ideas and theories, although you should be aware that his ideas developed further in the course of his writing. Try Chapter 1, 'Bourgeois and Proletarians'.

Pierson, Chris (1996) *The Modern State*, Routledge.

> A useful introduction to what the state is, how it has developed and how it operates.

Dimensions of modern social life

Part 3 focuses on some of the remaining important aspects of society that have been researched and debated by sociologists. It begins with a couple of topics – the family and education – which you will have some familiarity with from the inside. It then moves on to look at a number of other key areas of social life – work, the media, crime, health and belief systems – which have attracted interesting and significant sociological argument.

These topics may not appear in the exact order in which they are covered in your course, but we have written these chapters in such a way that they can be read in the order that you, and your lecturers, prefer. Do follow up on our suggestions for further reading, both across chapters within this book, and in relation to other books. The more widely you read, the better an overview you will get and the more informed you will be when you have to develop your own arguments in class or in written assignments. You may particularly want to refer back to the chapters of Parts 1 and 2 in the process of your reading at this stage, as there are many connections to be made between these earlier chapters and the chapters of this section.

chapter **9**

Family life

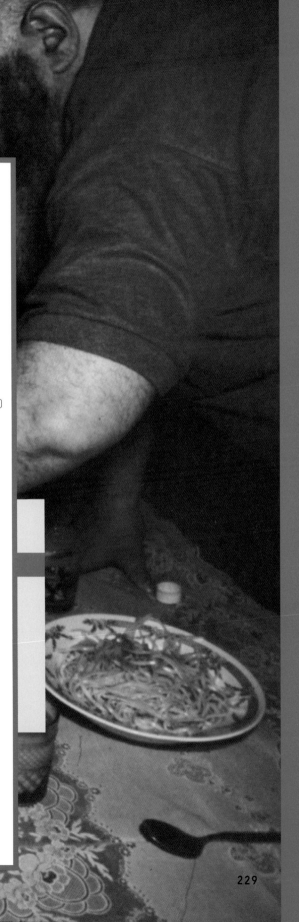

CHAPTER CONTENTS

Aims of the chapter

Most of us take living in a particular form of family for granted, assuming that most others have similar set-ups and experiences of family life. This chapter identifies the agencies at work in modern society that promote nuclear family living. Different perspectives on the virtues of this form of family are examined, and the assumptions about individual freedom and obligation underpinning these are explored. Our place within the family is located in the social institutions that have the power to shape and intervene in what is supposed to be the most intimate of social formations. Recent evidence about an increase in diversity in family living offers an opportunity for alternative theories of modern family life to be explored, and this is done in the chapter's concluding section.

By the end of the chapter, you should have an understanding of the following concepts:

- Nuclear family
- Extended family
- Reconstituted family
- Dysfunctional family
- Reserve army of labour

- Reproductive technologies
- Pro-welfarism
- Pro-natalism
- Liberationism

Introduction

Nuclear family
A household unit composed of a man and a woman in a stable marital relationship, and their dependent children.

Extended family
A group of kin comprising more than two generations.

Single-parent family
A household unit where only one parent, often the mother, resides with her children.

Nuclear family life is something that many people living in modern industrial societies take for granted, seeing it as normal or desirable. Although other forms of family – such as **extended families, single-parent families** and **reconstituted families** – are increasingly common, most people still hope or expect to live in nuclear families. Yet it is a form of family living that is culturally and historically specific. Historical and cross-cultural evidence testifies that, in other times and places, family lives were very different; indeed, some were so different that to use the word family to describe them almost renders the term meaningless. Anthropologists, whose interest is in making sense of the enormous cultural variations among the various societies of the world, usually talk about **kinship groups** rather than families. This is because about the only thing these groups have in common is that they are made up of people who are related by blood or marriage.

Before the rise of modernity in Europe, the nuclear family did not occupy the privileged position it tends to be given today. Among property-owning groups, there was concern about inheritance and transmission of property and privileges, and about the social standing of their 'house'. For all classes, the family was an important economic unit, involved in the production of goods and services upon which survival depended. But the nuclear family was closely embedded in the community, and not regarded as separate from the rest of society.

Ariès (1973) points out that from the fifteenth to the seventeenth centuries, the family did not occupy a special place in people's hearts and minds. People married and had children, but marriage tended to be seen as an alliance, important for the

Reconstituted family
A family unit that includes one or more step-parents as a consequence of divorce and marriage.

Kinship groups
An anthropological term referring to groups who are related by marriage or blood.

Conjugal relationship
The relationship between husband and wife in marriage.

connections it established with others rather than being the central relationship in people's lives. Marriage did not have the religious importance it later acquired; as Ariès puts it, 'sexual union, when blessed by marriage, ceased to be a sin, but that was all' (ibid., p.345). Nor did parents' lives revolve around children. In many European countries, it was common practice to send one's children away at the age of seven or so to be apprenticed. They would live for up to seven years in another house, where they would perform menial chores, be instructed in manners and morals, and perhaps learn a trade. This was regarded as a more suitable preparation for adulthood than being cosseted in the bosom of one's own family. Thus, child rearing was not the prerogative of the child's biological parents. Nor were families isolated from the wider community.

Ariès argues that the integration of the family into community life was reflected in housing, particularly that of comfortably-off citizens in towns. Daily life centred on a series of social and business encounters, so that business life, social life and family life overlapped. Houses sheltered a shifting population of servants, apprentices, friends, employees, clergy and clerks, as well as parents and children themselves, rooms were used interchangeably for eating, sleeping, entertaining and arranging business deals. Many people slept together in one room – parents, children, servants and friends alike. The home was definitely not a private place reserved for family and intimate friends; nor was the family a private and privileged unit devoted to the **conjugal relationship** between husband and wife and the rearing of their children.

We can summarise this by saying that nuclear families at that time were less privatised – less detached from the wider society – than they are in modern societies. Since home and workplace were often one and the same before industrialisation, child-rearing groups overlapped with groups concerned with production. Children grew up and worked and played alongside a range of kinfolk, acquaintances and friends. Socialisation was a natural by-product of community life, rather than a specialised activity taking place in isolation from the public sphere.

In pre-industrial Europe, then, family life was significantly different from family life now. Moreover, anthropological studies of tribal societies show that there are many different ways in which family life can be organised (Fox, 1967, p. 40). Edholm (1982, p. 177) summarises this evidence:

> " There are in all known societies social units concerned with childbearing, with sexual activity and with the daily activities of eating and sleeping; but these social arrangements differ from one society to the next – in terms of the composition of the largest cohesive groups, the composition of the domestic group, the links with the rest of the society, the authority patterns and division of labour within the 'family' – and these differences may often be dramatic.
>
> The family, particularly the nuclear family, can be seen, through comparative analysis, as just one very specific means of organising the relationships between parents and children, males and females. It is not, as has so often been claimed, some kind of 'natural', instinctive and 'sacred' unit. "

Because there are so many family forms, we need to investigate why nuclear families became the norm in industrial capitalist societies. After the Second World War, the most popular explanation of this was the structural–functionalist theory developed by Talcott Parsons (1902–79). Cheal (1991, pp. 3–4) calls this approach 'standard American sociology', because its 'domination of the American discipline in a formative period of growth meant that it had deep and lasting effects. … The influence of standard American sociology also extended far outside the US, since its rise coincided with the high point of American prestige in the period immediately after the Second World War.'

BOX 9.1 Functionalism and the family

Functionalism maintains that the persistence of any social institution can be explained in terms of the benefits it provides for both individuals and the society in which they live. Functionalists thus believe that families perform vital functions for their members, and for society. Furthermore, when a society's structure changes over time, its key institutions are reshaped to ensure that the society's needs continue to be met. Functionalist theorists of the family have thus been most interested in the 'fit' between the family and society. They argued that the reason why modern industrial societies are characterised by nuclear family life is that this form of family best satisfies the particular needs of an industrial economy.

CONNECTIONS An account of functionalism as represented in the work of Durkheim is provided in Chapter 17, pages 470–6.

Talcott Parsons: the fit between the nuclear family and industrial society

The theory most often associated with the idea of a fit between industrial society and the nuclear family is that of Parsons (1954,1955). His argument – that the nuclear family system is uniquely well adapted to the needs of industrial society – has two parts. First, he suggested that the economic differentiation (many different occupations, with different incomes and lifestyles attached) that characterises industrial societies is incompatible with the extended family but ideally served by the nuclear. If the family is restricted to a small nuclear group with a single primary breadwinner who is also head of the family, potential conflicts between members of an extended family working in different jobs are avoided. Such conflicts might be over where the family should live, or emerge from differences in incomes and lifestyles associated with occupations. Parsons suggested that only the nuclear family system can eliminate economic differentiation within the larger family and thus prevent the competitive elements of industrial wage-labour from undermining family solidarity. At the same time, the nuclear family is a small enough unit to be geographically and economically mobile, as an industrial economy demands.

BOX 9.2 Nuclear family relationships and identities

To consider that the nuclear family is the best way of organising domestic, sexual and parent-child relationships means prioritising:

- Heterosexuality over other sexual orientations and identities.

- Coupledom over remaining unattached.

- Monogamy over having more than one sexual partner.

- Marriage over cohabitation.

- Parenthood over childlessness.

- A preference for biological parenthood leading to social parenthood (the mother and father being responsible for the upbringing of their children) over other sorts of child-rearing.

- Waged work for the husband and domestic (unpaid) work, particularly mothering, for the wife over other domestic divisions of labour.

- Households comprising only parents and their children over other sorts of domestic arrangements.

Public sphere
Based on the notion of a public/ private dichotomy, this refers to the arena outside the home and family, including activities associated with paid work.

The second part of his argument concerns the need to resolve the conflict between the values that underpin economic and public activities in industrial societies and those which characterise family relationships. According to Parsons, families are characterised by values such as ascription (an emphasis upon who people are) and particularism (priority for special relationships). For example, it is expected that parents should love and care for their own offspring above all others, regardless of how successful or attractive they are by public standards. Parsons argued that ascription and particularism are unacceptable and harmful in the public sphere. For example, at work, hiring, firing and promotion are supposed to take place according to individual merit only. In other words, for Parsons, the efficient operation of the public sphere needs the values of achievement and universalism – the opposite of those that characterise kinship relations.

Domestic sphere
Sometimes referred to as the private sphere, this refers to the arena of activity associated with the household and family life.

Disruption would occur at work if kin and occupational obligations overlapped – for example, if one member of the family was a supervisor and another a labourer in the same firm. Such conflicts are avoided, Parsons argued, by (1) segregating the nuclear family from other kin, and (2) segregating the nuclear family from the **public sphere** (except for the father as the principal breadwinner). Intrusion of family values into work is thus avoided, and work values do not disrupt the solidarity of the family; people do not have constantly to choose between loyalty to kin and the impersonal standards demanded by their occupational roles.

CONNECTIONS The consequences of this separation for women was first explored in Chapter 2, pages 39–40. See also Chapter 6, pages 141–3.

Instrumental
In relation to the family, the term used by Parsons (1954,1955) to describe the husband's role of making material provision for his family.

In addition, Parsons argued that the nuclear family performs two main functions for its members – the socialisation of children and the 'personality stabilisation' (or tension management) of adults. Resources are provided by the husband/father, while the wife/mother runs the **domestic sphere**, caring for the emotional needs of family members. Parsons described the male function as **instrumental** and that of the female as **expressive**. This gendered division is based on a presumption about women's 'natural abilities': 'The particular tasks assigned to the sexes are, in Parsons' opinion, due to the primacy of the relationship between a small child and its mother. The special nature of that relationship, he claimed, is a consequence of the unique capacities of women for bearing and nursing children' (Cheal, 1991, p. 6).

QUESTION How convincing do you find Parsons' case for a fit between the isolated nuclear family and the needs of modern industrialised society? Give reasons for your answer, citing any counter-arguments you can think of.

Expressive
In relation to the family, the term used by Parsons (1954,1955) to describe the wife's role of catering to the emotional needs of her family.

Clearly this is both a modernist theory – it specifies how family life should be lived – and an idealised model of family life. We all know that families do not always conform to this model, and, of course, Parsons did too. Wives are battered, marriages break down, single parenthood is becoming more and more common, children are unhappy, mistreated and abused, and so on. But Parsons was above all else a modernist. He was concerned to specify, through his theorising, the sort of family it is worth aiming at because of its potential benefits for individuals and for society. So what happens when particular families fall short of the ideal, and what should we do to prevent such an occurrence? Nuclear family supporters in the Parsonian tradition advocate outside intervention, both to prop up ailing families and to prevent others going the same way. Their

Figure 9.1 Supporters of the nuclear family often point to the adverse impact on children of divorce. Research has found that marital breakdown is more likely to plunge children into poverty than a change in their parents' employment status.

enthusiasm for intervention reflects the main aim of the project of modernity – the application of theoretical knowledge to achieve improvement in people's lives. The development of family therapy theories and the establishment of powerful social service agencies to assist families 'in danger' are prime examples of the modernist project as it affects family life.

In order to make sense of the kinds of institutional intervention that have become part of modern family life, it is helpful to turn to the work of French historian and philosopher Michel Foucault (1926–84) and his characterisation of modern society.

Michel Foucault: discourses and social life

As we saw in the previous chapter, according to Foucault, human societies are best understood as places in which discourses – forms of knowledge that circulate in the process of social interaction – promote certain kinds of people and behaviour. For example, family discourses tend to favour the nuclear family as the most appropriate model of family life. Human societies also develop regulatory apparatuses to police and discipline their members to conform to these discourses, such as when homosexual activity is criminalised by the justice system because it is seen as a threat to the primacy of the nuclear family. For Foucault, the most important discourses in modern societies were those concerned with constituting and regulating the body in prescriptive ways, identifying, for example, approved and forbidden expressions of sexuality.

Foucault's materialist focus had two main features: first, he examined the kinds of discourse that have emerged in modern times to control the individual body. These discourses are concerned with 'anatomo-politics' – power over the individual body.

Second, he looked at discourses that exercise power over bodies in the aggregate, as a mass of bodies occupying a physical and social space. These discourses are concerned with the 'bio-politics' of a population, that is, the control of large numbers of individuals.

Foucault's perspective on social life is thus fundamentally concerned with power. Prevailing forms of knowledge or discourse exercise power over us because they provide us with the language we use to think about the world, and thereby 'know' about it. These discourses constitute us (make us what we are and what we think) because we have to use their vocabularies to make sense of events and phenomena. 'For Foucault we know or see what our language permits, because we can never apprehend or know 'reality' outside of language. Nothing occurs outside the language. … Different societies and different historical periods have different (languages) and therefore different realities' (Turner, 1987, pp. 10–11).

These discourses constitute our identity and construct our behaviour. That is, they define who we become as persons, and we live our lives in the way we do because our actions have been subjected to their determining influence. It is important to recognise that discourses do not suppress, deny or prevent ways of living. It is not a matter of 'Thou shalt not' but 'Thou shalt'. Disciplinary devices (or apparatuses such as the education system) promote discourses, and how successfully a discourse shapes our identity and constructs our behaviour reflects the regulatory power of these devices. Finally, the outcome, in terms of identities (who we are) and behaviour (what we do), gives power to particular groups in society, whose interests are best served by these specific forms of behaviour.

From this perspective, we can look at the development and characteristics of modern family life by considering three questions:

- What are the forms of knowledge that constitute family identities and construct family behaviour?
- What are the disciplinary devices used to promote these discourses?
- Who gains from their influence/power in society?

To answer these questions, we have to identify the definitions of the 'normal' family that prevail at any time, how these versions of normality are enforced and who are the beneficiaries of these discourses about 'normal' family workings. In the UK since the Second World War, two discourses in particular have emerged that promote nuclear

---

BOX 9.3 The Child Support Act 1991

The Child Support Act … [established] an agency to take responsibility for setting and enforcing maintenance payments for children … and … determining levels of maintenance according to a fixed formula. Thus the Act shifted child maintenance away from a system of judicial discretion to a system of administrative procedures, with the aim of producing 'consistent and predictable results'. … What these proposals do is to try and reproduce traditional family and gender relationships after couples have separated. The separated family is treated almost as if the relationship had not broken down at all. Thus, the men are to fulfil their traditional role as financial provider and the women are to fulfil their traditional role as mother. … In a way the government is trying to 'turn back the clock' and make policy on the assumption that the traditional gender division of labour within the family can continue even when other aspects of the family, such as marriage, have begun to disappear.

Source: Millar (1999), pp. 253–4.

family life. First, the 'medicalisation of family life' suggests that the family has been subject to intervention and constitution by medicine and medical practitioners. Second, 'family policy' refers to the state-instituted practices that various governments have used to construct a family life of which they approve (see Box 9.3 for an example). To understand their contemporary significance, we first need some historical background.

Pre-modern family life and religious discourses

Historically, religious discourses have played a significant role in constituting family members and constructing particular forms of behaviour in families, and religion has been particularly important in discourses on female sexuality. An example of the role of religion in this respect was the 'witchcraft craze' in Medieval Europe. According to Turner (1987, p. 86), this was a device to regulate the behaviour of women, and the attack on women as witches was principally 'a critique of their sexuality'. 'Women were closely associated with witchcraft, because it was argued that they were particularly susceptible to the sexual advances of the devil. …Women were seen to be irrational, emotional and lacking in self-restraint; they were especially vulnerable to satanic temptation.'

Turner argues that attempts to regulate female sexuality through religious discourse have, in the case of Western Europe, to be understood in the context of concerns about managing private property and ensuring its continuity. Thus, for the land-owning aristocracy, the point of marriage was to produce a male heir to the property of the house-hold. Since child mortality was common, women had to be more or less continuously pregnant during their marriage to guarantee a living male heir. Furthermore, this heir had to be legitimate, if disputes over inheritance were to be avoided. This legitimacy could only be ensured by the heads of households marrying virgins and ensuring the chastity of their wives for the duration of the marriage. Equally, daughters had to be sexually pure if they were to be eligible for marriage to other property-holding families. Such marriages were prompted solely by the need to produce children and had none of the elements of eroticism and sexual compatibility of contemporary marriages.

In pre-modern Europe, these interests were reflected in the character of marriages. They were private, arranged contracts that could be easily dissolved in the event of child production being compromised by the woman's infertility or infidelity. With the entry of the Church into marriage arrangements, different definitions of marriage emerged. Life-long marriages were demanded, but with a concern to regulate sexuality, particularly the sexuality of women.

> " Since the Church regarded marriage as a necessary evil against fornication, the Church argued that married couples should not enjoy their sexual relationship, but regard it merely as a system of reproduction. The Church also established a rigid set of conventions regarding sexual positions, homosexuality, perversions and various forms of deviance. Women came to be seen increasingly as a major threat to the stability of these social relations of marriage, since the Church regarded the woman as the weaker partner. It was assumed that the woman would be more susceptible to temptation and deviance. The Church therefore provided a powerful ideology for controlling women through such institutions [regulatory apparatuses] as the confession " (ibid., p. 96).

As Foucault suggested, we have to understand such discourses as being mainly concerned with the management of the body: 'Because the government of the body is in fact the management of sexuality, the issue of regulation is in practice the regulation of the sexuality of women' (ibid., p. 98). Furthermore, both bio-politics and anatomo-politics are being exercised here: such discourses were designed to manage bodies en masse (in order to control population growth) and individual bodies by controlling individuals' sexual desires.

Control of the body became even more important with the emergence of modern urban society. However, the secularisation of such societies involved a transfer of discursive power (the power to formulate discourses). While body management and the control of female sexuality remained priorities in nineteenth-century societies, a change in the basis of disciplining women took place. Medical discourse became the main medium for this, defining women as potentially sexually subversive and therefore in need of regulation. Rather than sanctity and purity being the main guards against sexual deviance, it became a matter of ensuring women's 'health' by controlling and disciplining their base and dangerous natural propensities through medical intervention.

CONNECTIONS Chapter 15, pages 418–29, provides an account of the decline of religious influence over social mores, a process called secularisation.

Modern family life and medical discourses

Foucault used the nineteenth-century notion of the 'hysterical woman' as evidence of the emerging dominance of medical discourse at that time (Turner, 1987, pp. 88–9):

> " The hysterical woman, rather like the 19th century masturbating child and sexual pervert, was a product of the all-pervasive ideology of sex, which came to cultural predominance in the 19th century. For Foucault, the discourse of sexuality produced the hysterical woman as the object of a detailed medical discourse and a medical practice . "

Supposedly originating in female physiology (the term hysteria is derived from the Greek word *hystera* or uterus), the condition gave rise to weeping, screaming, fainting, an arched rigid body, temper loss and so on. According to nineteenth-century medicine, this illness was brought on by lack of family membership, and thus was typically suffered by young single women, divorced women, widows and women who pursued careers instead of experiencing normal sexual fulfilment in a stable marriage. The implication of this illness was that women could only be healthy if they lived 'normal' family lives – being sexually connected to a man in a marriage whose aim was child production. A similar 'illness', nymphomania, befell women who pursued sexual satisfaction outside marriage. Such medical construction acted to promote family life. To avoid the danger of ill-health, it was argued, women should use their sexuality only to achieve pregnancy inside marriage and should not delay this goal by, for example, pursuing educational qualifications or establishing a career prior to motherhood. In this way, a particular way of life was defined as normal and all alternatives as deviant. Medical discourse provided the vocabulary for, and medical practitioners acted as the regulators of, these definitions, and the principal beneficiaries of their enforcement were men.

Twentieth-century changes in the position of women – achieved through an increase in employment opportunities, growth in the provision of education and, particularly, the spread of contraception, enabling women to have greater control over their fertility – altered this picture. Despite such changes, medical discourse still constructs family life and promotes a definition of womanhood that has strong echoes from the past. As we have said, the power of discourses lies in the definitions they promote. They do not simply intervene in an already existing reality, they also construct this reality – things become what the discourse defines them as being. So medical intervention in family life is important not just because it is concerned with returning a family to a state of health, but also because it defines what families are, or should be. This is why families need professional intervention. Because of their monopoly over medical knowledge, it is the experts' view that counts, not that of the patients. Two good examples of contemporary medical regulation of the family are the 'medicalisation of motherhood' and 'family therapy' – what Morgan (1985) calls the 'medicalisation of marriage'.

Reproductive technologies and the medicalisation of motherhood

According to Stanworth (1987), there are four kinds of contemporary technological intervention in the process of human reproduction. The first concerns contraception – fertility control. The second concerns the management of labour and childbirth, and the explosion of technical intervention methods associated with the hospitalisation of the process. Third, intervention to monitor the progress of the foetus has become routine in the ante-natal period. Fourth, the most controversial kind of intervention involves technologies designed to rectify infertility and promote pregnancy.

At first glance, these technological advancements would seem to be of considerable benefit to women, allowing them a real chance to influence and control their biology. But, as Stanworth points out, the interventions enabled by such technological developments have had the opposite effect, as they have placed the management of motherhood securely in the hands of professionals, the great majority of whom are men. As she puts it (ibid., p. 13):

> " New technologies help to establish that gynaecologists and obstetricians 'know more' about pregnancy and about women's bodies than women do themselves. When the majority of the profession is male, it is perhaps not surprising that medical practitioners have been attracted to techniques that enable them to brush aside a woman's own felt experience of menstruation, pregnancy and birth. "

In Foucauldian terms, the medical discourse that defines what it sees as healthy/ normal reproduction dictates how pregnancy and childbirth should proceed for women by constructing motherhood in a particular way. It also constructs pregnancy and childbirth in ways that benefit the (predominantly male) medical profession. This discourse of biological motherhood goes hand in hand with a view of normal women as mothers. It is assumed that all women instinctively desire motherhood – 'woman' equals 'mother' in this discourse, as it has traditionally done in **naturalistic** family theory – and healthy mothering has to take place within a normal family context. In effect, the discourse says that married women must be mothers while unmarried women must not. So, although married women who deny their maternal instincts are defined as selfish, deviant or clearly unwell, the medical promotion of healthy motherhood is selective (ibid., p. 15):

Naturalistic
Pertains to nature, for example a naturalistic theory is one that explains human behaviour in terms of natural instincts and drives.

> " The idea of maternal instinct is sometimes used to override women's expressed wishes with regard to childbearing – discouraging young married women from sterilisation or abortion, for example – while denying single women the chance to have a child. In other words, a belief in maternal instinct coexists with obstacles to autonomous motherhood – obstacles, that is, to motherhood for women who are not in a stable relationship to a man. According to ideologies of motherhood, all women want children; but single women, lesbian women (and disabled women) are often expected to forgo mothering 'in the interests of the child' . "

By such means, the so-called liberating potential of reproductive technologies serves to reinforce a particular view of family life as normal, and a particular view (ibid., p.4) of a normal woman as a married mother:

> "On the one hand, [reproductive technologies] have offered women a greater technical possibility to decide if, when and under what conditions to have children; on the other, the domination of so much reproductive technology by the medical profession and by the State has enabled others to have an even greater capacity to exert control over women's lives."

One powerful critique of reproductive technology concentrates on the power that medical manipulation confers on men. Medical control of fertility has become an essential modern device whereby women continue to be regulated by men. From this point of view, contemporary medical discourse and intervention operate in the same kind of regulatory way as did older religious discourses, and in the interests of the same beneficiaries.

QUESTIONS What is your own moral position on the use of reproductive technologies such as test-tube babies, cloning and surrogate motherhood? How does this moral position fit into a sociological view?

Family therapy and the medicalisation of marriage

Given the definitions of normality and deviance that successive family discourses have promoted, it is unsurprising that twentieth-century medical discourse has attempted to construct marriage in a similar way. Though the language has changed – it now deals with health and sickness rather than virtue and sinfulness – the aims have not. The 'discursive injunction' is still to be happily married and to receive emotional fulfilment from family life. However, in medical discourse, failure to secure these benefits is evidence of pathology, and this requires medical intervention to restore health. The medicalisation of marriage thus uses medical discourse to define marital normality and deviance. The best-known version of this intervention is family therapy.

Thus, intervention in the sexual relationship of an adult couple presumes a definition of normal sexuality that is reinforced by the intervention. This almost always means promoting genital contact between heterosexuals, leading to orgasm. Inability to achieve orgasm is usually defined as a dysfunction. Defining this as a problem springs from a normative ideal that sex should be equally pleasurable to both participants. Such an ideal, however, is culturally and historically specific. Indeed, the whole basis of such a discourse rests on an essentially modernist assumption that marital sexual relations are capable of being improved with the assistance of knowledgeable experts. Furthermore, it is also assumed that there are objective standards by which the sexual performance of particular individuals can be judged. Notions such as 'sexual adequacy' and 'reproductive competence' abound in family therapy discourse and illustrate Foucault's insistence that such discursive definitions should be understood as promoting and prescribing the lives and identities of human beings. In seeking to match the ideals of sexual adequacy, family members reinforce the power of the family therapy discourse and the institutions and individuals that promote it. Further promotion of this ideal is carried out by the state when formulating family policy.

CONNECTIONS For another view of Foucault's approach, see Chapter 13, pages 365–6, where you will be introduced to such concepts as surveillance.

The state and family life: the politics of family policy

A significant element in the history of the British family in the second half of the twentieth century was the state's endeavours to promote the nuclear family. Though Parsons expected that people's lives would conform to the nuclear pattern because of the needs of the system, historical analysis testifies that the script he wrote has not always been acted out by family actors. As a result, state intervention has increasingly been necessary to prop up the nuclear family. The activities of the state in areas such as family life, health care, education and so on are summarised in the term the **welfare state** – that is, those areas of social life in which governments take some degree of responsibility for the well-being of their citizens. In the UK, the welfare state has been the main means of intervening in and regulating family life. How has this been done?

Since the Second World War, propping up the nuclear family via welfare policies has taken two distinct forms, representing two different political philosophies. Between 1945 and 1979, a consensus prevailed among successive Conservative and Labour administrations about the need for state intervention in family life to achieve as much equality of provision as possible for families living in unequal material and social circumstances. This consensus is known as welfarism. After 1979, however, the state attempted to support the nuclear family for very different political purposes. Instead of targeting the needy, Thatcherite promotion of the nuclear family was motivated by a desire to reward individualism, self-help, enterprise and initiative, thereby reducing the state's involvement in people's lives. This is known as New Right thinking.

Welfare state
A system of government where the state is responsible for providing its citizens with a wide range of welfare benefits.

Welfarism, 1945–79

Although a radical left-wing Labour government came to power in 1945 (the prime minister was Clement Attlee), successive Conservative and Labour governments in the 1950s, 1960s and 1970s practised policies that could broadly be described as centrist or middle-of-the-road. Putting aside left and right-wing radicalism, these governments pursued essentially similar political agendas, with welfarism as a central element. The aim was to use welfare state provision to promote and practise benevolence – intervening in people's lives to achieve a more equal distribution of life chances among a population made up of unequally advantaged groups. Welfarism was thus based on the view that impoverishment and disadvantage were not matters of individual failure but socially constructed conditions characteristic of a stratified society that needed state intervention to ameliorate them. The use of welfarism to prop up nuclear family life was believed to be the most effective way to reach those most in need of support.

Anti-welfarism: the New Right, 1979–90

With the election of Margaret Thatcher's radical Conservative administration in 1979, a different orthodoxy, echoing nineteenth-century liberal thinking, was born. The New Right saw the use of the welfare state to promote welfarism as costly, unnecessary and morally repugnant. They believed that welfarism was financially crippling the successful (the able) in order to feather-bed the lives of disadvantaged (less able) members of society. For Thatcherites, individuals were responsible for their own successes or failures, and it was no business of the government to intervene to equalise the rewards given to citizens for their abilities and hard work. Human beings were unequally talented, and the success of a modern economy depended on the industrious and able receiving their just deserts. Since welfare state spending depended on taxation, and since taxation was government-sponsored theft of individuals' private property, Thatcherism attempted to 'roll back the frontiers of the state' and reduce its impact on people's lives.

For the New Right, the nuclear family was still an essential political instrument, since it was the most effective means of pursuing anti-welfarist, radical conservative ends. The radical right prioritised individualism and wished to dismantle the **nanny state** and the 'dependency culture', thus freeing individuals to take responsibility for their own lives and the lives of those for whom they had a moral duty to care – children, the non-hospitalised sick and infirm, and the elderly. The family was of crucial political import-ance in this process of deregulation by the government. Such a philosophy was neatly summarised by Thatcher's infamous assertion that 'There is no such thing as society. There are only individuals, and their families' (cited in Kingdom, 1992).

Nanny state
A pejorative term used to describe the welfare state, implying that the welfare system is overprotective and does not encourage individual responsibility.

BOX 9.4 The New Right perspective on welfarism

Throughout the second half of this century the state has seized control of all those essential services which socialists have tricked us into defining as 'wel-fare'. Sooner or later, this bizarre system will have to be replaced by more efficient arrangements, ones better suited to a free society. I believe that we shall look back on the welfare state with the same contempt with which we now view slavery or feudalism ...

Even if we could afford it in economic terms, its cost in moral and psychological damage to the population is intolerable. The 'hand-out culture' of state wel-fare, with its exaltation of rights without responsibilities and its celebration of egalitarian envy, is turning hard-working people into conformist yet ungovernable underclass serfs. It is paralysing the spirit of enterprise.

Worse still, it is subverting our freedom and corrupting our most precious institutions –

marriage and the family fore-most among them. It is proving a more destructive 'enemy within' of the values of our civilisation than national or boleshevik socialism ever were from the outside ...

A small and changing minor-ity of people needs safety-net support from time to time. The vast majority does not. We should turn the whole machinery of state welfare over, gradually and by voluntary choice, to the market and voluntary agencies. Envisage wholesale liberal-isation and straightforward privatisation of education, health care, housing, pensions, un-employment insurance, income protection, postal services, tran-sport and most local government services. All these functions would be taken over by the commercial insurance industry, mutual associations, trade unions, profit and non-profit schools, colleges, hospitals, and clinics, and other specialist com-

panies competing in a free market of welfare.

As far as the bulk of the population is concerned, the state's role should be restricted to regulation. Enormous reduc-tions in taxation should be possible. Most people could look after themselves and their families, with prudent self-reliance, out of their own moral and economic resources, insur-ing against misfortune, planning for their future, choosing freely among competing suppliers of real welfare.

For those – very few – people who are incapable from time to time of looking after themselves and their families from their own resources, the state should remain responsible. This does not require the massive machinery of the welfare state. Modest help organised through the tax system and by means of small-scale organisations at local level, mak-ing maximum use of voluntary agencies, would be sufficient. ▶

In order to minimise dependency, loans should be preferred to grants, and help should not be provided except in return for effort – workfare, participation in training, therapy where appropriate.

The whole system should be based on need – which should be demonstrated and closely monitored – rather than on fictitious rights. The exclusive objective and justifying mission of the programme should be to restore clients as quickly as possible to self-reliance. The welfare state, by contrast, with its stage army of rights-obsessed social workers, positively encourages unemployment, single-parenthood, spurious invalidity, fraud, criminality, and underclass dependency.

Source: David Marsland, *The Times Higher Education Supplement*, 17 May 1996, p. 5.

Hence, although New Right supporters were profoundly committed to promoting the nuclear family, they claimed that true freedom for family members involved reducing welfarism as much as possible. This was because welfarism was seen as positively destructive of the family, in that it involved the regulation of what individuals should rightly decide and arrange for themselves.

Three criticisms can be made of the New Right perspective. First, despite the 'freedom for the individual' version of modernity reflected in New Right discourse, it would seem that freedom for individual women to do other than perform family functions was a freedom too far. The emphasis of the New Right on the traditional family restricted the choices available to married women. Second, from a Foucauldian point of view, New Right thinking, while claiming to liberate individuals, was in fact a new form of regulation, prescription and control. It was a discourse that used the withdrawal of state provisions as a disciplinary device to make us feel we should live in nuclear families and fend for ourselves. Finally, we should note the important link with economic, laissez-faire, individualistic thinking here. 'Fending for ourselves' not only meant taking moral and social responsibility for our kin. It also insisted on the virtue of using privately financed welfare provision to help us meet those obligations.

Hence, although the aims of these two political discourses – Welfarism and anti-welfarism – were very different, both were committed to the Parsonian nuclear family model as an effective instrument to serve their respective political ends. Despite their contrasting aims, in regulatory practice both discourses attempted to reproduce exactly the same kind of family members and the same kind of family lives. Underpinning both types of policy making on the family was the distinction between Parsons' expressive and instrumental roles, sometimes called the private and the public. This distinction assumed that male family members would perform breadwinning functions, and that women's natural destiny was to take responsibility for the private domestic, familial aspect of human life. As Helen Crowley (1992, p. 70) puts it:

" In the process of slow but profound change traced by the emergence of the modern social formation out of the pre-industrial, agrarian society it replaced, the lines of demarcation between the work undertaken by women and the work undertaken by men were drawn and re-drawn, and gradually emerged in a division of the social world into public and private spheres, with women's work being firmly positioned in the latter. One of the dominant explanations for the positioning of women in the private sphere of the family and men in the public sphere of work and polity was, and remains, that women are 'naturally' suited to mothering and caring. "

The dominance of such naturalistic assumptions in both welfarist and New Right discourses in clearly illustrated in examples of family policies from both eras – post-war 'pro-natalism' and 1980s government policies designed to promote care in the community.

Pro-natalism

Pro-natalism
The view that everything should be done to encourage wives to have children.

Pro-natalism emerged as a significant discourse in the 1930s, when it was feared that the birth rate had gone into terminal decline. Although this fear proved unfounded, it gave rise to a concerted effort to promote child production, especially in the 1940s and 1950s, with profound consequences for the lives of women (Cheal, 1991, p.58).

> " The language of pro-natalism included unquestioned linkages between concepts of 'woman' and 'mother', and between 'maternity' and the 'family'. In the immediate post-war period the importance of locating maternity within a stable family environment was strengthened by popular psychological writings about the positive consequences of 'attachment' and the negative consequences of 'separation' between mother and child. New anxieties about 'maternal deprivation', which drew upon psychoanalytical research, reinforced beliefs about the proper location of women as mothers within the family – and not working for wages outside the home. "

Much of the theoretical backing for this idea came from the work of John Bowlby (1965, 1971, 1975), who produced a number of studies on how human beings form attachments, and how they experience grief and loss. Bowlby suggested that from infancy human beings have a predisposition to form a deep and overwhelmingly important attachment to one person – and that person will probably be the mother. Disruption of the child's relationship with the mother by prolonged separation will produce anxiety in the child and an effect similar to grief for the loss of a loved one. This experience may colour the child's later emotional make-up, and may interfere with his or her ability to form emotionally stable relationships. Thus, **maternal deprivation** in childhood was believed to have severe and lasting effects.

Maternal deprivation
The psychological damage said to be experienced by a child as a result of being separated from its mother.

Bowlby's work was a significant force in pro-natalism, whose welfarist support came in the form of family planning and family allowance policies. The effect of the discourse of pro-natalism was a tendency – still apparent today – for mothers to be criticised for working in paid employment, and even for having the occasional evening out. As Elizabeth Wilson (1977) argues, the idea that femininity was indivisible from motherhood was central to the purposes of welfarism and offered a unique demonstration of how the State can prescribe what woman's consciousness should be. This is exactly what Foucault meant about the constituting role of discourse. As Crowley (1992, p. 77) puts it: 'The Welfare State, in other words, was structuring not just the conditions of motherhood but women's identity as mothers. Motherhood was defined as a labour of love, private and unpaid, although socially supported and recognised.'

Care in the community

Care in the community
A range of informal and professional services to care for the elderly, disabled and sick in the community rather than in hospital or institutional settings, but typically undertaken by female relatives.

From 1979, the same kind of naturalistic assumptions about women informed the New Right's response to the sharp increase in the number of dependent elderly people. The assumption that expressive, caring capacities were unique to women was applied to dependency in the later stages of life as well as in childhood. The New Right's policy of **care in the community** in effect meant caring by women. Women's 'natural ability' for caring was commandeered by policy makers, and women were expected not only to perform the maternal function but also to provide care for the frail elderly. The implications of the discourse of care in the community were illustrated by the fact that it was not until the late 1980s, following a successful appeal to the European Court of Justice, that the UK government allowed non-waged women caring for elderly relatives to receive an attendance allowance – the sum paid to non-related community carers for doing the same work.

New Labour welfarism

With the victory of New Labour in the 1997 and 2001 general elections, at least some New Right ideas were shelved, and a version of welfarism is back on the government's agenda. This is clear from the following extracts from a Home Office leaflet promoting New Labour's 'Supporting Families' programme:

1.   Families are at the heart of our society and the basis of our future as a country. That is why this Government is so committed to strengthening family life.

2.   But they are under stress, and although most families do not want interference, they do want advice and support to be there when they need it.

3.   Our family policy is based on three simple principles:

- **Children must come first.**
We should aim to ensure that the next generation gets the best possible start to life.

- **Children need stability.**
There are many successful kinds of relationship outside marriage, but we share the belief of the majority of people that marriage is the surest way for couples to bring up their children.

- **Families raise children.**
The role of governments should be help and support, not to try to substitute for parents. The state should only intervene in extreme circumstances, for example where the welfare of family members is at stake …

Strengthening Marriage

22. Families do not want to be nannied themselves, or be nagged about how to raise their children. But they do want support to be there when they need it: advice on relationships, help with overcoming difficulties, support with parenting and, should the couple's relationship breakdown [sic] irretrievably, a system of divorce which avoids aggravating conflict within the family.

23. The Government believes that marriage provides a strong foundation for stable relationships. This does not mean trying to make people marry, or criticising or penalising people who choose not to. We do not believe that Government should interfere in people's lives in that way. But we do share the belief of the majority of people that marriage provides the most reliable framework for raising children.

24. We plan to **strengthen the institution of marriage**, including an enhanced role for marriage registrars, and to **improve support for all families**, including better advice on adult relationships (Home Office, 1999, pp. 1, 5–6).

For both welfarism and anti-welfarism, then, the nuclear family has been of fundamental political significance: for welfarists, it has helped administer social justice, while for the New Right it has enabled the welfare state to be rolled back.

Thinking about the nuclear family: sociological responses to welfarism

In the same way as New Right thinking is revealed by its attitude towards the welfare state, so post-war contributions to family sociology can usefully be considered as responses to welfarist discourses. Two distinct kinds of response are apparent: one arguing for more welfarist support and the other totally against it. We can call the first response pro-welfarism or social conservatism, and the second anti-welfarism or liberationism.

Social conservatism draws support from the centre of the political spectrum, including centre-left Conservatives and centre-right Labour and Liberal-Democrat supporters. Social conservatism considers the nuclear family to be an inherently weak unit and criticises welfarist policies for doing too little to support it. Supporters of this position point to a number of problems nuclear family members have faced when trying to live this kind of life, and to the strategies families have been forced to employ in the absence of the welfarist support they need. Their argument is that because nuclear family life is difficult in the absence of proper support, the rapid family changes in recent years – for example, the sharp rise in the number of divorces, single-parent families and working mothers – must reflect the failure of welfarism to do its job properly.

Liberationism rejects welfarism, though from a range of viewpoints and for very different reasons. Since the 1960s, a variety of sociological critics of welfarism have attacked state involvement in post-war family life. Marxists and feminists (and some-times writers who are both Marxist and feminist), as well as writers on sexual liberation, have argued that the policy of promoting the nuclear family as the source of social justice and social cohesion is flawed. It fails to recognise that this kind of family is in fact a site of disadvantage, subordination and oppression for its members, particularly women. For such theorists, nuclear family life subjugates its members, and therefore welfarism is an instrument of their subordination.

Here, then, is a nice irony: theorists from both the liberationist left and the radical right, though holding each other's views in contempt, are nonetheless united in defining welfarism as the source of individual lack of freedom. Liberationists' version of modern-ity is very different from that of Parsons and his supporters. Instead of seeing progress as exemplified by the nuclear family contributing to social cohesion by promoting social justice, liberationists see modernity as the enablement of individual freedom and self-fulfilment, above all else. The relationships between these perspectives on welfarism and the nuclear family are summarised in Figure 9.2.

	Pro-welfarism	Anti-welfarism
Pro-nuclear family	Social conservatism	New Right
Anti-nuclear family	—	Liberationism

Figure 9.2 Perspectives on welfarism and the nuclear family

Social conservatism: pro-welfarism in sociology

This approach is rooted in the ideas of Émile Durkheim (1858–1917). He believed that in all social worlds there is a constant threat of individualism running out of control. Durkheim described the human individual as, in essence, selfish and hedonistic, with limitless desires and constantly pursuing personal gratification.

Peopled by such inherently self-centred, anti-social inhabitants, social collectivities such as societies are threatened with disorder and disintegration unless their members' behaviour can be constrained and directed for the good of the social whole. The individual has to be liberated from the influence of base instincts and converted into a social being whose ambitions and desires are for the good of the group.

This is why socialisation has such a crucial role. For those in this tradition, social order cannot be guaranteed or individual happiness promoted unless the members of the social collectivity fully absorb the social rules (the norms and values) that hold it together. By proper socialisation, particularly in the family, a consensus on how people ought to behave is transmitted from one generation to the next. The individual is incorporated into a community of similarly socialised and therefore like-minded others. Through this shared set of beliefs and expectations, a collective conscience is created that guarantees social and individual health. Without norms to constrain behaviour (Durkheim, 1974, p.72):

> " humans develop insatiable appetites, limitless desires and general feelings of irritation and dissatisfaction. ...The individual submits to society and this submission is the condition of his liberation. For man, freedom consists in the deliverance from blind, unthinking physical forces; this he achieves by opposing against them the great and intelligent force which is society, under whose protection he shelters. "

Writers in this tradition often bemoan evils such as 'loss of social cohesion', 'loss of a sense of community' and 'lack of shared values' in a population. In the UK, this is arguably why Prime Minister Tony Blair has consistently preached the need to promote civic responsibility among British citizens, under the slogan 'responsibilities as well as rights'. He wishes to foster in citizens a sense of partnership with and obligation towards each other, and to encourage a move away from narrow, self-centred agendas.

Such contemporary projects are unequivocally rooted in the Durkheimian fear that modernity inevitably promotes individualism. Present-day social conservatives rail against anything that can undermine the group, the community or the collective. They rage against those who claim the right to pursue their own personal agendas regardless of everybody else. They are also wholly contemptuous of the postmodernist position (see later in this chapter) that all judgements and values are relative and thus the pursuit of a collectively held set of standards by which to live is a pointless task and an infringement of the freedom of others to be different.

This is why social conservatives are so concerned about the nuclear family. The intimacy of this type of family, with its major role in the primary socialisation of children, is a crucial bulwark against selfish, anti-social tendencies. It is the principal place to learn that rights should be subsumed under obligations, where a sense of responsibility for others can be fostered, and where the needs of the collectivity are promoted ahead of the desires of the individual. From this perspective, anti-social behaviour and deviance leading to social disorder are a consequence of cultural failure. The dysfunctional family and its inadequate socialisation of children into the collective conscience is the main

BOX 9.5 The problem with over-emphasising the 'death of the family'

While social conservatism stresses the growth of self-interest as a factor in undermining the solidarity of the family, empirical studies point to the continued strength of family networks. As McRae (1999) puts it, 'families still matter'. Various large-scale surveys (McClone et al. 1999; Grundy et al. 1999) have demonstrated that contact between family members is being maintained, even across large distances. These contacts suggest a continuing emotional tie between family members, but also the existence of practical support networks amongst family members. There may be increasing ambiguity about the nature of relationships in more complex family forms, such as reconstituted families, but the continued strength of traditional feelings about the importance of the family should also be recognised.

Communitarianism
Echoing Durkheimian thinking, a political philosophy of the 1990s that stressed the importance of community and shared values for social order and stability.

cause of this failure (but see Box 9.5 for a note of caution about the idea of the demise of the family). This Durkheimian perspective prospered in post-war sociology, particularly in the US with the work of functionalist associates of Parsons. In more recent times, British sociologists such as Norman Dennis (1993a, 1993b) and the **communitarian** ideas of American Amitai Etzoni (1995a, 1995b, 1997) have exhibited classic Durkheimian preoccupations. In more public discourse, the writings of journalist Melanie Phillips (of the *Observer* and then *The Sunday Times*) are also firmly in this tradition.

Since the nuclear family is based on marriage, threats to marital stability are squarely in social conservatives' sights. This means that 'divorce is a Bad Thing', since it compromises good parenting and the social construction of good citizens. In Box 9.6, note how Etzioni advocates the use of 'family experts' to help marriages to work, precisely the types of quasi-medical players in the modernist drama that, according to Foucault, sculpt our lives. In effect, Etzioni is saying that families are like organisms, and that family doctors need to intervene to prevent illness or heal pathologies, for the benefit of the ultimate organism – society. This is a neo-Durkheimian diagnosis and prescription (see Chapter 17). At the end of the extract, Etzioni attacks what he sees as the money-saving motives behind New Right methods of promoting the nuclear family.

BOX 9.6 The parental deficit

Underlying many of today's concerns is a sense that the quality of parenting has fallen. Millions have left to work outside the home, to be replaced by inadequate, poorly paid and insecure childcare workers. This isn't the fault of the women's movement. All women did was demand what men had long taken for granted, and few expected that women's emancipation would produce a society suffering from an acute parenting deficit, in which all adults would act like men who in the past were inattentive to children.

So tackling the parenting deficit does not mean a return to having women at home and men working outside the household. But those concerned with the quality of parenting cannot be oblivious to the rising divorce rate. While it is true that some single parents do as good a job or better than two parents, it is not the case across the board. American studies show that children from broken homes are more likely to have intellectual (learning) and social (behavioural) problems than children from intact families. They also have worse criminal records. Critics say that this is because single parents have a lower income, which is partly true. But even this is also in part caused by divorce. It simply costs more to run two households than one.

Above all, bringing up a child is a labour-intensive mission. There are never enough hands and voices to do what needs to be done. Africans say that it takes a whole village to raise a child. In the past, the extended family helped the two-parent family: today, when both parents work outside the household, they have a hard time finding enough time and energy for their children. A single parent is more likely to be beleaguered.

To make families stronger, we need to teach interpersonal skills in schools. Findings show that stable couples fight about as often as unstable couples, but they fight better. One can teach people to attack the issue and not the person, to set aside a cooling-off period before issues are tackled, and not to bring up everything that ever happened before at each opportunity.

We also need more marriage preparation sessions. In the US, churches and synagogues provide sessions so that prospective marriage partners can discuss basic issues – such as how family finances will be handled, whether or not to have children, and what to do if one partner gets a job in another city. Family counselling and mandatory delays for those who have elected to divorce also help. What matters even more than these arrangements is the change in culture they signify: marriage is not *passé* and family is important – for the sake of the children and the society that ▶

▶ must live with the consequences when children are not brought up right.

It is always better to provide people with positive messages and incentives than to coerce them. Firstly, if simply punished, they will often not comply. (Penalties on welfare mothers in the US have little influence on how many children they have and how they are treated. There is very little a welfare mother can do to make a teenager attend school, or to stop him dealing drugs.)

Second, the penalties fall on innocent children when benefits are cut. Last but not least, it is easy to tell when penalties on parents on benefits really aim at changing their behaviour, and when they are aimed at saving money for the state: if the goal is behaviour modification, the income penalties generated should be dedicated to providing incentives for those who 'behave'. When this is opposed, the champions of welfare penalties reveal what is uppermost in their mind.

For communitarians who want to shift the balance back from the radical individualism of the eighties towards the needs of the community, the priority is to work both on the side of culture and on the economy. The communitarian agenda calls for a change in values and for new measures to provide jobs and encourage flexible working. It seeks to motivate people to do their duty and favours penalties only as a last resort. Above all, it recognises that nothing is more important for society than that parents should be urged, and enabled, to be good parents.'

Source: Amitai Etzioni, *Guardian*, 15 October 1993, p. 20.

QUESTION According to your own experience and sociological evidence, how valid is Etzioni's portrait of family life in late modern society? In your answer, use the specific features of social and family life that Etzioni refers to in his argument.

 ## The liberationist critique of social conservatism

Liberationist objections to this perspective on the family are clearly made by journalist Polly Toynbee in her alternative account of the meaning of twentieth-century changes to family living (Box 9.7).

BOX 9.7 Happy families: a game of charades

On one thing most politicians and social theorists agree – family breakdown is A Bad Thing and Something Must Be Done. The right call for a return to lifelong fetters in divorce law, the left for counselling and mediation. Some look westwards for their social inspiration and call for birth outside wedlock (among the poor and genetically challenged) to be punished by a variety of Dickensian measures, mothers locked up in barracks, their offspring in orphanages ...

Marriage rates are at their lowest since records began 150 years ago. One in three births occur outside marriage. One in four new marriages will end in divorce. One in five families with dependent children are headed by a lone parent. Social mayhem, push the moral panic button, crank up your instant indignators, ... and blame it all on the 1960s.

Let me say it out loud – the permissive society is the civilised society. ... These figures represent the fruits of freedom. Current social problems make us forget history all too easily. A brutal past is blotted out in nostalgia for the golden days of the family when Darby and Joan ▶

▶hobbled contentedly into the sunset, never a cross word between them ...

The word Family is a dangerous political talisman. Family, community, nation. ... A whiff of something faintly suspicious can be caught, from time to time, wafting from Tony Blair's camp. According to Amitai Etzioni, the guru of communitarianism, 'the United Kingdom has not yet reached the levels of moral anarchy we witness in the United States, but the trends are clear. Increases in rates of violent crime, illegitimacy, drug abuse, children who kill and show no remorse and political corruption are all significant symptoms.'

Etzioni talks of 'grave social ill health' and the cracking of moral and social foundations. If the family is the building block of a stable society, the implication is that if we put it back together again, with everyone behind the right front doors, all will be well. There is a curious mismatch between the real world of our friends, relations, colleagues, soap operas on television, the gossip we read and indulge in – in short, the life we live – and the words of concern about the family that trip so readily off the tongues of policy makers. Have they no daughters, step-daughters, sisters, lovers, ex-wives? Is there no divorce all around them, too? Some may even have sons who are having affairs with older women. Public morality has always been a code for the morals of the poor. In other words, it isn't about moral-ity at all, but about money, and how to pay for the poor.

Three times more children are poor than in 1979. Thirty-two percent of children now live in families with less than half [the] average income, and that is due in part to divorces and single parenthood. Society is still modelled on a system where the man works and the woman minds. When the man departs, the woman is largely helpless, since women still earn only 75% of men's wages. The huge growth in working women is mainly in part-time jobs as second earners. Few can earn enough to become breadwinners. The single mother problem is really a problem of inequality between women and men.

Source: Polly Toynbee, *The Independent*, 22 February 1995, p. 19.

Here Toynbee has shifted the emphasis away from the social conservatives' overwhelming preoccupation with ideas – norms, values and socialisation – to the impact that advantage and disadvantage has on our lives. This alternative focus finds its most coherent and systematic expression in the analyses of modern family life of the three main structural liberationist approaches – those of Marxists, radical feminists and sexual liberationists.

There are two strands to this position: the first stresses the need to understand the facts of people's lives and the resources they possess; and the second stresses the need to recognise the importance of ideologies. Firstly, liberationist perspectives demand that we appreciate not only the role of ideas in structuring family lives, but also the crucial influence of material disadvantages. No matter what ideas they learn, lone mothers on benefit are grossly disadvantaged. No matter what ideas they learn, the so-called 'under-class' of families of the long-term unemployed live in poverty. No matter what ideas they learn, families of breadwinners in casual work, low-paid work, part-time work or work with no sick pay or pension benefits are all economically disadvantaged. No matter what ideas they learn, women who are economically dependent on their husbands or partners are usually disadvantaged compared with women in work. No matter what ideas they learn, elderly people who have to survive on the state pension are disadvantaged. No matter what ideas they learn, disabled people who cannot work are economically disadvantaged.

CONNECTIONS For a more detailed exploration of the issue of poverty and its effects, see Chapter 4, pages 72–82.

Mode of production
A Marxist concept that refers to the structured relationship between the means of production (raw materials, land, etc.) and the relations of production (the ways humans are involved in production).

Labour power
In Marxist theory, a commodity to be bought and sold; refers to workers' ability to produce goods.

The second element of the argument accepts that socialisation is a principal feature of human social existence and that the ideas of humans are largely predetermined. Liberationists accept that ideas are cultural and social constructions. But it is the role of these systems of belief as instruments of power – functioning either to obscure or to legitimise inequalities – that is ultimately important. By definition, a primary socialising agency such as the nuclear family, insofar as it promotes a consensus that allows power to remain with dominant groups such as capitalists, men or heterosexuals, is in fact an ideological device. The nuclear family helps to structure an agreement about ways of living and thinking that masks and legitimises the realities of power and disadvantage. These inequalities should be challenged and overturned in the name of individual liberty and social progress.

Liberationist anti-welfarism (1): Marxism and the nuclear family

For Marxists, capitalist society is best understood as being based on a particular kind of economy – a class-based way of producing goods. This is described by Marxists as a **mode of production** in which a dominant class of capital owners exploit the **labour power** of a subordinate class of commodity producers. In return for their labour, workers are given wages of much less value than the market value of the goods they produce.

Traditional Marxist analyses of social life in modern industrial capitalist societies seek to demonstrate that the ways in which people live always have benefits for capitalism, however remote from economic life these may appear to be. Thus, Marxists are interested in identifying those features of nuclear family living that have direct pay-offs for capitalist commodity production. They also explore the methods used to encourage people to live in a way that is economically beneficial to capitalist production. These methods include encouraging people to live a particular sort of family life by arranging things so that they have little or no choice. The ideas that capitalist social-isation uses to persuade people that this is the right way to live, or that seek to hide from their gaze the realities of capitalist exploitation, are called ideologies. This two-pronged approach is interested in both the structural features of the nuclear family and its ideological supports. What is there about contemporary nuclear family life that Marxists could use to demonstrate their case? The following arguments have been levelled:

- Capitalist commodity producers are exploited labourers. Encouraging them to value family life above all else diverts their attention away from the realities of their work experiences.

Reserve army of labour
Workers such as women who are brought into the workplace during times of labour shortage. When women are no longer needed, they are encouraged by the prevailing ideology to return to the home.

- Women are encouraged to be wives and mothers and to believe that this is their nature-directed destiny. Marxists – and Marxist feminists – say that such ideo-logical coercion produces enormous benefits for capitalism at no cost. The domestic labour performed by wives and mothers is unpaid. If commodity producers (usually men) had to purchase domestic services, their employers would have to pay far higher wages to cover these costs. Furthermore, child-rearing, from the capitalists' point of view, produces new generations of commodity producers at no cost to themselves.

- Women constitute a **reserve army of labour**, available to be used as commodity producers in times of crisis and dispensed with when they are no longer needed. When women are surplus to requirements, naturalism (the belief that women's natural place is in the home) is reinvoked to encourage them to return to the domestic sphere.

- Because a wife is seen as economically dependent on her husband, when she does enter the waged labour market, she is likely to be treated less favourably than a male labourer. She usually is paid less than a man, denied access to the better-paid jobs, consigned to part-time, casual or seasonal work and denied entitlements such as sick pay, holiday pay, pension rights, incremental rewards and a proper career structure. She may also be denied maternity leave, or denied the chance of a job at all because of her child-producing potential.

- Some Marxists argue that children and the elderly are similarly disadvantaged. Entry to and exit from the labour market are manipulated for these categories of people and disguised as humanitarianism and benevolence. Thus, childhood is socially constructed to deny young people the chance to earn a wage until reaching a particular age, and this is typically portrayed as being in the child's interest. Forcing children to remain the responsibility of their parents for a long time encourages the internalisation of values that are beneficial to employers, such as acceptance of authority and of the normality of gendered life chances. Similarly, older people are forced to leave paid employment at a certain age, and this is justified by invoking ideologies of ageing and dependency. By these means, the unemployment rate is manipulated and reserve armies of labour are put in place, to be called upon in the event of labour shortages.

Liberationist anti-welfarism (2): radical feminism and the nuclear family

Radical feminists have attacked the gender prescriptions or rules inherent in the naturalistic family discourse. For them, welfarism, however well-meaning, is effectively an instrument of women's subordination because it is aimed at propping up a particular version of family life. For radical feminists, the nuclear family is a prime site for the exploitation of women. Therefore, activities and ideas designed to reproduce and strengthen this family form are by definition social and cultural weapons to oppress women.

The personal is the political
A phrase coined by radical feminists to draw attention to issues of sexuality and violence in male–female relationships.

For radical feminists, the shackling of women in this way is part of a general system of oppression called patriarchy, or rule by men. They consider that women are oppressed in non-capitalist societies as well as capitalist ones, and hence they seek to identify a much more general source of the oppression of all women. For many of them, the culprit is family life based on a heterosexual partnership, because the nuclear family is the repository of patriarchy in modern societies. Radical feminists acknowledge the important part played in the construction of patriarchy by other ideologies that serve to discipline family life, as we have already described. But in recent years, some radical feminists have stressed that intra-familial male–female relationships are the root cause of patriarchy. Arguing that **the personal is the political**, some radical feminists assert that sexuality and violence in male–female relationships are both the engine (its cause) and a mirror (a symptom) of patriarchy.

Compulsory heterosexuality
This concept implies that heterosexuality is not necessarily the natural form of sexual preference but is imposed on individuals by social constraints.

For example, Adrienne Rich (1984) speaks of the **compulsory heterosexuality** that underpins the male–female relationship in nuclear families. She also problematises the naturalistic discourse that normalises heterosexuality. Why should penetrative sex, which involves the male exploiting the body of the female, be deemed natural while other forms of sexuality are not? Masters and Johnson (1996) having established that the vaginal orgasm is a physiological myth, radical feminists argue that the promotion of penetrative sex as normal is therefore a patriarchal device to ensure the satisfaction of male sexual needs. Indeed, heterosexual relations are, according to many radical feminists, essentially power relations, as indicated by the kind of language employed to

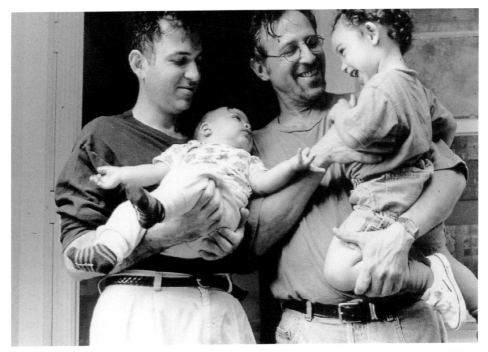

Figure 9.3 Non-heterosexual families highlight questions of commitment and responsibility but can also offer new possibilities for developing egalitarian relationships and can embody a powerful commitment to childcare.

describe them. Typically, they see the woman's body as being 'colonised' and 'occupied' by the man for his pleasure, with the sexual act symbolising the subjugation of the woman's life, mind and identity under patriarchy. This symbolic violence in male–female sexual relations leads directly to the actual physical and mental violence often inflicted by men on their wives in modern nuclear families.

CONNECTIONS Another account of compulsory heterosexuality is provided in Chapter 6, pages 153–6.

Separatism
An idea put forward by some radical feminists as a solution to patriarchy. Based on the conviction that the sexual act embodies patriarchal exploitation of women, it proposes that women should live separate lives from men.

Radical feminists therefore advocate separatism as a solution to patriarchy. That is, they call on all women, both heterosexual and lesbian, to live their lives separately from men, since only then can they be liberated from the patriarchal construction of heterosexual penetrative sex as normal.

Liberationist anti-welfarism (3): sexual liberationism

Writers on sexual liberty argue that the naturalism inherent in welfarism's view of normal family life is not restricted to mothering and caring for the elderly – it also suggests that a normal sexual relationship can only be monogamous and heterosexual. This, it is argued, ignores the diversity of sexual practices engaged in by humans. Moreover, it categorises such practices as deviant – as abnormal or perverse, thereby denying legitimacy to alternative sexual lifestyles and their practitioners. By promoting monogamous heterosexuality as a normal practice in normal families, practitioners of other forms of sexuality such as homosexuals, lesbians, masturbators, those with multiple sexual partners (or at least if they are female), sado-masochists, and rubber or bondage enthusiasts are marginalised and stigmatised. The language employed in this discourse of sexuality powerfully illustrates its normalising consequences: queers, poofs, and dykes, wankers and tossers, sluts and tarts, perverts and fetishists. All these bodily practices are condemned as abnormal by a dominant ideology that promotes a particular form of sexuality in a particular form of family. Nobody describes enthusiastic monogamous heterosexuality as perversion or fetishism! The liberationist argument is that while love and affection may be a precondition for individual happiness, there is no reason to suppose that it can only be experienced by adults in stable, monogamous, heterosexual unions.

QUESTION What contribution can sociologists make to the debates on sexuality described above? What sociological evidence can you find to illuminate these issues?

Difference and diversity in modern family life

Theorists of modernity may disagree about the meaning of progress and about the route humans should take to find their individual utopias, but they do not disagree about the possibility of such progress – as long as we organise ourselves in the way they tell us. Thus, social conservatives, the new right and liberationists all provide us with a meta-theory or meta-narrative of the family. Despite their differences, they all propose a grand, all-embracing solution to the problems posed by family life in modern society.

However, other theorists of the modern family do not claim to have a set of universally applicable solutions to these problems. They demand that we stop thinking of contemporary family problems as susceptible to generalised solutions. Instead, we should acknowledge that humans today differ in the construction of their identities as men, women and children, husbands and wives, mothers and fathers, grandmothers and grandfathers. For these critics of modernity realise there is no one right answer to the problem of living a human life. The pursuit of the modernist holy grail – the key to unlock the door leading to human happiness – is pointless. Instead, we should acknowledge the pluralism and diversity of the contemporary human condition and abandon the idea that one single narrative or story can help us to fulfil our potential and live secure and contented lives.

CONNECTIONS For an account of pluralism in politics, see Chapter 8, pages 198–201.

The problem for modernist family theorists is that recent research seems to support the pluralist view. People in modern societies today seem to be living very different family lives from each other – and the differences seem to be growing larger (Allan and Crow, 2001, p. 23).

" [T]here can be no doubt that in Britain and in other Western countries, the period since the mid-1970s has seen very significant shifts occuring in a number of key aspects of people's family and household experiences. In particular, patterns of household and family formation and dissolution have altered in ways which are quite different from the trends which dominated the first three-quarters of the twentieth century. "

We can find evidence of this characterisation by looking at recent changes to the patterns of divorce, lone-parent households, cohabitation and marriage.

Divorce

There was a dramatic rise in the divorce rate in England and Wales between 1969 and 1991 – from 4.1 per 1000 marriages in 1969 to 13.4 per 1000 in 1991. The actual number of divorces over this period increased from 51 310 in 1969 to 158 745 in 1991, (marriage, divorce and adoption statistics). Allan and Crow (ibid., p. 25) argue that in the UK, if divorce rates continue to increase as they have been doing, divorce, far from being an unusual ending to a marriage, will in fact become the norm. A similar picture emerges from international data:

- In the US, the divorce rate doubled between 1960 and 1997, when there were just under 1.2 million divorces (FASTATS, 1999; Kamerman and Kahn, 1997).

- In Canada, divorces per 1000 increased from 38 in 1951 to 270 in 1991.

- In Belgium, the divorce rate doubled between 1970 and 1990, while in France and Holland, it increased threefold over the same period (Goode, 1993). Current projections for most Northern European countries are that around a third of all marriages will end in divorce.

Single-parent households

One of the consequences of the higher divorce rate is an increase in the number of single-parent households. The number of such households in the UK rose from 570 000 in 1971 to over one million in 1986 and an estimated 1.6 million in 1996 (Haskey, 1996b, 1998). Today, approximately one in five dependant children are being raised by one parent. According to Allan and Crow (2001, p. 26), similar changes have been observed in most other Western countries: for example, in the US, the number of lone-parent households rose from under four million in 1976 to over 10 million in 1991.

The great majority of these households are headed by women – about 90 per cent since the early 1970s, according to some sources (Haskey 1995b, 1998), with a similar proportion in other developed countries (Duncan and Edwards, 1997). Other statistics show that an increasing proportion of these households are headed by never-married women. Between 1971 and the early 1990s, the number of such households in the UK increased from 15 per cent to 35 per cent of all single-parent households. Clearly, the days when the stigma of illegitimacy automatically ensured that pregnancy meant marriage are fast dying out.

Cohabitation

The available evidence shows that a similar shift in attitude has occurred with regard to what used to be called living in sin. Though the picture is somewhat patchy – for example, among British Asians cohabitation is still rare (Berrington, 1994; Heth and Dale, 1994) – it is clear that cohabitation, either before marriage or instead of it, is now extremely common.

In the late 1960s, only 5 per cent of first-time brides had lived with their future husbands before their wedding. By the late 1980s – the last period for which these particular data were collected – this was becoming a common practice, with 50 per cent doing so (Allan and Crow, 2001, p. 29).

While strongly Catholic countries, such as those in Southern Europe, are changing more slowly in terms of cohabitation, the data show that the rising trend is an international phenomenon. Denmark and Sweden have always had high levels of cohabitation, but other Northern European countries – such as Austria, France, Germany and Holland – are now exhibiting the same trend as the UK, as are Australia and Canada. In the US, the increase was from just over 500 000 cohabiting couples in 1970 to 3.5 million in 1993 (Graefe and Lichter, 1999).

Marriage

Although cohabitation still often leads to marriage, fewer people are marrying. Between 1965 and 1975, on average there were nearly 400 000 marriages a year in England and Wales. By the mid 1990s, this had fallen to less than 300 000, despite the larger number of second marriages. To put this more precisely, between 1981 and 1991 the marriage rates per thousand unmarried men and women fell by some 25 per cent and 30 per cent respectively (Haskey, 1995; Allan and Crow, 2001).

Furthermore, as in most of Europe and North America, in England and Wales people are getting married later in life. In 1965, the average age of marriage was 23.5 for men and 21.3 for women, while in 1997, these averages were 28.6 and 26.7 respectively.

Life-cycle or life-course?

Life-cycle
The social changes encountered as a person passes through childhood, adolescence, mid-life, old age and death. In the context of the family, the life-cycle includes courtship, child rearing, children leaving home and so on.

Life-course
This concept stresses the diversity of experiences during the course of people's lives. It suggests that contemporary experience is more diverse and less predictable than the concept of the life-cycle suggests.

Such evidence of difference and diversity in contemporary family life has led to calls for the traditional concept of the family **life-cycle** to be replaced with that of the **life-course** of the individual. Life-cycle theory rests on the belief that normal families go through normal stages of birth, growth and decline. Marriage initiates the family, the arrival of children develops and expands it, their departure contracts it, and it ends with the death of one of the spouses. At each stage in the cycle, specific problems emerge that need managing – these are sometimes described as the developmental tasks of the normal life-cycle. Progress and fulfilment for the family – both for its members and for the society of which it is part – depend on each of these tasks being successfully completed. This is an essentially modernist approach. It echoes the medicalist assumptions of family therapy in arguing that social scientific knowledge should be used to assist families to cope with the various demands that the life-cycle places on them. Family therapists claim, for example, that family stress is greater during the transition from one stage in the cycle to another, and that it is at these times, such as the teenage years or retirement, that the intervention of specialist knowledge can be most helpful.

Life-course proponents reject the assumptions of life-cycle theory, arguing that the contemporary diversity in people's lives has negated any validity it may once have had, because it can only work if male and female family lives are predictable. The growth in delayed marriages, female employment, single parenthood and marital and occupational instability, together with the large variety of educational and occupational opportunities available throughout life and the dissolution of the traditional distinctions between people of different ages, means that we now have to conceptualise family life in a different way. Thus, life-course theory 'recommends that we adopt the individual rather than the family as the basic unit of analysis ... the focus ... is on the individual's passage through a sequence of social situations, and on how each individual is affected by the passages of others' (Cheal, 1991, p. 139).

By what means can we theorise diversity in contemporary family living? Two options present themselves: action theory and postmodernist theory. According to action theory, contemporary family pluralism reflects the capacity of actors to choose and negotiate alternative lifestyles in line with their circumstances and as their structural conditions allow. In contrast, postmodernist theory holds that family pluralism is a consequence of the fact that social worlds today are made up of complexes of competing and contradictory discourses. These discourses act upon humans in different social and cultural circumstances, thereby constituting them and constructing their identities in different ways. In summary, action theory focuses on human agency to explain pluralism and difference in modern social life; while for postmodernists, pluralism and difference are the consequence of a new complexity in discourse-directed social existences.

CONNECTIONS The postmodernist perspective is explored in more detail in Chapter 19, pages 514–33.

Human agency and the family

Instead of the Durkheimian view that individuals are inevitably, but beneficially, constrained by the normative content of the culture they acquire through socialisation, action theorists point to the fundamentally creative capacities of social beings. Action theory emphasises the choices in role playing available to individuals and the crucial role of interpretation and negotiation in the management of identity and specific social occasions. Both symbolic interactionism and ethnomethodology insist that individuals are subjects, purposefully managing and negotiating their lives according to their views of their circumstances – referred to as their 'definitions of the situation'.

This tradition in family theorising sees family life as a fluid process, with roles not set in concrete by an implacable (albeit benign) collective consensus, but as a reality constantly renewed and redefined by specific members of specific families. We should reject a static, determined picture of family structure, with predetermined roles, as this overestimates the determining nature of external social forces. Rather, we should focus on individuals' ability to impose meaning on the world and to choose how to live their family lives in the light of these meanings.

Thus, describing a group of people as 'living in a nuclear family' tells us nothing about the ways in which they actually negotiate and manage their relationships. According to action theory, the fault of structural theories is that they homogenise social life, as though roles are played in the same way in similar-looking groups. In fact, each social group will have unique characteristics that an adequate sociological account must acknowledge and investigate. Each nuclear family will have its own interpersonal dynamics and its own personal history – a unique, never-finished story, collaboratively authored by the actors concerned.

Janet Finch (1987, pp. 155–6) emphasises the relevance of action theory to family sociology, arguing that the study of family obligations is 'part of the central task of understanding ... the puzzle of human agency' in contemporary societies:

" On the one hand, family obligations can be seen as part of normative rules which operate within a particular society, and which simply get applied in appropriate situations. On the other hand, they can be seen as agreements which operate between specific individuals and are arrived at through a process of negotiation ... using the concept of 'negotiation' very much in an interactionist sense ... a full understanding of what family obligations mean and how they operate almost certainly contain elements of both. "

To illustrate her argument, Finch asks us to consider the position of siblings who know that their ageing parents will eventually need some sort of care. British family norms place an obligation on children to care for their parents if it becomes necessary. However, Finch argues that theorising on the basis of such norms alone cannot tell us the whole story. Probably without realising they are doing it, children in such a position will negotiate among themselves the manner in which the obligation should be fulfilled. As she puts it (ibid, pp.156–7):

" it is unlikely ... that the three siblings will wait until the time comes when their parents actually need care, then open up round-the-table talks to decide precisely how each will fulfil his or her responsibilities. Probably such overt negotiations will never be necessary, because over a period of time – probably covering many years – it will gradually become 'obvious' to all concerned that when the time comes, one particular sibling (almost certainly a daughter) will actually be the one to provide daily care, another will perhaps provide some financial support, and the third will take the parents for a month in the summer. In this instance, concrete obligations between specified individuals have been arrived at in some way through a process of negotiation, but these negotiations themselves are shaped by the general normative prescriptions about children taking responsibility for their elderly parent. I see it as a central tack of any empirical work in this field to explore the relationship between moral norms and negotiation of obligations, and to understand the processes through which such arrangements ... become 'obvious'. "

Interpretive
Having an interest in the meanings underpinning social action. Synonymous with social action theory (see *social action*).

Finch argues that an **interpretive** element must always be added to the normative analysis of family life, and on this basis rejects the structural orientation of lifecycle theorising and of monolithic modernist approaches to family life. In the case of neither the individual nor the family is it satisfactory to use an approach that depicts life as progressing through predictable stages. Instead, because individual and family biographies are constructed through time, there is a need to build in 'an understanding of the social, political and economic contexts in which obligations are negotiated, honoured and abandoned' (ibid., p. 168). Finch thus endorses Abrams' (1982, p. xiii) view that sociological analysis must recognise that 'history and society are made by constant and more or less purposeful human action and that individual action, however purposeful, is made by history and society'.

CONNECTIONS The general theories that together make up interpretivism are detailed in Chapter 18, pages 498–509.

Postmodern theorising and the family

Modern societies do not just become modern and then stay still, for modernity is a process of continuous change and development. Indeed, for a society to be modern, constant change and the pursuit of what is believed to be progress has to be one of its features. That is why subjects such as sociology have been so much a part of modernity. Sociological theorising involves humans reflecting on their social circumstances and explaining them. These explanations make it possible to change things in order to make improvements and build a better society. Pre-modern theorising was aimed at revealing some sort of divine plan – with humans working out what their supernatural superiors had had in mind when they created them and their world (see Chapter 16). There was no possibility of changing or improving this world, since its features were not human creations. Modernity means the opposite. With the rise of reason and science, it became possible for humans not just to reveal how things had come to be, but also to use this knowledge to control, predict and improve. This is known as the 'project of modernity': the never-ending pursuit of knowledge by humans to achieve progress in their lives by their own efforts.

Each of the modernist meta-narratives about the family in this chapter has this goal of diagnosis, prescription and betterment. Social conservative, New Right, Marxist, structural feminist and sexual liberationist family theories seek not only to explain the nature of family structures and relationships but also to improve the life of family members and the societies in which they live. Claims such as 'the nuclear family best suits the needs of industrial society', or 'a child needs to be brought up by both its parents', 'housewives are oppressed', or 'domestic labour is unpaid labour benefiting capital' and 'gays should have the right to get married and parent children' are typical of modernist family meta-narratives.

Postmodernists attack this view, since for them, no human can ever acquire object-ive, certain truth about anything. For postmodernists, all knowledge is relative – true only of the time and place in which it is found. Underpinning postmodernist relativism is a theory of knowledge called post-structuralism.

Post-structuralists point to the centrality of language and discourse in social life. Like all living things, humans experience reality via their senses, but they alone know what these experiences mean. This is because they have systems of knowledge – for example, languages – that provide them with such meanings. However, despite being uniquely empowered in this way, there is a problem, for no human has any choice about the meanings contained in the language he or she learns. For example, we only find out that something is coloured blue when we are taught the word blue. Thus, pre-existing languages determine our knowledge for us. So, although we are empowered and enabled to be human because of languages, paradoxically, we have no control over which languages/knowledge we learn. For those in this tradition, most notably Foucault, all knowledge systems – which Foucault calls discourses – work like languages. Thus, we know that mad people are ill and not, for example, bewitched, because medical knowledge tells us so. We know that homosexuals are not sick or criminals, because our laws tell us so.

Such pieces of knowledge are cultural features that have emerged out of previous ones, just as ordinary languages have done. Therefore, just as it would be a mistake to claim that one language we have learnt is better, more accurate or truer than another, so we should realise that forms of knowledge that differ from our own are not better or worse than ours, or more accurate at depicting reality – they are just different ways of knowing. Our knowledge is our way of defining our world, but it is no nearer the truth than anyone else's. Hence, those subjected to other discourses in other cultures 'know' different truths. For example, the members of many cultures know that marriages are contracted for economic and political reasons rather than romantic ones. The members of many cultures 'know' that young girls should be circumcised or infibulated in order to ensure their chastity before marriage. The members of many cultures 'know' that polygyny (having more than one wife at a time) or polyandry (having more than one husband at a time) is the right marriage arrangement.

According to the post-structuralist view, all human ideas are **relative** to the time and place in which they arise. No one can stand aside from the social and cultural influences that have formed them and their ideas. All ideas, all theories, all knowledge

Relativism
An approach that denies the existence of absolute truth and maintains that beliefs, values and theories are relative to time and place. Accordingly, traditions and ways of life can only be judged in the context of the age or society that has produced them.

are the creation of a particular time in history and a particular cultural context, and they can never be objectively true. So, meta-narrative statements such as 'all women are repressed by men', 'female circumcision is evil' and 'it is unnatural for homosexuals and lesbians to marry and raise children', even if they are subscribed to by all or most members of a society, are merely judgements that are considered appropriate by people subjected to the particular influences of the specific world in which they happen to live.

As in the case of languages, the more complex a society, the more it is made up of groups with different cultural traditions and different, sometimes opposed, forms of knowledge. As electronic communications continue to shrink our world and bring us into contact with other ways of knowing things, we will become subject to more various and contradictory influences. This is what postmodernists mean when they say that contemporary social worlds are increasingly made up of complexes of competing and contradictory discourses that constitute humans and construct their identities in different ways.

This modernist–postmodernist debate is central to many contemporary arguments about the family. Modernists argue that it is not only possible but also essential to identify what is good and bad about adult relationships, domestic arrangements, child rearing and so on. Postmodernists insist that no one should be allowed to impose on others their view of how to live family life. We should be able to live as we wish and choose our own lifestyle, as long as others are not harmed or inconvenienced. We should be free from restrictions and regulations, which simply reflect the selective viewpoints of others, presented as objective truths.

Postmodernists argue that difference and diversity are the only certain characteristics of contemporary human life. Thus, postmodern family life is inevitably a world of contrasts and oppositions. No one form of sexuality, partnership, marriage or child rearing can be judged to be superior to any other – or at least not by another human being, whose judgements are themselves directed by discourse.

Does this solve the matter, then? Is it a case of 'anything goes – of doing our own thing and letting others do theirs? This presents both practical and moral problems. What if others doing their own thing prevents us from doing ours? Do we let them? Can we let them? Surely humans can only live their lives by acting according to their judgements, morals and values? Should we not fight for our versions of the decent life, even if we recognise the relativity of their foundations? In effect, do we encourage tolerance of dogmatism and bigotry, or should we respect conviction and commitment against indifference? What do you think? Are you modern or postmodern? (See Chapters 16 and 19 for further discussions of these issues.)

Chapter summary

- Family forms vary enormously, both historically and cross-culturally.

- The functionalist theory of the modern family argues that the nuclear family best meets the needs of an industrial economy.

- The ideas of Michel Foucault have made it possible to identify modern discourses that have promoted nuclear family life and fostered nuclear family identities.

- The principal discursive agencies designed to do this have been medicine and state-sponsored family policies since the Second World War.

- Social conservative and New Right political philosophies have, for different reasons, emphasised the importance of the nuclear family in modern societies.

- Liberationist objections to the nuclear family, and to the discourses that promote this family form, focus on the lack of individual freedom and empowerment experienced by nuclear family members.

- Recent evidence shows a rapid increase in alternative forms of family living.

- Theoretical explanations of this differentiation are offered by action theory and postmodernism.

 ## Questions to think about

- Foucault's contribution to the debate on the nature of late modern or postmodern society has been to provide us with concepts such as discourse, disciplinary regime, anatomo-politics and medicalisation. How confident are you that you fully understand these concepts? To demonstrate your grasp, write a paragraph on each one, including a definition and an example taken from the sociology of the family, but without reference to the above.

- Does the state have too much power to intervene in the lives of families? In your answer, identify the powers and limits of the state in deciding to intervene. Say whether you think this power should be stronger or weaker than it is, and why.

- Do you find the Marxist or the feminist theoretical position on the family most convincing, and why? Is some sort of amalgamation possible or desirable? Are the labels of Marxist and feminist too broad for you to come to a conclusion?

 ## Investigating further

Allan, Graham and Graham Crow (2001) *Families, Households and Society*, Palgrave.
    This is quite British in orientation, but it provides a very useful overview of how family life was changing at the turn of the century.
Cheal, David (1991) *Family and the State of Theory*, Prentice Hall.
    This is a clear and readable run-through of sociological theories of the family, with a focus on modernity, feminism and postmodern theory.

Somerville, Jennifer (2000) *Feminism and the Family: Politics and Society in the UK and USA*, Palgrave.

> This elegantly written book examines the problematic relationship between the women's movement and the family. Chapter 3, for example, offers a useful summary and critique of the work of Betty Friedan, Germaine Greer, Kate Millett and Shulamith Firestone.

10

Education

CHAPTER CONTENTS

Aims of the chapter

After the family, education is one of the most important social institutions in an individual's life. In this chapter, we explore the major sociological issues in education. One of our main concerns is to explain differences in educational attainment between social groups defined by class, gender or ethnicity, or all three in combination. A basic question to be raised in this respect is, are these simply differences or are they inequalities? We shall review a wide range of approaches that sociologists have adopted to address this issue. We shall also consider the wider social and historical context in which the modern education system has emerged, and investigate whether it is best accounted for in terms of the development of the economy or more closely associated with state formation. Our third broad area of discussion concerns the way in which different approaches view the pupil: are they based on an essentially passive model in which the pupil is acted upon by various external forces, or are pupils seen as actively engaging with their schooling according to their own values and aspirations under changing social conditions?

By the end of the chapter, you should have an understanding of the following concepts:

- Meritocracy
- Inequality and difference
- Functionalism
- Correspondence theory
- State formation
- Habitus
- Cultural capital
- Cultural deprivation
- Credential inflation

Introduction

When we think about education, we conjure up a vision of pupils waiting their turn for the scissors, revising anxiously for a biology test or having a laugh with friends when the teacher's back is turned. Through our shared experience of schooling, we have a taken-for-granted picture of what education is – so taken for granted that we may fail to realise just how recent, in historical terms, the institution of mass, universal schooling is. In the UK, it is not much more than a hundred years old. Yet its main feature – its universal, compulsory character – has become accepted as perfectly normal. However, even in the early twentieth century, it was not unusual for middle-class children to receive their early education in the home from private tutors. Today, home education is the fastest growing form of alternative education. This suggests that we need to (1) keep a sense of historical perspective as far as mass schooling is concerned, (2) observe that education need not simply mean schooling, and (3) remember that if things have changed before, they are likely to change again.

Educational policy and educational reform

In the West, the second half of the twentieth century was marked by two successive and competing perspectives on the nature and purpose of education: in the early postwar decades, 'equal opportunities' was the catchphrase; in the 1980s and 1990s, 'employ-ability' moved to the fore.

CONNECTIONS The problem of gender differences in education should be seen as a world-wide phenomenon. See Chapter 6.

Before the Second World War, education in the UK was, on the whole, unashamedly gender-biased and class-confirming. In the words of Halsey (1977, p. 176), education was 'the stamp put on the social character of individuals whose jobs and life-styles were predetermined by social origin'. In contrast, post-war education was heralded as a ladder of opportunity for the working class. Equal opportunity in education was seen as the key to a more open society – a **meritocracy** in which people would move up or down the occupational hierarchy according to personal merit (merit = ability + effort). The education system would ensure that individuals were allocated by ability; being born into a humble home would be no barrier to success, and being born into a wealthy or powerful family would provide no cushion against failure. Politically, these views were social democratic – and with differing emphases – they were largely shared by the main-stream parties, both left and right. This modernist social democratic perspective under-pinned a number of policies that broadened educational access. The 1944 Education Act entitled all children to a secondary education. The expansion of educational provision by raising the school leaving age (to 15 in 1947 and 16 years in 1971–72) and offering greater access to higher education was dramatic enough to warrant the term 'edu-cational explosion'. By 1970, 18 per cent of 18 year olds were in full-time education, compared with three per cent in 1938.

Meritocracy a society characterised by equality of opportunity in which occupation or position is allocated according to merit (intended ironically by the man who coined the term: Lord Young of Darlington).

The equal opportunities ethos fuelled the move away from a system of secondary education where pupils were divided between grammar schools, secondary modern schools and, in some areas, technical schools (the bipartite or tripartite systems), and towards a comprehensive system, and it also played a part in shifting the curriculum of primary schools towards a child-centred model in which the pace of learning was more closely geared to the current interests and capacities of individual pupils. The dominant factor in the educational philosophy of the 1950s and 1960s was the widespread belief in the positive power of education. Education was seen as more than a means to indi-vidual advancement: it was also seen as the solution to social problems such as delinquency and poverty, and as the key to a more civilised, democratic and prosperous society.

In the mid 1970s, however, this approach became the subject of energetic criticism. Critics from the New Right claimed that British education was a failure. It was accused of being expensive, insufficiently attentive to parents and ineffective in preparing children for work. With these criticisms in mind, Conservative governments after 1979 initiated sweeping changes, the key elements of which were as follows:

- The imposition of a national curriculum.
- The introduction of tests of basic skills and knowledge throughout pupils' school careers.
- Arrangements to make the results of testing widely known.
- The devolution of budgets, so that individual schools rather than local authorities became accountable for the effective use of resources.
- Emphasis on consumer choice for parents.

- Incentives for private education.

- Provisions to ensure greater parental and business involvement in the government of schools.

What these disparate elements had in common was their connection to a set of educational priorities that were very different from those of the 1950s and 1960s. Concern for equal opportunities had given way to anxiety about standards and assessment.

Free market
A form of trade or business environment free from outside interference or restrictions.

During the 1980s and 1990s, schools and universities, along with hospitals and primary health care centres, were enjoined to take the **free market** as their model. Local management of schools and provisions for parental choice were intended to make schools operate more like businesses, on the assumption that competition between schools would promote greater efficiency and wider choice for the consumer. Several measures, such as the pressure applied to universities to obtain more of their funding from corporations, were designed to forge a closer relationship between business and education.

Functionalist perspective
A theoretical perspective, associated with Durkheim and Parsons, based on an analogy between social systems and organic systems. It claims that the character of a society's various institutions must be understood in terms of the function each performs in enabling the smooth running of society as a whole.

However, at the same time, more and more aspects of the educational curriculum were brought under the direct control of the state. After 1979, centralisation speeded up dramatically, culminating with the 1988 Education Reform Act. It may seem contradictory that government intervention was championed by Conservative governments who prided themselves on rolling back the state. But as Kirk (1991) explains, antagonism towards local government (responsible for education) and hostility towards the teaching profession (whose constancy of purpose in the 1985–86 industrial dispute shook the government) made intervention attractive. Even more than that, Conservative governments, confronted with a stubborn recession and rising unemployment, hoped that education and training, rapidly reformed, would provide the quality of labour needed to revive the economy.

These shifts in educational philosophy – from education for the sake of a fairer society to education for the sake of the economy; from equal opportunities and child-centred learning to unequal assessments and common standards – highlight the discontinuities in education after 1944. Yet, as we shall see, there were also significant continuities. These changes were invariably the cause of major public debates, and you might like to reflect on where you would have stood on the issues at different times.

QUESTION   Do you think your own education prepared you for a role in the economy, or was it broader than this? Give examples to support your case.

The social context of education

Conflict perspective
A theoretical approach, such as Marxism, focusing on the notion that society is based on an unequal distribution of advantage (e.g. conflict of interests between advantaged and disadvantaged).

The growth of educational provision during the 1950s and 1960s was paralleled by an explosion of research on the sociology of education. The bulk of this was aimed at monitoring the effects that educational expansion was having on equality of opportunity, and much of it was informed by a **functionalist perspective** (which we discuss further in Chapter 17). However, since the 1970s, many writers have found an alternative **conflict perspective** useful for analysing the place of education in modern society. The two perspectives draw on similar data on the relationship between education, the economy and social equality, but they interpret them in radically different ways. Both perspectives link the education system to the industrial capitalist economy, but other researchers argue that we should look to state formation rather than the economy for the historical emergence of education. This alternative approach also directs attention to a factor that is particularly relevant to education: status.

CONNECTIONS The tension between the concepts of class and status is a recurrent theme in sociological discourse. For a fuller account of the idea of status, drawing on the Weberian approach, see Chapter 5, pages 102–3. Education is only one of the areas of social life in which class and status are intertwined.

Whereas the focus on education and the economy prioritises hierarchical class differences, the focus on the state and status highlights the significance of a major division within the middle class – between those (mainly professionals) who owe their position to high-status qualifications and those (based in industry and commerce) whose position depends on the organisations for which they work. Hence, we shall contrast economistic accounts with those that examine education, the state and status.

A structural-functionalist account

The structural-functionalist account underpinned the more general view of advanced industrial society that prevailed in the 1950s and 1960s. Perhaps the most distinctive feature of this society was its liberal progressive optimism. This reflected the view that the new social and economic order that emerged after the Second World War marked a radical break with the past – especially with the economic instability, mass unemployment and poverty that had led to fascism and to the war itself. Social divisions would be progressively eroded and everyone would become middle class. Education would play a key role in facilitating this development.

From a structural-functionalist perspective, the changes connected with industrialism gave rise to specific 'functional imperatives' – needs that had to be met if any society was to survive. The education system performed three vital functions on behalf of society.

First, it helped to develop the human resources of an industrial nation, especially white-collar, technical, professional and managerial workers. Second, the fact that industrial societies had a plurality of occupations requiring varying levels of skill, necessitated a sophisticated mechanism to select individuals according to their talents and train them for the jobs they could most effectively perform. Education therefore had a vital selection or allocative function. Third, it was argued that schooling contributed to social cohesion by transmitting to new generations the central values of society. A standardised curriculum exposed all pupils – whether their parents were Jamaican, Irish or Polish, whether they were working class, middle class or upper class – to their 'common cultural heritage'.

The functionalist approach has been attacked from several quarters. The assumptions on which it is based appear to be highly problematic:

Ascriptive characteristics Traits or characteristics that are inherited (e.g. age, colour, sex, height), rather than being the result of personal achievement.

- The degree of 'fit' between the skills taught in school and the technical requirements of efficient production was far from clear. Critics from the New Right have focused strongly on the charge that schools and colleges failed to prepare people for jobs.

- Though schools undoubtedly did sort pupils into successes or failures, it is not clear whether this selection was related to the intellectual merit of the pupils themselves, or to **ascriptive characteristics** such as their ethnic or social class backgrounds, or their sex.

- The notion of a common cultural heritage was difficult to sustain. Many content analyses of curricular materials have revealed racist, ethnic, social class and sexist biases.

In practice, the project of advanced industrial society faltered in the late 1960s and failed in the mid 1970s not so much because this approach had got things wrong, but because the world had changed. The idea of advanced industrial society was based on the existence of a nation-state with a national economy that a government could directly influence and manage. The transformations associated with globalisation (see Chapter 3) rendered the institutions of the social democratic welfare state no longer viable.

A conflict account: correspondence theory

One of the features of structural-functionalism was that it viewed the economic organisation of advanced industrial society in purely technical terms. It believed that modern industry could be rationally organised for optimum efficiency by a new breed of professional managers, who, unlike capitalists, would not be driven purely by greed for profit. Functionalism projected the idea of 'the logic of industrialism'. By contrast, the conflict model has retained the view that advanced industrial society obeys the 'logic of capitalism' (Goldthorpe, 1996). Whereas the functionalists saw economic relations as technically neutral, conflict theorists see them as reflecting class interests and divisions.

One of the best-known conflict models is that proposed by Bowles and Gintis (1976). Bowles and Gintis emphasise that the social relations of production under capitalism are characterised by rigid hierarchies of authority and by fragmentation of tasks. Apart from a minority of professionals and executives, most workers perform mundane tasks, allowing little scope for initiative, responsibility or judgement. Most people have minimal control over what they do and how they do it. The explanation for this lies not in the demands of technology itself, but in the capitalist need to control workers in the interest of profit.

Capitalism
An economic system in which the means of production are privately owned and organised to accumulate profits within a market framework, in which labour is provided by waged workers.

Bowles and Gintis argue that schooling operates under the 'long shadow of work': the education system reflects the organisation of production in **capitalist** society. For example, the fragmentation of work processes is mirrored in the breaking-up of the curriculum into packages of knowledge. Lack of control over work is reflected in the powerlessness of pupils to decide what and how they learn in school, and the necessity of doing unfulfilling jobs for pay is paralleled by the emphasis in schools on learning to obtain certain grades, rather than learning for its own sake. Bowles and Gintis therefore claim there is a correspondence between the nature of work in capitalist societies and the nature of schooling.

Bowles and Gintis (ibid., p. 42) also point out that schools are not uniform, rather 'schools do different things to different children. Boys and girls, blacks and whites, rich and poor are treated differently. Affluent suburban schools, working-class schools, and ghetto schools all exhibit a distinctive pattern.'

Streams
Within a school, the division of cohorts into separate classes that are ranked according to perceived ability, e.g. lower stream, upper stream.

Schools (or **streams**, or tracks) that cater largely for working-class children emphasise obedience and adherence to rules; pupils may be closely supervised and subjected to the same sort of discipline they will later experience in factories or shops. Schools that cater for the privileged emphasise leadership qualities for a future elite. Thus, the emphasis in Bowles and Gintis's account is on the personality characteristics that schools foster and reward.

Schools therefore play an active part in reproducing inequality across generations by moulding pupils to slot into a labour force that is divided along lines of social class, gender and ethnicity. At the same time, education helps to legitimate that inequality. It justifies inequality in people's minds and reconciles them to their position. How does schooling do this? As long as most people believe that education gives everyone a fair chance, then inequality may appear to be justified by different levels of educational attainment. The successful ones view their privileges as a well-deserved reward for ability and effort, while subordinate groups are encouraged to personalise their failure.

CONNECTIONS See Chapter 4, pages 81–6, and Chapter 5, pages 102–18, for an account of the way that educational experiences, social exclusion and labour market position are related. The intersection of social background, educational achievement and employment is a crucial factor in modern societies.

While correspondence theory contains a vivid analysis of the relationships between education, the economy and social equality, many sociologists of education have voiced criticisms. Three issues in particular have given rise to doubts:

- Some aspects of education reflect reforms won through the efforts of working-class people, community groups, feminists and others. The campaigns that led to the development of the education system involved compromises, some of which, in the words of Apple (1988, p. 123), 'signify victory, not losses' for the majority. Many ordinary people value education for its mind-broadening effects as well as for its occupational returns.
- Bowles and Gintis concentrate on social class to the neglect of other forms of inequality. They do not consider the part played by education in structuring race and gender.
- It is doubtful whether the concept of 'correspondence' is adequate to describe the relationship between education and its social context. The notion that the education system reproduces economic relations and class inequalities automatically through correspondence is rejected by other writers from the conflict tradition, who see education's part in the reproduction of inequalities as involving challenge and negotiation.

Macro-level
A level of sociological analysis which focuses either on large collectivities and institutions or social systems and social structures (see structures).

Despite their differences, functionalism and correspondence theory share a number of things in common. Both emphasise the **macro-level** of analysis – the wider relationship between education and other social institutions – and neglect the dynamic interactions between teachers and pupils in schools. Both give enormous weight to the power of education to shape pupils' minds and lives. Both concentrate more on the structure of education than on its content, but, as Moore (1988) points out, the education system is the principal site in our society for the generation of knowledge. Finally, both have been criticised for positing too tight a fit between education and the economy, and for exaggerating the extent to which schools act as providers of a ready, willing and able supply of labour.

In part, the reason why two such contradictory theories can be advanced is that modern societies are neither so closed nor so open that the evidence unambiguously supports one over the other. In combination, these problems suggest that theories that link education with the economy only tell half the story. To complete it, another dimension needs to added.

Education, the state and status groups

Consideration of the link between education and state formation offers not an alternative account to that of the economy but a complementary one. The state and the economy are interrelated: the state is itself an employer; it creates the space within which the economy flourishes, while the economy provides the wealth that enables the state to pursue its policies and provide public services.

The first reason for considering state formation is that the evolution of modern education systems did not follow the same sequence as industrialisation in Western Europe and North America. According to Andy Green (1990), the central factor linking state formation and education was centralisation. There were two educationally significant consequences of extensive state centralisation. First, the state required its own functionaries: literate, educated bureaucrats and administrators. Second, it required a relatively well-educated population, that was able to carry out the projects it initiated. This relates to Green's second main factor: the rapidity of modernisation. When states had to respond to special circumstances such as military defeat, significant transitional events such as the American War of Independence and the French Revolution, or economic competition from a neighbour, they rapidly had to transform their infrastructures or forge new models of citizenship. It was through the provision of education that these could be achieved. These two factors, centralisation and the rapidity of modernisation, better account for the emergence of education systems than does economic development.

Following on from this, the education system then contributed to class formation. In particular, the education system brought into being an important section of the middle class that served the bureaucracy. The great majority of the population, however, received only a basic elementary education that offered no possibility of progression to higher levels. The teachers in nineteenth-century elementary schools were quite distinct in background and education from the elite of the universities. The university elite, from which the class of administrators was drawn, underwent a particular kind of education, known in the German tradition as *Bildung*: 'education for cultivation', producing a person steeped in literature and the arts, engaging in a refined style of life and receiving respect and deference from the rest of the population. Fritz Ringer (1979) refers to this group as 'the German Mandarins'. Top civil servants in the UK are also commonly called mandarins for the same reasons. The Chinese reference is deliberate. Ringer's study was much influenced by Max Weber's (1964) classic work on the religions of China and the Chinese literati – the classically educated Confucian scholars who manned the Chinese imperial bureaucracy. Weber defined this 'education for cultivation' as one of the major types of education. He contrasted it with technical training, which was purely instrumental in purpose and did not carry the 'distinction' (as Pierre Bourdieu calls it) of *Bildung*.

Status groups and social closure

Status
The social honour or prestige accorded to individuals or social groups by others.

The relationship between class differences and education is hierarchical: on average, the higher the class the greater the amount of education. The relationship between **status** and education, however, relates to a horizontal difference within a class. It is not to do with the amount of education, but with the type of education. An important feature of the 'education of cultivation' is that, because of its concern with the whole child, it initiates the individual into a particular culture. It develops sensibilities and tastes that will be shared by those who have experienced such an education and provides the framework for a distinctive lifestyle. This shared lifestyle was central to Weber's idea of a status group (exemplified, for him, by the *Bildung* section of Germany's cultivated, middle-class elite). Educationally acquired status becomes the basis for group identity and solidarity, expressing itself through strategies of social closure (see p. 105), whereby the group attempts to enhance its market capacity.

CONNECTIONS For a more comprehensive account of the strategy of social closure and how it has fared under the impact of economic globalisation, see Chapter 5, pages 105–18.

Data for the UK, for instance, show that since the 1960s, the professional segment of the middle class has not only become significantly better educated than the commercial segment, but that this difference has actually increased over time (Savage *et al*,. 1992, p.152). The disproportionate improvement in the position of the professional segment might mean that it is becoming increasingly self-recruiting, thus making it more difficult for those born outside it to join. This could reflect a strategy of social closure, whereby this section of the middle class is effectively utilising its educational resources and cultural capital to safeguard its interests and those of its children in an increasingly competitive educational market. What this can involve is illustrated by a study carried out by Diane Reay (1998). She interviewed 33 mothers in two contrasting primary schools in London, one predominantly working class and multicultural, the other predominantly white and middle class. Box 10.1 presents Reay's account of the kinds of activity some were engaged in outside school.

The first observation is the amount of extra work these mothers and children put into the activity of schooling. While this primarily involved mothers, presumably there was a male partner in full-time work. Although the material advantages of the middle-class families were obvious, there were also crucial cultural advantages: the capacity of the middle-class women to network and organise; and recognition of the importance of what Reay calls the 'charismatic' qualities associated with artistic and cultural accomplishments. These things represent the advantages of cultural capital (see p. 107), itself derived from education. Reay also highlights the collective impact that the middle-class parents had on the school by insisting that it conform to their expectations, given their aspirations for the children's future. In terms of the more general discussion above, what this example illustrates is that status advantage is not simply automatic – it is something that has to be worked for and at.

BOX 10.1 Working at closure

A third of the children [in the sample] in both schools were currently receiving paid tuition, two working-class and nine middle-class. A further working-class mother talked of embarking on a course of paid tuition but being forced to abandon it when she ran out of funds. In all, over half of the middle-class families were paying for extra tuition for their children with four children having two sessions a week. However, tuition constituted only a small part of some of these children's paid out-of-school activities. For example, Manju's daughter, Negar, attended art and poetry classes and Islamic school, as well as having a personal tutor for mathematics and English. Clare's daughter, Sophie, went to Kumon mathematics classes, attended dance and drama classes and had a tutor for English. Sonia, who tutored Riva herself, paid for her to attend three classes a week in dance, drama and music. Some of the middle-class families were spending £100 a week, more than a number of the working-class lone mothers received in total to support themselves and their child for the same period of time. One child had five paid out-of-school activities a week, while four attended four sessions weekly. The organisation and servicing of these out-of-school activities was primarily the mothers' responsibility. Children's access to the wide range of out-of-school activities was heavily dependent on elaborate mutual arrangements whereby one mother dropped off a group of children and another mother collected them at the end of the session.

Source: Diane Reay (1998, p 201).

Review

Theories of the education system point in two directions: outwards, by means of comparisons with other countries in terms of relative participation and economic competitiveness (a theme of considerable concern to governments); and inwards at the pattern of social differentiation in education – the relationships between social groups. These two dimensions are, however, related, in that it is generally assumed that the more open and meritocratic an education system is internally, the more effectively it contributes to economic efficiency and international competitiveness. In the UK, the New Labour government has set a target of 50 per cent of pupils progressing to higher education. This reflects a long-standing view that the UK lags behind other countries in this respect. Expanding higher education will improve social opportunities for individuals and boost economic competitiveness. It is to these issues that we now turn.

Education and economic and social 'decline' in the UK

Education's role in promoting economic growth and efficiency was often invoked during the twentieth century. In 1976, the Labour Prime Minister Jim Callaghan initiated a 'great debate' on education, one focus of which was the alleged unpreparedness of school leavers for employment (Ahier, Cosin and Hales, 1996). This event signified a turning point in education in the UK: it marked the moment when the positive view that had characterised the earlier post-war period gave way to one that was increasingly critical. Since then, education has frequently been blamed for failing to provide the discipline and technical skills needed to prepare young people for the world of work.

This negative approach to education has been termed 'declinism' (Edgerton, 1996). The concern is that since the middle of the nineteenth century, the UK has been in steady economic decline relative to other countries, such as the US. Some writers (for example, Wiener, 1981; Barnett, 1986) attribute this to the perpetuation of anti-modern and anti-industrial values in the national culture, and especially in the education system (Mathieson and Bernbaum, 1991). Both in its traditional academic form and in its child-centred progressive form, the UK educational tradition and the wider culture are accused of a backward-looking rural nostalgia, as expressed, for instance, in the *The Wind in the Willows*. But as John Beck (1998) points out, declinism is not restricted to the economic. There have also been strong criticisms of moral and social decline, most often from conservative sources. Again education – especially 'progressivism', which is equated with permissiveness – is held responsible. However, does it make sense, sociologically, to blame the lack of competitiveness of the UK economy, or more general social decline, on the shortcomings of schools?

There is little evidence that educational shortcomings are at the root of youth unemployment. Educational qualifications play only a small part in the recruitment of new workers in the UK. For example, employers often prefer older workers, hoping to capitalise on their experience and the fact that, with homes to keep up and children to support, older workers may be more stable. Likewise, there is an enthusiasm amongst employers (especially in the rapidly growing financial services sector) for mature female 'returners' to work because of their inter-personal skills (see Ahier and Moore, 1998). Studies of the labour market suggest that the crisis of youth unemployment is due not to a lack of employable skills, but to wider changes in the job market (Coffield *et al.*, 1989; Ahier and Moore, 1998).

In its broadest form, the declinist position argues that education is responsible for (1) the UK's relative economic decline, (2) its moral and social decline and (3) the reproduction of outmoded class divisions through its elitist and narrowly academic curriculum (usually a leftist or 'moderniser' position, see Young, 1998). Whatever the ideological orientations of these various declinist perspectives, from a sociological point of view, what is significant is their assumption about social causality – the broader social effects attributed to education. It may well be that, if in the positive, social democratic period, too much was expected of education in advanced industrial society, in the period of backlash, too much blame is heaped upon it!

A number of anomalies suggest that declinist accounts should be approached with some scepticism. First, the direct relationship between educational levels and economic productivity has never been convincingly established. John Beck (1998) notes that declinist arguments appear to have more to do with the rhetoric of political agendas than anything substantial. Secondly, as other commentators have argued (for example, Edgerton, 1996), perhaps the situation is not that bad. The UK is still the world's fourth largest economy. In fact, the argument could be put the other way round – what is remarkable about the UK is precisely how productive it remains and how innovative it is in the areas of science and technology. Thirdly, the UK education system is one of the most meritocratic (or open) in the Western world – a point noted as long ago as 1960 by the American sociologist Ralph Turner. As Turner (1961) pointed out, working-class representation in the UK 'selective' system of higher education exceeded, proportionately, that in the US 'mass' system.

Finally, research on education casts severe doubts on the claim that there has been a permissive, progressive revolution, as the conservative perspective suggested. If there has been a national moral and social decline (a highly problematic concept), it cannot be attributed to a progressive revolution in schools, because it never occurred. We can see that there are no simple answers to the question of what an ideal education system should be like.

QUESTION What do you think are the main lessons to be drawn from this history of change and reform?

Education, social inequality and difference

In order to pursue these issues further, we shall consider the relationship between educational and social differences. This relationship is the most fundamental issue for the sociology of education and has obvious relevance to the general public, as well as to politicians and policy makers. Hence, this is an area of sociological work with substantial public implications. First, though, an important question needs to be addressed: what is the difference between inequality and difference, and how can we tell them apart? In the first instance, social differences should be seen as such – whether or not they are also inequalities has to be established.

Implicit in a great deal of sociological theorising is an existential assumption about the status of individual decision-making. For instance, school teachers are usually committed to the idea that their job is to develop their pupils' full potential and widen their horizons to the opportunities open to them (the ideal of meritocracy). Especially for lower-class students, this will involve encouraging them to be upwardly mobile, thus leaving behind their class of origin and its intimate associations with family, friends and community. In the case of female pupils, it might be equated with their adopting non-traditional gender roles – following professional careers rather than being wives and mothers. Certain kinds of pupil choices will be valued and assumed to be autonomous, authentic or liberated while others will be dismissed as stereotyped and simply the product of socialisation.

This is both a professional issue for teachers, to do with respect for pupils' individual values, and a theoretical and research issue for sociologists when deciding which so-called problems need explaining. Why, for instance, should it be considered a problem that fewer girls than boys take physics? Why should males' decision to study physics be unproblematic, whereas females' decision not to do so causes concern? How many people of either sex should take physics? In itself, this is entirely arbitrary, and the final answer rests on value judgements about the desirability or benefits of studying physics. In a similar fashion, why should we prioritise the traditional male 'destiny' of breadwinning above the female 'destiny' of caring for the home? Perhaps we would all be much better off as human beings if we spent more time at home and less at work!

The distinction between inequality and difference also influences what is to count, sociologically, as an explanation. The two things imply different views of the social actor. If we see things as differences, then this has to do with the exercise of personal preference. If we see things as inequalities, on the other hand, we seek explanations in terms of forces acting on individuals to prevent them from doing what they would otherwise choose to do. Hence, we can distinguish between explanations according to whether they operate with an active or a passive (acted upon) model of the subject. Virtually everyone in a contemporary society has been a pupil, so we can reflect on our own experiences as a way of evaluating these models. Were you an active or a passive pupil – or is this too simple an opposition?

Educational social differentiation: class, gender and ethnicity

Although for analytical purposes the major social dimensions of class, gender and ethnicity are often treated separately, it is important to be sensitive to their interactions. Each is qualified by the others in ways that make it dangerous to generalise about groups simply on the basis of one dimension. It is also important to recognise that descriptions of social differences tend to be based upon the average for a group – its arithmetic mean. There is invariably a considerable degree of spread (or variance) around that mean. Large numbers of working-class people, for instance, are highly successful educationally. It is not only necessary to qualify generalisations about this fact, but it also needs explaining – why is it that some working-class people do better in education than is the norm for their group?

Class differences in education

Historically, class was the earliest of the three major dimensions of social difference to be investigated sociologically, and in policy terms it was the main reason for educational reform. It is still the case that class is the main factor in social differences. Although more and more people have received extended education, educational achievement continues to be systematically linked to social background. Among those who possessed a degree at the beginning of the 1990s, 32 per cent had fathers with professional occupations, and about 6 per cent had fathers who were engaged in manual or service-sector work (Office for National Statistics, 1993).

The central fact that needs explaining is that although the lower social groups have consistently improved their absolute level of attainment, they have not changed their relative position.

BOX 10.2 Meritocracy in post-war Britain?

CHART 10.1 Participation in higher education by social class, 1991/2–1997/8 (per cent)

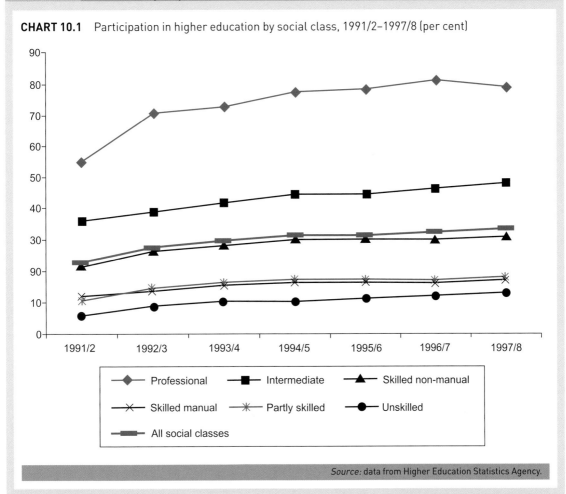

Source: data from Higher Education Statistics Agency.

Halsey *et al.* (1980), whose study *Origins and Destinations* reconstructed the educational careers of 8 529 men, concluded that the expansion of secondary and higher education in the 1950s and 1960s did little to iron out social class differentials. In fact, it may have benefited middle-class people more than the working class. For example, a boy from the service class (see Chapter 5), compared with a working-class boy, had:

- four times more chance of being in school at age 16;

- 10 times more chance of being in school at age 18;
- 11 times more chance of entering university.

This remains true today, as reflected in Chart 10.1.

Although participation in higher education expanded considerably, the variation between socio-economic groups changed little during the 1990s. All groups improved their participation levels, but more or less in step with each other, so that no groups significantly improved their relative advantage.

Based on a comparison of the oldest cohort of men in their sample with the youngest and most recently educated cohort, Halsey *et al.* refute the idea that the working class has caught up with other groups. Class differentials in educational attainment do not appear even to have narrowed over time, let alone equalised.

During the period analysed, the proportion of working-class boys entering university increased by 2 per cent, but that of boys from the intermediate ▶

▶ class (clerical workers, small proprietors, foremen) and the service class increased by 6 per cent and 9 per cent respectively. The expansion of university places resulted in greater absolute gains for the middle class than for the working class, so the differentials between the classes were preserved. Halsey *et al.* (ibid., p. 210) conclude that 'the 1944 Education Act brought England and Wales no nearer to the ideal of a meritocratic society ... Secondary education was made free in order to enable the poor to take advantage of it, but the paradoxical consequence was to increase subsidies to the affluent.'

This conclusion is all the more persuasive because it is consistent with the findings of other investigations, not only in the UK but in other countries as well. While there is disagreement about the reason for persistent social class inequality in education, the existence of that inequality is not in dispute. Education's role as a promoter of social mobility for the working class has been outstripped by its effectiveness in confirming the privileged location of children from middle-class homes.

QUESTION How difficult was it for you to get to university? Do you think that your home background and educational experiences helped or hindered you? Write a paragraph explaining your answer.

Figure 10.1 Social class influences both whether people go into higher education and the type of university they attend: about half the intake of the elite British universities of Oxford and Cambridge come from fee-paying schools.

Gender differences in education

As far as gender differences are concerned, the story is the exact opposite of that for class. The most significant event in education in the last quarter of the twentieth century was the improvement of the position of females *vis-à-vis* males, such an improvement that they overtook males at every level! Sociologically this is perhaps even more intriguing than the persistence of class differentials, and it might be that understanding how gender relations have changed could throw light on why the class gap has not.

It is no exaggeration to refer to these changes as an 'educational revolution'. Until the 1970s, little attention was paid to gender differences (see Arnot *et al.*, 1999), but then feminist researchers and teachers did much to highlight the issue (Weiner, 1994). Initially, the concern was with the under-achievement of girls relative to boys in secondary schooling and beyond. It is important to remember that until then it had been very much taken for granted that girls would do less well than boys, and that this was no more than the natural course of things. Hence, the major changes that occurred well deserve the term 'revolution'.

More broadly, feminist researchers were concerned with whether this under-achievement was related to the reproduction of traditional sex roles in a patriarchal and sexist society, and if so, in what ways. This involved investigating not only the differences in attainment, but also whether education was gendered, for instance, in terms of which subjects were typically studied by which sex. Stereotypically, arts and humanities subjects

(English, history, geography and so on) and languages were seen as female subjects, and maths and the natural sciences (especially physics and chemistry) as male. Sociology held the middle ground.

Much work had to be done to break down the taken-for-granted assumption that these divisions were natural. The introduction of the national curriculum was significant in this respect, because it defined a common curriculum for all pupils regardless of sex. This in turn reflected the idea that all pupils were entitled to a particular body of knowledge and that it was the responsibility of schools to transmit this knowledge. This common 'entitlement' curriculum replaced the gendered curriculum of earlier times. Hence, it is necessary to consider changes in (1) levels of participation and attainment, and (2) subject choice.

Chart 10.2 shows the changing relationship between male and female pupils obtaining 2 or more 'A' levels or 3 or more Scottish Highers and is representative of the general trend at other levels above and below. As can be seen, there was a consistent trend in female relative improvement. It is also useful to note that the 20-year period covered by the graph contained a variety of educational changes, but there are no sudden divergences in the graph to suggests that these changes had a significant independent effect. In the first part of the 1990s, girls began to overtake boys at A level. According to the Equal Opportunities Commission, 'Men and women now perform as well as each other in most subjects at A level and in [Scottish] Highers. In those subjects where men

CHART 10.2 The changing position of male and female pupils, A level and Scottish Higher passes, 1975/6–1996/7

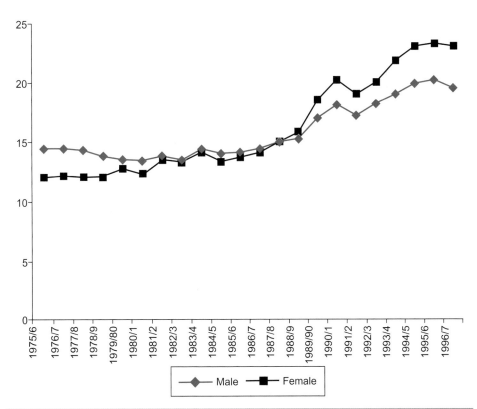

Source: data from Higher Education Statistics Agency.

continue to perform better than women, the gender gap is narrowing' (EOC, undated, p.3). This had important implications for university entrance and reflected females' superior GCSE performance.

Chart 10.3 illustrates how this improvement at GCSE level was also associated with the virtual elimination of gender difference in subject choice. Girls not only did better than boys, they also moved into traditionally male subject areas and began to outperform them there as well! They also extended their superiority in the traditionally female subjects.

CHART 10.3 Male and female passes for GCSE maths, science, modern languages and English 1988–96 (per cent)

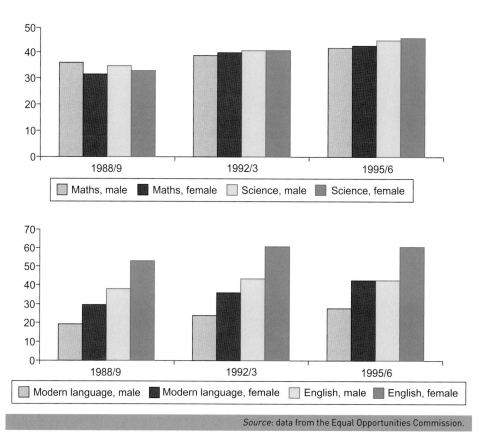

Source: data from the Equal Opportunities Commission.

A similar trend took place in higher education. Whereas women made up only one third of undergraduates in 1975, by 1999, their representation had risen to 54 per cent (Higher Education Statistics Agency). The distribution of degrees between the sexes in 1996/7 is shown in Table 10.1.

By 1998/9, the percentage of women receiving first-class degrees or upper seconds was 55 per cent compared with 46 per cent of men. In 1994/5, 36 per cent of students graduated in the sciences, and 38 per cent of these were women. In 1999, 38 per cent were science graduates, of whom 43 per cent were women.

Hence, in the last quarter of the twentieth century, there was a major change in the position of females with regard to education. This both reflected and had implications for gender relations, identities and expectations in society at large. Accounting for this educational revolution may hold the key to understanding much more.

TABLE 10.1 Performance at first degree level, 1996/7 (per cent)

	Female	Male
First	6.9	8.5
Upper second	48.4	40.2
Lower second	37.7	39.4
Third/pass	7.0	12.0

Source: derived from data available at Equal Opportunities Commission (undated).

CONNECTIONS Gender differences are expressed not only in educational achievement but also in a whole range of social processes and divisions. See Chapter 6, pp. 141–8, for a fuller account of the differential position of men and women in the labour force.

Ethnic differences in education

It is not possible to produce any broad generalisation about the relationship between ethnicity and education. In a pluralistic, multi-cultural society such as the UK, ethnic diversity is so great that no uniformity can be expected between groups. This is particularly so in the case of education. One immediate consequence of this observation is that the assumption that black pupils tend towards educational underachievement must be rejected. The actual situation is much more complex (see Chapter 7), and this is an area where the interactions between ethnicity, class and gender are especially important. Table 10.2 represents the highest qualification levels attained by ethnic groups for different ages.

However, this situation become more complicated when gender is taken into account. The Commission for Racial Equality (1997, p. 3) summarises the situation as follows:

" *Education*
47% of 16–24 year old ethnic minority women were in full or part-time education in winter 1995/96, compared with 32% of White women. White women were the least likely of all to be full-time students. Chinese women between 16 and 24 had the highest participation rate of women from all ethnic groups (66%). Black Caribbean women were least likely of all minority women to become full-time students (32%).
Qualifications
Women from all ethnic groups, except Black Caribbean, were less likely to have higher qualifications than men, in 1991. The proportion of Black Caribbean women with a higher qualification was twice that of Black Caribbean men. A greater proportion of ethnic minority women had higher education qualifications (13%) than White women (12%). Over 20% of Chinese and Black African women had higher qualifications – the highest proportions of women from any group. The lowest proportions were of Pakistani and Bangladeshi women (4% and 3% respectively). "

The table and the data above illustrate the above average attainments of some groups and the significantly lower ones of others. The effect of gender is striking. For instance, Asian women are significantly over-represented in the group with no qualifications (although so also are Asian males – see below). It is also the case that different groups tend to follow different courses. For instance, 40 per cent of black 16 year olds in full-time education in 1996 were pursuing vocational courses compared with 30 per

TABLE 10.2 Highest qualification held among people of working age, by ethnic group and age, spring 1997.

	White Minorities	All ethnic	Black	Indian	Pakistani and Bangladeshi	Other
25–59/64 years	%	%	%	%	%	%
Degrees	14	16	14	19	10	19
Higher below degree	9	7	11	7	2	8
A-level	23	12	15	11	7	11
GCSE grades A–C or equivalent	20	13	19	12	8	11
Other qualifications	15	29	25	30	26	36
No qualifications	20	23	17	20	47	15
16–24 years	%	%	%	%	%	%
Degrees	7	6	*	9	*	8
Higher below degree	4	2	*	*	*	*
A-level	27	24	24	29	19	26
GCSE grades A–C or equivalent	37	34	37	38	30	30
Other qualifications	10	15	15	*	17	19
No qualifications	10	17	18	12	24	15

Numbers less than 10 000; estimated percentages not reported.

Sources: Labour Force Survey, spring 1997; Commission for Racial Equality (1998, table 1, page 2, Education and Training in Britain, London: CRE).

cent of whites and 27 per cent of Asians (Commission for Racial Equality, 1997). In contrast, 41 per cent of Asians were following academic courses, as were 38 per cent of whites and 30 per cent of blacks. It is also notable that black women were most likely to hold higher education qualifications other than degrees, reflecting their involvement in the health and caring sector.

Table 10.2 highlights an additional issue that arises when considering ethnic groups: that of definition and categorisation. The single term 'Asian' incorporates people of Indian, Pakistani and Bangladeshi heritage. This, of course, disguises a massive amount of cultural and regional diversity, as well as significant educational differences between these groups. Among the UK population aged 25–64, for instance, 19 per cent of Indians hold degrees, compared with 14 per cent of whites and 10 per cent of Pakistani and Bangladeshi people (ibid.) Pakistanis and Bangladeshis also account for a much higher proportion in that age range with no qualifications: 47 per cent, compared with 20 per cent for Indians and 20 per cent for whites. It is always important to question the categories used in the presentation of data on ethnicity, as the hidden hand of class is often behind such differences.

CONNECTIONS For a fuller consideration of the impact of racism in society, see Chapter 7, especially pages 165–81. Education is only one of the areas in which ethnic identity plays a significant part.

Educational and social differentiation: Summary

This review of educational differences in relation to the major social dimensions of class, gender and ethnicity has stressed the complexities of the issue and the even more complex question of their inter-relatedness. In the case of class, the pattern is straightforwardly hierarchical. On average, the higher a person's social class, the higher his or her level of education. In the case of gender, there has been a crossover between the sexes in educa-tion. In the case of ethnicity, the picture is essentially kaleidoscopic. No generalisations can be made, and, in fact, it is important not to do so. As stated at the beginning of this section, not only do the three dimensions come together in real life situations, but there is also a significant variation in the group averages. These variations reflect the things that people actually do. Sociologically, we cannot disconnect explanations of mean differences from accounts of how significant numbers of people manage to be other than average. Together, these factors present a major explanatory challenge to sociology.

Explaining social difference and educational attainment

Sociologists are concerned not only to monitor the persistence of the relationship between educational attainment and social difference, but also to explain it. These explanations fall into two broad types. *Intra-school* explanations explore the impact of particular features of the educational regime – the curriculum, school organisation, teachers' expectations and classroom dynamics (that is, factors internal to the school). Such explanations point to the power of schools to influence the social distribution of achievement. The second group of explanations focus on extra-school influences that social groups carry into the school (that is, factors external to the school). These explanations assume that educational inequality is due to social differences that schools are relatively powerless to change.

Extra-school explanations: naturalistic and cultural

Extra-school explanations fall into two main types: 'naturalistic' ones that account for differences in people's innate qualities; and 'culturalist' ones that focus on aspects of the pupil's home and social environment. These two approaches have been locked together in what is known as the 'nature versus nurture' debate about whether biology or the environment, (that is, genetics or social conditioning) exert the greater influence. Most commentators see this distinction as far too simplistic, as nature and nurture interact in complex ways, and it is not possible accurately to separate them, let alone attach relative values to each. As a matter of common sense, we should expect both to be playing their part. Proponents of both explanatory extremes run the risk of producing explanations that are equally reductionist and mechanistic. It is necessary to preserve a sense of the individual as an active rather than simply a determined being. We shall contrast examples from each of these approaches. The first is the naturalistic argument that social inequal-ities reflect innate intelligence, a position assumed by Herrnstein and Murray in their controversial book *The Bell Curve: intelligence and class structure in American life* (1997), and the second is the culturalist theory of Pierre Bourdieu (1997) and his concept of habitus.

Intelligence quotient
A measurement of intelligence based on the ratio of a person's mental age (as measured by IQ tests) to his or her actual age.

Naturalistic explanations: who's a clever boy, then?

In the 1970s, Herrnstein and Murray (1997) argued that the class structure of American society reflected IQ (**intelligence quotient**) differences between social groups.

According to these authors, this was especially problematic at the lower end, in that the inferior intelligence of lower-class people expressed itself in violence, crime, family breakdown, inadequate parenting, drug use and other kinds of dysfunctional and anti-social behaviour. This argument had a special resonance for Americans because the US class structure was associated with ethnicity and colour. Many people interpreted *The Bell Curve* as a disguised attack upon black Americans, carrying a racist message of black inferiority and sanctioning the dominance of the WASP (white Anglo-Saxon Protestant) elite on the ground of its innate superiority. In so doing (something they themselves vigorously denied), Herrnstein and Murray seemed to be echoing a similar claim by Jensen (1969), who had sparked off a furious row when he asserted that the higher average IQ score of white Americans over black Americans was due largely to genetic differences, and that this justified different approaches to educating white and black pupils.

The existence of a correlation between IQ score and educational performance may appear to lend scientific weight to the common-sense idea that social groups who succeed in school do so because they are naturally bright. But there are serious problems with the notion that IQ scores reflect natural abilities and hence explain educational attainment.

First, it has to be recognised that however we choose to define intelligence, no measurement test of it can separate natural ability from cultural influence. Tests of intelligence therefore cannot be said to measure natural ability; at best, they can only test whether a person's intelligence develops in interaction with a particular environment.

Second, many factors besides IQ enter into the social distribution of achievement. Studies demonstrate that working-class pupils are educationally disadvantaged compared with middle-class pupils even when the two groups' IQs are identical.

Third, cultural factors influence different social groups' IQ test performance. Lack of experience with timed tests, distrust of the tester, and fear of failure are just three of the many variables that, experiments have shown, can lower the IQ score of a group (Kamin, 1977). For these reasons, many sociologists and educationalists are convinced that IQ tests put a naturalistic slant on differences between pupils that are in fact socially created.

BOX 10.3 Race, heredity and intelligence

The arguments advanced by Jensen (1969) and Herrnstein and Murray (1997) depend on four basic assumptions about the relationship between intelligence and genetics – 'that intelligence can be described by a single number; that it is capable of ranking people in some linear order; that it is genetically based; and that it is immutable' (Fraser, 1997, p. 781). Intelligence is no longer simplistically understood as a 'thing' that we have more or less of, and that can be represented by a numerical value.

Scientists now think in terms of 'multiple intelligences' of different kinds, variously developed in particular individuals. UK records show that educational attainment steadily improved during the twentieth century. If educational attainment reflects IQ levels, are we to assume that the nation became collectively more intelligent over the century? The answer is self-evidently no. In principle, people at the beginning of the twentieth century were well able to match the educational levels of those at

the end of it. The fact that they did not is an historical contingency – there simply was not the same degree of educational provision. The population has become more educated, not more intelligent.

There is also the issue of variance. Even if it could be established that there were mean differences between classes, races and the sexes, they would only be tiny in comparison with those within each group. There are no measured differences between men and women, for ▶

▶ example, that exceed the differences within each sex. Think here of shoe size. On average, men take a larger shoe size than women, but the difference within each group is so large that the overlap between the two groups is far greater than the difference between their means.

Ironically, even if the IQ argument were true, nothing of any consequence could follow from it, because there could be no justification for treating every member of a group as if they were representative of the average member. This would be like insisting that all men wear only the average size shoe for males and all women the average for females.

Finally, there are questionable policy implications which follow from the concern with inheritance of IQ. One politically contentious suggestion is that if IQ proved to have a large genetic component, this would entail a reduction in educational support for low IQ groups. Even if it were the case that certain groups were genetically disadvantaged in terms of IQ, and that IQ accurately reflected intelligence – neither of which has been properly demonstrated – this would provide a powerful argument for devoting extra resources to them.

These points are not intended to dismiss the notion of natural ability, but to indicate the problem with certain generalising types of argument that fail to take proper account of the complexities of the issue. Some of these also apply to the culturalist approach.

Culturalist explanations: who's a pretty boy, then?

The work of Pierre Bourdieu is complex, and to designate his approach as culturalist is problematic: part of his purpose has been to produce a theory that would overcome or integrate traditional distinctions such as macro and micro, objective and subjective, economic and cultural. However, for the present purposes, the culturalist label can be justified because of the role that culture plays in his theory, especially when he turns his attention to education. It is necessary to understand his key concepts of cultural field, **habitus** and cultural capital.

CONNECTIONS The notion of cultural capital was introduced in Chapter 5, page 107, where the university background of individuals is used as an example of cultural capital.

Habitus
Pierre Bourdieu's term for the everyday habitual practices and assumptions of a particular social environment. People are at once the product of, and the creators of, their habitus.

In his essay, 'The Forms of Capital', Bourdieu (1997) argues that the cultural field, especially in its high or elite form, must be understood as a transformation or 'transubstantiation' of the economic field and its relationships. This is because its principle is the opposite of the economic. Whereas economic exchanges and relationships are based on profit, gain and self-interest, culture is said to be disinterested, in that it is an end in itself and justified intrinsically by aesthetic value. The cultural is at a higher level than the economic field in the same way as the sacred is to the profane.

However, Bourdieu argues, that this is in fact an illusion, and the status accorded to high culture in reality has everything to do with the tastes cultivated by the ruling class. Rather than art objects themselves generating a sacred aura, they only become appreciated when individuals acquire the tacit codes for understanding them and are able to talk about them in an appropriate manner ('the rules of the game'). When we visit an art gallery, we have to know how to look at a picture, if we are to see what is held to be significant about it. Bourdieu's research indicates that lower-class people tend to discuss and evaluate paintings in terms of how life-like they are, or sentimentally in terms of what is portrayed. Higher-class people, in contrast, tend to discuss paintings in relation to each other, as schools or movements of varying originality or significance.

In a similar fashion, people who 'go to the pictures' often list their favourite films in terms of the stars who appear in them, whereas those who 'watch movies' talk in terms of directors and genres. The sociology of 'taste' and its social distribution is a central concern in Bourdieu's work.

Taste is acquired first in the home through the acquisition of a class habitus. Habitus has the qualities of both habit and habitat; that is, it is a predisposition to act in certain ways by virtue of one's environment. But habitus differs crucially from a mere habit, in that a habit is simply the repetition of the same piece of behaviour – for example, someone might say, 'I'm in the habit of singing in the bath'. Habitus, in contrast, is a generative capacity that predisposes us to classify things and act in distinctive ways. It is more like learning the rules of grammar than learning a vocabulary. The habitus of different groups is revealed in distinctive aspects of their life-styles: the papers and books they read, what they drink, where they go on holiday. Although these things are all socially produced and distributed, marking out the positions that people occupy in the social field, they appear to be and are treated as natural – habitus is, Bourdieu says, like a second nature. The mark of distinction associated with a cultivated habitus (*Bildung*) is precisely the ease with which those who possess it exercise it. Their good taste seems entirely natural, a superior attribute of the person him- or herself.

The different forms of habitus correspond to the social relations of capitalist society. According to Bourdieu, we classify ourselves in the same way as we classify the world, the positions we take indicate the positions we occupy. The structure of the cultural field parallels that of the social field and its economic base, but not as a simple reflection. The whole point about art for art's sake is that it does not represent any external social or economic interest. Habitus is crucial in relation to education, and it is through education that habitus is strengthened and refined for some, while systematically excluding others.

Although one culture (or habitus) is not intrinsically superior to another, the power enjoyed by the dominant classes enables them to impose their own framework of meaning on the school as if it were the only legitimate culture. Through this 'symbolic violence', the dominant class succeeds in defining which topics are worthy of consideration – in effect, the dominant class defines what counts as knowledgeable or intelligent activity. Even when schools treat all pupils equally, Bourdieu argues, through the selective tradition in the curriculum, the school legitimates the success of pupils from particular social backgrounds and the failure of others by making these socially produced principles of selection appear entirely natural.

As pupils move up the educational ladder, those from the dominated class are progressively eliminated or shunted into less prestigious forms of education; in contrast, the habitus of children from the dominant class provides them with cultural capital, which is translated into academic and eventually occupational success. The education system acts 'neutrally', but only in the sense that it evaluates all pupils according to their mastery of the dominant culture – those who have inherited a cultural capital that accords with the culture of the school (those who know the rules of the game) will appear naturally more gifted. As Lareau (1997) and Brown (1997) argue (drawing on Bourdieu), schools translate working-class culture into working-class failure and deficiency.

Thus, schooling reproduces relations of inequality between the classes and other social categories. In the process, it validates the superiority of dominant groups, and confirms for others their own sense of worthlessness, their distance from 'what really counts'. By employing the term cultural capital, Bourdieu is suggesting that culture, despite its claim to disinterestedness, ultimately serves an economic function and operates in the same way as economic capital by 'purchasing' social advantages for certain groups. Thus, economic advantage can be translated into a social advantage that, as a family habitus, can be transmitted between the generations. Because habitus is embodied in us (that is, it is imprinted on our consciousness and physiology – how we talk and move as well as think), once we have acquired it, unlike economic capital, it cannot be taken away from us.

Bourdieu's approach is the opposite of naturalistic approaches not just because of the priority he gives to culture in his analysis, but also because he sees culture as acting decisively upon nature, transforming us from natural to social beings. We are social precisely to the extent that we are not natural, and it is education (in the broadest sense) that causes this transubstantiation of the self. Despite this, Bourdieu's culturalist approach has similar problems to the naturalistic approach.

Bourdieu derives social and cultural relations from economic ones. However, questions of aesthetic judgement and discrimination resolve into 'position takings' and strategies to pursue social advantage. Bourdieu's model thus slides into reductionism and a relativism that the rhetoric of his intentions and claims denies (see Alexander, 1995, ch. 4). As we shall see, this is especially significant in the case of education.

In much the same way as the naturalists reduce social differences to IQ, so Bourdieu resolves them into differences in habitus. Although habitus is a more sophisticated concept, it effectively does much the same thing, in that it ranks people into a linear order. Given that habitus is in the first instance acquired in the parental home (the cultural equivalent of the genetic code), as with IQ, it becomes difficult to account for variance within a category. As with Bowles and Gintis's (1976) correspondence theory, the cultural capital theory of education satisfactorily explains social reproduction, but, precisely because of this, it makes non-reproduction difficult to account for. Bourdieu does have a response to this. He argues that any position has a range of possibilities (or social trajectories) associated with it that are expressed as an 'objective probability structure', distributing life-chances between classes. Unfortunately, it is not possible to theorise in advance what these will be (or why). Hence the argument has an underlying circularity – if x per cent of working-class pupils proceed to Oxbridge (despite lacking the necessary habitus), then this is because x per cent was the objective probability of the number of working-class pupils who would do so.

Finally, just as in naturalist accounts, individuals simply live out their biological destiny, so in Bourdieu's account, they live out a cultural one. In a sense, the theory explains too much, in that everything appears to be accounted for once we understand (1) an individual's background (primary habitus), (2) the condition of a field at a particular time in terms of relations, probabilities and trajectories, and (3) the position in the field occupied by that individual at a particular moment and the 'position takings' available to him or her. In short, the theory lacks the contingent qualities of spontaneity and chance that are present when individuals are truly active subjects.

Intra-school explanations: school organisation and school culture

Explanations that concentrate on educational factors focus on the organisation of the education system and the school (for example, the tripartite system and streaming) and on educational processes (for example, teachers' expectations and the hidden curriculum). What these approaches share is the view that factors of this type have educationally and socially significant implications for pupils' self-image and sense of identity. They draw upon a long tradition of thinking about the self that has its origins in symbolic interactionism (Jones and Moore, 1996).

CONNECTIONS For a full account of symbolic interactionism and its concepts of looking-glass self, definition of the situation, significant other, generalised other, I and Me, see Chapter 18, pages 501–4.

The 'looking glass' theory of the self holds that our sense of identity and personal worth is constructed through our impression of how others see us. Consequently, children construct positive or negative images of themselves or their group. Black children in a white racist society encounter numerous negative stereotypes that can lead to low self-esteem and educational under-achievement. A working-class boy placed in the C stream will come to see himself as an educational failure. These processes produce effects that apparently confirm the stereotypes held by dominant groups – black and working-class children will 'fail', and hence will appear inferior: a self-perpetuating, self-fulfilling prophecy. This approach has its origins in psychological studies of black under-

---

BOX 10.4 Comprehensive reform

The logic of the approach discussed above is that if educational organisation and processes have certain effects, then changing them should produce different effects. A great deal of the reform that occurred in the second half of the twentieth century reflected this thinking. Those arguing in favour of comprehensive schools stressed the damaging effects that the tripartite system had on the majority of pupils who did not gain entry to grammar schools:

- Errors made with the 11-plus examination resulted, according to Yates and Pidgeon (1957), in approximately 70 000 children being allocated each year to the wrong type of school.

- These errors tended to bear most heavily on working-class children.

- Secondary modern schools – with their stigma of failure, their less academic curriculum and their lack of preparation for national examinations – depressed the overall performance of pupils.

- The tripartite system contributed to the low rate of entry to higher education in the UK compared with its economic and political rivals.

All this led to a groundswell of opinion in favour of wholesale reorganisation, and by 1984, 82 per cent of state secondary pupils in England (and 96 per cent in Scotland and Wales) were in comprehensive schools. The new system would, it was hoped, raise the overall level of educational attainment, narrow class differentials in education, and help to dismantle the social and cultural barriers between the social classes. In the 1980s, the policies of the New Right reversed these principles. Today, New Labour's policy is to move towards a greater variety of schools catering for different needs and specialisms, but without the rigidity of the old tripartite model.

One thing is clear: during the period of wholesale reorganisation, standards – measured in terms of examination successes – did rise. More pupils than ever

before succeeded at school and gained qualifications. On the other hand, it is less clear that the reorganisation served to narrow class differentials. It should be noted that research in Scotland suggests that the effects of comprehensive schools on class differentials may have been greater there (McPherson and Willms, 1997).

In a similar fashion, in the 1980s a great deal of effort was put into examining stereotypes of girls and ethnic minorities in school texts and replacing negative or outmoded ones with more positive images (Jones and Moore, 1996). Multi-cultural, anti-racist and anti-sexist education were concerned with raising people's consciousness about discrimination and challenging their stereotyped assumptions. In this case, the emphasis was more on processes within education than on the organisational features of schooling. But, again, it is necessary to raise the issue of what is being assumed about how such educational processes create the effects attributed to them.

achievement in the US that advanced the view that black children had a negative self-image (Reeves and Chavannes, 1988).

Labelling theory and classroom processes

Sociologists working in the **social action** tradition argue that schools do not react to pupils in a neutral way; pupil identities (such as 'less able' or 'disruptive') are not fixed in childhood. Success or failure is the product of a career moulded over a long period, the outcome of which is never guaranteed. The relative failure of boys of Afro-Caribbean origin or of working-class children is not determined solely by their ability or attitudes, because teacher–pupil interactions play a significant part. Even in the most progressive infant classes, there exists what Bernstein (1977) calls an 'invisible pedagogy' – hidden criteria of judgement – according to which pupils will be approved of or not. In subtle ways, educational 'codes' act selectively upon pupils in terms of how effectively they are able to recognise the special demands that the school is tacitly making of them.

Teachers do not always react in the same way to instances of rule breaking. Their response depends initially upon how they interpret the action (Is it serious? Will it spread?), and then upon the view or typification that they have of the pupil concerned (Hargreaves *et al.*, 1975). Pupils become typecast on the basis of earlier impressions or reputations. By analysing how teachers arrive at such judgements, researchers have found that teachers are implicated in the process of pupil failure. Classroom observation studies in a variety of settings testify that, on the whole, teachers tend to give more of their time to pupils whom they believe to be bright; it may be partly the case that these children learn more than their classmates because of this extra attention.

Figure 10.2 During the many hours they spend at school, children absorb much more than what is just in the formal curriculum. Teacher expectations and teaching strategies also play their part in shaping students' values, attitudes and ambitions.

Stratification
The division of a population into unequal layers or strata based on income, wealth, gender, ethnicity, power, status, age, religion or some other characteristic.

Ethnocentric
The description of the inability to understand the validity or integrity of cultures other than one's own.

A process of **stratification** occurs in classrooms, with teachers meting out different treatment to more or less favoured groups of pupils. When analysing interactions in three junior and three middle schools, Green (1985) found that teachers with highly **ethnocentric** attitudes taught black pupils and white pupils in sharply differing ways. Likewise, Brah and Minhas (1988) found that some Asian girls were typed as 'passive', leading to their being overlooked and underestimated in class. In general, teachers' expectations have tended to reflect the priority given to males in our culture. Teachers in secondary schools have tended to prefer teaching male pupils, and expected boys to be more critical, more forthcoming and more enthusiastic than girls. Even when girls have been more successful than boys, the excellence of their work has sometimes been attributed to a desire to please rather than to creativity or intellectual promise (Clarricoates, 1980). Expectations – because they involve ideas about what 'such and such a group' are really like – mean that stereotypical assumptions about ethnic groups, social classes, and genders may shape relations between pupils and teachers in the classroom. Today, perhaps, teachers may have higher expectations of girls than of boys (Warrington and Younger, 1996).

Such expectations have often been associated with cultural deprivation theory. This theory differs from more general culturalist accounts (such as Bourdieu's) in that it pays less attention to the lack of congruence (or distance) between educational and home values. Rather, it argues that certain kinds of family are actually lacking in crucial cultural attributes such as basic linguistic skills. Such families are viewed as 'pathological' – as suffering a kind of cultural illness that makes them socially incompetent in general as well as in educational terms. For this reason, the children of these families, or the communities in which they live, require 'compensatory education', where the school attempts to supply the basic cultural competences said to be lacking in the home. A good example of this type of thinking can be found in Lady Plowden's influential report on primary education in England and Wales (1967). This way of categorising certain kinds of pupil can give rise to stereotypical expectations that influence how teachers react to them and address their presumed needs.

Children who are deemed to be culturally deprived may be bright enough, but they can be held back by values and attitudes that are not conducive to educational success. In the early post-war period, cultural deprivation was linked to social class. The Plowden Report argued that in such cases it was the entire family that needed educating, not simply the child. Teachers should join up with social workers and home health visitors in an attempt to help these families achieve normality. Theorists targeted various aspects of working-class culture, including an inability to defer gratification, lack of parental interest in children's education, and lack of ambition. Since the 1970s, it has been black and Asian pupils who have been seen as culturally deprived. Theorists have proposed a range of cultural obstacles to educational success, including 'mother-centred' families, lack of parental interest, low self-esteem and culture clashes.

One problem with cultural deprivation theory is that it uses a single model of the educable child – primarily white and middle class. The educational failure of certain groups is explained by the degree to which they deviate from this model. But instead of asserting that children who do not conform to the model are less well prepared for school, we could easily argue that the school is less well prepared for them – that the education system is insufficiently responsive to their gifts and their needs.

The above approaches to the effects of school organisation differ in the extent to which they emphasise psychological influences on identity formation and self-image, or see them as creating structural conditions to which different groups adapt in different ways. This difference reflects the degree to which pupils are seen as passive or active.

The more passive model associated with the symbolic interactionist position has been strongly criticised by the black sociologist Maureen Stone (1981). The passive model tends to depict the pupil as strongly influenced by pressures such as teacher expectations and the content of the curriculum, rather than as actively engaging with them and even rejecting or subverting their assumptions. Stone examines the psychological assumptions and experimental data upon which these ideas are based and finds both to be flawed. She concludes that there is actually no difference in the degree to which black and white pupils have negative or positive self-images, and that this approach is patronising in its assumption that black people are influenced by the racist views of whites. She also argues that the approach can disadvantage black pupils by encouraging teachers to see their needs as therapeutic rather than academic. This leads teachers to concentrate on activities such as multi-cultural education to boost self-esteem, rather than helping black children to get the good academic qualifications they really need.

In general terms, past approaches that sought to determine the effects of the tripartite system, streaming and teacher expectations were associated historically with the concern about class differentials. Although later work on gender and ethnicity shared some of the assumptions of the earlier approaches, they also differed in important respects. In particular, they focused upon the ways in which sexist and racist preconceptions might be a taken-for-granted aspect of school knowledge. The factors typically investigated as possible causes of gender and racial differentiation include the following (Weiner, 1994):

- Biases in school texts; a taken-for-granted use of sexist and racist (or ethnocentric) language.

- Teacher stereotypes and expectations; the domination of staff hierarchies by white men; the failure of teachers to see sexist and racist behaviour by children as a problem.

- More broadly, sexist and racist aspects of education policy and hostility towards anti-sexist and anti-racist initiatives.

QUESTION Are anti-sexist and anti-racist initiatives in schools just a case of political correctness gone too far? Support your answer with a reasoned argument.

The last of the above points was controversial in the 1980s, with high-profile public battles taking place between the New Right, the neo-conservative government and the more liberal or radical local education authorities, especially in London.

By showing how teachers can act (wittingly or unwittingly) as agents of differentiation, researchers working in the social action tradition have helped to illuminate the impact of schooling on the distribution of achievement. But one problem with this approach is the tendency to see the classroom in splendid isolation, divorced from the wider processes of social control. Hence some researchers, by combining structural and action approaches, have attempted to set classroom interaction within a broader framework. Examples of this are considered below.

Educational differentiation: descriptions and explanations

We have reviewed a range of approaches that attempt to explain the social and educational differences identified. A basic distinction has been made between extra-school explanations which advance either naturalistic or cultural causes, and intra-school explanations, which focus on aspects of educational organisation or processes.

Another distinction has been made in terms of 'active' and 'passive' pupils. It is now necessary to pull these things together. It will probably come as no surprise that there is no simple truth that can make complete sense of something this complex. We have to say that all of the explanatory approaches reviewed here do account for parts of what is going on, but none can convincingly explain the whole. However, some general observations can be made and conclusions drawn that may point us in the right direction.

First, if we consider intra-school accounts of the processes that cause differentiation, it seems fair to suggest that factors of this type have not made a major contribution to the patterns that have been observed empirically over time. The reasons for this are as follows.

During the course of the twentieth century, the organisation of schooling underwent considerable change, often with the explicit policy intention of reducing class-based differentials in education. But we know that these differentials remained more or less intact. The moves from tripartite to comprehensive, from selection and streaming to mixed ability and other progressive approaches are not associated with a significant change in class relativities. A century of changes in these aspects of education is probably long enough for us to conclude that they have not made much of a difference in this respect. But, at the same time, the mean level of attainment for each class has consistently improved. Perhaps the successive reforms have been responsible for this? Again, this is unlikely. The improvement was consistent and gradual and therefore cannot be associated with drastic reforms, such as those which followed the 1944 and 1988 Education Acts.

As for the effect of educational processes on gender and ethnic differentiation, the considerable success of women in the last quarter of the century and the high levels achieved by many black minorities suggests that hostile sexist and racist educational environments have not prevented females and blacks from becoming educationally more successful than white males. Arnot *et al.* (1999) conclude from their major review of the gender gap that explanations drawn from education alone cannot account for what has happened. For the same reasons that negative intra-school processes have prevented these achievements, anti-sexist and anti-racist initiatives (whatever other good they did) have not caused them.

This is not to say that schools do not make a difference, they do (see Mortimore, 1997, for a review of 'school effectiveness' research). But the kinds of difference they make do not contribute significantly to (or are not capable of generating) the observed macro patterns of change or significantly affect relations between groups. Many people, however, will say that their school or a particular teacher had a big impact on their lives – again, you can usefully reflect upon your own experiences here.

We shall conclude by considering a final stream of research that might point towards an explanatory framework.

Active and passive pupils: pupil identity, schools, culture and the labour market

The basic question to be addressed here is: is there some other dynamic at work between education and society that can plausibly be seen as generating the observed differentials in a way that substantively fits the facts? To answer this question, we shall explore studies that have treated pupils as active within the school and introduce the process of 'credential inflation' in the labour market, whereby over time the same jobs demand higher and higher qualifications. We shall illustrate the former by means of a study by

Heidi Mirza (1992) of Afro-Caribbean girls in London secondary schools, and the second by means of the structural dynamic model developed by the French sociologist Raymond Boudon (1974, 1977).

The active pupil and strategic decision-making

In this section, we focus upon the efforts of pupils – conceived as actors who deploy cultural resources related to their gender, ethnicity and social class – to *actively* create their own identities. The analysis draws heavily upon **ethnographic** traditions of research.

> **Ethnography**
> A research technique based on direct observation of the activity of members of a particular social group or given culture.

Mirza (1992) undertook a study of Afro-Caribbean girls in two inner London comprehensives. She located her work within a research tradition that goes back to a classic study of white working-class boys by Paul Willis (1977). However, Mirza aimed to extend this tradition by taking account of a wider range of structural and cultural features. In particular, she wanted to emphasise the structural context to understand and reassess the black family and black womanhood. This entailed a move from a passive model of the pupil (acting out internalised cultural models of identity) to an active one, where the pupil is a strategic decision maker.

In her book, Mirza emphasises the high levels of educational attainment among Afro-Caribbean women in the UK. She considers it strange that this success has been rendered virtually invisible in some studies of black women, which have chosen to present them as victims and have concentrated on the problem of low achievement amongst Afro-Caribbean males. She takes the educational successes of black women as her starting point. She notes that it would be very difficult to attribute this success to the schools in the study, which were less than ideal educational settings for any pupil.

Mirza's account draws together the complex interplay between choice and constraint, between cultural values and structural circumstances, between pupils being positioned by external discourses and conditions but, crucially, also positioning themselves in terms of their desires and strategic calculations.

Although the particular case that Mirza investigated was that of Afro-Caribbean girls, the model she constructed is of general relevance. Differences between groups

---

BOX 10.5 The educational strategies of Afro-Caribbean girls

The explanation produced by Mirza (1992) can be summarised as follows.

The female Afro-Caribbean pupils in Mirza's study positioned themselves in relation to the school rather than being positioned by it. They did so on the basis of their long-term social aspirations: upward mobility through education and work, leading to economic independence. Their approach to this target was pragmatic, advancing one step at a time by the best means available. As far as their school was concerned, although alienated from it as a social institution, they nevertheless conformed sufficiently to gain the qualifications they needed to progress to the next stage.

After leaving school, they would initially enter sectors such as nursing and social work, where black women were already established. This was not because they had internalised a gendered notion of 'women's work' in a caring profession, but because they wished to avoid discrimination elsewhere in the labour market. Their aspirations were supported by Afro-Caribbean cultural values, which affirm women's right to work outside the home and be economically independent, and make little distinction between men's work and women's work. An important feature of these girls' orientation was that they combined high aspiration with a high expectation of success. This was in contrast to the white working-class girls in the study, who also had high aspirations but did not expect to realise them.

could be presented in terms of why they differ. For instance, the aspirations of the Irish Catholic girls Mirza interviewed reflected a different cultural tradition in respect of womanhood, and the relative under-achievement of boys might have related to changes in the employment structure. From an explanatory point of view, it is not necessary to produce a set of explanations for each group, for they tend to be all doing essentially the same kind of thing, but under differing conditions and from differing starting points.

For example, Willis's (1977) analysis of a group of white working-class boys attending secondary modern school suggests that their disaffection with school was not merely a reaction to failure. Pupils go to school already equipped with class cultures, and the culture of Willis's group rejected academic success in favour of manual labour (or 'graft') as a celebration of masculinity. The eventual failure of pupils such as these is not merely a result of economic forces beyond their control, as correspondence theory seems to imply. Schools, Willis suggests, are partially independent of economic forces, and so are their pupils, who act creatively, often in ways that contravene expectations. Thus, schools do not merely reproduce the social relations of capitalism, as within schools there is resistance, rejection, innovation and change. The boys in the study deliberately chose 'failure' by asserting their preferences for laddishness. Willis suggests that, despite their very best efforts, there was little their teachers could do about this.

Working-class culture may have enabled boys in Willis's study to re-interpret and resist the ethos of the school, but they also drew on a particular culture of masculinity. Their scorn for office jobs, for example, and for the qualifications that lead to such jobs, was a way of affirming their masculinity as well as their class commitment. Similarly, Measor and Woods (1988) describe how a group of girls made an enormous fuss about the school regulation requiring them to wear safety glasses during physical science work. Distancing themselves from the physical sciences was as important to them as a demonstration of their femininity as scorn for office jobs was for the boys in Willis's study.

Mirza's (1992) Afro-Caribbean girls, on the other hand, were in a situation where some degree of compliance was necessary. The strategies that pupils develop to reconcile their educational aspirations with aspects of their gender, ethnic and social class identities need not involve wholesale confrontation. The crucial point about both Mirza's girls and Willis's boys is that they were making choices under certain structural conditions and within certain cultural traditions and value systems. The boys were aware of this and told Willis about when they decided to join 'the lads', and why they did so.

Interestingly, sometimes 'lads' reverse their decision and decide to rejoin the mainstream as exam time approaches. Clearly the concept of choice is difficult and problematic, but the studies discussed here present the pupil as an active subject. In historical terms, it could be said that the approach to the subject has moved away from the use of rather simplistic or one-sided models to more complex and multi-faceted models of the pupil and the educational process. Do you think that sociologists are now better able to make sense of what is going on in schools than they were in the past?

Credential inflation and the labour market: the macro dimension

The studies considered in the previous section provide subtly nuanced accounts of the micro processes of schooling and their contextualising influences. But how can they be related to the macro structures of differentiation? The model developed by Raymond Boudon (1974, 1977) was designed to account for the fact that class differentials in educational attainment have not lessened in advanced industrial society, contrary to the expectations of the meritocratic model. Boudon demonstrates that there is no reason why they should have. Changes in educational opportunities do not necessarily generate changes in social opportunities. The reasons for this can be summarised as follows.

Imagine a situation in which

- education is expanding,
- educational standards are rising,
- educational qualifications are the main requirement for occupational placement, and
- most people acquire qualifications in order to get jobs.

This combination of factors produces 'credential inflation' in the labour market. That is, unless qualifications are formally linked to occupational structures (which they are only in special cases, for example, medical qualifications are needed to practise medicine), as more and more people obtain qualifications at a certain level, the value those qualifications in the labour market will decline. The same job will require higher qualifications as time goes by. As Randall Collins (1977) has demonstrated, this is not because the technical requirements of the job have increased, rather it is a market effect reflecting growth in the supply of qualified people. This sets in train a seemingly unending upward educational spiral, with everyone needing to become more highly educated simply to maintain their existing status; for example, to stay middle class will require greater investment in education for each generation than it did for the previous one. Although the overall educational level will improve, no one will experience a net gain because it will improve equally for everyone.

Rather than educational levels being pushed up by educational reform, they are pulled up by credential inflation in the labour market (Moore, 1996). A consequence of this process is that qualifications at the lower level (for example, GCSEs) will be so widely distributed (virtually everyone will have some GCSEs) that there will be something close to educational equality at that level. However, this will have no impact upon social opportunities, because these qualifications will have no labour market value. Hence, there will be a genuine decline in educational inequality at the lower end, but without any corresponding decline in inequality of social opportunity. Educational differentiation will be subject to a process of 'upward translation', whereby the same social differences are reproduced at ever-higher levels of the system.

Halsey *et al.* (1980) have found that Boudon's model fits their data on class exactly and accounts for the empirical trends they have discovered. Hence, this structural-dynamic model appears to have the capacity to account both for the peculiar persistence of class differentials and for the improvement in absolute levels, but can it explain the reversal of the gender gap? It may well be able to do so, because the second step in his model has to do with educational decision-making. Decision-making is central to Boudon's account. The macro effects are the unintended consequence of the aggregated decisions about education made by individuals on the basis of their occupational aspirations. Boudon begins with an important observation about accounts that attribute educational differences to deficiencies in culture. He points out that this approach wrongly uses a common baseline against which to measure things such as degree of social aspiration. In fact, the son of a dustman who aspires to be a dustman himself has the same degree of aspiration as the son of a doctor who aspires to be a doctor. It is necessary to consider where people are starting from, rather than to impose a common (middle-class) standard, against which the working class is automatically held to be deficient. Making this move can radically change our understanding of education.

On this basis, the classes are more alike than they are different. By and large, the majority of people in all classes aspire to maintain their existing status, perhaps with some upward mobility relative to their parents but preferably within their class group. Relatively few aspire to extensive upward mobility (but fewer still want to suffer demotion). This is well illustrated in a study by Phillip Brown (1987). Brown took Willis's (1977) study as his starting point and observed that Willis's 'lads' were not typical working-class pupils, as the majority wanted to 'get on' within the working class and, like Mirza's (1992) Afro-Caribbean girls, sufficiently accommodated themselves to the school to achieve their purposes. Another minority (also as atypical as the lads) aspired to get out of the working class altogether. The basic dynamic of decision-making described by Boudon (1974, 1977) fits the case of Mirza's Afro-Caribbean girls (and, indeed, girls in general) as well as it does Willis's lads.

The observed continuities in class reflect the relative stability during the 1950s and 1960s of a certain kind of labour market for male work and its connection with a traditional family structure. However, these two things became increasingly vulnerable towards the end of the century. As we saw in Chapter 5, the traditional forms of Fordist male employment went into rapid decline, and the new areas of employment favoured female workers, whilst women themselves increasingly redefined their roles and aspirations in relation to work and family. These broader changes in the social situation of groups were associated with changes in their aspirations and educational decision-making.

Finally, this general approach recognises the importance of the economy, but not in the mechanistic fashion of technical-functionalism or correspondence theory. As with Weberian approaches that focus on status (Collins, 1977), the relationship between education and the occupational system is seen as a 'refracted' one – its link is mediated by conditions in the labour market and by labour market dynamics such as credentialisation (with more and more jobs requiring qualifications) and credential inflation.

 ## Conclusion

Mass education – the provision of universal schooling, with the elaboration of clear educational paths that lead to predictable occupational futures – is rooted in modernity. As David Hartley (1997, p.155) puts it, 'State education is a monument to modernity.' The expansion of educational provision was stimulated by – and helped to consolidate – the creation of national cultures. The education system helped to produce, validate and disseminate secular knowledge and an individualistic and materialistic culture. Moreover, mass education has played an important part in the structuration (see Chapter 5) of social classes and the consolidation of distinctive racial and gender divisions, contributing to the reproduction of complex patterns of asymmetrical life chances.

But none of these educational activities has remained uncontested. Different groups with different agendas have constantly challenged the nature and purposes of education. Since the 1980s, this questioning has included reduced expectations of what education can deliver: fewer people see education as the simple instrument of progress it was presented as in the early post-war decades. Education, like the notion of progress itself, has had to accept a more tentative and less grandiose role. And yet some of the contemporary changes that have shaken modernity owe something to, or have been dependent on, education. For example, education is crucial to the growth of knowledge workers in an increasingly service-oriented labour force. It is an important arena in which social pluralism and cultural complexity are expressed and created.

The impact of globalisation on education is contradictory. On the one hand, more highly qualified people are required for the economy, but as a result of the pressures exerted by global financial markets, governments are seeking to hold down public expenditure. Consequently, the individual and the family are having to assume a greater financial burden, with the introduction of student loans and the other costs of an increasingly competitive educational market at all levels. This is calling into question the status of education as a right, and is also threatening with increased instrumentalism the claims of liberal scholarship to autonomy and disinterestedness. At the same time, credential inflation is requiring individuals to extend their education, but with no guarantee of extra returns. These insecurities have been intensified by labour market changes associated with post-Fordism (see p. 56) and the demand for greater flexibility. The decline of traditional male jobs in heavy industry has had a depressing effect on the educational performance of boys. The expansion of the service sector has favoured women, whose 'educational revolution' was the outstanding event of the latter part of the twentieth century. But service sector work functions on a very different basis from traditional work – jobs are no longer 'for life', but are defined by the deregulated and flexible labour market. Hence, both nationally and for the individual, education is an imperative, but one associated with considerable costs and insecure returns.

Other developments also pose problems for education as a modernist project. The move towards multi-culturalism and social pluralism are making it difficult to know what to teach. Just as equipping pupils and students for the world is becoming more difficult, what is worthwhile or of value is becoming harder to define. These problems lie not only at the level of the values and culture that schooling should transmit, but also at the level of knowledge itself. Postmodernists, with their relativist nihilism (however dressed up as 'playfulness'), have called into question the entire foundation of the educational knowledge that has emerged from the rationalist ideals of modernity. Paradoxically, this loss of faith by some intellectuals has occurred at a time when science and its rational application are transforming the world and bringing into being, through the Internet, an entirely new realm of knowledge, communication and experience. Postmodernism is only one description of these times. Others, such as Giddens (1990a), prefer to talk of 'late modernity', while Alexander (1995) speaks of 'neo-modernism'.

CONNECTIONS Different sociologists have their own preferred terms for the state of society at the end of the twentieth and beginning of the twenty-first century. For some of these and the differences between them, see Chapter 19, pages 514–20 and 528–34.

The alternatives offered retain a crucial sense of continuity as well as attempting to delineate the major patterns of change. It is too soon to say whether these changes will fundamentally alter the form of education in society, whether mass schooling will continue or – in response to greater flexibility and fragmentation in the arenas of work, family and culture – lose its taken-for-granted status and be replaced by new forms of education.

It was pointed out at the beginning of the chapter that the mass education system is a recent phenomenon. Today, growing numbers of people are choosing to educate their children at home, and family and working lives are changing in significant ways – could it be that the education system should also change, become more flexible and less based on the school as an institution? What impact might the Internet have on the way we go about learning? Will we still need schools?

Chapter summary

- Schooling is important for the skills and knowledge it conveys and develops, and for the part it plays in the construction of identities.

- The shifts in educational philosophy since the Second World War – away from education for the sake of a fairer society and towards education for the economy, and then from equal opportunities and child-centred learning towards unequal assessment but common standards – have involved both continuities and discontinuities in educational policy and practice.

- The significant expansion of education has not been associated with a redistribution of social opportunity. Class differentials in educational attainment have remained largely the same.

- In contrast, girls and women have made major educational gains in recent years and now have higher attainments than boys and men at virtually every level, though some gender differences remain in subject choices.

- There is a great deal of variation in educational performance across ethnic and racial groups, especially when gender and social class are also taken into account. Although many ethnic minorities have above average levels of attainment, some are still disadvantaged and are over-represented in school exclusion figures.

- It appears that approaches that focus on factors internal to education are unable to account for the macro patterns of continuity and change over time. Similarly, naturalistic and culturalist approaches that assume a passive model of the pupil fail to capture the complexities of the education process and its relation to the wider social context.

- The most productive approaches are those which recognise pupils as active beings operating in accordance with a complex set of constraining and enabling conditions, including changes in the family structure, in relations between the sexes and in labour market dynamics.

Questions to think about

- From what you have read, do you consider economic factors or state formation to be more important in determining the shape of education systems?
- Which social characteristic – class, gender or ethnicity – do you think has the greatest influence on educational outcomes? Give reasons for your choice.

- How much freedom of choice do you think pupils have in the contemporary education system? Identify those areas where they have real choices and those where choices are limited.

Investigating further

Ahier, J., B. Cosin, and M. Hales, (eds) (1996) *Diversity and Change: Education, Policy and Selection*, Routledge/OpenUniversity.

> Here the focus is on social policy and the ways in which it affects educational outcomes. The sections divide concerns into international comparisons, the relationship between economic change and education, ideologies and policy.

Cosin, B., and M. Hales, (eds) (1997) *Families, Education and Social Differences*, Routledge/Open University.

> This book explores the relationship between family background and educational attainment. It covers such issues as socialisation, early years, special needs, inequality and stratification, gender and ethnic issues. A range of views is represented, from New Right to liberal.

Halsey, A.H., H. Lauder, P. Brown, and A. Stuart-Wells, (eds) (1997) *Education, Culture, Economy, Society*, Oxford University Press.

> A useful reader, bringing together nearly 50 essays by academics in the field – well worth dipping into.

chapter **11**

Work and non-work

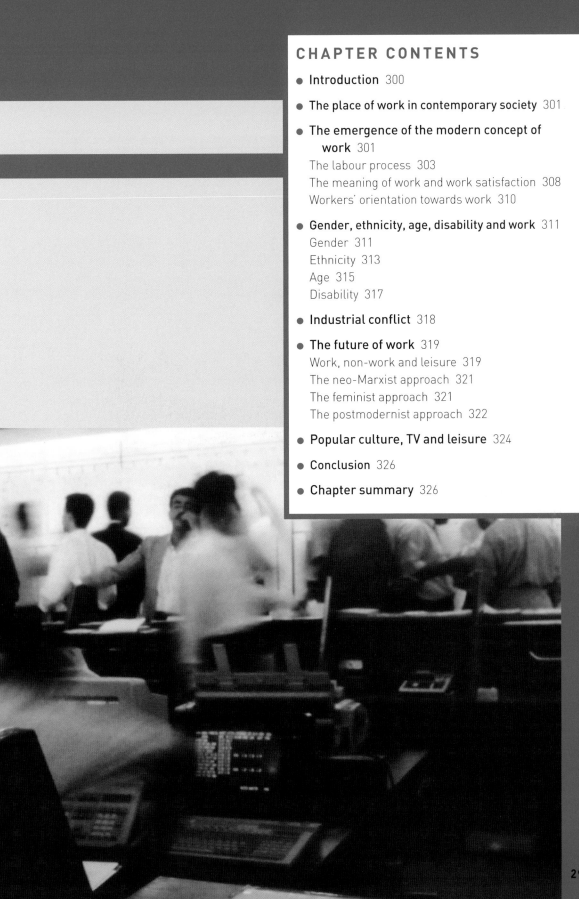

CHAPTER CONTENTS

Aims of the chapter

Work is of central interest to sociology because much of our social and material fabric rests on the work we do, whether paid or not. It is also a major component of our adult experience. Increasingly, leisure is also a central life interest for individuals and it makes up a large section of the social fabric. In this chapter, we examine the relationships between work, and non-work, and the variety of experiences associated with both, especially as mediated by gender. We shall see that the boundaries between work and non-work are becoming increasingly blurred, as the importance of work as a source of personal identity declines.

By the end of the chapter, you should have an understanding of the following concepts:

- Labour process theory
- De-skilling
- Casualisation
- Alienation
- Affluence
- Hidden work

Introduction

This chapter focuses on work and non-work and the relationship between the two. 'Work' and 'non-work' refer to forms of social behaviour that, in broad historical terms, are relatively recent and associated with the onset of industrialisation and the Great Transformation. In the past, not only were work and non-work (and the forms of leisure accompanying them) much less easy to distinguish, they were also less tied to specific times, places and **social framing** than is the case today. In modern society, many of us go to work at a certain time in a certain place, and then return to relax at another time and in another place. It is true, of course, that not all participate in this ritual – for example, the unemployed, domestic labourers, the retired, some of the disabled and people who work at home.

Social framing
To place within a bounded social context.

While this ritual can still be seen each day on the commuter trains of London, New York and other major cities, the pattern of work and non-work for commuters is beginning to change. The security and stability of doing the job for which one trained is rapidly being eroded as the nature of the labour market changes, along with the sorts of skill required. Many former commuters now stay at home, since it has become their place of work. Leisure is defined by participation in a consumer lifestyle with new leisure pursuits created (almost on a daily basis, it seems) for an individuated but nevertheless mass market of people desperately trying to fill their free time. Work on the fabric of the house – as in DIY – is also defined as leisure. Making full use of your leisure can be hard work!

The boundary between work and non-work has always been unclear, especially when both provide similar forms of satisfaction and pleasure. But now it is even more blurred, as time away from formalised work has become something to be bought or sold as a commodity. The commercialisation of leisure means that people have to spend a considerable amount of money to enjoy their 'free' time. Today, the leisure market is one of the largest commodity markets in the economy, and many people are working hard to provide the goods and services demanded by those in search of leisure.

The place of work in contemporary society

If you are looking for work, what is it you are doing? The obvious – though not necessarily the only – reply is, trying to get a job. We need a job to earn enough to buy the things that are necessary for survival – and more. This tells us immediately that work is not merely a physical and mental activity but also a social and economic one that typically produces some product or service for others. But what of those working for pleasure or without pay, as domestic workers such as housewives do? Is their work any less a form of work simply because it occurs outside the labour market?

As a social activity, work also provides us with identity and status, so that even if we lose our job, we may still define ourselves through our work – 'I am an unemployed miner', 'I am an out-of-work actress' and so on. Self-employed workers may regard themselves as being in work all the time, even when work is scarce, while some types of work – such as that of priests, artists or novelists – is regarded more as a calling than work. To call oneself an unemployed priest or novelist might be seen as rather odd. Some people may never work in any of these senses – for example, because they are very rich or desperately poor and excluded from normal social and economic exchange.

All this illustrates the difficulty of tying down precisely what is meant by work. Typically, of course, having a paid job is probably how most people would define the term. Nevertheless, it is clearly a restricted notion and one that says nothing about the variety of work in which people engage. It also says nothing about the way work is viewed. Two workers doing the same job may respond to it in very different ways, and this may in part reflect their particular gender, home situation, age, ethnicity, educational career and so on. The meaning of work is not uniform for any group of workers. Grint (1998, p. 6) stresses the heterogeneous nature of the meaning of work:

> " Work tends to be an activity that transforms nature and is usually undertaken in social situations, but exactly what counts as work is dependent on the specific social circumstances under which such activities are undertaken and, critically, how those circumstances and activities are interpreted by those involved. Whether any particular activity is experienced as work or leisure or both or neither is intimately related to the temporal, spatial and cultural conditions of existence. This does not mean that the search for the meaning of work is the equivalent to the quest for the Holy Grail, nor that one person's definition of work is as influential as any other. "

Caste system
A system of social division and stratification, influenced by Hinduism on the Indian subcontinent, in which an individual's social position is fixed at birth.

There are both negative and positive images of work, and both have a long history: work as drudgery, as demeaning, as merely a means to a more important end; as opposed to work as rewarding, as a route to salvation, as a source of pleasure and interest. Of course, both images are closely associated with the emergence of industrial society and modernity – from the negative image of 'dark satanic mills' to the more positive 'Heaven helps those who help themselves'. Note how each of these contrasting images is charged with religious and moral symbolism: work is as much a moral as it is a productive activity. This is perhaps most clearly expressed in the Indian **caste system**, where different castes and their trades, *jati*, are equated with different degrees of religious purity.

 The emergence of the modern concept of work

Historically, the notion of work as paid labour – a job – emerged when the wage started to become the main source of people's livelihood. In pre-industrial agricultural societies, wage labour was only part of a range of livelihood strategies. People might sell their labour on an occasional basis, but they were more likely to engage in share-cropping, subsistence farming, tenant farming, barter arrangements and so on. Similar strategies – and more – are utilised in the poorer parts of the world today. But as modernity developed and industrialisation and urbanisation took place (from roughly the eighteenth century onwards), families and households became increasingly reliant on wage labour precisely because other forms of livelihood were denied them and they could no longer sustain themselves as productive units. The household became a consumption unit instead. In the early nineteenth century, the centrality of the wage labour market became apparent with the first recognition of a clearly defined part of the population as 'unemployed'.

As we saw in Chapter 2, as factory production developed, work regimes became more regulated by factory owners keen to ensure control over labour. The relationship between time and work – whether related to clocking-in, shiftwork or time-and-motion studies – assumed central importance. Work came to be regarded as something done during a certain period in adult life – not during childhood or in retirement. In addition, the location of work became more clearly defined – the factory, the office, the mine – and separated, particularly in the case of males, from the home. It was this last development, the separation of home from work, that led to the gender differences that prevail today, inasmuch as women, even when not confined to the domestic sphere, tend to be mainly responsible for work within the home.

By the twentieth century, the conventional view of work was very different from that of the pre-industrial era. Work was now performed outside the home, was waged and was performed predominantly by men. Indeed, the sociology of work has largely focused on the waged and salaried labour of males. In Chapter 5, we saw that the same male orientation is evident in some of the traditional approaches to social stratification. In recent years, however, there has been a growing awareness of the inadequacy of this approach. Firstly, social scientists acknowledge that a task can be completed not only in the formal economy (the wage labour market) but also in the household economy, the communal economy and even the **black economy**. Only the first of these would show up in statistics on work.

Black economy
Denotes unofficial economic activity; for example, work carried out for payment in kind or cash payment for tax avoidance purposes.

Secondly, feminists have examined the work that women undertake in the home and shown how extensive and diverse this is – cooking, cleaning, caring for family members (especially children and older people) and other domestic tasks. And, as Schwartz Cowan (1983) has suggested, improved domestic technologies and equipment have not eased the burden of this but have merely raised expectations of cleanliness, food preparation and so on. Oakley (1974) calculated that an average working week for a housewife was 77 hours. The wage equivalent for such labour was estimated at over £18 000, and is probably substantially higher than this today. Some feminists have called for housework to be rewarded by a wage, but other feminists point out that this would confirm housework as women's work.

The constraints on women entering the labour market on terms equal to those enjoyed by men means that they are – as we saw in Chapter 6 – concentrated in specific occupations, often ones that mirror their domestic labour responsibilities – that is, the caring, nurturing, teaching and secretarial 'pink-collar' jobs. Hence, it is apparent that there is a strong relationship between the arenas of work and home: though separate physically and culturally, the one feeds back on the other. Often, however, the separation of the two spheres, with a strong boundary between the home and the workplace, is much less evident. For many women, the household has become a place of both paid and unpaid work, as Crompton and Sanderson (1990) observed:

> "Much of women's paid work has been carried out by offering domestic services within the home, for example, child-minding, or taking in laundry, or within the homes of others as full time domestic servants. The latter was the single most numerous occupation for women until the 1930s. Taking in lodgers is an economic activity that exists on the very boundary of the public and private spheres. ... Davidoff ... has emphasised the very different connotation attaching to the word 'landlord' (one who owns property and collects rent) as compared to 'landlady' (one who, usually living on the premises, provides houseroom and services for cash). "

For women, the establishment of a new household and formalising this through marriage is often the beginning of their being marginalised from or restricted within the labour market. Conversely, for men, it is more likely to be – especially in the case of professional middle-class men – the base upon which to build a respectable career. Oakley's (1974) classic study of the housewife shows how this role not merely constrains women but is 'basic to the structure of modern society and the ideology of gender roles that pervade it' (ibid., p. 24). She claims that housework is in many ways similar to manual industrial labour – repetitive, routine, tedious and so on. Over 75 per cent of her sample of young mothers expressed resentment and dissatisfaction with their lives, even though they viewed their work as of value to the home.

CONNECTIONS For a detailed discussion of the issues associated with the traditional view of women's work, see Chapter 6.

The labour process

Overall, then, work patterns today should not be thought of simply as descriptions of different types of job that map out modern livelihood strategies. More fundamentally, they are a description of the way the occupational labour market is structured to favour some over others, to give some more autonomy and security than others, to allow some to experience work as a career and others to experience it as drudgery, and to reproduce gender divisions at work and in the home.

Nevertheless many sociologists routinely divide work into types of job, often into four broad categories that carry different levels of material and cultural reward in terms of pay, job security, perks, skill and power (Table 11.1).

Broad summaries such as this are of limited value, for they say nothing about the informal black economy, domestic labour, the experience and meaning of work or the variation of work within these broad categories. For example, it is women who predominate in the cleaning and textile sectors of blue-collar work, not men. Nevertheless, the broad pattern of occupations over time reveals a changing labour market structure

TABLE 11.1 Broad types of work

Category	Power/status	Gender	Example
Professional	High	Male-dominated	Accountant
Managerial	High	Male-dominated	Executive
White-collar	Middle	Female-dominated	Secretary
Blue-collar	Low	Male-dominated	Car worker

TABLE 11.2 The move towards post-industrial society

Industrial society		Post-industrial society
Manufacturing	⟶	Dominance of service sector
Labour supply	⟶	Knowledge supply
Blue-collar workers	⟶	White-collar/technical staff
Machine technology	⟶	Information-based technology
Industrialists	⟶	Technocracy/technical elite
Business firms	⟶	Flexible organisational structures

Post-industrial society
A society in which industrial manufacturing has declined, giving way to rapid growth in the service and information sectors.

in industrial capitalist states. For example, some sociologists, following the American Daniel Bell (1973), believe that we now live in a **post-industrial society** where the more important jobs are those requiring technical and professional qualifications. Table 11.2 summarises Bell's image of the shift towards a post-industrial society.

As we saw in Chapter 3, the contemporary dynamics of globalisation have in some ways confirmed Bell's broad proposition of structural changes in the labour market. However, the flexible new work patterns are generating job insecurity for all, which Bell never properly envisaged. We shall return to this issue later when we look at the future of work.

QUESTION To what extent do you think that Bell's idea of the post-industrial society has come to pass in the society you live in today?

In the UK, decline in manufacturing and growth of the service sector has been a key trend in the postwar period. Chart 11.1 opposite shows how this trend has affected the UK labour market.

Between 1978 and 2000, service sector jobs rose by 36 per cent, from 15.6 million to 21.2 million. Over the same period, manufacturing jobs fell by 39 per cent, from 7.0 million to 4.2 million. Importantly, virtually all of the increase in women's jobs was accounted for by the service sector. The total number of male jobs was 15.1 million, compared with 13.0 million for women. It is important to note that the statistics in Table 11.3 represent jobs rather than people – some people might, of course, have had more than one job. The most common jobs for women were still in the clerical and secretarial sphere, followed by personal and protective services (illustrated by Table 11.3 on page 314). For men, there was a fall of four percentage points between 1991 and 2000 for those working in craft and related jobs. The proportion of male managers and administrators was almost double that of women.

As waged labour, work involves working for someone else, the employer. The employer may be a large or small organisation, public or private, in an industrial, service or other sector, and so on. As a worker, a person experiences work as a labour process, with a particular type of work carrying its own social, technical and economic requirements, to be completed properly, be this writing a book or ploughing a field. The onset of industrialisation brought significant changes to the labour process, most importantly with regard to workers' control over the work done and the reward it produced.

Marx (1954) was one of the first writers to consider the impact of capitalist industrial growth on the labour process, and thus on the experience of work. He argued

CHART 11.1 Employee jobs[1] in the UK: by gender and industry

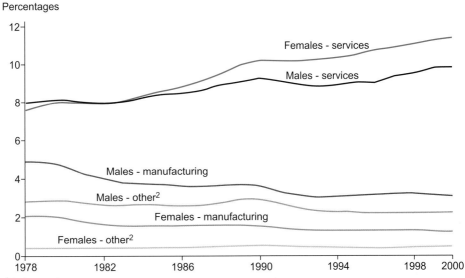

Percentages

¹ At June each year.

² Includes agriculture, construction, energy and water.

Source: Office for National Statistics (2001a, p. 80).

that the advent of machinery and automation gradually removed workers' control over the labour process by enabling their overall skills to be broken up to suit the new machines they tended, or by the machines taking over those skills. The knowledge and skills required for the completion of tasks thereby come under the ownership and control of the capital that bought the factory, ran the machines and employed the workforce. In this way, capitalists gained a virtual monopoly over knowledge and therefore

TABLE 11.3 Employees[1] in the UK: by gender and occupation, 1991 and 2000 (per cent)

	Males		Females	
	1991	**2000**	**1991**	**2000**
Managers and administrators	16	19	8	11
Professional	10	12	8	10
Associate professional and technical	8	9	10	11
Clerical and secretarial	8	8	29	25
Craft and related	21	17	4	2
Personal and protective services	7	8	14	17
Selling	6	6	12	12
Plant and machine operatives	15	14	5	4
Other occupations	8	8	10	8
All employees[2](= 100%)(millions)	11.8	12.8	10.1	11.0

¹ At Spring each year. Males aged 16 to 64, females aged 16 to 59.

² Includes a few people who did not state their occupation. Percentages are based on totals which exclude this group.

Source: Labour Force Survey, Office for National Statistics (2001a, p. 81).

control over the labour process. These arguments were developed in later years by labour process theorists (see for example, Braverman, 1974).

Braverman (ibid.) argued that the labour process was characterised by de-skilling and the degradation of work. Work tasks no longer required the application of a range of skills developed through apprenticeship and job experience, but merely the completion of mindless, repetitive and very limited tasks in pace with a machine-based manufacturing process. Braverman blamed these developments on the application of 'scientific management', inspired by the managerial philosophy of Frederick Taylor, whose impact was first felt in the 1910–20 period. Taylor (1911) argued that management was responsible for deciding how work tasks should be completed, and to this end should specify every detail of a task and the time needed to complete it: from this was born the 'time and motion' study so often used to orchestrate labour and ensure its efficiency on the assembly line. This approach sought to remove any reliance on workers' skills, which were often tacit and variable in the way they were applied to complete a particular job. Instead, these skills were deconstructed and reduced to a series of codified, regulated and therefore controlled actions that any worker could undertake.

Braverman's attack on the capitalist labour process was simultaneously an attack on the class inequality inherent in worker–manager relations: while managers were not necessarily the owners of capital, they did act on behalf of capitalist interests, either those of remote shareholders or proprietors of firms. But Braverman also noted that all occupational groups, including white-collar management, were subject to the same process of de-skilling and control, as capital sought ever greater efficiencies in all aspects of the labour process, including its management. Indeed, later sociological work in the US and Europe provided evidence of the de-skilling of office and clerical work.

Braverman's **neo-Marxist** analysis had a significant impact on the sociology of work during the mid to late 1970s. There were many who regarded his attack on the labour process under capitalism as timely and well-founded. But since then, an increasing number have challenged his account on both theoretical and empirical grounds. A number of criticisms have been raised.

First, a key criticism is that the notion of de-skilling depends on the existence of a clear benchmark of what skill actually is, so that we can then judge how far or in what way it has been de-skilled. Yet Braverman provided only a very limited – and in a sense non-sociological – notion of skill as 'craft mastery', of a technical competence associated with the use of tools and machinery. However, sociologists have shown that skill is a much more fluid notion than this: what a skill is and how it is rewarded depends on the social negotiation between workers and their employers. We can see this, for example, in the way that typing skills have been redefined as keyboard skills associated with word processors, and (especially when used by men) accorded a higher status than before. Professional and occupational groups and trade unions are striving to sustain and secure a definition of their skills over time as the labour market changes.

Second, even if the fragmentation and de-skilling of work is in some sense occurring in the way described by Braverman, this is only one of a number of strategies used by contemporary employers to secure the compliance of workers. Indeed, Friedman (1977) argues that rather than trying to reduce worker involvement in work tasks, many firms secure better worker efficiency by offering greater rather than less involvement. Edwards (1979) takes this further, suggesting that managers increasingly resort to a form of bureaucratic control over workers, where workers' compliance and commitment is obtained through the implementation of rules and regulations throughout the organisation, as well as incentive schemes that act as an 'elaborate system of bribes' (ibid., p. 145). The current practice of total quality management (Webster and Robins, 1993),

Neo-Marxism
School of thought based on the further development of Marxist philosophy.

Figure 11.1   Staff at call centres (a significant area of employment growth) work on shifts for low wages. The work follows a strict format dictated by computer software and is typically very closely monitored by managers.

where all firm members are expected to conform to a range of clearly defined measures of efficiency and product quality in return for bonuses and profit sharing, is an extension of this strategy. One can see this, for example, in the computing, engineering and aerospace industries, where the quality of a complex product design is crucial to eventual market success.

Third, others suggest that work now demands a broader range of flexible skills – technical, social and organisational – based on higher levels of training and educational achievement. US studies of engineers (Spenner, 1990) and dock workers (Finlay, 1988) confirm the findings of European studies (Bottrup and Clematide, 1992) on the impact of new technologies and management strategies. These show that in certain occupations, a re-skilling of work tasks has been conducted to suit the new technologies acquired by firms. Dockside crane operators, for example, have had to develop new skills to contend with containerised cargo shipments. Similar conclusions have been drawn in studies of clerical workers (for example, Crompton and Sanderson, 1990).

Gallie (1991) has shown how important it is to approach the question of skill from a social class perspective. In his study, the majority of non-manual, intermediate and skilled manual workers believed that their work had come to demand a higher level of skill, but the majority of manual workers felt that the responsibility and skill involved in their work had either remained the same or declined. This shows that we need to be careful of Braverman's claim that new technologies in the workplace necessarily lead to de-skilling. Much depends on the wider social context in which employers introduce that technology. As this context changes, so the broad impact of the technology might be very different, as noted by Green and Ashton (1992, p. 288):

" When introducing new technology, managers face a clear choice: they can use it as an opportunity to increase the skill level in the labour force, by involving the workers in the control of technology, or they can utilise the technology to further centralise control over the production process and simplify and fragment work tasks. International comparisons suggest that whether managers choose to upskill the work force or deskill it will depend in part on the national system of vocational education and training and the structure of the firm. In Germany, where workers have a relatively high level of intermediate skills, managers tend to utilise the new systems of programmable automation to further enhance the skills of the labour force. ... In Britain, where the level of training and hence skills of the labour force are lower ... the tendency has been to use programmable automation to increase the control managers have over the production process. One consequence of that is the further de-skilling of the tasks of workers. **"**

We can gain a better understanding of the impact of technologies by locating them within the contemporary labour market and the globalised innovation and production system. We saw in Chapter 5 that this system has produced a polarised occupational structure in modern industrial capitalist states, where those in secure work are more likely to be competent in a range of technical skills. Meanwhile, those working in the growing range of casual, insecure jobs may use new technologies, but in a routine and uniform way (such as the check-out assistant in the supermarket). This view is borne out by Gallie's (1991) UK-based study mentioned above. Furthermore, international comparative studies of class and occupational structure have shown a growing differentiation in the way in which skill is perceived as important while confirming the trend towards polarisation of the labour market. Overall, therefore, these various studies do not suggest that the workforce as a whole has been subject to de-skilling

This last point has important implications for another of Braverman's (1974) arguments: that the homogenisation of the labour process would encourage a greater sense of political solidarity among the working class. While **worker resistance** is still apparent, this has not necessarily led to strengthened solidarity. Some workers – typically white, male, technical or professional employees – are in a much better position to resist management control than others, and because of this, may be quite reluctant to carry others along with them. While the dynamics of the labour process are important in shaping the context in which work is experienced, they do not determine the meaning of that experience, which varies greatly, not least by gender, age and ethnicity.

Worker resistance
Strategies employed by workers to subvert the labour process.

CONNECTIONS For a discussion of the relationship between work and ethnicity, see Chapter 7.

The meaning of work and work satisfaction

There are, broadly speaking, two ways in which we can understand the meaning work has for and the satisfaction it gives to people. On the one hand, one could say that the experience people have of work depends on the nature of work itself, with boring work producing a bored worker with little or no job satisfaction. On the other hand, one could also say that the attitudes workers bring to their jobs are more important in determining work experience and what they expect of work. In this case, workers might find their jobs boring but because they expect little else, they are satisfied with the work they do. It therefore seems sensible to try to understand both the nature of work and the orientation workers have towards it.

Employees' conditions of work consist of a wide range of factors – their level of pay, the physical nature of the job they do, the surroundings in which they work, the level of autonomy they have in their job and, of particular importance, the sort of technology it involves. The term technology in this instance refers to the socio-technical relations that characterise a manufacturing, service or other job. For example, in car manufacturing, the Japanese just-in-time (JIT) production system is a complex system in which workers, components, the physical layout of plant, the information technologies managing the flow of materials and work patterns, and so on, are all orchestrated to ensure that quality products are produced as needed (without excess stock having to be held) and on-time for a well-targeted market. The spread of this type of production in Western Europe and the US has been called the Japanisation of production. Workers are subject to considerable surveillance and are used in a flexible way to meet changing production schedules and objectives. This experience of work is rather different from that of, say, a farm worker toiling alone in a field.

The notion that the particular type of technology – or socio-technical system – workers are exposed to shapes their experience was most forcefully argued in a classic study by Blauner (1964). Blauner argued that some work is more alienating than other types because of the different technologies workers are required to use. **Alienation**, according to Blauner, has four dimensions: powerlessness, meaninglessness, isolation and self-estrangement. Individuals are powerless when they cannot control their own actions or conditions of work; work is meaningless when it gives employees little or no sense of value, worth or interest; work is isolating when workers cannot identify with their workplace; and work is self-estranging when, at the subjective level, the worker has no sense of involvement in the job.

Blauner applied his model to four different industrial sectors using different technologies:

Alienation
Originally utilised by Marx to describe the feeling of estangement experienced by workers under industrial capitalism. Now more generally employed to describe people's feelings of isolation, powerlessness and self-estrangement.

- Printing – craft-based technology.
- Textiles – machine-tending technology.
- Car production – assembly-line technology.
- Chemicals – continuous process technology.

Of these four, the technology most likely to produce alienating work is assembly-line technology. The powerlessness of the work is reflected in the way the worker follows a routine set of tasks at a constant pace on the line; the job is mind-numbingly meaningless, and – with the worker isolated from co-workers – dull and monotonous. Chemical process work, on the contrary, is much less alienating, as workers have more control over their highly automated plant and considerable responsibility is attached to their jobs.

There are many problems with Blauner's claims, not least his failure to recognise that the same technology – such as that in an assembly plant – can be experienced in a variety of ways. For an example, we shall look at JIT production, which came to typify the car industry a few decades after Blauner's study.

A vast number of workers are now engaged in JIT production, but we should not assume that they all share the same work experience. Studies have shown that local cultural differences with regard to management–union relations, levels of hierarchical control, and reward and performance appraisal policies mean that the experience of JIT work can vary considerably between countries and firms (Jenkins, 1994). For example, workers in the French car industry are not subject to the high levels of surveillance and job control exercised by US corporations. Much depends on the social organisation of work and the 'psychological contract' that management makes with workers. In return for meeting JIT demands, individual workers are rewarded with good pay and career advancement. Indeed, in recent years, work experience has been increasingly shaped by the individualisation of the job contract (for those who have one), as unions' negotiating power has been undermined by anti-union legislation. This means that what a worker wants out of work is less likely to be collectively defined.

The individualisation of work and the need for individual workers to have more flexible skills in order to respond to technological changes means that Blauner's characterisation of work experience is out of date. Assembly lines still exist, of course, but they are very different from the ones described by him.

In car production these days, it is more common for workers to work in a team that assembles each car from start to finish. This can alleviate workers' sense of alienation because they are involved in the entire process, rather than just putting a screw in to a passing car frame on its way to a distant part of the factory. Even where the assembly line remains a part of the production process, automation has often removed the drearier chores. Today's car workers are different from the 'small cog in a large wheel' employees of the 1960s, being much more likely to maintain and repair their own machines, set and monitor their own quality control, and switch jobs regularly to reduce boredom.

Automative technologies and computerised work systems have typically enhanced workers' job satisfaction and skill deployment in the better-paid, secure public and private sector jobs. But in more casual. non-skilled manual work, they have merely perpetuated job dissatisfaction, especially for the many women engaged in this type of work. Perhaps for such poorly paid, vulnerable workers, it is rational not to look for intrinsic reward in the work they do. Therefore we should – as with all jobs – be particularly interested in the attitudes people bring to their work.

> **QUESTION** Think of a job that you have had (full- or part-time, permanent or casual) – what technology did you use, what skills did you employ and how satisfying was the work? Base your answer on concepts presented in this chapter.

Workers' orientation towards work

Privatism
A focus on the home and family life.

Instrumentalism
An approach to work in which workers derive satisfaction not so much from the job itself, but from benefits it brings, such as good pay or secure employment.

Rather than presupposing, as did Blauner, that workers' experience is a direct consequence of the technology they use, other sociologists stress the orientation of the worker towards his or her job. In another classic study, Goldthorpe *et al.* (1968) explored the attitudes towards work of Luton-based Vauxhall car workers in the UK during the early 1960s. The authors suggested that although the monotony, fragmentation and de-skilling of jobs on the assembly line meant that workers derived little intrinsic satisfaction from their work, they were not looking for this in the first place. The job was principally a means of securing a relatively good wage that would enable them to enjoy the sort of life they wanted outside the factory. Work was simply an instrument to achieve this end. In short, the workers had an instrumental orientation towards their jobs. Outside work, they sought **privatism** on the new housing estates of Luton. The terms **instrumentalism** and privatism lie at the heart of Goldthorpe *et al.*'s findings.

The importance of their study is that it revealed how workers' attitudes can be more fully understood by looking beyond as well as within the factory or other place of work. Workplaces are not closed systems but relate to and are experienced in terms of external – especially domestic and household – structures and expectations. The study also revealed the way in which the workers' orientation affected their political loyalties and attitudes. Instrumentalism and privatism, it seemed, weakened the workers' sense of class identification and their bond with trade unionism. Again, the significance of the world of work went far beyond the factory gates.

Snowball sampling
A research technique that asks existing respondents if they can suggest other similarly placed individuals who could be contacted as part of the on-going research.

Despite the valuable contribution made by Goldthorpe *et al.*'s study, it has been subject to a number of criticisms. One of the criticisms comes from Devine (1992). She too looked at car workers in Luton, this time in the very different circumstances of the late 1980s, a period of recession and, for this area in particular, growing unemployment. Some of this downturn was related to the restructuring of industry discussed in Chapter 5.

Rather than trying to reconstruct the original randomised sample of workers, Devine focused on 30 couples, ranging in age from the mid 20s to the late 60s, a group identified via **snowball sampling** (see Chapter 16). Her respondents painted a rather different picture from that produced by Goldthorpe *et al.* in the 1960s. Rather than instrumentalism and privatism continuing to prevail, she found that couples were more concerned about their working conditions. Their main concern was job security rather than pay. Moreover, the links that households had with others around them depended very much on which stage of the life-cycle they were in, whether both partners were earning or just one, whether Luton-based relations could help them to find work, and so on.

Much of this might, of course, have reflected the wider socio-economic changes experienced in the Luton housing and labour markets. But Devine believes that Goldthorpe *et al.*'s study exaggerated the degree of instrumentalism and privatism among the car workers. She also found that the workers still felt a broad sense of working-class solidarity, even if the means by which this could be expressed – unionism – had been dismantled by the anti-union legislation introduced by the Thatcher government in the 1980s. Most of the workers saw themselves as being in the same boat, one that was likely to tip them into the rising sea of unemployment. That this did not trigger off worker radicalism or resistance does not mean that the workers were prepared to acquiesce to poor working conditions, but rather that they had adopted what might be called realistic pessimism in light of the changing labour market.

Orientations towards work must therefore be seen as reflecting a number of factors:

- The nature of the technology used by workers.
- The relationship between home and work.
- The life-cycle stage of the household.
- The relationships between paid work and domestic labour.
- The wider labour and housing markets.
- The wider political milieu.

Gender, ethnicity, age, disability and work

So far, our account of workers' attitudes towards work has said little about how these are shaped by gender, ethnicity, age or disability. These significant variables influencing the experience, conditions, security and benefits of work will now be addressed.

Gender

Chapter 6 discussed the dynamics of gender in considerable detail and raised the question of how women's work patterns and their more general participation in the labour market differ from those of men. Women are disproportionately represented in work that can be viewed as an extension of their domestic life. In the US and UK, for example, a significant proportion of women work in secretarial, teaching, catering and retail jobs.

Figure 11.2   The rising number of women entering middle class occupations has created a 'crisis in social reproduction' for work-rich, dual-career families, leading to a resurgence in demand for waged domestic labour.

In recent decades, women have moved into other occupational positions, and in the UK women now account for almost half of all jobs.

One key factor restricting women's participation in the labour market is marriage. Married women are less likely to work, and even when they do work, they tend to give up their jobs if their husbands secure new employment elsewhere. If both partners have strong careers and intend to pursue them, the household structure and roles therein are usually very different from those of the conventional nuclear family.

Evidence from the US (Roos, 1983) suggests that the declining fertility rate (the number of offspring per woman) is resulting in married women returning to the labour market more quickly. There is also related evidence that women are returning to work more quickly after the birth of a child so as not to lose their 'labour market position' (what a Weberian might call their 'market situation' – see Chapter 5). Much depends here, of course, on employers' policies towards maternity leave and the terms on which mothers can rejoin their company (McRae, 1994).

Research by the Joseph Rowntree Foundation (2001) shows that mothers who spend less time with pre-school children because of full-time work face a trade-off between raising the family income and risking the impairment of their children's long-term achievement at school. This finding has led some researchers to conclude that welfare to work policies might better be focused on encouraging new parents to take up part-time work rather than returning early to full-time employment.

Even though there have been some improvements for women in the labour market, the constraints of domestic responsibility and subordination to male partners' priorities still mean that women have a greater problem securing the continuity and experience of work that is so important to employability. As a result, career advancement tends to halt at the so-called 'glass ceiling', providing an effective barrier to higher earnings.

Advancement is also hampered by women having fewer contacts with people who could help them to find better work, and at work, they generally receive less training and have less access to staff development programmes (Wholey, 1990). In part, this reflects the perspective common among certain types of male manager that women are less interested in careers, even when the evidence points to the contrary. The US is often cited as a country in which women have managed to break through the glass ceiling. However, in 1994, only 4 per cent of senior executive posts were held by women. As Grint (1998) notes, those who do break through tend to work in one of the 'triple-P' departments: purchasing, publicity and personnel. Roberts (2001) argues that 'glass ceilings have been cracking in most businesses and professions', but makes the important point that while the proportion of women in some senior positions is increasing spectacularly in percentage terms, the baseline is very low. In the case of professorships, for example, just 2 per cent of university professorships were held by women in the 1970s; although there are now roughly seven times more, this is still only about 14 per cent.

We have seen that technology has been associated with both the de-skilling and the re-skilling of work, and many commentators believe that new-technology-based work is particularly disadvantageous to women. Some feminist analysts believe that technology is itself gendered to work against women. As Frissen (1992) puts it: 'In feminist analyses, technologies are often described as "toys for the boys". According to these approaches an important reason for difference in access to technology between women and men, is that the value system underlying technological practices is fundamentally masculine.'

Not all agree with this view, however, since closer examination of the relation of men and women to technologies in general and machines in particular suggests no simple male/**technophilic**, female/**technophobic** dichotomy (see Packer, 1996). This does not, however, imply that, when women do feel comfortable with and are skilled at using new technologies, they will be promoted in recognition of this, be their workplace the laboratory, the office or the factory. In such a situation, technical skills may be accorded less importance by (predominantly) male managers who identify other skills as necessary for promotion. Again, we can see here how the definition of skill (and hence its reward) is socially constructed, this time based on a gendered view of competence. In this situation, women may experience considerable job dissatisfaction as their skills are undervalued and underrewarded.

The **gendered division of labour** still firmly benefits men to the detriment of women. Although women's proportional representation in the labour market is increasing and the range of jobs they do is broadening, the demands inherent in the domestic division of labour are continuing to prevent any fundamental change for most women in respect of work.

Ethnicity

For various cultural reasons (undoubtedly including discrimination) and age considerations, economic activity rates (those in employment plus those seeking work) vary between ethnic groups in the UK (Table 11.4).

In overall terms, the lowest female activity rates are in those of Bangladeshi and Pakistani women, at 22 and 30 per cent respectively in 1999–2000. The activity rates of these women are low at all ages compared with other ethnic groups. While the rates for Bangladeshi and Pakistani men aged 25–44 are comparable to those for most other non-white groups, the rates for younger and older men are low. The highest rates are those for Indian and white men aged 25–44.

Technophilic
Having an aptitude for and willingness to engage with technology.

Technophobic
Having a fear of and reluctance to engage with technology.

Gendered division of labour
The division of work roles and tasks into those performed by men and those performed by women.

TABLE 11.4 Economic activity rates[1] in the UK: by ethnic group, gender and age, 1999–2000[2] (per cent)

	Males				Females			
	16–24	25–44	45–64	All (16–64)	16–24	25–44	45–59	All (16–59)
White	78	94	78	85	70	78	71	74
Black Caribbean	77	89	65	80	63	78	72	75
Black African	50	84	77	76	40	65	71	61
Other Black groups	78	83	--	81	59	72	--	67
Indian	62	95	74	82	56	69	56	63
Pakistani	56	89	62	74	35	31	21	30
Bangladeshi	55	81	40	65	36	--	--	22
Chinese	--	83	73	63	--	63	64	57
None of the above[3]	55	86	79	76	50	56	65	57
All ethnic groups[4]	76	93	77	85	68	76	70	73

[1] The percentage of the population that is in the labour force.
[2] Combined quarters: Spring 1999 to Winter 1999–2000.
[3] Includes those of mixed origin.
[4] Includes those who did not state their ethnic group.

Source: Labour Force Survey, Office for National Statistics (2001a, p. 77).

As we saw in Chapter 7, ethnicity and race are key determinants of social inequality. Racism in the workplace and in recruitment tends to result in ethnic and racially defined minorities experiencing chronic disadvantage. This is despite the fact that the members of these groups often have the same credentials as ethnic (chiefly white) majorities. As with women, Afro-Caribbean, Indian, Pakistani and other racially defined groups tend to be found in a limited range of lower-paid jobs, although some groups – notably male Indians – tend to find greater success in the labour market. Not surprisingly, black women are most likely to be restricted to undesirable, low-paid work.

Prejudice and discrimination in the labour market lead to the racist equivalent of the glass ceiling experienced by women. Sometimes, as in the case of slavery and more recently South Africa apartheid, this ceiling is formally installed by state law. In such cases, certain jobs are closed to non-white workers, as is living and working in certain areas of the country. Surprisingly, perhaps, the assault on formalised racism in South Africa did much more to improve the position of black and coloured people than all the anti-discriminatory legislation passed over the years in liberal democracies.

Ethnic minorities in Europe and the US suffer from discrimination in the workplace for a variety of reasons. Some analysts stress the demand for cheap labour by private capital, others the failure of (ethnic majority) trade unions to support minority workers' interests to the full, while others – focusing on the 'outsider' status of many ethnic minority workers – stress the positional weakness of those seeking jobs as migrant labourers – for example, the Turkish workers employed in Germany and the Vietnamese in the United States. For these people, employment rights are often completely ignored, and as Piore (1979) has argued, such workers are unlikely to insist that their rights be honoured, as they regard their jobs as temporary and merely a way of securing income that can be taken back home. In a sense, migrant workers probably provide a better example of 'instrumentalism' than the Luton car workers in Goldthorpe *et al.*'s (1968) study.

It should be noted, however, that in the last decades of the twentieth century, black workers, particularly in the US, began to break out of the subordinate labour market ghetto they had occupied for so long. For example, Hout (1984) has shown that by the 1980s, African-Americans were occupying a much more diverse range of jobs across the social classes than they had in the 1960s, and he suggests that the growth of public sector work has been an important vehicle for social advancement. Nevertheless, compared with other ethnic immigrant workers such as the Irish, Koreans and Italians, black Americans are still structurally disadvantaged in the US labour market.

In the UK, the labour market prospects of the various ethnic groups vary considerably. For example, African Asians and Chinese are more likely than whites to earn more than £500 per week, and to have unemployment rates that are as low as or lower than that of the general population.

For many other ethnic minorities, though, both in the US and the UK, insecure and low-paid work, often in harsh physical environments, has resulted in limited job satisfaction. For ethnic minorities, work is much more likely to provide job satisfaction and a feeling of autonomy when kin, extended kin and the wider ethnic group combine to construct a mutually supportive **micro-economy**. Asian communities in the UK, for example, are characterised by a large number of (typically male run and owned) small businesses tied to the local community.

Micro-economy
The productive activities of small section of the wider macro-economy.

Age

Most people spend a large proportion of their lives in the workforce, but this proportion has been falling owing to the longer time spent in education, increased longevity and, as a result of the latter, longer retirement. The likelihood of being economically active varies with age (Chart 11.2). In 2000, about 66 per cent of women aged 16–24 were active in the labour market, almost the same as in 1971. For women aged 25–44 (the main child-bearing and child-rearing years) in 1971, there was a marked dip to 54 per cent, but by 2000, participation had risen to 76 per cent. For men of all age groups, labour market participation was lower in 2000 than in 1971.

Demographic age profile
The size and structure of the population based on age.

The **demographic age profile** of all industrialised countries is changing, with a growing proportion of retired people. Among the working population, certain types of work are more likely to be undertaken at particular stages of the life-cycle than others. For example, younger people are disproportionately represented in more physically demanding work, such as in warehouses, the police or the construction industry, or in work that depends on the acquisition of new skills to handle new technologies, such as computer programming. In some occupations, as Kaufman and Richardson (1982) have shown, there is a U-shaped distribution of younger and older workers in jobs that are low-paid and without career prospects, such as gardening, operating lifts and cashier work.

An important age-related phenomenon in recent decades has been the widespread redundancy of middle-income middle managers who have been encouraged to take early retirement. The restructuring of industry discussed in Chapter 5 has not only led to the polarisation of the workforce but also to substantial numbers of older workers experiencing unexpected vulnerability in their jobs. However, national (as in the US) and international (as in the EU) legislation has been implemented to counter discrimination against workers on the basis of age. Furthermore, the cost of paying off older workers has risen, and can be more expensive than keeping them on. As a result, the speed at which older workers have been removed from the labour market has declined, although the practice has not stopped. Many early retirees have drawn on their contacts and networks to establish small consultancy businesses, often acting on a casual basis on

CHART 11.2 Economic activity rates in the UK:[1] by gender and age, 1971 and 2000

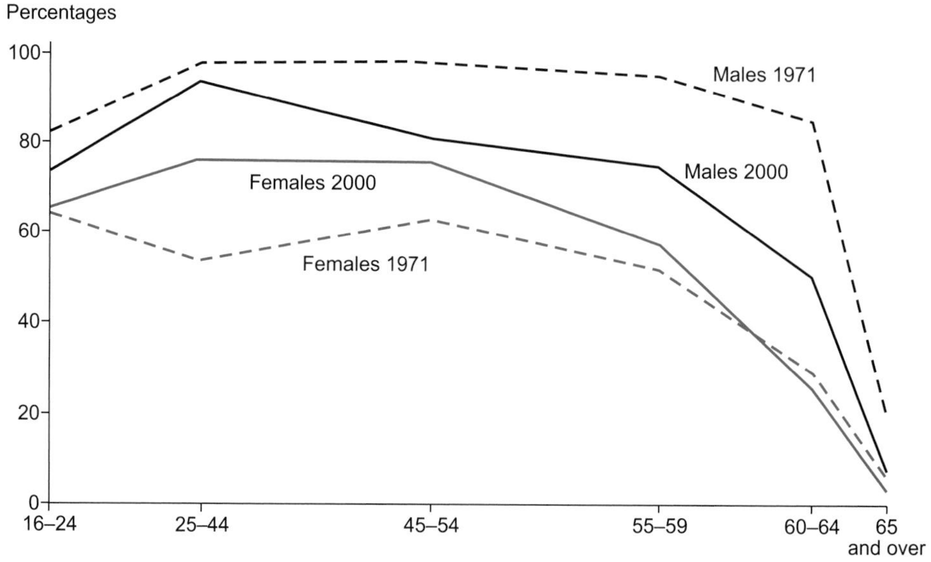

Percentages

[1] The percentage of the population that is in the labour force. The definition of the labour force changed in 1984 when the former Great Britain civilian labour force definition was replaced by the ILO definition which excludes members of the armed forces.

Source: Census and Labour Force Survey, Office for National Statistics (2001a, p. 76).

behalf of their former employers. This is especially true of former managers of the privatised public utilities in the UK. The production of business cards for the middle-aged self-employed has no doubt been a growth industry during this period of restructuring!

According to Scase (1992), because of all this restructuring, the traditional manager responsible for administering a business division is no longer seen as essential to a company's managerial strategy. Instead, the responsibilities of such managers are sometimes outsourced or subcontracted to smaller and cheaper business advisory firms. Stripping out middle management in this way is also related to the growth of **information technology** (IT), which has enabled greater control by the centre and a more horizontal (as opposed to hierarchical) management structure. The combined effects of this **downsizing** of the labour force and the fragmentation of large corporations into smaller, more flexible units (Shutt and Whittington, 1987) means that many thousands of people aged 45–50 cannot find work but will have to wait many years to draw their pensions in the future.

Governments in Western Europe are seeking to equalise the official retirement age for men and women. In the UK, universal retirement at the age of 65 is to be phased in between 2010 and 2020. At the moment, many retirees engage in part-time work, not merely to supplement their typically low state and (sometimes) company pensions, but also to try to sustain the sense of identity that work had brought them. During the 1990s, about one third of males in Western Europe worked after their official retirement (CEC, 1994), even though this work had a lower status than their previous jobs.

We saw in Chapter 5 how changes in the structure of the labour market are likely to result in secure, long-term careers being restricted to perhaps a third of the working population, irrespective of social class. The uncertainties experienced by middle man-

Information technology
Computerised, electronic technology to gather, record and communicate information.

Downsizing
Management term for reducing the number of employees.

TABLE 11.5 The employment effects of flexible employment and labour market regulation

| | Percentage of all in employment | | | |
	1979	1984	1990	1997
First-time employees	76.7	69.7	67.1	65.2
Full-time permanent	n.a.	67.4	64.8	61.7
Full-time temporary	n.a.	2.3	2.3	3.5
Part-time employees	16.1	18.8	19.4	22.2
Part-time permanent	n.a.	16.5	17.2	19.2
Part-time temporary	n.a.	2.3	2.2	3.0
Full-time self-employed	6.5	9.4	11.3	9.9
Part-time self-employed	0.7	1.9	2.1	2.6

Notes: Excluding those on government schemes and unpaid family workers. Robinson points out that although data on temporary employment are not available before 1984, it can be inferred that in 1979 about 74–75 per cent of all those in employment were full-time permanent employees.

Source: Robinson (1999).

agers in recent years are likely to become the norm for many in service-based occupations, and increasingly so for those engaged in manufacturing and related activities.

The proportion of the UK workforce with full-time permanent jobs has fallen significantly since 1979 (Robinson, 1999), as illustrated in Table 11.5. Work will no doubt be different in the future, and sociologists will need to explore the implications of this for occupational and class identity. Handy (1985, p. 37), argues that society must become less 'job-fixated' and consider the 'array of possibilities [available] if we start to play around with the conventional notion of the 100 000 hours lifetime job'.

Disability

According to Colin Barnes (1996), institutional discrimination against disabled people affects all areas of their life, including employment. In relation to work, Barnes notes that unemployment and under-employment are consistently higher among disabled workers than among their non-disabled contemporaries, with disabled young adults experiencing particularly acute problems.

QUESTION Why do you think that much of the legislation aimed at securing equal employment rights for disabled people has been largely ignored by employers and the state?

An important survey carried out by the Institute for Employment Studies in conjunction with NOP Social and Political (1998) produced nationally representative data on disabled people's participation in the workforce. The main survey (conducted between July and October 1996) involved 2 015 people of working age (women aged 16–59, men aged 16–64) who either had a long-term disability or health problem or had had such a disability, in line with the definition of disability presented in the Disability Discrimination Act. Of the 2 015 interviewees, 1 440 were economically active. The following are some of the key findings:

● Unemployed disabled people overwhelmingly agreed that getting a job was important to them, with 64 per cent agreeing strongly and 29 per cent agreeing.

- More than one quarter of the disabled people who had left their job because of their disability said that adaptations would have enabled them to remain in work, but fewer than one in five had been offered such changes.
- One in six disabled people (16 per cent) who were or had been economically active said that they had experienced discrimination or unfair treatment in a work-related context.
- Employed disabled people were more likely to work in manual and low-skill jobs.
- Disabled ethnic minority people were more likely to be out of work than their white counterparts.
- At £196 per week, the average take-home pay of disabled employees was lower than that of non-disabled employees (then £212).

Next we turn our attention to how workers are responding to the changing labour market, how trade unions are coping with the fragmentation of work itself and the traditional places of work, and whether this is likely to result in new forms of industrial conflict in the future.

CONNECTIONS For a further discussion of the relationships between gender, ethnicity, age and disability, see Chapter 4.

Industrial conflict

In the past decades, there have been significant changes in the way in which workers have tried to protect their jobs and their position in the labour market more generally. Worker resistance to management decisions on pay, conditions, rights and so on was traditionally expressed through strikes, absenteeism, sabotage, pilfering or negotiation through official trade unions or professional associations. We saw in the preceding section that the restructuring of the labour market has sometimes resulted in increased unemployment for both public and private sector workers. Jobs have also been lost to cheaper workers in overseas countries. State legislation has eroded worker and union rights, and traditional sites of union power, identity and leadership – such as coal mining – have been weakened. As a result, industrial conflict, which clearly reflects wider socio-political conflict, has experienced something of a decline when measured in terms of strike action, as workers have found it increasingly difficult to act in unison on a national basis via their trade unions. Unemployment – both official and hidden (unemployment among those who are looking for work but are excluded from the statistics) – is at a relatively high historical level in some European countries. The notion of full employment, once considered by many political parties as a desirable goal, is now receiving less cross-party support. That said, the UK Labour government, elected for a second term in 2001, has its sights on something approximating full employment.

This situation has a number of implications. If the fragmentation of work continues, we might expect to see the fragmentation of unions, or at least the further erosion of union power. Moreover, there is likely to be further growth in new jobs in part-time, casual sectors such as retailing and catering, where unionisation has been traditionally weak. Furthermore, such jobs are highly feminised, and as such are less likely to be union-oriented. The shift away from national bargaining over conditions and pay has resulted in plant bargaining and – more worrying for unions – individual contracts for members of staff. The power of large public sector unions has been eroded by privatisation, and at the local level, new forms of management and trustee ownership have been set up to take the state out of negotiations on pay and conditions.

In short, the traditional labour movement appears to have lost much of the momentum it built up during the pre- and post-Second World War periods. The collectivism it once expressed – although this was always somewhat over-romanticised by the movement itself – is proving difficult to sustain as the labour market's polarisation is splitting workers into a core, secure, privileged stratum and a large, casualised, insecure mass of workers.

In this situation worker resistance can be either bought off quite quickly or simply dismissed by bringing in new workers. Alternatively employers may threaten to relocate production elsewhere. Given this, from both the workers' and the employers' perspective one of the most important factors shaping the future of working conditions is the European Union (EU), which has introduced minimum levels of pay, workers' rights, and equality of opportunity. In the UK in the early 1990s, the Conservative government sought to opt out of these requirements, but many multinational corporations decided to adopt the same conditions throughout their European operations, including those in the UK. (The following Labour government eventually introduced minimum wage legislation.) Institutional protection of workers' rights is seen as very important in the EU and will help to shape the future industrial conflict in Europe. At the same time, the EU is keen for European industry to be competitive *vis-à-vis* that of the Pacific Rim and the US. So it will continue to juggle the interests of workers and private capital, and no doubt legislation on the European statute books will sometimes pull in conflicting directions.

CONNECTIONS The ability of multinational corporations to relocate their operations is a crucial element of their power – see Chapter 3.

The future of work

As work patterns change and the notion of full-time, secure work recedes, the nature of work is likely to change dramatically. Whether this change will be in the direction of Handy's (1985) rather Utopian vision of job-sharing and, by implication, leisure-sharing across all social classes, where the distribution of income will be much more even and people will willingly accept this, or in the direction of increased polarisation, growing unemployment and social deprivation, with more being spent on social control and video surveillance (in and out of work), will depend on society's response to the political options sketched out in Chapter 8.

Work, non-work and leisure

Before examining leisure in more detail, it may be useful to attempt to distinguish (as far as is possible) between work, non-work and leisure. As we have seen, work is an activity that produces goods and services (for example, building ships and parenting). Some work is paid, while some is unpaid. Non-work is an activity (such as reading a newspaper) or a non-activity (such as sleeping) that occurs before an individual starts paid or unpaid work (for example, during childhood), or during time off from paid or unpaid work (for example, at the weekend), or after an individual ceases to engage in paid or unpaid work (for example, when unemployed or retired). Leisure is not straightforwardly defined and is often seen in negative terms as non-work. Put more positively, leisure (normally) relates to recreational activities undertaken during non-work time (for example, having a swim at the weekend) where there is no compulsion and where there is autonomy and control over what is being done. Handy calls this 'discretionary time'. Like work, leisure activities take place at particular times and in particular locations (such as the cinema, the theatre, the home, the sports centre and so on).

The boundaries between the above three categories are sometimes clear, but at other times, they may be blurred or even overlapping. Take, for example, cultural perceptions of work and leisure. For instance, in countries where DIY is popular, is doing up the home a job or a leisure activity? One way to find out may be to ask people who do it. If they are enthusiasts, it is arguably leisure, but if they do it out of necessity, it is probably work.

BOX 11.1 Work, non-work and unemployment

In official terms, there are sometimes no clear-cut distinctions between work and non-work, especially when the measurement of employment and unemployment enters the fray. In the UK, for example, governments have traditionally measured unemployment on the basis of the number of jobless people claiming unemployment benefit. However, the Labour Force Survey takes into account all jobless people who are looking for work, not just those in receipt of benefit – a broader measure of unemployment often preferred by economists. So, for example, the number of UK benefit claimants fell by 10 000 in April to 976 000 (3.2% of the workforce), while the number of people looking for work but unable to find it fell by 64 000 in the first quarter of 2001 to 1.497 million (5.1% of the workforce).

But however we define work and leisure, we can see that the historical development of paid work has been paralleled by the development not only of unemployment (where jobs are available or unwanted) but also of leisure time, free from the demands of paid labour. Leisure activities have grown, especially in the last 50 years, as a result of a number of factors, including:

- A rise in the disposable income of many workers.
- A reduction in the number of hours worked per week (notably, since the 1960s, the institutionalisation of the five-day week and the free weekend).
- Holiday pay (from the early 1970s in Western Europe).
- The commercialisation of leisure, such that more opportunities and outlets for leisure pursuits have become available.
- A contraction of the working life as a result of longer schooling, and earlier retirement, primarily by those with good occupational pensions.

This last point means that the leisure industry has two very important age groups to target – youths and young adults, and older people. The recent demographic shift has resulted in an increase in the proportion of men and women aged 60–75, many of whom seek some form of leisure activity. The growth of leisure time does not mean, of course, that everyone is in position to take it up. The unemployed find it particularly difficult to convert free time into leisure, as they have little money and restricted social contact, combined with a sense of lost identity, self-esteem and personal status. They also have too much time on their hands for leisure to be enjoyable. Having paid work, then, is central to our enjoyment of leisure. Moreover, as domestic labourers, women's leisure is often circumscribed or experienced through that of others – their partner's, their children's and so on.

According to Glyptis (1989), there are three ways in which the relationship between work and leisure is characterised in sociology. The first, referred to as the 'extension' or 'spillover' approach, looks at the ways in which an individual's personality and attitudes are expressed in both work and leisure. The second, the 'oppositional' approach, sees leisure as entirely antithetical to the world of work, as a means of forgetting work, or at least compensating for it. The third approach views the two spheres as unconnected with each other: this is called the 'neutrality' approach. These broad characterisations have all found supportive evidence, such that the way in which work and leisure inter-relate is dependent on context, personality and opportunity.

There are also very different predispositions to leisure. Perhaps one way of illustrating this is by means of McGoldrick's and Carter's (1982) classification of the types of leisure activity undertaken by households where the principal (male) breadwinner has recently retired. They categorise these men as 'rest and relaxers', 'home and family men', 'hobbyists', 'good timers', 'committee and society men', 'volunteers', 'further education men', 'part-time jobbers' and 'new jobbers'. These categories are useful in providing us with an array of pursuits that people define as leisure. However, they do not enable us to understand leisure in its wider social context. For this, we need a more theoretical argument.

There are three principal theoretical approaches to leisure: neo-Marxist, feminist and postmodern. We shall look at each one briefly.

The neo-Marxist approach

This approach (see, for example, Clarke and Critcher, 1985), as one might expect, ties leisure to the interests of capitalism. Leisure is appropriated by private capital, which commodifies it and sells it to a mass market that has little knowledge of the way in which its leisure is being pre-packed and made ready for consumption. Moreover, while contemporary capitalist leisure is geared to a mass market, it is highly class-based, in that it carries the structured inequalities of capitalist society. The market for commercial leisure goods is growing constantly, so that eventually people will only experience a sense of leisure if they have bought it – through the theme park, the health club, the holiday abroad, the latest leisure shirt from a mail-order catalogue and so on. Sport, so central to leisure, is a vehicle both for social control and the sale of goods – the latest team shirt, for example. Sports men and women have themselves become commodified as promotors of the wares of sponsoring companies, oil companies or tobacco companies.

However, other sociologists (for example, Rojek, 1995) argue that leisure cannot be reduced to the interests of capital in this way. Some forms of leisure, such as tending a suburban vegetable allotment, are completely outside the circuit of capital and indeed are often explicitly hostile to it (Crouch, 1994). Other forms have offered women new opportunities – such as aerobics – that were denied them in the male-dominated past. Similarly, popular forms of leisure such as bingo, working men's clubs and 'rave' music nights are localised activities that cannot be conceived in terms of the class interests of capital.

Despite these criticisms of the neo-Marxist account, the commercialisation of leisure is an important and defining feature of contemporary society. This notion is taken up in a rather different way by those who adopt a postmodern perspective on leisure, as we shall see later.

The feminist approach

This approach, as Deem (1986, p. 11) observes, 'places women at the forefront of its analysis and sees them as an oppressed group with certain experiences and interests in common'. Not only is women's leisure more restricted than that of men, but women are typically the providers of leisure for men (ibid, p. 13):

> " Women service men's leisure activities, by undertaking domestic work and childcare, so that men are free to go out to the pub or to have leisure time out of the house. ... [M]any sites where leisure takes place are barred or made unattractive to women (football, rugby, working men's clubs, many pubs) by admitting them on male terms. ... Men see leisure as a right; women do not and are not encouraged by men to do so). "

Deem studied female leisure activities in Milton Keynes, a new town in the south of England. She studied two groups, one made up of women who regularly engaged in leisure pursuits outside the home and belonged to various organisations and clubs, and a random sample of women, most of whom had limited or no involvement with external organisations. While noting differences between the two groups, she shows how close their experience of leisure actually was (ibid., pp. 39–40):

> " Both groups have problems and constraints which it is necessary for them to overcome if they are to have any leisure of their own. Whilst some of those constraints and problems are of necessity individual and idiosyncratic, many of them are both structural and ideological and there is a limit to which individual women can challenge such constraints. ... Even women who are able to challenge or resist some of the constraints surrounding the possibilities of achieving leisure outside the home and inside it are limited by the extent to which male dominance permeates society. Whether it is the difficulties women face in being able to escape from the household tasks in the evenings or weekends, the places and activities with which they feel comfortable, vulnerability when travelling across a city, or the extent to which women are made to feel that sport and physical activity are unfeminine, it is male dominance, in its many forms, which stands at the roots of these constraints. ... Where women are active in leisure pursuits outside the home it is usually within a range of 'suitable' and 'gender appropriate' activities – women's organisations, caring and community activities, evening classes, keep fit and yoga groups, bingo – which are enjoyable, but are also where women feel and are perceived by men to be 'safe' and 'women in their place'. "

Deem identifies a number of factors that enable women to participate in leisure activities, including:

- Access to private transport.
- An independent source of money.
- Some form of work.
- A self-confident approach to life.
- A sense of a legitimate right to leisure.
- A social support network.

In the light of this, Deem argues that three changes need to be made if women are to enhance their experience of leisure: an improved environment for women's leisure by means of an integrated public policy that combines leisure provision with better public transport, childcare facilities and support for women's organisations; increased (non-commercial) leisure provision in general, the nature of which should be determined by women; and changes to the domestic division of labour and the relationship between work and leisure that derives from this division.

The postmodernist approach

This final theoretical approach to leisure draws on a much wider perspective within the sociology of postmodernity. As we shall see in Chapter 19, **postmodernism** claims that in today's society, the boundaries between social institutions and social structures, morality and immorality, and the right and wrong ways of doing things are breaking down. Postmodern culture, it is argued, is breaking down the tired, hierarchical

Postmodernism
Often perceived as a cultural phenomenon associated with contemporary arts, it combines apparently opposing elements to subvert meaning and fragment totality. It is characterised by a pastiche of cultural styles and elements, but implies a deep scepticism about order and progress. Instead, diversity and fragmentation are celebrated.

traditions of modernity and opening up new opportunities for self-expression and self-realisation. Featherstone (1991b, p. 65) puts it as follows: 'If we examine definitions of postmodernism we find an emphasis on the effacement of the boundary between art and everyday life, the collapse of the distinction between high art and mass/popular culture, a general stylistic promiscuity and playful mixing of codes.'

What has this got to do with leisure? For the postmodernist, leisure cannot be conceived of as simply an activity that takes place in a certain place at a certain time, for this is to assume that we experience leisure as a sort of social package, clearly defined and bounded. Instead, the boundaries are continually being dismantled, principally through our immersion in **consumerism**. But this consumption is an active rather than a reactive process, as Willis (1990, pp. 17–18) observes:

Consumerism
A culture based on the promotion, sale and consumption of consumer goods.

> "[S]ymbolic work and creativity mediate, and are simultaneously expanded and developed by the uses, meanings and 'effects' of cultural commodities. Cultural commodities are catalyst, not product; a stage in, not the destination of, cultural affairs. Consumerism now has to be understood as an active, not a passive process. Its play includes work. "

Unlike neo-Marxists, some postmodernists celebrate consumerism as a vehicle for creative cultural activities, rather than viewing it as a means of capitalist profit making. Leisure is, as Fiske (1992) argues, now part of a 'semiotic democracy' in which we can invest different meanings and different lifestyles, and which we choose to buy into.

CONNECTIONS A fuller account of postmodernism is provided in Chapter 19.

Clearly, the postmodernist approach raises questions about the relationship between the production of leisure by consumer industries and the terms on which their products are consumed. There is tension in the fact that the culture industries – such as the media, and especially TV – produce images and products geared for niche markets and others that are sold on a mass basis, such as the Game Boy electronic toy. It is clearly the case that leisure and the audio-visual technologies that have played a key role in shaping it have become increasingly individualised and privatised. The leisure industries have defined and exploited niche markets for 'discriminating categories' of individual consumers for whom a particular form of leisure activity creates a sense of personal identity. Even when a leisure facility caters for a large number of people – such as a swimming centre – this is still geared to a range of distinct, targeted needs. In Western Europe, the leisure chain Centre Parcs provides a suitable illustration of multi-faceted leisure provision.

It is important to explore how free we are to create our own meanings of these cultural objects. Some within the culture industry itself – for example, Madonna – help reproduce that industry but challenge its images and ideologies. Madonna's post-feminist challenge to gender stereotypes has been conducted through the very industry that has been most responsible for constructing sexist images of women.

Seen in these postmodernist terms, the Marxist and feminist notion that enjoyment of leisure is constrained by class or gender barriers is thrown into question. However, the wider claims of postmodernism are also open to challenge. Hence, this remains an important arena for sociological debate, tied into wider debates on the nature of consumption and the experiences we have as consumers.

CONNECTIONS Return to Chapter 2, pages 29–32, for a discussion of the complex relationship between culture industries and consumers. Chapter 12 also debates these ideas in relation to media audiences.

A topic that has been extensively worked over is the relationship between leisure, TV and popular culture more generally. We shall consider this in the next section.

Popular culture, TV and leisure

Raymond Williams (1980) describes TV as enabling mobile privatisation, whereby 'the public world is made available in new and extensive ways within the private sphere of the home: we travel imaginatively and stay put simultaneously'. To achieve success, TV producers have had to construct both the messages and the audiences for them: in a sense, audiences are told how to view the media. As Hartley (1987, p. 121) observes:

" Since audiences don't exist prior to or outside of television, they need constant hailing and guidance in how-to-be-an-audience – hailing and guidance that are unstintingly given within, and especially between, shows and in the meta-discourses that surround television, the most prominent among which, of course, are those publications aptly called 'television guides'. In fact, so numerous are the nightly programmes available on US TV (up to 500 options) that choosing one becomes something of a viewer's nightmare: hence all the technological peripherals that are now being developed to help you 'channel hop'. "

Likewise, Goodwin (1994, p. 134) comments:

" TV technologies are focussing on ways of making the choices more accessible: the remote control unit, gadgets which allow easier programming of video-cassette recorders, and TV screens with additional windows which permit the viewer to preview one channel while watching another. Indeed, there is now a cable TV channel, the prevue Channel, devoted exclusively to telling the viewer what is on the other channels. "

Text
Any form of symbolic representation that takes on a physical form; for example, books and films.

Sociologists have examined the various TV genres that have created a strong visual **text** for specifically targeted audiences. These genres include soap operas, game shows and children's TV.

Studies of soap operas (for example, Ang, 1985, 1991; Buckingham, 1987; Geraghty, 1991) show that from their inception, all UK soaps are targeted at the 'privatised' upper working class: as Turner (1990) remarks, it is ironic that upper-middle-class TV producers 'feel they know what will make a show successful even if they would never be caught dead watching one'!

Soap operas invite their audiences to identify with particular characters, to follow the ups and downs of their lives, to expect twists and turns as one cliff-hanging episode follows another. Newspaper coverage of soap opera events, characters and actors adds to viewers' knowledge of what is going on, where and with whom. The early soaps, such as the still-running *Coronation Street*, were more community-focused, and the plots and characters were more romanticised. Today's soaps indulge in gritty realism, and the community, rather than being revered, is problematised, divided along class and family lines. A number of soaps challenge some stereotypes while confirming others. For example, the US *Cosby Show* presents a positive image of a prosperous, professional black family, but this image conforms to the stereotype of the highly consumer-conscious white nuclear family (Miller, 1989).

The debate about the meaning and impact of soaps, game shows and the like echoes the debate described earlier between those who regard contemporary leisure as serving capitalist interests, and those who believe that individual consumers are able to resist capitalist images and messages to construct their own texts. Smythe (1987), who adopts the first of these views, has provided a powerful analysis of the logic of TV consumerism, a logic in which TV prepares audiences to be consumers of advertisers' products. The

TV station 'delivers' the audiences to those corporations which advertise on its channel. Product placement in programmes is a less explicit but nonetheless powerful advertising technique.

Other writers, for example, Morley (1992), argue that we need to be aware of the polysemic character of TV messages, that is, programmes and their surrounding adverts can be interpreted in numerous ways. This is illustrated by the very different receptions that *The Cosby Show* has had (Goodwin, 1994, p. 149):

" For many African-Americans, Cosby represents a bold effort to break down stereotypes and provide white and black viewers alike with an improved role model of the black American. But for many white viewers Cosby was used to show that racial discrimination was a thing of the past and that social equality had now been achieved. Since it can be empirically demonstrated that this was not the case, Cosby was allowing its white audiences to believe that which was wrong but nevertheless comforting, whilst at the same time, the very same episodes sent a positive message to many African-Americans. This is an important example of the multiple interpretations that are possible, especially when a mass medium is central to such a diverse and multicultural society. If television is polysemic – containing many meanings – anywhere in the world, then it will certainly be polysemic in the United States. "

QUESTION How important are soap operas to you? Can sociologists learn anything from watching them?

Morley (1992) also recognises that the meaning given to TV programmes depends on the context and circumstances in which they are viewed. In this regard, he acknowledges the feminist critique of TV: TV viewing is often determined by what the man wants to see, primarily because of the patriarchal attitude that defines the home as a place of rest, recreation and leisure for men but a place of (domestic) work for women. As McGuigan (1992, p. 136) comments: 'women are rarely permitted to watch [TV] with undivided attention: that is one of the reasons why the fragmented and repetitive structures of soap opera are so popular with the female audience'.

Debates about the message, context and audience of TV programmes are part of a much larger debate about the media themselves. As the quote from Williams (1980) at the start of the section suggests, the media not only send multiple messages but also provide us with indirect experience of events and processes happening beyond our own social world. We broaden our learning through TV, films, radio, the Internet, the press, books and magazines, but as implied earlier (and in our more extended commentary on the media in Chapters 3 and 12), the mass media do not necessarily provide neutral information on the world. Rather, information is structured and packaged in such a way that we make sense of the world through others' interpretations. News broadcasts, for example, have been shown to present explicit and implicit views of events that favour one reading over others.

As commercial organisations, global media companies develop media products and media vehicles to capture as large a market as possible. This involves structuring news programmes (to be shown in the home, the cinema, on a plane or on the Internet) to maximise sales and thereby attract advertising business. Not surprisingly, the message we receive – whether in our own lounge or that at the airport – is of a society broadly happy with itself, enterprising, and concerned about the environment, the value of the major currencies and who is likely to win the next major sports event. We are much less likely to see programmes that offer a critical perspective on society, revealing social inequalities, offering radical solutions to them and so on (Murdock, 1989).

CONNECTIONS There is a good account of the development of the global media in Chapter 12.

The more, then, that our leisure time is mediated by TV and other audio-visual technologies – such as MTV at the fitness centre – the more leisure will become a conduit for powerful social conventions and ideologies. Even if audiences are able to reject media messages (see Hall, 1993), the overall interpretive and informational flow tends to favour a constructed consensus and the status quo.

Conclusion

This chapter has examined the sociological analysis of work and non-work. It is clear that work and non-work share similar features. First, they are not easily defined and their boundaries can overlap. Second, both are centrally related to the dynamics of capitalism through the labour process and what might be called 'the leisure process' – the incorporation of leisure through consumerism into the capitalist market. We have also shown that the meaning of work and leisure varies according to context and the social position – for example, gender – of the social actor.

We have considered the idea that work has become subject to a de-skilling process, and concluded that this is not a general phenomenon but one that depends on social class, gender and ethnicity, as well as the context in which skills are deployed. On the other hand, some types of work have clearly involved re-skilling, as new technologies have affected jobs in both public and private organisations.

It might be worth considering whether leisure has been subjected to similar processes of de-skilling and re-skilling. The new technologies associated with leisure activities – especially computer-based ones – indeed do require the development of new skills to handle the **software**, surf the Internet and so on. The potential for audience involvement in and interaction with TV programmes has already been demonstrated, with over seven million people voting for which housemate should win the *Big Brother* 2001 prize.

What is clear is that one of the most important sources of personal identity – the work one does – seems to be declining in significance, or is at least being paralleled by personal identity constructed through consumerism.

Software
Computer programmes, manuals, instructions and other materials in written or numerical form that can be used in computer systems.

Chapter summary

- Industrialisation brought about the separation of paid work in the formal labour market from non-work. Women's domestic labour is extensive but materially unrewarded (or ungenerously rewarded).

- Gender division in the labour market both reflects and perpetuates gender division in the household.

- Labour process theorists who adopt a neo-Marxist approach to the labour market argue that there has been a general de-skilling of work across all occupational group.

- Against this, more recent analyses suggest that while some de-skilling has occurred, there is also evidence of re-skilling to meet the demand for flexible labour.

- The meaning of work and work satisfaction has to be understood in terms of the technology sector and the advent of new production regimes such as JIT.
- Orientations towards work cannot be identified simply by looking at the experience of work itself, as they reflect a number of factors outside work.
- Gender, age, ethnicity and disability affect opportunities for work and the rewards it brings.
- There are three main approaches to the relationship between work and leisure: Marxist, feminist and postmodernist.
- Leisure and the consumption of leisure goods – especially via the media – are important sources of social and personal identity, and for many they are more important than the identity bestowed by work.

Questions to think about

- To what would you attribute the decline in worker militancy since the 1980s? Identify and describe at least five factors and rank them in order of importance, justifying your choices.
- Applying what you have learned about discrimination on the grounds of gender, ethnicity, age or disability in relation to employment, what do you think sociologists would find if they explored the issue of sexuality and work?
- How important do you think leisure has become in contemporary societies? Give reasons for your answer.

Investigating further

Bradley, Harriet, Mark Erickson, Carol Stephenson and Steve Williams (2000) *Myths at Work*, Polity Press

> This accessible text focuses on some of the key debates on work and employment in contemporary society, and questions the accuracy of some widely held beliefs. With discussions of issues such as globalisation, the feminisation of the labour force, the skills revolution and lean production, it offers a good introduction to a number of topical debates.

Critcher, Chas, Peter Bramham and A. Tomlinson (1994) *Sociology of Leisure: A Reader*, Routledge

> An anthology of classic readings covering a range of debates on leisure and society.

Dunne, Gillian (1997) *Lesbian Lifestyles: women's work and the politics of sexuality*, Palgrave

> Based on original research, this book examines how women's experience of work and the domestic sphere is profoundly affected by sexuality, with consequences for the patterns of power and inequality throughout society. Chapter 5, which focuses on paid work, offers a range of fascinating debates, data and quotes from the women interviewed in the research.

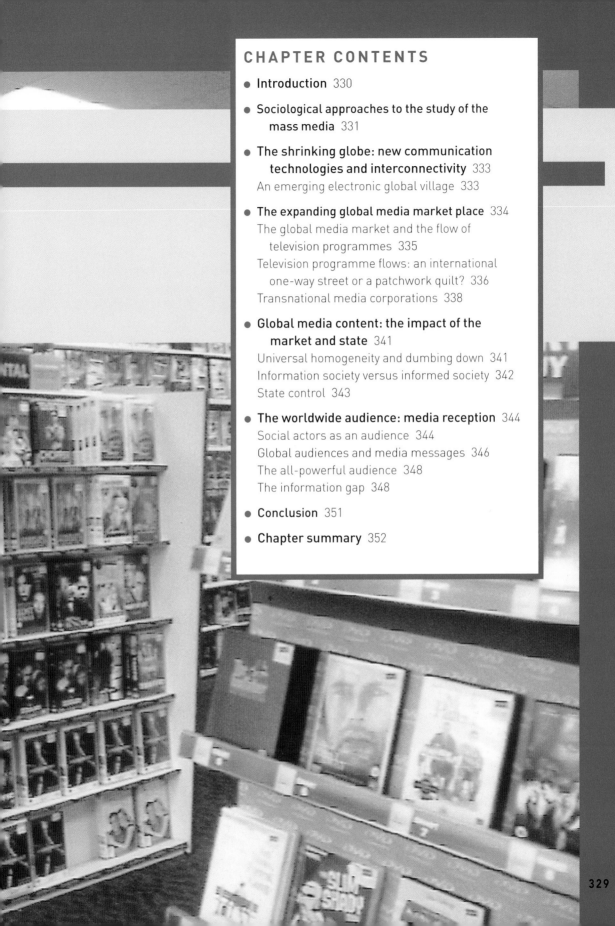

CHAPTER CONTENTS

Aims of the chapter

The mass media are hugely important in contemporary societies. This chapter provides an insight into the media as a common feature of globalisation. It provides you with an introduction to traditional sociological approaches to the media, up-to-date empirical data on the usage of the media and an overview of the latest research developments, as well as introducing the main debates in the field.

By the end of this chapter, you should have an understanding of the following concepts:

- Public sphere
- Reception theory
- Passive/active audience
- Ideology
- Information rich/poor
- Global interconnectedness
- Conglomeration

Introduction

Communications technologies have become an integral part of all modern societies. Social actors are surrounded by a great diversity of communication technologies – telephones, fax machines, mobile phones, cinema, radio, records, CDs, videos, television, computers and the Internet, to name but a few. These technologies are a taken for granted part of our everyday lives (Silverstone, 1990), and we use them on a daily basis. A recent study of a sample of young people in the UK (Livingstone and Bovill, 1999, p. 5) found that:

- On average, 99 per cent spent two and a half hours a day watching television.
- 88 per cent spent two hours watching videos two or three days a week.
- 36 per cent spent the same amount of time on a personal computer.
- 19 per cent used the Internet, the majority doing so once a month or less at school.

Each of these technologies acts as a facilitator of content distribution (Tomlinson, 1999), that is, as a means of communicating the content of programmes, news, financial data, texts and so on between a vast array of institutions and actors over large distances. They also act as an intermediary between sender and recipient, by constructing and conveying messages. So, by interacting with communication media, social actors are not only provided with instant access to information and entertainment and exposed to a vast number of images and texts from around the world, they are also able to communicate with individuals across great distances.

Sociological analysis of the mass media is interested in the impact of new communication technologies on societies, and in how societies use such technologies. For example, it is interested in the production and distribution of media products, as well as their reception by social actors. While individuals may own the technological means of reception, the contents are produced by organisations in an ever-growing media industry, shaped by the environment in which they operate. What individuals watch or read is increasingly produced by global corporations and takes place communally, with family and friends, or on their own.

The theme of this chapter is the global diffusion of communication technologies and media products, and their local appropriation (Thompson, 1995). After introducing traditional sociological approaches to the media, it examines how information and communication technologies enable greater global interconnectedness between social actors in countries around the world. It then discusses the global flow of media products, the increasingly transnational nature of media organisations, their patterns of ownership and the consequences of this. The focus then turns to the audience and local reception of globally produced media products. Finally, national and global inequalities in respect of access to the media are discussed.

When focusing on the various aspects of media globalisation, the chapter will examine a series of important questions relating to the production, distribution and reception of media content. Who determines media content? Is ownership concentrated? Whose interests do media organisations serve? How do audiences make sense of media messages? In answering these questions, the chapter will illuminate the ongoing debates between different sociological perspectives in the study of the media.

Sociological approaches to the study of the mass media

The history of sociological approaches to the media in some ways mimics the development of media technology. From a fairly simple understanding of the way in which the media impact on the audience, sociological approaches have grown more complex, and not just as a result of the proliferation of media types and outlets in society. The factors that have to be taken into account when exploring the media from a sociological point of view have also increased and now include the producers of media content and the audience for media products.

Audience
A term used to denote the receivers of the media messages contained in texts, broadcasts and so on.

Research in the middle of the twentieth century tended to start from the assumption that the effects of the media on the **audience** were relatively straightforward and direct, with passive receivers absorbing media messages in a relatively unproblematic way. This 'hypodermic syringe' approach (see, for example, Cantril, 1997) focused on politics on the one hand – propaganda and the impact of political campaigns during elections – and violence on the other. The interest in violence stemmed from the fear that some media were taking up too much of young children's time and having an undesirable effect on them (Bandura, 1965).

Over the course of the second half of the century, more sophisticated models of media effects were developed. These suggested that the interplay between media content and the audience was more complex than had been thought. For example, it was recognised that the receivers of media messages had prior experiences and other important influences on their lives that they brought to bear on their media experiences. A classic example of this was the two-step model of media communication, in which opinion leaders shaped the reactions of others to media messages (Katz and Lazarsfeld, 1955).

By the end of the twentieth century, approaches such as reception theory had recognised the audience as active players in the communication process, manipulating media usage and content for their own purposes, such as information gathering, entertainment and as a focus for interaction with significant others. The emphasis in reception analysis is on the way in which individuals 'read' media texts, for example, there are differences between the male and female ways of reading television content. Class and ethnicity were also found to be important variables in people's approach to media content (Morley, 1986).

Figure 12.1 The experience of watching TV can be subject to gender inequalities: men are often found to take charge of the remote control, while women combine TV watching with domestic chores. See table 12.3 on p. 344.

Other theoretical approaches focused on different but often related issues. A major topic of debate between Marxist and pluralist theorists was the influence that the owners of media industries brought to bear on the content of media messages. There were several versions of the Marxist assertion that the owners of the means of communication had tremendous power to influence the audience through the messages that their media empires put out. These ranged from the direct influence model (Miliband, 1968), which cited cases of direct interference in the editorial process, to more indirect approaches that focused on 'allocative control', whereby owners determined the broad thrust of media content (Golding and Murdock, 1991). Conversely, pluralists argued that the influence of the owners was negligible because the media had to respond to audience needs or go bankrupt. The content of the media was therefore determined not by what the owners wanted, but by what the audience demanded (Whale, 1977).

CONNECTIONS For a description of the pluralist model in politics, see Chapter 8, pages 198–201.

Feminists had a substantial impact on the sociological study of the media during the second half of the twentieth century, particularly with regard to the way in which women were portrayed by the media. Because the media promoted images of women that reflected a patriarchal view of women's role in society, they were seen as reinforcing traditional stereotypes of feminity. This claim was clearly related to the debate about effects, as it was assumed that long-term exposure to consistent images would lead the audience to absorb hidden messages (see Signorelli and Morgan, 1990).

The debate about the impact of media images on the audience has since been broadened with the development of postmodernist approaches. Postmodernists stress the centrality of the media in the postmodern condition, arguing that the media are the main source of images of the world in which we live. The media therefore constitute a world of hyper-reality, in which the strong but partial images of the world they put forward structure our reality (Seidman, 1994). With the proliferation of global technologies, the issues of audience effects and the way in which the media may be structuring our reality have assumed prime importance.

The shrinking globe: new communication technologies and interconnectivity

Examination of the development of communication technologies provides important insights into how these technologies have globalised communication between social actors. Studies of the historical impact of such technologies by Williams (1976), Meyrowitz (1985), Giddens (1991), Thompson (1995) and Tomlinson (1999) emphasise the way in which they have enabled the distribution of political, social and economic information, ideas and attitudes over ever greater distances at ever increasing speeds.

In early modern societies, information, ideas and attitudes were mainly spread via face to face contact between social actors, or during public gatherings. However, the widespread diffusion of printing presses in the fifteenth century meant that for the first time, ideas could be disseminated over large distances without the need for personal contact. While the oral dissemination of information at public gatherings continued, it was now supplemented by 'mediated distribution', that is, literate individuals could learn of events by reading newspapers and periodicals, and political and economic information, attitudes and ideas could flow to distant individuals.

However, there was still a reliance on physical distribution – information was physically conveyed to newspaper offices, and newspapers had to be transported from their place of production to their point of sale. The development of electronic communications, in particular the telegraph and Morse code, in the mid-nineteenth century meant that information distribution was no longer linked to physical transportation and was virtually instantaneous over large distances. In the 1850s, underwater cabling technology enabled rapid international information distribution. In the 1860s, the first underwater cable was laid between the US and the UK. The laying of cables continued, linking the UK and the other European powers to the various parts of their empires. For example, at the end of the nineteenth century, individuals living in Manchester could not only find out about events in London by the next day, but could also receive information from around the world, as the telegraph enabled the fast transfer of information to individuals in printed form.

An emerging electronic global village

New electronic communication technologies continued to transform the nature of the information that could be transmitted over distance and led to a further shrinkage of time and space (Giddens, 1991). Telegraphic communication was essentially a code-based, business-to-business communication device, but the broadcasting technology developed in the 1920s allowed first sound and then images to be carried instantaneously over large distances into the homes of individuals. From the early days of broadcasting, British listeners were exposed to novel dialects and regional cultures as well as the high arts and classical music.

Today, satellites and the Internet allow social actors in any locale to obtain instant information on national and global events and distant cultures. Satellites and the Internet have made it possible for individuals to become 'direct audiences' (Held, 1995,

p. 123); they have enabled senders and receivers to 'overcome geographical boundaries which once might have prevented contact; and they create access to a range of social and cultural experiences with which the individual and group may never have had an opportunity to engage' (Giddens, 1991, pp. 84–5). Hence, these two communication technologies in particular have led to greater global interconnectedness.

Broadcasts by satellite differ from conventional broadcasts, in that the signals are delivered to homes via a satellite dish. Rupert Murdoch's News Corporation was a pioneer in this field, launching Sky TV in the UK in 1989. There has been a strong take-up of satellite television, not only in the UK but also in countries such as India, where News Corporation launched the first foreign-owned satellite system (Star TV), followed quickly by rival satellite stations. Thompson (1995) argues that such broadcasting is inherently global, as the area where the signal is received does not necessarily correspond to national boundaries. Satellite broadcasting has enabled people in different locales around the world to witness events such as the Tiananmen Square massacre (1989), the Gulf War (1991) and the funeral of Princess Diana (1997) as they happened. Hence, as Held (1995, p. 124) argues, 'events … in distant localities came to impinge immediately and directly on everyday life in many parts of the world'.

This interconnectedness between different cultures and countries was further enhanced by the development of the Internet. The Internet, a network of interconnected computers, was developed by the US Defence Department and military establishment in the 1960s, but the introduction of browser software in the early 1990s made it suitable for the general public and led to its global spread (Herman and McChesney, 1997; Golding, 1998). The Internet has enhanced the potential for shared experiences regardless of distance, and increased the immediacy with which a wide variety of information can be disseminated.

QUESTION How has the Internet affected your life? List the different ways in which you use it.

The more recent arrival of digital technology promises to transform global mass communication even further. Digital technology has enabled the fusion of delivery systems, that is, 'all signals whether they carry sound, data, or pictures, can converge into digital formats. They thus become, however different in substance, identical in the technical sense' (Hamelink, 1995, p. 52). Signals are converted into a series of ones and zeros and transmitted via phone lines, satellite or cable between all networked computers and a new generation of televisions with 'set-top boxes' and mobile phones, at speeds that dwarf the older delivery systems. Digital terrestrial and satellite broadcasting started in the UK in 1999, combining hundreds of television channels with Internet features such as e-mail. In the case of Sky Digital, for example, 550 000 homes have already registered for its free e-mail service, and approximately 100 000 additional subscribers sign up each month (Price, 2000, p. 2). Other digital broadcasters such as ITV-digital have also launched e-mail services.

The expanding global media market place

Audiovisual market
The market for television programmes, films and music.

There is a continuous trade of media products between producers and distributors around the world, with an annual turnover of billions of US dollars. It is helpful for the sake of analysis to depict the global media market place as a series of submarkets or sectors (Hamelink, 1995). There is the global **audiovisual market**, the global news market, the telecommunications market, and the computer and software market.

Programmes, news, information, financial data, software and texts are produced, sold and traded in the same way as other commodities in the capitalist world economy. Here we shall focus on the television market. We shall examine its emergence, some of its main characteristics, and the dominant role played by giant transnationals. We shall also consider debates about the consequences of such trade and the activities of global media corporations.

The global media market and the flow of television programmes

The global television market started with a series of trade connections between various countries, confined by the international political contours of the Cold War. After 1945, in most developed capitalist societies, there were one or two programme producers broadcasting on a fixed number of channels within a set geographical area, with limited exchange of programmes between countries. As noted by Held *et al.* (1999), from the 1950s, there was a gradual increase in the ownership of television sets and a rise in the number of television channels in these countries. The UK was not untypical in this respect. For example, in 1946, 15 000 homes had a television set, and there was one broadcasting channel. By 1955, 4.5 million homes had televisions and a choice of two channels. By 1981, there were around 21 million televisions and four channels. Today, 23 million homes have around 55 million sets, and there are hundreds of channels.

This growth in television ownership and channels was naturally accompanied by an increase in programme production in capitalist countries, and international trade in programmes grew accordingly. In the US, the Hollywood studios dominated the production of television programmes from the 1950s, supplying not only the American networks but also television stations in other countries. Global programme trade takes several forms:

- Traditional programme purchases and sales.
- The international transfer of programme ideas. Many game shows and soap operas are now part of numerous countries' programme schedules.
- Co-production by two or more programme makers in different countries.

The dramatic growth in the volume of cross-border trade was due to a number of factors. Firstly, the arrival of satellite TV, the Internet and the new digital technology meant that the number of channels on which programmes could be seen was almost infinite. In addition, the falling cost of reception television sets meant that more people could afford them, and therefore the global audience increased substantially.

The second was government activity. In the last decades of the twentieth century, the governments of Western capitalist countries as well as many in the developing world took steps towards economic liberalisation (Hamelink, 1995; Herman and McChesney, 1997; Held *et al.* 1999; Murdock, 2000). As part of this process, tightly regulated media markets served by one or two suppliers were opened up to competition. Many governments also loosened their regulatory laws on media cross-ownership, enabling media corporations to own both newspapers and broadcasting operations. The process also involved the entire or partial privatisation of publicly owned telecommunication corporations. In the UK, government legislation in the 1990s, underpinned in part by neo-liberal ideas on freedom of choice and consumer sovereignty (Curran and Seaton, 1992; Murdock, 2000), led to the liberalisation of commercial television, the easing of programme standards, reduced ownership regulation and the growth of independent programme production. In the twenty-first century, the UK mass media system consists of a highly competitive and expanded print sector and an enlarged and less strictly regulated commercial broadcasting sector, with commercial satellite broadcasting, new digital terrestrial and satellite channels and the Internet.

The third factor was the collapse of the Soviet bloc. The governments of many of the former communist countries subsequently liberalised their media systems, allowing private ownership for the first time and resulting in increased demand for media products. Fourthly, global trade tariffs have fallen to the their lowest level for centuries (Held *et al.* 1999), and international bodies such as the World Trade Organisation (WTO) have aided multilateral trade by insisting on the removal of non-tariff trade restrictions between countries. As a consequence, many Third World countries have been forced to open up their media markets to Western imports (Thussu, 1998).

CONNECTIONS For a more general account of the effect of the collapse of the Soviet bloc, see Chapter 3, pages 60–4.

Television programme flows: an international one-way street or a patchwork quilt?

There has been vigorous and long-standing criticism of the cross-border flow of programmes, news, information, financial data, software, and so on. Critics have consistently argued since the 1960s that these one-way flows from producers in capitalist countries, most notably the US, to developing countries constitute a form of **cultural imperialism**. Studies of the audio-visual market and the sale of television programmes have confirmed the asymmetric flow of programmes from the Western core to the developing periphery. For example, in the 1970s, Nordenstreng and Varis (1974) found that American programmes accounted for '40% of programme hours exported worldwide, including 44% of hours imported by countries in western Europe' (quoted in Barker, 1997, p. 49). In another study, conducted in the 1980s, Varis found that there had been little change in the pattern of programme exports. 'In terms of programme hours … the US shares of exports [were] 77% for Latin America, 44% for Western Europe, 42% for the Arab countries, 47% for Africa (south of the Sahara)' (quoted in Barker, 1997, p. 49).

Critics of cultural imperialism argue that there are four key reasons for the US and Western dominance of the audio-visual market:

Cultural imperialism
The aggressive promotion of Western culture based on the assumption that its value system is superior and preferable to those of non-Western cultures.

- Their highly developed media industry (Schiller, 1976; Tunstall, 1977; Herman and McChesney, 1997).

- The support of successive governments.

- Media corporations subsidise the cost of programmes, effectively dumping programmes on the media markets of the developing world and preventing competition by indigenous companies. For example, US producers still sell popular television series at discounted prices to broadcasters in Third World countries (Thussu, 1998).

- The global dominance of the English language. According to Held *et al.* (1999), although some 5 000 languages are spoken in the world, just 10–12 of these are spoken by 60 per cent of the world's population. Held *et al.* argue that the global spread of certain languages has eased 'the transmission of cultural products and ideas' (ibid., p. 335). In particular, English 'has become the central language of international communication in business, administration, science, academia as well as being the language of globalised advertising and popular culture' (ibid., p. 346), and, one should add, the language of the Internet.

How convinced are you that the West, and the US in particular, is engaging in cultural imperialism? Does your own television viewing support this idea?

While US television producers are still the largest global exporters, their position is declining. As Table 12.1 shows, Europe and the rest of the world's share of international programme exports grew between 1987 and 1995, while that of the US slowly declined.

One of the factors driving the growth of Western European programme exports has been co-production, in which programme producers in different countries share the cost of production and benefit from economies of scale by producing programmes for domestic and global audiences. Television programmes are increasingly being produced with foreign markets in mind. In the UK, television exports amounted to £234 million in 1996, 53 per cent of which was accounted for by the BBC (Clarke, 1998, p. 6). Exports are increasingly taking the form of advanced sales. For example, the serial costume dramas *Pride and Prejudice* (BBC, 1996) *Moll Flanders* (ITV, 1997) and *Far From the Madding Crowd* (ITV, 1997), as well as a number of natural history programmes, were sold to overseas broadcasters, particularly in the US and Europe, before they were produced. In other words, global marketing now takes place before production even begins.

Studies of television programme flows in the 1990s by Sinclair *et al.* (1996) and Straubhaar (1997) have shown that the flow has become less unidirectional and more complex – a patchwork quilt, shaped not only in terms of economic dominance but also by linguistic, historical and cultural closeness. As Cunningham *et al.* (1999, p. 178) put it, instead of the image of the West at the centre dominating the peripheral Third World with an outward flow of cultural products, we can see the world as divided into a number of regions which each have their own internal dynamics as well as their global ties'.

Geo-linguistic regions
Regions linked by cultural and linguistic similarities as well as historical ties. Such regions often transcend national borders.

These regions are termed **geo-linguistic regions**. For example, there is an English-speaking geo-linguistic region, a Spanish-speaking one, an Arabic-speaking one, a Hindi-speaking one and a Chinese-speaking one. Cunningham *et al.* argue that there is a preference for programmes produced by other countries in the same region rather than those produced outside it, with the result that trade in television programmes is being shaped by cultural and linguistic similarities between trading countries. Of course, there are nations whose media industries dominate their region, but this does not necessarily translate into global dominance. Regional production centres have been developed in Egypt, Hong Kong and India, producing and distributing programmes to countries with cultural and linguistic ties and to migrant communities in other countries.

TABLE 12.1 Estimated revenue from international programme exports, 1987–95

	1987	1989	1991	1993	1995
Exports ($ millions):					
US	1119	1696	2096	2521	3005
Western Europe	161	426	660	910	1175
Others	194	273	393	566	815
Total	1474	2395	3149	3997	4995
Percentage of total:					
US	76	71	67	63	60
Europe	11	18	21	23	24
Others	13	11	12	14	16

Source: Parker (1995, p. 39).

CONNECTIONS For a brief account of global migration since the Second World War, see Chapter 7, pages 165–6.

Migrant communities often seek out programmes from their countries of origin. In the UK, there are satellite channels, video shops and cinemas catering for all the major ethnic minority groups and providing them with programmes produced in their countries of origin. For instance, there are 14 satellite and cable channels, mostly subscription based, broadcasting to 500 000 people in Asian languages such as Urdu, Bengali and Hindi (Barakrishnan, 2000). The largest audience shares are held by Zee TV and its rival Sony Entertainment Television. Many of the programmes they screen are imported from India, where there is a well-established production centre.

The international trade in pirate or illegal video copies of films, TV shows and music further complicates the examination of flow patterns. While these flows are mainly limited to the largely unregulated audio-visual markets of the developing world (Sreberny-Mohammadi, 1991), pirated products have also penetrated the protected national media systems of the West.

Transnational media corporations

The global media market is dominated by large transnational corporations that produce and distribute media products. These global giants, many of which are American in origin (Sreberny-Mohammadi, 1991), have emerged since the Second World War through a process of national and international conglomeration (Herman and McChesney, 1997) or consolidation (Hamelink, 1995), in which national media corporations have merged with and/or acquired their rivals. Herman and McChesney (1997) and Hamelink (1995) argue that this process has been aided by lax national and international regulation. At the beginning of the twenty-first century, conglomeration has become more pervasive than ever as transnationals in all sectors are seeking access to newly emerging markets. However, other researchers point to the existence of countervailing trends, such as de-aggregation. Cunningham and Jacka (1996, p. 33) note that in the audio-visual market, there has been a growth of 'small specialised firms which are often geographically, even globally, dispersed and which provide components for the big firms'.

The global news market, too, has come to be dominated by global giants. In 1979, 80 per cent of global news came from five major Western news agencies (Barker, 1997), but by 2001, three corporations had largely seized control of the global flow of news and video footage: Associated Press (US owned) and its television film provider, APTV; Reuters (British) and its subsidiary, Reuters TV; and Agence France-Presse (French) (Boyd-Barrett, 1997). These organisations have the resources to provide much of the images and text used by national news media (Paterson, 1997). However, while they do have a dominant grip on the news market, they are facing challenges from niche players. Bloomberg provides specialised global business information, and specialist news agencies such as Gemini News Service focus on providing information about the developing world. The giants also face competition from global news retailers such as CNN International, BBC World and news channels such as Sky News. Nonetheless, Boyd-Barrett (1997) and others suggest that the main agencies' dominant position is guaranteed by their global news-gathering reach and their exclusive contracts to supply foreign news to the national news outlets in most countries.

The audio-visual market, according Herman and McChesney (1997) and McChesney (1998), is dominated by ten transnational conglomerates: AOL/Time Warner, Disney,

TCI, Bertelsmann, Viacom, News Corporation, PolyGram, Seagram, Sony and General Electric. These first-tier firms sit at the top of about 50 second-tier global media corporations in the audio-visual market (Herman and McChesney, 1997). All of the first-tier firms are genuinely transnational, that is, they are no longer predominantly based in one country. Rather, they have subsidiaries in numerous countries and an international management structure, and they are willing to relocate anywhere to obtain the highest profit. They can also afford the services of major global advertising firms to devise global promotional strategies.

These companies are vertically integrated, that is, for each one, the global production and distribution of a film, from the formulation of an idea, to the making of the film, its mechandising and the cinema it is screened in are controlled by the corporation. These corporations also tend to be horizontally diversified, with alliances and holdings in other product areas. As Hamelink (1995, p. 52) notes, 'Although ... it is still possible to distinguish computer manufacturers, telephone service companies, publishing houses, broadcasters, and film producers as separate industrial actors, they are rapidly converging into one industrial activity.' McChesney (1998) agrees that one of the most striking features of the advance of digital communications has been horizontal diversification and alliances between corporations in different media markets. He notes that AOL/Time Warner is connected to American telecom giants Bells and AT&T, and News Corporation is partially owned by telecom giant MCI.

Boxes 12.1 and 12.2 illustrate the extent to which two of the first-tier corporations – AOL/Time Warner and News Corporation – have diversified. The world's largest media transnational, AOL/Time Warner, has subsidiaries in many countries around the world, and where it does not, it deals with second-tier media companies. Time Warner was formed in 1989 with the merger of Time Inc. (publishing) and Warner Brothers (films), and in 1996, it acquired Turner Broadcasting (the owners of CNN). In 2000, it merged with the American Internet giant AOL (America Online) to form AOL/Time Warner, valued at $337 billion (Bell, 2000, p. 6).

News Corporation was established by Rupert Murdoch in Australia in the 1960s and grew through merger and acquisition from an Australian newspaper group into a transnational media corporation. It first expanded through the purchase of British national newspapers in the 1970s and early 1980s, and diversified with the purchase of

---

BOX 12.1 AOL/Time Warner

- Music: Warner Music Group (with artists such as Madonna, REM, Simply Red, Alanis Morissette).

- Film: Warner Brothers film studios (produces box office films and television serials such as *The Larry Sanders Show* and *The Sopranos*) and a global chain of cinemas – Warner Village.

- Television: US cable television channels, including HBO, Warner Brothers Network and the news channel CNN, and the second largest cable system in the US.

- Publishing: Time Life Books (the second largest global publisher) and 24 magazines such as *People*, *Time*, *Sports Illustrated* and DC comics.

- A global chain of theme parks and retail stores.

- Internet: AOL (the largest Internet provider in the US) and CompuServe.

- Catalogue: a library of some 6000 films and 25 000 television programmes.

- Joint ventures with Viacom, TCI, Sony, News Corporation, Bertelsmann, and Disney. Second-tier media firms: Kirsch (Germany), United News and Media (UK), Hachette (France).

Sources: Bell (2000); McChesney (1998).

BOX 12.2 News Corporation

- Film: Twentieth Century Fox.

- Terrestrial television: US Fox television network (the fourth largest US national TV network), 22 television stations, Fox News Channel, two Latin American TV channels (El Canal Fox and Fox Sport Noticias), 50 per cent stakes in Fox Sports Net and Fox Kids.

- Satellite television: controlling interest in British Sky Broadcasting (BSkyB), Asian star TV and India Sky Broadcasting, partial stake in Latin Sky Broadcasting, Zee TV and El TV (India), Japan Sky Broadcasting, Star Chinese channel and Phoenix Chinese channel.

- Publishing: 130 daily newspapers, concentrated in Australia (*The Australian* and 21 metropolitan newspapers) the UK (*News of the World*, the *Sun*, *The Times* and *The Sunday Times*), the US and China; 25 magazines, including a US TV guide; book publisher HarperCollins.

- Internet: News Technology Group, including News Electronic Data, Delphi Internet and News America New Media.

- Catalogue: 2000 films.

- Joint ventures with first-tier firms AOL/Time Warner, Viacom, TCI, Universal, PolyGram, Sony and Bertelsmann; second-tier firms Canal Plus (France), BBC, Granada and Carlton (UK), Globo (Brazil), Televisa (Mexico).

Figure 12.2 Rupert Murdoch, founder owner of the fourth largest media empire in the world, after AOL Time Warner, Disney and Viacom.

Source: McChesney (1998).

the US film studio Twentieth Century Fox. It was one of the pioneers of satellite television in Europe.

QUESTION   How healthy do you think it is for society for the media to be dominated by a handful of giant organisations? Construct a sociological account of both sides of the argument.

Despite this domination, some writers (for example, Cunningham *et al.*, 1998) point to fragmentary trends in the audio-visual market. These giants face competition not only from each other but also from smaller producers. TV Globo in Brazil and Televisa in Mexico are the main producers and exporters of television programmes in the Spanish-speaking geo-linguistic region (Sinclair *et al.*, 1996). TV Globo in particular is a major producer and exporter of soap operas. The Bollywood studios in Mumbai are the main producers of films in the Hindi geo-linguistic region. National producers are increasingly involved in the exportation of media products, including co-productions. For instance, BBC Worldwide, the BBC's commercial arm, was formed in 1994 to organise commercial ventures with television producers in various countries. As with the news market, there has been a growth of small production companies delivering specialised niche services, especially via the Internet. Redbus Film Group in London uses the Internet to provide a large amount of background information and interactive services for film viewers who subscribe to a video-on-demand television system.

However, Herman and McChesney (1997) and Golding (1998) argue that there is little competition between these corporations in the international arena. Many of the largest corporations 'share major share holders, own pieces of each other, or have inter-

locking boards of directors' (McChesney, 1998, p. 32). Their global strategies mean that they are predisposed to alliances and joint ventures with each other and with second-tier global corporations and nationally based producers and distributors. Hence, there is minimal competition between corporations of all sizes.

CONNECTIONS A general account of the power of transnational corporations is provided in Chapter 3, pages 54–60.

Global media content: the impact of the market and state

The deregulation of the global media market, dominated by a profit-oriented culture industry, has implications for programmes and audiences around the world. This section focuses on these consequences. Critical sociologists on the left, particularly the critics of cultural imperialism, see the consequences as essentially negative for audiences. Deregulation of the commercial television market will lead to increased emphasis on low-quality entertainment programmes. In Keane's (1991, p. 89) words, markets 'restrict freedom of communication by generating barriers to entry, monopoly and restrictions upon choice and by shifting the prevailing definition of information from that of a public good to that of a privately appropriable commodity'. The concentration of media owner-ship in increasingly fewer transnational corporate hands is limiting the range of infor-mation and opinions conveyed to social actors, and favours some views over others (Boyd-Barrett, 1997; Paterson, 1997; Thussu, 1998). This section also examines the way in which democratic states have sought to control the flow of information to their citizens.

Universal homogeneity and dumbing down

There has been almost continual concern amongst critics of cultural imperialism about the onslaught of American television programmes and other cultural products. Some of these critics argue that a deregulated global media market dominated by American transnational corporations will lead to the global homogeneity of output by crowding out locally produced material. If we look at the film market both in the developed and the developing world, then the domination of US-produced films is obvious. However, if we consider a particularly popular television genre – the soap opera – then a different picture emerges. Although this was originally an American genre, research shows that it has been subject to increasing **hybridisation** (Straubhaar, 1997). For instance, soap operas in the US and the UK are quite different. In the US, they are seen as cheap fillings for daytime TV and tend to be escapist or fantasist in nature (Tunstall, 1977), whereas in the UK, they are shown at peak viewing time and tend to portray the gritty realism of everyday life (Barker, 1997). While both UK and US soaps tend to have a continuous story line and are of indeterminate length, Latin American telenovelas – extremely popular soaps screened in prime time – are finite, with each soap opera finishing after about 200 episodes (Reeves, 1993).

Hybridisation
Adaptation of a genre to fit the cultural circumstances of a particular country.

Other critics argue that despite this heterogeneous picture, low-cost populist genres have the same purpose in every media environment – to maximise audiences and therefore advertising revenue. Some sociologists (Curran, 1991; Keane, 1991) argue that the reliance on advertising revenue and the consequent emphasis on audience maxi-misation is leading to reduced diversity and lower quality, with entertainment-oriented programmes increasing at the expense of educational programmes throughout the world. Peak viewing time in the UK and other countries with a commercial broadcasting system is dominated by soaps , serial documentaries (docu-soaps) and game shows, with a consequent decline in more thought-provoking programmes such as current affairs.

There are, however, exceptions to this trend. In some Third World countries, soap operas are used not only to entertain but also to disseminate information on health and educational issues. In Kenya, despite the recent growth of commercial television, radio still has far greater audiences, particularly in rural areas. The agricultural radio soap *Tembea na Majire* ('Move with the Times') is modelled on the BBC radio soap *The Archers*, and with 70 per cent of Kenyan households having a radio, it regularly attracts nine million listeners. It gives advice on agricultural techniques and covers social issues – for example, female circumcision, male alcoholism and Aids – and basic women's rights. All these are interwoven into the story of everyday life in an African village.

Information society versus informed society

With the advent of 24-hour satellite news channels and the Internet, individuals around the globe gained instant access to news and information on an infinite variety of subjects. While some argue that information networks and media content are still subject to control by the state, others point out that control increasingly lies in the hands of transnational corporations. Direct satellite broadcasting around the world has largely been a transnational enterprise (Thompson, 1990). Encryption technology, which scrambles satellite signals, limits viewing to those who possess decoding equipment, that is, those who are prepared to pay for it.

McChesney (1998) argues that the Internet is also being developed along commercial lines. Golding (1998) notes that the number of Internet sites devoted to commercial use rose from 4.6 per cent of the total number of sites in 1993 to 50 per cent in 1996. The Internet service providers have become large companies. The AOL/Time Warner merger reinforced the views of those who argue, as Herman and McChesney (1997) and McChesney (1998) do, that the Internet has provided a new distribution mechanism for transnational media corporations to exploit when marketing their goods and services. Critics of cultural imperialism argue that, far from allowing greater diversity, the control of global news and information gathering and distribution by a few global firms is unacceptably restricting the information individuals receive.

Global news and information is an essential resource, keeping individuals fully informed about events in the world. The foreign news that audiences receive in both the developed and the developing world is almost exclusively provided by large news agencies situated in the developed world. The two main television news agencies, APTV and Reuters TV, provide a significant proportion of the foreign news footage screened around the world (Paterson, 1997). The **news values** these companies deploy to determine which international event will or will not be covered directly affect what individuals at home are able to see. The foreign news provided by news agencies tends to focus on the powerful nations of the world, and these countries are routinely prioritised in news bulletins. This means that the poorer nations of the developing world tend to be ignored. A study commissioned by the Department of International Development on UK television news programmes found that during the three months of the study, of the 137 developing countries, 67 of them received no coverage, and of the countries that were covered, 16 were only included because they were being visited by prominent Westerners (Snoddy, 2000, p. 27).

News values
The criteria that determine which news stories are chosen to be shown to the public.

The need of broadcasters to attract large audiences means that TV news coverage of foreign events is dominated by stories that are 'easily accessible, dramatic and visually arresting' (Thussu, 1998, p. 70), such as compelling pictures of war, pestilence, famine or other natural disasters such as floods and earthquakes (Snoddy, 2000, p. 27). There is rarely any background explanation or follow-up coverage of these events. Thussu (1998) argues that, as a consequence, Western TV viewers receive a narrow and often stereotypical view of the developing world. In the UK, news coverage of developing countries, particularly those in Africa, tends to be driven by Malthusian values. A key means of providing the viewer with additional information is the current affairs programme, but according to Stone (2000), the amount of airtime devoted to the developing world in current affairs programmes on UK terrestrial television has declined, particularly in the case of the commercial networks – ITV, Channel 4 and Channel 5 (Table 12.2).

TABLE 12.2 Number of hours per year devoted to developing countries in current affairs programmes

	BBC1	BBC2	ITV	Ch.4	Ch.5
1993–94	2	13	3	2	–
1996–97	3	15	7	1	–
1998–99	3	8	1	0.5	–

Source: Stone (2000, p. 11).

State control

State censorship is an important determinant of what individuals watch, listen to and read. For example, the Chinese state goes to considerable lengths to control the information its citizens receive via satellite and the Internet (McChesney, 1998; Held *et al.* 1999), and similar control is exercised by other authoritarian regimes around the world, such as that in Iran. But the desire to control media content is not limited to authoritarian regimes. For instance, the French state has sought to preserve the French language and culture by establishing special laws and organisations, and a quota has been placed on the amount of American music that can be played on French radio stations.

The British state has a well-deserved reputation for restricting media freedom, as successive governments have sought to limit freedom of expression by the media and to control the transmission of information to citizens on a wide range of issues. Franklin (1994) argues that there has been a sustained attack on the media in the UK. Legislation designed to prevent or inhibit the disclosure of information includes the Official Secrets Act and the Prevention of Terrorism Act, and all films for general release first have to go before a classification board. The current government is updating or introducing further pieces of legislation aimed at restricting the flow of information.

CONNECTIONS For a more detailed sociological view of the state, see Chapter 8, pages 215–24.

The Regulation of Investigatory Powers Act (2000) allows the state to monitor and intercept all e-mails in order to combat terrorism, child pornography and organised crime. The authorities need only the Home Secretary's approval to intercept e-mails, and if messages are encrypted, the Act gives customs and exercise officials, chief constables, magistrates, judges and the Home Secretary the power to demand the key to decrypt the code. The burden of proof is on the defendants, and forgetting the key or mislaying it is not accepted as reason for non-provision. The Act requires all internet service providers to install a remote-controlled black box that relays all messages passing through the service provider to a special monitoring centre, the Government Technical Assistance Centre, at an estimated cost of £17 million to the service providers.

> **QUESTION** To what extent do you think the state should control the flow of information to its citizens?

The worldwide audience: media reception

This sections focuses on the delivery of cultural experiences across borders by the mass media. If we assume that access to the mass media is universal, what sense do social actors make of television programmes from other cultures? What effect does media content have on an audience? A large amount of research has been carried out on the mass media and audiences, underpinned by various social theoretical positions. This section examines the habits of the UK audience and then looks at the impact of imported media content on social actors.

Social actors as an audience

The media audience can be depicted in simple terms as an aggregate of social actors interacting with media content. As a social group, it consists of actors from different classes, races, genders and age backgrounds. Before looking at the appropriation of media products, it is worth examining some audience trends in recent years (Table 12.3). As can be seen, media consumption by men and women has changed over time. Both men's and women's consumption increased between 1977 and 1997, with the proportion of men and women watching television and listening to the radio rising in line with each other. While both read more, women read more books than men, and the percentage of women who read books increased at a higher rate than that for men.

TABLE 12.3 British men and women over 16 who watch TV, listen to the radio and read books, 1977–97 (per cent)

	1977	1987	1996–97
Men			
TV	97	99	99
Radio	87	89	90
Books	52	54	58
Women			
TV	97	99	99
Radio	87	86	87
Books	57	65	71

Source: Office for National Statistics, Social Trends (2000a, p. 210).

CHART 12.1 British men and women over 15 who read a national daily newspaper, 1981–99, (per cent)

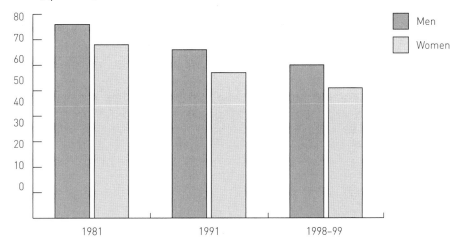

Source: Office for National Statistics (2000), p. 213.

When it comes to the reading of national daily newspapers, the reverse seems to be true. As Chart 12.1 shows, more men than women read a daily national newspaper, and over time the number of both men and women readers has fallen. That the national daily newspaper audience is shrinking has been confirmed by other researchers (Franklin, 1994; Tunstall, 1996).

While watching television is more a popular leisure activity than listening to the radio and reading, particularly newspapers, certain types of programme are more widely watched than others. It is not possible to ascertain the difference between men's and women's preferences, but Table 12.4 shows the proportion of viewers who watch different types of programme. During the 1990s, there was a bias towards popular programmes (drama followed by light entertainment), and while documentaries, features and films rose in popularity, interest in sport and news declined.

TABLE 12.4 Types of terrestrial TV programme watched by UK audiences aged four plus, 1990–97 (per cent)

	1990	1994	1997
Drama	24	25	25
Light entertainment	17	18	16
News	21	11	15
Documentaries and features	8	13	14
Films	11	15	13
Sport	11	11	8
Children's programmes	7	5	5
Other	1	3	3

Source: Office for National Statistics (1992, p. 178; 1996, p. 217; 1999, p. 211).

Global audiences and media messages

There are two approaches to examining the relationship between media messages and audiences. The first, effects studies, is interested in the impact that media content has on behaviour. Within this approach, there is a difference of emphasis between those who hold a holistic view of society – particularly orthodox Marxists – and those who hold an atomistic view, with an emphasis on human agency – particularly behaviourists. The second approach, reception studies (or new audience research), is interested in how audiences interpret media content. Drawing on interpretive methodology, adherents of this approach argue that individuals are active to different degrees in creating meaning and resisting dominant definitions.

Effects studies

Views on the characteristics of an audience vary between the different sociological positions. Critics of cultural imperialism have traditionally seen audiences as a large, passive, monolithic mass, with little if any diversity (Boyd-Barrett and Newbold, 1995) – an alienated part of a divided and inequitable class-based society. This view of audiences has been attacked by behaviourist sociologists as crude. They see the audience as a 'tissue of inter-related individuals' (Gitlin, 1995, p. 23), as part of a heterogeneous society bound together by norms and values. Their empirical research suggests that audiences are not passive dupes but selective users of the media.

The Marxist view is that media content has a strong and identifiable, society-wide effect, uniformly shaping social action. Critics of cultural imperialism argue that US media transnationals' dominance of the global media and the one-way flow of media products is leading to the substitution of indigenous cultures in developing countries by a Western capitalist – mainly American – consumer culture. The media, as 'carriers of cultural meaning' (Barker, 1997, p. 183), act as a cultural/ideological battering ram. The values contained in imported programmes and advertisements are injected into the minds of the audience, converting them into Americanised capitalist consumers.

False consciousness
Ways of thinking about the world or understanding reality that are defective and obscure the truth.

In other words, media imports inscribe Western ideological/cultural messages into the minds of a passive and alienated audience (Gitlin, 1995; Boyd-Barrett and Newbold, 1995). The messages impart a **false consciousness** and legitimise the dominant position of transnational corporations and the Western capitalist nations. For instance, Dorfman and Mattelart, in their 1975 study *How to Read Donald Duck*, demonstrate that the Disney cartoon strip contains the 'ideological assumptions that support American imperialism' (Barker, 1997, p. 114; see also Reeves, 1993). Other research (see Schiller, 1976) has also highlighted the impact of the cultural meanings contained in imported media products.

Sociological research in the behaviourist tradition firmly rejects the notion of a uniform, society-wide effect and stresses that the impact of media messages can only be identified by measuring changes in the behaviour of those exposed to the media. Many of the studies in this tradition conclude that the media have little if any effect on the audience, and that any effect is limited by a series of variables or filter conditions. As Gitlin (1995) notes, many researchers pay considerable attention to establishing what these variables are – in particular, audience selectivity, the resonance of the message to personal experience, and so on. The key point is that these and other variables act as a brake on the media's ability to affect an audience. This approach can be seen in research on the impact of satellite television on the children of the tiny island of St Helena – a British colony in the South Atlantic 1 000 miles from the nearest land mass.

The St Helena research project focused on the playground behaviour of 3–8 year-old children on the island. It was interested in establishing whether television programmes beamed onto the island led to increased pro- or anti-social behaviour. To establish this, the researchers compared observations of playground behaviour in the years before and after the introduction of television in 1995. Around 60 hours of sport was broadcast each week, including football, and there was an increase in the incidence of children playing football. However, in terms of the children's behaviour, the researchers found no increase in anti-social conduct (such as hitting, fighting, kicking, pushing and pinching) in the five years following the introduction of television, and pro-social behaviour (such as playing games and using play equipment) remained much the same as its 1994 level. This was considered to be due to the existence of strong filter conditions, such as the effective supervision and control of children within families, schools and the wider community. It was this supervision that prevented children from engaging in anti-social behaviour learned from television programmes (Charlton, 2000).

Reception studies

Whereas effects studies assume that the meaning of media messages is unambiguous, reception studies see meaning being actively constructed by social actors while engaging with the media. In this sense, content does not determine how individuals interpret a particular story or text. The 'production of meaning does not ensure consumption of that meaning' (Baker, 1997, p. 117). Rather, a wide range of social and cultural factors determine interpretation. These include the class, educational level, occupation, gender, ethnicity and age of the social actor, and 'the structure of the text, the social context within which the text is read, the cultural affinities of the readers and the ways in which [these] factors influence their reading competencies, predispositions, opportunities and likes and dislikes' (Boyd-Barrett and Newbold, 1995, p. 499). These factors help shed light on why individuals agree or disagree with the media content they encounter.

Reception studies research is based on qualitative analysis of audience readings of popular media output, particularly soap operas. The notion of non-determined interpretation stands in strong opposition to the assumptions about the cultural and ideological impact of the media held by the critics of cultural imperialism. These critics saw the popular American soap opera of the 1980s, *Dallas*, as conveying particular American cultural values around the world. For example, Moores (1993, pp. 45–6) notes that at the height of its popularity, it was 'regarded as more evidence of the threat posed by American-style commercial culture'. However, studies of audiences' interpretations of soap operas show that this is a complex process, and interpretations vary between audiences from different cultures. Of the studies that sought to explore interpretations of *Dallas*, perhaps the best known is that by Liebes and Katz (1988), who, through a series of focus groups, investigated the interpretations made by cultural and ethnic groups in Israel, the United States and Japan. They found that the cultural background of the groups largely shaped their readings of the narrative. Likewise, Miller's (1995) study of viewers of the American soap *The Young and the Restless* in Trinidad and Tobago revealed 'the ways in which the soap opera is localised, made sense of and absorbed into local practices and meanings' (Baker, 1997, p. 123).

However, with the arrival of new means of global programme distribution, such as satellites, the Internet and video recorders, and the more complex flow patterns between countries, viewers are no longer restricted to the imported offerings of the main national television channels. Immigrant communities in Western Europe and the US have ready access to programmes produced in their countries of origin, either on video tape or on satellite channels. There have been a number of studies of the viewing habits of such communities in the UK, such as that by Gillespie (1997) on the Punjabi community in Southall, London (Box 12.3).

BOX 12.3 The viewing of Hindi films on video in Southall

Gillespie (1997) found that viewing imported Hindi films on video was a regular activity in the Punjabi community and a way of reinforcing their cultural traditions. Audience gatherings were often family-based, intergenerational and exclusively female. The dominant theme of nearly all the videos watched collectively was 'the "clash of tradition and modernity" in Indian society; which was normally resolved at the expense of the latter (ibid., p. 324). Gillespie found that the different generations of women responded differently to the content, and viewing was followed by discussions and debates on the theme of tradition and modernity. Young family members' interpretations of films, which affirm tradition as against modernity, provoke discussion with female elders, many of whom, as their children and grandchildren say "are living in the India which they left 20 years ago" and are unwilling to embrace change' (ibid.) Imported US films and UK programmes were viewed by the young separately from other family members. This, Gillespie suggests, was 'partly due to the texts of such films and, given parental reservations about their morality, or lack of it, the values [that the films] are seen to endorse.' (ibid.)

The all-powerful audience

The notion of non-determined interpretation reaches its extreme in the work of postmodernists (see Chapter 19). The act of reception is seen in terms of viewing a flow of images embedded in programmes and the spaces in between, such as advertising breaks. Individuals inhabit a mediated world of symbolic imagery, a collage of **polysemic** symbols. Social actors metaphorically generate new symbolic associations and unexpected meanings as they surf the net or 'zap' between an increasing number of channels, between different genres and programmes from different locales and cultures. According to postmodernists, national audiences are fragmenting. The days of the national 'did-you-see' culture, when individuals talked about common viewing experiences, have come to an end, as audiences now tune into a diverse offering of programmes on an abundance of digital channels. The number of homes in the UK with digital television is set to grow substantially from the present 3.5 million (Price, 2000, p. 2).

The new generation of Internet-linked digital televisions will be interactive, enabling the viewer to decide not only which programmes to watch but also when, undermining the notion of traditional television schedules. For example, in the UK, a 'video on demand' system has been launched, and British Telecom and the cable companies NTL and Telewest offer subscribers 24-hour access to the films and programmes of their choice. Viewers can also interact with the programmes, send their views to the producers via e-mail, examine in more detail the characters in a film or soap, and interact with other fans via Internet chat rooms. The first interactive advertisement has already been shown on SkyDigital: an advertisement for 'Chicken Tonight' invited viewers, by clicking on an icon on their television screen, to tour the Creative Kitchen service, where they could order a money-off voucher or a recipe book (ibid.) In the view of postmodernists, the audience is all-powerful, and the new digital technologies have empowered them further. The individual viewer is engaged in 'semiotic guerrilla warfare', actively resisting dominant meanings and able to subvert them in a continually changing and fragmenting media environment.

> **Polysemic**
> An almost an infinite number of possible meanings that can be interpreted in many ways.

The information gap

One criticism levelled at both reception studies and the postmodernist approach is that questions of inequality are drowned out by their over-emphasis on viewer enjoyment and empowerment. Access to media hardware and new information technology is unequal within individual societies and between nation states. The 'information gap', as it has been termed, is a feature of all societies. It is the notion that 'the educationally and socio-economically advantaged are able to enhance their advantages via communications media, whose distribution and consumption are such as to ensure that such social divisions widen' (Golding, 1990, p. 96).

In the UK, according to Peter Golding (ibid.), there is a big difference, in terms of access to new technology, between the top and bottom social classes. 'Entrance to the new media playground is relatively cheap for the well-to-do. … For the poor the price is a sharp calculation of opportunity cost, access to communication goods jostling uncomfortably with the mundane arithmetic of food, housing, clothing and fuel' (ibid., p. 90).

TABLE 12.5 Households in selected income groups that have access to information and communication facilities, 1997–98 (per cent)

Gross weekly income	TV	Telephone	Video	Satellite	PC
Under £100	95	86	51	11	10
£100–200	97	88	64	15	8
£200–300	98	95	82	23	17
£300–400	99	97	90	29	25
£400–500	99	98	93	36	34
£500–600	99	99	95	36	39
£600–700	99	100	97	39	45
£700 and over	99	100	96	39	59

Source: Department of Social Security (1999, Table 3.8, p. 58).

Table 12.5 shows that Golding's assertions are valid. Personal computers and satellite reception are concentrated among higher income households, whereas television has a near universal reach across income groups. Similarly, Chart 12.2 shows that use of the Internet is 'highest amongst individuals whose households are headed by someone from a professional occupation and lowest amongst those living in a household headed by someone working in an unskilled occupation' (Office for National Statistics, 2000b, p. 2).

The findings of a study by Livingstone and Bovill (1999) on the usage of media and information technology by a sample of 6–17 year olds from different social background provide a similar picture. Sixty-eight per cent of the middle-class children in the study had access to a PC at home, compared with 40 per cent of working-class children; 46 per cent of middle-class children but only 19 per cent of working-class children had a multimedia computer at home; 19 per cent of the middle-class children had access to the Internet at home, compared with only 2 per cent of working class children; and a further 6 per cent of middle-class children used the Internet at a friend's or relative's house, compared with only 3 per cent of working-class children (ibid., p. 16).

CHART 12.2 UK adults who have used the Internet, by social class of head of household, July 2000, (per cent)

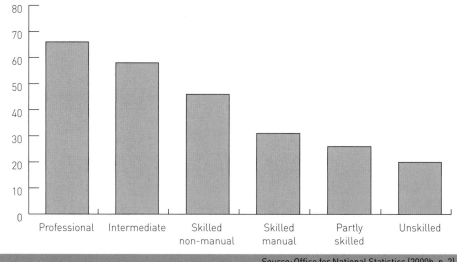

Source: Office for National Statistics (2000b, p. 2).

While all the children had televisions in their homes, video recorders were slightly more common in the middle-class homes, and cable and satellite were more common in the working-class homes. The working-class families were more likely to have a TV linked to a games machine: 'Working-class families are as or more likely to own screen entertainment media. Middle-class families are more likely to own most other media' (ibid., p. 12).

There is a marked information gap between individuals in the rich developed world and those in the poor developing world. Eight times more printed material is produced per capita in developed countries than in developing countries (Golding, 1998). In addition, substantially fewer individuals have access to communication technology such as the Internet in developing countries compared with developed countries.

Chart 12.3 shows that both television ownership and Internet connections are more concentrated in developed countries than in developing ones. The US alone has more televisions and Internet connections than Malaysia, Mexico, Zimbabwe, Kenya, Pakistan and India combined. Any talk of social actors in the Third World regularly inter-acting with the media is misguided: 'Half of humanity has never made a telephone call' (Thabo Mbeki, quoted in Golding, 1998, p. 145). However, the table also shows that the Third World is not uniform in this respect. Citizens of countries such as Singapore, South Korea and Malaysia have significantly better access to communication tech-nologies than those of Africa and the Indian subcontinent, who, in effect, are con-demned to a life of information poverty on the hard shoulder of the global information superhighway.

CHART 12.3 Number of computer systems connected to the Internet per 1000 people (1998) and television per 1000 people (1996), selected countries.

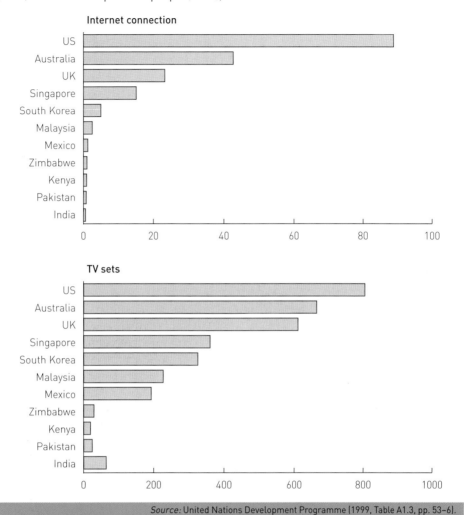

Source: United Nations Development Programme (1999, Table A1.3, pp. 53–6).

Conclusion

This chapter has explored some key aspects of the globalisation of the mass media: the global media market, the flow of media products, the dominance of transnationals, and the appropriation of media products by audiences. The chapter has sought to provide an insight into the main theoretical debate on each of the above issues in order to show that the consequences of media globalisation are essentially contested.

The differences can be clearly seen when examining the global trade in media products. Critics of cultural imperialism highlight the unequal flow of media products from the developed to the developing world, aided by governments' trade liberalisation policies. Other sociologists, for example, Sinclair *et al.* (1996), argue that the flows of media products are more complicated than the simple core–periphery model assumes.

According to the critics of cultural imperialism, many of the cultural products that audiences around the world consume are produced and distributed by giant media transnationals. These powerful corporations largely determine what audiences view and read, the content reflecting their values, which are consumerist and culturally American. The values contained within media products are seen as being appropriated uncritically by audiences around the world, but particularly in the developing world. These critics also point to how Western commercial media systems have been exported to the developing world, driven by a worldwide programme of liberalisation that is undermining countries' attempts to develop. However, there is evidence of counter-trends, of the rise of non-American media transnationals, the growth of specialist media organisations occupying market niches, and cultural and linguistic barriers to Western transnational dominance.

In terms of audiences around the world, critics of cultural imperialism argue that the media act as instruments of manipulation that reinforce the values of capitalism through their output. Reception studies, adopting an interpretivist methodology, focus on how social actors interpret media messages and the complex process through which meaning is produced. For them, the impact of media output is not predetermined. The notion of audience autonomy is strongly promoted by postmodernist writers. Numerous criticisms have been levelled at both reception studies and the postmodernist approach. Critics of cultural imperialism argue that they dilute criticism of market capitalism and tacitly reinforce the liberal pluralist argument of consumer sovereignty. Questions of programme quality are diluted to a matter of individual taste and descend into relativism. The wider social position of the actor is ignored. Reception is determined by the individual's social position, and for many people, access to information through the media is restricted by economic reality. Therefore, any discussion of the interpretation of media messages and resistance to these messages must take account of the social conditions in which viewing takes place.

Chapter summary

- The speed at which information travels over large distances has steadily increased over time, referred to as the shrinking of time and space. Modern societies are increasingly interconnected by communication technologies.

- The development of mass media systems over time has been shaped by social, political and economic factors. The trade in media products has increased with the development of media systems. In the 1990s, the liberalisation policies of Western nations led to an increasingly deregulated global media market. In the global audio-visual market, the dominant one-way flow of products has given way to complex patterns. Nationally produced programmes are increasingly being produced for an international market.

- A series of mergers and acquisitions has given rise to giant media transnationals operating in numerous countries and dominating the global media market place. This domination has consequences for what the audience is able to see.

- These corporations are mainly interested in revenue maximisation. In terms of television, this translates into an emphasis on the production and distribution of popular entertainment programmes at the expense of educational and information-oriented programmes.

● There are different methods of assessing the impact of media content. Reception studies have challenged effects studies and shown that viewers are active creators of meaning and not passive recipients, and that meaning is socially constructed through interaction with the media.

● Although reception studies have cast doubt on the cultural imperialism view of the impact of commercial media systems, they pay little attention to the question of unequal access to the media between classes and between the developed and developing world.

Questions to think about

● Do we, as a society watch too many American produced television programmes? If we do, what adverse effects are possible?

● Do you find reception studies or effects studies the more convincing? Give reasons for your answer.

● What are the possible consequences of the division between the information-rich and the information-poor?

Investigating further

Abercrombie, Nicholas (1996) *Television and Society*, Polity Press.

> A good all-round introduction to debates about television, this book looks at issues of representation and programming, the structure and organisation of the television industry, and perspectives on the audience.

McQuail, Denis (2000) *Mass Communication Theory: An Introduction*, 4th edn, Sage.

> A comprehensive survey of theoretical debates on the media, covering the rise of the mass media, cultural theory, media institutions, organisational cultures, media content, audiences and media effects.

Thompson, John B. (1995) *The Media and Modernity*, Polity Press.

> This large book very usefully focuses on the emergence and development of the media in the modern world.

chapter

13

Health, illness and medicine

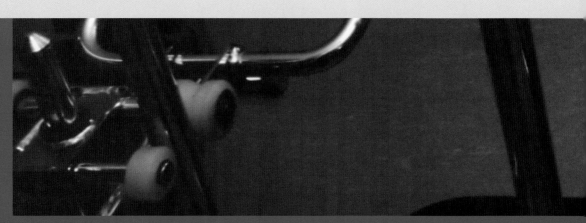

CHAPTER CONTENTS

Aims of the chapter

Health and illness are consistent human preoccupations, and sociologists are not immune to this fascination with the state of our bodies. This chapter introduces you to the main sociological approaches to health, illness and medicine. We show how the distribution, experience, definition and treatment of illness cannot be under-stood simply in physical or biological terms. Health, illness and their medical management are part of the wider cultural system and are closely associated with social control by professions and the state. The sociology of medicine also has strong links to analyses of the sociology of the body.

By the end of this chapter, you should have an understanding of the following concepts:

- The sick role
- The clinical gaze
- Epidemiology
- Iatrogenesis

- The biomedical model
- Total institution
- Labelling theory
- Professionalisation

 Introduction: the social basis of health, illness and medicine

To say that health and illness have a social basis may at first seem to be an example of sociological arrogance, claiming for 'the social' more than can be credibly accepted. Health and illness are, surely, simply biological descriptions of the state of our bodies. When we're ill, we're ill. A more refined version of this common-sense view underlies the long-standing **biomedical model** of disease, which is based on the following assumptions:

> **Biomedical model**
> A model of disease and illness that regards them as the consequence of certain malfunctions of the human body.

- Disease is an organic condition: non-organic factors associated with the human mind are considered unimportant or are ignored altogether in the search for biological causes of pathological symptoms.
- Disease is a temporary organic state that can be eradicated – cured – by medical intervention.
- Disease is experienced by a sick individual, who then becomes the object of treatment.
- Disease is treated after the symptoms appear – the application of medicine is a reactive healing process.
- Disease is treated in a medical environment – a surgery or a hospital – away from the site where the symptoms first appeared.

This model has dominated medical practice because it has been seen to work. It is based on a technically powerful science that has made a massive contribution to key areas of health (for example, vaccination). The anatomical and neurophysiological structures of the body have been mapped out, and the genetic mapping of the body is being undertaken through the Human Genome Project. The search for the fundamental – that is, genetic – basis of human pathology is on, whether the target is cancer, AIDS or Alzheimer's disease. This ever closer and more sophisticated inspection of the body – or as Foucault (1977a) would say, the **medical gaze** – has brought considerable power and prestige to the medical profession. It has also established a large and profitable market for major pharmaceutical companies such as Glaxo-Wellcome, Zeneca and Merck. The biomedical model also underlies the official definition of health and disease adopted by state and international authorities. National governments and international agencies such as the World Health Organisation (WHO) proclaim their long-term health goal to be the eradication of disease. Sometimes they have been successful, as in the global elimination of smallpox.

The rational application of medical science is therefore a hallmark of modernity, inasmuch as it has depended on the development over the past two centuries of a powerful, experimentally based medical analysis of the structure and function of the body and the agents that attack or weaken it. During the course of this, scientific medicine has effectively displaced folk or lay medicine. Modernity is about expertise, not tradition; about critical inspection, not folk beliefs; about control through scientific and technical regulation of the body, not customs and mistaken notions of healing.

Medical gaze
A concept employed by Foucault (1977a) to denote the power of modern medicine to define the human body.

CONNECTIONS For a description of the growth of rationality in the modern world, see Chapter 2, pages 30–3.

This application of 'rational medicine' has also reduced reliance on patients' own accounts of their illness (Stacey, 1989). Unlike in the eighteenth and nineteenth centuries, doctors rarely rely on descriptions by or the demeanour of the patient for diagnosis. Instead, clinical instruments – ranging from the stethoscope to NMR (nuclear magnetic resonance imaging) – are used to expose deep-seated disease. This distancing from the patient is part of the rationality of medical practice, as well as an important device for cultivating a mystique of professional expertise. It also means that – by means of patients' records, X-rays, scans and chromosomal profiles – cases can be handled by teams of doctors, many of whom may never meet the patient in the flesh.

Beck (1992) points out that the improved capacity to diagnose illnesses has not necessarily been accompanied by 'the presence or even the prospect of any effective measures to treat them'. Distinguishing between acute (short-term) and chronic (long-term) illnesses, he points out (ibid., pp. 204–5) that:

❝At the start of this century, 40 out of 100 patients died of acute illnesses. In 1980 these constituted only 1% of the causes of mortality. The proportion of those who die of chronic illnesses, on the other hand, rose in the same period from 46 to over 80%. ... A cure in the original sense of medicine becomes more and more the exception. ... Yet this is not the expression solely of a failure. Because of its *successes* medicine also discharges people into illness, which it is able to diagnose with its high technology. ❞

Moreover, the growing technical sophistication of medicine exposes patients to an array of equipment and therapeutic techniques that have to be used frequently to justify their expense, and, as Richman (1987, p. 87) notes, 'the criteria of referral are continuously being adjusted to keep specialists in work'.

QUESTION What do you feel about the last interaction you had with your doctor? Do any of the above observations about the power and status of the doctor *vis-à-vis* the patient ring true for you?

Yet the power and status of the medical profession and the health industry in general should not deflect us from asking about the social basis of health and illness. In fact, the position of medical professionals is itself a result of the socially institutionalised power to define the experience of being 'ill' and decide what treatment is required. More reflective doctors will acknowledge that their definitions of health and illness are not always shared by their patients and therefore have to be promoted through education, socialisation and expensive advertising. Symptoms that, according to the biomedical model, should force us to go to the doctor or take a pill are not necessarily seen as signs of illness by people themselves. Among a household of smokers, for example, the morning 'smoker's cough' is unlikely to be seen as abnormal or a sign of ill-health: indeed, it is often calmed by a good pull on the first cigarette of the day. Among many Westerners, a suntan suggests health and good looks rather than leading to wrinkled skin or skin cancer. Among the Madi of Uganda, illness is often associated with failure to deal properly with interpersonal relations, so that social or moral – rather than biomedical – repair is needed (Allen, 1992) Alternative or complementary remedies for ill-health often take a **holistic** approach to understanding the cause of illness and its remedy. Studies in the US have shown that patients present themselves to 'the medical gaze' more rarely than doctors would expect or like. Table 13.1 shows the relatively infrequent rate at which people visit a doctor for a range of symptoms.

Holistic
Involving a focus on the whole rather than on specific parts or aspects.

In short, people's perception of health and illness is culturally variable, highly context-specific, dynamic and subject to change. Crucially, there is no clear-cut relationship between the existence of a physical or emotional feeling and the judgement that this indicates illness (that it is a 'symptom'), requiring consultation with a doctor and becoming a patient.

Sociologists, anthropologists and historians have described the social basis of health and illness in a wide range of studies, including ethnographies of specific communities. They have explored issues of health care, performance of 'the sick role', the construction of mental illness as a disease, the wider creation of medical belief systems and the relationship between these and the exercise of power and social control.

CONNECTIONS Chapter 16, pages 456–60, considers the techniques of ethnography as a way of exploring the social world.

The sociology of *health and illness* is concerned with the social origins of and influences on disease, rather than with exploring its organic manifestation in individual bodies. The sociology of medicine is concerned with exploring the social, historical and cultural reasons for the rise to dominance of medicine – especially the biomedical model – in the

TABLE 13.1 Ratio of symptom episodes to consultations

Headache	184:1
Backache	52:1
Emotional problem	46:1
Abdominal pain	28:1
Sore throat	18:1
Pain in chest	14:1

Source: Banks *et al.* (1975).

definition and treatment of illness. These fields are closely related, since the way in which professional (or orthodox) medicine defines and manages illness reflects wider social dynamics that shape the perception and experience of disease.

Theoretical approaches

The sociology of health and illness is informed by five theoretical traditions:

- *Parsonsian functionalism* looks at the role the sick person plays in society. The focus is on how being ill is given a specific form in human societies so that the social system's stability and cohesion can be maintained.
- *Symbolic interactionism* is concerned with examining the interaction between the different role players in the health and illness drama. The focus is on how illness and the subjective experience of being sick are constructed through the doctor–patient exchange. The argument here is that illness is a social accomplishment among actors rather than just a matter of physiological malfunction.
- *Marxist theory* is concerned with the relationship between health and illness and capitalist social organisation. The main focus is on how the definition and treatment of health and illness are influenced by the nature of economic activity in a capitalist society.
- *Feminist theory* explores the gendered nature of the definition of illness and treatment of patients. Its main concern is the way in which medical treatment involves male control over women's bodies and identities.
- *Foucauldian theory* concentrates on the dominant medical discourse, which has constructed definitions of normality (health) and deviance (sickness). This discourse provides subjects in modern societies with the vocabulary through which their medical needs and remedies are defined. The source and beneficiary of this discourse is the medical profession. Foucauldian theorists also argue that medical discourse plays an important role in the management of individual bodies (what Foucault called 'anatomo-politics') and bodies *en masse* (bio-politics), Medicine is not just about medicine as it is conventionally understood, but also about wider structures of power and control.

Parsonsian functionalism and 'the sick role'

Although Parsons (1951) was interested in several aspects of the management of illness, he is best remembered for his emphasis on the social importance of the sick role. Parsons stressed the motivation involved in being sick and getting better. That is, people have to decide that they are sick and in need of treatment. Since being sick means choosing to withdraw from the normal patterns of social behaviour, it amounts to a form of deviance, and hence the efficient functioning of the social system depends on the sick being managed and controlled. The role of medicine is to regulate and control those who have decided they are sick so that they can return to their normal tasks and responsibilities. In short, the sick role enquires a commitment on the part of those who feel unwell to return to normality as soon as possible. Four features define the sick role:

- Sick people are legitimately exempted from normal social responsibilities associated with work and the family.
- Sick people cannot make themselves better – they need professional help.
- Sick people are obliged to want to get better – being sick is only tolerated if there is a desire to return to health.
- Sick people are therefore expected to seek professional treatment.

As for the role of doctors, in return for the trust placed in them, doctors are obliged to act in the best interests of their patients, applying their skill and expertise according to professional codes of conduct. Conformity to these codes gives doctors unusual rights – the right of authority over their patients' health, the right to examine their patients' bodies, and the right to obtain personal details from their patients.

There have been a number of criticisms of Parsons' model. First, it assumes that recovery is always possible, but during the twentieth century, there was a growth in chronic rather than acute conditions. Second, a number of researchers have pointed out that arrival at the doctor's surgery is often the last stage in the construction of sickness. For example, according to Scambler (1991), the majority of patients consult widely with lay (non-medical) contacts before deciding to visit the doctor. Thus, it is perfectly possible to be a sick person without becoming a patient. For this reason **epidemiological** statistics on the distribution of illnesses, which derive from doctor–patient consultations, should be treated with caution. The sociological question here is why it is that some sick people and their illness remain under-reported or are dealt with primarily within the lay arena, while others are not.

Epidemiology
The study of patterns of disease.

Third, Parsons assumes that patients will be sufficiently knowledgeable about and sensitive to their condition to know that they should consult a doctor, but will be naive and compliant once inside the surgery. In return, doctors are expected to treat all patients equally, but research shows that the class, age, gender and ethnicity of patients can have a considerable bearing on the kind of treatment provided. For instance, higher social classes are given more consultation time and a more comprehensive explanation of their illness than are lower classes. There is also a tendency to treat female patients' problems as 'typical' feminine neuroses and complaints, while similar problems among male patients are viewed as the product of work-related stress (MacIntyre and Oldham, 1977). Doctors in UK casualty wards have a private language for classifying newly arrived patients, including the acronym 'T. F. Bundy' ('Totally fucked, but unfortunately not dead yet'). These are just a few examples of the variation in practice among doctors.

Despite these criticisms, Parsons' notion of the sick role enabled exploration of the construction and career or 'occupation' of being ill (Herzlich, 1973; Pollock, 1988). Many patients cope with illness by defining it as a 'job', to be successfully managed by hard work, cooperation with others (doctors and kin) and sharing information about the state of the illness. According to Pollock (1998), for people suffering from chronic forms of mental illness such as schizophrenia, this 'illness as a job' option is not available, as they are seen by others as having no control over their illness: the notion of positive coping is not seen as credible in their case. This example tells us much about the interactive nature of illness and the social accounting processes surrounding it, which has prompted sociologists from the symbolic interactionist school to look more closely at the interaction between doctor and patient.

Symbolic interactionism and the social construction of illness

According to the symbolic interactionism thesis, identity is created through interaction with others. Learning to become a social being means learning to achieve control over this process by managing the impressions others have of us (see Chapter 18).

This creative capacity is evident when we play the role of patient in our encounters with health-care practitioners. Practitioners also attempt to create impressions of themselves for us. Given this interpretive element of the social encounter, doctor–patient interactions do not follow the script laid out by Parsons (1951). Instead, we should expect a considerable variation in the interactive play.

Byrne and Long (1976) present a continuum of interactions, with exclusively patient-centred communication at the one extreme and exclusively doctor-centred communication at the other. Most studies show that the power element in doctor–patient relations is significant, with doctor-centred interactions being the most common. Stewart and Roter (1989) have constructed a similar classification, contrasting the situation where the patient dominates (as a consumer of medicine, especially in private, market-based health care) with that where the doctor dominates, exercising a strong paternalism over subordinate clients. Morgan (1997, p. 53) suggests that the relationship between practitioner and patient moves between these two states during the various stages of an illness: 'At an acute stage of illness it may be necessary or desirable for the doctor to be dominant, whereas at later stages it may be beneficial for patients to be more actively involved, as they are responsible for the everyday management of their condition.'

QUESTION Have you ever manipulated an illness for your own ends, such as taking more time off work than is strictly needed for recovery? If you have, what part did the sick role or labelling play in this process?

Total institutions
Employed by Goffman (1968), this term refers to all institutions that assume total control over their inmates, such as prisons and mental hospitals.

Labelling
Describes the process where socially defined identities are imposed or adopted, especially deviant identities. Such labels can result in the individual being trapped in that identity (see *stigmatise*).

The power element in doctor–patient relations is particularly significant when a patient is obliged to enter hospital. Following the classic analysis of institutionalisation by Erving Goffman (1968), interactionist research into hospital life often focuses on the claim that the hospital regime is designed to restrict the opportunity of patients to fashion their own identities. Hospital life mirrors life in other **total institutions** such as prisons, mental hospitals, convents and so on. Patients' power to control their identity is reduced as much as possible, a process that starts as soon as they are admitted.

Most patients are compliant, but some do resist and attempt to maintain their personal autonomy and identity, for example, by refusing to comply rigidly with the ward rules, whereupon they become 'difficult patients'. This shows the potential for conflict between medical practitioners and patients. Conflict also arises from the power of others to impose their definition of 'being ill' on the patient. That is, there is a **labelling** component in illness, whether through medical diagnosis or through the way in which a sick person's friends, relatives and others treat him or her. For example, a cancer patient may be labelled a cancer patient above all else, no matter how the sufferer tries to persuade others that he or she is still a friend, a lover or a mother who just happens to have cancer. Interactionist analysis draws attention to the often overwhelming influence of the stigmatic label. Indeed, the illness to which the label is attached may even be interpreted as a sign of personal weakness or culpability (Sontag, 1979). Rosenhan *et al.* (1973) have shown how difficult it is to resist the imposition of a label for those defined as mentally ill. Likewise, Horwitz (1977) has shown that the greater the social gap in terms of class and status between the labeller and the labelled, the more difficult it is for the latter to resist the illness stigma. Lemert (1974) asserts that the imposition of a stigmatic label – especially that of being 'mentally ill' – is a serious assault on a person's sense of self. Such people are effectively being told that their (mental) capacity for self-knowledge is damaged and their feelings about themselves are probably delusory. The end result is that the patient, whether mentally ill or not, finds it impossible not to believe in the reality of the illness. It is at this stage – of 'self-realisation' – that the labellers, especially the medical staff, start to feel hopeful about eventual recovery!

Labelling can work in other ways, too. For example, in the case of elderly people who are physically very fit, preconceived notions about the state of being elderly discount the way they really are.

In summary, the interactionist approach focuses on power relations in the construction and management of health and illness. It draws attention to the unequal distribution of the resources available to health practitioners and patients, whether in home visits, in the surgery, at the outpatient clinic or on hospital wards. However, interactionism offers neither a theory of power nor a theory of patterns of inequality. Rather, it explains power and inequality as functions of the relative strength of the personalities of the parties to the medical encounter. We have to turn to other approaches to provide a theoretical explanation of such inequality.

CONNECTIONS For the main features of interactionism and criticisms levelled against it, see Chapter 18, pages 501–5.

Marxist theory

As we have seen elsewhere, Marxist theory is concerned with the way in which the dominant economic structure of society determines inequality and power, as well as shaping the relations upon which the major social institutions are built. Medicine is a major social institution, and in capitalist societies, it is shaped by capitalist interests. Marxist accounts of capitalist medicine have been developed by a number of sociologists and health policy analysts, notably Navarro (1985). According to Navarro, there are four features that define medicine as capitalist, or as he puts it, that point to 'the invasion of the house of medicine by capital' (ibid., p. 31):

- Medicine has changed from an individual craft or skill to 'corporate medicine'.
- Medicine has become increasingly specialised and hierarchical.
- Medicine now has an extensive wage-labour force (including employees in the pharmaceutical industry and related industrial sectors).
- Medical practitioners have become proletarianised, that is, their professional status has gradually been undermined as a result of administrative and managerial staff taking over responsibility for health care provision.

These four processes mean that medicine has become a market commodity, to be bought and sold like any other product. Furthermore, it has become increasingly profitable for two dominant capitalist interests: the finance sector, through private insurance provision; and the corporate sector, through the sale of drugs, medical instruments and so on. The power to direct and exploit the medical system has been seized by large corporations that enjoy monopolistic control over related market sectors. This process is characteristic of (late) capitalism as a whole: 'Monopoly capital invades, directs and dominates either directly (via the private sector) or indirectly (via the state) all areas of economic and social life' (ibid., p. 243). The last point illustrates Marxists' claim that just because medicine is organised as a national system of health care (as in the UK), this does not mean it is free of capitalist influence. Rather, it is part of the medical–industrial–state complex, involving close relations between large firms and state agencies. The state buys drugs and other equipment from large firms, subsidises their research through university laboratories and maintains a large hospital infrastructure that requires their goods.

Marxists also claim that health problems are closely tied to unhealthy and stressful work environments. Rather than seeing health problems as the result of individual frailty or weakness, they should be seen in terms of the unequal social structure and

Figure 13.1 Are wrinkles part of the natural ageing process or a condition of 'photodamage' which can be treated with commercial pharmaceutical products?

class disadvantages that are reproduced under capitalism. Patterns of mortality and ill-health (morbidity) are closely related to occupation, especially in the case of the industrial working class. For example, industrial carcinogens (asbestos, heavy metals, chemicals and so on) are responsible for over 10 per cent of all male cancers. While accidents at work may be regarded as the result of human error, research has shown that they also reflect pressure on workers to complete tasks at speed in risk-laden environments (Tombs, 1990; Wright, 1994). Legislation to control hazards in the workplace has been introduced over the years, and this has reduced the rate of death, injury and illness among workers. However, such legislation can only be fully effective if it is policed properly, and in the UK there has been considerable under-policing of sweatshops and similar workplaces. Moreover, Health and Safety Executive reports show that it has been difficult to reduce injury levels below a certain threshold, suggesting that these statistical levels represent the structural – and not the accidental – character of occupational injury and mortality.

Navarro argues that medicine is in a state of crisis, in that its growth is matched by an increasing inability to meet society's needs. Despite more and more money being spent on health care, more and more people are experiencing the system as ineffective. The state's response has been to deflect attacks on the medical–industrial–state complex by declaring that health problems are the problem of the individual, and that any difficulty coping with this is not the fault of the system but of the individual. The individual must be taught to become a discerning consumer of medicine, to take out extensive (and expensive) private medical insurance, allowing the state to reduce the burdensome cost of universal medical provision. This latter strategy will cause problems for the medical–industrial complex, since a reduced state budget will hit the secure drugs market enjoyed by the pharmaceutical industry. According to the Marxist view, this is to be expected in medicine as elsewhere, since in late capitalism there is never complete coincidence between the interests of powerful corporations and those of the state (see Chapter 3). The danger for the state is that larger multinational corporations will seek secure markets and cheaper labour overseas, so reducing the overall contribution they make to the state's GNP. We shall return to this global dimension later in the chapter.

Critics of the Marxist view of medicine focus more on its inadequacy than its practice of locating medicine firmly within capitalism. That is, it should pay more attention to the dynamics of the medical process, the experience of illness and the state of being a patient. In addition, as Turner (1987) argues, the Marxist **political economy** of health needs to address how the diversity of capitalist societies relates to medicine, health and illness. As he notes, 'there are major differences between the USA, the UK and Sweden, despite the fact that all three societies are quite distinctively capitalist' (ibid., p. 194). The welfare state, of which medical care is a key part, operates on a different basis in each of these countries. Moreover, Marxists are accused of underplaying the genuinely progressive features of the health sector under contemporary capitalism, arguing that the measures taken are ameliorative rather than solving people's health problems. Navarro (1986) does acknowledge that medical practitioners play a useful role in delivering health care, but argues that their primary purpose is to regulate the working classes and the popular masses. Finally, the Marxist account is criticised for downplaying the gendering of health and medicine, that is, the professional process that has sub-

Political economy An approach that embraces the concepts of social class, the value and division of labour, and moral sentiments.

ordinated women of all social class backgrounds to patriarchal medical control. This leads us to the feminist approach to health and illness.

Feminist accounts

In general, feminist analyses of inequality have focused on the construction and mainten- ance of female subordination. It is not surprising that medicine, health and illness have been central to this analysis, as they concern the body, the site where most gendered interaction takes place. Nor is it surprising that feminists have paid great attention to birth and maternity, an area where patriarchy is acute and the links between sexuality and reproduction are biologically and socially intertwined. As Turner (1987) notes, the regulation of women's bodies by controlling their sexual expression and reproductive capacity is now conducted through medicine, whereas in the past religion played this role (see Chapter 15). For women, a healthy body is tied to healthy sexuality and reproduction within the confines of lawful marriage.

The feminist critique concentrates on the male-dominated medical profession and the way in which, over the past century, it has medicalised events that are natural to women, including menstruation, pregnancy and childbirth. Medical intervention in these areas – which in the past were handled by women themselves in conjunction with family and female friends – originally arose from the desire by the newly emerging medical profession to create a medical market. Not only was there little real benefit in having a physician in attendance at child birth, but there is also evidence to show that physicians had little idea about the birth process and that medical intervention often endangered both mother and child.

CONNECTIONS A general account of feminist theories is presented in Chapter 17, pages 488–94.

By the mid 1950s, pregnancy had become a fully medicalised condition (Oakley, 1984). Midwifery had gradually been excluded, in the US by state legislation. This removal from women of control over their bodies, both personally and professionally, means that the majority of obstetricians and gynaecologists are men – about 80 per cent in the US and about 85 per cent in the UK. Medical training, textbooks and journals perpetuate the patriarchal attitude towards women. For example, Jordanova (1989) has shown, through an examination of medical journals and magazines, and especially the advertisements, how the classification of illness by gender is commonplace. 'Depression, anxiety, sleeplessness and migraine are likely to be associated with women, while disorders that can inhibit full movement and strenuous sporting activities are associated, metaphorically, with masculinity' (ibid., p. 144).

The sexual division of labour in medicine reflects the subordination of women. Despite health matters being seen as closely tied to women's caring, nurturing role in a patriarchal society, this does not mean that women have a high position in the medical hierarchy. Thus, while many women work in medicine, the bulk of them are in para- medical or nursing jobs with poorer pay and occupational status. Feminists believe that the gradual increase in the proportion of female physicians, while welcome, will not bring about any major change, since at medical schools they are indoctrinated with the same patriarchal attitudes as their male colleagues.

Malestream
Used to describe institutions or practices that are male dominated.

Feminists argue that only by breaking with the **malestream** of orthodox medicine can women regain control over their bodies. Hence, there has emerged a feminist health movement (led by writers such as Ehrenreich, 1979) that is challenging the medical establishment and promoting a philosophy of self-care and healing by and for women.

The relation between health, its definition, care and control and how this relates to the regulation of bodies and sexuality in wider society was also recognised by Foucault, whose theory we consider next.

Foucauldian analysis

Foucault (1977a) insisted that in order to understand the role of medicine in society, we have to see it as part of a wider social requirement for the regulation and surveillance of bodies. He used the term bodies both in the physical sense of individuals' bodies and in the more abstract sense of bodies of populations. According to Foucault, the demand for regulation grew as society became more complex – especially as it became urbanised and brought people together in one large mass. Urban areas have both public and private 'spaces' that dictate appropriate behaviour for the bodies that occupy them.

Medicine, and especially the medicine of the asylum, the clinic and everyday public hygiene, has to be understood within this broader context of public control. Foucault argued that medicine plays not merely a clinical but also a moral role, especially with regard to 'proper' forms of sexual expression, as he described in his *History of Sexuality* (1977b). This recounts the way in which medicine has played an increasingly important role in establishing a regimen of acceptable sexuality. Here the concept of 'discipline' is important. The emergence of 'rational' modern disciplines – such as economics, urban planning, penology and notably medicine – was central to the disciplining of people as public and private bodies. In their different ways, each of these disciplines legitimated forms of social control and regulation over people. They constituted powerful forms of social discourse.

Foucault's concept of discourse was central to his analysis. As discussed in other chapters (especially Chapter 19), discourses are ways of knowing about or of representing, and so giving some control over, reality and social behaviour. Medical discourse is one of the most powerful discourses, because it defines, organises and controls human bodies from the cradle to the grave. This discourse first appeared during the nineteenth century: 'A medico-administrative knowledge begins to develop concerning society, its health and sickness, its conditions of life, housing and habits, which serve as the basic core for the "social economy" and the sociology of the 19th century' (Foucault, 1980, p. 176). For Foucault, medical discourse and the medical profession that sustained it had displaced the religious, clergy-based discourses that dominated in previous centuries. Scientific, secular medicine provided a powerful means of social discipline and control. As Turner (1987, pp. 37–8) suggests:

> "Put simply, the doctor has replaced the priest as the custodian of social values: the panoply of ecclesiastical institutions of regulation (the ritual order of sacraments, the places of vocational training, the hospice for pilgrims, places of worship and sanctuary) have been transferred through the evolution of scientific medicine to a panoptic collection of localised agencies of surveillance and control. Furthermore, the rise of preventive medicine, social medicine and community medicine has extended these agencies and regulation deeper and deeper into social life."

Religious mortification and denial of the body have been replaced by health regimes, diets and exercise as the modern forms of self-regulation and public regulation of our bodies. The clerical gaze has been replaced by the clinical gaze.

Foucault's work on medicine requires us to relate analyses of medicine and the body to historical changes in the ways in which the regulation of bodies has been secured in society, at both the micro (individual) and the macro (population) level. Medicine cannot be seen merely as an activity associated with clinical healing; the medicalisation of the body has to be understood as a process of social control. Croft and Beresford (1998) have provided an example of this when looking at discourses on dying (Box 13.1)

BOX 13.1 The discourse of dying

[T]he following seem to be some of the key terms in which we are conventionally encouraged to conceive of death and dying... . [M]edical victory; the medical profession and associated medical research overcoming disease through skill, science, knowledge, technology and wisdom. This is linked to the medicalisation and technisation of death; medical dominance in death and dying. A high percentage of dying takes place in medical institutions, yet this is coupled with a low priority of palliative care in medicine ...

The response of the dominant medical discourse on dying is often unsympathetic at [the] individual level to the concerns and approach of its subjects. For example, the focus of some people who are dying on the life they have, rather than on addressing dying, is interpreted in negative terms of people being 'in denial', and not facing or accepting that they are dying.

The dominant medical discourses on ... dying are deeply rooted in the scientism and rationalism of the nineteenth century. But the emergence of new discourses from the disabled people's and social service users' movements have strongly challenged this tradition.

Source: Croft and Beresford (1998, pp. 107–8).

Combining perspectives: Turner's contribution

The sociological perspectives discussed above are based on distinct theoretical assumptions about how best to understand health, illness and medicine in society. Parsons (1951) suggests that illness and disease create structural and behavioural problems that society needs to resolve through normative, rule-governed role performances. In contrast, interactionists stress how the definitions of illness and the appropriate behaviours surrounding it are elastic and precarious because they are constructed through interaction. Marxists emphasise the political economy of health, in that there is considerable inequality in the ways in which health and illness are defined and managed, and this reflects the wider social structures of capitalism. Feminists insist that gender should be incorporated into the analysis of role relations and the definition of health and illness, and point to the institutionalised patriarchy that characterises the health care system. Foucauldian analysis ties the issue of medical control to the question of how the individual and the wider collective body are subject to bio-social surveillance and regulation.

It is possible to argue that these discrete traditions cannot be merged into a single theoretical model. However, Turner (1987) considers them to be reconcilable, as they focus on different aspects of the same phenomena. Each has something to contribute to the sociological analysis of health, illness and medicine. He begins by distinguishing between three levels of analysis – the individual, the social and the societal. At the level of the individual, we are interested in the experience of illness and disease. Here, interactionism plays a valuable role in drawing attention to the perceptions that people (and patients) have of their illness. Secondly, at the level of the social, we concentrate on institutional dynamics (for example, of hospitals and asylums) and the way in which professionals (doctors) define and regulate sickness and disease (whether physical or mental). Here, the Parsonian and more institutionally oriented interactionist analyses (such as that by Goffman) are appropriate. Finally, at the societal level, we turn to the wider macro or systemic structures that pattern health care systems. Here, feminist analysis, Marxist political economy and Foucault's exploration of power and discourse are important. Turner (1992, p. 237) describes the accommodation of these different perspectives within a single theory as a 'strategy of inclusion': 'Rather than being forced to choose between [these] particular competing paradigms, one could see them as addressing very different issues at rather different levels'.

Turner has built on these different traditions to produce an integrated theoretical approach. His strategy relies on tying the sociological analysis of medicine to the sociology of the body. He agrees with Foucault that we can distinguish between the body as an individual entity – as a person – and as a collective entity – as a population. The desires, demands and pathologies of the body at both these levels are regulated, especially those relating to sexuality. Turner is particularly interested in understanding the social and societal management of the HIV virus, where sexual and biological pathologies are explicitly interlinked. The personal and public hygiene that those in dominant positions demand for the regulation and checking of the virus has both a biological and a moral form: hence the **homophobic** term 'gay plague'.

> **Homophobia**
> Hatred or fear of homosexuals (including lesbians).

 ## The medical profession and the power of orthodox medicine

All the above perspectives highlight the power of the medical establishment. How did medicine become so powerful? To answer this question, we need to trace the evolution of the profession, especially since the late nineteenth century. Its roots lie in the general **professionalisation** of a number of occupational groups, which took place at different rates in different fields (Rich, 1974). Professionalisation involved three related processes (Turner, 1987):

> **Professionalisation**
> The process by which the members of a particular occupation seek to establish a monopoly over its practice. Typically, this is done by limiting entry to those with certain qualifications and claiming that those who lack these qualifications do not possess the requisite expertise.

- The creation and defence of a specialist body of knowledge, typically based on formal university qualifications.
- The establishment of control over a specialised client market and the exclusion of competitor groups from that market.
- The establishment of control over professional work practices, responsibilities and obligations while resisting control by managerial or bureaucratic staff.

In short, professions are skilled occupations with a relatively privileged position in the occupational hierarchy whose members employ an ideology of expertise and client service to legitimate their advantaged position. Professional status can only develop when there is sufficient demand for the skills in question (Johnston and Robbins, 1975). The demand for the healing powers of medicine has always existed, but its professionalisation is much more recent. The Western medical profession developed within two distinct contexts during the nineteenth century. In the first, medical research and career opportunities centred on the university, where the role of clinical practitioner/teacher and researcher was formally established as a salaried occupation, first in Germany and then in the US. The international standing of German medicine is indicated by the fact that between 1870 and 1914, 15 000 Americans studied medicine in German universities and took the German model back to the US.

The second context was that in England. According to Wright (1979), the current medical system is the product of three centuries of dominance by the Royal College of Physicians (RCP), whose monopolistic practices, legitimated by royal charter and government legislation, allowed it to control if not eliminate competition by other medical groups, such as the apothecary companies and guilds. Wright points out that the dominance of orthodox medicine did not reflect superior technical or scientific practices compared with other forms of healing, such as astrology. Typically, doctors would use bleeding and purging in their treatment, neither of which were likely to have any beneficial effect on the patient. When more reliable and effective medical techniques were developed, many doctors resisted them, as scientific medicine might compromise their client-oriented practices and the patronage these attracted. The most important factor in the professionalisation of medicine was the expansion of the medical market during the nineteenth century. There was a growing demand for doctors by rich city dwellers and the new urban middle classes. There was also an increased demand for social regulation (for example, of urban prostitution and working-class slums), which the medical profession could help deliver.

The growth in demand for medical services caused key players such as the RCP to seek to consolidate their control – backed by the government – over the health market. The result was the Medical Act of 1858, which established the first national register of recognised practitioners, set the qualifications for registration, restricted the terms of entry to the profession and gave doctors a legally sanctioned monopoly. New recruits to the profession were limited by the terms of entry, so although the population of England and Wales grew by 30 per cent between 1861 and 1881, there was only a 5 per cent increase in the number of medical practitioners.

There were striking differences between the British and US patterns of medical professionalisation, one indication of which was the relative absence of general practitioners and a preponderance of specialists in the US. The two professional systems began to diverge as early as the turn of the twentieth century, so their present-day distinctions do not merely derive from market forces in the US and national health care in the UK. Indeed, they have more to do with the historical structure and character of the profession in the two countries and the distinct medical markets within which practitioners operated. In the British case, formal medical practice can be traced back to the sixteenth century, when guilds of physicians, surgeons and apothecaries provided care for the embryonic middle classes (merchants, other professionals, early civil servants and so on), while the lesser number of elite practitioners attached to the Royal College (of Surgeons/Physicians) attended to the upper classes and acted as principal medical officers for charitable hospitals catering to the very poor. Developments during the latter part of the nineteenth century consolidated this split between the specialised, hospital-based elite and the larger number of general practitioners. The position of the latter group was secured by the 1911 National Health Insurance Act, which guaranteed them a market among the poorer social groups to supplement their growing middle-class market in the cities. The welfare state provided further support for this two-tier specialist and general practice structure.

Today in the UK, GPs control patients' access to primary health care, while specialist consultants control hospital provision. Once seen by a specialist, the patient is referred back to his or her GP for the next step – be this the discontinuation of treatment or referral to another specialist, and so on.

In contrast, in the US, the professional class structure that was so evident in British medicine was virtually absent. There were no equivalents of the guilds and the Royal Colleges to provide a framework for the broader medical structure. As Rosemary Stevens (1980, p. 110) notes, 'American medicine was a profession without institutions', and therefore its institutional base had to be built from scratch, using institutions such as universities and medical colleges, new technologies and the like, with a strong emphasis on competitive specialisation. The culture of nineteenth-century and early-twentieth-century US medicine was in stark contrast to that of the UK. In the latter, there was hostility towards new techniques such as anaesthesia, which was seen as an affront to the professional skill of surgeons who were practised in the art of rapid and therefore relatively pain-free surgery. In the US, the social context of medical practice encouraged the many competing specialists to look to new treatments, techniques and therapies to demonstrate their specialist skills. This specialist competitive dynamic also encouraged much greater emphasis on research in the US than in the UK, and this has remained broadly true ever since. Commenting on this difference in the earlier part of the twentieth century, the American physician Flexner (1910, p. 30) observed that research and clinical standards were poor in the UK, while the guild-based professional structure was 'admirably calculated to protect honour and dignity, to conserve ceremony, and to transmit tradition'.

Whatever the historical variations in the professionalisation of medicine, the power of the profession to control its position and reward in the labour market has been carefully documented, especially by sociologists such as Freidson (1988) and Johnson (1972), who sought to lift the lid on client-oriented professional ethics that claimed to benefit patients but were in fact occupational ideologies that enabled professionals to secure considerable autonomy and distance from their clients. As Johnson (1972, p. 25) says: 'The professional rhetoric relating to community service and altruism may be in many cases a significant factor in moulding the practices of individual professionals, but it also clearly functions as a legitimation of professional privilege.'

CONNECTIONS For a general discussion of the issue of power, see Chapter 8, pages 194–206.

The power of the profession can be understood by considering the medicalisation of lay forms of coping with illness and natural physical processes, such as ageing, previously handled within the community. Medicalisation can take three forms.

The first is incorporating and redefining lay approaches to illness and physical processes so that they fall under the 'medical gaze' – that is, they are redefined as a form of illness open to medical intervention. Mental illness was medicalised in this way in the late eighteenth century. Deviant or unusual mental states that had been seen in communities as signs of witchcraft or possession (divine as well as evil) were gradually redefined as psychiatric conditions, with religion gradually ceding territory to the newly established psychiatric profession. Ageing is another area where medicalisation has occurred. The old tend to be treated as a homogeneous group by the biomedical model of declining health. Unlike other areas of medical discourse, the ageing of the body is seen as incurable. As such, ageing does not fit the conventional biomedical 'curative' discourse. However, the pressure to medicalise ageing is increasing because the necessary community and family structures are no longer in place to take on responsibility for the aged, whose number is growing rapidly: for example, in 1994 in the UK, over nine million were aged 65 or over.

BOX 13.2 The medicalisation of pregnancy

Common medical procedures associated with pregnancy:

- Regular ante-natal check-ups.
- Iron and vitamin supplements.
- Vaginal examinations during pregnancy.
- Ultrasound monitoring of pregnancy.

- Hospital birth.
- Enemas or suppositories in the first stage of labour.
- Shaving of the pubic hair during labour.
- Artificial rupture of the membranes.
- Pharmacological induction of labour. ▶

- ▶ Vaginal examinations during labour.
- Bladder catheterisation during labour.
- Mechanical monitoring of the foetal heart.
- Mechanical monitoring of contractions.
- A glucose or saline drip during labour.
- Epidural analgesia during labour.
- Pethidine (meperidine) or other pain-killing/ tranquillising injections during labour.

- Birth in horizontal or semi-horizontal position.
- Episiotomy.
- Forceps or vacuum extraction of the baby.
- Cutting the umbilical cord immediately after birth.
- Accelerated delivery of the placenta by injection of ergometrine and/or oxytocin and pulling on the cord.

Source: Oakley (1979, pp. 17–18).

The claimed efficacy of scientific medicine is the second element of medicalisation. Better drugs, surgical techniques, therapies, anti-viral agents and antibiotics are heralded as proof of the scientific progress of medical research and clinical practice. While the evidence here is very persuasive, some have stressed the need for caution when evaluating the impact of medicine. Cochrane (1971), a former director of the UK Medical Research Council's Epidemiology Unit, produced a powerful critique of the effectiveness of medical treatments, citing poor monitoring and the failure to conduct rigorous comparisons of one technique against any other. When the latter was done, quite unexpected results appeared: 'Possibly the most striking result [was the trial] in Bristol in which hospital treatment (including a variable time in a coronary care unit) was compared with treatment at home for acute ischaemic heart disease. The results do not suggest that there is any medical gain in admission to hospital with coronary care units compared with treatment at home' (ibid., p. 74).

Moreover, the benefit of scientific medicine is challenged by the growing incidence of **iatrogenic illness**, that is, doctor-induced illness and disability. According to Illich (1976, p. 24), 'the pain, dysfunction, disability and anguish resulting from technical medical intervention now rival the morbidity due to traffic and industrial accidents and even war-related activities, and make the impact of medicine one of the most rapidly spreading epidemics of our time'. Illich's strong attack on medicine might seem to be overstated, but it becomes credible when looked at in the light of the damage done by the side effects of drugs such as thalidomide, the dangerous contraceptive techniques devised for women and general malpractice. In large, impersonalised hospitals, however, the personal responsibility of physicians is less clear. Malpractice and negligence may be defined as merely technical breakdowns in the system rather than ethically questionable behaviour by practitioners.

The marginalisation of alternative medical therapies is the third aspect of medicalisation. Despite the strength of orthodox medicine, lay medical treatment still plays a part in all health care systems. It is important to recognise that the dominance of orthodox medicine in the formal health care sector does not encompass the whole of what Kleineman (1973) calls the cultural health system. The relationship between orthodox and alternative medicine in terms of patient involvement varies: some may always turn to alternative medicine when ill, while others seek alternative treatment because of the perceived failings of orthodox medicine.

iatrogenic illness
Illness or disability caused by medical treatment.

QUESTION Why, in your opinion, has alternative medicine become so popular? Use appropriate sociological concepts to construct your response.

Since the early 1980s, there has been a steady rise in the popularity and availability of alternative treatments such as acupuncture, chiropracture, osteopathy, homeopathy, herbalism, reflexology, shiatsu and the Alexander technique. These differ in the extent to which they claim to offer a complete alternative to orthodox medicine or serve as a complement to it.

Saks (1992) estimates that in the UK about 11 000 therapists are registered with alternative medical associations, with another 17 000 non-registered practitioners. Popular support for complementary medicine has led to political support in parliament, forcing the government to appoint junior ministers with responsibility for alternative medicine (AM). Despite this, AM has yet to establish itself as an organised health care movement. This is partly because of splits among AM practitioners in terms not only of what strategy to adopt professionally but also of how to describe their medicine. Saks notes that there are 'eighty-eight organisations in Britain covering seventeen or more alternative therapies' (ibid., p. 16).

According to Stanway (1982), there are five main reasons for the steady growth in the number of AM patients:

- People believe that orthodox medicine is failing in certain fields, for example, cancer.
- People are afraid of the iatrogenic effects of Western medical treatment (see above).
- Some have religious/philosophical reservations about what is being offered by orthodox medicine.
- Some want to protest about what is available in the orthodox system.
- Some want to experiment with new medicine.

Figure 13.2 Despite their 'alternative' status, complementary therapies – like orthodox medicine – lay the emphasis of health care on the individual and tend to ignore wider social and environmental factors.

In broader terms, Coward (1989) argues that the interest in AM is linked to a 'new philosophy of the body, health and nature'. AM offers 'a new consciousness of the value of involving the individual in her and his well-being and a new sense of being natural'. AM can be seen as part of a wider shift towards a naturalistic approach that contrasts lay versus expert, natural versus synthetic, organic versus chemical and holistic versus mechanistic. In a wider cultural context, this relates to the green movement and the 'natural system' idea of contemporary ecology. If it is natural, it must be good, and homeopathy makes much of this claim in its treatment.

Although more and more patients may vote with their feet and seek treatment from AM practitioners, the institutional entrenchment of orthodox health care is unlikely to be dismantled. One reason for this is that orthodox practitioners may simply incorporate AM into their practice and turn a threat from competitors into an advantage for themselves. This is especially true in Western Europe, where doctors have the right to use whatever medical technique they regard as valuable when treating patients – prescription medicine, physiotherapy, acupuncture, endoscopy and so on. Their response to AM tends to vary according to circumstances.

AM practitioners face a number of dilemmas when orthodox doctors adopt aspects of their traditional medicine. Incorporation usually involves the following:

BOX 13.3 Forms of control by orthodox practitioners over competitors

- Incorporate on own terms competing ideas and skills; for example, mesmerism/neurohypnology (hypnosis).

- Competitors practise in subordinate position in law; for example, radiographers (when practice first developed in 1920s).

- Reject competitors completely; for example, chiropractors.

- Competitors accept dominance of medical profession; for example, osteopaths.

- Wider acceptance of AM by the public and the possibility of referral by GPs. This poses a threat to the beliefs and therapies upon which AMs are based, as they lose their alternative identity (the very claim that makes them so attractive).

- AM practitioners gain access to a new medical market but they have to develop a working knowledge of orthodox medical terms to reassure new patients.

- Recognition provides formal state blessing but on terms that require AM associations to police their members.

- New research support may be provided, but developments are likely to be orchestrated by orthodox researchers rather than AM practitioners themselves.

The success of AM will depend as much on patient disaffection with orthodox medicine as on the capacity of AM lobbies to establish themselves in the medical system.

In terms of one of the key themes of this book, one might wonder whether the AM movement, with its challenge to rational scientific medicine, is part of a postmodernist critique of established medicine. Inasmuch as it proposes a wide range of alternative therapies and distances itself from the authoritarianism of the professional elite, AM is another illustration of the deconstruction of traditional forms of social authority (the medical profession) and conventional expertise (medical knowledge). Its popularity might reflect a wider desire to challenge powerful modernist practices and certainties.

To the extent that AM achieves these goals – and its victories have been small and rather insignificant to date – it might be seen as another indication of the onset of postmodernism. However, a different view is that while AM challenges orthodox medicine, the knowledge it offers as an alternative is far removed from the unstable, shaky and ephemeral world of the postmodernist. AM promotes the image of a natural, holistic medicine that is grounded in a set of strong, overarching principles about nature and our place in it, reminiscent of some of the fundamentalist beliefs of left-wing environmentalists.

To secure a foothold in the health care system, many AM groups have adopted similar strategies to those utilised by early Western medical practitioners to establish their modernist credentials. Hence, many of the advances that AM groups have made have depended on professionalising themselves rather than on demonstrating the success of their treatment. For example, professional bodies have been created to set standards, monitor members and prevent undesirables practising. In the UK, the Council for Complementary and Alternative Medicine sets standards of AM care that mimic those of the General Medical Council.

As stated above, there is little evidence of AM posing a major threat to professional entrenchment. If it continues to expand, it is likely to be through orthodox medical practitioners adopting it as a useful, cheap and patient-centred form of health care. Whatever the form of medicine delivered, chronic inequality between various sectors of the population in respect of general standards of health is likely to remain. It is to this issue that we now turn.

Health inequalities

In Bethnal Green in 1839, the average age of death was as follows: gentlemen and persons engaged in professions and their families, 45 years; tradesmen and their families, 26 years; mechanics, servants and labourers and their families, 16 years (Chadwick, 1842). Although the general standards of health have improved dramatically since then, the prevalence of chronic sickness still varies according to social class, as Table 13.2 shows.

TABLE 13.2 Chronic sickness rates by social class, UK, 1994 (per cent)

Socio-economic group	Male 0–15 yrs	Male 65 and over	Female 0–15 yrs	Female 65 and over
Professional	16	57	11	53
Unskilled	28	68	8	65

Source: Office of Population Censuses and Surveys (1994, p. 86).

The continuing inequality in morbidity and mortality across social classes has been explored in detail by Townsend and Davidson (1982), who argue that the most important factors affecting health are income, occupation, education, housing and lifestyle. They examined four explanations that have been offered to account for the statistical trends.

- First, health inequality as an artefact. Here, health differences are claimed to be a statistical fiction, artificially created as a result of the way in which data are gathered and analysed. There is no real causal relationship between class position and the quality of an individual's health.

- Second, health inequality as a process of social selection. In this explanation, there is acceptance that health and class inequality are related, but that the independent variable is health itself. Good health promotes upward social mobility, while bad health results in downward mobility. Therefore, health is seen as a determinant of class position.

- Third, health inequality as material deprivation. Against the second view, this position argues that poverty is a direct cause of ill-health. In the 1970s, a major survey of poverty in the UK (Townsend, 1979) found that 7 per cent of households (3.3 million people) received an income that was lower than the Supplementary Benefit level, while 24 per cent of households (almost 12 million people) were on the margins of poverty. Since Townsend's study was published, the figures have remained steady or worsened, especially in the case of single pensioners and single-parent families, whose chance of being in poverty has increased by 60 per cent. While these two groups reflect changing demographic patterns in society, the majority of those who are poor are so because they cannot secure work that will provide an adequate wage. Millar (1993) relates this to high unemployment, the growth of low-paid work and the increase in part-time casual labour.

  The evidence suggests a direct relationship between these groups and high levels of illness and disease. One measure of this is high prescription rate for people living in poor inner-city areas. Poor nutrition, inadequate hygiene facilities, exhaustion from long working hours (especially on night shifts) and the general struggle to make ends meet make for poor health, especially among the very young and very old.

- Fourth, health inequality as cultural deprivation. The argument here is that poor health has more to do with cultural practices and beliefs than material disadvantages. The

Cultural deprivation
An approach that claims that lifestyle choices determine ill-health. It offers an explanation of the greater incidence of ill-health among working-class people by directly relating it to factors such as smoking, alcohol consumption and diet.

focus is on the relative cultural ability of social classes to use knowledge about health and the health services. Smoking is one practice that might be used to illustrate this point. Why do people smoke despite the evidence of its damaging effects? Why is the incidence of smoking higher among lower social classes, such that more working-class people die from smoking-related lung cancer than any other social group?

It is argued here that certain social groups experience **cultural deprivation** throughout their lives in terms of knowing how best to manage their health needs. In addition, ethnic minority groups and the working class might be less likely to regard their illness as worthy of a doctor's attention. Finally, it is conceivable that smoking for the working class – and increasingly for women – is a symbol of defiance: a vehicle to assert their identity and personal control in social situations. Tobacco companies, of course, rely on just this sort of association being made, be it by the newly assertive woman, the 'Westernising' East European (smoking Western cigarettes) or the Third World entrepreneur stocking the latest line in T-shirts promoting Camel cigarettes. Smoking is clearly a social statement that brings pleasure as well as a chesty cough and lung cancer.

CONNECTIONS Other disadvantages experienced by the lower social classes are outlined in Chapter 4, pages 72–82 and Chapter 5, pages 110–18.

These four interpretations of the health statistics have been subject to sociological and medical debate for many years, and, in broad terms, the last two – the material and cultural accounts – are the favoured explanations of the patterns of morbidity and mortality. The issues they raise are not simply the concern of academics and the medical profession: there is a strong governmental interest in using certain interpretations to support particular health policies. A particularly attractive line for governments in periods of reduced state expenditure is that health should be seen as a matter of personal responsibility, a view not far removed from the ideas underlying the cultural deprivation approach. Health services and insurance companies in advanced countries are penalising smokers because of this. This is given greater momentum by the growing importance of health economics as an expert discipline – a highly modernist approach to the rationing of health care that provides 'scientific' grounds for deciding who should and who should not receive medical attention (Ashmore *et al.*, 1989). The ultimate decision on treatment is taken by the managers and professionals working in state and private health care. In the UK, it is those working in the National Health Service who have this responsibility, as discussed in the next section.

QUESTION What impact do industries such as the cigarette industry have on the general health of society? Do you think that all industries affect the health of their workers, their customers and their neighbours? If so, provide examples.

The contemporary health care system

The principal health care system in the UK is national in scope and state-sponsored. The main actors involved are the various professionals, their 'consumers' (primarily their patients) and the state, which provides the basic funding for the system while subjecting it to continual monitoring and evaluation. The National Health Service (NHS), founded in July 1948, is a medicalised health care system, in that medical professionals are the principal providers of health care (although there are high levels of self-healing). The

BOX 13.4 Characterising the US health care system

'Third world medicine at super-power prices' – in such terms did Gavin Esler, then the BBC's chief US political correspondent, describe the state of health care in the United States. This view of a system that mixes deprivation with excess is shared by many commentators on the US. US citizens have access to very expensive treatment for rare, life-threatening diseases and are offered the most advanced operations, but there are no mass vaccination programmes to provide cheap preventative medicine at $3 a shot. The US spends more than any other country on its health care – about 14 per cent of GDP, more than twice that spent in the UK. Yet over 30 million out of the 250 million US citizens have no health care provision whatsoever – public or private. That so massive an expenditure is failing to provide basic health for millions poses a social and a political problem for the US government. The policy problem is to reduce the bill while improving the provision of health care. The political problem is that achieving this will require a state-led attack on the powerful institutions that benefit from the system: the medical and legal professions, the insurance sector and the pharmaceutical industry.

The latter, for example, is being pressed to reduce the price of drugs because the profit margins are excessive, while insurance companies are under attack from firms whose duty to provide private sickness benefit for employees has forced up the cost of insurance and eroded corporate profits. The spiralling costs have caused many firms to set up a form of self-insurance for their workers' health needs, thus removing the costly third party – the insurance company – from the scene. It is evident, then, that major economic interests – not always convergent with each other – are tied into the US health care system. It is also evident that private provision does not necessarily work more effectively than collective public provision.

founding assumptions of the NHS were that expert, scientific medicine was good in itself and had collective approval, and that primary care should be provided by doctors and hospitals. This set of assumptions is found in most industrialised countries, but far less so in developing countries.

As the NHS has traditionally provided free health care, it has tended to be the primary vehicle for medical treatment for the bulk of the population. In fee-paying systems, patients shop around for treatment, and, as a result, the medical market is more competitive, and litigation is common.

The NHS has a sort of 'protected species' status among the British public, and any governmental threat to its existence is regarded as political suicide. This is partly because it is free at the point of delivery: no one wants to pay for treatment. But it is also because of a well-rooted belief that health care is safer when it is not commercialised, and is therefore transparent, accountable and reliable. While this belief may rest on an oversentimental attachment to something that has never lived up to its image, it has nevertheless been a powerful myth that both professionals and consumers have helped to reproduce over the years.

Yet the NHS is still under government attack, albeit disguised by the rhetoric of efficiency and patient choice. During the 1980s and early 1990s, a number of crucial changes were made to the operation of the NHS that affected its essential character:

- Community care: while this was claimed to be a progressive policy promoting de-institutionalisation, in practice it meant a shift from care *in* the community to care *by* the community.
- Marketisation: the promotion of patient choice and the introduction of fund-holding for doctors.
- Privatisation of services within hospitals.

- Resource costs: stress on new managerialism and health economics; an increase in health charges (for example, for prescriptions and dental care); the introduction of self-governing trust hospitals.

- Ideology: a shift in emphasis from public health care to private health care, with the individual being responsible for her or his own well-being.

Together, these developments resulted in a qualitative change to the NHS, and one that was not necessarily coherent: for example, community care seemed to work against patient choice by denying any real alternative to domiciliary care. Moreover, health care needs were redefined and placed within more restricted boundaries, while social needs such as respite care and community care were made the responsibility of social services and/or the family. There was also a **de-medicalisation** of health care – especially for the elderly – in that social services were expected to take on more responsibility for the sick.

The above developments confirm that the definition and satisfaction of health needs are as much political as medical matters. Who decides what needs are, how they should be met and at what level are questions for political debate, especially when the health care system is ostensibly based on an equitable distribution of resources provided free of charge.

The **marketisation** and privatisation of the NHS under consecutive Conservative governments was based on the separation of those who purchased health care (fund-holding doctors and local health authorities) – the famous purchase/provider divide – from those who provided health care (public, private and charitable hospitals and health services). The idea was to create efficiency-generating competition between providers, but many commentators argued that it would lead to additional administration costs and a two-tier system in which some people would receive an inferior service. At the same time, the broader issue of health inequality, one of the main reasons for the establishment of the NHS, was neglected in favour of cost reduction and the efficient use of resources.

The New Labour government elected in 1997 pledged to abolish the purchaser/provider divide, to base health care on partnership rather than competition, and to tackle health inequality by reducing inequality in general. (It had long been recognised that people in countries with lower overall levels of inequality, such as Sweden and Japan, enjoyed better than average health and a lower mortality rate.) In practice, however, New Labour policies showed continuities as well as breaks with previous policies. For example, the government abolished fund-holding by general practices but set up new commissioning authorities, which meant that the two-tier system of health care within the NHS was eliminated, but there was still a separation between those who purchased health care on behalf of patients and those who provided care. The health care model adopted by the previous Conservative administration had been designed to operate on market principles, and there remained an element of this in the new system.

Under New Labour, links have been established between the public and private health care sectors through the private finance initiative (PFI) and the increased use of private sector beds for NHS patients. PFI is based on a partnership between the public and the private sectors, an example of which is the construction of a new general hospital in Norwich by a private company that will lease it to the NHS upon completion. One criticism of PFI is that it will only work for projects that serve the interests of private corporations, and that this will distort planning for the health care needs of patients. The increasing use of vacant private sector beds for NHS patients is portrayed as a means of meeting the demand for NHS care without having to build new NHS hospitals or enlarge existing ones. Commentators are divided over whether this amounts to the creeping privatisation of NHS care or represents a sensible 'mixed economy' of provision.

De-medicalisation
The process whereby orthodox medicine loses its ability to define and regulate areas of human life (see *medicalisation*).

Marketisation
An economic concept that describes the process of exchange and the distribution of services and goods by private individuals or corporate bodies, based on the dictates of supply and demand.

BOX 13.5 Health policies and individual risk

In 'The New Politics of the NHS', Klein (1995) has argued that ... in the 1990s (we have) 'a new health policy paradigm'. In short, the government finally acknowledged that it had responsibilities for the health of the population that went beyond the provision of a health-care system. It argued that the main health problems of the twentieth century were due to personal health behaviours. The 'Health of the Nation' White Paper and subsequent documentation set out the government's strategy to improve the nation's health. The risks to health were conceptualised as predominantly those associated with individual behaviours and lifestyles – especially the holy trinity of risks: smoking, exercise and diet. Within the health literature there appears to be an emerging consensus that health and medicine work within a new framework or paradigm – one which is governed by notions of surveillance and risk.

Source: Nettleton and Burrows (1998, pp. 156–7).

A further aspect of New Labour policy is the idea of a partnership in prevention. In its early days in office, the government identified a number of 'health action zones' where high levels of material disadvantage needed to be addressed in order to improve the health of the inhabitants. More generally, however, the government's approach to prevention has been couched in terms of Tony Blair's 'third way', in which the provision of public health care resources has to be accompanied by responsible (healthy) citizenship. People are expected to adopt healthy practices and abandon those which pose a risk to their health. This resurrects the old preoccupation with giving up smoking, drinking sensibly, taking exercise and eating a healthy diet, and reflects the individualistic, potentially victim-blaming focus that has long been a tradition in UK health policy (see Box 13.5).

Finally, New Labour has intimated that spending on health care in the UK will rise to European levels. (The UK currently spends around 6 per cent of its GDP on health care, while countries such as France, Germany and Sweden spend 8–9 per cent.) However, this is dependent on the continued growth and prosperity of the UK economy.

Managerialism
A process of increased managerial control.

The rise in the level of state support for national medical provision is a problem shared by many advanced industrial states. Solutions to the problem involve a mixture of increased **managerialism**, an emphasis on health care via the market, and, despite the growth in the bureaucracy that oversees medicine, a tendency to rely on carers in the community – a responsibility that falls most heavily on women.

 ## The globalisation of health, illness and medicine

In Chapter 4, we saw how the contemporary world can be regarded as a global system, shaped by major cultural and economic players, notably Sklair's (1991) transnational classes. It should come as no surprise that patterns of morbidity and mortality also have a globalised dimension. The more the world economies are integrated in terms of production and consumption, the more similar the international structures of class inequality will become; and the more the culture of the West (notably in its American form) comes to predominate, the more similar the global patterns of health and illness, good and poor nutrition, and access to health care will become.

CONNECTIONS The general impact of globalisation is discussed in Chapter 3 – see pages 54–64 in particular.

According to Turner (1987), the global patterns of morbidity and mortality are converging, with cancer, strokes and heart disease predominating whatever the national context. Similarly, there has been a globalisation of the institutional responses to the demand for health care, that is, highly bureaucratic, 'rational' systems of medical delivery that go beyond national boundaries. Finally, as a feature of modernity common to all industrialised states, medicine is playing an important scientifically and professionally grounded role as a regulator of individual and collective bodies in all societies.

The globalisation of common forms of medical practice and their associated technologies – such as scanning devices, the paraphernalia of intensive care units and so on – reflects the existence of an international network of medical practitioners who share similar requirements and standards. It also reflects the way in which modernity has encouraged the standardisation of technologies and instruments (not only in medicine but also elsewhere). Major suppliers of equipment, drugs and other medical items are under pressure to pursue the same technical innovations in order to remain competitive, while conforming to quality standards set by international regulatory agencies. Because the major drugs companies are merging to become truly global firms – such as SmithKline Beecham and Glaxo-Wellcome – the drugs they develop are geared to global markets. The GATT (General Agreement on Tariffs and Trade) agreement encouraged this by ensuring that the proprietary rights of drug companies were observed in a wider range of countries, thus securing and stabilising world markets for them.

In addition, the communication and information technologies that are crucial to the globalisation process are playing a growing role in medical science and medical practice. In the field of medical research, access to international databases is important for keeping up with new developments and exchanging information quickly in standardised formats, as in the Human Genome Project. From practitioners' perspectives, the digitalisation of patients' records allows doctors to discuss cases over the Internet without meeting the patient. Not only does this encourage greater international standardisation of symptomatology and diagnosis, it also opens up intriguing questions about doctor–patient relations and the continuing relevance of the bed-side manner!

At the same time, the globalisation process has prompted resistance at the local level. For example, transnational pharmaceutical companies have had their global dominance checked by small competitor companies in Southern states that are keen to cut their health care bills. Moreover, indigenous or traditional forms of medicine in Africa, Asia and the Pacific Rim countries are still popular and are often practised alongside modern medicine: indeed, in China, this was openly advocated by the government until recently. Even in Western societies, alongside alternative medicine there are lay remedies for coping with illness – such as 'feed a cold and starve a fever' – and prescriptions for remaining healthy, such as 'don't go out with your hair wet'. It is doubtful whether either of these are global injunctions!

 ## Conclusion

This chapter has explored the theoretical and empirical basis upon which the sociology of health, illness and medicine is built. It should be clear that the role of the medical profession involves more than curing sickness. It also shapes the definitions of health and illness and is closely tied to major economic and political interests. However, its curative and healing powers are often less effective than its modernist self-image would have us believe. Sociologically, therefore, the social basis of health and illness is evident, at both the micro and the macro level of analysis.

Chapter summary

- Sociology challenges the biomedical model of health and illness by demonstrating the social bases of both.
- The development of rational, scientific medicine is associated with the growth of professional medical expertise and state-sponsored institutions of health care, both of which exemplify the impact of modernity on the health care system.
- There are five main theoretical approaches to health, illness and medicine: the functionalist, interactionist, Marxist, feminist and Foucauldian approaches.
- Turner (1992) has developed a valuable model that attempts to integrate these approaches by analysing at the level of the individual, the social and the societal.
- The medical profession has established itself as the principal authority in the medical market, although there are differences – between the UK and US, for example – in the way this power is expressed and in its historical origins.
- Alternative medicine challenges orthodox medicine but cannot be seen as a postmodern critique.
- Health inequalities reflect wider social divisions, although there are a number of possible interpretations of the health statistics used to back this assertion.
- The NHS, like state-sponsored health care elsewhere, is undergoing fundamental change, although its full privatisation seems unlikely.
- Health has global dimensions, in terms not only of patterns of morbidity and mortality but also the convergence of forms of treatment, drugs and equipment. However, local resistance to this convergence is apparent.

 Questions to think about

- Which of the five theoretical models of health and illness do you find most convincing, and why?
- If you had the power to construct a medical system for the twentieth century, would you look to the US or UK model for your inspiration? Justify your answer.
- Given the existence of health inequalities, should more resources be targeted at the chronically ill? Produce an argument for both sides of this question.

 Investigating further

Doyal, Lesley (1995) *What Makes Women Sick: Gender and the Political Economy of Health*, Palgrave.
> This book offers a useful critique of the medical model, focusing on global patterns of health and disease among women.

Evans, Mary and Ellie Lee (eds) (2002) *Real Bodies: A Sociological Introduction*, Palgrave.
> Some of the chapters in this collection are more demanding than others but they include some interesting discussion of how much our bodies are 'real' or 'constructed'. Try the chapters on 'the disabled body' and 'the body in pain' as a starting point.

Nettleton, Sarah (1995) *The Sociology of Health and Illness*, Polity Press.
> A good, clear overview text, with chapters on medical knowledge and lay beliefs about health, the relationship between the public and the medical profession, health inequalities, disability and the body.

chapter **14**

Crime

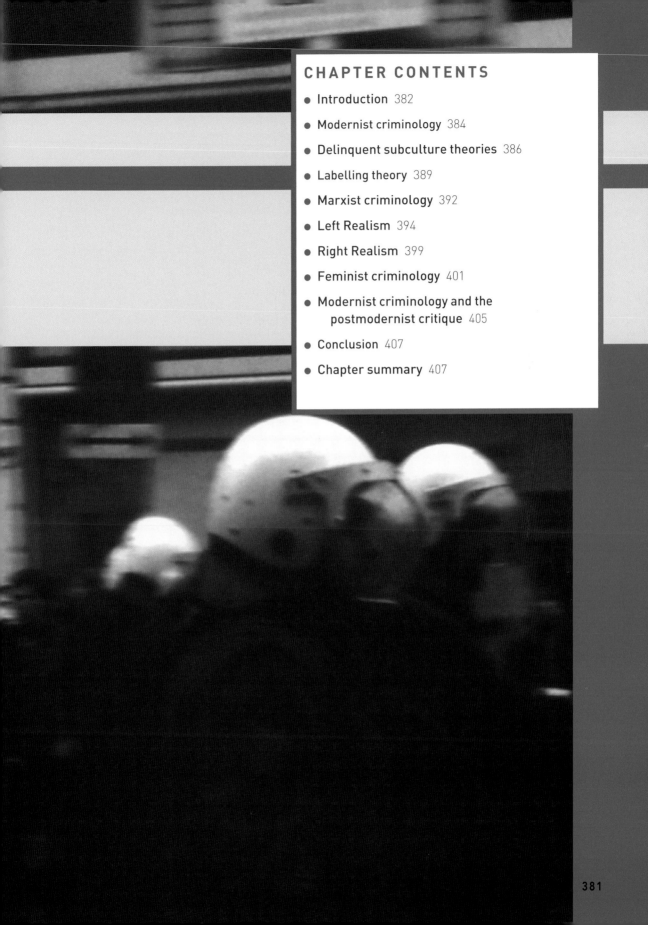

CHAPTER CONTENTS

Aims of the chapter

Like health, crime has been a central policy concern for government and a constant subject of media fascination. This chapter examines the diverse sociological explanations of crime and compares them along a number of dimensions. While highlighting key differences between these approaches, we explain how they have a common commitment to the modernist project – that is, they believe in the possibility and legitimacy of constructing a valid explanation of crime, and hence of developing strategies for doing something about it. In line with one of the central themes of this book – the debates about modernity and postmodernity – we introduce you to the postmodernist critique of criminology.

By the end of this chapter, you should have an understanding of the following concepts:

- Subculture
- Deviance amplification
- Stigmatisation
- Self-report study
- Left Realism
- Right Realism
- Biologism

 Introduction

At the beginning of the twenty-first century, perhaps as never before, crime stands at the centre of public consciousness and political debate. The mass media serve up a regular diet of stories of rising crime, vulnerable victims and uncaring offenders. The public persistently voice their fear of crime in opinion surveys and official government and local area studies, prioritising the issue alongside such fundamentals as the state of the economy, unemployment and redundancy. Political parties are vying with each other to establish their credentials on the question of law and order. The success of the police in dealing with crime in general and with particular types of criminal and criminal activity is coming under ever more scrutiny, and the effectiveness of the criminal justice and penal systems is the subject of apparently never-ending controversy.

Crime, then, is clearly a major realm of societal concern, a spectre that preoccupies the state and its agencies as well as ordinary people. It is important, however, to keep that spectre in proportion. For instance, the crime problem in the UK pales into insignificance in some ways when compared with that of the US, where there are more than 20 000 murders a year compared with the UK's 700–800. However, the UK and many other countries witnessed substantial increases in recorded crime in the last decades of the twentieth century. In England and Wales, for example, recorded crime tripled between the early 1970s and the early 1990s, peaking at about 5.5 million offences in 1992 and remaining around the five million mark in subsequent years (Chart 14.1). Although those data allow us to draw no simple conclusions about changes in actual criminal behaviour, we can be fairly confident that there have been real, if not precisely measurable, increases in criminal activity in Western Europe, North America and elsewhere.

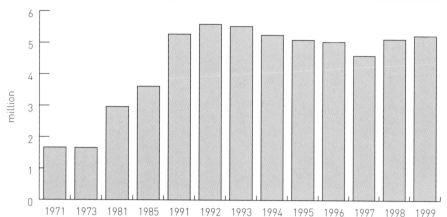

CHART 14.1 Recorded crime in England and Wales, indictable/notifiable offences, 1971–99

Closer examination of the statistics reveals that crimes against property (in the form of theft and handling stolen goods, burglary and criminal damage) comprise the vast majority of recorded offences (Table 14.1). While violent offences such as robbery, assault and woundings cannot be dismissed lightly, they form the minority of recorded crimes.

But, as numerous self-report studies and national and local victim surveys over the years have confirmed, far more crime occurs than the official data indicate. For example, the British Crime Surveys, conducted regularly since 1982, provide some indication of the scale of hidden or unrecorded crime. The 1998 survey estimated that 16.437 million crimes were committed against adults in households in England and Wales in 1997 and that 34 per cent of adults were the victims of at least one crime (Table 14.2).

These findings confirmed those of previous surveys in that, for every crime recorded by the police, there were anywhere between three and four times as many unrecorded offences, although even this figure varied considerably according to offence (Chart 14.2). For example, while the vast majority of vehicle thefts and burglaries were reported to or

TABLE 14.1 Recorded indictable/notifiable offences, England and Wales, 1985–96 (thousands/per cent)

	1985	1992	1996
Violence against the person	121.7 (3.4)	201.8 (3.6)	239.0 (4.7)
Sex offences	21.5 (0.6)	29.5 (0.5)	31.0 (0.6)
Robbery	27.5 (0.8)	52.9 (0.9)	74.0 (1.5)
Theft/handling stolen goods	1884.1 (52.2)	2851.6 (51.0)	2384.0 (47.3)
Fraud/forgery	134.8 (3.7)	168.6 (3.0)	136.0 (2.7)
Burglary	866.7 (24.0)	1355.3 (24.2)	1165 (23.1)
Criminal damage	539.0 (14.9)	892.6 (16.0)	951 (18.9)
Drugs	8.0 (0.2)	13.8 (0.2)	22 (0.4)
Other	8.7 (0.3)	25.6 (0.5)	34 (0.7)

Source: Home Office Criminal Statistics for England and Wales, Cmnd 4162 (London, HMSO, 1997).

TABLE 14.2	**Estimated number of crimes committed against adults, England and Wales, 1997 (millions)**		
Burglary (actual/attempted)	1.639	Mugging (robbery and snatch theft)	0.390
Car-related theft	3.483	Wounding	0.714
Bicycle theft	0.549	Common assault	2.276
Other household thefts	2.067	All violent offences	3.381
Other personal thefts	2.397	Vandalism (against vehicles and other property)	2.917
All property thefts	10.134		

Source: 1998 British Crime Survey.

CHART 14.2   Comparison of BCS and police counts of crime, England and Wales, 1997.

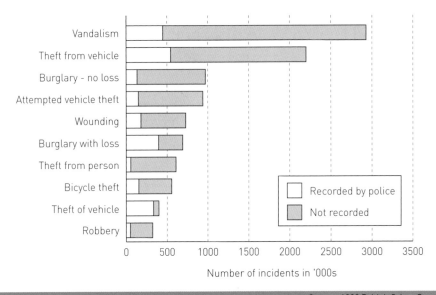

Source: 1998 British Crime Survey.

recorded by the police, only a small proportion of robberies, acts of vandalism and theft from individuals appeared in the official figures.

QUESTION   Crime statistics cannot cover all incidences of law-breaking. Suggest three reasons why some crimes do not appear in government statistics.

 ## Modernist criminology

Anxiety about crime is not peculiar to present times. Indeed, consecutive generations stretching back into the nineteenth century have been preoccupied with the problem of crime and the 'criminal classes', and academic analyses of crime have a similarly long history. In Western Europe and North America in the nineteenth century and for much of the twentieth, attempts to understand and explain crime were dominated by academic approaches other than sociological ones – most notably by biological and psychological explanations. It was not until the 1950s that a serious sociological challenge to those individualistic explanations was made.

Despite their incompatibilities, these non-sociological and sociological approaches have a fundamental thing in common – that is, a commitment to the modernist project. Modernity brought a distinctive position on the nature of knowledge and the part it could and should play in the lives of human beings and human societies. Modernists were committed to the idea that it was possible to attain rational, verifiable, cumulative knowledge of society and to construct from that knowledge theories with which social phenomena could be represented and explained. Competing theories or narratives could be evaluated by an appeal to logic and by the testing of their claims – that is, a particular theory or narrative could be proved right. Thus, modernism held the promise of revealing the truth about human behaviour. Moreover, modernists believed in the idea of progress through knowledge – that the accumulation of knowledge could be acted upon to emancipate human beings and enrich their lives, to improve society and to achieve progress and a better future.

CONNECTIONS To further your knowledge of modernism, see Chapter 2.

In the study of crime, this meant a belief in the possibility of establishing verifiable knowledge about crime, criminals and criminality that would provide a rational basis for controlling crime through strategies of prevention or reduction and/or methods of punishment, deterrence or rehabilitation. As Heidensohn (1989, p. 181) says:

> " Sociologists have played major parts directly and indirectly in strategies linked to altering levels of criminality. It is, after all, inherent in the nature of the sociological approach, deriving as the discipline does from intellectual reactions to and theories of social change, that its practitioners believe that states can be altered, institutions restructured and communities be redeveloped. "

We shall highlight some of these sociological approaches and their modernist orientation by examining them along four axes, which, while neither exhaustive nor immune to alternative construction, provide useful bases for comparison and contrast:

- First, we shall locate them in their theoretical/political contexts by identifying their theoretical origins – that is, where they came from and where they stood theoretically – and examining the socio-political circumstances of their emergence. While it is too simplistic to see theories simply as 'children of their times', they are connected with the prevailing socio-political climate.

- Second, we shall identify their central concerns – what they see as the most important aspects of the study of crime, what criminology should be about.

- Third, we shall highlight their substantive themes – the key distinguishing ideas that characterise their explanations.

- Fourth, we shall show that in criminological theorising, important connections have been made, sometimes explicit and sometimes implicit, between explanations of social phenomena and the policy solutions offered. Particular approaches to crime therefore often contain unstated assumptions about what should be done about crime.

Delinquent subculture theories

A challenge to individualistic, non-sociological explanations of crime was provided by delinquent subculture theories in the US during the late 1950s and early 1960s, notably in the work of Albert Cohen (1955) and Richard Cloward and Lloyd Ohlin (1960). These theories, although differing from the non-sociological approaches in the key variables used to explain crime, were rooted firmly in the positivist theoretical tradition. Positivists saw the social world as an objective entity that could be directly observed, just like objects with regular features in the natural world. Human behaviour was considered to be subject to the same principles of cause and effect that typified the behaviour of physical objects: human beings reacted to external social forces that constrained them to behave in certain ways. Hence, the explanation of social behaviour centred on the social causes that determined that behaviour.

Within that tradition, delinquent subculture theories identified an unproblematic reality for their subject matter. Crime and criminals were social phenomena and subject to relations of cause and effect. They were 'out there' waiting to be examined and explained. Criminals and delinquents were social actors whose behaviour was determined for them and who were different from non-criminals, and hence sociologists should seek the causes of these differences.

The political position of this approach was essentially liberal positivism, in that it blamed the prevailing social order for crime, but the critique was essentially a mild one, which identified malfunctions in the social order but saw them as rectifiable without the wholesale restructuring of society. The social order was relatively viable, if somewhat flawed. Such a view chimed well with post-war liberal optimism about the possibility of social engineering by means of programmes of social reform, social welfare and education, and with the gradual recognition (particularly in the US) of the value of the social sciences and their potential for problem solving.

When we look at the central concerns of delinquent subculture theories, we can see how their acceptance of a given, relatively non-problematic social reality shaped those concerns. It led them to accept as real the official picture of crime provided by government statistics of recorded crime, and to accept the need to explain a distinctive social pattern of crime and delinquency – that crime was a particularly male, adolescent, working-class, urban phenomenon. For delinquent subculture theorists, these were the social facts of crime, and their positivist orientation led them to conclude that these social facts must have social causes, that social structural arrangements were the key crime-producing agents. Their central concern, then, was to identify the social causes of criminality in social environments and social experiences.

This marked an important step away from the conception of criminality as a property of individuals towards a view of crime and delinquency as rooted in social systems and therefore explicable in terms of social systems. That is, delinquent subculture theories rejected the idea that the causal factors of crime and delinquency lay within individuals who were somehow abnormal or different in their biological or psychological make-up. Rather, they were normal social actors whose motivations were shaped by their (unfavourable) social circumstances and experiences. More specifically, crime and delinquency were seen as resulting from the way in which society worked – or, more accurately, from the way in which it was not working perfectly.

Many delinquent subculture theorists took their inspiration from Robert Merton's (1949) reworking of Durkheim's (1952) notion of **anomie**. For Durkheim anomie implied a state of normlessness in society. For Merton, too, anomie involved a

Anomie
For Durkheim (1952), a social condition where the norms guiding conduct break down, leaving individuals without social restraint or guidance (see *norms*).

BOX 14.1 Crime, gender and age

Although official data do not include the class backgrounds of those found guilty or cautioned, they do provide a gender and age profile for convicted offenders. As the data in Table 14.3 reveal, young males figure most prominently among those dealt with by the police and courts.

By definition, of course, these figures consist only of known offenders involved in recorded and solved crimes, and, as such, they do not allow us to draw any firm conclusions about the perpetrators of the much larger number of unrecorded and recorded but unsolved crimes.

TABLE 14.3 Offenders found guilty of/cautioned for indictable offences, by gender, age and type of offence, England and Wales, 1998 (rate per 10 000 population)

	Age 10–15		16–24		25–34		35+	
	Males	Females	Males	Females	Males	Females	Males	Females
Theft/handling stolen goods	133	73	221	75	88	30	18	7
Drugs	15	2	177	18	70	10	9	1
Violence against the person	31	11	74	12	33	5	8	1
Burglary	40	4	66	3	18	1	2	–
Criminal damage	11	1	18	2	8	1	1	–
Robbery	6	1	11	1	2	–	–	–
Sexual offences	3	–	4	–	3	–	2	–
Other indictable offences	11	3	104	21	61	13	12	2
All indictable offences	250	95	674	131	282	61	53	12

Source: Office for National Statistics (2000a).

disjunction or breakdown in social arrangements, and more specifically a lack of balance between elements of a society's culture and its social structure.

CONNECTIONS For a fuller account of Durkheim's work, see Chapter 17, pages 470–6.

Building on Merton's ideas, delinquent subculture theorists argued that crime and delinquency were a product of the imbalance between society's culturally prescribed goals and its opportunity structures. The ideology of success had permeated Western liberal democratic societies, with status and material rewards being presented as an attainable outcome for anyone who worked hard. Thus, the good life was attainable even for those from the most humble backgrounds if they put their backs into it.

But for some social groups – notably young working-class males – there was a chasm between their lived experiences and the American Dream to which they were exhorted to aspire by the state, the education system, the mass media and other institutions. That is, there was a gap between the culturally prescribed success goals and the availability of legitimate opportunities to achieve them. This gap generated a sense of frustration and strain. Working-class male youths were bombarded with images of success and exhortations to 'make it', and they came to share a common commitment to high aspirations and ambition. But cold reality revealed that they were unable to take advantage of the legitimate opportunities available, largely because their family socialisation had left them ill-prepared for succeeding in the middle-class environment of the school and college.

Young working-class males had to find a way to come to terms with this, and they did so by forming delinquent subcultures that provided a collective solution to the problems of status frustration and thwarted aspirations by constructing alternative criteria of status and success. As Cloward and Ohlin (1960, pp. 19–20) put it: 'Delinquents have withdrawn their support from established norms and have invested officially forbidden norms of conduct with a claim to legitimacy in the light of their special situation.' Members of delinquent subcultures, then, rejected conventional values. They might not have been able to succeed in terms of the middle-class standards of school and college, but they were good at what the delinquent subculture valued – they could excel at fighting, doing 'dares', flouting the rules and causing trouble at school, vandalism, petty theft and the like. In so doing, they gained status among their peers and were able to raise two fingers to respectable society and its values and standards. Embracing the delinquent subculture allowed 'the explicit and wholesale repudiation of middle-class standards and the adoption of their very antithesis' (Cohen, 1955, p. 130).

Turning to the fourth axis of our analysis (the link between explanation and policy solutions), the liberal origins of delinquent subculture theories were apparent in their proponents' belief that the social structural defects that were generating the strain experienced by young working-class males could be eradicated by partial social repair work. Tinkering with social arrangements – by way of ameliorative social reforms designed to re-socialise or rehabilitate alienated youths and allow them to compete successfully – was seen as legitimate. If the problem was inequality of opportunity and the consequent formation of groups committed to delinquent values, then the solution was to bridge the gap between aspirations and achievement by expanding the opportunities available to them, such as better educational opportunities and social enrichment

BOX 14.2 The delinquent subculture

[I]t may confidently be said that the working class boy ... is more likely than his middle class peers to find himself at the bottom of the status hierarchy whenever he moves in a middle class world, whether it be of adults or of children. To the degree to which he values middle class status, either because he values the good opinion of middle class persons or because he has to some extent internalised middle class standards himself, he faces a problem of adjustment and is in the market for a solution...

The delinquent subculture offers him status as against other children of whatever social level, but it offers him this status in the eyes of his fellow delinquents only.... He can perfect his solution only by rejecting as status sources those who reject him. This, too, may require a certain measure of reaction-formation, going beyond indifference to active hostility and contempt for all those who do not share his subculture ...

The problems of adjustment to which the delinquent subculture is a response are determined, in part, by those very values which respectable society holds most sacred. The same value system, impinging upon children differently equipped to meet it, is instrumental in generating both delinquency and respectability.

Source: Cohen (1955, pp. 119, 136–7).

programmes to combat the value systems that encouraged delinquency. This line of thought found practical expression in the US in the early 1960s with the Mobilisation for Youth project and the War on Poverty project of the Kennedy and Johnson administrations respectively.

Labelling theory

Labelling theory of the late 1960s was distinct from delinquent subculture theories and had a different theoretical/political basis. The theoretical underpinnings of this approach derived from social action theory and **symbolic interactionist** approaches – notably in the work of George Herbert Mead (1934) and Charles Cooley (1909). It emerged as part of the interpretivist critique of positivist and structural sociology.

Symbolic interactionism
A theoretical approach focusing on the role of symbols and language in human interaction.

Whereas positivist sociology saw social reality as something absolute and directly observable 'out there', labelling theory adopted an anti-positivist relativism in which social reality was not straightforward, pre-given and absolute but was socially constructed, problematic and open to interpretation. It is illuminating to identify the socio-political context of its development and hence the reason for its attraction to many theorists. The 1960s were marked by challenges to authority and official views of the world in the form of political protests, radical youth subcultures and alternative lifestyles and value-systems. The anti-Vietnam War movement, hippies, radical students and others were unwilling to sit back and accept the official interpretations of the world. Rather, they saw them as merely one version of social reality (albeit a powerful one) that could be tested and contested.

CONNECTIONS The interactionist approach is explained in more detail in Chapter 18. See pages 501–5 in particular.

Labelling theorists such as Howard Becker (1963) and Edwin Lemert (1961) reflected that relativist stance in their approach to crime and deviance. Their aim was to counteract the deterministic assumptions of traditional positivist accounts of crime, and they rejected both the legitimacy and the practical utility of any simple search for the causes of crime. Their position was anti-etiological, that is, they moved the central focus of the study of crime away from causal motivational questions ('what makes them do it?') to questions of definition ('which behaviour and whose behaviour is defined/labelled as crime and why?'). They analysed the processes and consequences of interaction and reaction among the key social actors involved, and an examination of labelling theory's substantive themes reveals their central concerns.

One key notion stands out – that the labelling of individuals as 'criminals' is essential a selective and not a universal process. We all commit crimes at some time or other, but not all of us are caught. Moreover, those who are caught are not all labelled as criminal – their behaviour may be ignored, excused or subject to a caution by the police. Thus, the distinction between criminals and non-criminals (the basic starting point for positivist approaches) is fortuitous and highly problematic, and hence a quest for some magical differentiating feature between them is doomed. So, how does labelling happen? How does the behaviour of some people come to be officially designated as criminal?

Labelling theory's answer is that labels emerge from the interaction between those who have committed offences and a range of other people involved in the process – victims, witnesses, police officers, social workers, judges and lawmarkers. Subtle (and not so subtle) exchanges and perceptions are at work in shaping the outcome of

BOX 14.3 The application of labels

Social groups create deviance by making the rules whose infraction constitutes deviance, and by applying those rules to particular people and labelling them as outsiders. From this point of view, deviance is not a quality of the act the person commits, but rather a consequence of the application by others of rules and sanctions to an 'offender'. The deviant is one to whom that label has successfully been applied; deviant behaviour is behaviour that people so label.

Source: Becker, (1963, pp. 8–9).

Deviance amplification
A spiralling sequence of interaction between deviants and those reacting to their behaviour (typically agents of control, such as the police), which generates further deviance and therefore further punitive responses.

Self-fulfilling prophecy
The situation where social actors construct their self-image from the reactions of powerful and persuasive others, thereby acting out or living up to the characteristics attributed to them, thus confirming the original evaluation.

'deviance situations'. These perceptions influence whether suspected offenders find themselves receiving the label 'criminal'. Factors in these exchanges include suspects showing lack of respect to police officers, whether the victims are articulate, assertive and socially influential, police officers' and judges' images of typical offenders, and so on.

This emphasis on interaction means that as much attention has to be paid to the activities of those conferring criminal labels as to those on whom they are conferred. Hence, understanding crime involves studying the police, the courts, and other agencies of social control as well as offenders, particularly since labelling theorists stress the importance of power in both the enforcement and the construction of laws. Those with power benefit from it, and those without power are disadvantaged when laws are constructed and enforced. Law enforcement by the police and courts is a selective process in which certain social groups are more vulnerable to arrest, prosecution and punishment. They tend to be those of lower social class, those with a non-white ethnic background, and the young – groups with less power and fewer social resources to resist labelling (see Box 14.4). We should also look at how legal rules defining crime come about, and at the definers of crime – that is, those involved in the making of laws. For labelling theorists, laws reflect the interests, moral concerns and ideological assumptions of those in positions of power in society.

Labelling theorists' interactionist inclinations have led them to focus on what happens to labelled individuals. In their view, social control through the application of criminal labels has adverse consequences for recipients and society alike. Being labelled a criminal and treated as such damages individuals' social identity and self-image – it places them outside conventional society, seriously restricts their chance of a normal life and undermines their self-esteem. The likely results are deeper involvement in criminal activities and subcultures, and conformity to the negative label that has been applied – that is, labelling leads to **deviance amplification** and the realisation of a **self-fulfilling prophecy**.

BOX 14.4 Selective law enforcement – stop and search

The police practice of selectively stopping and searching suspected offenders has long provoked controversy in the UK and elsewhere, not least because ethnic minority people, particularly young Afro-Caribbeans and Asians, are disproportionately (in terms of their representation in the total population) stopped and searched, as various studies and the data below reveal. According to Statewatch (1999), black people in Britain are 7.5 times more likely to be stopped and searched and four times more likely to be subsequently arrested than white people. The proportion of people 'of ethnic origin' stopped and searched in London in 1993/4 was 42 per cent of the total there, and ethnic minority people accounted for 21.6 per cent of the national total.

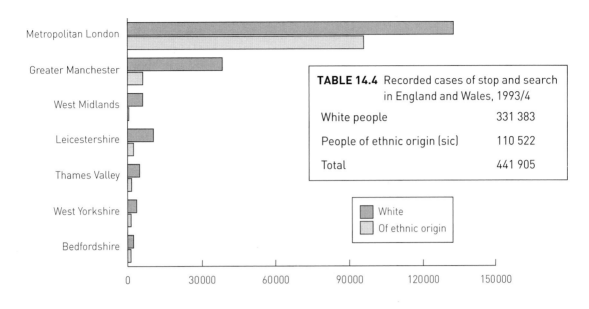

CHART 14.3 Stop and search, by police force, England and Wales, 1993/4.

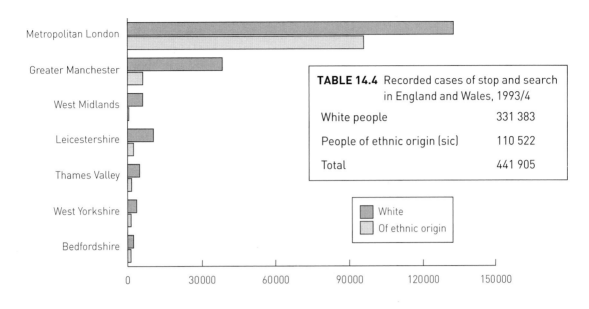

TABLE 14.4 Recorded cases of stop and search in England and Wales, 1993/4

White people	331 383
People of ethnic origin (sic)	110 522
Total	441 905

Source: *Statewatch Bulletin*, vol. 6, no. 2 (March/April 1996).

The connection between explanation and policy prescription in labelling theory follows directly from this. Put baldly, negative labels are more trouble than they are worth, both for those on the receiving end and for society and the social agencies charged with the responsibility of affixing them and administering the punishment and sanctions associated with them. So the solution is to do something about the negative labelling process, to eliminate or significantly reduce the **stigmatising** effects of criminal labels.

One logical strategy is to get rid of such labels altogether – that is, to de-criminalise certain offences. For example, in the sphere of drug taking, labelling theorists argue that those using (soft) drugs do no one any harm and that their criminalisation, prosecution and labelling is counter-productive, because it forces them to commit other crimes to pay their fines, buy more drugs and so on. Similarly, the criminalisation of prostitution has generated spin-off problems such as kerb crawling, exploitative pimping and so on.

Advocates of de-criminalisation clearly face the problem of how far such a policy should go – for example, would it be appropriate to apply it to robbery and personal violence? Hence, some supporters of labelling theory advocate reducing rather than eliminating the label of criminal by de-escalating the punishment administered to convicted offenders. Typical strategies include alternatives to continuous imprisonment (which cuts offenders off from socially integrating interactions with family, workmates and friends), such as community service, weekend imprisonment and so on.

While labelling theory's emphasis on the problematic nature of social reality and on the socially constructed dimensions of crime and deviance has had a powerful impact on the agenda of criminology, its micro-sociological inclination and its underdeveloped analyses of structures have been seen by some as limiting its explanatory power.

Stigmatisation
The process in which social behaviour or an attribute becomes subject to social disapproval and is discredited, resulting in spoiled identity in the eyes of others and possible exclusion from normal social interactions.

QUESTIONS When walking down a lonely street at night, would you feel more uncomfortable if a group of young men or young women were approaching you? Would it make any difference if they were black? Write a paragraph on how media representations of criminals and criminality might have affected your answer to these questions.

Marxist criminology

Dissatisfaction with labelling theory's failure to provide an adequate structural analysis of crime in the 1960s was highlighted by the development of a Marxist criminology in the 1970s, as seen in the work of Frank Pearce (1976), William Chambliss (1976) and Richard Quinney (1980), among others. As we have suggested in other chapters, Marxist approaches employ a structural-conflict model of society and social relations, assigning central importance to economic arrangements and seeing societies as characterised by divisions of interest and class conflict. The Marxist criminologists of the time shared this same broad theoretical orientation. Once again, a distinctive theoretical–political context is evident, in that the late 1960s and early 1970s saw a resurgence of interest in Marxist theorising in sociology. Moreover, that interest reflected the social, economic and political ferment of the time. It was an era in which consensus politics was eroded and radical social and political movements became more prominent. Strong trade unions were pressing for and defending workers' rights in a climate of intense industrial conflict and militancy, Western capitalist countries were experiencing a decline in economic growth and a problem with competitiveness, and the less acceptable face of capitalism – class division, inequality, poverty, Third World exploitation and imperialism – was exposed to critical scrutiny.

The central concerns of Marxist criminology reflected much of the above, with a stress on fundamental social and class divisions and rejection of the myth of a sound society built on a value consensus. These theorists were concerned to develop a materialist analysis, a political economy of crime – that is, one that had as its central structural framework the economic base of society and that located crime within the systems and social relations of capitalist production. Moreover, they sought to rectify a major omission in traditional positivist criminology, namely that it had managed to produce an analysis of law breaking – the violation of the state's legal rules – without constructing a theory of the state and the legal system. For these Marxists, there were political dimensions to crime, which necessitated a central place being given to the role of the state and the legal system in any explanatory framework. Thus, the study of crime could not merely be a matter of uncritically analysing behaviour that violated legal norms, since that would mean ignoring those political dimensions and perpetuating the pluralist myths of impartial law and a simple 'arbiter' role for the state.

In the substantive themes of this approach, there is a strong emphasis on the connection between crime and capitalism. High levels of crime in capitalist societies are unsurprising, because capitalism is a crime-creating *system* by virtue of the motivations and aspirations it encourages in people and the class relations and inequalities that characterise it. It promotes and prioritises self-interest, personal gain and the accumulation of wealth and material possessions as supreme virtues and goals. It persuades (through a culture of advertising and media fiction) that life is incomplete without expensive clothes, the latest stylish car, and high-tech leisure items and domestic appliances, and in doing so it motivates individuals to accumulate by both legal and illegal means. People set out to achieve these goals with the resources and options they have at their disposal. Upper-class businessmen have more legal means to realise their material desires (though, as Marxists argue, they frequently use illegal ones), but working-class people have fewer options available to them, one of which is crime. So, if some working-class people resort to crime, this is because they are at the sharp end of the unequal distribution of resources that typifies capitalist social and economic arrangements. According to Taylor *et al.*, (1975, p. 34):

> Property crime is better understood as a *normal* and conscious attempt to amass property than as the product of *faulty* socialisation or inaccurate and spurious labelling. Both working class and upper class crime ... are *real* features of a society involved in a struggle for property, wealth, and self-aggrandisement. ... A society which is predicated on unequal right to the accumulation of property *gives rise* to the legal and illegal desire to accumulate property as rapidly as possible.

In any case, the official picture of crime and the typical criminal is distorted by the fact that laws are not neutral – they do not embody a widespread value consensus and they do not work impartially for the benefit of everyone. While laws are occasionally used against powerful groups, they essentially reflect partisan class interests: they predominantly benefit and secure the interests of a dominant class, and largely work against subordinate groups. The designation of certain kinds of behaviour as 'criminal' is the outcome of the dominant class successfully enshrining its definition of crime in legal statutes. This definition simultaneously legitimises the status quo, criminalises activities that threaten the reproduction of capitalism and conceals its inequalities.

BOX 14.5 Crime and capitalism

An understanding of crime ... begins with an analysis of the political economy of capitalism. ... Those who own and control the means of production, the capitalist class, attempt to secure the existing order through various forms of domination, especially crime control by the capitalist state. Those who do not own and control the means of production, especially the working class, accommodate and resist the capitalist domination in various ways. Crime is related to this process ...

[W]hen work is thwarted as a life-giving activity, the way is open for activity that is detrimental to self and others. At the same time, some of the behaviours that follow from alienated work are an attempt to set things right again. Some behaviour is a conscious rebellion against exploitation and inhumane conditions. And there is the responsive activity which, in a reproduction of capitalism, is pursued for economic survival or gain. Activity of a criminal nature becomes a rational and likely possibility under the conditions of capitalism. All of this is to say that crime – including both crime control and criminality – is a by-product of the political economy of capitalism.

Source: Quinney (1980, pp. 66–7, 100–1).

Thus, for Marxist criminologists, laws primarily protect capitalist property. They are disproportionately directed against shoplifting, burglary, car theft, vandalism and so on, rather than financial swindles, business crime, tax evasion and industrial pollution by multinational companies. Large corporations and business leaders are sufficiently powerful to avoid criminal labels being attached to their activities. The (limited) prosecution of corporate and white-collar crimes sustains the illusion that the law is non-partisan. However, a second illusion is created by this selective construction and enforcement of the law: working-class street crime, rather than upper-class 'suite' crime, comes to epitomise the crime problem, both officially and in the minds of working-class people themselves.

When addressing the question of what to do about crime, the Marxist policy solution is simple yet monumental: if capitalism creates crime, then the solution is clear – get rid of capitalism in a root-and-branch restructuring of society through wholesale social, economic and political change. Anything else would be insufficient, and would represent irrelevant tinkering with an essentially irredeemable system. Piecemeal social reforms would be inadequate because they would not confront the real basis of crime – the capitalist social, economic and political structure. For example, reform of the penal system might make life marginally more comfortable for prison inmates, but it would do little to alter the fundamental inequalities brought about by capitalism and its criminal justice system. What is required is the restructuring of society to transform it from capitalism to socialism.

Left Realism

One reaction in the mid 1980s to the Marxist approach and Right Realism (which we shall examine shortly) came from theorists such as Jock Young, John Lea and Roger Matthews, who called themselves Left Realists (Lea and Young, 1984; Young, 1986, 1992). These writings provided an analysis of crime that started from a structural theoretical position. They maintained that it was important to locate the roots of crime in fundamental social and economic relationships, but they accorded structural factors less importance in the causation of crime. Left Realism emerged in a political context in which the New Right was dominant. Those on the left were on the defensive politically and intellectually, as political parties wedded to **neo-liberal** economic and political philosophies had won a series of electoral victories in the UK, the US and elsewhere, while the communist regimes of the Soviet Union and Eastern Europe, originally founded on Marxist ideas and principles, had become progressively unstable and ultimately collapsed.

The Left Realists chose their title deliberately to distinguish themselves from their Marxist predecessors. The latter, in their view, had over-simplified the criminological agenda into one in which a big, bad capitalism and its biased, dominant-class-orientated legal and criminal justice system exploited the working class and disproportionately labelled as criminal those working-class people who committed offences. The Left Realists aimed to correct the 'left idealism' of that approach, because it risked under-estimating how much of a problem crime actually was. Because substantial increases in crime had occurred, they sought to re-emphasise the reality of the crime problem, the rational basis of people's fear of crime, and the need to do something about it. In other words, they stressed the need to take seriously both the problem of crime and the problem of crime control.

For Left Realists then and now, a full understanding of crime can only come through a consideration of what they call the 'square' of crime – the state, the public at large, offenders, and victims – and the interplay between them. For example, the relations between the state and the public will shape policing priorities and the degree of public cooperation, and therefore police effectiveness. Similarly, the relations between the state and offenders, in the form of penal policies, will influence the rates of **recidivism**.

Neo-liberalism
A form of right-wing philosophy associated with Thatcherism and laissez-faire liberalism (see *Thatcherism* and *laissez-faire liberalism*).

Recidivism
The tendency for those who have committed crimes to lapse into further offending after release from prison, for instance.

Figure 14.1 Although young men are much less likely to admit to fear of crime than women and older people, they are far more likely to be involved in criminal or violent incidents.

> **QUESTION** Does imprisonment work? Consider the arguments for and against extended imprisonment as a means of controlling crime. You should include in your arguments concepts such as recidivism, deterrence, rehabilitation, protective custody and revenge.

In their substantive themes, Left Realists suggest that the Marxist/radical position neglects one important fact: that victimisation is unevenly distributed among the population, that crime is a real problem for the working class (and for ethnic minorities and women) because they are its principal victims (see Box 14.6). So, instead of seeing crime predominantly as a problem of the capitalist system, we should recognise that it is concentrated in inner cities and on working-class housing estates, and that it is committed *by* working-class people *against* other working-class people – that is, most crime is intra-class. Left Realists acknowledge that the official picture of crime does not tell the complete story: that white-collar and corporate crime is under-represented in official data and that the police and the criminal justice system may well discriminate against certain categories of offender at certain times. But they reject the idea that the crime problem is simply a social construction, fashioned by official bias. For example, although police and judicial practices may exaggerate the involvement of black youths in crime, Left Realists insist that the higher levels of officially recorded black crime are a reality and not merely the product of racist law enforcement, prosecution and sentencing.

But what causes crime? Left Realists share with their Marxist counterparts an emphasis on structural inequality as a key component of crime causation, but they avoid the dangers of a narrowly materialist or economic reductionist theorising. For them,

BOX 14.6 Unequal risk of victimisation

Local and national crime surveys have revealed that the risk of being a victim of crime is not equally distributed across the population. The 1998 British Crime Survey found that those with a relatively young head of household, single parent families, those with a low household income and/or no work, those living in privately rented or local authority or housing association accommodation, and those living on council estates and/or in inner cities were disproportionately at risk of burglary, vehicle-related theft and violence (see Tables 14.5, 14.6 and 14.7).

The 1996 survey suggested that ethnic minorities, especially Pakistanis and Bangladeshis, had a statistically higher risk of being victims of crime than white people, partly because they were younger, of lower socio-economic status and more likely to live in high-risk areas in rented/local authority accommodation (see Chart 14.4).

TABLE 14.5 Proportion of all burglary incidents experienced by high risk groups

	Proportion of households in sample	Proportion of all burglary incidents experienced
Head of household aged 16–24	4%	12%
Single parent household	5%	14%
Head of household unemployed	3%	5%
Private renter	12%	20%
Inner city area	13%	21%
Council estate area	17%	28%
High physical disorder	12%	27%

Source: 1998 British Crime Survey.

TABLE 14.6 Proportion of all vehicle-related thefts experienced by high risk groups

	Proportion of households in sample[1]	Proportion of all vehicle-related thefts experienced
Head of household aged 16–24	3%	4%
Single parent household	4%	5%
Head of household unemployed	2%	3%
Private renter	11%	13%
Inner city area	9%	16%
Council estate area	13%	17%
High physical disorder	9%	14%

[1] Based on vehicle-owning households.

Source: 1998 British Crime Survey.

TABLE 14.7 Proportion of all violent incidents experienced by high risk groups

	Proportion of adults in sample	Proportion of all violent crime experienced
Men aged 16–24	5%	25%
Women aged 16–24	7%	13%
Single parent	5%	8%
Respondent unemployed	2%	5%
Private renter	12%	29%
Inner city area	13%	18%
Council estate area	17%	23%
High physical disorder	12%	18%

Source: 1998 British Crime Survey.

CHART 14.4 Risk of crime in 1995

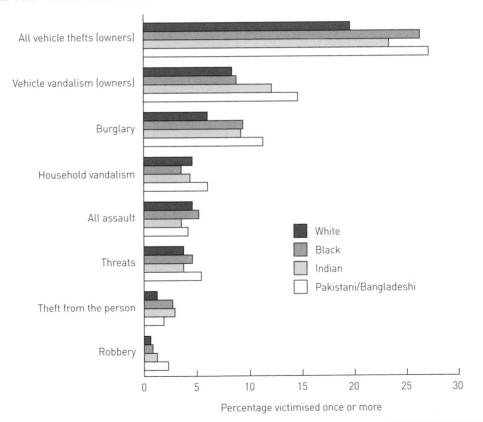

Percentage victimised once or more

White
Black
Indian
Pakistani/Bangladeshi

Source: 1996 British Crime Survey.

crime is not simply related to structural inequality: there is no straightforward correlation between poverty, material deprivation, unemployment and involvement in criminality – if that were so, far more working-class and black people would be engaged in crime. Rather than seeing offending in simple deterministic terms, we need to consider the subjective understandings and choices of those involved in crime.

Left Realists echo the themes of delinquent subculture theories by arguing that crime is produced by relative deprivation and marginalisation. It is committed predominantly by those who find themselves on the edge of society, who have a sense of being worse off than others and who feel that their situation is fundamentally unjust. While such sentiments are likely to be felt more keenly and frequently by working-class and black people, they are not exclusive to these groups. The feeling of relative deprivation can exist throughout the social structure, thus motivating criminal behaviour among the better-off, and such motivation might be intensified by changing economic circumstances or shifts in the prevailing political ideology which intensify individualism, competitiveness and a 'me-first' culture.

However, Left Realists see some groups as particularly and increasingly vulnerable to relative deprivation and marginalisation, most notably young people from working-class and ethnic-minority communities in the inner cities. Such groups have a sense of exclusion, resentment and grievance at their lack of opportunity to realise their expectations and satisfy societally defined needs. Black Afro-Caribbean youths are especially susceptible: they are predominantly working class and they have the additional disadvantage of being on the receiving end of racial discrimination and prejudice. The result is that they enjoy less success in education and in the competition for good jobs, and they suffer higher levels of unemployment. This leads to a sense of alienation and marginalisation and a greater likelihood of involvement in both petty and serious crime.

As for the policy solutions advocated by Left Realists, they espouse a rather different approach from that of Marxist criminologists, whom they characterise as offering only utopian solutions (for example, getting rid of capitalism) and as being unwilling to involve themselves in policy debates about crime. Left Realists argue that this runs the risk of leaving a vacuum in the policy debates on crime and allows others of less acceptable political persuasions to dominate the policy agenda. Hence, they point to the practical possibility, social desirability and political necessity of devising ways of doing something about crime, and to the legitimacy of modest, marginal improvements when doing so.

For them, dealing with the crime problem requires multi-level strategies. At the macro level, the pursuit of social justice is essential, requiring the government to improve material rewards, employment opportunities, housing and community facilities by making fundamental shifts in its economic and educational policies. At the intermediate level, it requires more enlightened penal policies that will reduce the prison population and replace imprisonment, when appropriate, with non-custodial alternatives. It also requires more democratically controlled and accountable police forces that are sensitive to the communities in which they work. This necessitates the police rethinking and amending their methods of operation and their style of interacting with sections of the public (for example, with black youths). Such changes will forge greater public trust and co-operation and improve the chance of both clearing up and preventing crime. At the immediate level, it requires 'target-hardening' strategies based on environmental and design changes that will inhibit the ability to commit crime, such as better security measures in housing developments, better street lighting and even changes to the design of phone boxes to make them more vandal-proof.

QUESTION What other target-hardening measures, beyond increased street lighting, could be tried? If you were in charge of a tower block estate and had unlimited funds, how would you alter the design of the estate to make it harder for criminals to operate?

BOX 14.7 Left and Right Realism

Left realism then is the opposite of right realism. Whereas realists of the right prioritise order over justice, left realists prioritise social justice as a way of achieving a fair and orderly society. Whereas right realists descend to genetic and individualist theories to blame the 'underclass', left realists point to the social injustice which marginalises considerable sections of the population and engenders crime ...

Right realism is a new right philosophy: left realism stems from the current debates in democratic socialism. Thus it argues that only socialist intervention will fundamentally reduce the causes of crime, rooted as they are in social inequality; that only the universalistic provision of crime prevention will guard the poor against crime; that only a genuinely democratic control of

the police force will ensure that community safety is achieved.

Thus on the one hand, left realism takes an oppositional political and theoretical stance from that adopted by the realists of the right, while on the other, it consciously avoids collapsing into the romanticism and idealism of much of the radical and critical criminological literature of the 1970s.

Source: Matthews and Young (1992, p. 6).

Right Realism

A common feature of all the approaches so far is that they have been committed to a sociological explanation of crime. Right Realism or New Right criminology, represented most notably in the work of James Wilson (1975) and Ernst van den Haag (1975), departed significantly from that pattern. It first emerged in the 1970s and was developed further in the 1980s as an explicit critique of liberal sociological theorising about crime. While right realists frequently expressed hostility towards attempts to develop theories of crime, distinct theoretical assumptions are evident in Right Realist approaches, based on notions of an essential human nature, combined with voluntaristic conceptions of human action and versions of control theory.

These approaches arose and flourished in a distinct political context – the era of the New Right and the neo-liberal political and economic philosophies of Reaganism and Thatcherism in the US and UK. The emphasis was on limited state intervention in economic affairs and welfare provision, reduced dependence on the 'nanny state', and greater individual responsibility or 'standing on one's own feet'.

The central concerns of Right Realists stemmed from their disdain for sociological criminology, and so they attempted to shift the balance away from (in their view) over-sophisticated and essentially unproductive theorising to the practical business of containment and control. They were thus concerned with devising realistic and workable strategies for dealing with street crime and those who perpetrated it. While they were not optimistic about fully preventing and controlling crime, they maintained that its impact could be limited by appropriate strategies of deterrence. This did not mean greater responsibility for the state in dealing with the crime problem. Instead, Right Realists were anxious to shift the balance of responsibility for confronting the crime problem away from state intervention and towards a partnership between state and citizens.

When we examine the substantive themes of Right Realist analysis, their misgivings about sociological approaches and their antagonism towards the idea of crime as a product of social circumstances stand out clearly. Indeed, they poured scorn on such theorising, arguing that it had been a wasteful and damaging enterprise, taking the study of crime in directions that were both theoretically unproductive and practically undesirable. Liberal and other sociological criminologists had focused on issues of opportunity, deprivation, poverty and so on. For Right Realists, even if it could be established that links between crime and such social variables existed, they were variables that were difficult for the state to manipulate. Moreover, they were variables in which the state had no business intervening – it was not the job of the state to attempt to change social conditions. But in any case, we should be deeply sceptical about those explanations, since there was no real evidence that these social factors were the causes of crime. In fact, Western capitalist societies had seen unprecedented improvements in material prosperity and the opportunities open to people, while at the same time experiencing ever-increasing levels of criminal activity. Thus, the extension of welfare services, poverty reduction policies and education reforms, far from reducing crime, formed the backdrop to a large increase in crime. The growth of welfare had actually contributed significantly to that increase by weakening people's sense of individual responsibility, breeding a culture of dependency and undermining the bonds holding society and communities together.

CONNECTIONS For a critique of the concept of the underclass, as associated with the New Right, see Box 5.5.

This indictment of sociological criminology and welfarism was closely linked to Right Realists' conception of human nature to account for the rising levels of crime. They had a fairly unflattering view of human nature: for them, humans were motivated by self-interest, and high levels of crime were a product of ineffective constraints on their naturally anti-social inclinations and desires. A culture of permissiveness and indulgent self-expression had developed, fostered by over-liberal parenting and by educators and social workers who had failed to inculcate proper morality and the virtues of self-restraint and self-control. The result was a spiralling of street crime – petty theft, vandalism and criminal damage, car theft, physical assaults, burglaries, robberies and the like. Such activities were doubly damaging, in their view: as well as being intrinsically harmful and inconveniencing in themselves, they were also responsible for undermining social order and causing the collapse of people's sense of community. For that reason, such crimes constituted the key problem to be attacked.

Turning now to the Right Realists' policy solutions for crime, their prescriptions contrasted strongly with more sociological approaches. Given their ideas about human nature and people's motivations for criminality, they were under no illusion about the magnitude of the task of reducing crime and accepted that only a certain amount could be done about it. Their policy solutions followed inexorably from their central premise – that is, policies for dealing with crime had to be based on an understanding of human nature. It was necessary to attack those dimensions of the crime problem that could be rectified by practical strategies of deterrence.

If people were motivated to commit crime because of their self-seeking and self-interested nature, then two fundamental strategies were necessary. One was to deter

BOX 14.8	Situational contexts of crime

Essentially, (situational) theories assume that there are always people around who will commit a crime if given a chance, so they do not explain the motivation to commit a crime. Rather, they explain the situations and circumstances in which motivated offenders find that they have the opportunity to commit a crime. Therefore, these theories sometimes are called 'opportunity theories' of crime.

For example, looting often accompanies large-scale disasters such as floods, earthquakes, violent storms, wars and riots. Home owners and store owners flee the disaster, leaving their property unprotected. The police often are busy with more pressing matters, such as saving human lives. Many people who normally would not commit crime take advantage of the opportunities in the situation and

steal whatever they think they can get away with. ... In general, motivated offenders consider ease of access to the target, the likelihood of being observed and caught, and the expected reward. This perspective assumes that offenders are largely rational in their decision-making processes, so it is associated with 'rational choice' explanations of crime.

Source: Vold *et al.* (1998, p. 153).

them from committing crime by increasing the risks associated with it, so that the costs of offending would outweigh the benefits; the other was to reduce the opportunities for offending. Hence, severe punishment in the form of longer custodial sentences in an uncomfortable and demanding prison regime was required, with very long sentences to isolate and incapacitate recidivists and dangerous individuals. However, while severe punishment was important, it was not sufficient. It was also necessary to increase the certainty of detection and punishment by means of more extensive policing.

This was not simply a matter of employing more police officers, but also of how they should carry out their policing tasks to enforce the law and maintain order. Indeed, many Right Realists prioritised the maintenance of order because of what they saw as a vicious circle, in which street crime led to disorder in and the decay of communities, which in turn led to more street crime. They regarded it as vital for the police to be given sufficient powers to enforce the law when it was being broken, and to control the streets by dealing with even trivial instances of unruly behaviour (such as rowdiness, drunkenness and begging). This was epitomised in policies such as 'zero tolerance', where the police confronted anti-social behaviour by applying heavy law enforcement measures. If some rough justice was occasionally meted out, this was an unfortunate but justifiable by-product of maintaining order on the streets, restoring and maintaining public confidence and preserving the community.

Right Realists also insisted that some of the burden of controlling crime and maintaining order should be shouldered by ordinary members of the community. 'Active citizens' should play their part by disciplining and morally educating their children (preferably by reverting to traditional practices in home and school), by working collectively in the community to prevent crime and disorder (through, for example, Neighbourhood Watch schemes), and by diligently protecting their own property (with better domestic security devices and systems).

Feminist criminology

All the approaches examined so far (with the partial exception of Left Realism) focused on males and male crime and made no great attempt to incorporate female offenders into their analysis. Feminist criminology was developed to rectify that omission.

The title 'feminist criminology' is something of a misnomer, as there have been a number of feminist perspectives on the problem of dealing with crime, but in terms of their theoretical–political orientation, they have all been part of the more general critique of sexist and masculinist theorising in sociology and other social sciences. Feminists have argued that the study of crime has been persistently characterised by theories that claim to be general and comprehensive explanations of behaviour, but which in reality have only considered males and male crime.

The political context of this critique was the growth in the 1970s and 1980s of feminist ideas and movements. Their core notion was that women, both historically and contemporarily, had been and continued to be subordinated on the basis of their sex, and that action directed towards the elimination of that subordination was an urgent priority. The principal concern of feminist criminology, as represented in the work of Carol Smart (1976), Ann Campbell (1981), Frances Heidensohn (1985) and others, was to broaden the scope of the criminological agenda in a number of ways. They aimed to expose the absence of women and girls from mainstream (or, as it was sometimes dubbed, 'malestream') criminology, both as offenders and as victims (Walklate, 2001). In so doing, they sought to develop fully sociological analyses of female crime and delinquency, and at the same time to sweep away the tendency to discuss female crime within highly individualistic frameworks that represented women as crude stereotypes and perpetuated sexist images and ideologies. They also sought to highlight sexism in the treatment of women in the criminal justice system and penal policy. Finally, they stressed that bringing women into criminology required greater attention to be paid to them as victims and to the processes and consequences of victimisation.

In their substantive themes, the feminists' main complaint about much sociological and non-sociological work on crime was that it had been conducted as though women were non-existent, so that theories of criminality had predominantly been developed by studying males. They acknowledged that female offending was less frequent (and generally less serious) than that of males. (Official data, for instance, reveal lower recorded crime rates for women and girls, with a male to female ratio of around four to

CHART 14.5 Offenders found guilty of or cautioned for notifiable offences, England and Wales, 1995–99 (thousands)

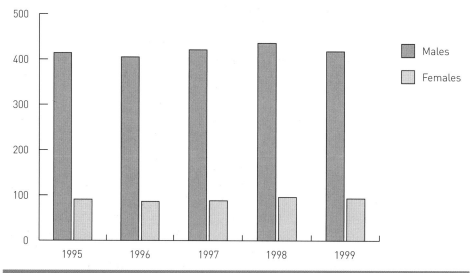

Source: Office for National Statistics (2000a).

Self-report studies

In the context of crime research, these involve questioning people about criminal acts (detected or otherwise) they have committed. The aim of such studies is to amplify the picture of recorded crime provided in official criminal statistics.

Biologism

A form of biological determinism that claims human behaviour is determined by biological or genetic characteristics (see *biological determinism*).

one – see Box 14.1 and Chart 14.5 – though data from some **self-report studies** suggest a lower ratio). But feminist critics argued that this could not justify the marginal attention accorded to female offending and the exclusion of women and girls from criminological theorising. For them, any adequate theory of crime had to take account of the criminal behaviour of both men and women.

They also drew attention to the fact that when female crime was considered in any detail by mainstream criminology, all women were represented in a highly stereotypical and sexist fashion. At the core of much of that theorising was a crude **biologism**, in which explanations of female conformity and criminality rested on highly dubious, biologically based conceptions of women's special or unique 'nature' and/or their individual pathology. Hence, the conforming woman – the 'normal' woman – was by nature passive, virtuous, domestically inclined and respectful of authority, while the non-conforming woman's criminality was determined by biological or physiological abnormality, or biologically founded psychological/emotional disturbance of a hormonal, chromosomal or psycho-sexual kind. While male crime and delinquency were cast in the context of blocked opportunity structures and peer group solidarity, of selective labelling processes or even of capitalism's crime-generating structures, for a long time such social and economic influences remained absent from explanations of female criminality.

For feminist criminologists, it was not simply a matter of amending or converting existing sociological theories to take account of women. Those theories were fundamentally flawed and partial, since they were a criminology of men pursuing 'an exclusive interest in male criminality in a comfortable world of academic machismo' (Heidensohn, 1985, p. 143). A fully social theory of crime had to be capable of reflecting men's and women's behaviour and of highlighting factors that operated similarly on men and women and those which operated differently. Thus, if crime was to be explained as a product of particular social environments, and if males were more frequently involved in crime than females, then it was necessary to identify which social environmental factors exerted a more powerful influence on males and to explain why that was so. Or, as Heidensohn (ibid.) argued, as much attention may need to be paid to female conformity as to female non-conformity if female criminality was to be understood and explained. Either way, any explanation offered had to account for both male and female behaviour and provide an adequate analysis of crime, sex and gender.

As well as highlighting the sexism in much criminological theorising, feminist criminologists sought to broaden the study of female crime by examining the workings of the criminal justice and penal systems. In their view, men controlled women through a variety of mechanisms, agencies and institutions, and the criminal justice and penal systems were no exception. Their studies uncovered evidence of widespread sexism and discrimination in judicial and penal policies towards women offenders. They pointed to the ways in which traditional gender role expectations and perceptions of female offenders as biologically or psychologically abnormal persisted in court decisions and sentences. For example, being judged a 'good mother' could have a significant bearing on the outcome of a court appearance, women offenders were more likely to be viewed as 'disturbed' and in need of medical treatment than men, and girls were frequently penalised or institutionalised for behaviour that was condoned if not encouraged in boys (such as sexual activity or running away from home).

Feminist criminologists were also influential in extending the criminological agenda from an emphasis on offender-orientated studies to a more focused analysis of the victims of crime, particularly the analysis of female victimisation in the realms of domestic violence and sexual offences (Heidensohn, 2000). They showed that women experienced far greater victimisation than was previously acknowledged, and that the incidence of domestic violence and sexual offences against women was far higher than suggested by official data and national crime surveys (see Box 14.9). They were also responsible for highlighting women's fear of crime and the resultant constraints on life-style and life-choices (for example, the difficulty of going out alone or travelling on public transport at night).

BOX 14.9 Hidden victims – domestic violence against women

Feminists describe domestic violence against women as one of the archetypal 'hidden crimes', and one that is all too rarely regarded as a serious offence. Victim surveys have consistently identified domestic violence (of which 80 per cent of victims are women) as the single largest category of assaults:

- The 1998 British Crime Survey estimated that women had been victims of over 580 000 domestic violence incidents in 1997, a year in which the total number of officially recorded cases of violence against the person had been just 250 827.

- On 28 September 2000, in order to obtain a snapshot of the impact of domestic violence, a number of service providers in the UK, including the police and organisations such as Victim Support, Refuge and Women's Aid, were asked to count the number of times they were contacted by domestic violence victims. That day, the police received more than 1300 calls – roughly one every minute – and a larger number contacted Refuge and Women's Aid (Domestic Violence Data Source, 2000).

- In a study conducted by Mooney (1994), 30 per cent of women had suffered physical violence that was more severe than being grabbed, pushed or shaken by their partners or husbands at some point in their lives. Twelve per cent had experienced physical violence in the previous 12 months, of whom 30 per cent had experienced it on six or more occasions.

Of course, as such surveys acknowledge, even estimated figures fail to capture the full extent of domestic violence, as many women are unwilling to report such incidents to researchers or even to define their experiences as domestic violence.

With regard to the fourth dimension of our analysis – policy solutions to crime – the feminist position is less straightforward than those of the other approaches, because there is no single feminist theory of crime, and because the feminist agenda for criminology is more diverse. However, some insights into policy prescriptions can be gleaned.

Firstly, because crime is predominantly a male activity, many feminists consider that the problem is essentially one of (aggressive) masculinity and that no significant inroads into crime can be made until something is done about that. Many radical feminists point to the irredeemability of men, and even the more optimistic think that wholesale reconstruction of the attitudes, values and behaviour of males is an unlikely prospect. Failing that, many feminists advocate the need for male crimes against women to be taken more seriously by the criminal justice system and to be punished appropriately. Greater attention should also be paid to the needs of female (and other) victims of crime and to the procedures for dealing them (for example, the handling of victims of rape and sexual assault).

Feminist policy solutions to female crime tend to focus on strategies for improving the treatment of female offenders. Firstly, rejecting the idea that women criminals are somehow 'abnormal', they insist on abandoning the tendency to medicalise women's crime in the judicial and penal systems. Secondly, feminists question the assumption that penal programmes aimed at turning female criminals into good mothers and homemakers will deflect them away from crime and onto their 'true path'. Finally, many feminist criminologists, recognising that the legal system is fundamentally sexist, call for the removal of gender biases in the construction of laws and their enforcement. For example, women arrested for soliciting are more likely to be prosecuted than their male clients (who may be persistent nuisances as kerb crawlers) or their male pimps (who may be exploiting them financially, coercing them and threatening or perpetrating violence against them).

CONNECTIONS Compare the work of feminists on crime with that of feminists on the family in Chapter 9, pages 251–2.

Modernist criminology and the postmodernist critique

We suggested at the beginning of this chapter that competing approaches to crime between the 1950s and 1990s shared a commitment to the modernist project. Positivist criminology, both sociological and non-sociological, enthusiastically engaged in what David Matza (1964) called 'the search for differentiation' and what David Garland (1994, p. 18) designated 'the Lombrosian project ... that tradition of inquiry, begun by Lombroso, which aims to differentiate the criminal individual from the non-criminal'. While labelling theory, Marxist criminology and Left Realism rejected such differentiation as simplistic, they were still wedded to the modernist principle of a privileged master narrative of crime, a verifiable 'knowledge' of crime that was superior and more truthful than other accounts. They also insisted on the legitimacy of applying that knowledge to the business of doing something about crime. That is, they maintained that knowledge about crime could be used to tackle the crime problem. Right Realists, too, despite their proclaimed disdain for theorising about crime, embraced distinct theoretical positions that underpinned and informed their prescriptions for dealing with crime. Similarly, the feminist critique, while strongly critical of the partial and frequently sexist character of malestream criminology, nevertheless advocated the construction of a (gender-adequate) theory of crime.

However, the debates within feminist criminology were partly responsible for the beginnings of a postmodern critique of criminology, as advanced by Carol Smart (1990) and others. Postmodernists, as we have suggested elsewhere, reject modernist conceptions of the social world, of knowledge about it, and of the pursuit of progress and a better future. They reject the possibility of large-scale theoretical interpretations of universal application offering unified representations of the world – meta-narratives or totalising discourses, as they call them. Such overarching grand narratives are no longer credible: there is no social totality and hence there is no possibility of a universal social theory in a postmodern world that is diverse, fragmented and indeterminate. Rather, there are multiple claims to truth – a plurality of discourses – competing with each other but having no justification for claiming privileged access to truth (see Box 14.10 for an application of this view to the judicial process). Moreover, such meta-narratives are no longer credible, they cannot serve as guides for human conduct, and the idea of progress and improving the human condition – the basis of the modernist project – goes out of the window.

Smart (1990, p. 77) argues that criminology is particularly vulnerable to the postmodernist critique because 'both traditional and realist criminological thinking are especially wedded to the positivist paradigm of modernism'. That is, they believe in the

BOX 14.10 Discourses and the criminal justice system

Postmodernist criminologists point out that, once people assume one of these 'discursive subject positions' [for example, the police, juvenile gang members, drug dealers, court workers, lawyers – each with their own language systems] then the words that they speak no longer fully express their realities, but to some extent express the realities of the larger institutions and organisations. Because people's language is somewhat removed from reality, people are described as *decentred* – i.e. people are never quite what their words describe and always are tending to be what their language systems expect or demand.

For example, women who have been raped must present their stories to prosecutors, who then reconstruct and repackage the stories into the language of the courts – i.e. 'legal-ese'. The woman may testify at the trial, but her testimony may not deviate from the accepted language system without jeopardising the chances that the defendant will be convicted. Even when the defendant is convicted, the woman who has been raped may leave the court with a deep and dissatisfying sense that her story was never fully told, her reality never fully seen, her pain never fully acknowledged. The language of the court system expresses and institutionalises a form of domination over the victim, and this is one reason that victims so often are dissatisfied with the courts.

Source: Vold *et al.* (1998, p. 272).

need to establish verifiable knowledge or truth about crime and its causes, and to construct explanations that will provide the basis for solutions or strategies of intervention. But, according to Smart, criminology commits the modernist errors of essentialism and totalism. It attributes some essential unity and totality to its objects of study (crime and criminals) and assumes that definitive statements in the form of a general theory of crime can be made about them and solutions applied to them. But they share no unity other than happening to involve infringements of the law. Thus, rejecting crime and criminals as essentialist concepts means, for the postmodernist, that any notion of criminology as a unified discipline or discourse is undermined because the central objects of study are dissolved, and particular categories of crime (such as theft, murder, rape and so on) disappear or become disconnected. The deconstruction of crime means the deconstruction of criminality. According to Smart (ibid., p. 77):

> The whole *raison d'etre* of criminology is that it addresses crime. It categorises a vast range of activities and treats them as if they were all subject to the same laws. ... The thing that criminology cannot do is to deconstruct crime. It cannot locate rape or child abuse in the domain of sexuality or theft in the domain of economic activity or drug use in the domain of health. To do so would be to abandon criminology to sociology; but more importantly it would involve abandoning the idea of a unified problem which requires a unified response – at least at the theoretical level. ... The core enterprise of criminology is profoundly problematic .

This loss of certainty and the rejection of progress has had an impact on crime in postmodern society. For example, Morrison (1995) argues that an underclass has emerged that is disconnected from the mainstream values of consumerism by virtue of unemployment. With the financial support offered to the poor by mainstream society being cut back, their stake in society is falling. The constraint on criminal activity that was exercised through adherence to mainstream moral values is being undercut by the loss of certainty in moral codes. In the postmodern world, with its competing discourses, there is no compelling argument for observing the law in all circumstances. Moreover, the 'discourse of progress', which offered the hope of a better future for the poor, has also been undermined. In such circumstances, the members of the underclass are likely to turn to illegitimate means of obtaining the benefits denied them, such as activity in the black economy or engaging in criminal behaviour.

CONNECTIONS The central ideas of postmodernism are set out in Chapter 19. See especially pages 514–20.

In postmodern societies, this potential for criminality is subject to 'the intensification of resentment' (Denzin, 1984). When expectations, fuelled by pervasive media messages, remain unfulfilled, those in subordinate positions in society increasingly direct their resentment towards those who seem to achieve more. This leads to an increase in violence towards the self and others. While it is difficult to investigate sociologically such subjective feelings as resentment, Morrison (1995) and Denzin (1984) have attempted to apply the insights of postmodernism to the study of crime.

QUESTION So far, postmodernists have offered few policy recommendations on the control of crime. Based on the understanding of postmodernism you have gained from reading this book, suggest three reasons why this might be so.

Conclusion

This chapter has shown that the study of crime is firmly embedded in the modernist project. It has also shown that a number of approaches within this tradition, while differing significantly in their emphases, share a belief in the legitimacy of a definitive narrative on crime and an accompanying programme of social intervention. But the apparent insolubility of the crime problem may well have shaken faith in the effectiveness of these narratives to tell the crime 'story', and indeed in the validity of attempts to do so.

For some, therefore, interest in explanations of crime has given way to concern with a more amorphous array of crime issues, such as fear of crime, victims of crime and media representations of crime, all of which are stimulating and fruitful topics in their own right. This trend towards fragmentation of the criminological project could be seen as confirmation of the postmodernist critique of criminology.

But criminologists who are sceptical about the postmodernists' arguments continue to insist that there is a reality to crime for actors on the ground, and this has consequences for them as victims, members of communities, suspects and offenders in terms of the quality of their lives and their sense of security and safety. The consequences of crime for those living in inner-city areas, for instance, are all too real, be they loss of or damage to property, personal injury, a climate of fear, or a feeling of unease about the policing of their community. Furthermore, the consequences of imprisonment for those convicted of crime – for the juvenile offender sent to a youth custody institution, or for the street prostitute imprisoned for non-payment of a fine – are as real as ever, both during incarceration and upon release.

Chapter summary

- Crime as a social problem has been and remains a major focus of public, political and academic concern.

- Explanations of crime can be usefully compared in terms of their theoretical and political contexts, their central concerns, their substantive themes and their policy prescriptions.

- Delinquent subculture theories have attributed crime to the lack of opportunities available to young working-class males.

- Labelling theorists have stressed the negative consequences of selective labelling, which tends to push labelled offenders into criminal careers.

- Marxist criminologists have blamed the capitalist system for the existence of crime and see it as the main obstacle to solving the crime problem.

- Left Realists have emphasised the need to take crime control seriously and to see relative deprivation and marginalisation as central causes of crime.

- Right Realists have rejected the utility of sociological theorising about crime and stressed the need for policies based on an understanding of human nature to deter people from committing crimes.

- Feminists have accused criminological theorising of being overly concerned with males and of neglecting women, both as offenders and as victims.

- Postmodernists have questioned the viability of criminology's modernist orientation, based on a commitment to using reliable knowledge and theories to construct solutions to the crime problem.

 ## Questions to think about

- Which of the theories of crime considered in this chapter do you find most convincing, and why?
- Given the gap between the male and female crime rates, can differences in the nature of men and women account for this? If not, why not?
- Crime is not only always with us, it also seems to be increasing, despite growing affluence. What policy solutions would you offer for its control?

 ## Investigating further

Hobbs, Dick (1998) *Doing the Business: Entrepreneurships, the Working Class and Detectives in the East End of London*, Oxford University Press.

> A classic and highly readable ethnographic study of the policed (petty criminals) and the police by a partial insider who engaged in both overt and covert observation to further his research, and did a lot of drinking in pubs and some thieving in the process.

Maguire, Mike, Rod Morgan and Rob Reiner (eds) (1997) *The Oxford Handbook of Criminology*, 2nd edn, Oxford University Press.

This large collection of contributions to the field offers a wealth of material, both theoretical and empirical. Well worth dipping into.

Morrison, Wayne (1995) *Theoretical criminology: from modernity to post-modernism*, Cavendish Press.

This book provides an overview of competing contemporary theories in criminology.

Walklate, Sandra (1997) *Understanding Criminology: Current Theoretical Debates*, Open University Press.

This is a clear, concise and readable overview of contemporary criminological theory.

15

Knowledge, religion and belief

Aims of the chapter

This chapter examines one of the major questions about the emergence of modern social life: does rationalism, represented by scientific thinking and practices, mean that we, as modern human beings, have access to a way of thinking, and consequently a kind of knowledge, that is superior to any other kind? Or should science be seen as just one more human endeavour, whose knowledge claims are no better and no worse than other kinds? Science is often counterposed to religious thought and knowledge, and we shall consider whether there has been a decline in religious beliefs and practices, or whether they have just changed under conditions of modernity. This debate between forms of knowledge can be described as the 'Great Divide' between supporters of rationalism, supporters of non-rational belief systems and supporters of relativism.

By the end of the chapter, you should have an understanding of the following concepts:

- The Enlightenment
- Positivism
- Hypothetico-deductive method
- Dependent variable
- Independent variable

- Falsification
- Epistemology
- Secularisation
- Rationalism
- Relativism

Introduction

The Enlightenment
An 18th-century philosophical movement based on notions of progress through the application of reason and rationality. Enlightenment philosophers foresaw a world free from religious dogma, under human control and leading ultimately to emancipation for all humankind.

It is only human to want to acquire knowledge one can be sure of. It is also only human to have wishes and desires, hopes and dreams. How, then, can humans discover the truth about their world? Is it possible to find out how things really are, or will our feelings about the way we would like things to be get in the way? According to supporters of science, it is only by using scientific thinking and practices that humans can reveal the truth about the world. While there have always been alternative accounts of how and why the world is as it is, such as religious or magical explanations, advocates of science insist that only science can prove the truth of humans' knowledge claims. According to this view, the emergence of science as a way of thinking and acting represented a great leap forward for humankind. The realisation that humans could think rationally and therefore act scientifically was the defining moment in the history of human thought. The name given to this historical moment is **the Enlightenment**, and it is claimed that the Enlightenment allowed humans, for the first time, to know the real nature of things. According to rationalists, it was during the Enlightenment that humans crossed the 'Great Divide' and moved from ignorance, guesswork and faith to certainty and truth.

Great Divide thinking

A good example of Great Divide thinking can be found in the work of the philosopher and anthropologist Ernest Gellner (1992). Gellner distinguishes between:

- A non-rational knowledge/explanatory system, such as a religion, that 'believes in a unique truth and believes itself to be in possession of it' (ibid., p. vii).

- Relativism, which denies the existence of a unique, objective truth, arguing that all beliefs and knowledge claims have equal validity.

- Rationalism, which (1) believes in the existence of an objective truth but does not think that humans can ever acquire this knowledge for certain and (2) claims that it is superior to any other form of knowledge, not because it argues for the supremacy of any particular set of ideas, but because of its uniquely effective method of producing knowledge.

This is how Gellner (ibid., pp. 56–7) describes relativism, which, for him, totally fails to portray knowledge in the modern world:

> "Relativism ... postulates a symmetrical world. Culture A has its own vision of itself and of culture B, and, likewise, B has its own vision of itself and of A. The same goes for the entire range of cultures. A must not sit in judgement on B nor vice versa, nor must B see A in terms of itself. . .
>
> Often members of both A and B are likely to be somewhat ethnocentric, given to thinking that their own concepts capture the world as it really is, and that the Other should see himself and everything else in their own terms, and is being silly if he fails to do so...
>
> The truth is that all cultures are equal, and no single one of them has the right to judge and interpret the others in its own terms ... above all ... it must not claim that the world is correctly described in its own terms ."

According to Gellner (ibid., p. 57), relativism bears no relation to the actual state of knowledge in modern societies:

> "The world we actually inhabit is totally different. Some two millennia and a half ago, it did perhaps more or less resemble the world the relativist likes to paint ... there was a multiplicity of communities, each with its own rites and legends. It would have been truly absurd to try to elevate one of them above the others, and, still more, to claim that the truth about any one of them was only to be had in the terminology of another ."

Then the world was transformed. The Great Divide occurred when rationalism – a secular, non-religious, non-magical way of thinking – emerged, producing knowledge we now know as natural science. Scientific ideas and practices are unique:

- The knowledge science produces can be applied to any cultural setting.

- When this knowledge is applied to achieve particular ends, it totally transforms human existence.

- Scientific knowledge is indifferent to culture and morals. Indeed, it often contradicts our most deeply held desires and hopes, giving us an account of reality that persistently fails to comfort or console. Nor does science reassure us that things really are the way we would like them to be. This is in direct contrast to previous forms of knowledge.

Unlike relativism, rationalism holds 'all men and minds but *not* all cultures and systems of meaning, to be equal' (ibid., p. 37). Every human mind is capable of discovering the truth, but only by employing the correct method to do so. Rationalism argues that 'there are an awful lot of meanings and opinions about, that they cannot all be right, and that we'd better find, and justify, a yardstick which will sort the sheep from the goats' (ibid., p. 38). The Great Divide opened up when this method was devised. How does it work? What is unique about scientific knowledge production?

CONNECTIONS For a general account of the growth of modernity and the creation of the Great Divide, see Chapter 2, pages 24–40.

What is science?

Positivism
A doctrine that claims that social life should be understood and analysed in the same way as scientists study the natural world. Underpinning the notion that phenomena exist in causal relationships and that these can be empirically observed, tested and measured.

Science operates with specific assumptions, usually associated with the term **positivism**, which can be summarised as follows. Things (phenomena whose existence is identifiable by the human senses) are situated in an endless chain of causation. Anything that the human senses can detect is as it is because it has been caused by some other thing, which our senses also allow us to recognise. However, science deals with abstract phenomena too. Concepts such as volume, pressure, temperature and so on are significant aspects of the reality dealt with by science. But scientists always try to give such concepts physical indicators that are identifiable by the senses. So, a thermometer renders temperature visible, a barometer does the same for pressure and so on. This is called the operationalisation of concepts. To be sure of a cause and effect relationship between things, we have to be able to demonstrate this relationship to other humans. Scientists insist that we can be certain of the causes of phenomena only if we can prove their existence. Such proof can only be acquired through empirical evidence – evidence that the human senses can recognise. That is, scientific knowledge is based solely on facts. How can science guarantee the exclusive factual basis of its knowledge claims?

Science does not claim to make facts – its aim is to reveal their existence. That is, facts are objective in that they exist, whether we like it or not. We may not like the fact that grass is green, or that a full bladder requires emptying, or that smoking is likely to cause lung cancer, but they are natural and biological features of our existence that we can do nothing about. Of course humans are capable of being subjective too. They have opinions and exercise judgements about facts. However, positivism demands that this human ability to have a viewpoint and feelings about how things ought to be must be ignored by scientists when producing knowledge based on empirical evidence. To rely on scientific evidence and trust its account of reality, we must be sure that whatever scientists may personally think, they describe the facts they uncover objectively, ignoring any feelings, favourable or unfavourable, they may have about reality.

Karl Popper (1902–94) was one of the most famous philosophers of science. According to Popper, only one kind of methodological procedure could ensure such an objective, value-free disclosure of the facts of reality. He called this the hypothetico-deductive method. This involves breaking down the world into individual cause and effect relationships and trying to produce empirical evidence about each relationship in isolation from all the others. This aspect of science is sometimes described as the atomisation of reality. Scientists use the term hypothesis to describe a particular cause and effect relationship that is as yet uninvestigated. In the natural sciences, hypothesis testing usually involves the physical isolation in a laboratory of the phenomena

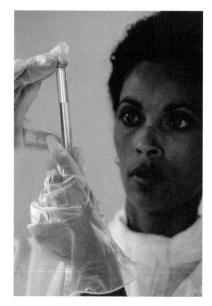

Figure 15.1 Popper argued that hypotheses can never be proved true for all time: instead, scientists must work to refute them, even if this goes against significant personal and professional investment in the ideas.

believed to be in a causal relationship. Laboratory research takes the form of an experiment, which involves measuring, or quantifying, the extent to which something – the independent variable in the experiment – causes something else – the dependent variable.

CONNECTIONS For the impact of science on sociological methods, see Chapter 16, pages 446–50.

According to Popper, however, we can never be sure that things will always remain as the facts suggest at the time we uncover them. As he said in a famous example, just because we have always seen white swans coming round a river bend, this does not prove that a black swan will not appear next time. This inability to be sure of the future means that our knowledge, even if factually based, can only be seen as provisional. Because of this, Popper insisted that experiments must take a definite form. Instead of endlessly repeating the same experiments in the belief that the more times a relationship is demonstrated the nearer certainty we are, the scientist should always try to disprove an hypothesis. Although Popper acknowledged that this goes against a natural human desire to be convinced our ideas are correct, proper science must involve a ceaseless attempt to court failure. That is, science must constantly find new ways of trying to falsify a belief about the world. (As Einstein said, 'While thousands of scientists can't prove me right, it only takes one to prove me wrong.') For Popper, then, the only way science can justify its claim to be superior to other forms of knowledge is to rely on this unique form of cognition, or method of producing knowledge.

Popper acknowledged that in non-scientific thought, such as religions and magic, humans are typically so enthusiastic and reassured by these explanations of reality that they avoid putting them to any real test: 'Popper is of course fully aware that man is, cognitively speaking, addicted to cowardice. Men and societies do put forward theories about the world, but they generally fortify and insure them for all they are worth' (Gellner, 1974, p. 171).

Popper acknowledged that some, if not most, scientists are guilty of the same lack of courage. (The work of Thomas Kuhn explores this tendency in science.) However, Popper was not describing what actually happens in science, but what should happen. Although timidity and wishful thinking are apparent in much scientific work, there are elite scientists who do exhibit courage in their thinking, whose **epistemology** and methodology do match Popper's ideals. For rationalists, when science is practised properly and scientists do invite failure, we have the ultimate form of cognition and knowledge production – distinct from all other forms. This is why science represents such a leap forward (Gellner, 1974, p. 171):

Epistemology
The theory of knowledge and the study of its validity, scope and methods.

" Its success is due not to the fact that it is more certain ... but, on the contrary, that it is less certain, that it accepts and rejoices in uncertainty, seeks it out, and possesses devices, such as accurate and unambiguous formulation, which increase the exposure to risk . "

So, it is the shift from beliefs based on faith and commitment to beliefs based on criticism that produced the Great Divide.

QUESTION How much of this description is familiar to you from your own experience of science, perhaps in school? Were you ever introduced to these ideas in science education? Do you think, therefore, that science is really like this?

Science, rationalism and disenchantment

While appreciating the uniqueness and cognitive power of post-Enlightenment thinking, rationalists are only too aware of the drawbacks of living life on this side of the Great Divide. There are two big problems:

- There is the loss of what Weber called enchantment – a loss of mystery, imagination and faith in the unknown. It is a world in which objectivity triumphs over subjectivity. Things are what they are, not as we would wish them to be; science reveals a cold, inhospitable world where we have no choice about the way things are. According to Weber, a rational world, however efficient and ordered, is a disenchanted world for its inhabitants. Truth is a matter for assessment by employing one yardstick only – the facts. Any other criteria, more human, more personal, almost certainly more comforting, fulfilling and rewarding, are irrelevant: 'Truth is *not* beauty; nor virtue, nor utility, nor the advancement of any political cause' (Gellner, 1979, p. 144).

- Furthermore, although, like everyone else, scientists would like to know how best to live, they cannot expect the knowledge they produce to help them. Science does not provide a 'charter for social arrangements' (Gellner, 1974, p. 184). Not only are our feelings, judgements, values, hopes, aspirations and fears irrelevant for the rational investigation of the world, but scientific evidence about this world cannot tell us how to organise ourselves. Cognitive truths are not moral truths, and knowing what is cannot help us to decide how individuals should live or how human societies should be organised.

Other knowledge systems, though unable to explain the world accurately, at least make humans feel at home in the world. Indeed, as we shall see in the next section, for many thinkers this is precisely the advantage of these systems. Whether religious, magical or whatever, such systems give their believers comfort and succour. The stories they tell are of a universe to which humans naturally belong and in which they have a particular and usually elevated place. Such belief systems not only explain the world, they also tell humans how they should live their lives; they provide both explanatory accounts and morally prescriptive ones.

However, with the rise of science, we leapt the Great Divide. We came to know the falsehoods contained in these other accounts. Uniquely, it is post-Enlightenment, modern humans who can know real truth – but only at a huge cost, because modern humans are denied any moral guidance from their knowledge. This is the double-edged sword of rationality; it arms us with the means to know what really is but provides us with no prescriptions about how we should live. Despite attempts to do so, such as the French Revolution, Nazi Germany and communism, scientific knowledge can never be employed to construct Utopia, and such projects are doomed to failure. Science, though born of specific religious influences, is not a secular religion. It merely presents us with cold reality in a hard-nosed way: 'it desecularizes, disestablishes, disenchants everything substantive: no privileged facts, occasions, individuals, institutions or associations. In other words, no miracles, no divine interventions ... no saviours, no sacred churches or sacramental communities' (Gellner, 1992, p. 81).

Perspectives on scientific and non-scientific knowledge

Symbolic anthropology and phenomenology

For some writers on the sociology of knowledge, the inability of science to offer psychological and emotional comfort explains the presence and influence of non-scientific knowledge in human lives, even in a rational world. The important thing about non-scientific beliefs is the reassurance they give to believers.

Symbolic anthropology and some versions of **phenomenology** argue that all humans require reassurance that the world is a safe and ordered place – that is, they have a need for **ontological security** (Giddens, 1991). Therefore all societies have forms of knowledge that perform this psychological task. Furthermore, unlike secularisation theories, these perspectives do not see non-scientific knowledge as becoming less and less important in modern societies. Since scientific knowledge fails to satisfy the human need for ontological security, we should expect other forms of knowledge to be as influential in rational, scientific cultures as they were in pre-modern ones. Here is a sociology of knowledge that, unlike the believers themselves, cares little about the content or truth of systems of knowledge. It concentrates instead on the benefits they provide for those who do the believing.

Functionalism

Functionalist perspectives also show little interest in the content of beliefs but are in favour of examining their effects. However, unlike symbolic anthropology and phenomenology, functionalism points to the benefits for social organisation which non-scientific belief systems provide and which scientific knowledge fails to deliver. Belief systems are seen as encouraging social order and social stability in ways that rationally based knowledge cannot. From this point of view, the existence of non-rational accounts of reality can be explained by the benefits they offer to society. We should therefore not be surprised to find science and non-science co-existing in our modern world, since they are different kinds of knowledge, performing different functions.

The phenomenological and functionalist perspectives therefore argue that although science is able to tell us how things actually are, it does not tell us how to make our social world a nicer place. Since non-scientific stories do this (albeit at the expense of the truth), they co-exist with science. However, the problem is that those who believe in such stories do think they tell the truth.

CONNECTIONS For a more detailed explanation of the phenomenological approach, see Chapter 18, pages 504–7.

Rationalism

Rationalist writers object to the phenomenological and functionalist approaches, arguing that they fail to explain why believers in systems of non-scientific knowledge do think they tell the truth and that their ideas are right, even though science has shown them to be wrong. We cannot explain forms of knowledge in terms of the beneficial psychological or societal effects that an outside observer may see them as producing. We have to look at the point of view of those who believe in them. People do not believe in God, practise magic or think that witches cause misfortune because they think they are providing themselves with psychological reassurance, or to achieve greater cohesion for the social groups to which they belong. They do so because they think their beliefs are correct – that they tell them the truth about the way the world is. For scholars in this rationalist tradition, the problem of non-scientific knowledge is why people believe in falsehoods.

Nineteenth-century rationalist writers, reflecting the **evolutionist** spirit of their times, tended to explain the lack of rationality and the dominance of false beliefs in pre-modern

---

Phenomenology
In sociology, a focus on the taken-for-granted knowledge that social actors share and which underpins everyday life. It is part of tradition, which focuses on consciousness and meaning rather than on structural social phenomena.

Ontological security
A stable mental state derived from a sense of continuity and order.

Evolutionism
A doctrine based on the notion that historical, biological and social changes are subject to development and progressive unfolding (see *Darwinism*).

worlds in terms of the deficient mental equipment of their inhabitants. Such peoples were seen as possessing a pre-logical, or non-rational, mentality. Twentieth-century rationalist thinking generally rejected such a view, subscribing à la Gellner to the Great Divide position that pre-modern people did not possess inferior minds, but lacked the social and cultural conditions, described by Weber, needed to promote rationalism. Rationalists saw the history of modern societies as the inexorable rise of scientific knowledge and the subsequent decline in non-rational belief. Some of these beliefs – magic, witchcraft – had disappeared, while others – such as religion – had become marginalised. This rationalist perspective has led to secularisation theories of various kinds.

Relativism

The final perspective on knowledge, relativism, takes a different line, questioning the basic claim of rationalism/Great Divide thinking that science provides truth. According to relativists, close inspection of scientific thinking and practices reveals that they are more like those found in non-scientific systems than rationalists claim, and therefore science will not displace non-science in the modern world. This is because science cannot perform the task it sets out to do – to give us objective truth. Relativists focus on scientific method – on how scientific knowledge is produced. They claim that, since scientists are social beings too, scientific activity is so suffused with the social and cultural influences of the scientists engaged in it that, although there may be a true story about reality to be told, scientists can never hope to tell it. This relativist position that all human stories are of equal validity and that the pursuit of objective truth is a doomed project, has led to the critique of the Enlightenment/modernism/rationalism known as post-modernism.

The characteristics of the four perspectives on knowledge, and their relationships with each other are summarised in Table 15.1.

TABLE 15.1 Perspectives on knowledge

	Science	Non-science	Conclusions
Symbolic anthropology, Phenomenology	True	Beneficial for the believer	Co-existence of science and non-science
Functionalism	True	Beneficial for society	Co-existence of science and non-science
Rationalism	True	False	Secularisation in modern societies
Relativism	Flawed	Flawed	Postmodernism

One of the main aims of post-Enlightenment rationalist thinkers is to show how incorrect, non-scientific knowledge is bound to lose significance in proportion to the increase in true (scientific) knowledge in the modern world. According to this position, the secularisation of knowledge is an inevitable feature of modern societies, leading to the marginalisation or even total elimination of unfounded, false beliefs.

 ## Theories of secularisation in modern societies

Secularisation theorists define modernity as the replacement of pre-modern forms of knowledge by science. Non-science does not die out completely, but progressively loses its significance and becomes increasingly marginalised. Different secularisation theorists place a different degree of emphasis on the part played by scientific knowledge in the decline of religion, ranging from those who see science and religion in direct competition to those who reject the role of science in the decline of religion (see Box 15.1). What is not in dispute is that the UK, along with most of Western Europe, has seen a marked decline in religious observance. Church attendance declined from 4.7 million in 1989 to 3.7 million in 1998, or just 7.5 per cent of the population. This is not to say that the Church has no significance – many of us attend church at some time during the year, if only for formal events such as weddings and funerals. Nor should we forget the opportunities for religious observance offered by minority faiths, or by Christian sects that do not appear in official attendance counts. Nevertheless, as a characteristic of the social fabric, church-going no longer has the importance it once had.

BOX 15.1 Science, religion and secularisation

The second big mistake is to suppose that science played a large part in the decline of religion (and hence any weakening in the social standing of science enhances the plausibility of religion). Christianity was not defeated by Enlightenment philosophers and rational scientists. The real explanation of secularisation ... lies in the combination of cultural diversity, competing religious ideas and increasing democracy that brought about an increasingly neutral State and society, while at the same time causing most people to lose certainty in the authority of their religious beliefs and to reflect the weakening of commitment in the liberal attitude towards the socialisation of their children. Over the twentieth century, an increasingly large proportion of children were not raised in a strong religious culture and such vague beliefs as they retained were not constantly reinforced by the social pressure to conform and by living in a world that gave constant background support.

Source: Bruce (2001, p. 15).

Bryan Wilson

Wilson is a writer on secularisation who is alarmed about the nature of life in a society dominated by scientific knowledge. His work is in the tradition of Weber, who saw modern societies as places in which rationality dominates life and thought. Weber saw rationality as concerned with identifying causes and working out technical efficiency, with a focus on how things work and with calculating how they can be made to work more effectively, rather than why they are as they are. According to Weber, such rational worlds are disenchanted. **Existential** questions about the mysteries of human existence, about who we are and why we are here, have become less and less significant.

> **Existentialism**
> A philosophy that espouses free will and responsibility for one's own actions.

Wilson (1982) insists that non-scientific systems – and religious ones in particular – have experienced an irreversible decline in influence. He has engaged in a long debate with those who dispute the secularisation thesis – those for whom religious beliefs and practices in modern societies remain significant. Some of these critics argue that traditional religions, such as church-centred ones, have become displaced by a proliferation of non-traditional ones, for example, cults and sects of various kinds. Others argue that religion has become an individual rather than a collective, organised affair. Still others suggest that functional alternatives to traditional religion, such as nationalism and patriotism, have emerged to promote social solidarity. Wilson does accept the presence of a large variety of non-scientific forms of meaning and knowledge in modern societies, but he argues that this is actually evidence of the decline of religion. The increase in the number and diversity of such systems is evidence of the modern marginalisation of religion – its removal from the central structural location it occupied in pre-modern times. As Hamilton (1995, pp. 172–3) puts it:

> " The situation where one can choose between one religious interpretation and another, where rival interpretations and organisations compete in the 'market place' of religions as Berger puts it, is likely to result in a devaluation or loss of authority for the religious view generally. The pluralistic situations where one can choose one's religion is also a situation where one can choose no religion at all. "

BOX 15.2 The characteristics of a secular society

According to Wilson (1982), secularisation in modernity involves the following features:

- The taking over by political powers of the property and facilities of religious agencies.

- A shift from religious to secular control of the activities and functions of religion.

- A decline in the proportion of time, energy and resources that individuals devote to super-empirical or spiritual concerns.

- The decay of religious institutions.

- The supplanting, in matters of behaviour, of religious commands by demands that accord with strictly technical criteria.

- The gradual replacement of a specifically religious consciousness that ranges from dependence on charms, rites, spells or prayers to a broadly spiritually inspired ethical concern.

- The abandonment of mystical, poetic and artistic interpretations of nature and society in favour of matter-of-fact description and the rigorous separation of emotion from cognitive processes.

Source: Wilson (1982, p. 189).

Wilson (ibid., p. 88) has an alarming vision of the potential consequences of secularisation:

> " At present, in the West, the remnants of religion are, if receding, as yet still in evidence, but generally it may be said that western culture lives off the borrowed capital of its religious past. It is by no means clear what sort of society is coming into being as religious values wane. The consequences, not only for the arts and high culture, but also, and perhaps more importantly, for the standards of civic order, social responsibility, and individual integrity, may be such that the future of western civilisation itself may be thrown into jeopardy. "

Ernest Gellner

As we have already seen, unlike Wilson (and Weber), Gellner (1974) acknowledges that there are drawbacks to living in a world whose main form of knowledge is confined to facts we can do nothing about and that provides us with no guidelines on how to live and how to organise ourselves. In this respect, we are worse off than premodern people, whose knowledge, while incorrect, at least provided them with prescriptions for living. However, Gellner insists that these disadvantages are far outweighed by the enormous technological advances modern societies have experienced as a result of the application of scientific knowledge.

Gellner does not claim that non-scientific knowledge is in the process of dying out. For example, he accepts that religions in various forms continue to attract adherents. He also acknowledges that other forms of belief and meaning, such as those provided by art, music, literature, popular culture (a specifically modern phenomenon), dropping-out, drug taking, political protest and so on are important for many people. But he rejects the relativist interpretation of this situation – that in modernity, scientific knowledge is just one of many accounts of existence, all of which have equal validity. This is because, for Gellner, such alternatives to science are profoundly insignificant when it comes to the

BOX 15.3 Ironic cultures and the meaning industry

'Modern societies are not systematically and consistently secularised; luxuriant, self-indulgent, cosy or ecstatic faiths are present in a thousand forms, new, old or revivalist. It would be most rash to say that they are on the decline. ... But ... all this is froth rather than substance...

'Why is it ultimately superficial? Society continues to be based on a productive, administrative, and order-enforcing technology which is scientific, which transcends cultural boundaries. ... The new pseudo-cultures continue to rely on this technology for a standard of living to which its members are accustomed and which they are certainly not seriously prepared to forego. ... It is precisely because the basic and assured standard of living is so fabulously high that so many can 'opt out' and sacrifice some marginal benefits. ... Such conspicuous abstention from these marginal extras is one thing, and a genuine return to the squalor of pre-industrial poverty would be

quite another. There is no sign whatever that anyone is genuinely willing to opt for the latter; and that whole populations should choose such a course is unthinkable.

'And as it continues to live by and rely on powerful, manipulatively effective, scientific knowledge, society also habitually turns to it in real need, in any field in which this type of knowledge is genuinely established. ... It is only in the residual sphere, where nothing very serious is at stake, that the scientific vision has become optional...

'When serious issues are at stake – such as the production of wealth, or the maintenance of health – we want and expect real knowledge. But when choosing our menu or our rituals, we turn to culture and religion. In these frills of life, we ... must use some culture or other, and select it in some other way. (We must, because our truth no longer generates or selects its own.) But all this is not serious. ...

Culture remains rich and human and is even, in various ways, more luxuriant than it used to be; but it is no longer all of a piece with the serious and effective convictions of a society. ...

'It is for this reason that the Weberian disenchantment thesis is in partial error. What is true is that modern cognition does bureaucratise nature, and must necessarily do so; but, serious cognition need not pervade all aspects of daily life. ... Real knowledge is to be found elsewhere; and it does have the cold forms which ... Weber discerned and anticipated. But more colourful, human, cosier worlds and thought-styles are at the same time available to envelop our daily life, and they have reached their quiet accommodation ... with the island of truth. The world in which we think is not the same as the one in which we live. ... The colder the one, the more fanciful the other, perhaps.'

Source: Gellner (1974, pp. 191–207).

crunch. We have to remember that non-scientific accounts are technically impotent – only science can do things and improve our physical and material circumstances. We are only able to deal with existential questions about meaning, life, death and eternity – 'Who am I?' 'Where am I going?' 'What's it all about?' – because we can take for granted the kind of world that science has constructed for us. It is this that makes Gellner a secularisation theorist. He sees the modern preoccupation with meaning and being as a self-indulgence that is only possible because scientific knowledge has enabled our world to advance so far. Unlike those in pre-modern worlds today, whose overriding priority is to get hold of scientific knowledge in order to begin to develop, we can afford to sit back in the luxury of our well-appointed world and concentrate on navel-gazing. However, when things really matter, we know on which side our bread is buttered.

Michel Foucault

As we have seen elsewhere (see especially Chapter 9), Foucault was a **post-structuralist** who saw human existence as being dependent on forms of knowledge – discourses – that

Post-structuralism A development in French theory that follows on from linguistic structuralism but goes further by treating social life as a 'text' that can be analysed without reference to any author (or creative subject/ actor) (see *deconstruction*).

work like languages. Languages/discourses define reality for us. In order to think at all, we are obliged to use these definitions. The knowledge we have about the world is provided for us by the languages and discourses we encounter in the times and places in which we live out our lives. Thus, who we are, what we know to be true and what we think are discursively constructed. That is, our knowledge and thoughts – our identities – are fashioned by definitions of reality that lie outside our control. In post-structuralist terminology, we are constituted by discourses.

Foucault defined history as the rise and fall of discourses. Social change is about changes in prevailing forms of knowledge. The job of the historian is to chart these changes and identify the reasons for them. Unlike rationalists, however, Foucault saw no element of progress in this process. The replacement of one way of knowing reality is not a victory for truth but simply the result of politics – the existence of power. He had a relativistic view of knowledge that was similar to Kuhn's about scientific knowledge. For Kuhn (1970), scientific knowledge was relative to particular paradigms; while for Foucault, human knowledge in different cultures and times in history was relative to discourses. For both, the production of knowledge was a political process – the outcome of the exercise of power.

The question of power is at the heart of Foucauldian thinking:

- Power is exercised by discourses over subjects (people) because in order to think at all – to 'be' – they have to do so in the terms provided by a discourse: they are subject to the power of the discourse.

- Power is exercised to achieve dominance for particular discourses: they are promoted and sustained by discursive practices – disciplinary or regulatory apparatuses, as Foucault called them, such as those operated by the medical profession.

- Power is exercised because of the dominance of specific forms of knowledge – different groups benefit unequally as a result of the power of a particular discourse.

CONNECTIONS For another view of Foucault and power, see Chapter 8, page 196.

These features are central to Foucault's account of the rise of modern society. What is distinctive about modernity is the ascent of discourses concerned with the control and regulation of the body: 'If Foucault's epistemological work represents analyses of knowledge/power, his historical inquiries centre on the body/society. The object of these investigations is the emergence of ... practices by which the body is organised and controlled within social space' (Turner, 1991, p. 130).

According to Foucault, the rise of body-centred discourses necessarily involved a process of secularisation. Pre-modern discourses were dominated by religion, where things were defined as good or evil, and social life was structured around these concepts. With the emergence of modern urban society, scientific discourses took over, and medical science was a crucial element of this new knowledge. Modern life became increasingly subject to medical control – the medical gaze, as Foucault called it and as we saw in Chapter 13.

The rise to power of science, and of medicine in particular, coincided with a progressive reduction of the power of religious forms of knowledge. For example, normality and deviance became more a matter of health and illness than of good or evil, and the doctor/physician took over from the priest the role of defining, promoting and treating deviance.

Materialist
For Turner, following Foucault, a focus on the body as an object of analysis.

Superstructure
A Marxist term for social forms other than the economy (for example, politics and culture) that are determined by the economic base.

Bryan Turner

Turner (1991) offers a **materalist** theory of religion and secularisation in the tradition of Foucault. Although he is interested in the effects of religious beliefs rather than their content, he dismisses both Durkheim's functionalist 'social cement' thinking and phenomenology's subjective interest in religion. He argues that the role of religion and its decline in modernity is closely linked to the two main material aspects of human existence – the production of goods and the management of the body. He sees the pre-modern role of religion as controlling the sexuality of the body for the benefit of the economy. When this was no longer economically necessary, there was a decline in the significance of religion.

While Turner sees strong links between religion and the economy, he is no Marxist. For Marxists, religion is a significant feature of class societies, especially feudal ones. Marxists see religion as an important element of the **superstructure** – an ideological device to encourage the members of an exploited class to acquiesce to their subordination in this world in the expectation of liberation in the next. It functions, as Marx put it, as the 'opiate of the people'.

For Turner, in contrast, it is religion's influence on sexuality that is its *raison d'être*. Like Wilson, Turner insists that the growth in the number of small, marginalised religious organisations and the individuation of religious belief is evidence of religion's loss of structural significance and therefore of secularisation.

BOX 15.4 Property, sexuality and secularisation

'[R]eligion has the function of controlling the sexuality of the body, in order to secure the regular transmission of property via the family. ... In feudalism, religious control of sexuality, especially the sexuality of wives and sons, was crucial to the control of private feudal rights to land; the confessional, penance and other sacraments were important in the social control of women and the production of legitimate offspring. In competitive capitalism, religious control of sexuality was again important in the distribution of property, where the capitalist family was the primary source of further investment for accumulation. . .

'In late capitalism, where there is a degree of separation of ownership and control, the importance of the family for economic accumulation declines and there is less emphasis on the importance of legitimacy and monogamy ... there is no longer an economic requirement for sexual restraint among property-owners since the public corporation rather than the family firm dominates the economy. There is, however, still the need for the regulation of urban populations in time and space, in order to achieve public order and to secure taxation.

'Traditional religious controls over the body are now transferred to public disciplines which are exercised within the school, factory, prison and other 'total institutions'. ... Religion may continue within the private sphere of the body of an individual, but the public sphere of the body of populations is now subordinated, not to the conscience collective (Durkheim), the sacred canopy (Berger) or the Civil religion (modern functionalists) but to secular disciplines, economic constraint and physical coercion.'

Source: Turner (1992, p. 9).

 ## Anti-secularisation perspectives

The co-existence of science and non-science in pre-modernity

When anthropologists began to study contemporary pre-modern societies, they found no evidence of intellectual deficiencies among their inhabitants. On the contrary, they realised these people used both science *and* non-science to make sense of and attempt to control their world.

Evans-Pritchard (1937) described such a collaboration of scientific and non-scientific knowledge in a pre-modern society in his study of the Azande of the Nile/Congo basin. The Azande explain misfortune by means of witchcraft beliefs. Witchcraft – called *mangu* – is believed to be a physical phenomenon that enters the bodies of unsuspecting persons and causes them to harm others, their victims usually being those living in close proximity to them. To explain a misfortune, such as damage to property, an accident, illness or whatever, the Azande begin by assuming it is the result of witchcraft. Although they know how things happen – how canoes are damaged by hippos, or how fragile items such as pots are shattered by a fall – the Azande ask 'Why should this misfortune happen to me?' 'Why do things happen to particular people and not others?' While we can only answer such questions with reference to concepts such as luck, fate, or chance, the Azande, because of their knowledge of witchcraft, not only have an explanation for misfortune (as we do), they also have the means of doing something about it (which we do not).

In the event of misfortune, the Azande speculate about who might be the witch and take steps to confirm or falsify their suspicions by consulting an oracle. The most effective Zande oracle is *benge*, or poison-oracle, mediated by a witch doctor. The poison is asked whether the suspected person is indeed the witch, and the oracle replies by killing or not killing a young chick to whom the poison is administered by the witch doctor. If the questioner asks the poison to kill the chick if the suspicion is correct, the death of the chick is all the proof needed. If the chick does not die, another suspect has to be thought of. The interrogation of the oracle continues until the witch is identified. When told of the results, the identified witch will normally apologise profusely and ritually spit out water to expel the *mangu*. This is enough to explain a misfortune such as an accident. In the case of illness, the ritual is supposed to restore health. Since most ill people get better anyway, the system is seen as working. In the case of persistent illness, either the witch is believed to have been insincere in his or her attempts to expel the *mangu*, or it is assumed that a new witch has become involved. These investigations and ritual expulsions continue until the sick person recovers. In the case of a fatal illness, a witch doctor is employed to identify the witch who has caused the death. The next Azande in the locality to die is believed to be that witch, killed by the witch doctor's magic.

As we shall see later, some writers argue that there are strong parallels between the logic of Zande thinking on witchcraft and the logic of scientific activity. Both are designed to maintain confidence in the system for the benefit of those who depend on it for their knowledge.

QUESTION Examine your own beliefs. Do you hold non-rational, 'magical', quasi-religious or religious beliefs? Write a paragraph on your belief in superstitions, astrology, aromatherapy, lucky charms, God, the after life, ghosts, spiritualism, reincarnation, resurrection, the wheel of life and Paradise. What does your answer tell you about the survival of non-rational belief in society?

Anthropological accounts of the use of both scientific and non-scientific knowledge to explain and manage events leave important questions unanswered. Do the Azande make a distinction between scientific and non-scientific beliefs and practices, or is it only apparent to us? Do they know whether one works and the other does not? If they do not recognise the difference between empirical and mystical explanations, why not? If they do know, why do they continue to retain beliefs and use techniques that do not work? To answer such questions, contemporary anthropology concentrates on the non-instrumental benefits of technically impotent actions and beliefs, and argues that such an approach explains the benefits of non-scientific thinking in modernity too.

People retain these beliefs and techniques not because they fail to recognise that they do not work, but because they do work on a non-technical level. Non-scientific beliefs either provide psychological and emotional benefits for the believer or perform important integrative functions for the culture in which they exist, or both. We should therefore expect to find scientific and non-scientific knowledge co-existing in all societies, however modern or scientifically developed. Religious thought and practices have not declined in modern societies because they continue to perform important functions for individuals and society as a whole. For example, postmodern theories of religion emphasise that fundamentalist religions have gained importance under the conditions of postmodernity because they meet the emotional needs of many of those who feel most challenged by these conditions (see Box 15.5).

BOX 15.5 Fundamentalism and postmodernity

Fundamentalism is a thoroughly contemporary, postmodern phenomenon. ... It makes possible a full enjoyment of modern attractions without having to pay the price they demand. The price in question is the agony of the individual condemned to self-sufficiency, self-reliance and a life of never fully-satisfying choice. ... The bitter experience in question is the experience of freedom: of the misery of life composed of risky choices, which always mean taking some chances while forfeiting others; of incurable uncertainty built into every choice; of the unbearable, because unshared, responsibility for the unknown consequences of every choice; of the constant fear of foreclosing future and yet unseen possibilities; of the dread of personal inadequacy. ... And the message arising from that experience is: no, the human individual is not self-sufficient and cannot be self-reliant; one cannot go by one's own judgement, one needs to be guided, and directed, and told what to do.

Source: Bauman (1998. pp. 72–3).

Religion is what religion does (1): knowledge and the search for meaning

The role of knowledge in this tradition is to provide the individual with ontological security – a sense that the world is a meaningful, ordered and coherent place. Symbolic anthropologists focus principally on the construction of meaning in pre-modern worlds; phenomenologists look at the search for meaning as a universal human project.

Symbolic anthropology

Life always throws up threats to ontological security – suffering and misery, calamities and disasters, the inhuman actions of some of our fellow beings and so on – that are hard to explain. From this perspective, non-scientific knowledge and beliefs are necessary to help us make sense of such senseless features of our lives. They do this in two ways: they give us explanations that help us to cope; and they offer us ways of behaving that allow us to express our desire for meaning and order in our world. Symbolic anthropology argues that ritual, for example, should be seen as a kind of language, allowing those who engage in it to symbolise their feelings about the world – it enables them to articulate, through action, the way they would like the world to be. Therefore, even if a rite seems to be aimed at a particular goal, and even if its participants describe this as its purpose, its real significance lies elsewhere. That is, rituals work in the same way that any language works – as a means of expression (Beattie, 1964, pp. 203–4).

> "[T]he whole procedure, or rite, has an essentially expressive aspect, whether or not it is thought to be effective instrumentally as well. In every rite something is being said as well as done. The man who consults a rain-maker, and the rain-maker who carries out a rain-making ceremony, are stating something; they are asserting symbolically the importance they attach to rain and their earnest desire that it should fall when it is required. . .
>
> [O]nce the essentially expressive, symbolic character of ritual ... has been understood, it becomes easier to answer the question often asked: how is it that so many people continue to believe in and practise magic, without either noticing its ineffectiveness or attempting to test it empirically as they test their practical techniques? It is simply that there would be no point in doing so, for if and insofar as the rite is expressive ... it would be inappropriate, even meaningless, to put them to the kinds of tests which might disprove them. "

Clearly, religious beliefs and rituals are useful for generating meaning and reassurance, since religious rituals are meant to be exclusively symbolic, and recognised by believers as such, differing from magic in that they rarely aim at any practical result as well.

Phenomenology

Phenomenology is a form of sociology whose interest lies in the human activity of attaching meaning to reality. People need to make sense of their experiences, for without the capacity to do so, human life would not be possible (see Chapter 18). It is this theoretical interest that has led some phenomenologists to take a special interest in religion.

Phenomenological definitions make religion universal. Religious ideas and practices are defined in terms of their effects, and if these effects exist, so must religion. Phenomenologists define being human as having the ability to attach meaning to reality. If religion is defined as the activity of making reality meaningful, then, by definition, being human means being religious – a human being must be a religious being.

The idea that there is an inherent religiosity in being human underpinned the work of Peter Berger, whose book *The Social Reality of Religion* (1973) dominated the sociology of religion in the 1970s. Berger argued that knowledge and religion are inextricably linked. For humans to know and understand the world, they need to allocate meaning to events. This is done symbolically – mainly through language, although other forms of representing meaning, such as ritual or artistic images, are also important. The creation of such a symbolic world is, according to Berger, what being religious means. That is, being religious involves the construction of a 'sacred canopy' or religious system of meaning, under which we can shelter and live out our lives. The canopy, created by ourselves, gives us confidence that the world is a meaningful and intelligible place.

Thomas Luckmann (1983) developed this argument further and argued that the evidence of a modern decline in established, structurally central, religious belief and practice (secularisation) is in reality only a decline in one form of religion in such societies. All that has happened in modernity is that new forms of religion have emerged, away from the collective membership of religious organisations and towards the individual search for meaning. According to Luckmann, being religious in the modern world is usually about the search for one's self – the construction of a meaningful identity. As he puts it: 'The social structure is secularised – but the myth of secularisation fails to account for the fact that the individual is not secularised' (ibid., p. 132). However, as we shall see in the next section, the emphasis on religion in

Inclusivist
A definition of religion that includes systems of beliefs and practices that, while different in content, produce similar effects.

Exclusivist
A definition of religion that excludes any beliefs and practices that do not conform to very specific criteria.

modernity as an essentially individual affair could not be further away from the functionalist explanation of the phenomenon.

Religion is what religion does (2): religion, integration and solidarity

The functionalist approach to non-scientific knowledge is closely bound up with the Durkheimian tradition in sociology. Functionalists explain the existence and persistence of such knowledge in terms of its beneficial effects. They concentrate on religious beliefs and practices, defining religion as any institutionalised form of thinking and acting that serves to integrate the social collectivity in which it is found. According to functionalist theory, if the continued existence of any collectivity depends upon its integration/ solidarity, then religion must be a universal phenomenon. From such an **inclusivist** point of view, and unlike **exclusivist** definitions, two other aspects of religion are relatively unimportant: the content of its beliefs, and the meanings that its beliefs and practices have for individual believers. According to functionalism, it does not matter if the beliefs and practices of different religions are not the same, nor does it matter if the followers of different religions think themselves to be different. What is important is that all religions can be explained in the same way – with reference to the integrative functions they perform for the social worlds in which they are found.

CONNECTIONS See Box 1.1 for a basic account of Durkheim and Chapter 17, pages 470–6, for a fuller account.

Durkheim (1976) based his theory on his analysis of totemism among the Arunta, an indigenous Australian people who divided themselves into bands and clans. The bands consisted of small groups of Arunta living together, while the clans were much larger groups of several bands who believed themselves to be related. Routine contact between clan members was very limited. However, on rare occasions, clan-wide gatherings took place to carry out a ceremony, at the centre of which was the clan emblem – its totem. The totem of an Arunta clan was an object from natural life, for example, a plant, animal or bird. The aim of the ceremony was to ensure that the totem thrived and multiplied. Arunta clan members treated their totem as a special object that demanded respect and awe when they came upon it during their day-to-day lives. According to Durkheim, for the Arunta clan, their totem was a sacred object – special, set apart and different from all other profane things.

Durkheim argued that totemism was essential to the survival of the Arunta identity. Since day-to-day life was lived out in the band, unless there was some way of reminding the Arunta of their membership of the wider society, their sense of themselves would be restricted to their band membership. Without this sense of identity, there would be no solidarity. Members of different Arunta bands would feel no allegiance to one another, and there would be no sense in which the Arunta could be described as – or recognise themselves to be – an integrated unit. For Durkheim, the totem and the clan's existence were dependent on each other. The sacred object – the totem – provided the motive for clan-wide association, and encountering it and treating it as set apart from other (profane) things reminded band members of their clan's existence. In effect, it was only the symbol of the clan that made its continued existence possible.

According to Durkheimian functionalists, the same features can be found in all religions, and religions are found wherever there are social groups. There will be objects that are believed to be sacred – emblems that symbolise the collectivity of members – and there will be occasions when the members collectively celebrate (worship) the

Conscience collective
The shared beliefs and values of a collectivity that are a prerequisite for social integration, promoting a sense of belonging for the individual.

existence of the symbols. This combination of symbols and collective action serves to integrate the group by promoting in its members a recognition of the group's existence and of their membership of it. Theoretically, Durkheim argued that the sharing of common sentiments – a **conscience collective** as he called it – is the basis for social life itself. By defining religious beliefs and practices as the source of such sentiments, he was saying that religion is a precondition for social survival. The fate of the group and the fate of individual members are bound together – the members depend on the group to survive, and the group's survival depends on its members recognising their membership. Religion ensures that this occurs. Religious symbols represent the group, and the worship of these symbols by the group reproduces its existence. Thus, religious worship of the sacred is in fact a celebration of the group itself.

> **QUESTION** From your own experience of religion and your own spiritual life, if you have one, to what extent are you convinced by the arguments of the phenomenologists and of the functionalists?

Civil religion
Associated with non-supernatural religious objects whose existence promotes solidarity for the group and a sense of belonging for the individual.

This definition of religion is inclusivist because it allows for all sorts of collective commitment and activity to be called religion, on the ground that religion is what religion does. Religiosity has been identified by contemporary neo-Durkheimians in such apparently disparate sources of collective identity as membership of nations, political movements and even sports clubs and associations. This tendency is apparent in the claim by Robert Bellah (1967) that **civil religion** performs the required functions in present-day America. As Wallis (1983, p. 44) says:

Figure 15.2   Are sporting events purely entertainment or – with their emphasis on collective ritual, symbolic objects and intense shared emotions based on spectacle and belief – do they manifest some of the characteristics of a quasi-religion?

" Bellah finds evidence for the existence of civil religion in such events as Presidential Inaugurations. Inaugural addresses tend to be couched in a religious idiom, referring to God in general terms and to the travails of America as a modern Israel led out of Egypt. This stylised rhetoric is taken as indicating a real commitment on the part of participants to symbols and values, which unify and integrate the community and provide sacred legitimation for its affairs. Other more frequent ceremonials such as Thanksgiving Day and Memorial Day are similarly held to integrate families into the civil religion, or to unify the community around its values. "

Scientists are human too: demystifying scientific rationality and objectivity

Interpretive sociologists base their ideas on the *lack* of similarity between nature and society. Unlike natural phenomena, humans try to make sense of their world and act in the light of their interpretations. Post-structuralists, too, see human lives as the product of allocating meaning, though they differ crucially from interpretivists by seeing the content of thought and interpretation as the outcome of the influence of language. Either way, these sociologies draw a fundamental distinction between the natural world and the social world. Therefore, the distinctive aspect of human existence – the use of consciousness – cannot be explained by the methods used to explain the natural sciences.

This raises an important question touched on at the beginning of the chapter. Since scientists are human too, the most important factor in their lives and work must be the use of their minds to make sense of the world. These meaningful accounts, like all human accounts, cannot be seen as objectively true, but only true as far as the owner of the mind is concerned. This is because human theories, including scientific accounts, can only ever be relative – relative to particular occasions of social interaction, or to the cultures or languages that underpin their creation. This raises some important questions. How can human scientists produce objective, value-free accounts of nature if these accounts are inevitably the products of the use of their minds? How can human scientists suspend their socialness and remove themselves from the influence of the social and cultural factors that make thought and social life possible? How can scientists produce knowledge that is uncontaminated by the effects of social interaction, language or culture?

For many sociologists of science, the answer to these questions is that scientists cannot do these things because science is a social product, like any other humanly created knowledge. If this position is correct, then it is obviously devastating for the post-Enlightenment claim at the heart of Great Divide thinking that humans *are* capable of producing objectively true knowledge and that it is science that enables them to do so. This belief, that scientific knowledge amounts to just one more account of the world, is known as relativism. How does this sort of sociological analysis of scientific activity lead to relativism?

Wishful thinking: non-rational thinking in science and magic

Evans-Pritchard (1937) argued that Zande beliefs about witchcraft do not form a perfectly consistent or rational set of ideas. Within its terms, the Azande reasoned logically and coherently. Thus, for example, the Azande would laugh at a European who asked whether poison would kill the chicken without any accompanying address. 'If the fowl died they would simply say that it was not good "benge". The very fact of the fowl dying proves to them its badness' (ibid., p. 315). Any such 'test', then, would reinforce rather than undermine the Zande belief system. Again, if an oracle contradicted itself, it would simply be said to have been addressed or prepared improperly, and this would again reaffirm the basic assumptions of the belief system. These assumptions are used to account for the world, and to establish the point at which reasoning and further questions come to an end.

Evans-Pritchard's sympathetic treatment of the Zande belief system created an interest in comparing magic with science. Polanyi, for example, argued that there are similar implicit beliefs and assumptions at the heart of science, and that these have been screened from our eyes by the ideology of **objectivism**. Objectivism insists that scientific theories are built solely on the observation of empirical 'facts' and the systematic consideration of evidence. Peering behind this curtain of objectivism, Polanyi (1958) identified a number of features common to both witchcraft and science.

> **Objectivism**
> A doctrine that proclaims that scientific truth is a matter of factual evidence, not belief (see *objectivity*).

There are three features working together to ensure that any belief system – magical or scientific – is sustained by those who believe it, despite evidence to the contrary. The three features together guarantee that awkward questions, problems or issues will be unhesitatingly ignored. First, Polanyi pointed to the circularity of the ideas that constitute any belief system. Each idea in the system is explained by reference to another idea, and this other idea only makes sense by reference to the original idea. As symbolic systems, all languages include this circularity. For example, a dictionary defines a word in terms of another word, which is then used to define the original. Thus, 'marriage' may be defined as 'wedlock', which in turn is defined as 'a state of marriage'. This circularity promotes the stability of a system of ideas and beliefs. If one belief is doubted, it is justified by reference to another connected belief. Therefore, 'So long as each doubt is defeated in its turn, its effect is to strengthen the fundamental convictions against which it was raised' (ibid., p. 289).

CONNECTIONS Language is a main focus of Chapter 18, pages 509–11, and Chapter 19, pages 520–5.

Second, Polanyi suggested that all belief systems hold in reserve a supply of subsidiary explanations for difficult situations. For example, the Azande explain failure by the oracle in terms of the ceremony being wrongly conducted. Similarly in science, contradictory events or phenomena can be explained in terms of some auxiliary hypothesis. Thus, conflicting evidence is often referred to in science as an 'anomalous finding', a quirk of investigation that can be safely ignored. In physics and chemistry, many experiments are designed to show a constant relationship between two phenomena, which can then be plotted as a straight-line graph. Sometimes, one point on the graph is consistently out of line with the rest, but students may be told to ignore this anomaly, as it is the result of incorrect methodology at some point in the experiment. This is an explanation that an Azande student would find most appropriate!

Third, belief systems reject alternative views of the world by refusing to grant legitimacy to their basic assumptions. Thus, new ideas that challenge orthodox knowledge claims are suppressed as soon as they appear. Defenders of the new ideas are denied any respectability within the community of 'experts'.

According to Polanyi, these three features explain how contradictory evidence or inconsistent findings do not normally lead to the overthrow of a set of ideas, be it Zande magic or European science. Such evidence can be explained away, denied any validity and meaning, or simply ignored. All systems of knowledge rest on basic premises that are sustained by virtue of actors' commitment to them as 'true'. Ideas are reaffirmed as much by faith and trust as they are by any methodologically correct procedures – believing is seeing, as much as seeing is believing.

QUESTION Has your study of sociology changed the way in which you think about things? Or has it just reinforced what you already knew?

Polanyi's work has forced us to reconsider the way in which scientific knowledge is certified as correct by scientists. Most importantly, we have had to abandon the view that science is an activity that – by unbiased, neutral observation – accumulates evidence from which the universal laws of nature are derived. Instead, scientists' work is characterised by selective inattention to evidence or knowledge claims that do not conform to their picture of reality.

Science as a social product

Contributions to the sociology of science have explored the ways in which the production and acceptance of scientific ideas depend on social and cultural factors. The growth of this area of sociological research was partly due to the influential work of Thomas Kuhn. Kuhn (1972, p. 82) identified what he called 'the dogmatism of mature science', which he defined as 'a deep commitment to a particular way of viewing the world and of practising science in it'. As a scientific field such as physics becomes more mature, as the number of scientists increases, as education courses are established and textbooks produced, those working and training within it adopt a common ideological commitment to what it is to be a physicist and study physics. This dogmatic attachment provides scientists with the rules of the game, defining what is to be treated as a scientific puzzle and how it is to be solved. These rules constitute what Kuhn (1972, p. 93) called the **paradigm** of a scientific field:

> **Paradigm**
> Refers to the set of questions, practices and institutional arrangements that characterise scientific activity for a particular historical period. For Kuhn, (1970, 1972) paradigms produce forms of scientific knowledge that appear to be objective but in reality reflect very specific sets of interests.

❝ Their paradigm tells [scientists] about the sort of entities with which the universe is populated and about the way the members of that population behave; in addition, it informs them of the questions that may legitimately be asked about nature and of the techniques that can properly be used in the search for answers to them. ❞

Kuhn's notion of paradigmatic science can be set against the misleading notion that scientists test their theories by collecting observable facts that exist in nature and await observation and classification. Instead, scientists, armed with their paradigm, seek evidence that confirms it. As Kuhn (ibid., p. 96) argues, 'the challenge is not to uncover the unknown, but to obtain the known'. This parallels Polanyi's concept of the circularity of belief-systems, in that it suggests that scientific research operates in terms of a relatively closed system of ideas that are self-confirming. If evidence that contradicts the paradigm does appear, it is typically ignored as an anomaly, and for good reason. An anomalous finding or unexpected discovery is, by definition, potentially subversive. It threatens to change the rules of the game by which the paradigm works. So the paradigm is a source of resistance to innovation in science. This is in direct contrast to Popper's claim about the courage and lack of conservatism of real science. But major innovations in science do occur, such as the shift from Newtonian to Einsteinian science. However, innovation only takes place when anomalous findings become 'particularly stubborn or striking' so that they force scientists 'to raise questions about accepted beliefs and

BOX 15.6 Scientific thinking and scientific practice

Kuhn's analysis of the paradigmatic nature of science extended the general ideas raised by Polanyi. Polanyi showed how the logic of science is very similar to that sustaining the Zande belief system. Kuhn indicated the way in which aspects of the social institution of science – textbooks, curricula, research communities – continuously sustain the conceptual commitments of its practitioners, guiding their activities, interpretations and accounts of the natural world, and reinforcing the stability of their scientific belief system.

procedures' (ibid., p. 96). When the paradigm consistently fails to deal with an increasing number of anomalies, the scientific field experiences a major intellectual and social crisis, which is overcome by the formulation of a new paradigm.

This commitment to a particular scientific interpretation of the world also encourages resistance to new ideas or 'deviant' interpretations. A considerable body of literature in the sociology of science examines the way in which non-orthodox knowledge claims are received and evaluated by orthodox science (see, for example, Wallis, 1979). Case studies – for example, on parapsychology (Collins and Pinch, 1979) or acupuncture (Webster, 1979) – show how fringe groups that threaten the conceptual and social status quo of science have been dismissed, but not on the basis of open-minded, impartial scientific theorising and experiment. Instead, many scientists simply assert from the outset that the existence of the phenomenon in question is inconsistent with known reality, and therefore any findings, however carefully presented, must be the result of fraud or experimental error, and need not be taken seriously.

Interpretative sociology highlights another source of social and cultural contamination in scientific activity. The focus here is on the dynamics of local, small-scale interaction. Interpretivists argue that face-to-face interaction among scientists – in the laboratory, for example – is a matter of negotiated collaboration between the particular individuals involved, however routine the scientific work may appear to be. For **ethnomethodology** in particular, this has profound consequences for the nature of the knowledge produced. When scientists work together, it is a unique social event, with the outcome of the interaction inevitably being context-bound and contingent, or, as ethnomethodology calls it, indexical. The knowledge produced can only be understood by looking at the interpretive methods used by the participants to arrive at an agreement about the event, that is, to decide together what it means or what is going on. Like all social occasions, then, what matters is the work put in by those party to it to arrive at an interpretation of its meaning. The result of the work, the 'knowledge' produced, cannot be objective, since it is the end product of wholly subjective, interpretive effort by the participants. Thus, it is inevitably relative knowledge – relative to the occasion and to the sense-making efforts of the particular scientists involved. Only by the **ethnographic** study of particular scientific work can this inherently subjective knowledge be understood.

Post-structural sociology also points to the inevitability of scientific knowledge being contaminated by human interpretation. Here the interpretation is not the result of subjects creatively collaborating to produce an agreed account, but the result of the impact of discourse. For post-structuralists, meanings are imposed on subjects by the languages they are obliged to use to think. While humans experience reality for themselves, they can only know what this reality means if they are provided with pegs to hang the experience on. It is languages – systems of symbols representing meanings – that

Ethnomethodology
Associated with the work of Harold Garfinkel, this is an approach to studying the methods people use in their everyday lives to make sense of social life and enable meaningful exchanges with each other.

Ethnography
A research technique based on direct observation of the activity of members of a particular social group or culture in order to understand the meanings given to actions within that social group.

Deconstruct
To analyse texts in order to grasp their implicit meaning by exposing their underlying assumptions.

provide these pegs. For example, the sciences often use mathematical, statistical and chemical symbols, and what these mean is not the decision of the subject who uses them. Furthermore, others may take them to mean something different. As with all forms of human production, then, what scientific accounts mean depends on the language used. To understand their meaning, all we can do is to **deconstruct** the text that represents these meanings. Thus, scientific knowledge is not an objective account of things, but is as subjective as an artist's painting or a novelist's story.

 ## Relativism

The rationalist/Great Divide claim is that science is unique among systems of knowledge because of its particular method of producing knowledge. Since only this method can eliminate subjective influences, only scientific knowledge is objective, and therefore true. However, the sociology of science claims to have demonstrated that social and cultural influences are involved in the human practice of science, so that the knowledge produced by science is inevitably contaminated. This means not so much that all human accounts of reality are equally true, but that all accounts are equally flawed. This position is known as relativism.

Relativism involves the claim that all systems of meaning or accounts of reality produced by humans are equal. It also argues that because any criteria used to judge truth or falsehood are themselves provided by a system of knowledge, truth or falsehood cannot be objectively identified by human beings. Thus, for their believers, religions A, B or C are true; for their users, the ideas underpinning magical systems X, Y or Z are true; and for those who believe, produce or use it, scientific knowledge is true. Furthermore, since religions A, B and C, magical systems X, Y and Z and science use different criteria to determine truth and falsehood, no human can know the truth for certain, since we cannot know except by means of a specific system of belief.

This argument has led to a number of relativistic propositions about the nature of humanly produced knowledge:

Imperialism
Common form of Western colonial rule in the late nineteenth early twentieth centuries. Characterised by the extension of the power of the state through the acquisition, normally by force, of distant territories (see *colonialism*).

- Scientific knowledge is not powerful because it is true; it only seems to be true because it is powerful. It is politics that establishes certain accounts of reality as influential. Therefore, it is not the proximity to truth that explains the dominance of a system of knowledge in any time or place but the methods its supporters use to promote it.

- Since the exercise of power in human activity means there must be losers as well as winners, the dominance of one form of knowledge implies the marginalisation and subordination of others. Though justified in the name of truth, such domination should be recognised for what it is – the imposition of one way of making sense of the world at the expense of others. It is, in effect, the epistemological equivalent of **imperialism** – the use of political power to oppress the weak. Relativists have sometimes explicitly drawn this parallel.

- Modernity involved the pursuit of objective truth. Once armed with this truth, modernisers saw it as their duty to become missionaries – to oppose falsehoods. Thus, the standard bearers of science have marched against other forms of knowledge, crusaders on behalf of freedom from ignorance. According to relativism, to understand the meaning of this missionary project, we must remember that political colonialism – for example, by European states over the last few centuries – has almost always been justified in precisely these terms: pre-modern cultures could only progress through the influence of modernising forces. Because relativism believes it has demonstrated the impossibility of achieving objective truth in any sphere of human thinking, such claims to altruism are exposed for what they are. Rationalism and colonialism are revealed as cultural and political oppression cloaked in missionary garb, as elitist and racist attempts to subordinate or eradicate other belief systems and cultural traditions.

- Relativism provides the epistemological foundation of postmodernism. The inability of humans to produce true accounts of reality means that the project of modernity initiated by the Enlightenment – to employ rationalism to discover the way things really are – has to be abandoned. We have to accept that we can never suspend our humanity to produce a meta-narrative that gets at the truth. We have to accept that we live in a postmodern world, where different ways of creating knowledge and making sense of existence deserve equal respect and tolerance.

- Unlike rationalists, we should not assert the objective truth dominance of our form of knowledge, but accept the legitimacy of other ways of knowing and living. Although these may well seem odd or even repellent from our point of view, because they have as much meaning and virtue for their adherents as ours do for us, they have as much right as ours to an untroubled existence.

Responses to relativism

Ethnocentric
The description of the inability to understand the validity or integrity of cultures other than one's own.

Relativism argues that humans are creations of their culture, and that what they think is true and what they think is right are products of the times and places in which they live out their lives. This leads to the anti-provincialist or anti-**ethnocentric** position of Clifford Geertz (1984), which implies both moral relativism and cognitive relativism. Both moral systems (judgements about good and bad) and forms of knowledge are equally valid.

Objections to cognitive relativism

Like Gellner (1992), some rationalists insist that while it may not be possible to identify an example of morality as objectively correct, it is certainly possible to identify a form of cognition that is, and that scientific knowledge is the product of that form of cognition. The proof of this is that the knowledge produced has been applied successfully to transform lives in the developed world. To downplay these advances is to ignore the almost universal effort by non-advanced societies to get hold of this knowledge in order to achieve similar progress for themselves.

Objections to moral relativism

There are also major difficulties with moral relativism. If there are no standards that are objectively good, then no human has the moral justification to deny others the right to live their lives in whatever way they see fit. This could be seen as an affirmation of the importance of tolerance in human life. However, this position has disturbing implications.

Does moral relativism mean that we have to tolerate all the ideas or behaviour of others, however repellent they might seem to us? For example, should we accept racism, sexism or religious intolerance by others in our culture? Should we have accepted the right of Hitler to exterminate the Jews, or of Stalin and Pol Pot to annihilate millions in order to achieve their political ends? Furthermore, does it mean that we have to accept the cultural and historical relativity of ourselves? Are we entirely at the mercy of social and cultural sources of identity, so that who we are and what we think is right or wrong are entirely a matter of chance?

To avoid such problems, many thinkers adopt a human rights position and argue that there must be limits to tolerance, and that a civilised existence depends on the identification of correct, universally applicable values. The search for universal standards of behaviour – the ways of thinking and living to which all humans should subscribe, irrespective of historical or cultural circumstances – is apparent in the work of many contemporary thinkers, such as Habermas and Rorty.

CONNECTIONS You will find an account of the position of Habermas in Chapter 19, pages 530–2.

The idea that certain emotions and feelings are a universal part of being human is also present in the work of a number of contemporary advocates of rationalism and science. The claims of natural scientists such as Richard Dawkins and Francis Crick (1994) can be seen as part of an extreme rationalist project to deny any significant role for social and cultural influences in the formation of human personality and identity. For example Crick (ibid., p. 268) claims that 'Free will is located in or near the anterior cingulate sulcus. ... In practice, things are likely to be more complicated. Other areas in the front of the brain may also be involved.' Crick (ibid., p. 3) summarises his position as follows:

> " The Astonishing Hypothesis is that 'You', your joys and sorrows, your memories and your ambitions, your sense of personal identity and free will, are in fact no more than the behaviour of a vast assembly of nerve cells and their associated molecules. As Lewis Carroll's Alice might have phrased it: 'You're nothing but a pack of neurons'. "

Nihilism
The total rejection of all moral principles.

Reductionism
An outlook that explains phenomena in terms of a simple determining factor.

The implication of this is that the source of universal human emotions as well as differences is human biology. Similar claims about the genetic basis of human behaviour have been made by the rapidly growing science of evolutionary psychology.

For many sociologists, the real danger of relativism is that it will lead to **nihilism**. In such a moral void, the rationalist **reductionism** of Crick and others like him may become the dominant discourse. To avoid this, they insist that sociology must remain committed to the original modernist project – the quest for true knowledge and the pursuit of human liberation and fulfilment through the reconstruction of society. This leads us to ask: 'What is sociology for?' It is to this that we turn in the final chapters.

Chapter summary

- Great Divide thinking argues that the rise of rationalism, enabling the rapid growth of scientific knowledge, was the real motor behind modernity.

- Weber was concerned with emphasising the disenchantment of a world pervaded by rationalism.

- Symbolic anthropology and phenomenology argue that non-rational beliefs will always be important, even in modern scientific societies, because of the feeling of security they generate for individuals.

- Functionalist writers on religion argue that systems of religious belief will be present in all societies, even modern ones, because of the integrative function they perform.

- Rationalist writers disagree with both these viewpoints and claim that modern societies have become secularised.

- Sociologists of science have attempted to expose the inability of human scientists to provide a truly objective account of the world.

- This has led to relativism – the claim that scientific accounts are no nearer to objective truth than non-rational ones.

- This relativist position has given rise to postmodern accounts of human knowledge, with all the problems this entails.

 ## Questions to think about

- To what extent do you agree with the relativist contention that there is no such thing as absolute truth? When composing your answer, consider both the rationalist and the relativist case before coming to a conclusion.

- In the cases for and against secularisation, which aspect do you find compelling and why?

- Does the human rights position offer a way out of the relativist/rationalist dichotomy? Give reasons for your answer.

 ## Investigating further

Aldridge, Alan (1999) *Religion in the Contemporary World: A Sociological Introduction*, Polity Press.

> A very useful and up-to-date overview of debates in the sociology of religion, with chapters on such topics as secularisation (its rise and retreat), religious fundamentalism and religious identity and belief.

Heelas, Paul (1998) *Religion, Modernity and Postmodernity*, Blackwell.
    A reader with a global perspective on developments in religion, drawing on work
    on Latin America, Japan, Indonesia and Europe.
Hunt, Stephen (2000) *Religion in Western Society*, Palgrave.
    A very clear and readable account of religion in its social context, with
    particularly helpful and interesting coverage of globalisation, postmodernity,
    cults and other new religious movements.

part 4

Sociological theory and method

Sociology would not exist as a discipline without a theoretical base and a more or less agreed set of methods by which researchers can investigate their subject at a practical level. Theory and research have been the bedrock of every chapter in this book, but in this section we look at the particular issues and debates that they raise. They are contentious subjects in their own right!

It is perhaps tempting to label theory as abstract and difficult but, by this stage in the book, you will have encountered a rich volume of theory in more applied contexts, and these last chapters of the book offer an opportunity to extend your wings a bit.

We begin with the more practical task of research, looking at the challenges sociologists face in obtaining meaningful and representative data about the society we live in. We then turn to look at the theoretical debates that have shaped the discipline, from its origins in the nineteenth century to debates that are still ongoing and vibrant today. We end by revisiting the question why sociology is important in understanding our rapidly changing world.

CHAPTER CONTENTS

Aims of the chapter

When researching substantive areas of social life, sociologists pay attention both to methodological and to theoretical matters. While it is important to recognise that theory and method should be considered together, this chapter concentrates on the methodological dimension. It introduces some of the basic principles of sociological research and discusses key concepts and concerns that have shaped sociological inquiry. It examines the basic methodological tools available to the sociologist, as well as the relationship between and assumptions behind the various theories and methods. It also discusses how conventional research approaches in the discipline have been challenged by feminism and postmodernism, though perhaps not fatally so.

By the end of the chapter, you should have an understanding of the following concepts:

- Methodology
- Reliability
- Validity
- Causal relationship
- Sample population
- Quantitative research
- Qualitative research
- Secondary data
- Ethnography

 ## Introduction

The discipline of sociology is precisely that: a disciplined understanding of society and the social processes that both reproduce and change it. As members of society, we experience and understand these processes in many ways, but rarely – as suggested in Chapter 1 – do we reflect on why or how they occur. Instead, we often make sense of our world by ignoring much of it, or by taking much of it for granted – not only our own behaviour but also that of others.

This chapter introduces the principal research methods used by sociologists and shows how they relate to wider theoretical principles. It describes the basic features of research design and discusses the strengths and weaknesses of various research approaches. It concludes with a discussion of feminism and postmodernism, which, in different ways, have challenged the conventional assumptions of sociological research that arise from sociology's link to modernity.

Sociological questions

Disciplined sociological research on human social behaviour requires a range of theoretical and methodological issues to be confronted before, during and after the research. This is not to imply that there is a rule book that all members of the profession typically follow – sociologists adopt various research techniques and often use different ones simultaneously in order to explore and explain some particular area of social life. This can lead to considerable debate about the appropriate choice of research method, conceptual framework and the like, as is illustrated by the range of approaches used to understand and explore crime in Chapter 14.

What counts as a sociological research problem can often surprise those new to the field. Often sociological research is most revealing when it delves into taken-for-granted aspects of everyday life. For example, taken-for-granted notions of the home have certain implications for who has rights to that home, and most importantly, who has inheritance rights to it and whether the home can withstand the social process of inheritance.

BOX 16.1 Inheritance and the idea of the home

'The home is the embodiment of the modern domestic ideal, a suitable place to be occupied by "a family". It is a place of security, privacy and comfort. The home is conceived of as something which is actively constructed through a process which turns the raw materials of a house plus possessions into a home. It offers significant opportunities for its occupants to express their individuality and their taste, through the way in which they organise and furnish it. It is therefore, in a meaningful sense, a personal creation, and probably the most significant material thing which many people ever create and certainly the most valuable ...

'Within this imagery the home belongs to the couple, both materially and symbolically. Though their children may also "belong" there when they are young, this is a temporary arrangement. They have not created the home, they do not have the same rights of ownership over it, and in a very real sense do not "belong" there once they have reached adult life ...

'Looking at inheritance, some interesting questions emerge. If the home is an intensely personal creation, which powerfully expresses individuality, what happens when its creator dies ... ? Does the house then cease to be a "home" and simply become "property"? Does the home die, along with the person who created it? Or is there a sense in which a home is – or can be – passed on as a home for someone else to occupy as their own?'

Source: Finch and Hayes (1994, pp. 417–18).

Many of the questions that shaped early sociology were concerned with the 'Great Transformation' associated with the development of modernity (see Chapter 2). The pace and scope of change in social structures encouraged social theorists to ask very broad questions:

Rationality
A preoccupation with calculating the most efficient means to achieve one's goals.

- How would social order and integration be maintained (Durkheim)?
- How would the new dynamics of capitalism affect production relations (Marx)?
- How would the dynamics of **rationality** spread throughout social institutions (Weber)?

CONNECTIONS You will find the basic concepts formulated by Durkheim, Marx and Weber in Boxes 1.1, 1.2 and 1.3 in Chapter 1.

These early analyses did not have the benefit of a sociological research manual, as research methods had yet to be developed as formalised tools of social inquiry. Work was often quite speculative and theoretical, with limited empirical investigation (although this did not prevent grand theorising, such as Herbert Spencer's [1820–1903] theory of cosmic and social evolution). There were some exceptions, such as Charles Booth's (1903) study of the poor in London and Durkheim's (1952) international study of suicide in the last decade of the nineteenth century.

These broad historical and comparative analyses of social change provided the basis for much of the focused empirical research subsequently conducted by twentieth-century sociologists. Some of the key concepts – such as culture, class, rationality and power – were reworked and redefined through many thousands of empirical studies. The absence of formalised rules of sociological inquiry in the nineteenth century prompted many of the founding sociologists to develop series of principles for conducting research, or at least principles that would help to identify and explore a specifically sociological – as opposed to a philosophical, biological or historical – problem. Durkheim set out his 'Rules of Sociological Method', while Weber developed and applied his notion of the **ideal type**, which he used to construct robust and useful concepts of social behaviour and organisational structure, such as 'bureaucracy'.

These attempts to provide a more rigorous basis to social analysis reflect the impact of modernity on sociology, for they were driven by the belief that the new discipline must be objective and scientific. As sociological research methods developed, so the demands for **objectivity** and reliability in research grew, and the methods became more defined.

Much of the discussion that follows reflects the sense in which sociology is a child of modernity. However, as we shall see, some contemporary theorists believe that modernity has been displaced by postmodernity. This has major implications for the sort of methodological approach that can be taken to social inquiry. But this is for later. We need to begin with some basic principles that have shaped sociological inquiry thus far.

One way of ordering the range of issues that are subject to the contemporary sociological gaze is to adopt Greer's (1969) classification. He divided sociological inquiry into three main areas:

- A sociology devoted to the analysis (and perhaps resolution) of *policy* problems – such as studies on poverty, crime and urban degradation.
- A sociology that examines the broad *dynamics of society* and social change, where the problems investigated reflect the sociologist's social and historical philosophy – such as debates about social stratification, the political sociology of the state and so on.
- A sociology that asks questions about its own *prior stock of knowledge*, to refine understanding, open new questions and challenge the assumptions of previous researchers. In this case, questions are generated as much by the discipline itself as by developments external to it.

In practice, these three types of sociology often overlap in a major piece of research. For example, Townsend's (1979) study of poverty located the problem within the broader aspects of contemporary capitalism, challenged prior notions of poverty that had been developed by previous research and recommended a range of policies for the measurement and alleviation of poverty.

Another way of identifying the range of issues that sociologists address is to leaf through any current sociological journal, noting what the articles are trying to explore and what methods they are using to do this.

We should not make the mistake of thinking that the topic under investigation inevitably governs the research method used. For example, it is perfectly possible that a number of sociologists will explore unemployment and the underclass from a range of perspectives using different techniques. These can range from the use of official statistics on unemployment as **secondary data** to produce statistical measures of the phenomenon, to more qualitative techniques – such as ethnography – to try to understand the experience of unemployment for those most marginalised in society. Both techniques have their strengths and weaknesses, and this is precisely why the researcher

Ideal type
A model or a set of exaggerated characteristics defining the essence of certain types of behaviour or institutions observable in the real world. 'Ideal' signifies 'pure' or 'abstract' rather than desirable.

Objectivity
An approach to knowledge acquisition that claims to be unbiased, impersonal and free from prejudice. Commonly associated with positivism.

Secondary data
Data, often in the form of official statistics or statistics from other printed sources, that have not been generated by the present researcher.

may choose one in preference to another. This tells us that researchers are looking for different types of data to answer different types of question.

Whatever the particular focus of the sociologist, research projects generally involve a number of research steps that require methodological and practical issues to be resolved. For example:

- What is the principal research question – what am I trying to find out, and how can I define this in a clear and unambiguous way so that I will know precisely what I am looking for? If I cannot do this, am I looking for something that is not there? Or do I need to adopt exploratory research techniques to test my basic beliefs and ideas?

- Which theoretical and conceptual frameworks should be adopted which make best sense of the research question in relation to prior work and through which my analysis could best be conducted?

- What methods should be used to collect data, and how reliable and valid will these be as investigative tools for my particular project?

- How should the data be analysed in order to produce coherent conclusions that other researchers will be able to evaluate and use?

Secondary questions include the following. Does the research have any ethical implications? How will the findings be disseminated? Who will be the users and beneficiaries of the research?

The answers to all these questions will clearly vary because different data-collection techniques are used to address similar research problems. There is no one preferred method of sociological fieldwork, even if there is broad consensus on the steps that should be taken in the interest of good research design. It has long been important to produce results that can be regarded by others as reliable and valid, but as the volume of sociological data grows (both quantitative and qualitative, including mixed toolbags) and becomes more easy to obtain from and exchange through electronic databases (see Table 16.1), the importance of producing reliable and valid information has become even greater. Reliability and validity are so intrinsic to debates about theoretical and methodological approaches to sociological research that it is essential to clarify what these concepts mean.

Reliability refers to the replicability of the research. That is, a reliable research project will produce results that have not been distorted by the process of collecting data with a particular research instrument (a survey, an ethnography or an interview) and will produce similar results if repeated on the same set of respondents. Put simply, reliability is a measure of the degree of repeatability of your findings. There are a number of ways of ensuring the reliability of data collection such as conducting a 'test retest', in

TABLE 16.1 Online social science databases: some examples

Social science gateway	www.sosig.ac.uk
National Statistics	www.statistics.gov.uk
ESRC national research database	www.regard.ac.uk
Social Sciences Data Collection, USA	http://ssdc.ucsd.edu
OECD data bases	www.sourceoecd.org/
Social Science Data Archives, NL	www.pscw.uva.nl/sociosite/databases

which data are collected on two separate occasions using the same instrument. The problem, of course, is that the subject(s) of the research may have changed, and so the second test cannot be seen as a reliable check on the first. This is clearly a problem for all research – even in the natural sciences (see Collins, 1985, and Chapter 15) – but it is especially problematic when the investigation focuses on ideas, attitudes and beliefs, all of which are liable to change over time. Another way of achieving reliability is to check 'internal consistency', which involves testing the extent to which items (for example, questions) relating to a particular issue (for example, depression) address this issue and no other.

Validity refers to the quality of the data obtained, which will govern the extent to which inferences, propositions or conclusions are valid. Researchers need to ensure that the data collection techniques used actually capture the data they need – what they intend to measure and not something else. Sometimes – often, in fact – the researcher is unsure of the precise questions that should be explored, and will conduct an exploratory pilot study before the main research in order to clarify matters. Even if it is clear from the start what is needed, it may be less evident how to obtain it and thus secure valid data on it. One may have to be very flexible during the fieldwork to secure valid data that relate precisely to the topic of interest. As Whyte (1984, p. 103) says of his own research experience:

> "In one interview with a union leader, for example, my opening question about a problem situation elicited a response of about 500 words. No doubt the informant considered this a full response, as indeed it was, by ordinary conversational standards. However, I was dealing with a problem of some technical complexity as well as one of specifying people and process. It took me eighteen questions or statements before I felt I had the problem adequately covered. Even then, upon reviewing the transcription later, I found important elements I had overlooked."

It is perhaps not surprising that some sociologists prefer to undertake research that does not involve the uncertainties associated with collecting and interpreting respondents' views on the subject. For example, Inkeles (1993), in his study of the impact of industrialisation and modernisation on people's quality of life, explicitly avoided what he regarded as subjective measures. He preferred objective indicators 'which can be ascertained and rated by an outside observer *without* reference to the inner states of the persons presumably affected by the conditions observed' (ibid., p. 3). Such indicators included items such as how many square feet of housing each person enjoyed, what access to food and medicine they had and so on, rather than asking people how they felt about certain issues. Clearly, not all sociologists would agree with this method, and would suggest that data on the way people feel provide a more genuine picture of their quality of life. This issue highlights a major difference in sociological research, a difference that is based on very distinct methodological approaches.

QUESTION When trying to achieve a balance between reliability and validity, which do you think should have priority? Justify your response.

Theoretical approaches and research methodologies

Two broad traditions have shaped the research agendas of sociologists, although the gap that separates them now has many bridges, as researchers have recognised that each has a valuable role to play in exploring society. The first tradition is based on the belief that

Figure 16.1 Research has established a clear correlation between poor housing and ill health. But the precise dynamics of cause and effect are much debated.

Causal relationship
A relationship where one phenomenon has a direct effect on another.

Dependent variable
The term used in empirical research to denote a phenomenon that is caused by or explained by something else.

Independent variable
The term used in empirical research to denote a phenomenon whose existence causes or explains the presence of another variable.

Hypothesis
A set of ideas or a speculative theory about a given state of affairs that is to be subjected to empirical testing.

sociology should provide scientific and objective analysis of social phenomena. This tradition has its roots in modernist positivism, which we shall explore in Chapter 17 when we look at some of the key foundations of social inquiry. According to this perspective, social phenomena can be explained by showing the **causal relationship** between different phenomena, which are treated as distinct variables. There is the phenomenon that one is trying to explain – the **dependent variable** – and the phenomenon that is its likely cause – the **independent variable**. For example, if young women smoke more than other groups, there must be something about the state of being a young woman that causes this, since it is obvious that smoking does not produce young women! The phenomenon of a higher incidence of smoking among young women compared with men of the same age then has to be explored and any **hypothesis** about it tested against collected data. The data on both variables must be collected in a rigorous and reliable manner. When cause and effect analysis is untenable, positivists usually settle for prediction–outcome models.

CONNECTIONS There is a comprehensive account of science and its impact on modernity in Chapter 15.

Quantitative
Used to describe a form of data or data analysis that is based on precise measurement.

Quantitative research in the behavioural sciences (especially psychology) is often based on experiments. There are various definitions of what constitutes an experiment, but in a strictly scientific sense, the true (or classic) experiment involves two or more differently treated groups (experimental and control) and the random (chance) assignment of participants to these groups (Bowling, 1998). The experimental group is exposed to a variable, and then the experimental and control groups are investigated under identical conditions in order to find out if the variable has had an effect. In sociological research, it is often well nigh impossible to set up true experiments because most people do not live in laboratory-like conditions. Some social scientists (probably more often social psychologists than sociologists) use quasi-experiments as a compromise. The single most important difference between a quasi-experiment and a true experiment is that the former involves intact groups, that is, groups constituted by means other than random selection (Cohen and Manion, 1997). In the last few years, quite a lot of psychological experiments have been conducted via the Internet. Internet samples are often larger and more heterogeneous but typically less well controlled for than those used in laboratory (or laboratory-like) conditions.

When conducting quantitative research, most sociologists opt for the survey rather than the experiment. Surveys often yield statistical measures of variables and their correlation across a sample population – a sample so constructed that it is representative of a broader population. This allows the researcher to generalise across a range of similar cases. For example, the relationships and regularities found in a specific study – say, on the attitudes of a sample of school leavers in a particular region towards the labour market – can be said to apply to all school leavers in similar circumstances elsewhere.

The second major approach derives from a rather different tradition within sociology and in many ways is rooted in the ethnographic traditions of social anthropology. This approach depends first and foremost on gaining an in-depth understanding of the cultural meanings, subjective perceptions and intersubjective dynamics of social behaviour in order to make sense of it. (The broader theoretical tradition within which this approach is located is discussed more fully in Chapter 18.) It does not seek to convert these meanings into some statistical representation or try to correct or translate the subjective meanings and perceptions of the social actors involved. Rather, it is thought that careful, close observation will enable the meaning of behaviour to be understood by and made accessible to others. This approach is heavily dependent on **qualitative** data collection techniques such as **participant observation**, which allow the sociologist to share in the culture under examination. Goffman's (1968) study of the St Elizabeth State Mental Hospital in Washington DC is a classic example of the use of this technique. Goffman spent over a year at the hospital, immersing himself in the everyday life of the wards, gradually building a full picture of the interaction between staff and patients.

This second tradition is distinct from that inspired by the positivist approach, and has been termed anti-positivist, or more appropriately, interpretivist. Hughes (1976, p. 25) summarises the interpretivist position:

> "Human beings are not things to be studied in the way one studies rats, plants or rocks, but are valuing, meaning-attributing beings to be understood as subjects and known as subjects. Sociology ... deals with meaningful action, and the understanding, explanation, analysis, or whatever, must be made with consideration of those meanings. ... To impose positivistic meaning upon the realm of social phenomena is to distort the fundamental nature of human existence."

Table 16.2 contrasts the two broad approaches to society and what each regards as the most appropriate way of studying it.

Researchers acknowledge that all data rely for their meaning on the interpretive inferences of the sociologist: no data can speak for themselves', not even these collected by those of a positivist inclination. As Jones (1985, p. 57) has said, 'the analysis of data about the social world can never be "merely" a matter of discovering and describing what is there. The very process of deciding "what is", and what is relevant and significant in "what is", involves selective interpretation and conceptualisation.' This is further complicated by the fact that some concepts that describe social behaviour have no directly observable or measurable indicators by which to register them, such as the

Qualitative
Information that is not always quantified, but which has a 'text'.

Participant observation
A research method where the researcher takes part in the activities of the group or community being studied.

TABLE 16.2 The broad methodological differences between positivism and anti-positivism

	Positivist	Interpretivist
Basic view of society	Society is a system of social phenomena that are causally linked together	Society only exists as a result of meaningful social interaction
Who best defines it	The external observer (as an expert sociologist)	The social actors themselves
How best to validate claims about it	Test hypotheses through rigorously collected quantitative data	Work towards an empathy with the actor through the sensitive collection of qualitative data
Likely method	Survey	Observation

concept of modernity itself. Such concepts have to be translated into other concepts that are observable. This might include features of modern society such as the 'privatisation' of societal behaviour, which is a shift away from a public, communal form of social intercourse to one that is more individual and privately expressed. This indicator of modernity may have to be refined even further before reliable and valid data can be collected. It is here that the positivist/interpretivist divide is more apparent. A quantitative survey could be conducted to test a number of hypotheses about the onset of privatisation – for example, if privatisation was occurring, it could be expected that people would have a less strong sense of belonging to a wider community or group. The notion that underlies this hypothesis – that a shift is taking place in people's reference and membership groups – could also be explored through an in-depth qualitative study of a village, a family or whatever by the researcher, if he or she believed that privatisation could only be understood properly and accurately (that is, validly) by immersing him- or herself in the respondents' lives.

> **QUESTION** From a sociological point of view, what do you think are the risks of totally immersing yourself in the lives of others?

While the positivist/interpretivist divide still prevails in some important debates about the construction and direction of sociological theory, it is becoming increasingly less significant for many engaged in sociological research. For example, more and more sociologists are using a mixture of quantitative and qualitative methods of collecting data and explaining social behaviour. Indeed, the analysis of secondary data, a popular sociological method, can involve the extraction of quantitative patterns from qualitative sources. Moreover, primary qualitative data – for example, the narrative that unfolds during an interview – can be explored for the relative frequency with which certain observations or ideas are voiced by the respondent. Those using a computer software system, such as Nvivo and Atlas Ti, to manage large qualitative datasets often use the program to take such counts, and even to determine the correlation between various observations made by the respondent(s).

There has been a tradition among more quantitative-minded sociologists to use qualitative research in early stages of fieldwork in order to pilot surveys for later delivery, to sharpen up concepts and to refine empirical indicators. But today, it is more common to use a range of methods in tandem throughout a research project to gather different types of data that can be mutually supportive – the qualitative providing the detail and depth of observation, and the quantitative providing a greater sense of representativeness and reliability.

This combining of the two approaches, however, is never straightforward, since the variables being measured quantitatively may have no obvious expression in the rich qualitative data collected through in-depth interviews. Considerable inference across the two sets of data may have to be made by the sociologist. This difficulty has been experienced by many sociologists, for example by Ann Oakley and Linda Rajan (1991) in their study of the way women from different social classes secure support from kin, neighbours and friends during pregnancy. Quantifiable measures of social support networks needed to be blended with interpretive analysis of the women's experiences of the networks: the women's accounts of these experiences were sought in order to 'provide a description of "the meaning behind" associations between quantitative variables' (ibid., p. 37). In a sense, what was regarded as statistically significant could also have a qualitative significance, and at the same time qualitative checks could be made on quantitative findings.

Blending different research techniques in this way can be a demanding and problematic task, since the quantitative methods often tend to depend on the researcher defining what is to be measured in advance of the fieldwork, while qualitative methods often mean taking a step into the sociological unknown, obtaining insights during interactions with the respondents. Strictly speaking, therefore, the two techniques are not measuring the same thing. It is not, for example, the same as measuring a piece of wood in centimetres and then in inches, since the wood remains constant whatever the measure used. Rather, the different techniques measure different aspects of the general phenomenon under investigation and depend on individual judgements about what counts as a 'good measure'. We cannot add these different measures together to produce a more sophisticated mathematical measurement. Nevertheless, more and more sociologists are mixing their research techniques, as the rewards to be had from blending methods in a careful and rigorous way can be very great. We shall now consider some of the main data collection methods used by sociologists and how they have been used in various studies.

The survey

Surveys are an important means of gathering local, national and international information for agencies and organisations. They can cover a wide range of social, political and economic issues of concern to the government, the professions, academics and others who need to obtain reliable and representative information. In the US and UK, for example, there are regular national surveys of social trends, covering occupational changes, household and family patterns, income differentials, educational achievement and so on. In the UK, the General Household Survey (based on a sample of 12 000 households) has been conducted annually since 1971, providing a rich supply of statistical data with which trends can be mapped. There is a similar annual survey in the US, the General Social Survey, again initiated in 1971. The longest-running survey is the British National Census, which has been carried out every ten years (apart from 1941) since 1801. The data from national and international surveys (such as the International

Social Survey Programme) are often available from electronic databases. In the UK, the principal academic database, the Economic and Social Research Council's data archive, is held at the University of Essex.

BOX 16.2 Some useful statistical sources

- *Social Trends*: an annual review of social trends in the UK, produced by the Office for National Statistics. It provides a summary of and commentary on data derived from a large number of independent surveys. It covers population changes, household and family structure, education, employment, income and wealth, expenditure, health, housing supply, the environment, leisure, religion, crime and transport.

- *General Household Survey*: published in the UK since 1971 and based on a sample of about 12 000 members of the general population residing in private households. It is particularly

valuable as a source of detailed statistical data and is often used as secondary data for further analysis by sociologists.

- *Eurostat Annual*: an EU publication (since 1970) that presents EU member state data on demography, the labour force, economic activity and agriculture.

These sources tend to use different criteria to define the various categories, resulting in different statistics. For example, differences between *Social Trends* and Eurostat in defining 'unemployed' meant that in 1990, 400 000 were excluded from the unemployment count in the UK.

Social surveys have a long history in sociological research and go back to Booth's (1903) early statistical studies of families and poverty in London between 1889 and 1902. Many surveys, particularly those sponsored by national governments, are information-based, descriptive surveys, while those conducted by academic sociologists often have an analytical purpose, for example, to explore concepts, hypotheses, models and so on. Some classic UK examples of the latter are Townsend's *Poverty in the United Kingdom* (1979), Goldthorpe *et al*.'s *Affluent Worker* studies (1968, 1969) and Douglas's *The Home and the School* (1967); and for the US, we can mention Hirschi's *The Causes of Delinquency* (1969) and Elder's *Children of the Great Depression* (1974). More recent studies include those on social class (Marshall *et al.*, 1988), food and consumption (Fine, 1994) and racism and ethnicity (Sagger, 1992; Policy Studies Institute, 1997).

As with any research, all surveys must address the four questions, outlined earlier, that shape research design. The first question is perhaps the most important – what am I trying to find out, and how can I define this in a clear and unambiguous way so that I will know precisely what I am looking for? When doing any research, it is essential to identify precisely what one wants to explore. Not only is it necessary to distinguish one's new work from what already exists, which is crucial if the research requires funding, it is also necessary to translate the broad abstract issues under investigation into more concrete issues that can be explored by means of interviews and questionnaires. In other words, it is necessary to condense broad research topics into precise, researchable questions. For example, if one wanted to conduct a survey to ascertain the degree to which social class is still important, one might translate the broad notion of 'the demise of social class' into more precise issues such as patterns of association among different occupations, the sense of class loyalty in the workplace, people's sense of difference from other social groups, and so on. These topics can be translated into fairly specific questions for inclusion in the survey.

Surveys are normally planned as a series of steps:

- Identification of the topic to be addressed (the research question, its relation to prior work and, as appropriate, the proposition or hypothesis to be tested).
- Identification of the population of respondents to be surveyed.
- Selection of a sample of respondents who are representative of the total population.
- Dry run of, for example, the interview schedule to refine the questions to be asked and topics to be addressed.
- Preparation and implementation of the interview schedule.
- Follow-up interviews.
- Analysis of the data collected.
- Dissemination of the findings.

When defining the research question, it is important to locate previous work that might contribute to the survey. Earlier survey data, for example, will be of use, and the short-comings of such surveys can help to clarify what needs to be covered. Using secondary data in this way is a valuable and time-saving technique when developing one's own research agenda. However, such data must be used carefully, since they were produced in different circumstances for different theoretical or empirical purposes (this is particularly true of official government statistics). Furthermore, they might be based on different measures of the phenomenon under investigation. In other words, it is important to recognise that an established database can never 'speak for itself'. As discussed in Chapter 5, there is disagreement among sociologists over how to read data on social class and social mobility in contemporary Britain: different theoretical assump-

Figure 16.2 Official crime statistics reflect public, police and court definitions of crime and reporting priorities. They therefore tend to under-represent crimes such as rape, white collar crime and traffic speeding.

tions and ways of interpreting empirical data on class mean that the choice of secondary information is not straightforward. Bias in secondary information is not just linked to technical quality, it might also reflect faulty theoretical assumptions.

BOX 16.3 Official statistics as a secondary data source

At some point, all sociologists are likely to draw on official government statistics in their research. Official statistics are useful for a number of reasons:

- They are frequently the only available data on a particular topic (for example, hospital waiting lists).

- They are readily available (unless subject to some government embargo), so researchers do not have to spend their own time and money collecting the information on which they are based.

- They allow an examination of trends over time – or time series data – on a range of topics, such as income differentials, divorce, educational achievement and so on.

- They allow before and after comparisons to be made – for example, the effect that changes in legislation have had on the divorce rate.

However, they also have a number of drawbacks:

- They have been collected for a particular purpose, which has influenced how, when and from whom they were collected.

- They count phenomena using a set of assumptions that might differ from those adopted by the researcher – for example, the US and UK censuses define class by occupational category, a practice that some sociologists question (see Chapter 5).

- Data collected over a number of years may have been subject to alterations to the criteria used, so it is crucial to ascertain whether and how such modifications have been made.

- The status of official statistics – or, for that matter, any statistics – as facts begins to look shaky when one considers all the factors that have prevailed during the long process of data collection. Just who, for example, counts as a criminal in crime statistics depends on the law and its implementation, local policing policy, the capacity to defend oneself against a criminal charge and prosecution, and so on. In this sense, statistics are not objective figures that tell the real story, but the end result of a complex process of social interaction. Sociologists who are especially critical of statistics see them as merely social constructs that have to be deconstructed and demystified.

The sample of respondents to be surveyed has to be selected in such a way that the respondents are representative of the population in question. For example, if the population to be surveyed has a particular gender balance, this should be reflected in the sample, as should features relating to age and class. In order to ensure that the sample is representative, sociologists use (or construct one if a suitable one is not available) a **sampling frame**, from which respondents are selected using a randomising technique that ensures each potential respondent has the same chance of being included in the sample. One of the most frequently used sampling frames is the electoral roll or register. The sample is normally stratified (built up) to reflect the particular features under consideration before random sampling is undertaken.

Another technique is quota or judgement sampling. This is a quicker and more convenient way of obtaining a sample, but is arguably the least reliable. Typically, before interviewing takes place, the main features of the population are defined, such as sex, age, occupation, religion and so on. Interviewers are then given a quota of respondents from each of these categories to contact, the size of the quota being determined by what the research manager judges to be the relative proportion of individuals in each category in the population as a whole. Sometimes a clearly defined sampling frame is not readily

Sampling frame Used in sociological research, this is an accurate list of the subjects of a total population, such as an electoral roll. Research subjects are subsequently randomly selected from this list.

available, for in some research – such as that on deviance – there is no pre-established list of 'deviants' who can be surveyed. In such situations, snowball sampling can be used: the researcher begins with one or a few contacts, who then help to find others, and so on. While this is clearly an uncertain and contingent process, and therefore less reliable than other sampling techniques, there are some situations – such as the mapping of friendship patterns – in which it is particularly appropriate.

| QUESTION | Which of the sampling procedures would you find most useful and why? |

In a UK study of young adults leaving school and entering work, Layder *et al.* (1991, p. 454) describe how they chose their representative sample.

"The sample consisted of 1,786 18–24-year-olds interviewed in four local labour markets during the period October 1982–October 1983. The local labour markets were chosen to represent contrasting local labour market conditions but when aggregated also provided a socio-economic distribution which approximated the total population of 18–24-year-olds. Sunderland was representative of areas with a declining manufacturing base and high levels of unemployment, St Albans typified the more affluent South East with high-technology manufacturing industry, a strong service sector and a low level of unemployment. Leicester was chosen for its diverse industrial base and a level of unemployment close to the national average, while Stafford was selected for its average level of unemployment and high proportions of non-manual workers, to compensate for the above-average proportion of manual workers in Leicester. ... Within each of the localities interviewing was confined to certain electoral wards, chosen to provide a representative sample of the area in terms of the socio-economic characteristics of the population. The interviewer enquired at every fifth house or flat in the area to identify the respondents. If respondents were identified but not available, arrangements were made to call back. ... The questionnaire took between 45 and 90 minutes to administer."

Surveys can be based on face-to-face interviews of the sort conducted by Layder *et al.*, postal questionnaires or, as is often the case, a combination of the two, the interviews typically following postal data gathering. Postal questionnaires are a relatively quick and inexpensive way of collecting data from a large number of respondents, of whom a smaller number may be selected for a (more expensive and time-consuming) follow-up interview on the phone, the Internet or in person.

There are a number of problems with postal surveys. For example, the response rate is often quite low (a good response might average 30–40 per cent), respondents may misinterpret or completely ignore some questions, and overly long questionnaires can discourage some people from responding. In addition, as the questions have to be kept simple, they may provide clues to the answers being sought. Finally, there is no guarantee that the person who has completed the questionnaire is the one who was supposed to. Nevertheless, if the sample is representative and the response rate is around 30 per cent, valuable information can be derived from postal surveys, especially when the final sample is large (such as the 12 000 respondents to the General Household Survey).

While mail surveys are still commonly used for data collection, the use of fax machines and the Internet is increasing. Other self-reported data are collected by means of touch-tone telephone entries, and in some surveys, the researchers even set up their computers to 'talk' to the respondents' computers.

Face-to-face interviews can provide richer data for subsequent analysis because the researcher can discuss all the questions, clarify their meaning, probe for additional information on an unexpected issue that emerges during the interview, and gather responses from a much larger proportion of the initial sampling frame – perhaps as much as 80–90 per cent. To ensure consistency, it is important that the same interview schedule be used for all interviews.

Interviews do, however, have their own problems. These are of two main kinds: those concerned with the design of the interview schedule; and those concerned with the interview situation itself. With regard to the first, the interview must be designed so that the questions seem both sensible to the respondent and flow in a logical sequence. Moreover, because respondents often need to be 'warmed up', the first questions should be restricted to broad background information – such as the respondents' job, marital status, age and so on – rather than anything that is likely to be particularly awkward or embarrassing, such as intimate details of their sex life! The interview situation is also problematic in that it is self-evidently a form of social interaction, and, as such, the data it produces may be biased by the circumstances in which the interview was conducted – where it took place, what the gender interaction was, whether it was taped and so on. This is why the more positivistically inclined researchers prefer to avoid undue interaction with respondents, restricting the survey to precoded, **closed-ended questions** that permit only one of a limited range of responses. These can then be quantitively analysed by means of computer programs such as the Statistical Package for Social Science (SPSS). Responses to **open-ended questions** are more difficult to code in terms of tying them into the specific conceptual issues of interest – one has to make many more interpretive moves to do this.

While surveys can produce large volumes of data, it is important to treat the latter with caution. One cannot always assume that the respondents have accurately reported their attitudes, expectations, behavioural patterns and so on. What is essentially obtained in most cases is merely a claim to truth! According to Hughes (1976), for example, respondents have been found to give inaccurate replies on whether or not they have voted, relied on social welfare, practised birth control and so on. In addition, respondents may give answers that they think are more socially desirable, have a tendency always to respond in the affirmative, or simply get tired and give less thought to their answers than they might. It is because of this that some sociologists back up their survey data with observations of actual behaviour, or develop alternative observational instruments to secure more valid and reliable evidence. Table 16.3 summarises the basic strengths and weakness of surveys as methods of data collection.

Surveys that now enjoy classic status in the sociological research archive have gained their reputation not only for what they discovered but also how they went about it, and it was often the researchers' ability to recognise both the strengths and the

Closed-ended question
The most commonly used form of questionnaire question, the answers to which fall within a predetermined range and thus can be precoded.

Open-ended question
A type of question used in questionnaires to elicit narrative information from the respondent, the answer to which cannot be precoded.

TABLE 16.3 Advantages and disadvantages of surveys

Advantages	Disadvantages
Can handle large numbers of respondents	May have poor response rate
Based on reliable sampling	Can be expensive if large-scale
Standardisation of instrument allows others to replicate the research	Cannot control for the impact of the external environment on respondents
Allows rapid statistical analysis of large volumes of data	No guarantee that respondents actually act and think the way they say they do

limitations of the survey method that has made these classics especially valuable and convincing. One such study was that by Young and Willmott (1957) of families living in an East London suburb (Bethnal Green) who moved to a new housing estate during the early 1950s. The survey explored the changes in kinship networks and contacts that resulted from the move. Such has been the long-standing interest in the findings of this survey that sociological investigations into life in Bethnal Green have continued.

BOX 16.4 Surveying family life in east London

We obviously could not see all the people in these districts. In fact we saw not more than 1,000. But these were chosen rather carefully. We wanted, as far as we safely could, to talk about all the local people although we were seeing only some of them. This object was achieved by following the usual practice of sociologists and selecting 'samples' of people for interview. In Bethnal Green, for instance, we picked from the electoral register every thirty-sixth name appearing on it. We then called on each of the people whose name had come up in this way and asked if he or she would be willing to talk to us. Most of them were. These people were in what we call the general sample; in addition we interviewed a second or third time, and much more intensively, a smaller marriage sample of couples with young children ...

Both of us worked either in the borough or on the estate throughout the three years in which the research was done. One of us also lived in the borough with his own 'family or marriage' for most of the time, and both his wife and his children, who attended local schools, provided further sidelights on the place. ... As a result of this close connection with the district, we came to know well a number of local residents who gave us full accounts of their family relationships which helped us understand and assess the information given to us in the formal interviews. We also did what we could to check what people told us verbally by personal observation in homes, churches, clubs, schools, parks, public houses [bars], and street markets. But we should say, what is as obvious as it is important, that for the most part we can only report what people say they do, which is not necessarily the same as what they actually do.

Source: Young and Willmott (1957, pp. 13–14).

Observation

As we have seen, anti-positivists argue that the more sociological research immerses itself in the subject of investigation the more likely it is to produce a valid account of the meaning it has for the social actors involved. Not surprisingly, therefore, close observation of social action and even full participation in it are often the preferred methods of social research among interpretivists. The term ethnography (literally, the description of a people) perhaps best describes the art of detailed qualitative sociological observation. Ethnography, whose roots lie in early anthropological studies of marginal or isolated cultures during the time of European colonisation, has traditionally explored unusual cultures or social groups. Fielding (1993, p. 155) argues that, 'as a means of gaining a first insight into a culture or social process, as a source of hypotheses for detailed investigation using other methods, it is unparalleled'. As with surveys, however, in-depth observational methods have both strengths and weaknesses, and a number of methodological and practical problems have to be confronted.

CONNECTIONS The theoretical basis of interpretivism is described in Chapter 18.

Figure 16.3 Ethnography aims to shed light on the meanings and intentions behind social behaviour. For example, to what extent are youth subcultures a form of resistance to the socio-economic circumstances of young working-class people?

The first problem is that researchers have to conduct their observations in such a way as to secure a rich body of data without distorting the situation by being present. In what manner should the researcher join in? What is the best method of participant observation? There is no simple answer, for much depends on the situation being studied and the questions that have to be asked. Participant observation can be either overt – known to the actors under investigation – or covert – hidden or disguised in some way. Covert observation is less likely to disrupt or distort the situation being observed, since the researcher appears merely to be another member of the group. However, if the researcher's cover is blown, it will be difficult, if not impossible, to continue the project, as resentment and anger from those under observation might lead to the researcher being ejected from the group. In some areas of research, notably crime and deviance, being a covert observer may well drag one into activities that are legally or ethically compromising. More generally, all covert research raises the broader ethical issue of failing to obtain the informed consent of those under scrutiny. How can sociologists be accountable to their respondents in these circumstances, and how can they ensure that the results of their work will not adversely affect those who have been observed?

Clearly, much depends on the individual situation. Humphreys' (1970) covert study of homosexual behaviour in men's 'tea rooms' (rest rooms or public toilets) in the US was both ethically and legally problematic for him as researcher. Nevertheless (ibid., p. 25):

“ From the beginning, my decision was to continue the practice of the field study in passing as deviant. … [T]here are good reasons for following this method of participant observation.

In the first place, I am convinced that there is only one way to watch highly discreditable behaviour and that is to pretend to be in the same boat with those engaging in it. To wear a button that says 'I am a watchbird, watching you' into a tea room would instantly eliminate all action except the flushing of toilets and the exiting of all present. ... The second reason is to prevent distortion. Hypothetically, let us assume that a few men could be found to continue their sexual activity while under observation. How 'normal' could that activity be? How could the researcher separate the 'show' and the 'cover' from standard procedures of measurement? "

Whether overt or covert, it is clear that observation can work well in situations in which there is no pre-selected sample population, and where the behaviour in question is hidden or deviant. It is obvious that Humphreys would have made very little progress with his research if he had tried to collect data in the 'tea rooms' via a clipboard and closed-ended questionnaire! But it is also true that observation is useful for all situations, not only the unusual. For example, Fox (1990, p. 435) reports his use of participant observation in a fairly unremarkable situation – a group of business executives taking a course at one of the UK's major business schools:

" My research was an ethnographic investigation of the experience of executives studying on the school's part-time Executive Masters programme. I was a participant observer with one cohort of these students, a group of about twenty people most of whom were men. ... While they were busy taking notes on and seeking to learn about finance, statistics, marketing, corporate strategy, public sector management and more I was taking notes on and seeking to learn about them. "

It would have been possible to question the executives about what they thought about the course and its value to them. Yet Fox's participation in the class gave him an insight into the group's culture and behaviour that would have been missed in a survey: 'While ethnography, of the sort I was engaged in, is by its nature limited to the study of one case, it had the benefit of allowing the researcher access to a level of interactional minutiae ... which other methods cannot attain.' (ibid., p. 436). For example (ibid., p. 435):

" [A]lthough the managers were on the masters programme to learn about management from the faculty, in many cases they had much more managerial 'street credibility' than their teachers. This produced a degree of tension, for the students were in a sense paying customers with considerable experience and knowledge about that which they were paying to learn. If coffee arrived late or handouts were poorly organised, the students would jokingly question whether they could trust what the business school was teaching if it could not even manage to produce coffee on time. The ability or inability of the business school to practise what it preached became a theme which much of the part-timers' banter and joking worked upon. "

The ethnographic technique is likely to be the preferred choice when studying people who do not share the dominant (English-speaking) language-base that typifies most surveys and structured questionnaires. Ethnic minorities in inner-city areas, for example, not only have a specific subculture but sometimes use a private language unsuited to questionnaires, as illustrated by the following exchange between a principal of a Pittsburgh inner-city school and a black teenage pupil (quoted in Deutscher, 1970, p. 19).

Principal: Why are you stretched so thin by joy? Are you flying backwards?
Pupil: My special pinetop is smoking and wants to eyeball you fast.
Principal: I'm stalled. What is this all about?
Pupil: I wasted one of the studs for capping me. Teach blasted at me and told me to fade away to the hub and fetch you.
Principal: Don't put your head in the bowl and pull the chain.

Observation and reliability

Whenever observation is used as a research technique, the researcher has to make a large number of inferences about the meaning behind the phenomena under scrutiny. Can these inferences and accounts of behaviour be considered valid and reliable interpretations of what has taken place? Would two observers look at and see the activity in the same way? If not, would one account be better than the other, or would both be equally useful, revealing distinct aspects of the activity?

These questions take us to the heart of the methodological problems with observation. It is a selective process, and one that is dependent on the role and position the observer adopts while observing. Those who employ a participant strategy can overplay their role in the group and so affect the group's behaviour (and distort matters). There is also a danger of 'going native', becoming less an observer and more a full member of the group being studied – the observer being captured by his or her subject matter. The benefits of easy familiarity with respondents can turn into the disadvantage of over-familiarity, in the sense of developing more than a research relationship with them. This can compromise objectivity.

To be valid, non-positivist observational research has to produce accounts that the observed would recognise as accurate stories of their lives. Unlike Inkeles (1993), who distanced himself from anything that smacked of 'subjective indicators' in his study of the quality of life, qualitative observation and analysis involve getting as close as possible to such indicators. This may require the researcher's interpretations of events and behaviour to be checked out with those who have been observed, a common technique to ensure that the research is a valid reconstruction of the subjective meanings of social actors. Hessler (1992) calls this technique 'touching base' (Box 16.5).

BOX 16.5 'Touching base' – validating interpretive observation

When I was observing the development of a comprehensive health centre for the poor in a Chicano and Mexican-Indian community in a large southwestern city, I was fortunate to have met a very influential Chicano leader who must have seen some utility in taking me under his wing. I worked a bit at his candle factory, did some editing for him, and gave him one of my tape recorders. I lived for a brief time in his house along with his five children, wife, grandchild, daughter-in-law, and mother-in-law. The cultural nuances were very difficult for me to observe and record because I was a complete stranger to the community and because the Spanish spoken was a different dialect than the Spanish I had grown up with in Los Angeles. Touching base involved me getting some field notes together, making copies of them at the university across town, and blocking out names. I would sit with my informant and go over my more general recordings with him. Then I would ask him if I had observed the particular event or confrontation between a neighbourhood resident and the medical director correctly. I even checked my interpretations, which I had bracketed in the field notes. After several sessions, my informant began to get the hang of what I was trying to do with my study, and I began to get a feel for the quality and accuracy of my observations.

Source: Hessler (1992), p. 223.

Valid interpretation is an important requirement for good observational sociology. However, it can never be entirely free of distorting or biasing effects, since the observer is clearly not the observed. As Stanley (1990a, p. 624) has noted with regard to ethnographic observation, 'the project which drives the writing of ethnography is different from that which drives the doing of social life. Ethnographic description is actually not, and cannot be, literal description.' Rather than hide or gloss over this, some researchers turn it into a topic for debate, reflexively observing their own participation in the social activity (see Phillips, 1971). Gilbert and Mulkay (1984) argue that no one interpretation of social action can be better than another – whatever method is used to record or observe it – because all social actions have numerous meanings, each created by and dependent on the interactive context in which it is constructed. One sociologist's version of events is no more and no less valid than anyone else's, it merely describes particular features that the sociologist regards as important to him or her. This assertion has encouraged sociologists to explore the way in which accounts of social events and activities are constructed through the discourse and language that actors use. This has in turn led to increased use of the technique of conversation analysis, which is closely associated with the ethnomethodological school of social theory (see Chapter 18).

The use of observational methods is crucial if sociologists are to construct – even if only reflexively, as Gilbert and Mulkay (1984) would argue – cogent accounts of the interactive and subjective meanings of social actors. This is where their strength lies, as evidenced by the vast number of qualitative ethnographies and observer studies that have contributed to the sociological research base. The basic strengths and weaknesses of these methods are summarised in Table 16.4. When this table is compared with Table 16.3, it becomes obvious that the strengths and weaknesses of the observational and survey methods are the converse of each other. This is perhaps why sociologists are keen to combine the two approaches (when appropriate) in such a way as to maximise the benefits and minimise the limitations of each.

TABLE 16.4 Advantages and disadvantages of observational methods

Advantages	Disadvantages
Provide in-depth data on social actors' meanings and behaviour	There can be problems with representativeness and reliability
Can reveal deviant or non-conventional subcultures	Restricted in terms of the size of the research population that can be observed
Avoid the use of artificial research instruments to collect data	There can be problems with the observer role and 'going native'

QUESTION Can you think of any methodological problems that might be caused by combining interviews or questionnaires with ethnographic observational methods? How might these problems be overcome?

The case study

Before we end this discussion of the principal research tools used by sociologists, it is worth considering the case study, which can include both survey and observational methods of data collection. Case studies have continuing appeal in sociology despite their often hostile treatment in some research texts because of doubts about their reliability and representativeness.

Case studies involve the detailed exploration of one or a number of individuals, groups, communities, organisations or events that are thought to reflect or embody some phenomenon or set of processes that might throw light on a broader area of sociological concern. They are also used to explore new areas of inquiry and to put new issues on the sociological research agenda. Not surprisingly, they often use a qualitative approach to explore the case in as much detail as possible. A useful definition of the case study has been provided by Yin (1989, p. 23):

" A case study is an empirical enquiry that: investigates a contemporary phenomenon within its real-life context; when the boundaries between the phenomenon and the context are not clearly evident; and in which multiple sources of evidence are used. "

Getting close to one's subject matter is crucial if the experiences of the social actors under investigation are to be accurately portrayed. If more than one case study is undertaken, as in multiple case studies, this can only be regarded as replication, not sampling. Platt (1988) has provided a typology of case studies that moves from the specific to the more general in focus:

- Ideographic case studies: cases chosen because of their intrinsic interest and not because they necessarily point to a wider, more general phenomenon.
- Indicative case studies: cases that have a bearing on other situations that will need to be taken into account when conducting similar case studies.
- Representative case studies: here the researcher selects a case on the basis of rigorous criteria that will enable the case to be representative of other cases.

Platt suggests that most case studies lie towards the ideographic end of the research spectrum. She likens their role as exploratory vehicles to a 'social barium meal – whose progress through the [social] system illuminates it' (ibid., p. 10). For example, Townsend (1979), in his survey on poverty, used case studies of individual families' interactions with welfare agencies to show how the wider benefit system worked.

Clearly, the interpretive and qualitative aspect of case studies means they have been criticised for being less reliable than other research methods. However, Brewer (1994) argues that ethnographically based case studies can claim to be rigorous, reliable and representative if they conform to a number of research design principles. That is, a case study should:

- Identify the wider relevance of the setting and topic so that it can justificbly claim to be representative of other cases.
- Identify what it is focusing on and what is being left out and why, and the implications of this.
- Identify the theoretical framework used.
- Reinforce the authority of the findings by discussing problems that emerge during research, clarifying why the data were classified into certain types rather than others, and being open to rival interpretations.
- Show negative cases, if any, and how they impact on positive ones.
- Stress the contextual nature of the respondents' accounts.

Brewer's suggestions for improving the accountability of the case study are welcome and show how case studies can be a basis for generalisation and thus contribute to wider social theory.

 ## Feminist methodology and the critique of 'malestream' research

Ethnographic research methods have frequently been used by feminist sociologists. Ethnography starts with the premise that the meanings and ideas of those being observed are of paramount importance: they should not be stripped away or reduced to statistics. Letting the actor speak for him- or herself is a central principle in such research. As such, ethnography is an inherently collaborative and democratic form of research that does not seek to impose the observer's ideas on the observed, although, as in all research, the researcher will make his or her own interpretation of the subjects' accounts. In a similar fashion, feminist analysis claims to be collaborative and non-impositional. It is highly critical of mainstream (malestream) knowledge, which is considered to be expert-based, hierarchical and fundamentally patriarchal. The Australian sociologist Dale Spender (1985, p. 5) contends that:

> "at the core of feminist ideas is the crucial insight that there is no one truth, no one authority, no one objective method which leads to the production of pure knowledge. This insight is as applicable to feminist knowledge as it is to patriarchal knowledge, but there is a significant difference between the two: feminist knowledge is based on the premise that the experience of all human beings is valid and must not be excluded from our understandings, whereas patriarchal knowledge is based on the premise that the experience of only half the human population needs to be taken into account and the resulting version can be imposed on the other half."

Consequently, the methodology used by feminist researchers is designed to avoid the distinction between 'objective' and 'subjective' indicators of social action. Rather than seeing science and rationality as privileged forms of knowledge counterposed to the 'soft' and 'unreliable' discourse of subjectivity and experience, feminists insist that personal experience should be the foundation of all research. Women's experiences in particular have been ignored in male-dominated social research, reflecting the more general marginalisation and subordination of women in society.

CONNECTIONS See Chapter 17, pages 487–94, and Chapter 19, pages 525–8, for a more substantial discussion of feminist theories.

Hammersley (1992) has summarised the main features of feminist methodology and identified four main themes:

- Gender divisions and the subordination of women run through all areas of social life. They are not restricted to one particular arena of interaction, such as the domestic household or the workplace, but are a constant feature of all interactions. All research must therefore recognise and address this from the start.

- Rather than being unreliable, subjectivity and personal experience are the source of sensitive and profoundly insightful knowledge about the social world, a form of knowledge that women themselves are most able to understand and express.

- The research process must not lead to a hierarchical division between researcher and researched. Rather, the latter should be invited to help interpret the data. Those who are oppressed should be given the tools to help them understand this oppression and liberate themselves from it.

- The overall goal of feminist research is the emancipation of women, which is seen as the only valid basis for research. Feminist research is successful when it raises consciousness and transforms gendered relations.

These four themes mean that the feminist research agenda is very different from that of the more traditional approaches. Hammersley acknowledges the importance of the feminist challenge to conventional research techniques, and recognises the value of the work it has produced. It has placed gender at the centre of research and, by doing so, it has raised new questions. However, he believes that while these questions do need to be addressed, the claim that a distinct feminist methodology is needed or can be constructed should be rejected.

In response, feminists such as Ramazanoglu (1992) have asked how it is possible for Hammersley to accept the basic research findings of feminists and yet reject the methodology with which these findings were generated. Moreover, feminists have reasserted their belief in the need to dismiss the division between science and emotion, rationality and experience that has dominated Western thought since the Enlightenment and produced 'views on which western scholarship, science and universities have long relied [and which] are blatantly sexist and racist, and privilege middle class males' (ibid., p. 208). Against such a tradition, feminist research seeks neither to impose itself on others nor to claim some privileged position or way of accessing the truth of subjective experiences. Reinharz (1992, p. 243) argues that:

> " there is no single 'feminist way' to do research. There is little 'methodological elitism' or definition of 'methodological correctness' in feminist research. Rather there is a lot of individual creativity and variety. ... Feminist research is amoeba-like; it goes everywhere, in every direction. ... The amoeba is fed by the women's movement. The women's movement, in turn, is fed by women's outrage and hope. "

This specifically feminist call for multiple and creative research techniques might have more appeal to researchers who have yet to engage with the feminists' challenge. That is, the long-standing conflict between the theoretical traditions of positivism and anti-positivism might be superseded by a willingness to use new combinations of methods allied to new theoretical approaches to understanding social action and interaction. For example, Giddens' (1990a) notion of structuration (see Chapter 19) requires entirely new methodological strategies that will dissolve the conventional distinctions between structural and interpretive analysis. There will continue to be debate about the relevance of different research methods, but perhaps there will also be a greater preparedness to accept a much wider range of methods.

Postmodernity and research methodology

The challenge to the distinction between positivism and anti-positivism is indicative of the wider rejection of the dualisms prevalent in modernist thinking. There is a strong school of thought in sociology (and parallel schools in art, literature and philosophy) that we now live in a postmodern age. According to this view, the absolute forms of knowledge – including sociological knowledge – that characterised modernity have evaporated, along with the validity of accounts of society and culture based on rational and objective inquiry. There can no longer be privileged, expert accounts of the world. Postmodernism challenges not only certainty but also traditional disciplinary and methodological conventions. It seeks to replace them not with another convention, but with a limitless range of possible interpretations of the world around us. Feminism offered a different critical approach from that of mainstream sociological research, together with an alternative methodology. Postmodernism also offers an alternative, but one that in principle pulls the rug from under the feet of all methodologies.

One of the main reasons for this is that sociological inquiry is based on the core belief that it is possible to examine and explain the structure and meaning of social action. This rests on the assumption that there is a subject of social action, who – with other subjects (social actors) – gives meaning to social action. Weber (1970) argued that one of the first priorities of sociology was to understand 'subjective meaning'. By understanding the intended and unintended effects of social action, sociologists would be able to map out and explain, through disciplined inquiry, 'the social' – the specific patterns and dynamics of society. Postmodernism challenges the assumptions of modernist sociology by deconstructing the idea of 'the subject' or 'the self'. There is no stable meaning to 'the subject', the 'self' is uncertain, and 'the social', which sociologists believe they discover through research, is simply the creation of a sociological discourse – a particular type of knowledge that does not have a privileged position among other discourses.

Thus, from both the theoretical and the methodological viewpoint, postmodernism challenges most if not all the modernist assumptions discussed in this chapter. But this should not necessarily be regarded as unproductive or negative, for just as feminists have called on sociology to be self-critical, reflexive and open to new ways of engaging with and understanding culture and society, so postmodernism has sparked an interest in new approaches to social analysis. Much of this work is highly abstract and philo-sophically deep (see Chapter 19).

One recent methodological development inspired by both feminism and post-modernism is the interest in autobiographical forms of sociological inquiry. This interest in part reflects the wider concern in sociology with identity and the desire by many feminists to document and describe the lives of women from their own per-spective. As we saw in Chapter 1, our 'selves' are not single, stable identities but are multiple and change according to context and over time, and our memories and images of our past are shifting and unfixed.

A growing number of sociologists have seen the value of opening their analysis to the rich social vein that runs through the biographical and autobiographical accounts of social actors (Benstock, 1988; Bell and Yalom, 1990). Research sources now include dairies, memoirs, letters, films, videos and other forms of visual representation that help reveal the meaning of personal lives and the contexts in which they are lived. But what about the postmodernist stand against all methodologies? Postmodernists would argue that autobiographical inquiry cannot provide a new foundation for the discipline; it is merely another way of attempting to construct a version of reality when in fact there is no reality to be constructed. Against this strongly relativist position, many sociologists contend that sociology is able to acknowledge the ambiguities and uncertainties of the postmodern condition, and rather than collapsing into a methodological heap, it could help to reveal and explain these ambiguities and uncertainties. If this were not possible, the foundation of the sociological discipline and its critical edge would disappear.

Chapter summary

- Sociological research explores a wide range of questions about the dynamics of social change, matters of social policy and broader theoretical issues asso-ciated with the development of the discipline itself.

- Researchers have to define their principal research question and the conceptual framework to which it relates, as well as determine the most appropriate method of collecting data, and how these data can be rigorously analysed.

- Researchers have to ensure that their research is reliable, valid and, when appropriate, based on some form of representative sampling.

- The positivist and interpretivist approaches have shaped the theory and practice of research, but they are gradually being displaced by a more reflexive and pluralistic approach to social inquiry.
- Common research instruments are surveys (using questionnaires and/or interviews), observational techniques (such as ethnography and participant observation), case studies and the analysis of secondary data. Experiments are not commonly used by sociologists.
- Both feminism and postmodernism have posed major challenges to the modernist assumptions underlying traditional sociological research.

 ## Questions to think about

- How does the subject of a piece of sociological research influence the methods chosen to study it?
- To which research instrument(s) do you feel most drawn? Explain your response.
- Do you think that feminism and postmodernism have dealt a fatal blow to modernist methods of research? If so, why? If not, why not?

 ## Investigating further

Benton, Ted and Ian Craib (2001) *Philosophy of Social Science: Philosophical Issues in Social Theory*, Palgrave.

> Although primarily a theoretical book, this has very useful discussions in the early chapters on empiricism, positivism and interpretive approaches to social science.

Coleman, Clive and Jenny Moynihan (1996) *Understanding Crime Data*, Open University Press.

> A useful text for thinking about research and about crime in society. It offers a strong focus on the uses and limitations of data, as well as key issues in the interpretation of data.

Devine, Fiona and Sue Heath (1999) *Sociological Research Methods in Context*, Palgrave.

> Based on a series of case studies (in such areas as education, the family, crime and politics), this book looks at the problems and challenges of doing 'real life' social research. It would usefully supplement your reading of other chapters in this book.

17

Classical social theory, feminism and modernity

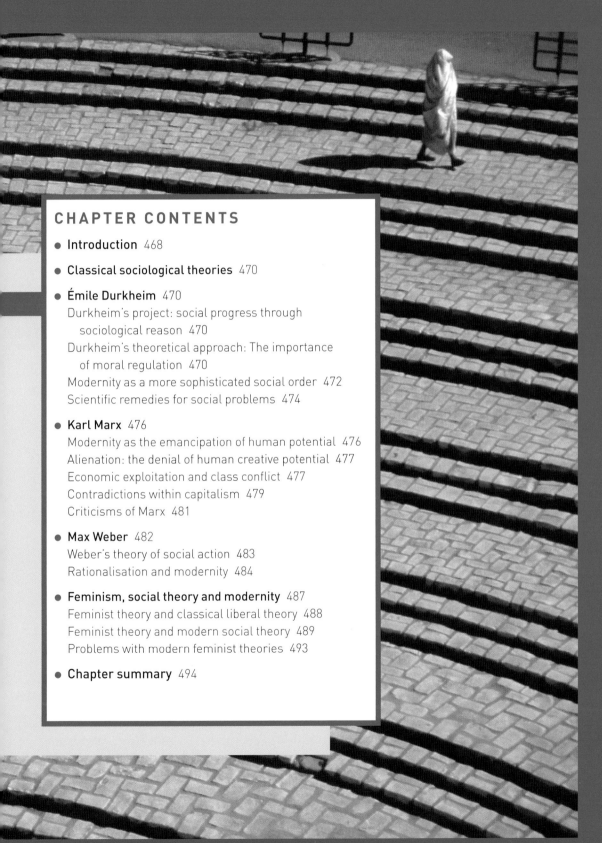

CHAPTER CONTENTS

Aims of the chapter

We open this chapter by returning to some of the themes of modernity discussed in Chapter 2 in order better to understand how the key founding sociologists shaped their theories in response to the Great Transformation. Focusing throughout on social structure, the chapter explores the contribution of the classical sociologists to the understanding of society and the relationship between feminist theory and modernity. By laying out the main ideas developed in these perspectives, we shall help you to consolidate your understanding of the basic concepts of sociology. By the end of this chapter, you should have an understanding of the following concepts:

- Mechanical solidarity
- Organic solidarity
- Social differentiation
- Anomie
- Conscience collective
- Infrastructure
- Superstructure
- Class consciousness
- Realism
- Ideal type

Introduction

The roots of sociology are entangled with the new form of society that began to emerge in the early nineteenth century. This new social world, or 'modernity', gave birth to a new area of knowledge – the systematic study of society that we call sociology. From the start, this new social science was part of a great and optimistic project. It was believed that human beings could know their world accurately and thus improve it. At the time, it was assumed that it was possible to control and shape the natural world, but it was a radical innovation to proclaim that the social world could be understood and reshaped in the same way.

Sociology began as part of the great project to achieve progress through reason – that is, to gain knowledge and use it to create a better social world. With access to truth, the early sociologists believed they could promote progress and bring about the good society. They recognised that knowledge gave humans the power to shake off the past and shape their destiny, and sociological knowledge would bring this power into the social world. One side of the early vision of sociology embodied all this: hope of progress, faith in knowledge and the sheer thrill of experiencing a rapidly changing society that seemed able to shake off its past. As Marx and Engels put it in the *Communist Manifesto* of 1848 (1967, p. 83):

> "All fixed, fast-frozen relations, with their train of ancient and venerable prejudices and opinions, are swept away, all new-formed ones become antiquated before they can ossify. All that is solid melts into air, all that is holy is profaned, and men at last are forced to face ... the real conditions of their lives and their relations with their fellow men."

But this was not the only side of the sociological vision. For, while celebrating the new, early sociologists also asked what would be lost in this transformation, this transition to modernity. Just how good was this future that society was rushing towards?

Sociologists always had grave doubts about the shape of modernity. This ambivalence is expressed by Marshall Berman (1983, p. 15) in a passage that has become a classic statement in its own right:

> "There is a mode of vital experience – experience of space and time, of the self and other, of life's possibilities and perils – that is shared by men and women all over the world today. I will call this body of experience 'modernity'. To be modern is to find ourselves in an environment that promises us adventure, power, joy, growth, transformation of ourselves and the world – and at the same time, that threatens to destroy everything we have, everything we know, everything we are. Modern environments and experiences cut across all boundaries of geography and ethnicity, of class and nationality, of religion and ideology: in this sense, modernity can be said to unite all mankind. But it is a paradoxical unity, a unity of disunity: it pours us all into a maelstrom of perpetual disintegration and renewal, of struggle and contradiction, of ambiguity and anguish. To be modern is to be part of a universe in which, as Marx said, 'all that is solid melts into air.' "

Ever since the birth of modern sociology, many key theorists have shared this ambivalence about social change. The disorder brought about by rapid social and political change led sociologists to propose solutions that would allow the social order to be recreated in a progressive way, without turning back the clock to a rigid, ranked, static society. The question was how to promote social progress and social unity at the same time. Different theorists with differing political and philosophical views provided dramatically different answers, as we shall see. For nearly two centuries, sociology's goal was to move through this transformation towards a new stability, where human needs would be fulfilled. Sociologists as different as Durkheim and Marx wished to resolve social disorder and bring about a higher, better form of society. As we shall see, the early feminists were also concerned with the idea of progress, although feminist theory came to the fore rather later in time.

CONNECTIONS At this point, you might wish to remind yourself of some of the key themes discussed in Chapters 1 and 2, particularly on pages 4–20 and 24–41.

Today, it is less usual to voice optimism about progress in society and about the benefits of science. At one level, we do have a vague sense of progress. Technology, communication and information systems are becoming ever more sophisticated, goods are being produced more cheaply, and we are filling our leisure hours with an increasingly diverse and imaginative range of activities. But to what extent are we confident that our social and moral life is improving, or that the planet can cope with the economic and military impositions of different national governments?

Certainly, the founding sociologists had doubts about the health and justice of the social system of their time. Each of them sought change – whether gradual reform or grand revolution – that would put society to rights. They did not share all our present-day concerns (such as the environment), but we still share many of theirs. So we shall re-visit the work of the classical sociologists – Durkheim, Marx and Weber – to see what light they can shed on our current concerns. In the second part of the chapter, we shall examine the place of feminist thought in understanding these issues.

QUESTION Based on your reading of Chapters 1 and 2, to what extent do you think that the 'promise of modernity' has been fulfilled? Support your answer with appropriate references.

Classical sociological theories

By the end of the twentieth century, sociology was facing many challenges to its ideas. Some argued that the discipline was out of date and unable to offer solutions to such pressing issues and problems as war and conflict, global inequalities, and prejudice and discrimination based on gender, sexuality, race, religion or class background. And yet it has proved impossible for sociology to break with its classic legacy. In trying to understand the key features of modernity, sociologists return again and again to the core ideas of the three founding fathers: Émile Durkheim (1858–1917), Karl Marx (1818–1883) and Max Weber (1864–1920). Although elements of their thinking have been rejected and superseded, sociology still draws on their conceptions of modernity and its problems and possibilities. For Durkheim, Marx and Weber, social scientific understanding was an urgent task – an indispensable weapon for engaging with all the problems and unfulfilled potential of modern society. All three had both positive and negative feelings about modernity, though they differed with regard to their degree of faith in the future and the extent to which knowledge of society could help create the good society. We shall look at these founding theorists in turn to consider their key ideas and the core tensions in their work.

Émile Durkheim

BOX 17.1 Émile Durkheim (1858–1917)

Born: Lorraine, France, 1858.
Education: Ecole Normale Superieure, 1879.
Career: Schoolteacher in philosophy, 1882–87; university lecturer, Bordeaux, 1887; taught sociology and education, Sorbonne, Paris, 1902; professor of Education and Sociology, 1913.

Main works: *The Division of Labour in Society* (1893), *Rules of Sociological Method* (1895), *Suicide* (1897), *The Elementary Forms of Religious Life* (1912).

Durkheim's project: social progress through sociological reason

Social integration
The unification of diverse groups of people in a community.

Moral consensus
Desire for and agreement upon a set of prescribed moral values.

One of Durkheim's prime ambitions was to establish sociology as a respectable academic discipline in universities. But more than this, he wished to apply sociological knowledge to social intervention by the state in order to create social harmony. Durkheim regarded himself as a progressive, pursuing reform guided by positive sociological laws. Indeed, he felt that his commitment to reform for the good of society made him a socialist. Paradoxically, the goal of his reformism was close to the traditional conservative aims of moral consensus and a stable hierarchy. Progress should be towards social order, rather than towards the emancipation of the individual human being. Durkheim's core concern was re-establishing **social integration** and **moral consensus** in the modern industrial world. He saw the science of sociology as providing a sound basis of knowledge to underpin social intervention that would bring society to a new state of harmonious health.

Durkheim's theoretical approach: the importance of moral regulation

At the heart of Durkheim's work was his belief in the importance of well-organised and harmonious societies in which individuals could flourish and live out their lives productively and contentedly together. He saw the individual subject as above all in need of control and regulation. Without some means of constraining and structuring the individual's needs and desires, personal misery and social disorder were all too probable.

According to Durkheim, both order and individual fulfilment were dependent upon proper socialisation. People must learn how to behave appropriately in different circumstances and acquire proper knowledge of the collective culture that binds them together like an invisible social cement. The beauty of efficient socialisation is that, while we think we are acting independently and autonomously as active agents in the creation of our own life stories, in fact our journey through life is structured by norms and values that existed before us and will continue to exist after we have left the stage (Durkheim, 1938, pp. 1–2):

> " When I fulfil my obligations as brother, husband or citizen, I perform duties, which are defined, externally to myself and my acts, in law and custom. Even if they conform to my own sentiments, and I feel their reality subjectively, such reality is still objective, for I did not create them; I merely inherited them through my education … the church member finds the belief and practices of his religious life ready made at birth; their existence prior to him implies this existence outside himself. "

Functionalism
A theoretical perspective based on an analogy between social systems and organic systems. It claims that the nature of a society's various institutions must be understood in terms of the function each performs in enabling the smooth running of society as a whole.

Durkheim is emphasising here the objective nature of norms and values – their existence outside us and independent of us as individual subjects. This is a fine example of a structural sociology – a sociology that emphasises how our lives are patterned by social forces outside our control. Durkheim insisted that we treat the social (collective) rules that govern our lives as facts, just like the facts of nature. 'Treat social facts as things', he demanded. Although the social structures of norms and values may seem to differ from the physical or biological facts that also structure our lives, they are just as real and objective. However, Durkheim went further, arguing that human society is not just made up of social facts, but that it also works as a social system, with particular institutions contributing to the smooth operation of the whole society. This theory is known as **functionalism** and is discussed more fully in Box 17.2. Drawing on a biological analogy, Durkheim suggested that sociology should use the same scientific techniques to explain the facts of society as the natural sciences did to explain the facts of the physical and natural world. For Durkheim, this meant that sociology should adopt the model of natural science explanation known as positivism.

BOX 17.2 Durkheim and functionalism

The health of an organism depends on all the organs that make up its system working properly together, each organ performing a necessary function for the organism's health. In the human body, for instance, the heart is needed to pump the blood around the body, the liver is needed to purify the blood, and so on. Furthermore, the performance of each organ depends on the others performing their functions properly. The performance of the brain depends on the efficient functioning of the lungs, which depends on the performance of the heart, and so on. An organic system is an integrated system of interdependent, functioning parts.

Durkheim draws an explicit analogy between an organic system and a social system. Ways of living and thinking that are firmly established in a culture are referred to in sociology as institutionalised behaviours and beliefs. Functionalism explains the existence of any institutionalised aspect of a society in the same way as a biologist explains the presence of an organ in the body – in terms of the function it performs in keeping the whole system in a stable state. Thus, the integration, solidarity and equilibrium of a society are maintained by its constituent institutions – such as the family, the political system, the education system –▶

performing their functions properly and interdependently.

This conception of a social system ties in precisely with Durkheim's emphasis on the externality of social facts. Just as humans do not decide to have a liver, or kidneys or a spleen, so the institutions that exist in a social system can be explained in terms of their ability to perform a function that maintain the whole. In fact, functionalist sociology is above all characterised by a lack of interest in actors' explanations for their ways of living and thinking. Whatever the members of a society may think about its cultural features – their manifest functions, as functionalists call them – the reasons for them are identifiable only by the perceptive functionalist observer who is able to recognise their latent functions. Nothing could be further from the world of action sociology, for which, as we shall see in Chapter 18, the subject matter of the discipline must be precisely those actors' theories which functionalists dismiss as irrelevant.

Modernity as a more sophisticated social order

Durkheim's earliest work was his doctoral thesis, *The Division of Labour in Society* (1893), which provides a key to his ideas on the problems of society and their possible solutions. In *The Division of Labour*, Durkheim focused on the distinction (common among evolutionists at the time) between traditional and modern society. The diversity and complexity of human civilisations was encompassed by this simple distinction, which stressed evolution away from the **mechanical solidarity** that characterised primitive societies, and towards the sophisticated **organic solidarity** that would provide the basis of harmonious integration in industrial society.

Primitive societies, he argued, were 'segmental', in that they were just the aggregation of kin groups into clans and tribes. These larger groupings had little real cohesion, since each unit could be self-sufficient as hunters or agriculturalists. Hence, like a worm, society was divided into similar segments that could survive perfectly well if separated from one another. Even within these segments, social cohesion depended on rigid collective norms governing behaviour in every detail, so that total conformity was ensured. If any transgression did occur, then the basic social response was revenge. The primary source of conformity, however, was the shared consensus about norms and values – the 'conscience collective' that was absorbed and reproduced by every member of society. Mechanical solidarity was the term Durkheim used to convey this rigidity of social formation.

In contrast to his contemporaries, therefore, Durkheim did not portray traditional primitive society as an ideal, harmonious, integrated unity, but as a collection of fragmentary units embodying repressive conformity. For him, modern society was not inevitably fragmented by the breakdown of traditional community. Instead, the evolution of society provided the potential for a more stable and sophisticated social cohesion. The key to this potential was social evolution, the functionalist explanation for social change. This would take the form of increased social differentiation, whereby society would develop specialised institutions to deal with distinct areas of social life (for example, religion or production). Just as the evolution of animals had produced more sophisticated, specialised organs to perform particular functions for the whole creature, so society would develop a range of distinct institutions that would cater more adequately for the particular needs of the social whole. Like anatomical organs, they would be mutually dependent for their survival, and their correct functioning would depend on the healthy functioning of each one and their continuing integration, or organic solidarity. If the component parts of society developed 'a lively sentiment of their mutual dependence', conflicts and crises could be swept aside. Once again, a new

Mechanical solidarity
For Durkheim, the form of social cohesion that binds people through conformity to norms, especially in traditional societies (see *norms*).

Organic solidarity
For Durkheim, the desirable form of social cohesion that binds people in societies of greater and specialised complexity.

moral consensus had to be constructed to bring forth order. Unlike that in primitive society, however, this moral order would be sufficiently flexible to cope with the diverse social roles in a complex society – the individual would have freedom within the social constraints. A prime task for sociology was therefore to construct a new civic morality that could be disseminated efficiently by a state education system. Durkheim was directly involved in the development of these educational aims and techniques in his academic work, and in the advice he gave to the French government.

Because Durkheim conceived of society as primarily a moral order, the goal of recasting moral values was central to his sociological project. But social reform also had to have an institutional basis, and Durkheim identified chaotic economic competition as the root of conflict and class struggle. Since unequal rewards must be given to different positions, conflict would be created if individuals did not obtain suitable positions. As a result, he advocated regulation of the economy and of the worker–employer relationship.

Some of these reforms were directed at overcoming anomie – that is, a lack of regulating norms. As we shall see in Durkheim's explanations of suicide, he regarded the lack of normative regulation as a key cause of social and individual ill-health. Without such norms, he argued, humans developed insatiable appetites, limitless desires and a general feeling of irritation and dissatisfaction. Modern competitive market society encouraged this and, despite its claims, condemned people to 'unfreedom'. The idea that 'unfreedom' was due to anomie rested on conservative assumptions about human nature. Without normative constraints, humans could only be uncivilised beasts, slaves of their own whims and passions. Individuals had to be subordinate to society; they had to play their humble part in the functioning of the social organism. The collective consensus would allow them some choice between roles, but once allotted their position, they had to conform or become pathological deviants. Durkheim (1974, p. 72) described his vision of the correct relation between individuals and society as follows:

> "The individual submits to society, and this submission is the condition of his liberation. For man, freedom consists in the deliverance from blind, unthinking physical forces; this he achieves by opposing against them the great and intelligent force that is society, under whose protection he shelters."

Thus, society is outside us and above us; it constrains us and shapes our lives and our physical responses. What is good for social integration is good for the individual. These are Durkheim's core themes and they led him to his solutions to social problems (Table 17.1).

TABLE 17.1 Durkheim's analysis of problems and solutions in modernity

Problems in modernity	Causes	Durkheim's solutions
Anomie: lack of moral regulation, limitless ambitions, sense of worthlessness, lack of meaning in life	Rapid social change, decline of moral authority (for example, religion), increased complexity in social roles and rules, fragmentation of work	A new non-religious civic moral order, promoted through the state, laws and education. Moral unity to be based on a sense of mutual social interdependence
Lack of social integration, excessive individualism	Unfettered market system, unregulated competition	Regulation of markets and working conditions
Class conflict	Unequal opportunity for natural talents	Equal opportunity, abolition of inheritance, fair distribution of rewards.

QUESTION How important is the issue of social order in contemporary society? Construct a case for and against its importance. You might want to draw on examples you encountered earlier in this book (such as crime or employment) to help formulate your arguments.

Scientific remedies for social problems

Durkheim's emphasis on externality and constraint was directly linked to his conception of scientific explanation. This was presented in *The Rules of Sociological Method* (1938), in which he developed his conceptions of the subject matter of sociology and its methodology, dictated by his view of science. Since sociology had to be established as a scientific discipline (thus enabling social intervention on the basis of positive knowledge), then science had to dictate its methods and concepts. The view of science that Durkheim adopted was a fairly crude, positivistic one.

BOX 17.3 Durkheim and positivism

The Enlightenment was the period in which thinkers stopped relying on religion to provide them with knowledge of the world and started to use reason, to think rationally. Many writers on the history of knowledge (see, for example, the account of Gellner's views in Chapter 15) identify the Enlightenment-sponsored emergence of rationalism as the defining moment in human intellectual history. This was when the 'Great Divide' opened up between pre-modern thought (typified by faith in religious doctrines) and modern thinking. For many, it was the rise of rationalism, and thereby scientific knowledge, that was the real springboard from which the key elements of modernity – the Industrial Revolution and capitalism – were launched.

Durkheim's enthusiasm for scientific sociology has to be understood in this context. If nature could be explained rationally by using scientific methods, then surely society

could be too? His account of the similarity between natural facts and social facts derived directly from his desire for sociology to blossom into a mature science equal to the other sciences. Durkheim's definition of sociology's subject matter as social structures of social facts stemmed from his determination that sociology would be positivist. Unless he defined social life as similar to natural life, this project would be doomed.

Positivism is the name given to the set of ideas that underpin most scientific work. As a philosophy, positivism includes three distinct principles:

- Reality is made up of cause and effect relationships – things are as they are because they have been caused by other things.

- These are facts – objective features – and, whatever our subjective feelings, we can do nothing about them. Whether

we like or dislike a factual state of affairs is irrelevant. Our judgements about reality must be ignored when revealing its factual character.

- We can only prove the existence of cause and effect relationships by demonstrating their existence empirically, by collecting evidence identifiable by the senses.

Thus, scientists assume that medical conditions such as cirrhosis of the liver must be caused by something natural. The knowledge that alcohol is a major contributory factor in this disease was discovered by testing various hunches (hypotheses). This was done by means of experiments that involved observing and measuring empirically the extent to which liver tissue was damaged by alcohol. This factual state of affairs is something none of us can change, however much we would like to; however much we wish that ▶

pouring pints of lager or bottles of red wine down our throats did not damage our livers, the fact is it does.

How did Durkheim make this philosophy suit the character and investigation of social life? Just as frogs do not choose to have bulging eyes and croak a lot, and people do not choose to have bladders that need periodic evacuation, so modern humans do not choose to live in nuclear families or go out to work for a wage. They think they choose, but the reality is that they do not, because the social facts of their world constrain and structure their lives – they learn to live as they do. Sociology's job is to collect empirical evidence of the extent to which normative structural forces determine social lives. Thus, Durkheim (1938) was able to claim that 'The laws of societies are no different from those governing the rest of nature and the method by which they are discovered is identical with that of the other sciences.'

Durkheim's model of scientific sociology was put into practice in his study entitled *Suicide* (1952), which followed two years after *The Rules of Sociological Method*. Firstly, the use he made of statistical correlation illustrates the importance he laid on empirical methods (even if later commentators criticised his dependence on official statistics). Secondly, given that the suicide rate in most societies remained fairly steady from one year to the next, and that there were marked but stable differences between societies, he argued that suicide was due to social influences rather than individual propensities. (Obviously, the individuals who figured in the suicide rate in one year were not the same as those who figured in the statistics for the following year!) Thus, Durkheim sought to explain the social fact of suicide solely and exclusively by other social facts, such as social cohesion and economic change. Most commentators agree that Durkheim's exclusion of all psychological and physiological explanations in his study of patterned suicide rates was productive only to the extent that it revealed the importance of social factors. It is, however, profoundly mistaken to divorce sociological explanations from other complementary ones. Suicide must be explained by a range of factors that fall within the remit of many disciplines, but this in no sense undermines the scientific status of any of these disciplines.

Thirdly, Durkheim's explanation of variations in suicide rates embodied his interest in collective solidarity. He identified three types of suicide – anomic, **egoistic** and **altruistic** – and linked the first of these to strains in the moral order (brought on by economic deregulation and fluctuation) and the second two to insufficient or particularly high levels of social integration respectively. Moral regulation, one must surmise from this, must have been considered by Durkheim to be too low, for the counterpart of anomic suicide – fatalistic suicide – has only a shadowy existence in Durkheim's conception. Thus, the two dimensions of the social group that mattered were social integration and moral regulation, and the element in society that most strongly influenced both was the moral order – usually embodied in religion.

For Durkheim, social life was built out of patterns of behaviour governed by norms and values. Although related to other aspects of society, culture remained the key force shaping individuals and governing human behaviour, and culture was intimately linked to religion. Religion was, as Durkheim put it, 'the most primitive of all social phenomena. It was the source, through successive transformations, of all other manifestations of collective activity: law, morality, art, science, political forms, etc. In the beginning all is religious' (quoted in Lukes, 1973, p. 232).

Thus, social organisation and cohesion could be explained by the presence of religion – a normative system shared by the entire social group. This led Durkheim and his followers to define religion extremely broadly and include all sorts of institutionalised systems of belief that promoted solidarity. Changes in this structure of norms and values

Egoism
Normally a reference to selfishness, it also refers to a social setting where individual self-interest is the basis of morality.

Altruism
Unselfish action in the interest of others.

did not reflect changes elsewhere, but were the prime movers of social adaptation. This was an approach that directed attention away from economic relationships, political and economic domination, and variations in class structure. The evolution of culture within the integrated organic society was seen as far more illuminating than the study of concrete structures of power, which varied according to historical circumstances. Rather than historical analysis, Durkheimian sociology sought to identify the universal laws governing social order and social evolution. This (functionalist) view stood in opposition to any form of Marxist economic determinism, as we shall see next.

CONNECTIONS Chapter 15 offers a more detailed account of Durkheim's view of religion – see pages 427–8.

 Karl Marx

BOX 17.4 Karl Marx (1818–83)

Born: Trier, Rhineland, 1818.
Education: University of Bonn, 1835, University of Berlin, 1836–41.
Work: editor, *Rheinische Zeitung*, 1842; Paris, 1843; Brussels, 1845; Germany 1848; London 1849–83.
Main works: *Poverty of Philosophy* (1847), *Communist Manifesto* (1848), *The Eighteenth Brumaire of Louis Bonaparte* (1852). *Grundrisse (Outline of a Critique of Political Economy)* (1857), *Preface to A Contribution to the Critique of Political Economy* (1859), *Theories of Surplus Value* (1862–3). *Capital*, volumes 1–3 (1863–7), *Critique of the Gotha Programme* (1875).

Marx's ideas have been hugely influential, not only because he was the great prophet of the end of capitalism, but also because he forged an original vision by critically drawing on three distinct intellectual traditions: **German idealist philosophy**, **French socialism** and **British political economy**. Marx responded to capitalism by reworking these traditions. He attempted to put socialism on a scientific basis by specifying how structural weaknesses built into the capitalist economic system created the necessary conditions for it. As a result, his theory was wide-ranging, but also a product of a specific period in the history of a particular part of the world.

German idealist philosophy
An approach based on the thesis that the only things that really exist are minds and their content. It proposes that human progress comes through the advancement of human reason.

French socialism
A political doctrine that emerged during the French Revolution and emphasised social progress led by a new industrial class.

Modernity as the emancipation of human potential

In his earliest writings, Marx displayed his philosophical training through abstract criticisms of the philosopher Hegel, whose ideas dominated German intellectual life in the 1840s. For Hegel, the development of human society had to be seen as uneven and fitful progress towards a state of true, full humanity. According to Hegel, it was the philosopher's role to subject the world to critique and discover in it the tendencies towards the fulfilment of true human potential. The state, as the home of law and justice, demonstrated higher qualities than the mundane **civil society**. Thus, in Hegel's philosophy, the Prussian state was the embodiment of reason, despite his critical stance towards the imperfect contemporary society.

Radical young Hegelians – including the young Marx – accepted the idea of the philosopher as an all-seeing liberator, but were more critical of the contemporary state.

British political economy
The economic and social analysis of early capitalism by writers such as Adam Smith and David Ricardo.

Civil society
An imprecise concept that normally refers to social institutions outside the political state.

Materialism
In its Marxist usage, an emphasis on economic and political relations.

However, Marx took things much further and rejected Hegel's idealism in favour of a **materialistic** explanation of history – that is, one based on humans' practical actions within the constraints of particular social structures. He came to see the state as a reflection of class relations in civil society, and these social relations as shaping human nature.

In his later work, Marx developed an economic and political analysis of capitalism in order to provide an understanding of the weaknesses of capitalism that would cause it to be superseded by an entirely new social order – socialism. Lying behind this, and throughout his work, was a vision of what humans could and should be if social conditions would allow. This is set out schematically, together with Marx's proposed remedies, in Table 17.2.

Alienation: the denial of human creative potential

Marx believed that what singled humans out from other species was their capacity to shape their world by creative activity. Only humans could develop a conception of what they wished to create and bring it to fruition. Work could therefore be the expression of humans' intellect and creative capacity, providing it was not alienating, either by being concerned merely with survival or by being socially organised in such a way that it became debased. The alienation of labour reached its worst, Marx argued, under industrial capitalism, for here workers were tied to machines to perform meaningless tasks that were only part of a larger process. They were forced to sell their ability to work (their labour power) to the employer as a marketable commodity. Human creativity was therefore turned into a commodity, to be bought and sold in the labour market for the going rate. The product of this labour was owned and sold by the capitalist, and the harder that workers laboured, the more they were exploited by the capitalist. The conditions that would allow true humanity were therefore those which would bring an end to alienated labour. These must include abundance, abolition of the division of production into meaningless tasks, and the termination of economic exploitation.

To overcome alienation, the basic economic relations that created it must be abolished – by revolutionary means. The whole structure of society must be transformed.

Mode of production
A Marxist concept that refers to the structured relationship between the means of production (raw materials, land, labour and tools) and the relations of production (see below).

Forces of production
The tools and techniques of production.

Relations of production
A Marxist term that refers to class relations that produce an unequal distribution of economic benefits and political power.

Economic exploitation and class conflict

Functionalist social theorists tend to regard economic activity as merely a mundane necessity to support the cultural structures that depend upon it. For Marx, the reverse was true: the rest of society more or less directly reflected economic relations. The key to understanding a particular society was its predominant **mode of production**. This consisted, firstly, of the equipment and raw materials needed in the production process – the means or **forces of production** – and, secondly, the resulting **relations of production** between the workers and those who owned the means of production. The relations of production constituted class relations, which in all non-communist societies produced an unequal distribution of economic benefits, political control and ideological domination by an elite. In this broad sense, Marx and Engels (1967, p. 67) argued that 'the history of all hitherto existing society is the history of class struggles'.

For Marxists, in all societies other than communist ones, the production of goods is structured in such a way as to produce great benefits for a minority – the dominant class – at the expense of an exploited majority – the subordinate class. Modern capitalist society differs from historical non-communist productive systems simply because the classes involved have changed. In ancient times, masters exploited the labour power of the slaves

TABLE 17.2 Marx on capitalist modernity and the socialist solution

Crisis/Social problem	Cause	Marx's solution
Chronic social conflict, class struggle	All social relations in capitalism embody exploitation and domination, reflecting the underlying relations of production	A new social organisation of production to end capitalist social relations. Social justice would become possible, with material abundance and an end to exploitation: 'From each according to their ability; to each according to their need'
Alienation	Capitalist economic relations	Socialist economic relations
Alienation from work	Labour is a commodity, bought and sold	Work and products cease to be commodities
Alienation from the products made in work	The tools and products are owned and controlled by the employer	An end to the rigid division of labour, especially between mental and physical work
Alienation from fellow human beings	Cooperation is destroyed	Full development of every person's potential
Alienation from the human potential for creative, constructive activity	Workers are prevented from controlling their work and being creative	
Systemic crises of capitalism: collapse of capital accumulation; monopolies replace competition; worker resistance becomes more effective	Falling rate of profit stops investment and hence growth; large capital displaces small; workers brought together in large workplaces and cities, with common interests as a class	The proletariat take advantage of economic crises to build class struggle and destroy capitalist economic and social relations by revolution. They then begin to build socialism. For the first time in history, the subordinate majority gain power, so class exploitation and domination cease

Proletariat
The Marxist term for wage earners, the propertyless class under capitalism.

Bourgeoisie
The Marxist term for the property-owning capitalist class.

they owned. In feudal times, landlords were able to exploit the productive labour of serfs because they owned the land on which the serfs scratched out a living. Under capitalism, a working class – called the **proletariat** by Marx – produces goods for the benefit of a dominant class of owners of capital – the **bourgeoisie**. This capitalist class exploits the labour of its employees by paying them wages that are lower than the market value of the goods they produce. This is not because of deliberate evilness on the part of capitalists – as a productive system, capitalism can only work if wage earners earn less than the value of the goods they produce. Without the profits generated by this relationship, enabling further investment, the system simply could not function.

Marxism is not just a theory of systems of production, it is also a theory of systems of ideas. Because class-based production involves exploitation that generates gross inequality between the classes, the system is inherently fragile. Capitalism can only survive as long as the disadvantaged wage earners put up with their situation. Why do they?

Economic base
The Marxist term for the economy, which has a determining effect on the superstructure (see *superstructure*).

According to Marxists, the **economic base** or infrastructure of a class society – the exploitative way it produces its goods – creates the superstructure – its non-economic institutions and systems of belief. As these terms suggest, Marxists see non-economic life in a class-based society as intimately bound up with the system of production: the economy is the base upon which culture is built. Thus, typical Marxist accounts of family life, education, the mass media and so on demonstrate their benefits for capitalism, even though at first glance they may have little connection with the economy. The same is true of ways of thinking. Marxists are interested not only in identifying features of the social structure that have direct benefits for capitalist commodity production, but also in the methods used to encourage people to live in this way. The most important of these methods in modern societies is socialisation. A crucial aspect of the superstructural support for capitalism is that people are encouraged to hold ideas that prop up the system. Such systems of ideas are called ideologies by Marxists.

So far, so structural. Like Durkheim, Marxists seem to focus exclusively on social forces external to the individual subject (class membership and ideological indoctrination) when explaining social behaviour. It is the theory of the system that matters. The ideas that actors have about their world are almost certain to be wrong, because of the power of ideology. Thus, rejection of Marxist analysis by the working class – the people the theory is designed to liberate – can be put down to ignorance and the mystification wrought by dominant beliefs: Marxists call this condition false consciousness.

But unlike Durkheim's ideas, Marx's theory of social change depends on the introduction of agency, or creative action. Whereas functionalists liken social change to the evolutionary adaptation of species to new environmental conditions, most Marxists see change as subject-inspired. Social change requires meaningful action by people who gain consciousness through struggle. Their position is half way between implacable structuralism and action theorising (a tradition of social thought that will be examined in more detail in the following chapter).

Capitalism, according to Marxists, has within it the seeds of its own destruction. The more it evolves as a system, and the more that capitalists seek ever-more efficient ways of generating profits (as they must), the more they create the conditions that will enable workers to see the truth about their lives. For Marxists, this is one of the internal contradictions of capitalism. While it is a system locked into the ceaseless pursuit of profit, at one and the same time this cumulatively disadvantages wage earners whose preparedness to accept their lot is essential to capitalism's survival. That is, the immiserisation of the proletariat produces increasing discontent among them, thus placing the system in jeopardy. Faced with the stark facts of their world that ideology can no longer obscure, the exploited workers abandon their false consciousness and become conscious of themselves as a class. Armed with this new insight, they take action to overturn the system that they now see has always oppressed them.

The replacement of false consciousness by class consciousness, then, can only come about because of changes taking place within the system at the structural level; but once this happens, creative action to overthrow the system is taken by subjects working collectively. As Marx and Engels (1968, p. 96) put it, 'Men make their own history, but not under circumstances of their own choosing'.

Contradictions within capitalism

Marx used the term contradictions to refer to the stresses and strains that weaken the social structure from within. Contradictions are not simply matters of logic. This idea is expressed in Marx's assertion that capitalism not only creates its own gravediggers (in the shape of the proletariat) but also destroys its distinctive character through the logic of its own development. We could call these two dimensions 'social contradictions' and 'systemic contradictions'.

Social contradictions are given direct expression in collective action. The economic relations of capitalism require domination and exploitation in the workplace, although this is disguised by the apparent fairness of the wage contract and the impersonal logic of the market. Nonetheless, there will always be struggle between the capitalist class and the proletariat because class relations are all about power and inequality. That is, class conflict is built into capitalism as a social contradiction. Whether this conflict can actually change anything, however, depends on the degree of systemic contradiction. Is capitalism generating crises that will give workers the chance to achieve real change? Can systemic contradictions and social struggles combine to create the conditions for successful revolution?

According to Marx, systemic contradictions work at two levels: first, the actions of capitalists themselves undermine profits, and then the competitive, atomised nature of capitalism is gradually transformed into a more organised, socialised form. Profits fall because workers are replaced by technology. Without wages, people cannot afford to buy goods, so low profits fall, re-investment falls and capital accumulation collapses. Furthermore, as capitalism develops, the expansion of share ownership and the growth of monopolistic firms foreshadow the emergence of a socialised economy.

Today, of course, we have the benefit of hindsight. We know that capitalism has not only survived but has rapidly developed into a voracious global system. So, it is very tempting to dismiss Marx's analysis as being without merit. But we can interpret the progress of capitalism over the course of the last hundred years in a way that is more sympathetic to Marxism. For example, it could be argued that, as a system that constantly generates crises, capitalism has had to adapt and transform itself in order to survive. But no survival strategy would have been able to save capitalism if the state had not helped out when necessary – for example, by reducing social conflicts through

Figure 17.1 Marxist thinking focuses on the conflict inherent in a capitalist economy. Who is making a profit at the expense of whom?

welfare provision. For these reasons, it is a mistake to write off Marxism as outdated. The challenge for Marxists is to understand the current form of capitalism and identify its potential for contradiction and change. However, this is not to say that there are not real problems with Marx's account of capitalism and modernity.

CONNECTIONS See Chapter 11, pages 304–8, for some insights into the Marxist analysis of work and the impact of capitalism on it.

Criticisms of Marx

Marx's later writings put so much emphasis on the economy as a separate area of social life that they encouraged almost exclusive concentration on the material conditions for change. Focusing attention on economic activity in this way is certainly valid under capitalism, since it operates with a logic and dynamic of its own, through capital accumulation, expansion and competition. However, it is less applicable to pre-capitalist modes of production, where economic domination was hard to separate from military, political and ideological relations. It is much harder to see a 'logic of development' for a social structure deriving from the economic base. We therefore need a more complex account of the relations between the economic, political and ideological aspects of social life under capitalism.

We also need to build clearer theories linking social action to its structural consequences, though Marx did begin to move towards this. For example, his account of the rise of capitalist class relations stressed the deliberate creation of new economic relations by the capitalist gentry. So we must conclude that the social structure can only control our actions once it is established as a dominant system with specific dynamics and tendencies. Then the capitalist is constrained almost as much as the proletarian. At the same time, these structural features create the conditions needed for the recapturing of control by those who seek to transform the social structure. Hence, there is a complex relation between human action and the underlying social structures. According to Marx, the causes of social phenomena lie at a level of structural causation that cannot be seen by looking at individual events or experiences: that is, Marx employed a realist perspective. These structures are, however, constantly changing, and they develop in uneven, contradictory and crisis-ridden ways. They always generate new possibilities for historical change and thus for intervention by groups of actors.

There is a real problem with this relationship between ideology and politics, however. We need to know not only what Marxists make clear – the material conditions that enable such change – but also how the working class can take advantage of its historical opportunity. For example, is revolutionary consciousness a spontaneous phenomenon, or is the leadership provided by a political party necessary for it to happen? Without better accounts of politics and ideology, we are in danger of viewing consciousness as an automatic by-product of material change. The continuing survival of capitalism, the collapse of state communism and the defeat of the left in Western Europe have intensified the pressure on Marxists to provide an adequate theoretical answer to these questions, but they have been bitterly divided over the issue. Marx's own writings provide no real answer.

Despite these misgivings, as a sociological perspective, Marxism can still provide us with questions to help make sense of our times:

● Is the focus on the production of goods the best way to analyse society?

● Is capitalism the defining feature of modern societies?

- Is class membership the most important fact of our lives?
- Are ideas inextricably bound up with economic forces and processes?

QUESTION   To what extent is Marx's analysis of the ills of capitalism in his own time relevant to contemporary capitalist societies?

 ## Max Weber

BOX 17.5 | Max Weber (1864–1920)

Born: Erfurt, Thuringia, 1864.
Education: University of Heidelberg, 1882; University of Berlin, 1884–85; University of Gottingen, 1885–86.
Career: Taught law, Berlin, 1892; professor of political economy, Freiburg,1894; professor of economics, Heidelberg, 1896.

Main works: *Methodological Essays* (1902), *The Protestant Ethic and the Spirit of Capitalism* (1902–4), *Economy and Society* (1910–14), *Sociology of Religion* (1916).

Although Weber died only a few years after Durkheim, in some ways he seems much more a figure of the twentieth century than either Durkheim or Marx. This is due to Weber's doubts and fears, and the anxious pessimism that underlay his view of modernity. His view of what lay ahead – a 'polar night of icy darkness' – foreshadowed the more sceptical mood of our time. Although Weber was committed to the values of knowledge and individual liberty, he had no faith in the future. For him, modernity was irreversible, and, while it brought material gain and increased power, it did not necessarily serve human needs. A system that expanded economic and political power so dramatically could have the perverse consequence of trapping humans in a debased and inhuman society. As he put it in the bleak conclusion to *The Protestant Ethic and the Spirit of Capitalism*: 'Specialists without spirit, sensualists without heart; this nullity imagines that it has attained a civilisation never before achieved' (Weber, 1930, p. 182).

One of the reasons why *The Protestant Ethic* became such a classic text is that it made large claims about the importance of belief systems and religious world-views in social life. Weber argued that people's practical economic behaviour changed if they adopted a particular belief system (in this case, Puritan Christianity), because a change in their values changed the motives for their actions. Furthermore, to pursue their goals, they had to conform to the rules and norms of their new belief system – in the case of Puritanism, these were particularly strict and demanding. This meant that a large-scale phenomenon such as a change in religion strongly affected the actions of individuals by transforming their goals, their motives and the norms they followed. However, for Weber, this structural emphasis was not enough by itself to explain social behaviour. Individuals and their actions mattered too – after all, many individuals deliberately chose to be Puritans because Puritanism's belief system fitted in with their lives. Unfortunately, Weber did not succeed in fully reconciling his structural and historical sociology, which operated on a grand scale, and his interest in individual action. In exploring this, we shall look first at his account of the systematic study of individual action.

Weber's theory of social action

As we shall see in the next chapter, the main standard-bearers of the action tradition in twentieth-century sociology – symbolic interactionism and ethnomethodology – typically focused on small-scale interaction. They did this to tease out the interpretive methods used by subjects to fashion their own identities and to establish order in the specific social events in which they are involved. Weber, like his late-nineteenth-century peers, was preoccupied with the nature of modernity and was thus interested in the broad sweep of history and social change. But his focus was on action in modernity: the question for him was not 'how do modern social systems work?' but 'what are the kinds of action that typify modern social life?'

He classified social action into four types, each distinguished by the particular motivations or goals of actors. Different societies at different times in history were characterised by different forms of action.

- *Traditional* action occurred when actors chose to do things because they had always done so.
- *Affective* action occurred when actors could not help but do something or other for emotional reasons.
- *Value-oriented* action occurred when one principle or purpose overrode all others.
- *Rational* action occurred when actors weighed up, or calculated, the most efficient way of achieving specific ends – not 'I'll do this because I want that', but 'I'll do this because I reckon it's the most efficient way of getting that'.

Rationality
A preoccupation with calculating the most efficient means to achieve one's goals.

Bureaucracy
An organisation run by officials and based on hierarchical authority for the efficient pursuit of organisational goals.

Rationalisation
A way of thinking regulated by reason (rather than, say, intuition, emotion or tradition) and based upon clear, objective ideas, that can be demonstrated and understood by other intelligent human beings.

According to Weber, modernity was about the triumph of narrow **rationality** over all other forms of action. Only in modern capitalist society could efficiency be the over-riding motive – more important than tradition, emotion or principles.

For example, capitalism involves the relentless pursuit of efficiency to increase profitability. Running things in an efficient, business-like fashion – a modern capitalist notion – implies the subordination of goals thought important in other times and places. There is no room for sentiment, principles or tradition here. Science itself is harnessed to construct new production technologies that can eradicate waste and promote efficiency, whatever the human and social costs. **Bureaucratisation** is the exemplar of **rationalisation**: 'not my job, mate'; 'you'll have to go to another department'; 'sorry, more than my job's worth'. The marketisation of what used to be the principled provision of public services in the UK in the 1980s and 1990s is another exemplar; a world in which students and NHS patients are 'consumers' – 'units' to be 'throughputted' the production process, in which accountants dominate. Management theory deter-mines action, with 'downsizing', 're-structuring', outsourcing and so on as buzz-words.

It is the hegemony of this sort of value orientation that Weber feared when he wrote so pessimistically about the modern world. He despaired of a world in which humans were locked in 'an iron cage of bureaucracy'. For him, this was a world of spiritual barrenness: a world lacking mystery, imagination and awe, in which enchantment was lost; a world whose inhabitants were condemned to the 'polar night of icy darkness' created by the never-ending, ruthless, rational pursuit of efficiency.

Unlike Durkheim and Marx, Weber did not think that sociological diagnosis of the ills of modernity could lead to a prescription for their cure. For Durkheim, anomie could be prevented or eradicated by the application of sturdy regulation through socialisation – by society's commitment to maintaining a strong collective culture properly passed on to its members. For Marx, a Utopia free from the diseases of class exploitation and alienation could be achieved as long as the correct medication – Marxist theory – was prescribed and taken. For Weber, however, there was no cure for what he saw as the plague of modern social life – rampant rationalisation.

Rationalisation and modernity

Weber devoted most of his formidable scholarship to placing modern capitalism in its historical context. Born into an academic family, he pursued an intellectual career that encompassed economic history, law, sociology and philosophy. Despite psychological illness, his output was prolific, but his body of work has often been seen as fragmentary; Weber does not appear to have any central organising theory to guide his work in the way that Marx did. However, certain guiding interests do unify the diverse themes in his work.

His first major concern was with the political paradoxes facing German society at the turn of the twentieth century. Weber was acutely aware that although Germany had become a strong capitalist state, the bourgeoisie had not secured independent political power. As a result, Germany lacked democratic institutions. Instead, traditional status groups such as the Prussian Junker aristocracy and their highborn functionaries in the army and state bureaucracies ruled Germany. At the same time, the German working class was the most highly organised in Europe and was nominally Marxist. Weber was deeply committed to the pursuit of a liberal-democratic bourgeois regime, but was haunted by the threats from Marxism on the one side and the all-powerful bureaucracy on the other. As a result, he engaged in passionate attack on the theories of Marxism, although he did accept that the world could only be understood by means of economic and historical analysis.

His other interest was in the historical conditions for the rise of modern capitalism and science in the West. 'Through what combination of circumstances did it come about that precisely, and only, in the Western world certain cultural phenomena emerged which represents a direction of development of universal significance and validity?' (Weber, 1978b, p. 331)

For Weber, science and modern capitalism were both part of a broader cultural development - the rationalisation process. Unlike other areas of the globe, the evolution of Western Europe away from its ancient civilisations involved the gradual abandonment of magic and superstition, which ultimately undermined the basis of spiritual faith. Instead, social institutions and individual actions began to show a more calculating, instrumental rationality. Law, administration and economic activity became formalised and rationalised, while the associated rise of science undermined the power of religious elites. The rise of rational knowledge, moreover, was linked to the rise of rational economic behaviour, institutionalised in the structure of modern capitalism.

For Weber, any pursuit of profit through exchange could be regarded as capitalistic, and therefore he saw most societies as containing some element of capitalist activity. In the modern West, however, the economy had come to be dominated by capitalism of a new form, the distinctive feature of which was the rational capitalist organisation of (formally) free labour – proletarians employed as propertyless wage earners by an industrial bourgeoisie. This employing class pursued capital accumulation (the continual growth of capital through profits) by means of rational calculation, which Weber argued was only possible with free wage-labour (as opposed to serfs or slaves). For him, the emergence of this particular form of capitalism was the central problem in a universal history of civilisation. With this in mind, he embarked upon his vast comparative study of the economic, legal and religious institutions of countries outside the

West, guided by the question: Why was it in general that in those countries neither scientific nor artistic nor political nor economic development followed the path of rationalisation that is unique to the West?' (Weber, 1930, passim).

As we have seen, one of Weber's principal interests was the role of belief systems in social life. At the most general level, therefore, the explanation Weber provided for the lack of rationalisation lay in the institutionalised world-views encouraged by non-Western cultural traditions. According to Weber, the rulers and intelligentsia of other cultures were prevented from pursuing the road of rationalisation by the doctrines and intellectual orientations they themselves produced. For example, the Buddhist monk withdrew from all worldly activity in order to achieve spiritual elevation, while the Confucian Mandarin engaged in administration on the basis of highly traditional and non-scientific knowledge. Only in the West did a cultural orientation emerge that favoured rationalisation.

Weber described and explained the development of rationalisation in the West in *The Protestant Ethic*. In his view, rationalisation came about because Puritanism demanded sober worldly activity – doing one's duty in line with one's calling. If this produced riches, it was a sign of God's favour and demonstrated good work. However, this worldly wealth should not be consumed, as it had been in non-capitalist societies. Rather, it should be re-invested to create the basis for further dutiful work. This was required by the ascetic demand of Puritanism that the godly should reject all earthly pleasures. Locating virtuousness in this combination of asceticism and worldly work was seen by Weber as a unique cultural development, and one that fitted perfectly with capital accumulation. Wealth was amassed, but it was continually reinvested to accumulate further wealth. No other religious movement had ever demanded this from its believers. None had revered worldly work so highly for its own sake. Weber therefore argued that the origins of modern rational capitalism must lie in Western culture, and above all in Puritan Protestantism.

This is the most famous example of Weber's thesis that general world-views had a crucial effect on the intentional actions of individuals, and that these world-views derived from the doctrines produced by religious elites who held positions of intellectual dominance. Although the content of religious ideas and the extent to which they were accepted might be influenced by economic or political interests, they had to be accepted as independent causal elements in their own right (Weber, 1930, p. 277, n. 84):

> " For those to whom no causal explanation is adequate without an economic (or materialistic as it is unfortunately still called) interpretation, it may be remarked that I consider the influence of economic development on the fate of religious ideas to be very important. ... On the other hand, those religious ideas themselves simply cannot be deduced from economic circumstances. They are ... the most powerful plastic elements of national character and contain a law of development and a compelling force entirely their own . "

Instrumental calculation
The process of using the most efficient means to secure a particular goal.

Although Weber went on to suggest that the next most important factors were political and not economic, he nevertheless discounted any move towards socialism. Even if Germany did move in a socialist direction, he argued, the rationalisation process could not be reversed. As a result, humanitarian goals (whether liberal or socialist) were doomed by the inexorable and irreversible growth of rational bureaucratic administration. Sober **instrumental calculation** would dominate all social life, and individuals would be stifled by the constraints of the 'iron cage of bureaucracy': 'More and more the material fate of the masses depends upon the steady and correct functioning of the increasingly bureaucratic organisation of private capitalism. The idea of eliminating these organisations becomes more and more utopian' (Weber, 1978, p. 988).

Humanism
A position that
stresses the
importance of
human needs and
rejects the
existence of a
supernatural deity.
It implies a belief
that humans have
the potential for
goodness.

Utopian doctrines of all kinds were pathetic delusions, for rationalisation would create a world of technical efficiency and undemocratic administration that could not be transcended, a world in which the **humanistic** values generated earlier would be derided.

This dismal account of contemporary problems demonstrates Weber's opposition to Marxist economic determinism, for he insists on viewing culture as an independent factor. One might think that this placed Weber close to Durkheim, who stressed the primacy of cultural phenomena, but this proposition is not easy to sustain. Durkheim focused on the general process of socialisation and its beneficial consequences for integration, with little regard for the actual content of belief systems. In marked contrast, Weber approached culture in a grounded, historical way, examining the specific kinds of ideas institutionalised in particular societies by their respective intellectual elites. As such, his was a materialist account of the role of ideas.

CONNECTIONS For a Weberian account of social class, see Chapter 5.

Weber also differed from both Marx and Durkheim in regarding social institutions as ultimately reducible to individual acts, even though these acts were shaped by the social context. As we said earlier, Weber failed to reconcile grand historical studies with a philosophy of social action that stressed the deliberate intentions and motives of the individual actor. As a result, he addressed social structures and types of social organisation in an analytical and descriptive manner, and did not offer structural explanations deriving from an account of society as a system, as did Durkheim and Marx.

One reason for this was his approach to history, which he saw as a 'meaningless infinity'. Seeing pattern and order in this infinity of unique events could only be accomplished by imposing ideal types to make comparisons. He rejected any notion of universal causal laws governing society, and was therefore not a positivist. However, because of his view of history, he resisted making distinctions between different types of society. He may have described the basic features of capitalism and acknowledged that competition constrained the capitalist, but he made no attempt to analyse the possible sources of change within capitalism as a system. As a result, he displayed a curiously fatalistic pessimism about the inevitability of being trapped in materialistic and bureaucratic capitalism. Since capitalism embodied rationality of technical means, it was inescapable. Curiously, Weber failed to acknowledge the potential for change generated by the failings of both capitalism and bureaucracy.

Weber's vision of the possibilities available in modern society were far from optimistic, as Table 17.3 shows. His proposed reforms were modest, and his solutions purely individualistic. It seems that there was no hope of escape from this monolithic, rationalised world of bureaucratic capitalist domination. Humans could only try to impose some countervailing democratic controls whilst retaining some private, personal space to escape the burdens of modernity.

QUESTION To what extent do you share Weber's pessimism about modernity? What features of modernity lead you to your view? What arguments can you muster in opposition to your general conclusion?

If all this seems depressing, it is important to emphasise that some of the assumptions Weber made may be erroneous. He seems to have envisaged an inescapable trend towards impersonal, bureaucratic forms of power and organisation, with an increasing concentration of control. However, this does not take account of the rich variety of

TABLE 17.3 Weber's dilemmas in modernity and rationalisation

Apparent benefits of modernity	Actual negative consequences	Weber's solutions
Increase in human powers	Enslavement to new forms of domination	None
Choice and control over society and nature	Impersonal control over individuals; Bureaucratic power	Control of bureaucracy through parliament; Government by elected elite
Secularisation, liberation from forced belief	Crisis of belief; loss of meaning and ethical rules	Personal preference for humanistic liberal values, Sects and cults may revive faith
Rational reason: end of uncritical faith	Relativity of values; loss of ultimate values; dominance of mundane material goals	Remain true to one's own individually held values; pursue scientific knowledge in an ethical manner; charismatic leaders may inspire new faith in their followers.
Reflexive sense of self; individuality.	Others may be treated as instruments or objects.	Defend individual human creativity.
Rational approach to mind and body.	Loss of sensuality, physicality, eroticism.	Protect private love/desire.
Dynamic expansionism of capitalism	Domination by impersonal market forces	None

Source: adapted from essays in Whimster and Lash (1987).

organisational forms that may be rational for different purposes. A profitable record company is likely to operate in very different ways from a food manufacturing firm, for example, and even the food manufacturer is likely to make innovations in working practices and management structures in order to remain competitive. In other words, the dynamics of capitalism throw up great diversity, and there is no one deterministic model of power or organisation. As we saw in Chapter 3, the forces exerted by globalisation can add further to the variety and complexity of capitalist forms of organisation. Moreover, our sense of self and identity is not shaped simply by our experience of more or less bureaucratic institutions. A number of sociologists have pointed to the scope that modernity offers for choosing from a wide spectrum of possible roles, redefining ourselves, or acting out particular identities in ironic or playful modes. Weber may have been right to emphasise the power and force of modern institutions, but modernity has also meant greater individual freedom for many. The women's movement offers a particularly vivid illustration of this, and it is to the body of theory that emerged to address questions of gender that we now turn.

Feminism, social theory and modernity

Looking at the development of sociological theory in the late nineteenth and early twentieth centuries, it is striking how little gender and sexual inequality figure, despite the fact that the changes brought about by processes of modernisation were shaped by pre-existing patterns of gender inequality. For example, women's labour was essential to the early growth of industrial capitalism. In the US, women were the original wage workers and the first factory employees (Bose, 1987, p. 272). As Bradley (1989, p. 68) explains:

> " from the *beginning* of industrial development the labour process was not only 'capitalist' but also 'gendered'. That is, as capitalists introduced new techniques and reorganised the process of production they in fact created 'men's' and 'women's' jobs, utilising the characteristics that were socially ascribed to men and women as workers; the 'skill' and 'technological expertise' of men, the 'cheapness' and 'adaptability' of women. "

Although they would have had access to the literature and theories of contemporary feminist movements, neither Marx nor Weber nor Durkheim properly addressed the gendered dimensions of the process of modernisation, tending to draw instead on more traditional ideas about women – ideas that associated women with an unchanging nature, instinct and conservative or traditional family values. It was only relatively recently that the political and economic significance of gender relations was recognised by mainstream sociology. We can identify three broad phases in the development of modern feminist thinking, each one drawing on particular mainstream theories that were criticised, adapted and recast by feminists to address sexual differences and inequality as social and political issues. The theories were:

- Classical liberal theory.
- Modern social theory.
- Post-structuralist and postmodern theories.

We shall look in detail at the first two of these in this chapter, and the third in the final chapter.

Feminist theory and classical liberal theory

The first phase of feminist theory emerged in the eighteenth century, and feminists were concerned with extending the central concept of classical liberalism – the doctrine of individual freedom – to apply to women as well as men. Freedom was 'defined as freedom from coercion, as moral determination, or as the right to individual happiness' (Seidman, cited in Marshall, 1994, p. 10). In accordance with this doctrine, which underpinned Enlightenment thinking, only rational beings were capable of exercising freedom – rationality being the characteristic that distinguished humans from animals. But the catch for women in this theory was that they were not considered to be as rational as men. Everything implied by the word human was applicable to both sexes, but women were actually credited with very different (and inferior) intellectual and moral qualities from men by classical liberal thinkers.

One of the earliest feminist thinkers, Mary Wollstonecraft, writing in 1792, referred to the liberal framework, in which rationality was identified as essentially human, and argued that it was irrational not to apply it to women too. Women might seem to be less rational (Wollstonecraft was notoriously rude about the behaviour of her bourgeois and aristocratic female contemporaries), and they might appear to wallow in empty-headed vanity, frivolity and sentimentality, but that was because the sharply segregated system of education had taught them to behave in that way in order to attract men. At the very least, she argued, non-segregated education should be introduced to allow women to

Figure 17.2   Wollstonecraft was reviled in her day as 'a hyena in petticoats' but her outspoken views on women's education, for example, proved visionary, as we saw in Chapter 10.

develop their minds. All of society would reap the benefits of harnessing women's talent, which was otherwise going to waste.

Successive generations of feminist thinkers have incorporated liberal feminist ideals. For example, the argument for the social utility of removing man-made obstacles to women's full participation in society was deployed by women in the suffrage campaigns in the UK and the US in the late nineteenth century, and it is still employed by contemporary liberal feminists in campaigns for equal opportunities in education and paid work.

Wollstonecraft's work illustrates the fact that the revolutions of 1780–1830 shaped the core concerns not only of sociology but also of feminist thinkers. She adopted the central modern belief that reason should be applied to human affairs to promote progress, and she applied it specifically to women's subordination. The tyranny of men over women should be viewed as another case of unreasonable, unjustified privilege that was ripe for removal.

Feminist theory and modern social theory

Whereas in classical liberal theory the individual was seen to pre-exist society, classical sociological theory saw the individual as constituted by society. Second-wave feminism – that is, the feminist movement that took off in the late 1960s and 1970s, subsequent to the achievement of female suffrage in the US and Europe in the early part of the twentieth century – drew on this classical sociological legacy because, by pointing to the power of society to shape the individual's values and behaviour, it helped to debunk the idea that sexual inequality was a natural and therefore unchangeable fact of life. Second-wave feminist theorists made much of the distinction between sexual difference – which they regarded as rooted in nature – and socially constructed gender difference, which, as we saw in Chapter 6, was seen as much more malleable and therefore a good target for political campaigning.

We also saw in Chapter 6 how the study of gender has contributed to the socio-logical understanding of central aspects of contemporary life, from the structure of the labour market to the development of sexual identity. The foundations of these analyses of gender were laid in the late 1960s and 1970s, after a more radical approach to investi-gating power and inequality had become established within sociology. This radicalism attracted activists in the feminist movement who wanted to investigate the causes of female oppression. Their rallying cry was 'the personal is political'. They wanted to extend the analysis of women's subordination to include matters that were usually treated as private, such as the sexual division of labour in the home, and sexual relation-ships. Aspects of women's subordination that were usually accepted without question, such as unequal pay and discrimination in the labour market, domestic violence, rape and other forms of assault predominantly experienced by women, were also identified as important topics for sociological research and as targets for social change. It was important to many of this generation of feminist activists that all these facets of women's subordination be recognised as sociological in the strict sense of the word – as explicable by the organisation of society, and therefore able to be solved by reorganising society. The priority they gave to this helps explain their attachment to social theories that were seeking to explain how society was structuring the lives of its individual members.

However, before sociological tools could be used to understand the social organisation of gender and the sexual inequality it produced, feminist social theorists had to re-draw the basic map of social life used by conventional sociology. This map located gender and sexual inequality at the margins of social life. The conventional mapping of society delineated two separate spheres of life:

- *The public sphere* was viewed as the arena of male activity, made up of paid work, the market, the state and politics, and was seen to be characterised by objectivity or impartiality.

- *The private or domestic sphere* was considered the domain of women, set aside for child-rearing and taking care of other family members. This sphere was characterised by emotional attachment rather than impartiality, tied closely to nature and instinctual behaviour, and the arena in which the next generation was equipped to play a full part in society.

According to this schema, the only connection between the two spheres was the fact that men lived in both. Women's lives and behaviour were understandable only by reference to the private sphere, their role as wife and mother, and the dictates of their reproductive biology. The public sphere was seen as the more important field of interest for sociology, and the sexual division of labour and gender related issues were therefore pushed to the outer edge of sociological interest.

This map was handed down, largely intact, to twentieth-century sociology from classical liberal theory via the classical social theorists we have looked at in this chapter, and the relationship between the two spheres tended to be treated as unchanging in all societies at all times. Feminist and gender theorists spent the last three decades of the twentieth century remapping the sociological domain, with the two spheres being treated as historical and shifting zones of social action. They produced a comprehensive body of knowledge on how the two spheres were connected to each other in the lives of women as well as men. Issues that were once deemed private and outside of the field of sociological interest came to be regarded as central to the explanation of power and privilege in society as a whole.

There were important differences between second-wave feminist analyses in respect of the relationship between the public and private spheres, its political significance for women, and how the two dimensions of social and political life should be reorganised. These differences were commonly presented as neatly demarcated academic models, as liberal, Marxist, radical and socialist theories. However, while there were significant theoretical differences between these models, they should also be seen as expressions of differences in political strategy within the women's movement as a whole. It is also important to appreciate the extent to which these feminist theories shared concepts and analyses. They all agreed fundamentally on the idea that the private realm needed to be opened up to scrutiny, and that conventional sociological concepts needed to be recast to explain how and why this should happen.

Liberal feminism

The influential second-wave liberal feminist Betty Friedan (1965) drew upon Talcott Parsons' distinction between instrumental and expressive values (see Connell, 1987,

p. 33). According to Friedan, women were driven into depression and drug abuse by being expected to confine their activities and interests to the private sphere. Furthermore, giving men exclusive responsibility for paid work limited their ability to lead fulfilling lives. Hence, the cultural values and norms internalised by men and women had to be more flexibly distributed between the genders. The political strategy of liberal feminists such as Friedan focused on legal reform to remove discriminatory practices in all areas of the public sphere, including the education system, politics and the labour market. They emphasised the extent to which both genders were restricted by conventional sex roles and sought to make the barrier between the public and private realms more permeable, so that men and women could build their lives around activities in both spheres.

Other second-wave theorists had a much starker conception of the power relationship between the genders, so that what Friedan saw as gender difference they treated as the concealment of gender inequality. These theorists argued that activities in the two spheres were not valued equally, and that encouraging women to live and work primarily in the private sphere was an important means of perpetuating male supremacy.

Radical feminism

The emphasis on the collective and systematic nature of male oppression of women was particularly evident in the radical feminist theories of the time. Radical feminists took the conventional sociological distinction between public and private and reversed the terms of the hierarchy, so that the 'private sphere' became fundamentally political. There were different kinds of radical feminist theorist, but they all tended to share a core belief that men had an interest in controlling women's reproduction and sexuality (see for example, Millett, 1977; Rich, 1976, Dworkin, 1981). Shulamith Firestone (1979) identified a world-wide system of patriarchy (or male domination of women) that had been in operation from the earliest stages of human history and provided the model for all subsequent forms of exploitation and oppression. Specific groups of men deployed various tactics (actual or threatened) to control women, ranging from rape (Brownmiller, 1975), genital mutilation and foot binding (Daly, 1978), to wife battering and sexual harassment (MacKinnon, 1987). Hence, radical feminist political strategy was clearly shaped by the belief that the defining characteristic of society was the patriarchal control of female sexuality, childbearing and childrearing. 'On this view, "sexual politics" means not only that the relations between the sexes are political, it also means that any permanent and far-reaching change in that political situation requires a transformation of human sexual arrangements' (Jaggar, 1983, p. 105).

The radical feminist argument that these aspects of life that might be considered the most personal were in fact the most political offered a rigorous challenge to the conventional definition of politics. However, the feminist theorists influenced by Marxism (to whom we turn next) argued that radical feminism offered an essentialist analysis of gender relations that suggested that patriarchy was universal and unchangeable. Its portrayal of gender conflict as entirely connected to reproduction and men's desire to control it was seen as neglecting the sphere of economic production and the impact of class on gender relationships.

Marxist feminism

The Marxist feminists of the period in question used the framework of the Marxist analysis of capitalism to establish the basis of women's oppression. They argued that women's oppression and exploitation was a symptom of capitalism. For example,

Michele Barrett (1981) argued that the household was fundamentally shaped by the needs of capitalism, and she identified the family as the crucial site of women's oppression. Marxist feminists tended to explain women's oppression as arising from the fact that women engaged in unpaid work in the household and paid work outside the home. Trying to balance both kinds of work left them disadvantaged in each situation: they shouldered more than their share of domestic work, and they were undervalued and underpaid in the paid workforce (see Lydia Sargent, 1981).

In bringing together paid and unpaid work to analyse how women were oppressed under capitalism, Marxist feminism usefully broadened the conventional sociological definition of work to include activities that took place in both the public and the private sphere. However, because it tended to concentrate on the links between the household and the capitalist economy to explain women's subordination, it has been criticised for neglecting other aspects of gender relations, and in particular the interest men may have as men, rather than as capitalists, in the continuing subordination of women.

So, both radical and Marxist feminist theorists developed a connection between the public and private spheres, which they believed explained the root cause of the subordination of women. However, while radical feminists did this by conceiving issues connected with sexuality and reproduction as political, Marxist feminists argued that the division of labour and the gendered structure of power in the household and the work place reflected the needs of the capitalist economy.

Socialist feminism

Socialist feminist theorists attempted to synthesise elements of both of the above theories, believing that women's oppression must be explained in terms of the combined forces of capitalism and patriarchy. Zillah Eisenstein (1979) was representative of socialist feminist theorists in her criticism of radical feminism's exclusive focus on the male domination of women at the expense of examining the impact of other sources of social inequality, such as class and race. According to Eisenstein, Marxist feminism paid too much attention to the impact of capitalism and ignored other ways in which women were oppressed. Socialist feminists aimed to develop an analysis of how gender relations operated in all domains of social life, including the very different ways in which a white, university-educated, professional woman without children and a black school leaver expecting her first child and living on an inner city estate experienced the combined forces of capitalism and patriarchy. Socialist feminist theory arguably offered the most thorough deconstruction of the separate-spheres schema of society set out by conventional sociology.

Socialist feminists developed two distinct models of the relationship between capitalism and patriarchy: dual-systems theory, which saw capitalism and patriarchy as two distinct forms of oppression (see for example, Mitchell, 1975; Hartmann, 1979); and unified-systems theory, which argued that capitalism and patriarchy were so inextricably linked that they should be conceptualised as one system (see Young, 1981).

CONNECTIONS See Chapter 6, pages 139-46, for an overview of Walby's theory of patriarchy and a discussion of the sexual division of labour.

However, all socialist feminists shared the belief that gender relations were ubiquitous and threaded between the public and private spheres, connecting them in different ways for different groups of women (see Walby, 1990, for a synthesis of socialist and radical feminism that includes housework, waged work, sexuality, culture, violence and the state as interconnected dimensions of patriarchy).

In conclusion, we can see that there were significant similarities between these theoretical positions. All drew on mainstream sociological theories, including structural functionalism and, particularly, Marxism. Each theory re-worked concepts from traditional sociology. Liberal feminists criticised the exclusive association of women with expressive or nurturing sex roles and of men with instrumental roles in functionalist theory; radical feminists saw reproduction rather than production as the central locus of power struggles; and Marxist and socialist feminists developed distinct points of departure by broadening the notion of work and upgrading the importance of the household to the capitalist economy.

All of these theories have helped to bring women's experiences into our understanding of modernity. Be it the liberal feminist emphasis on changing discriminatory beliefs and attitudes, the Marxist and socialist feminist focus on the relation between capitalism and gender inequality, or the radical feminist attention to sexual practices and beliefs that leave women vulnerable to violence, all have enabled us to examine the structures of society that shape gender relations, so that we can intervene to change them.

Problems with modern feminist theories

Many fruitful connections with social theory have been forged by feminist theories. They have transformed the public/private model to make it a more accurate reflection of how real women and men live, and have re-theorised key sociological ideas of who and what should be included in the category of the individual, of labour and of politics. At the same time, though, feminist theories may have been subject to some of the weaknesses of mainstream sociological theory.

Any social theory, but particularly one that claims to be committed to social transformation, has to be able to theorise freedom and constraint in relation to each other. It must do so without neglecting the impact of structures such as class, gender and race inequality, but without construing members of society as passive victims of the social system. Have the various feminist theories we have examined managed to keep this balance? In their concern to uncover the social, economic and cultural sources of women's subordination, radical, socialist and Marxist feminists may have lost sight of the other vital point of feminist theory: the development of liberation strategies. At times, their analyses of the social constraints facing women leave little room for what sociologists call women's 'agency' – the creative potential of all members of society to understand, adapt and transform their social context (this subject will be re-examined in the next chapter). Liberal feminism, on the other hand, with its emphasis on role adaption and individual choice, underplays the impact of power relationships and the social structures that limit our choices and perpetuate chronic cycles of deprivation and inequality (see Connell, 1987, Part 1).

Feminist theory has been sceptical about the ideals of modernity and the Enlightenment heritage, questioning how rational the Enlightenment concept of reason really is when it involves unfounded, irrational beliefs about women. At least two feminist responses to this combination of rationality and prejudice in the social theories of modernity can be identified. One response, as we have seen, has been to tackle this problem by criticising, reforming, and expanding the concepts and theories so that they can be used for women. Conversely, the other response, that of postmodern and post-structuralist feminism, argues that theories of modernity are beyond salvage for feminism because they are irredeemably connected to the attempt by white Western males to dominate and control 'the other', whether the other is defined as women, nature, or racially oppressed groups. We shall review this approach in Chapter 19, after looking in more detail at action theories (sometimes called theories of agency) in Chapter 18.

 Questions to think about

- 'As contemporary sociologists, we have nothing to learn from the classical sociologists.' To what extent do you agree with this proposition?
- Choose either Durkheim, Marx or Weber and, drawing on what you have read in earlier chapters of this book, describe the ways in which sociologists have built upon the body of knowledge provided in his work.
- What are the strengths and weaknesses of second-wave feminist theorising?

 Chapter summary

- The founding sociologists were all aware of the profound transformations inherent in the shift to modernity, but they differed greatly in their views on the possibilities and pitfalls presented by this new society.

- Among those committed to social progress, some were reformist (for example, Durkheim) while others sought radical change (for example, Marx). In both cases, there was optimistic belief that modernity could bring about 'the good society'.

- The fears about the consequences of modernity expressed by Weber have strong resonance today.

- Classical social theory neglected questions of gender and sexual inequality, and mainstream sociology has only relatively recently recognised the significance of gender relations, largely as a result of the impact of a variety of feminist theories.

Investigating further

Craib, Ian (1997) *Classical Social Theory*, Oxford University Press.
Pampel, Fred (2000) *Sociological Lives and Idea*, Palgrave.
    These are both useful general texts on the theories of Durkheim, Marx and Weber, as well as Simmel (in the case of Craib) and Simmel and Mead (in the case of Pampel). Craib takes a more thematic approach and looks at some key issues in social theory in relation to the work of these classical sociologists. The chapter entitled 'What's the Point?' is a very good starting point. Pampel looks at

the theories in the context of the life and times of the theorists and presents vivid textual portraits of the men themselves.

Tong, Rosemary (1989) *Feminist Thought: A Comprehensive Introduction*, Routledge. This is one of a number of good introductions to feminist theory.

18

Making
social life

theories of action and meaning

CHAPTER CONTENTS

Aims of the chapter

This chapter explores the range of action theories developed by sociologists, high-lighting what they have in common and what separates them from each other. A contrast will be made between structural theories and these action-oriented approaches. We shall emphasise that the social actor is a creative agent, and the issue of language will be used to illustrate this. Finally, we shall consider the theory of post-structuralism as a bridge to more contemporary social theories.

By the end of the chapter, you should have an understanding of the following concepts and theories:

- Reflexive actor
- Life-world
- Phenomenology
- Ethnomethodology

- Symbolic interactionism
- *Verstehen*
- Indexical
- Post-structuralism

Introduction

As human beings, we make and remake society through our own actions, but we do not do so in circumstances of our own choosing. This statement (paraphrased from Marx – see Chapter 17) expresses one of sociology's most fundamental puzzles. Can we portray the nature of social life in a way that reflects not only human creativity but also the power of society to shape human actions? Many sociologists are committed to emphasising the uniquely creative abilities of humans – the fact that, unique among living things, humans have the capacity to interpret their world and make choices about how to behave. Sociology should therefore concern itself principally with this capacity for action, or agency, by creative actors or subjects. Other sociologists, as we saw in Chapter 17, are more concerned with explaining people's behaviour in terms of a structure of external circumstances and societal influences. They stress that we cannot act as we please, because there are always social constraints and limited possibilities, and that we do not have total free will, because we have been fashioned into social actors while growing up in society. Clearly, the structural and action approaches can each furnish us with important insights that will help us to see the whole picture. The question is, to what extent can we as social actors re-make social situations and re-form our own social identities?

As we saw in Chapter 17, structural sociology emphasises how society pre-exists the individual. Predetermined social roles and powerful belief systems socialise the actor into conforming to an existing culture that is stronger and longer lasting than any individual. In contrast, social action theories point out that social life could not continue at all without people acting and interacting. One area of dispute is whether this small-scale action merely reproduces the wider social setting, or whether it can transform it. Central to this are the consequences of action. Whatever the meanings and intentions actors may have, the consequences of their actions may escape their control or under-standing. Social action theorists who focus on the immediate social setting may have little interest in this, but theorists of structure see the **unintended consequences** of action as a key dimension of the reproduction of society.

Unintended consequences Repercussions or outcomes that result from actions initiated for other purposes.

As we shall see, there is little agreement among the various social action theories when it comes to the relationship between action and society. The more radical accounts, such as ethnomethodology, deny the existence of wider structures – except as convenient fictions that help us to act in routine ways without bringing every situation into doubt. Others, such as the symbolic interactionist G. H. Mead (1934), see the acting self as a social product, uniquely individual but only existing through socialisation into the socially available roles and symbols that make action possible. So, even such basic terms as 'social action' and 'meanings' are used in diverse ways by different theorists. One way to think of this is to imagine a continuum between those who see society as largely shaping action, and those who regard small-scale action as the true source of social life.

Actors and their meanings: varieties of action theory

As we saw in Chapter 17, a key part of Weber's argument in *The Protestant Ethic* (1977) was that changes in the belief system led to changes in the world-view held by groups of people. This in turn led them to act in ways that were guided by new ideas. So, people began to behave differently in practical ways, becoming rational, calculating and self-denying, and imbued with the work ethic. But Weber did not restrict himself to this purely structural analysis; he also recognised that there was an independent action element to the story. Thus, he saw an affinity between the economic interests of certain groups and their religious need to make sense of their lives in congenial ways (their 'ideal interests'). The new beliefs made sense of their economic lives and legitimated them, but the new ideas also pushed them towards new ways of acting and thinking.

Therefore, a change in the belief system has a direct effect on the values, goals and actions of the individual, as long as the new beliefs are accepted and adopted by all actors. As actors live in a society imbued with a certain culture and world-view, the latter will underpin their individual goals and actions. In this way, structural sociology has provided an account of action, but from a 'macroscopic' point of view, stressing the impact of the society or the wider belief system on the actor. Weber also developed a theory of individual action, but this did not come to terms with interaction, innovation and small-scale settings. These have been explored in an American theoretical tradition known as symbolic interactionism.

There are profound differences between the American and German traditions of action theory. The American tradition, rooted in Chicago, started from a humanistic focus on the creative, conscious actor. Deterministic, **mechanistic** explanations of behaviour (for example, inborn instincts) were rejected. Instead, actors were seen as possessing creative selves that initiated conduct. However, these creative actors did not act in isolation, for interaction and the practical negotiation of conduct was central to the constant renewal of social life. Symbolic interactionism grew as a practical approach based on fieldwork, with an apparently simple philosophical underpinning: the philosophy of **pragmatism** accredited both social life and social science knowledge with the same source: creative human interaction. Social actors defined situations and chose how to act. When this action included creatively seeking knowledge, then practical human debate considered concepts and evidence before agreeing that certain ideas should be regarded as knowledge. This seemingly simplistic philosophy became extremely influential, and many philosophers now insist that knowledge is a collective human product, with no timeless status as truth.

In contrast, German philosophy was more abstract and drew on traditions that were opposed to the positivist model of knowledge, especially in social science. One tradition was the neo-Kantian approach, which strongly influenced Weber. This stressed the gulf

Mechanistic
Used to describe behaviour that is determined by external forces or internal constraints.

Pragmatism
A philosophy of US origin that treats values and knowledge as means to practical human ends. Concepts and values are regarded as true only as long as they prove useful.

between the natural world and the human world. In social science, meanings and acts had to be understood by means of insight and understanding rather than empirical causal facts. An alternative tradition was idealism, which proposed that knowledge and truth were to be discovered in thought itself: that is, in the mind of the thinker, not through reference to an objective outside reality. The phenomenological approach grew from this idealist root and offered a view of the social world as consisting purely of human taken-for-granted meanings. Ethnomethodology was developed to put phenomenological ideas into practice. We shall look at these four action theories – Weber's social action theory, symbolic interactionism, phenomenology and ethnomethodology – in turn.

Weber's theory of social action

Weber's work spanned both structural and action sociology. He attempted to reconcile large-scale historical comparative studies with a methodology that began from the individual social act. Weber argued that historical trends and social institutions could ultimately be reduced to unique individual actions; but at the same time, actions would always have motives and goals, derived from the broader cultural context. For example, the instrumental, calculating rationality of Western individuals derived from a much broader trend of historical development (see Chapter 2). Weber also tried to reconcile scientific sociology with the special methodology needed for understanding social action. He did this by means of **verstehen** – a process in which the sociologist attempted to gain access to the meaning of an act for an actor.

For Weber, this meaning of the act for the actor was the motive present in his or her mind, and this motive was the cause of the act. Weber distinguished four types of motive:

- Traditional conformity to habit.

- Emotional behaviour.

- Rational behaviour oriented towards an ultimate value (such as salvation).

- Rational behaviour oriented towards a mundane goal (such as earning a living).

Scientific explanation involved using verstehen to understand the correct motive. It is true that this was done partly by locating the act in its context – for example, we know that a woodcutter chops wood for rational reasons connected with pay. In the end, however, this approach simply boiled down to making an informed guess about the actor's reasons for acting.

The problem with this definition of action is that it is excessively individualistic and fails to locate thought and action in any real social context. In particular, Weber's methodology does not encourage us to look for the social backdrop to motivated choice, nor to recognise that our actors may not know what these historical and structural influences are. The irony is that in practice, Weber investigated action in a much more social way than his methodology prescribed. In *The Protestant Ethic and the Spirit of Capitalism* (1977), he did relate motives and meanings to larger world-views and belief systems beyond the actor. However, at the theoretical and methodological levels, the connection between these and action was never adequately addressed. This was unfortunate, because it meant that critics of Weber's methodology – above all, Alfred Schutz (1976), in his theory of phenomenology – concentrated on developing action theory at the expense of attention to the historical and structural origins and significance of beliefs and meanings. As a result, twentieth-century studies of action tended to be devoid of considerations of structure, and Weber's interest in the context for action given by belief systems and historical social structures was largely forgotten.

Verstehen
A German term usually translated as 'understanding'. Employed by Weber to define his approach to the study of social life, namely the interpretative understanding of human agents and the meaning they attach to their actions.

Symbolic interactionism

The American social action tradition emerged early in the twentieth century, particularly in Chicago. It was distinctive for its stress on face-to-face interaction in small-scale social settings, as well as for its concern with social identity and the 'public face' that people presented to others. At the heart of this lay the notion of a creative, consciously acting self – even though the self was a social product developed in a social setting through learning and socialisation. This symbolic interactionist (SI) approach emphasised, indeed celebrated, diversity and difference in social life. This gave the tradition a liberal, humanistic character that refused to judge or condemn, and instead sought to understand social life on its own terms, through direct contact in the field. This had affinities with ethnographic studies of different ways of living, whether carried out by anthropologists or socially aware journalists.

Today, SI emphasises the diversity of social roles and subcultures and the way in which social rules and social identities are constructed by actors themselves through their interaction with each other. For example, Plummer (1975) has traced the process by which people come to establish their homosexual self-identity, while Becker (1963) has drawn attention to the powerful effect of labels that impose deviant identities.

CONNECTIONS See Chapter 14, pages 389–91, for an interactionist account of crime.

Looking-glass self
Coined by Cooley (1922) to convey how individuals perceive their identity through the responses of others.

Definition of the situation
A term used in symbolic interactionism to describe an actor's interpretation of an event or experience.

The 'I' and the 'me'
Terms used by Mead to refer to the impulses for social action ('I') and the socially constructed self ('me').

Significant other
A particular individual whose views, opinions and reactions contribute to and influence the conception we have of ourselves.

Generalised other
Expectations of general conduct in a social group: what is expected of you.

As mentioned earlier, the roots of SI lie in a reaction against mechanistic or biological accounts of behaviour based on instinct. Central to this was the humanistic idea of the self-conscious individual, actively choosing his or her actions. This self is not, however, pre-formed and in-built. Instead, selfhood – identity – is learnt through the responses of others. This is captured in Cooley's (1922) notion of the **looking-glass self**. Once we possess this conscious self, we create actions in ways that are not just simple reactions to stimuli. As Thomas (1928) put it, we actually respond to our interpretation or **definition of the situation**: if we define a situation as real, it is real in its consequences. Hence, a creating, choosing self stands between social influences and social actions. However, this is not a purely individualistic perspective. SI writers have also revealed the way in which we draw upon shared symbols that attach meaning and social significance to objects or actions: is this object a dining table or is it an altar? The answer rests in meaning and symbol, not carpentry.

Individuals monitor their own behaviour by conscious thought, and this thought can only operate through symbols learnt in a social context, largely through language. Shared language gives us access to shared meanings and social expectations. We come to know who we are and what we should do through the response of others to our actions – responses we have to interpret using our social knowledge of meanings. These general notions vary in sophistication from Cooley's looking-glass self to Mead's (1934) conceptions of the **'I'** and the **'me'**, but they all begin with face-to-face interaction. While Cooley portrayed society as an interlocking network of small groups, Mead acknowledged more general roles and patterns in society. Mead also stressed how our self has to develop in a social context through learning and socialisation. He described how the development of personality moves beyond the stage where the child responds to the demands of a **significant other** (for example, the mother) to where the adult is aware of the demands of the **generalised other** in the roles he or she plays. However, this world of roles is flexible because actors can always try to renegotiate the nature of the roles through interaction. Hence, the self is a social construction, but society is constantly being reshaped by the actions of social selves.

QUESTION Symbolic interactionism has been hugely influential in sociological theorising. Which of its features do you think theorists would find most attractive, and why?

Society is seen as consisting of interlocking interactions between individuals based on actors' perceptions and expectations of each other. The content of action depends on how the actors read or define the social settings in which they find themselves. To repeat our earlier reference to Thomas (1928), situations defined as real are real in their consequences. In other words, the nature of the social world ultimately depends on the shared definitions of roles and identities constructed through interaction. Both self and society are essentially fluid and adaptable, as Mead (1934, p. 182) suggests:

BOX 18.1 Erving Goffman and the politics of interaction: social life as theatre

Erving Goffman (1967, 1969) is probably the best-known SI writer, and his work is as well known and widely read outside the academic world as inside it. His ideas can be summarised as follows:

- Uniquely among living things, humans are interpretive beings, able to attach meanings to the world around them and to choose how to act in the light of these meanings.

- Humans are also social beings, and most of what they choose to do takes place in the company of other human beings.

- Inevitably, being human involves attaching meaning to each other's actions. Anything we parade during public (social) interaction can be interpreted as saying something about us.

- Language is the most important source of symbolic meaning in human social life, though other symbols – such as dress, demeanour, expression, even smell – are important too. Social encounters therefore necessarily involve other people interpreting what we are like. Anything we disclose in social encounters can and usually will be used by others to confer identities on us.

- Since this is so, we soon learn to attempt to sculpture or manipulate others' interpretations of us. We learn to become actors on the stage of life, but we write our own lines and use whatever props we can find in the metaphorical wardrobe mistress's cupboard to assist us.

Goffman uses this theatrical metaphor to illuminate the detail of local, small-scale encounters – to identify the usual and the unusual in the everyday rituals involved in being social. He calls our attempts to organise others' interpretations of us 'impression management' and 'presentation of the self', and he characterises the whole process as 'dramaturgy'. Essentially, he is describing everyday life or the social world (favourite SI terms) as places where countless little dramas take place – some serious, some not – and in which the humans involved are, quite literally, actors.

For SI, then, our identity, our sense of self, depends a great deal upon the management and outcome of the innumerable social encounters in which we are involved during our lives. We come to think of ourselves in the way we do because this self-image is confirmed or altered by those who comprise our audience. Clearly, some members of this audience occupy seats in the stalls night after night – our parents, siblings, partners, peers, teachers, friends and so on – while others may witness only one of our performances. That is, some of our audience are significant others in our lives, and others are hardly significant at all. Also, general cultural expectations, of the kinds concentrated on by functionalists, operate as constraints that we have to take account of when we walk on stage – a sort of generalised other that sets limits to our creativity. But this is no story of biographical forces outside individuals' control. This is the triumph of autobiography – creative actors writing their own life stories – the only real limits being set by the desire to hear the applause of an appreciative audience.

" The individual is continually adjusting himself [*sic*] in advance to the situation to which he belongs and reacting back upon it. The self is not something that exists first and then enters into a relationship with others, but is, so to speak, an eddy in the social current and so still a part of the current. "

The real strength of the SI approach lies not so much in its theoretical foundations as in the practical qualitative research it has generated. Writers such as Hughes (1958), Becker (1963) and Goffman (1967, 1969) pioneered qualitative research methods aimed at 'getting in where the action is' and 'telling it like it is'. In other words, we should try to understand the world as it is seen by our subjects – be they homosexuals, mental hospital patients or 'trainee' marijuana users. The task is to see how they make sense of the world and cope with others who have different expectations, or with those who have power over them (Goffman, 1974). Researchers must therefore use sensitive empathy and engage in participant observation.

CONNECTIONS See Chapter 16, pages 448–50 and 456–61, for a full account of interactionist techniques.

Goffman's works illustrate some of SI's key characteristics. For example, he shows how a similarity of form can be found in settings with quite different content (Goffman, 1961). Total institutions such as monasteries and prisons may insist on a **mortification of the self**, the stripping away of entrants' old identity by taking away their clothes, cutting their hair and renaming or numbering them. A new institutionally defined identity is then imposed. Implicit in this account is the importance of individual identity, and the powerful ways in which this can be distorted. Equally implicit is a commitment to individual autonomy and authenticity. This liberal, humanistic sentiment is at the

Mortification of the self
Rituals of entry, especially in total institutions, that debase the old identity in order to impose a new institutional identity (see *total institutions*).

Figure 18.1 According to Goffman, the self is not a cause but an effect of social behaviour. Props, such as the dress of these Tibetan Buddhist monks, are part of the dramatisation of identity to others.

heart of SI. Thus, Goffman shows how apparently irrational behaviour (such as the hoarding of useless objects by patients in mental hospitals) can be seen as having a sensible logic once it is understood on its own terms, in the context of that social setting. This approach generously assumes that actors' behaviour has its own rationality, and it follows that we have a duty to understand and accept it on its own terms. Interactionists often view themselves as subverting orthodox judgements about what is acceptable or reasonable behaviour: tolerance of diversity is their goal.

The concept of a 'career' guides SI accounts of the way in which a new social identity (as pot smoker, physician and so on) is negotiated. This involves learning appropriate behaviour, exercising initiative and possibly resisting unwelcome labels being imposed by others. For example, a teenager caught stealing might try to resist the label of 'criminal', but during the process of conviction and sentencing to a penal institution, this social identity will be imposed by others. This labelling (and its consequences for employment), together with the skills learnt inside prison, may result in acceptance of the criminal self-image by the person himself; this would be a completed 'deviant career' (see chapter 14). These qualitative methods used by symbolic interactionists are closely associated with sympathy for the underdog. SI often seems like a manual for individual resistance to pressures from powerful social institutions and a defence of the dignity and rationality of the individual actor.

Criticisms of SI

For all the attractiveness and plausibility of this account of social life, there are certain problems with it. The first and most obvious is that social structures are neglected. In a typical SI account, social institutions are acknowledged as a backdrop to interaction, but social systems and their related structures of economic and political power have only a shadowy existence. Certainly, the claim that social life consists solely of actors' definitions is not sustainable. The consequences of inequality, for example, are real, irrespective of whether or not the actors define them as real, and the consequences of actions in a complex social structure may be outside the control or knowledge of any actor. In order to understand such consequences, we need an account of structure (cf. Plummer, 1979). However, it is unfair to direct these criticisms only at SI, for they also apply to other action perspectives.

We can also question the adequacy of the approach's notions of self and action, since SI overestimates the degree of conscious monitoring of action and manipulation of situations. Social life is presented as a very consciously played game, and perhaps more scope should be allowed for unconscious drives and social action that is less consciously controlled. A quite different criticism has been levelled at SI's liberal tolerance of deviant diversity. This can be seen as humanistic when it comes to championing gay people or those with a social stigma, but can tolerance be extended to the rapist or the drug baron? Is any way of life really as good as any other? This liberal perspective can easily slip into always justifying action on its own terms, without concern for the wider consequences for others. Issues about the relativity and diversity of social life have become central topics of debate in the social sciences with the rise of postmodernist theorising, as we shall see in Chapter 19.

Phenomenological sociology

One of the leading figures in phenomenology was Alfred Schutz, an Austrian-born American philosopher who was best known for *The Phenomenology of the Social World* (1976). In this work, Schutz drew on the philosophies of Husserl (1931) and Bergson

(1913) to criticise Weber's methodology and construct a radical account of the nature of social action. In Schutz's view, Weber's theory of action was too individualistic. Schutz insisted that humans could only act by drawing upon a shared set of social concepts, symbols and meanings, and he argued that Weber's account of the relation between actions and reasons or motives was too mechanical.

As we have seen, SI shows how actors share definitions of situations and roles, how symbolic communication through language is fundamental, and how these things are built up out of interaction in a creative manner. Schutz's emphasis was quite different. He argued that the **life-world** is a precarious set of shared meanings available to the whole social group. It is a shared stock of **common-sense knowledge**, of taken-for-granted assumptions about society, other actors and the world. In effect, social life consists of these shared arbitrary assumptions and conceptions, and social order can only last as long as we collectively believe in them. However, the fragility of this shared definition of reality is not recognised by actors in normal circumstances, because they adopt the 'natural attitude'. That is, they see the world as solid, inflexible and constraining, even though it is really only a product of shared ideas. It is only by painful effort that the phenomenologist can suspend this common-sense knowledge and see the real nature of social life. For Schutz, the social world rests solely upon 'acts of establishing or interpreting meaning'. Phenomenologists therefore claim that conventional positivistic sociology suffers from the same commonsensical self-delusions as any ordinary member of society, because positivism assumes that there really is a constraining world of social facts out there.

Life-world
From Schutz (1976), the world of shared social meanings in which actors live and interact.

Common-sense knowledge
Schutz's term for the practical social knowledge that we take for granted as the basis for everyday actions.

CONNECTIONS For an account of the positivist position, see Chapter 17, pages 474–6, and Table 16.2.

In contrast to Weber's view of action, Schutz rejected the idea that single acts have particular motives. Instead, actors engage in a constant flow of action that takes place through the continuous use of 'recipe knowledge': practical knowledge of how things are done. They do not constantly reflect on future acts and clarify a goal (though they do have long-term projects): they just use their common sense and get on with things. Only sometimes do they look back at an act and give an account of their motives. In the course of their action, they employ assumptions about society and how it works, and they use *verstehen* in a crude way to predict the actions of others. This last point constitutes a major innovative departure from Weber, and perhaps also from SI. According to phenomenology, all actors are amateur sociologists if they are successful social actors. This raises profound questions about the relationship between common sense and sociology.

Equally important is the fact that phenomenologists insist we should understand the socially given meaning of an act in its context. This socially given meaning (for example, of a gesture at an auction) is quite separate from any motive the actor might have. For phenomenology, all the collectivities in which actors take part are universes of shared meanings.

QUESTION What criticisms could be made of the phenomenological approach?

Ethnomethodology

Ethnomethodology (EM) arose directly from Schutz's phenomenological work, but it is more committed to practical grounded research – the general aim is to demonstrate the truth of phenomenological arguments by means of practical experiments. EM, which emerged in the mid 1960s in the US, is a fusion of action research and phenomenology.

Harold Garfinkel was the founding father, and he coined the name ethnomethodology to express a particular aim: the ethnographic description and analysis of the methods used by actors to sustain social life. In other words, ethnomethodologists' objective is to show, by practical studies, how the social world is produced and reproduced by the practical actions of actors, on the basis of taken-for-granted assumptions – just as Schutz described.

Garfinkel (1967) developed EM as a new answer to the problem of order. Functionalism had addressed this problem by emphasising moral order, but Garfinkel rejected this in favour of a search for the processes that allowed orderliness to emerge out of the flux of everyday life. For Garfinkel, only this could capture the real nature of social life. The task of EM is therefore to expose the mundane everyday processes of social life as skilful accomplishments of the actors. Even in routine conversations, we use knowledge, skills and taken-for-granted assumptions. However, the crucial point is that we, as lay actors, are unaware of this. Only a painful effort, a disruption or an incomprehensible response from another can make us aware of just how much we are taking for granted. So, when Garfinkel asked his students to behave like boarders at home – polite, well-behaved and respectful – their families responded with incomprehension or even hostility. As in his other experiments, Garfinkel was arranging for **background expectancies** to be violated so that the social setting would cease to make sense to the actors. Thus, ethnomethodologists sought appropriate methods to turn Schutz's 'natural attitude' into a researchable phenomenon, exposing the organised, artful practices of everyday life. Because mundane interaction was treated as 'anthropologically strange', grounded observation and ethnographic description were deemed to be appropriate methods.

For many sociologists, insights provided by EM, though limited, are illuminating and should be added to the range of sociological perspectives available to be used (Goldthorpe, 1973). However, ethnomethodologists claim that, because the processes they expose tell everything about social reality that is capable of being told, EM has displaced conventional sociology altogether. For them, the typologies and structural concepts of conventional sociology are illusory. When they portray social processes as solid and constraining, they merely reproduce the natural attitude of the lay actor. EM dissolves away the patterns and regularities that are the focus of mainstream sociology, for all social phenomena are open to transformation in the flux of everyday life. What is more, social action and understanding only really operate in a particular social situation, since meanings are **indexical** or tied to the immediate context. This applies equally to the actor using understanding and the social scientist seeking to understand. Consequently, it is not clear that any account can make any definitive claim to truth or certainty: knowledge is relative and even arbitrary unless we can find a way to justify our interpretations.

Clearly this is a far cry from the project of modernity – the construction of rational, verifiable and objective accounts of social life so that this proven knowledge can be harnessed to improve the human condition. As Sharrock and Anderson (1986, p. 104) observe:

> " In short, ethnomethodology does not think of itself as telling either the whole or a part of the story, but of trying to examine the ways in which any story might be told, with the ways in which stories are projected and interpreted as intelligible, coherent, plausible, demonstrably correct and so forth . "

In other words, we cannot choose between stories, but we can show how stories come to be constructed and believed. Is this enough to satisfy those who want sociology to tell us something of substance about the world? As we shall see, this is precisely the objection that structural theorists have to another (and more influential) perspective that has sprung from relativism: postmodernism (see Chapter 19).

Background expectancies
Coined by Garfinkel (1967) to describe taken-for-granted assumptions and expectations about human behaviour in a given context.

Indexical
From ethnomethodology, the claim that meanings can only be gained in the context of their social setting.

BOX 18.2 Ethnomethodology and the contingency of meaning

Whereas SI focuses on the importance of *verstehen* – both in everyday life and in social research into the dynamics of this life – EM attempts to show how *verstehen* works. Arguing that since human understanding of any aspect of reality can never be objectively correct, but only correct for the individual subject doing the interpreting, EM claims that this must be true of sociological accounts. All knowledge of the world is bound to be subject-centred – relative to the subjects involved – whether they are sociologists or not. So, expert sociological accounts of how things really are cannot be achieved by humans, hamstrung as they are by their incapacity to see anything except from their personal, *verstehen*-generated point of view. Thus, the accounts of other sociologies, SI included, are dismissed as subjectivity masquerading as objectivity. EM argues that the discipline should instead concentrate on the one thing it can be objective about – the way in which humans, sociologists or not, use *verstehen*. For EM, *verstehen* itself is the topic: it is not the artist's painting that is to be objectively understood, but the way in which materials and brushes have been used to paint it.

Imagine an unoccupied classroom – all that fills it are desks, chairs, some tables perhaps, a blackboard and so on. Now picture the room filled with students and a teacher. How is order possible in such a situation? In principle, anything could happen during the 50 minutes or so the class exists as a social event. But lessons are almost always ordered occasions. Why? How? Structural explanations would point to role playing, norms, constraints, sanctions and so on. But EM argues a different case. If structural forces were the real explanation, most events in the lesson would be predictable and repeated week after week. But, as we all know from our own experience of education, this never happens. Each class is a unique event. Once the 'members' (the EM term for actors) of the occasion gather, the room is filled with communication and interpretation – language, laughter, gestures, actions, looks, signals and so on – the precise nature of which can never reoccur (or make sense if it did) on any other occasion, anywhere else, ever again! In effect, what is said or done can only make sense on the occasion and at the time when it makes sense to say or do it.

Action, then, is contingent or context-bound, or in EM terminology, indexical. The next time the class gathers, the only thing that will be repeated will be its physical presence: everything social will be constructed anew. Thus, EM stresses that each separate social occasion requires non-stop work on the part of its members to make it work – even though these members will not realise they are working at all! Furthermore, if each member of the class was asked, at the conclusion of a lesson, to describe what had happened during the lesson, how similar would the various accounts be? This is what makes EM suspicious of claims to objective authenticity by any sociological account, even SI accounts, which are also exclusively interested in action. How can anyone know how others see the world? How can one account be judged superior to others? The only thing we can be sure of is how members arrive at their personal subjective views, since all humans must make use of the same method – *verstehen* – to do so. Aside from that, all human accounts are of equal validity – or invalidity. They are inevitably relativist – in this case, relative to the subjects involved. In summary, the content of communication and interpretation during an event is indexical, and any understanding of it is subject-centred.

Summary: creative social action

From the above discussion of the development of social action theories, or theories of agency, it is apparent that the creative actor, or subject, is conceived in quite a variety of ways. Equally, consideration of the theories reveals that the social world is an arbitrary and relative construction.

Action theories give varying accounts of the ways in which social actors shape social life, and how the actor has the ability to do so creatively and competently (see Table 18.1).

TABLE 18.1 Actors, meanings and society

Example of action theory	Nature of meanings	Form of action studied
Weber on religion and action, Parsons' theory of action	Meanings derived from established culture/values/belief systems in the society or social group	Goals and rational motives for intended actions deriving from belief systems
Symbolic interactionism	Meanings and identity are constructed through social interaction, or imposed through powerful shared symbols and labels	Face-to-face interaction, the process of labelling and the negotiation of social identity
Weber's *verstehen*	Intentions held by an actor in relation to a separate act; goals for rational action	Individual acts; understanding the motive of the actor and the beliefs available to the actor
Phenomenology	Meanings are a common stock, used in a common-sense way to construct actions. They are taken-for-granted definitions of reality: 'common sense'	Meanings must be interpreted on their own terms, and seen as real to the actors and true in their setting
Ethnomethodology	Meanings are accounts of everyday life, by means of which actors make sense of their setting and achieve order within it	Context-specific speech and behaviour; routine social practices that sustain order and meaning in social settings

Subject-centred
An approach to social analysis that centres on the active, creative human subject.

Reflexive
Normally employed to describe a process of self-reflection that may modify beliefs and action (see *reflexivity*).

As we have seen, Weber stressed the human potential for goal-directed rational action, even if much of the time human action is governed by habitual, traditional or emotional motives. We have also seen that the wider belief systems in society may shape the goals of the individual and govern action through rules and norms. In Weber's modern society, actors are forced to be increasingly rational in their pursuit of increasingly mundane and worldly goals. In contrast, the symbolic interactionist's actor is a creative, reflexive self. Although socialisation shapes humans' social identity and develops their capacity to play roles and interact with others, once they are mature they can recast their identity and negotiate how to behave in social settings. Goffman and the labelling theorists showed how this could be a matter of power or resistance – for example, over the imposition of a deviant label. But behind this, there is a potentially autonomous actor with an integrity and a will that is under threat. Symbolic interactionism is thus an intensely humanistic, **subject-centred** perspective.

QUESTION To what extent do you agree that the actor in society is autonomous, with integrity and will?

Phenomenology and ethnomethodology place more emphasis on the tacit skills, knowledge and social skills that actors use without fully realising it. According to this view, actors creatively reshape society by drawing on taken-for-granted recipe knowledge and sustaining routines that preserve the illusion of a stable, solid social reality. In this sense, actors are not fully self-aware, **reflexive** subjects. However, there is an underlying assumption that all social actors are competent, unknowingly deploying great social skills, the greatest of which is language itself. The formation or development of these skilled actors is not explored: it is the processes of acting that count. However, not every sociologist would accept that using language is the most creative action that humans involve themselves in. So, we shall now turn to the issue of language and how important it has become for a sociological exploration of contemporary societies.

Language and social life: post-structuralism

The most influential figures in this tradition of looking at language are French – for example, the semiologist Roland Barthes, the literary analyst and critic Jacques Derrida and, most significantly for sociology, the historian and philosopher Michel Foucault. The influence of these writers is not confined to one academic discipline, but straddles all disciplines that deal with the role of language in human life, such as philosophy, English, history and sociology.

CONNECTIONS For a fuller account of the importance of language, see Chapter 19, particularly pages 522–5.

The conventional view of language is as a means of communicating ideas – the sophisticated resource that humans use to express themselves to each other in symbolic form. For example, the sounds we utter and the words we write are symbolic representations of meaning that can be understood by others who speak and read the language concerned. For action sociology, language is the main reason for the triumph of the subject and for the possibility of meaningful social interaction. It is the key means by which we can communicate to others what we wish them to know.

Post-structuralism turns this notion of the relationship between language and knowledge on its head, arguing that, far from language symbolising original creative thought, it actually dictates the thoughts we have: languages do not represent our meanings so much as construct them for us. To understand this approach, two of its principal features need to be understood:

- 'Experience' and 'knowledge' are different things. Although we all experience the world through our senses, we cannot know what these experiences mean until we learn a language. Although we feel pain, elation, sorrow, tiredness and so on as soon as our developing senses begin to work, we do not know what to call these experiences until we learn a language that defines their meanings. That is, languages dictate, demand or solicit certain meanings and interpretations from us; words and sounds create our ideas about reality.

- Languages – systems of meanings that construct our thoughts – are not just English, Spanish, Italian or whatever. The term applies to any system of meanings that elicits particular understandings when we encounter and use them. It therefore applies to scientific representations such as mathematical or chemical symbols, painting, sculpture and even architecture. Drawing a picture is not drawing a map of some sense data that we see. If we draw a 'free' or a 'sad face', what we are drawing is a representation of the idea of a tree or a sad face. We are communicating a concept, and that depends on meanings being shared by the person drawing and the person viewing the sketch. Whether it is words or pictures, we always communicate concepts through these signs. To use print to draw this picture – 'sad' – and to use it to draw this picture – ☹ – involves the pictorial production of symbols designed to elicit similar meanings for those who see them.

> **QUESTION** Do you see language as primarily a creative act by the individual, or a structural feature of society? Give reasons for your answer.

Post-structuralists use the term 'text' to refer to any symbols that organise meanings; texts construct and direct our knowledge of our world. Without a text to tell us, we cannot know what our experiences mean; however, once we use a text, it ends up controlling what we think. We all know that this is true of the arts: music, literature, paintings, sculptures, films and so on. We approach works of art in the expectation of having our thoughts pushed in one direction or another. Post-structuralists argue that it is the text that directs such thoughts – not the words the author employs to convey his or her meanings. Post-structuralists claim that their insights have resulted in the 'death of the author': no one who uses language to construct a text has any control over the meaning each of us reads into the symbols. In effect, we are all authors of texts when we encounter them – yet we are not the creators of our authorship, since we cannot think just what we like. The language used instructs us, 'telling' us what to think – soliciting from us certain responses rather than others, even though these may not be the responses intended by the authors of the text.

Furthermore, since who we are – our identities – can be defined as our thoughts, meanings and interpretations, and since these are linguistic constructions, then post-structuralists insist that the possibility of an autonomous subject creating a self or identity for him- or herself is a nonsense. The idea of the 'subject' is dead and buried. We are under the power that forms of knowledge exercise over us; our identities are constituted by languages. We are helpless in the face of the power of language; we are obliged to think in the directions it pushes us.

BOX 18.3 The historical relativity of the meaning of language

In medieval Europe, plump or fat bodies were considered to be beautiful, while slight, slim ones were not. A glance at any of the figures in paintings by Reubens demonstrates this clearly. It is still true of some African tribes, who use 'fattening sheds' to build up the bodies of girls so that they will be admired at the initiation ceremonies that mark their entry into womanhood. In the West, however, the reverse is true. Today, to be 'fat' is to be 'overweight' or 'gross', and this is considered so alarming and disfiguring, especially for females, that it has spawned a large slimming industry, as well as the modern illnesses of anorexia and bulimia.

However unfair we may believe it to be, it is difficult for us to escape the connection between 'fat' and 'ugly' that has taken root in Western culture. When seeing the words 'fat woman' printed on a page, it is difficult to resist feeling disapproval or pity, at least momentarily. Yet the conjunction of these words provoked the opposite response a few hundred years ago, when the words 'slim' and 'thin' would have had us turning up our noses in disapproval.

Post-structuralists therefore want to put languages, texts or, as Foucault calls such forms of knowledge, 'discourses' at the top of the sociological agenda. For them, any discipline that deals with the nature of identity and the reasons why cultures are as they are must focus principally on the representations of meaning that provide the knowledge of the world for their users. This means that, as in the case of ethnomethodology, forms of knowledge can never be objectively correct. Just as we do not rank ordinary languages – English is not a better way of talking about things than Welsh, even if it is used by many more people – so forms of knowledge that work like a language are not better or worse than each other, just different. Therefore, it can never be a matter of history ushering in new eras of 'progress' and 'improvement', as modernism suggests. History simply tells the story of the rise and fall of different discourses, all defining normality and deviance, all true for their time, and all untrue for different times and places.

Post-structuralism, then, is a relativist sociology, denying all possibility of humans possessing objectively true knowledge. Unlike ethnomethodology, however, this is not a subject-centred relativism, but a language-centred relativism. This is why post-structuralists are enthusiastic supporters of the idea of postmodernism. Since contemporary life is infused with a large variety of forms of knowledge, often electronically communicated around the globe, postmodernists insist that the project of modernity – the search for the truth, for the answer to the problem of human existence – should be abandoned. Instead, we should recognise and accept different accounts of reality, since there is no human way of judging their validity. It is to this debate that we turn in the final chapter.

 ## Questions to think about

- How much influence do you think that Weber's work had on the development of action theories? Make a case for and against the idea that his work was influential in this regard.
- Of symbolic interactionism, ethnomethodology and phenomenology, which do you think is the most valid, and why?
- Think of three important events in your recent personal life. How much freedom of choice did you have in shaping those events?

 ## Chapter summary

- A number of humanistic perspectives place their main emphasis not on structural causes and constraints but on the creative human actor who negotiates situations and identities purposefully and resourcefully in face-to-face settings.

- These approaches (for example, symbolic interactionism) tend to assume that actions make sense if they are understood on their own terms and in the context of their particular setting; consequently, these theories tend to advocate social tolerance of diverse norms and identities.

- Phenomenology and ethnomethodology place rather less stress on conscious motives and reflection by the actor. Instead, an essentially changing and precarious social world is maintained unwittingly through shared meanings and practical social skills.

- Post-structural theory 'decentres the subject' by proposing the self as a product of language rather than seeing language more conventionally as a resource of the self.

- Post-structuralists do not see language as creative social action. For them, language, texts and discourses construct and direct our knowledge of the world and shape our identities: the 'autonomous subject' is a fiction, and the search for 'truth' is fruitless.

Investigating further

Craib, Ian (1992) *Modern Social Theory: from Parsons to Habermas*, 2nd edn, Prentice Hall.

> A clear, thematic guide to such areas of theory as functionalism, action theories, structuralism, post-structuralism, postmodernism and the Frankfurt School.

Lemert, Charles and Ann Branaman (eds) (1997) *The Goffman Reader*, Blackwell.

> A useful compendium of extracts from Goffman's major works, including his writings on the presentation of self in everyday life, total institutions, stigma and frame analysis.

Swingewood, Alan (2000) *A Short History of Sociological Thought*, 3rd edn, Palgrave.

> This text covers sociological theory from Marx, Durkheim, and Weber onwards, and is very useful in the way it places more recent theories in the context of what has gone before. Try Chapter 8 on structuralism and post-structuralism.

chapter 19

Modernity, postmodernity and social theory

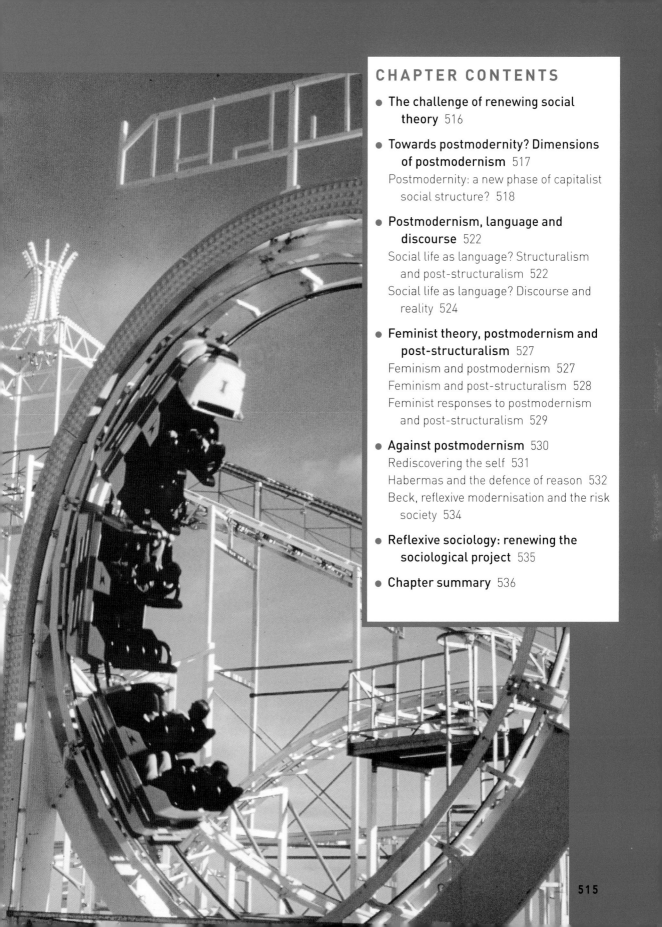

CHAPTER CONTENTS

Aims of the chapter

This chapter introduces a wide range of current theoretical approaches and shows the diversity of contemporary social theory. The various theories are organised around the theme of whether or not modern societies are undergoing profound change, and whether or not postmodernism is the best way of characterising this change. Postmodern and post-structuralist feminist theorists are considered, as are the ways in which a number of other contemporary social theorists have sought to extend and renew the classic sociological project (that is, using knowledge to help construct a better social world).

By the end of the chapter, you should have a basic understanding of the following theories and concepts:

- Postmodernism
- Meta-narrative
- Discourse
- Genealogical inquiry
- Identity
- Sign
- Individualisation

The challenge of renewing social theory

Sociologists have always been concerned to analyse their immediate time and place, even though this risks misrepresenting or misinterpreting aspects of social change because there is no benefit of hindsight. As societies change, sociological accounts inevitably change too in order to offer fresh understandings of salient social trends. However, at what point should sociologists decide that their established frameworks and concepts are no longer productive? When should they conclude that their established theories are proving a hindrance rather than a help to understanding the changes taking place in society?

In recent years, a number of sociologists have become sceptical about the value of the classical frameworks and concepts derived from studies of modernity. This scepticism has been fuelled by two main channels of thought:

- The argument that classical theories offer an inadequate framework for understanding many important issues in contemporary social life.
- The (much debated) claim that we are moving to a qualitatively new form of society known as postmodernity.

Adherents of the first viewpoint highlight the powerful influence on recent social theory of social movements such as feminism, environmentalism and (the largely anti-nuclear) peace movements. These have challenged previous priorities, highlighting how the focus of classical social theories on production, class and economic inequality seriously neglected such critical issues as warfare and nationalism, the impact of technology and social divisions of race and gender. As we shall see later in this chapter, some sociologists have recently worked to redress this imbalance and provide a less narrowly focused analysis of power, conflict and inequality.

Adherents of the second claim argue the case for a newly emerging postmodern society of a different order altogether from modernity. Instead of pointing to neglected issues, they insist that sociological frameworks and concepts should be recast to make them appropriate for the new social world. Social theorists are very divided on the merits of this claim. Bauman (1992, p. 188), for example, declares that postmodernity has its own distinct features rather than being just a version of modernity: 'a theory of post-modernity therefore cannot be a modified theory of modernity … it needs its own vocabulary'. On the other hand, Habermas, whose work we shall consider shortly, has emphatically rejected postmodern theory in his ongoing commitment to the Enlightenment goals of social progress and emancipation, and Giddens (1990a) has argued for a concept of 'radicalised' or 'late' modernity, which he sees as providing a more accurate description of contemporary social circumstances than postmodernity. We shall look in more detail at the work of these important writers later in the chapter. First, we shall consider what is meant by the notion of postmodernity.

Towards postmodernity? Dimensions of postmodernism

Postmodernity, it is claimed, is not an extension of modernity but a fundamental break from it. As Smart (1993, p. 13) puts it, postmodernity is 'a highly loaded term' that has been interpreted and used differently by different social and cultural analysts. Broadly speaking, however, it refers to an unstable and sceptical world in which anything goes, where traditional modernist boundaries, even of time and space and reality and its images, have dissolved. Postmodern thinkers emphasise the highly information-laden, media-saturated nature of our everyday lives in the West, in which we experience events virtually and instantaneously from around the world 24 hours a day, seven days a week. They claim that, as individuals, we are no longer defined in a structured way by the job that we do, but that we actively construct our ever-changing identities through what we consume, be this on the Internet, in shopping centres, on holiday or sitting in front of the TV. If the characteristic modern activity was manufacturing, the defining postmodern activity is shopping. In sum, the postmodern age is a global, post-industrial age of proliferating signs, hyper-reality and deep-seated scepticism and uncertainty.

It is generally claimed that modernism's purest expression was in architecture. Modernism pursued an ideal of unadorned, functional design where the economic use of materials ensured elegant simplicity of form. Great glass-walled skyscrapers and curving, gravity-defying bridges symbolised the conquest of the natural world's con-straints by applying rational design and scientific knowledge. In reaction to this modernist tradition, postmodernist artists and architects favour the mixing of decora-tive styles, and the ironic or witty combination of elements from incompatible times and places. Unlike modernism, with its emphasis on form following function, postmodern design neither despises commercialism nor dignifies it with cool grandeur. Instead, it just goes along for the ride.

We often experience such playful environments in theme parks or popular restaurants. One example is McDonald's in Cambridge. Once past the stone facade, customers find themselves in a modern-tabled eating area with mock seventeenth-century plasterwork, imitating the famous Pepys Library. A visual surprise follows when they walk into a fibreglass Roman coliseum to order their American meal. Fun and superficial, and with no apparent unity of design, this pastiche of styles is jumbled together with the highly controlled, labour-intensive processing of factory-produced food that is the super-commercial hallmark of McDonald's. While no one would claim this restaurant to be a gem of postmodern architecture, it does demonstrate some of the fundamental characteristics implied by Venturi (1977) when he advocated 'learning from Las Vegas' to his fellow architects. This postmodern approach is playful and full of self-parody, deliberately denying any seriousness of purpose.

More generally, postmodernism as a perspective demonstrates a deep reluctance to accept any all-embracing, 'totalising' explanation – or meta-narrative – of how society develops or what we should believe. As the influential theorist Jean-Francois Lyotard puts it, 'Simplifying to the extreme, I define *postmodern* as incredulity towards meta-narratives.' (1986, p. xxiv). For the postmodernist, such grand narratives are delusions that lead directly to authoritarianism, as these doctrines are imposed by those who claim to have the unifying key. Instead, postmodernists celebrate diversity and difference, since this can reinforce dislocation and offer an open, unpredictable future.

Behind their rejection of monumental political theories of progress (such as that developed by Karl Marx), there is a rejection of grand philosophies of knowledge. Claims to certainty and truth have been brought into question by a wide range of modern philosophers, but postmodernism goes further and regards all truth claims as competing narratives – or rival stories. Similarly, postmodernists distrust claims to political salvation and scientific certainty. Box 19.1 summarises the changing nature of culture and knowledge from early modernity to postmodernity.

Postmodernity: a new phase of capitalist social structure?

Capitalism has had no serious rival as an economic system since the collapse of Soviet communism in 1989. This is not to say that there are no alternatives, or that capitalism

---

BOX 19.1 Culture and knowledge: from early modernity to postmodernity

Seventeenth century
Foundations of rational science, for example, the philosophy of Descartes and the scientific theories of Newton.

Eighteenth century
The Enlightenment: rationalism, science and faith in reason. Political revolutions; faith in human rights and powers.

Early nineteenth century
Moves against urban industrial modernity, for example, the romantic movement in literature and art. Faith in progress through science: positivism.

Late nineteenth/early twentieth century
Doubt and fear about the consequences of modernity, as expressed in the philosophy of Nietzsche and the sociology of Weber.

Early twentieth century
Simple models of truth and reality are questioned. Relativity in science, for example, the work of Einstein. High modernism in art and literature: individual, original art of serious purpose, for example, the novels of James Joyce and Marcel Proust and the surrealist and avant-garde movements in art (for instance, the paintings of Picasso and Magritte).

Late twentieth century
Fragmentation, cultural diversity, plurality of identities. Post-structuralism in cultural theory, for example, the work of Derrida. Mass reproduction of images, for example, the work of Benjamin; super-abundance of signs, for example, the work of Baudrillard. Distinction between 'high art' and commercial culture weakens, as exemplified by Andy Warhol and the pop art movement. Post-modern art and architecture: playful, eclectic, ironic, superficial, for example, the architecture of Venturi.

Figure 19.1 In the hyperreal world of the postmodern, there is no longer a clear distinction between the 'real' and its 'representations'. Baudrillard argues that Disneyland helps us to believe the illusion that the rest of the US is real.

is the best imaginable system. It is simply a description of the contemporary world, where capitalist corporations are constantly increasing their global reach and ensuring that more and more of the world's activities involve commodities, bought and sold for a price.

> **QUESTION** Which social movements oppose capitalism today? Where are they coming from ideologically?

It is in this context of unparalleled capitalist dominance that a new set of social theories have argued that class is dead and that culture and consumption, not work, are the predominant shapers of people's lives (Gorz, 1982). If this seems paradoxical, then one answer lies in the idea that capitalism has entered a new phase, where the economic structures and mode of profit making are different from before. A number of terms are used by theorists to capture this idea: 'post-Fordism' (a term we first encountered in Chapter 3), 'disorganised capitalism' (Lash and Urry, 1987), 'flexible accumulation' (Harvey, 1989), all of which capture the sense of a new economic phase being born.

At the heart of these theories is an emphasis on the ways in which capitalism has simultaneously become more global and yet geographically more divided and separated. In the older industrial nations, manufacturing, manual employment and hence working-class politics are in decline. Production is shifting to newly industrialised countries. In the established capitalist economies, the old industrial centres are contracting and the service sector expanding.

CONNECTIONS See Chapter 3, pages 54–7, Chapter 5, pages 112–18, and Chapter 11, pages 303–8, to see how this employment development has unfolded so far.

These points are developed systematically in the Fordism/post-Fordism model, which derives from regulation theory – a branch of Marxist political economy (Lipietz, 1987). The contrast between these two capitalist 'regimes' is summarised in Table 19.1. In this view, a certain way of organising profitable production, a 'regime of accumulation', must be underpinned by a 'mode of regulation' – that is, a set of social and political arrangements that support and reproduce this way of organising production.

Fordist production characterised the post-war economic boom, which lasted for three decades. Most Western societies had state policies to promote welfare and full employment, and workers were tied to the system through this, as well as by rising

TABLE 19.1 Fordism and Post-Fordism

Regime of accumulation	Mode of regulation	Culture and world-view
Fordism		
• Mass production • Standardised products • Rigid bureaucracy • Routinised work • High productivity and wage growth • Strong, large trade unions • Wages bargained collectively	• State manages the economy for growth and full employment • Universal welfare provision • Redistribution of incomes • Strong interest groups influence policy and bargain with government	• Class is the central social and political identity • Work identity is more important than consumer identity • Collectivist class interests oppose groups with individualistic values in shaping politics · Modernist culture • Belief in social and technical progress • Emphasis on social justice as well as profitable production
Post-Fordism		
• Flexible specialisation in production, using global manufacturing • Goods designed and produced for market niches • Polarization of workers into core and secondary labour forces • Organisations devolved into delayered horizontal structures	• Private welfare for core workers, basic state provision for the rest • Resistance to planning or state coordination • Fragmentation of group interests • Diverse social identities and interests	• Self-expression through consumption and lifestyle • Non-class issues and identities are the focus of political action • New social movements · Postmodern culture • Commercial and artistic cultures overlap • Mass-produced images more significant than individual art • Image and surface appearance more important than structure

standards of living. Workers were able to buy the standardised goods they mass-produced, and they could afford to pay taxes to fund state welfare provision. All this bound the majority of people into a shared economic and political order, and few were marginalised.

Post-Fordism contrasts dramatically with this. Products are more diverse, and workers are much more divided by skill, reward, security and geographical location. Manufacturing is divided into simple and complex operations, with a global division of tasks across huge distances. A core of workers are rewarded very well for their flexible skills, but many others (perhaps in other countries) have had flexibility thrust upon them because of low wages, unemployment and low-skill work. Social groups have become divided from one another, and social differences have widened between the affluent and the dispossessed minority. In affluent countries, there is less of a shared commitment to paying taxes to cover universal state welfare. Instead, unequal private and state welfare is dividing people even further, and right-wing governments are appealing to individualism.

It is difficult for anyone in society to understand or form a picture of this emerging economic system. Although it is bound together by widespread and complex connections on a global scale, it has the appearance of being fragmented and disorganised. Particular social groups in particular places who are on the receiving end of this new and impersonal global system find it very difficult to visualise it – let alone know who to fight or protest against when their plant is closed or their jobs are scrapped. Since it is hard to understand the complex, diversified linkages of capitalism beyond one's own community or society, it is hard for people to have clear models of social class or opposed interests, or to identify those directly responsible for specific instances of social injustice or oppression. Class politics in the core industrial countries have become fragmented and disunited, and new forms of politics have emerged that are not purely economic in focus. Feminist and green politics are obvious examples of the latter.

CONNECTIONS Return to Chapter 8, particularly pages 206–15 and 218–24, to remind yourself of relevant contemporary debates on politics.

BOX 19.2 From economic modernity to postmodernity

Seventeenth to eighteenth century
Capitalism dominant in agriculture, finance and trade

1780–1830
Industrial Revolution and urbanisation. Modern class identities and organisations develop.

Late nineteenth century
Faster global communication by sea and telegraph. Monopoly capitalism. Imperialism.

Twentieth century
Air travel and radio reduce the problem of distance. Mass production and consumption. Consumer society and the welfare state.

Late twentieth and early twenty-first century
Instant electronic communication and mass air travel shrink time and space dramatically. Information revolution. Globalisation of manufacturing and finance. Growth of new service industries. Advertising/marketing: 'buying the image'. World markets, products designed for localised consumers.

Global political linkage: international institutions, for example, the EU, UN and IMF. Local political fragmentation: nationalism and regionalism.

Beyond the superpowers: collapse of communism, triumph of capitalism. Fragmentation of class politics. Rise of new social movements. New sources of political identity.

The interlocking features of the new economic and political structures are summarised in Box 19.2, which also gives a guide to the timing and development of these changes. Today, hardly any writers on contemporary global politics would wish to be associated with the ideas of postmodernism – culture and linguistic signs seem much less important than the brute reality of civil wars and terrorism on a global scale. However, these tragic symptoms of world disorder can be seen as powerful evidence of a shift to globalised postmodernity. Globalisation has contrasting consequences simultaneously: powerful forces for economic and cultural linkage co-exist with an upsurge of nationalist struggles and fragmentation into small nation-states. In addition, the importance of cultural difference has been obvious in the conflicts following 11 September 2001. Religious fundamentalism has frequently interlocked with popular resistance to cultural and economic domination by the West, first in the Iranian revolution and more recently in extreme terrorist networks. We have also seen the rise of emotive nationalism using potent symbols which have no real connection to religion – for example, Serb nationalism and ethnic cleansing in the former Yugoslavia. In the face of all this, it is hardly possible to maintain the modernist faith in a natural political progress towards the Western model of secular, constitutional and democratic states.

Recent theories have provided new twists to the debates about social reality and the actor (or subject). For a long time, a number of theories have emphasised the centrality of language in social life, as we saw in the previous chapter. Partly growing out of these theories, postmodernist theories add intense scepticism about the idea of human creative autonomy. Instead of the humanistic focus of action theories, postmodernist theories trace the ways in which particular discourses define and constitute knowledge, social reality and the nature of the subject.

CONNECTIONS An introduction to the issue of language and its importance in sociology is presented in Chapter 18.

Postmodernism, language and discourse

Social life as language? Structuralism and post-structuralism

Various approaches see language as the key to social life. This has two important aspects: (1) the form and structure of language are often seen as providing a key to the form and structure of society, and (2) language is seen as crucial to our thought and experience. Although we may be affected by physical events, we cannot think or speak about them without using the tool of language – and language is always rooted in society and social settings. In important ways, therefore, we are created as social actors by language.

Figure 19.2 sets out in simplified form the range of approaches to language and social life. Some approaches suggest that social life is itself structured like a language, and the key task is to understand these structures and patterns. This implies a very

Social life is structured like language	Social list is constituted by powerful discourses	Social life is a fragmented play of signs
French structuralism Winch	Discourse Theory Foucault	Post-structuralism Postmodernism

Figure 19.2 Society, language and meaning.

distinctive meaning for the term structure. In contrast, postmodernist approaches often portray social life as a limitless play of signs and symbols that seems to dissolve familiar meanings of the term structure. The figure also distinguishes approaches (such as Foucault's) that see social life as embodied in powerful discourses that define meaning, identity and reality.

French linguistic structuralism saw the structure of language as holding the key to the structure of social life. This was one of the most influential theories of the 1960s, and its application ranged from anthropology (Levi-Strauss, 1963) to psychoanalysis (Lacan, 1977). It grew out of Saussure's (1974) new science of linguistics, developed in the first part of the twentieth century. Saussure was interested in how language worked as a system. According to him, what made language work was its internal structure, the relationships and differences between its component parts. That is, we should not be concerned with the unique content of particular pieces of speech or text, or focus on the origins of the language – what matters is similarity of form and structure. We should be concerned with uncovering structural form, not with human actions and motives.

The dry formalism of this approach limited its influence among sociologists. Perhaps the most influential theory of the 1970s was Althusser's (1970) highly structuralist version of Marxism, which rejected humanistic notions of creative struggle in favour of a Marxist science that revealed the underlying, complex, structural determinants of social change (see Chapter 17). Althusser's 'hyper structuralism' produced strong critical reactions (Thompson, 1978).

More recent French writers, such as Derrida (1978), Lyotard (1984) and Baudrillard (1988), are part of the post-structuralist movement, which is an important facet of postmodernism. As we saw in Chapter 18, post-structuralism shifts the emphasis away from the actor's motives and exercise of free will. Active speech is not the important side of language, because there is nothing outside the text. In other words, meanings always escape the intention of their author (the actor) because they are interpreted by others in various ways. In this sense, our focus must always be on the process of interpretation – content and meaning are no longer stable and self-evident.

Inevitably, this relativises knowledge – there is an endless succession of interpretations, and 'truth' is forever deferred. Consequently, the old Enlightenment idea of achieving progress through knowledge is abandoned. Instead, there is only uncertainty; interpretations endlessly shift, analysis deconstructs apparent meaning and order. What is more, language is not grounded in any external point of reference. Language refers only to language, and signs only relate to other signs. For example, advertisements often conjure up a positive image by referring to other signs or symbols, such as evocative, 'feel-good' songs from another era that match the age of the target market, rather than referring to anything real about the product.

QUESTION   Is all knowledge relative? How do you know that the things you believe in are true?

Fundamental to all structural linguistic approaches is the idea that we inhabit a world of signs – words that represent the idea of the thing. We have to accept that we are surrounded by a multitude of signs and messages, none of which has any special priority. We are set adrift in an endless play of signs referring to other signs, and texts interpreting other texts (Callinicos, 1989, p. 44). This is profoundly unsettling for anyone who clings to old-fashioned notions of truth and knowledge. It is equally disturbing to those who (like Callinicos) want social knowledge to be committed to radical change in society. However, postmodernism (including post-structuralism) seems to celebrate the fluidity and flux of ceaselessly proliferating signs and endlessly deferred knowledge. We are invited to be playful and frivolous, celebrating diversity and subverting the idea of order.

Social life as language? Discourse and reality

In a particularly influential discussion of language and social life, Winch (1958) challenged functionalist and positivist ideas by reviving Weber's action theory and drawing on Wittgenstein's (1953) philosophy of ordinary language. Winch made a number of claims about the nature of social life that strongly challenged the prevailing notions of social science.

He started from the assumption that social reality consists solely of shared meanings: 'Social relations are expressions of ideas about reality' (ibid., p. 123). He went on to claim that sets of ideas are always related logically, so that sets of social relations ('forms of life') have an internal logic. In other words, a certain way of life is always logical and consistent and therefore has to be accepted on its own terms. It is pointless to bring in any analysis or judgement from outside. It is a mistake to look for external causes or explanations of this way of life – people just live that way because they share meanings and rules that are conventional among themselves. Thus, each form of life is a game with its own rules. If you do not follow the rules, you are not playing the game – picking up the ball and running for the goal line in soccer is not only against the rules, it also undermines the whole activity. Thus, for Winch, behaviour that is not rule-governed is literally meaningless.

There are many problems with Winch's ideas, and they have been much debated: Can 'forms of life' really be sealed off from one another so completely? How can we step into another form of life and understand it? Is it adequate to view society as composed purely of shared conventions? Is all our behaviour rule-governed, and why should we assume that rules are logical and coherent? Many more questions are prompted by Winch's highly relativist position, and by his rejection of the existence of anything 'real' in society beyond shared rules. But these questions can also be asked of many of the other theories discussed here.

More recently, discourse theorists have emphasised discourses rather than 'forms of life', but their basic claims are similar to Winch's. The starting point is the proposition that humans can only know the world, and act on it, by means of language. There is no room for direct experience or empirical data – we can only experience things through the medium of language. Laclau and Mouffe (1987) provide a clear example of this approach. While not denying that physical objects exist outside us, they argue that they only exist for us in terms of some concept or discursive framework: 'In our interchange with the world, objects are never given to us as mere existential entities; they are always given to us within discursive articulations' (ibid., p. 85). Thus, an activity such as building a wall involves both language (asking for more mortar) and non-linguistic acts (laying the brick), and the combination of the two makes up the discourse of wall building. This discourse, say Laclau and Mouffe, is a human construct: 'natural facts are also discursive facts' (ibid., p. 84).

CONNECTIONS There are good accounts of discourses in Chapter 9, pages 234–6, and Chapter 15, pages 421–2.

By saying that we can only experience the world through language, discourse theorists are making a basic anti-realist claim: the world only exists for us in and through the meanings we share. This claim, which is widespread in postmodern social theory, implies that we should not try to understand social life by looking for causes or patterns outside language and discourse, and nor should we look for the real effects of social structures.

This anti-realist stance is not beyond challenge, however. What if one brick fell down and hit the discourse theorist on the head? Certainly, she would need language to give an account of what has happened, but would the consequences for her head be altered by the language she uses? If not, then we could ask whether there are any social phenomena that would have a similar direct, unmediated impact on us – poverty, for example. This exposes the fundamental split between realist approaches and the anti-realist post-structuralism, discourse theory and postmodernism.

That is not to argue that discourses are unimportant. Much of what is interesting in social life relates to competing discourses – be these warring political ideologies or differing prescriptions for moral conduct. Stuart Hall (1988, p. 10), for example, has written influential accounts of political discourse, but as he emphasises, 'I do not believe that … ideologies are logically consistent or homogeneous; just as I do not believe that the subjects of ideology are unified and integral "selves".' Hall thus rejects the postmodern notion that discourses are unstructured and open-ended. Rather:

> " All discourse has 'conditions of existence' which, although they cannot fix or guarantee particular outcomes, set limits or constraints on the process of articulation itself. Historical formations, which consist of previous but powerfully forged articulations, may not be guaranteed forever in place by some abstract historical law, but they are deeply resistant to change and do establish lines of tendency and boundaries which give to the fields of politics and ideology the 'open structure' of a formation and not simply the slide into an infinite and never-ending plurality " (ibid.)

This is an interesting corrective to postmodernism, because Hall cannot accept that we have no means of knowing where social life is leading, or what is possible within the existing social arrangements. If politics is to retain any meaning, we need to be able to analyse the conditions for social change and seize practical opportunities. At present, though, we have no fully developed theory of how discourses might be constrained by practical conditions of existence.

To explore how discourse theory might be connected to these practical concerns about power and resistance, we need to examine the work of Michel Foucault. According to Foucault, we should turn to 'the historical analysis of discourse. Perhaps it is time to study discourses not only in terms of their expressive value or formal transformations, but according to their modes of existence' (Foucault, in Rabinow, 1984, p. 117).

In one sense Foucault's work is historical, for he traced aspects of modernity first through an 'archaeology of knowledge' (as in *The Birth of the Clinic: an archaeology of medical perception*, 1977a) and later through a 'genealogy' of power/knowledge (as in *Discipline and Punish*, 1979). But he rejected any straightforward narrative of events or any overarching explanations. He charted the development of powerful discourses (such as psychiatry) and their associated techniques of power (such as the asylum). These discourses are bodies of ideas, concepts and theories that define the phenomenon they describe (possession by spirits, or in a different discourse, schizophrenia) and make it exist for people in a certain form: that is, they constitute *social reality*. For example, today we 'know' that witchcraft does not exist, but it did exist until its credibility was undermined by science. Similarly, schizophrenia did not exist until it was categorised, defined and labelled as schizophrenia.

Hence, Foucault extended the notion that social reality is arbitrary and relative. Social reality is built from meanings, but these are analysed as historically developing discourses. It follows from this that there can be no theoretical key to social order or progress. In Foucault's work, as in other postmodern theories, this is proclaimed as a major argument against modernist theories that seek to explain social change structurally and hope to set the terms for progress and a better future.

For Foucault, it followed that our identity as subjects – who we are and what we are capable of – has been constructed or constituted through particular discourses. This is important, in that here Foucault went beyond theories of creative human action such as phenomenology and beyond structuralist theories such as Marxism. While he was opposed to structural explanations, he also rejected any notion of free, creative social action by autonomous subjects. Instead, their social identity is constructed through discourse and social practice. For example, nowadays in the West, everyone knows that women are independent, rational actors, capable of making choices beyond the dictates of instincts, hormones or emotions. Hence, women are eligible to exercise full legal and political rights as individual citizens; females are not simply extensions of their more rational fathers or husbands. However obvious this may seem, this conception of women is recent and precarious. For a long time, the discourses of individualism, citizenship and rational conduct were applied only to men. It took a considerable struggle to constitute women as really possessing these qualities in the eyes of society. Feminists had to make the existing discourses applicable to women (for example, citizenship) as well as trying to initiate their own discourses of feminism.

CONNECTIONS See Chapter 17, pages 487–94, for an account of feminist positions.

Thus, although discourses consist of meanings and language, this does not diminish their power. Discourses attain widespread power as soon as we take them for granted and live within their bounds. From a Foucauldian viewpoint, if we conceive of ourselves and our social world in terms of a particular discourse, then that is who we are and how we live. For example, prisoners may be forced to accept that in order to be rehabilitated (and be eligible for parole) they must admit their own guilt and responsibility for their actions. In Foucault's eyes, this was a more insidious form of control than torture, because it required prisoners to regulate themselves, and even to accept their punishment as legitimate. Through such examples, Foucault showed that discourses link to power in another way: they are a terrain for struggle and domination as they are established or resisted. The genealogy (or history) of a particular discourse (for example, penal policy) traces this process (Foucault, 1979).

To summarise, Foucault aimed to provide an 'archaeology' of the human sciences, tracing the development of distinct discourses about madness, the body and criminality, as well as charting the establishment of power/knowledge through institutional practices such as the design of prisons and the treatment of madness in asylums. Changing discourses define and constitute human qualities in different ways in different eras (for example, the concept of rehabilitating criminals, or notions of sexuality since Freud). These definitions of human qualities may also be enacted or enforced through the disciplinary techniques of power/ knowledge – the practical implementation of a powerful discourse. This in turn leads subjects (that is, conscious individuals) to define themselves and their nature in particular ways. Hence, we are constituted as humans through particular discourses and practices: our own subjectivity (our identity and will to act) is relative and constructed. This emphasis on the 'genealogical mode of enquiry' has been picked up by feminist postmodernists such as Butler (Butler and Scott, 1992), and it is to the relation between feminism and postmodernism/post-structuralism that we now turn.

 ## Feminist theory, postmodernism and post-structuralism

As we saw in Chapter 17, in the process of building its own body of sociological theory and research, feminist theory highlighted some of the strengths and weaknesses of modern social theory. More recently, feminist theory has engaged with key postmodernist and post-structuralist ideas. This has both contributed to postmodernist and post-structuralist thinking and helped to establish new areas of debate. One particular question that feminist theory can illuminate is whether the use of postmodernist and post-structuralist ideas will compromise sociology's commitment to producing knowledge that can be used by the members of a society to adapt and transform their society.

Modern feminist theory is explicitly committed to the removal of inequality in gender relations, and many of the modernist feminist theorists considered in Chapter 17 argue that postmodernist and post-structuralist theories threaten feminism as a collective political project. The debate between modernist and postmodernist post-structuralist feminists about the political implications of their respective views has thrown light on how postmodernist and post-structuralist thinkers understand their work in respect of it having a socially useful role.

Feminism and postmodernism

For some feminist theorists writing in the mid to late 1980s, the attraction of postmodernist thinking lay in its potential for resolving political differences and theoretical tensions within feminism. To understand why this was so, it is worth outlining some of these tensions.

From the beginning of the 1980s, the significance of experiential differences between women – particularly with regard to racism, ethnicity (see Amos and Parmar, 1984) and sexuality (see Jackson and Scott, 1996) – was highlighted by groups of women who felt unrepresented by second-wave feminism. It was argued that feminist theory was claiming a false universality for what in reality were white, middle-class, Western women's experiences of subordination.

For example, socialist and Marxist feminist theories that put the family at the centre of women's subordination and exploitation under capitalism were criticised for neglecting the extent to which, for black women, the family could be a source of political solidarity and emotional support in the struggle against racism. As Bhavnani and Coulson (1986) argued, feminist theory needed to analyse how racism, class and gender inequality interconnected with each other differently for different groups of women and men. A crucial point of this argument was not so much that black and Asian women experienced greater subordination than white women because of racism, but that racism changed the very basis of the experience of gender inequality.

This omission on the part of second-wave feminists could perhaps have been dealt with by adapting concepts and analyses to address diversity among women. However, it was argued by a number of feminist theorists that the problem was too serious to be dealt with in this way. Instead, fundamental questions needed to be asked about the relationship of feminism to the Enlightenment legacy and modernist thinking.

The postmodern feminist theorist Jane Flax's essay 'Postmodernism and Gender Relations in Feminist Theory' (1990) has been influential in questioning the usefulness of Enlightenment thinking to feminist theory. Flax singles out for criticism the key ideas upon which Enlightenment philosophies were built, and from which sociology has taken its brief. These include:

- The idea of a stable coherent self.
- The belief that reason can provide a reliable and universal foundation for knowledge.
- The idea that reason has transcendent qualities existing independently of physical and social experiences.
- The claim that knowledge can be used in a socially beneficial way to ensure freedom and progress.

She argues that such ideas are fundamentally incompatible with the interests of feminism because they have been used to justify and conceal the interests and power of white Western men. Feminist theory therefore 'more properly belongs on the terrain of postmodern philosophy' than on the 'apparently logical and ordered world of the Enlightenment' (ibid., p. 42)

According to Flax, the interests of domination and power are hidden in the recesses of an apparently neutral reason. This contamination of Enlightenment ideas means they cannot be used by feminists without involving them in the very domination they condemn. As Flax puts it: 'Perhaps reality can have a structure only from the falsely universalising perspective of the dominant group ... only to the extent that one person or group can dominate the whole will reality appear to be governed by one set of rules or be constituted by one privileged set of social relations' (ibid., p. 49).

So, rather than look for objective, universal knowledge or for causal theories of gender difference, feminists should embrace the postmodern celebration of uncertainty and instability and reject the need for order and structure: 'If we do our work well, reality will appear even more unstable, complex and disorderly than it does now' (ibid., pp. 56–7). Postmodern feminists such as Flax consider that the conflict between different groups of women within feminism is evidence that feminists should abandon their attempt to provide overarching structural theories of the causes of gender inequality. To impose any theoretical pattern on reality is inherently dominatory, suppressing the experience of those who do not fit into the pattern. Instead, the way forward for feminism is to deconstruct notions of gender identity whenever they appear.

Feminism and post-structuralism

Judith Butler is another influential theorist who wants to unmask the political interests hidden in apparently neutral or objective concepts such as reason or 'the universal'. She prefers to define her work as post-structuralist rather than postmodernist (Butler and Scott, 1992, p. 6). Post-structuralism has a narrower focus than postmodernism, and is chiefly concerned to expose the power that pervades theoretical concepts. Butler argues that post-structuralism can be of use to feminist politics because it shows how the universal category 'women' really only applies to certain groups of women. Post-structuralist analyses show that the unintended outcome of the use of Enlightenment concepts and participation in the political discourse of modernity has been to exclude particular groups of women, and the resulting conflicts between women are eroding the power of feminist politics.

Butler suggests that expanding the concept of women to include the experiences of those who were marginalised by earlier feminist theory, such as black and working-class women, will not solve the main problem. Philosophical or political concepts such as 'women', 'humanity' and 'the universal', which are apparently all-inclusive, actually covertly set limits to the classes of people to whom they apply. 'To define' also means 'to limit', and post-structuralist thinking tends to take this as more than just a semantic point.

Butler suggests that a much more fruitful direction for feminist theory would be to adopt the genealogical mode of inquiry developed by Foucault. This would involve undertaking a 'radical inquiry into the political construction and regulation of identity' (1990, p. ix). This genealogical inquiry would attempt to expose the way that concepts like 'the individual', or 'identity', or 'women', which seem to refer to our unique self or our inner emotional integrity, are really the tools of various organisations, from the Church to prisons, that are really concerned with managing and controlling the population. Butler wants to investigate the concealed interests of these various social institutions in ensuring the dominance of the heterosexual construction and regulation of sexuality that lie behind the concepts of sex, gender and sexuality.

She argues, as Segal explains, that, rather than these concepts referring to an inalienable inner essence, they are 'established in discourse only through a process of reiteration, or enactment in repeated cultural performances, that congeal over time to produce the effect of identity' (Segal, 1999, p. 57). Therefore, it is not really helpful for feminists to organise their politics on the basis of a notion of gender identity that is part of the process by which women are subordinated. Butler suggests that feminists should instead be working to reveal the artificial nature of these notions. In an argument that proved very influential in the development of 'queer theory', Butler points to the subversive power of activities such as drag performances and cross-dressing, which suggest that even the apparently natural expression of gender identity is 'a kind of persistent impersonation that passes as the real' (Butler, 1990, p. viii). The subversive power of drag performances lies in their destabilising 'the very distinction between the natural and the artificial, depth and surface, inner and outer through which discourse about the genders almost always operates' (ibid.)

For Butler, the post-structuralist deconstruction of political and philosophical concepts is of potential significance for feminist politics. It could help us to understand some of the personal interests invested in cultural identities such as 'woman' or 'heterosexual', and, 'more importantly to understand the interests and the power relations that establish identity' (in Nicholson, 1990, p. 339).

Here we see a feminist theory that views its contribution to feminist politics as subverting and undermining ideas of humanity, rationality and gender as foundations for emancipation, rather than trying to complete or renew them by making women part of these ideas. These subversions are aimed at generating new, more politically productive coalitions between diverse groupings, thus avoiding the conflictful and authoritarian consequences of organising on the basis of a shared identity and a common experience of oppression. As Denise Riley (1988, p. 113) suggests in a similar argument to Butler's, 'an active scepticism about the integrity of the sacred category "women" would be no merely philosophical doubt to be stifled in the name of effective political action in the world. On the contrary, it would be a condition *for* the latter.'

Feminist responses to postmodernism and post-structuralism

Commentators on postmodernism and post-structuralism within feminist theory tend to agree that there have been major changes in society in recent decades, and therefore feminism should not continue to slot itself into the old certainties, whether those of

Marxism (Walby, 1992) or of the more philosophical Enlightenment thinkers (Benhabib, 1994). But those who accept that we are living in changed times and need renewed social theories insist that feminist theory cannot remain coherent if it abandons structural analysis. According to them, if feminists adopt the post-structuralist ideas that humans are just effects of discourse, that there is no self behind the mask and that humans are no more than the sum total of their gendered performances, then the basis of feminist theory and politics will collapse. As Benhabib (1994, p. 80) asks, how can the project of female emancipation be thinkable without the 'ideal of enhancing the agency, autonomy and selfhood of women', qualities that postmodernism and post-structuralism suggest are dispensable theoretical illusions?

Those who are more sceptical of the claims of post-structuralism and postmodernism do admit that some of the insights of these theories could usefully be incorporated into the feminist project, but this should be done without replacing the structural analysis of patterns of inequality with discourse theory's portrayal of power as endlessly dispersed, and of individual identity and agency as illusions of discourse. As Lynne Segal (1999, p. 34) suggests:

> " Feminists need to pay heed to the normativities and exclusions of discourse, especially as they construct differences between women. But in a world of intensifying inequality, any concern with either gender justice or the fate of women overall must also engage us in social struggle for economic redistribution, alongside (and inevitably enmeshed with) issues of identity involving cultural recognition and respect. "

Against postmodernism

In this section, we shall examine arguments from a range of writers who wish to show that postmodernist ideas may profoundly damage sociology's commitment to know-ledge as a means of human empowerment. Just as many feminists have been critical of post-structuralists' reliance on the idea of discourse, the more sweeping claims of postmodernist writers have not gone unchallenged. Critics fall into two broad camps: those who reject the whole notion of postmodernity and postmodern philosophy (for example, Habermas, 1981); and those who accept the existence of widespread social change but propose a renewal of social theory to create a sociology of postmodernity (Bauman, 1992) or late modernity (Giddens, 1990b). Gregor McLennan (1992) provides a detailed account of the debates between the two camps.

As far as postmodernism as a social theory or philosophy is concerned, the key objections can be summarised under four headings:

- *Self-defeating rejection of knowledge.* One basic objection is that postmodernism itself offers an account of social development by referring to the transition from modernity to postmodernity. What is more, the notion of a clear and coherent postmodernist account of contemporary society is rather contradictory, since fragmentary incoher-ence and uncertainty are the hallmarks of the views put forward by Lyotard, Baudrillard and, to a lesser extent, Foucault (Giddens, 1990a). At the same time, the fact that postmodernists continue to write books shows that intellectuals will always offer claims to knowledge, however much these are described as partial and provisional. Denying the quest for knowledge is self-defeating.

- *Rejection of postmodernism's claims to novelty.* Many writers reject the way in which postmodernists take the Enlightenment dream of progress through scientific reason as the whole picture of modernity. Callinicos (1989) emphasises how there have been radical and questioning elements within modernism itself, for example, the innovative artists and writers of the early twentieth century, such as Picasso and James Joyce. They went far beyond surface realism or simple narrative to explore and experiment with the structure of their own craft – whether two-dimensional painting or language in the novel. This was a deeper, more serious questioning of reality than the postmodernists' superficial playfulness.

- *Defence of agency.* Most sociologists are seeking ways to renew our conception of human agency, not reject it (for example, Bauman, 1992, pp. 192–4; Giddens 1991), and hence they feel that postmodernist theorists go too far when they deny that humans are creative agents playing an active part in shaping their social settings. Often such claims are simply self-contradictory, as when a postmodernist authors a text that argues against the significance of authorship.

- *Denial of social reality.* A Marxist, or any other realist theorist who believes that social relations and social structures have direct consequences for human lives, is likely to be dissatisfied with the notion that the social world consists of nothing other than shared ideas of discourses. This realist objection rests on the idea that social structures have an independent impact on actors (for example, by affecting economic life chances). This is so irrespective of whether or not the actor discursively perceives that social structure and gives an account of it.

In terms of its political character and values, many writers who regard themselves as progressive see postmodernism as reactionary, if not dangerous. Two key issues provoke debate:

- *Relativity of values.* Although few modern theorists would justify particular values as correct on grounds of religion or human nature, the moral relativism of writers such as Foucault makes many people uneasy. Do we really have no grounds for condemning or condoning any conduct? Must we really abandon all commitment to universal principles about human rights and injustice? We should also remember that contemporary philosophies such as pragmatism argue that just because ideas about human rights and other values are acknowledged to be social, discursive constructs, this does not mean that these values are worthless or meaningless as guides to conduct.

- *Rejection of social progress.* Postmodernists dismiss the notion that human societies progress towards ideal goals (the so-called 'grand narratives'). The idea that humans progressively gain ever more self-consciousness and freedom of action is regarded as a delusion – or even a meta-narrative that justifies oppressive political action by those who claim that history is on their side. Against this is the residual commitment of many social theorists to the idea that human beings can move towards emancipation, with more reflexive control over their own future.

Rediscovering the self

Many postmodernist social theorists have engaged in a sustained assault on the humanistic idea of a willed, creative, choosing actor. As Foucault stressed, the very notion of the originating, free-willed actor or 'subject' is a historically specific construction; our ideas about human nature and human powers are socially constructed through powerful discourses, as we saw earlier. So, when we read Foucault's argument that 'it is a matter of depriving the subject … of its role as originator, and of analysing the subject as a variable and complex function of discourse' (Foucault in Rabinow, 1984,

p. 118), we have to remember that he also stressed the struggle and resistance that surrounds discourses as power/knowledge.

CONNECTIONS For an account of individuals as creative actors in respect of the structures they inhabit, see Chapter 1, pages 16–19.

Foucault's claim that our nature is constituted by discourse raises as many questions as it answers. If we really are constituted by discourse, do we acquire the powers of the witch if the discourse of witchcraft is dominant? Or to put it another way, have the discourses of modernity succeeded in making human beings into creative, acting individuals? If these are the dominant discourses, how could Foucault deny them? Foucault's wry, subversive scepticism about all discourses renders this ambiguous.

In his later writings, Foucault re-emphasised the constructed nature of identity, but this time as an aesthetic self-stylisation: 'We have hardly any remnant of the idea in society, that the principal work of art that one has to take care of, the main area to which one must apply aesthetic values, is oneself, one's life, one's existence' (Foucault in Rabinow, 1984, p. 362). This seems a narcissistic way to reintroduce the capacity of the individual to reshape and negotiate his or her identity. Foucault seemed to have a yearning for some departed self-autonomy that discipline and rationality had suppressed in modernity.

This contrasts sharply with the emphasis of some sociologists on self-identity, life history and autobiography (*Sociology*, February 1993). For others, such as Giddens (1991), human powers have been enhanced in modernity even if many dilemmas remain. Human beings do act on the basis of knowledge and think **reflexively** about their conduct and their society, and this need not be limited to small-scale social settings. Modern societies continually accumulate information and use it to influence the social world as well as the natural world. The increased openness of roles and identities in late modernity gives greater scope for re-negotiating social relations. For example, Giddens emphasises the flexibility with which we redefine familial roles after divorce, as well as the increasingly voluntary nature of family roles – as divorce exemplifies.

Of course, this can also be expressed in negative terms, as in Lasch's *Culture of Narcissism* (1980). Here narcissism refers to self-obsession, not self-love. If our identity and appearance are under our own control, then we must accept responsibility for them. A neurotic obsession with beauty, fitness and health may overtake us, with damaging effects. Giddens (1991) acknowledges some of this anxiety when referring to our need for **ontological security**, our need to protect ourselves against our vulnerability to disease, death or uncontrolled emotional violence. In the absence of established meaning systems (such as religion) to provide security, we face 'the looming threat of personal meaninglessness' (ibid., p. 201). Modernity destroys security at the same time as it enhances our powers. Despite the resources of knowledge we have, we find our fragmented world extremely difficult to understand. Powerful forces relentlessly commercialise it and build anonymous empires of influence that can leave us feeling powerless or inadequate. Giddens nonetheless appears to have faith in our capacity to learn and reflect, to resist, and to modify our conduct. According to him, we have the power to re-make ourselves and rebuild our social world.

Habermas and the defence of reason

The work of Jurgen Habermas is perhaps best located in the broad tradition of emancipatory reason, which has its roots in the Enlightenment. It draws on the German

Reflexivity
A process of examining, questioning and monitoring the behaviour of the self and others promoted by the social conditions and experiences of late modernity.

Ontological security
A stable mental state derived from a sense of continuity and order.

school of critical theory developed by writers such as Adorno, Horkheimer and Marcuse (see Held, 1980, or Jay, 1973, for general accounts), as well as bringing together numerous strands of European and American sociology. Some of Habermas's attempts to synthesise sociological theories into a theory of human progress combine unfashionable ideas in questionable combinations (Habermas, 1987, 1991). He has committed himself to an evolutionist account of culture in society (echoing nineteenth-century sociologists) and he works with a duality of structure and action. For Habermas, at one level, interaction and communication form the foundations of human social life (and knowledge); while at another level, the abstract systems theories of Talcott Parsons (1961) and the German theorist Niklas Luhmann (1982) serve to illuminate social structures.

Habermas asks some profound questions about contemporary society in very different terms from those of postmodernism. He followed Marcuse in building on Weber's concerns about rationalisation. According to Habermas, the narrowing of rationality into instrumental, technical matters destroys the potential for liberation through knowledge and instead serves capitalism. He goes beyond Weber's fatalism about rationalisation to demand a new commitment to practical reason (to do with social life and social order) and emancipatory reason (Habermas, 1972). He conceptualised Western societies as deeply alienating, due to **reification** and loss of human control. The impersonal institutions and social forces that make up the social system (such as the advanced capitalist economy) have colonised the life-world, removing scope for freedom and human control at the level of interaction. The increasingly complex and impersonal character of modernity, with its strong, faceless state institutions, provokes a degree of anomie and the danger of a 'motivation crisis' among the members of society (Habermas, 1976). New social movements try to win back human control over events in their struggle against this impersonal power. For Habermas, it is too negative and sweeping to treat all power as domination and to reject the possibility of gaining rational knowledge as a foundation for action.

Although a sharp critic of positivistic conceptions of knowledge, Habermas defends the pursuit of truth, but sees it as part of the very nature of human communication. Like many other philosophical thinkers (such as Rorty, 1982), Habermas defends a pragmatic conception of knowledge. Here, truth claims are made by human beings in dialogue and argument, mobilising models and evidence to support them, but ultimately determining knowledge through a process of human communication. For this dialogue on truth to take place, communication has to be on an equal and free basis, not distorted by domination or social exclusion. Distorted communication produces distorted knowledge. Furthermore, there is no great gulf between dialogue on scientific truth claims and normal social communication. Therefore, the pursuit of truth is intimately bound up with the pursuit of freedom and inequality in social life as a whole. The quest for truth is also the quest for the good society, characterised by freedom and non-domination.

Reify
To treat a social phenomenon as an independent entity, with its own qualities.

QUESTION Is it possible to have a clear idea about how humans should live, as opposed to how they actually live? Would such a clear idea inevitably lead to authoritarianism?

Not surprisingly, Habermas has published a number of sharp criticisms of post-modernism, which he sees as 'neo-conservative' (Habermas, 1981, 1985). His whole approach is at odds with postmodernism's scepticism about knowledge, progress in society and culture, emancipation from domination and humanistic values. Everything that postmodernism has condemned as domineering Enlightenment meta-narrative, Habermas defends as progressive.

Beck, reflexive modernisation and the risk society

When the Ukrainian nuclear power plant at Chernobyl exploded in April 1986, the easterly winds distributed radioactive fallout across Europe. Along with the nuclear weapons crises stretching back to the early 1960s and widespread concern about the ecological consequences of global warming and depletion of the ozone layer, Chernobyl made clear that the risks generated by advanced modernity were both life-threatening and global in scale.

It was in the shadow of these events that Ulrich Beck (a German social scientist and citizen of a country with a strong green movement) published *Risk Society* (1992). Beck argues that the threats and transformations associated with modernity cannot be accommodated within the existing system. Instead, a new phase of modernity must begin, a phase in which we shall become capable of confronting 'the problems resulting from techno-economic development itself.' This phase, dubbed 'reflexive modern-isation' is viewed as progressive – 'we are witnessing not the end but the beginning of modernity – that is, of a modernity beyond its classical industrial design (ibid., p. 10).

Risk
A term encapsulating the distinctiveness of people's experiences of danger in late modernity. Awareness of risk can undermine our confidence in abstract systems of knowledge, expertise and social organisation.

With strong echoes of Habermas, Beck argues that this new phase will involve a more rational, considered approach to **risk** and science. Instead of being helpless, we can apply reason and collective reflection to safeguard our future. Thus, emancipation from industrialism's threats is possible by means of collective, rational reflection. In this sense, Beck's approach is far removed from postmodernism. He invites us to regard these threats as real, not discursively constructed. His remedy for risk is more reason and rationality, not less. In this way, he is maintaining the tradition of seeking emancipation through modernity, however sceptical he may be of scientific progress.

Among those opposed to postmodernism, there is considerable scope for argument. Beck argues that many of the risks we face cannot be understood purely in terms of economics or class (for example, the nuclear threat). In contrast, Marxist writers such as Mike Rustin (1994, pp.10–11) point out that key aspects of the threats are driven by the logic of capitalism, not technology itself: 'Beck's critique … is directed towards "techno-scientific rationality", not to the institutional power of capital.' For Rustin, Beck's concept of risk is too abstract and generalised, and fails to take account of oppression, domination and scarcity. To take genetically modified foods as an example, the conversion of public scientific knowledge about genes into private, corporate-owned intellectual capital is at the heart of the issue. Here again is the argument about the key dynamics of (late) modernity. Is capital still in charge, driving the key changes? Or do events such as the terrorist attack on the World Trade Centre in New York on 11 September 2001 show that power, risk and religion have more dimensions than capitalism?

Rustin expresses some scepticism about the extent of emancipation that new political movements might bring: 'The new forms of mobilisation which Beck proposes are undoubtedly positive, but whether they are a match for the unending capitalist transformation of the world is another matter' (ibid, p. 11). Supporters of Beck respond that there are more dynamic drivers of change than capitalism alone, but they have yet to show how democratic control of these driving forces could be effective.

Beck's concept of reflexive modernisation refers to the capacity of society as a whole to learn and apply knowledge in response to problems. However, Beck also transfers these issues to the individual level. He declares that a process of individualisation is occurring, whereby we are moving out of the set social roles of industrial society (whether roles of gender, class or political identity) and moving into more open, uncharted terrain, where we will have to re-invent our own identities: 'Individualisation means first the dis-embedding, and second, the re-embedding of industrial society's ways of life by new ones in which the individuals must produce, stage and cobble together their biographies themselves' (ibid., p. 13).

After all that has been written about nineteenth-century modernity tearing people out of their traditional roles and into a modern state of mind, it seems odd that social changes at the turn of the twenty-first century have been described as the 'end of tradition'. But this is a theme in later work by Beck and Giddens.

Reflexive sociology: renewing the sociological project

Nearly a century ago, in his lectures on 'Science as a Vocation' and 'Politics as a Vocation', Weber (1970) argued that sociology could not tell the members of society what values to hold, but it could demonstrate the possibilities and constraints facing them within their social structure. This is a view with which sociologists such as Giddens are sympathetic. You will recall our discussion of reflexivity in Chapter 1 – that is, the way in which knowledge gained about society taps into and affects social values and social behaviour, whether embodied in the actions of individuals or in social institutions. In that chapter, we quoted Giddens as saying that the social sciences have had a profound and lasting impact on modern societies, which inevitably regularise themselves by drawing on social scientific knowledge in the face of rapid social change. As we have seen in this chapter and Chapter 18, the changing nature of discourses may mean that we can never know for certain (and this is arguably the important contribution of the relativising perspectives of postmodernism), but it does not follow that all social alternatives are equally capable of being realised, let alone being equally desirable.

For sure, sociology has abandoned any pretence of predicting the future, but we need not regard change in society as wholly arbitrary. There is a strong element of contingency in social change because of the unintended – and often surprising and even perverse – consequences of much human behaviour. However, as Hall (1988) asked of discourse theory, we can still ask what the conditions of existence are for certain developments and which outcomes are more possible than others. At the very least, sociology can study society to analyse 'the sum total of [the] resources for all possible action' that are available to actors as the 'inventory of ends and the pool of means' (Bauman, 1992, p. 191), even if some sociologists argue that this is a very minimal aspiration, given the claim of the discipline that the consequences of agency are patterned and non-random.

These debates are unlikely to be laid to rest; but if they divide sociologists, they also keep the discipline alive and vibrant. Social theorists may have become cautious about making claims for sociological knowledge, or any discourse that implies finality or authority, but a sociological perspective can be critical without being prescriptive. As Bauman says, sociological investigations can 'revitalise the existing interpretations of reality. ... The one right it claims to itself is the right to expose the conceit and arrogance, the unwarranted claims to exclusivity of others' interpretations, but without substituting itself in their place' (ibid., p. 214). So, it seems that we can question any argument that suggests our society or social arrangements have to be the way they are, but we should stop short of prescribing what they should become. Making the future is for the members of society to do.

Chapter summary

- This chapter has considered whether contemporary societies are acquiring a qualitatively new form of culture and social structure, and questioned whether these changes can be best understood through the theories of postmodernism.

- The general features of recent social change have been summarised, picking up on the themes of Chapters 2 and 3 of this book.

- Theories unified by a concern with language and discourse have been described, and have been shown to be key elements of the postmodernist approaches.

- The ways in which feminist theory has drawn on postmodern and post-structural social theory have been considered.

- Critiques of postmodernism and postmodern and post-structuralist feminism have been outlined, highlighting theoretical objections and political and value issues.

- The chapter has discussed a range of theories that are concerned, unlike postmodernism, to re-affirm agency and the self, as well as the reflexive use of knowledge by members of society to shape their own future. For some theorists, this shows the continuing possibility of progress through reason.

 Questions to think about

- If there are no meta-narratives, what future is there for sociology as a way of explaining social conditions?

- How convincing do you find discourse theory? What are its advantages and its disadvantages in explaining postmodern times?

- Does the concept of progress still have any attraction in the conditions of late modernity? Give reasons for your answer.

Investigating further

Elliot, Anthony (ed.) (1999) *The Blackwell Reader in Contemporary Social Theory*, Blackwell.
> A useful source book containing original texts, carefully contextualised and introduced by the editor.

Stones, Rob (ed.) (1998) *Key Sociological Thinkers*, Palgrave.
> This edited collection offers short essays on a wide range of theorists, from the classical sociologists to contemporary thinkers. Inevitably some chapters are

more accessible than others, given their different authorship, but the book helpfully tries to illustrate the application of theory to social life. The chapters in part three would be particularly useful as further reading on the topics in this chapter, and the chapters in the part one would supplement your reading of Chapter 17.

glossary

Agency Purposeful action. This term implies that actors have the freedom to create, change and influence events.

Alienation Originally utilised by Marx to describe the feeling of estangement experienced by workers under industrial capitalism. Now more generally employed to describe people's feelings of isolation, powerlessness and self-estrangement.

Altruism Unselfish action in the interest of others.

Anomie For Durkheim (1952), a social condition where the norms guiding conduct break down, leaving individuals without social restraint or guidance (see *norms*).

Ascriptive characteristics Traits or characteristics that are inherited (e.g. age, colour, sex, height), rather than being the result of personal achievement.

Audience A term used to denote the receivers of the media messages contained in texts, broadcasts and so on.

Audiovisual market The market for television programmes, films and music.

Autonomous motherhood The assumption of sole responsibility for childcare without the close involvement of a father. May be voluntary, as in the case of single mothers who choose not to involve the father, or involuntary.

Background expectancies Coined by Garfinkel (1967) to describe taken-for-granted assumptions and expectations about human behaviour in a given context.

Berdache A practice among the native peoples of North America to allocate male gender roles on the basis of cultural preference rather than on anatomical maleness (see *gender*).

Biological determinism A simple causal approach that explains human behaviour in terms of biological or genetic characteristics.

Biologism A form of biological determinism that claims human behaviour is determined by biological or genetic characteristics (see *biological determinism*).

Biomedical model A model of disease and illness that regards them as the consequence of certain malfunctions of the human body.

Black economy Denotes unofficial economic activity; for example, work carried out for payment in kind or cash payment for tax avoidance purposes.

Blue-collar worker A manual worker.

Bourgeoisie The Marxist term for the property-owning capitalist class.

British political economy The economic and social analysis of early capitalism by writers such as Adam Smith and David Ricardo.

Bureaucracy An organisation run by officials and based on hierarchical authority for the efficient pursuit of organisational goals.

Capitalism An economic system in which the means of production are privately owned and organised to accumulate profits within a market framework where labour is provided by waged workers.

Care in the community A range of informal and professional services to care for the elderly, disabled and sick in the community rather than in hospital or institutional settings, but typically undertaken by female relatives.

Caste system　A system of social division and stratification, influenced by Hinduism on the Indian subcontinent, in which an individual's social position is fixed at birth.

Cathexis　Originally employed by Freud to describe a psychic charge or an emotional attraction towards another person. More generally associated with the social and psychological patterning of desire and the construction of emotionally charged relationships.

Causal relationship　A relationship where one phenomenon has a direct effect on another.

Civil religion　Associated with non-supernatural religious objects whose existence promotes solidarity for the group and a sense of belonging for the individual.

Civil society　An imprecise concept that normally refers to social institutions outside the political state.

Class　A term widely used in sociology to differentiate between sections of the population. It is based on economic considerations such as wealth or income.

Closed-ended question　The most commonly used form of questionnaire question, the answers to which fall within a predetermined range and thus can be precoded.

Common-sense knowledge　Schutz's term for the practical social knowledge that we take for granted as the basis for everyday actions.

Communitarianism　Echoing Durkheimian thinking, a political philosophy of the 1990s that stressed the importance of community and shared values for social order and stability.

Compulsory heterosexuality　This concept implies that heterosexuality is not necessarily the natural form of sexual preference but is imposed on individuals by social constraints.

Conflict perspective　A theoretical approach, such as Marxism, focusing on the notion that society is based on an unequal distribution of advantage as is characterised by a conflict of interests between the advantaged and the disadvantaged.

Conjugal relationship　The relationship between husband and wife in marriage.

Conscience collective　The shared beliefs and values of a collectivity that are a prerequisite for social integration, promoting a sense of belonging for the individual.

Consumerism　A culture based on the promotion, sale and acquisition of consumer goods.

Consumption sector cleavage　A social division based on people's consumption patterns and their location in the private or public sectors of production and consumption.

Content analysis　Analysis of the content of communications; usually refers to documentary or visual material.

Cultural advantages　Life styles, religious beliefs, values and other practices that give people a greater chance of obtaining economic success and/or social status.

Cultural capital　The cultural resources, skills and qualities which individuals possess, such as linguistic ability, social style and manners. Associated with Pierre Bourdieu, who claims that the more cultural capital individuals possess, the more successful they will be in the educational and occupational system.

Cultural deprivation　An approach that claims that lifestyle choices determine ill-health. It offers an explanation of the greater incidence of ill-health among working-class people by directly relating it to factors such as smoking, alcohol consumption and diet.

Cultural imperialism　The aggressive promotion of Western culture based on the assumption that it is superior and preferable to non-Western cultures.

De-industrialisation　Decline of industrial manufacturing and concurrent increase in output and employment in the service sector.

De-medicalisation　The process whereby orthodox medicine loses its ability to define and regulate areas of human life (see *medicalisation*).

De-skilling　A term describing what Braverman (1974) believed to be a strategy by employers to reduce the skills of their labour force. This often occurs alongside the introduction of new technological processes into the workplace.

Deconstruct　To analyse texts in order to grasp their implicit meaning by exposing their underlying assumptions.

Definition of the situation　A term used in symbolic interactionism to describe an actor's interpretation of an event or experience.

Demographic age profile　The size and structure of the population based on age.

Dependent variable   The term used in empirical research to denote a phenomenon that is caused by or explained by something else.

Determinism   A simple, causal, reductionist explanation (see *biological determinism*).

Deviance amplification   A spiralling sequence of interaction between deviants and those reacting to their behaviour (typically agents of control, such as the police), which generates further deviance and therefore further punitive responses.

Diaspora   Originally used to describe the dispersion of the Jews from Palestine, it now more generally refers to any dispersed ethnic group, with a common culture or heritage.

Discourse   A body of ideas, concepts and beliefs that have become established as knowledge or as an accepted world-view. These ideas provide a powerful framework for understanding and action in social life.

Domestic sphere   Sometimes referred to as the private sphere, this refers to the arena of activity associated with the household and family life.

Double burden   A term used to describe black women's experience of both sexism and racism.

Double standard of sexual morality   The assumption that promiscuous or sexually assertive behaviours are to be expected or admired in men, but that the same behaviours are deviant in women. For example, there is no male equivalent of the term 'slag'.

Downsizing   Management term for reducing the number of employees.

Dual-sector model   A model of work that suggests there are both primary and secondary labour markets.

Economic base   The Marxist term for the economy, which has a determining effect on the superstructure (see *superstructure*).

Economic growth rate   Level of economic expansion.

Egoism   Normally a reference to selfishness, it also refers to a social setting where individual self-interest is the basis of morality.

Embourgeoisement thesis   An explanation of the decline of working-class solidarity. It claims that, because of increasing affluence, working-class people tend to adopt middle-class values and thus become absorbed into the middle class.

Enterprise culture   An environment that acclaims and rewards those who show initiative by setting up businesses and creating wealth.

Entrepreneurial   Used to describe activity in business or economic development based on the promotion of innovative ideas and decision-making.

Epidemiology   The study of patterns of disease.

Epistemology   The theory of knowledge and the study of its validity, scope and methods.

Essentialism   An approach that assumes some universal feature that identifies the phenomenon under study. Essentialist approaches to gender assume that all women share traits in common, as do all men.

Ethnic absolutism   An understanding of ethnic divisions as fixed and absolute, resting on unchanging cultural traditions.

Ethnicity   While the term 'race', emphasises biological differences based on skin colour, ethnicity denotes the sense of belonging to a particular community whose members share common cultural traditions.

Ethnocentric   The description of the inability to understand the validity or integrity of cultures other than one's own.

Ethnography   A research technique based on direct observation of the activity of members of a particular social group or culture in order to understand the meanings given to actions within that social group.

Ethnomethodology   Associated with the work of Harold Garfinkel, this is an approach to studying the methods people use in their everyday lives to make sense of social life and enable meaningful exchanges with each other.

Eugenics   A nineteenth- and early-twentieth-century pseudo-scientific movement concerned with the alleged 'genetic improvement' of the human species.

Evolutionism   A doctrine based on the notion that historical, biological and social changes are subject to development and progressive unfolding (see *Darwinism*).

Exclusivist   A definition of religion that excludes any beliefs and practices that do not conform to very specific criteria.

Existentialism   A philosophy that espouses free will and responsibility for one's own actions.

Expressive   In relation to the family, the term used by Parsons (1954,1955) to describe the wife's role of catering to the emotional needs of her family

Extended family   A group of kin comprising more than two generations.

False consciousness   Ways of thinking about the world or understanding reality that are defective and obscure the truth.

Fascism   An authoritarian and undemocratic system of government that emerged in the first half of the twentieth century. It was characterised by extreme nationalism, militarism, and restrictions on individual freedom. The will of the people was held to be embodied in the leader (for example, Mussolini in Italy).

Femininities   Various socially constructed sets of assumptions, expectations and ways of behaving that are associated with and assigned to women in a particular culture.

Feminisation of poverty   The increasing concentration of poverty among the female population.

Feudalism   A social and political power structure prevalent in parts of Europe during the twelfth and thirteenth centuries. Power was fragmented and enjoyed by a number of authorities including the Church, the monarchy and local lords.

Finance fraction   That part of capital, for example, banking, concerned solely with financial activities rather than production.

Forces of production   The tools and techniques of production.

Fordism   A form of industrial economy based on mass production and mass marketing that was prevalent in the postwar period. The techniques and processes were pioneered by Henry Ford in the manufacture and sale of Ford motor cars.

Free market   A form of trade or business environment free from outside interference or restriction.

French socialism   A political doctrine that emerged during the French Revolution and emphasised social progress led by a new industrial class.

Functionalism   A theoretical perspective based on an analogy between social systems and organic systems. It claims that the nature of a society's various institutions must be understood in terms of the function each performs in enabling the smooth running of society as a whole.

Functionalist perspective   A theoretical perspective, associated with Durkheim and Parsons, based on an analogy between social systems and organic systems. It claims that the character of a society's various institutions must be understood in terms of the function each performs in enabling the smooth running of society as a whole

Gender   Refers to the socially constructed categories of masculine and feminine that are differently defined in various cultures and the socially imposed attributes and behaviours that are assigned to them.

Gendered division of labour   The division of work roles and tasks into those performed by men and those performed by women.

Gendering   The process of differentiation and division according to gender.

Generalised other   Expectations of general conduct in a social group: what is expected of you.

Geo-linguistic regions   Regions linked by cultural and linguistic similarities as well as historical ties. Such regions often transcend national borders.

German idealist philosophy   An approach based on the thesis that the only things that really exist are minds and their content. It proposes that human progress comes through the advancement of human reason.

Glass ceiling   A metaphorical concept used to explain how women are prevented from reaching the top managerial, political or professional jobs.

Globalisation   The process whereby political, social, economic and cultural relations increasingly take on a global scale, and which has profound consequences for individuals' local experiences and everyday lives.

Habitus   Pierre Bourdieu's term for the everyday habitual practices and assumptions of a particular social environment. People are at once the product of, and the creators of, their habitus.

Hegemony   Refers to consent or acceptance of an ideology, regime or whole social system. Full hegemony exists when a social order is accepted as natural and normal.

Holistic   Involving a focus on the whole rather than on specific parts or aspects.

Homophobia   Hatred or fear of homosexuals (including lesbians).

Horizontal gender segregation   The separation of men and women into qualitatively different types of job.

Humanism   A position that stresses the importance of human needs and rejects the existence of a supernatural deity. It implies a belief that humans have the potential for goodness.

Hybridisation   Adaptation of a genre to fit the cultural circumstances of a particular country.

Hypothesis   A set of ideas or a speculative theory about a given state of affairs that is to be subjected to empirical testing.

Iatrogenic illness   Illness or disability caused by medical treatment.

Ideal type   A model or a set of exaggerated characteristics defining the essence of certain types of behaviour or institutions observable in the real world. 'Ideal' signifies 'pure' or 'abstract' rather than desirable.

Identity politics   A political agenda based on shared experiences and forms of self-expression (see *the personal is the political*).

Ideology   A set of ideas and beliefs about reality and society which underpin social and political action. Ideologies are often used to justify and sustain the position and interests of powerful social groups.

Immigrant–host model   An approach to racial inequality that saw assimilation as the solution to racial disadvantage, based on the view that the problems experienced by immigrants arose from their situation as new arrivals.

Imperialism   Common form of Western colonial rule in the late nineteenth early twentieth centuries. Characterised by the extension of the power of the state through the acquisition, normally by force, of distant territories (see *colonialism*).

Inclusivist   A definition of religion that includes systems of beliefs and practices that, while different in content, produce similar effects.

Independent variable   The term used in empirical research to denote a phenomenon whose existence causes or explains the presence of another variable.

Indexical   From ethnomethodology, the claim that meanings can only be gained in the context of their social setting.

Individualism   A doctrine or way of thinking that focuses on the autonomous individual rather than on the attributes of the group.

Informal economy   Includes unwaged work such as housework or labour-sharing between households.

Information technology   Computerised, electronic technology to gather, record and communicate information.

Institutional racism   The unwitting reproduction of racism by institutions. Implicit, taken-for-granted racism.

Instrumental   In relation to the family, the term used by Parsons (1954, 1955) to describe the husband's role of making material provision for his family.

Instrumental calculation   The process of using the most efficient means to secure a particular goal.

Instrumentalism   An approach to work in which workers derive satisfaction not so much from the job itself, but from benefits it brings, such as good pay or secure employment.

Intelligence quotient   A measurement of intelligence based on the ratio of a person's mental age (as measured by IQ tests) to his or her actual age.

Intergenerational mobility   The movement of individuals from their parents' position in the social hierarchy to another. Usually refers to occupational position or social class.

Interpretive   Having an interest in the meanings underpinning social action. Synonymous with social action theory (see *social action*).

Intragenerational mobility   The movement of individuals of the same generation from one position in the social hierarchy to another. Usually refers to occupational position or social class.

Islamic fundamentalism   A contentious, often pejorative term for strict adherence to the Koran and Islamic law.

Jobless growth   Economic growth that is not accompanied by rising employment.

Just-in-time production   A finely balanced and controlled manufacturing production system designed to produce goods to meet demand as and when required.

Kinship groups   An anthropological term referring to groups who are related by marriage or blood.

Labelling   Describes the process where socially defined identities are imposed or adopted, especially deviant identities. Such labels can result in the individual being trapped in that identity (see *stigmatise*).

Labour market   The supply of people who are willing and able to work.

Labour power   In Marxist theory, a commodity to be bought and sold; refers to workers' ability to produce goods.

Late modernity   A term that implies a change in the nature of modernity, characterised by increased reflexivity and globalisation, but without a qualitative shift to postmodernity. Similar terms are 'high modernity' and 'radicalised modernity'.

Lean production   A highly competitive, streamlined, flexible manufacturing process that operates with a minimum of excess or waste (see *just-in-time production*).

Life-course   This term encompasses the diversity of experiences and differences that people encounter during the course of their lives. It came into being because contemporary experience is considered to be more diverse and less predictable than the traditional concept of the life-cycle suggests.

Life-cycle   The social changes encountered as a person passes through childhood, adolescence, mid-life, old age and death. In the context of the family, the life-cycle includes courtship, child rearing, children leaving home and so on.

Life-world   From Schutz (1976), the world of shared social meanings in which actors live and interact.

Looking-glass self   Coined by Cooley (1922) to convey how individuals perceive their identity through the responses of others.

Macro-level   A level of sociological analysis which focuses either on large collectivities and institutions or social systems and social structures (*see* structures).

Malestream   Used to describe institutions or practices that are male dominated.

Managerialism   A process of increased managerial control.

Marginalisation   The process whereby specific population groups are excluded from mainstream activities because of lack of income, cultural bias and so on.

Market position/situation   Relates to the skills one has to sell in the labour market relative to others.

Marketisation   An economic concept that describes the process of exchange and the distribution of services and goods by private individuals or corporate bodies, based on the dictates of supply and demand.

Masculinities   Various socially constructed sets of assumptions, expectations and ways of behaving that are associated with and assigned to men in a particular culture.

Material advantages   Money and other material goods that offer people a greater chance of success in life than they would otherwise have.

Materialism   In its Marxist usage, an emphasis on economic and political relations.

Materialist   For Turner, following Foucault, a focus on the body as an object of analysis.

Maternal deprivation   The psychological damage said to be experienced by a child as a result of being separated from its mother.

Mechanical solidarity   For Durkheim, the form of social cohesion that binds people through conformity to norms, especially in traditional societies (see *norms*).

Mechanistic   Used to describe behaviour that is determined by external forces or internal constraints.

Medical gaze   A concept employed by Foucault 1977a to denote the power of modern medicine to define the human body.

Medicalisation   Increasing medical intervention in and control over areas that hitherto have been outside the medical domain.

Meritocracy   A society characterised by equality of opportunity in which occupation or position is allocated according to merit (intended ironically by the man who coined the term: Lord Young of Darlington).

Micro-economy   The productive activities of small section of the wider macro-economy.

Mode of production   A Marxist concept that refers to the structured relationship between the means of

production (raw materials, land, labour and tools) and the relations of production (the ways humans are involved in production).

Modernity   A term coined to encapsulate the distinctiveness and dynamism of the social processes unleashed during the eighteenth and nineteenth centuries, which marked a distinct break from traditional ways of life.

Moral consensus   Desire for and agreement upon a set of prescribed moral values.

Mortification of the self   Rituals of entry, especially in total institutions, that debase the old identity in order to impose a new institutional identity (see *total institutions*).

Multi-culturalism   An approach that acknowledges and accommodates a variety of cultural practices and traditions.

Nanny state   A pejorative term used to describe the welfare state, implying that the welfare system is overprotective and does not encourage individual responsibility.

Nation-state   A form of political authority that is unique to modernity. It comprises institutions such as the legislature, judiciary, police, armed forces, and central and local administration. It claims monopoly over power and legitimacy within a bounded territory.

Naturalistic   Pertains to nature, for example a naturalistic theory is one that explains human behaviour in terms of natural instincts and drives.

Neo-liberalism   A form of right-wing philosophy associated with Thatcherism and laissez-faire liberalism (see *Thatcherism* and *laissez-faire liberalism*).

Neo-Marxism   School of thought based on the further development of Marxist philosophy.

New racism   Racism based on ideas of cultural difference rather than on claims to biological superiority.

News values   The criteria that determine which news stories are chosen to be shown to the public.

Nihilism   The total rejection of all moral principles.

Norms   Socially accepted 'correct' or 'proper' forms of behaviour. Norms either prescribe given types of behaviour or forbid them.

Nuclear family   A household unit composed of a man and a woman in a stable marital relationship, and their dependent children.

Objectivism   A doctrine that proclaims that scientific truth is a matter of factual evidence, not belief (see *objectivity*).

Objectivity   An approach to knowledge acquisition that claims to be unbiased, impersonal and free from prejudice. Commonly associated with positivism.

Ontological security   A stable mental state derived from a sense of continuity and order.

Open-ended question   A type of question used in questionnaires to elicit narrative information from the respondent, the answer to which cannot be precoded.

Organic solidarity   For Durkheim, the desirable form of social cohesion that binds people in societies of greater and specialised complexity.

Outsourcing   The subcontracting of work, that is, passing on certain research and development tasks to external contractors that were previously undertaken inside the firm.

Pacific Rim   The rapidly developing South-East Asian economies that border the Pacific Ocean, such as Singapore, Taiwan, Hong Kong, Malaysia and South Korea.

Paradigm   Refers to the set of questions, practices and institutional arrangements that characterise scientific activity for a particular historical period. For Kuhn, (1970, 1972) paradigms produce forms of scientific knowledge that appear to be objective but in reality reflect very specific sets of interests.

Participant observation   A research method where the researcher takes part in the activities of the group or community being studied.

Patriarchal   Used to describe a system that perpetuates the dominance of senior men over all women and junior men.

Patriarchy   A term used by feminists to refer to an overarching system of male dominance, often involving the dominance of senior men over junior men as well as over women.

Phenomenology   In sociology, a focus on the taken-for-granted knowledge that social actors share and which underpins everyday life. It is part of tradition, which focuses on consciousness and meaning rather than on structural social phenomena.

Polarisation of the labour market   The deepening division of the labour market into jobs that are well paid and secure and those that are not.

Political economy   An approach that embraces the concepts of social class, the value and division of labour, and moral sentiments.

Polyarchy   A pluralistic view of the distribution of power that rejects the notion of class division. It sees power as emerging from the interplay of various social groups with multiple, cross-cutting political interests.

Polysemic   An almost an infinite number of possible meanings that can be interpreted in many ways.

Positivism   A doctrine that claims that social life should be understood and analysed in the same way as scientists study the natural world. Underpinning the notion that phenomena exist in causal relationships and that these can be empirically observed, tested and measured.

Post-Fordism   The use of sophisticated computer-controlled production systems, with an emphasis on flexibility and the production of specialised goods tailored to meet the demands of a competitive world economy.

Post-socialist states   The former Soviet states of Central and Eastern European countries that since the 1980s have abandoned or adapted socialist practices and principles in favour of capitalist ones.

Post-structuralism   A development in French theory that follows on from linguistic structuralism but goes further by treating social life as a 'text' that can be analysed without reference to any author (or creative subject/ actor) (see *deconstruction*).

Post-industrial society   A society in which industrial manufacturing has declined, giving way to rapid growth in the service and information sectors.

Postmodernism   Often perceived as a cultural phenomenon associated with contemporary arts, it combines apparently opposing elements to subvert meaning and fragment totality. It is characterised by a pastiche of cultural styles and elements, but implies a deep scepticism about order and progress. Instead, diversity and fragmentation are celebrated.

Postmodernity   For its supporters, the transformation of social, cultural economic and political arrangements that has taken society beyond modernity.

Pragmatism   A philosophy of US origin that treats values and knowledge as means to practical human ends. Concepts and values are regarded as true only as long as they prove useful.

Privatisation   The process of transferring state assets from public to private ownership.

Privatism   A focus on the home and family life.

Pro-natalism   The view that everything should be done to encourage wives to have children.

Professionalisation   The process by which the members of a particular occupation seek to establish a monopoly over its practice. Typically, this is done by limiting entry to those with certain qualifications and claiming that those who lack these qualifications do not possess the requisite expertise.

Project of modernity   A belief in the possibilities opened up by modernity, involving a commitment to social progress through rational and reasoned engagement with the word.

Proletarianisation   The process whereby some parts of the middle class become absorbed into the working class.

Proletariat   The Marxist term for wage earners, the propertyless class under capitalism.

Public sphere   Based on the notion of a public/ private dichotomy, this refers to the arena outside the home and family, including activities associated with paid work.

Qualitative   Information that is not always quantified, but which has a 'text'.

Quangos – Quasi-Autonomous Non-Governmental Organisations   Nominally independent bodies whose members are funded and appointed by central government to supervise or develop activities in areas of public interest.

Quantitative   Used to describe a form of data or data analysis that is based on precise measurement.

Rationalisation   A way of thinking regulated by reason (rather than, say, intuition, emotion or tradition) and based upon clear, objective ideas, that can be demonstrated and understood by other intelligent human beings.

Rationality   A preoccupation with calculating the most efficient means to achieve one's goals.

Recidivism   The tendency for those who have committed crimes to lapse into further offending after release from prison, for instance.

Reconstituted family   A family unit that includes one or more step-parents as a consequence of divorce and marriage.

Reductionism   An outlook that explains phenomena in terms of a simple determining factor.

Reflexive   Normally employed to describe a process of self-reflection that may modify beliefs and action (see *reflexivity*).

Reflexivity   A process of examining, questioning and monitoring the behaviour of the self and others promoted by the social conditions and experiences of late modernity.

Reify   To treat a social phenomenon as an independent thing, with its own qualities.

Relations of production   A Marxist term that refers to class relations that produce an unequal distribution of economic benefits and political power.

Relative autonomy   The situation where a link exists between two institutions, for example, the state and the economy, but each institution has a degree of independence in deciding outcomes.

Relative deprivation   Developed by Townsend in the late 1970s to conceptualise the deprived living standards of some people compared with the vast majority of the population.

Relativism   An approach that denies the existence of absolute truth and maintains that beliefs, values and theories are relative to time and place. Accordingly, traditions and ways of life can only be judged in the context of the age or society that has produced them.

Reserve army of labour   Workers such as women who are brought into the workplace during times of labour shortage. When women are no longer needed, they are encouraged by the prevailing ideology to return to the home.

Risk   A term encapsulating the distinctiveness of people's experiences of danger in late modernity. Awareness of risk can undermine our confidence in abstract systems of knowledge, expertise and social organisation.

Sampling frame   Used in sociological research, this is an accurate list of the subjects of a total population, such as an electoral roll. Research subjects are subsequently randomly selected from this list.

Secondary data   Data, often in the form of official statistics or statistics from other printed sources, that have not been generated by the present researcher.

Secular   Not concerned with religion.

Segmentation   The restructuring of social class boundaries, associated with the polarisation and fragmentation of occupational groups.

Self-fulfilling prophecy   The situation where social actors construct their self-image from the reactions of powerful and persuasive others, thereby acting out or living up to the characteristics attributed to them, thus confirming the original evaluation.

Self-report studies   In the context of crime research, these involve questioning people about criminal acts (detected or otherwise) they have committed. The aim of such studies is to amplify the picture of recorded crime provided in official criminal statistics.

Separatism   An idea put forward by some radical feminists as a solution to patriarchy. Based on the conviction that the sexual act embodies patriarchal exploitation of women, it proposes that women should live separate lives from men.

Sex/gender distinction   Early feminist sociologists, made a distinction between sex (the universal biological division between male and female) and gender (the social and cultural meanings that are attached to this distinction). Later theorists questioned whether there is anything outside the cultural constructions of gender

Significant other   A particular individual whose views, opinions and reactions contribute to and influence the conception we have of ourselves.

Single-parent family   A household unit where only one parent, often the mother, resides with her children.

Snowball sampling   A research technique that asks existing respondents if they can suggest other similarly placed individuals who could be contacted as part of the on-going research.

Social action   A perspective that usually concentrates on the micro-level of social life, in order to show how human interpretation, arising out of the interaction with others, gives rise to social action.

Social closure   Employed by Weber to describe the efforts made by social groups to deny entry to those outside the group and thereby maximise their own advantage.

Social construction   The process whereby natural, instinctive forms of behaviour come to be mediated by social processes. Sociologists would argue that most forms of human behaviour are socially constructed.

Social exclusion   The ways in which people are marginalised from society by having limited or no access to public services, and little participation in education and the political process.

Social framing   To place within a bounded social context.

Social institutions   Social practices that are regularly and continuously repeated, legitimised and maintained by social norms.

Social integration   The unification of diverse groups of people in a community.

Social mobility   The movement of individuals in a stratified society from one position in the social hierarchy to another. Usually relates to occupational position or social class.

Social movement   A broad alliance of people with common interests or goals acting collectively to promote or prevent some form of social change.

Social stratification   The division of a population into unequal layers or strata based on income, wealth, gender, ethnicity, power, status, age religion or some other characteristic.

Social/class reproduction   The process by which, over time, groups of people, notably social classes, reproduce their social structures and patterns.

Socialisation   The ongoing process whereby individuals learn to conform to society's prevailing norms and values (see *norms* and *values*).

Socialism   An economic theory or system in which the means of production, distribution and exchange are owned collectively, usually mediated by the state.

Software   Computer programmes, manuals, instructions and other materials in written or numerical form that can be used in computer systems.

Status   Prestige or social standing in the eyes of others. A term particularly associated with Weber.

Stigmatisation   The process in which social behaviour or an attribute becomes subject to social disapproval and is discredited, resulting in spoiled identity in the eyes of others and possible exclusion from normal social interactions.

Stratification   The division of a population into unequal layers or strata based on income, wealth, gender, ethnicity, power, status, age, religion or some other characteristic.

Streams   Within a school, the division of cohorts into separate classes that are ranked according to perceived ability, e.g. lower stream, upper stream.

Structural unemployment   Chronic, long-term unemployment due to changes in the structure of the economy.

Structures   Refers generally to constructed frameworks and patterns of organisation that serve to constrain or direct human behaviour.

Sub-proletariat   Used by some neo-Marxists to describe a socio-economic group in the lower echelons of the working class (see also *underclass*).

Subculture   The set of values, behaviour and attitudes of a particular group of people who are distinct from but related to the dominant culture in society.

Subject-centred   An approach to social analysis that centres on the active, creative human subject.

Superstructure   A Marxist term for social forms other than the economy (for example, politics and culture) that are determined by the economic base.

Symbolic annihilation   A term coined in 1978 to signify how, as a result of under-representation in the media, women have been dismissed and ignored in the public domain.

Symbolic interactionism   A theoretical approach focusing on the role of symbols and language in human interaction.

Technophilic   Having an aptitude for and willingness to engage with technology.

Technophobic   Having a fear of and reluctance to engage with technology.

Text   Any form of symbolic representation that takes on a physical form; for example, books and films.

The Enlightenment   An eighteenth-century philosophical movement based on notions of progress through the application of reason and rationality. Enlightenment philosophers foresaw a world free from religious dogma, under human control and leading ultimately to emancipation for all humankind.

The Great Transformation   The name given by Karl Polanyi to the historical moment – characterised by massive social, political, technological, economic and intellectual change – that marked the onset of modernity

The 'I' and the 'me'   Terms used by Mead to refer to the impulses for social action ('I') and the socially constructed self ('me').

The personal is the political   A phrase coined by radical feminists to draw attention to issues of sexuality and violence in male–female relationships.

The Poor World   (sometimes referred to as the Third World)   Poor countries not aligned politically with the large power blocs.

The Rich World   (sometimes inappropriately referred to as the First World)   These days, post-industrial capitalist societies, such as those of Europe, North America and Japan.

Total institutions   Employed by Goffman (1968), this term refers to all institutions that assume total control over their inmates, such as prisons and mental hospitals.

Transnational corporations (TNCs)   Large companies with economic activities in more than one country and with the flexibility to shift resources and operations between locations globally to increase their competitive advantage.

Underclass   A contested concept which describes those at the bottom of the social hierarchy who are economically, politically and socially marginalised from the rest of society.

Underlying structures   Associated with realism, this concept refers to organisational features of society that, while not observable, affect human behaviour.

Unintended consequences   Repercussions or outcomes that result from actions initiated for other purposes.

Values   Ideals and beliefs regarded as important by a society or social group.

Verstehen   A German term usually translated as 'understanding'. Employed by Weber to define his approach to the study of social life, namely the interpretative understanding of human agents and the meaning they attach to their actions.

Vertical gender segregation   The separation of men and women into higher or lower grades within the same occupation.

Welfare state   A system of government where the state is responsible for providing its citizens with a wide range of welfare benefits.

White-collar worker   A non-manual employee, for example, an office or junior administrative worker.

Worker resistance   Strategies employed by workers to subvert the labour process.

bibliography

Abbott, P. and R. Sapsford (1987) *Women and Social Class*, London, Tavistock.

Abercrombie, N. and J. Urry (1983) *Capital, Labour and the Middle Classes*, London, Allen & Unwin.

Abrams, P. (1982) *Historical Sociology*, London, Open Books.

Acheson, Sir D. (1998) *Independent Inquiry into Inequalities in Health Report*, London, HMSO.

Adkins, L. (1995) *Gendered Work*, Milton Keynes, Open University Press.

Ahier, J. and R. Moore (1998) 'Big Pictures and Fine Details', in J. Ahier and G. Eslands (eds), *Education and the Future of Work*, London, Routledge.

Alexander, J. C. (1995) *Fin de Siècle Social Theory*, London, Verso.

Allan, G. and G. Crow (2001) *Families, Households and Society*, Palgrave Macmillan, London.

Allan, T. (1992) 'Upheaval, affliction and health', in H. Bernstein, B. Crow and H. Johnson (eds), *Rural Livelihoods: Crises and Responses*, Milton Keynes, Open University Press.

Allmendinger, J. (1989) 'Educational systems and labour market outcomes', *European Sociological Review*, vol. 5, no. 3, pp. 231–50.

Althusser, L. (1969) *For Marx*, London, Allen Lane.

Althusser, L. and E. Balibar (1970) *Reading Capital*, London, New Left Books.

Amin, K. with C. Oppenheim (1992) *Poverty in Black and White*, London, CPAG.

Amos, V. and P. Parmar (1984) 'Challenging imperial feminism', *Feminist Review*, vol. 17.

Anderson, B. (1983) *Imagined Communities*, London, Verso.

Andreff, W. (1984) 'The internationalisation of capital and the reordering of world capitalism', *Capital and Class*, vol. 22, pp. 58–80.

Ang, I. (1985) *Watching Dallas – Soap Opera and the Melodramatic Imagination*, London, Palgrave Macmillan.

Ang, I. (1991) *Desperately Seeking the Audience*, London, Routledge.

Appignanesi, L. and S. Maitland (eds) (1989) *The Rushdie File*, London, Fourth Estate.

Apple, M. (1988) 'Facing the complexity of power: for a parallelist position in critical educational studies', in M. Cole (ed.), *Bowles and Gintis*, London, Palmer Press.

Appleyard, B. (2000) *Brave New Worlds*, London, HarperCollins.

Ariès, P. (1973) *Centuries of Childhood*, Harmondsworth, Penguin.

Arnot, M., M. David and G. Weiner (1999) *Closing the Gender Gap: post-war education and social change*, Cambridge, Polity Press.

Ashmore, M., M. Mulkay and T. Pinch (1989) *Health and Efficiency: A Sociology of Health Economics*, Milton Keynes, Open University Press.

Ashton, D. and M. J. Maguire (1986) 'Young adults in the labour market', Research Paper 55, Department of Employment, London, HMSO.

Ashton, D., M. J. Maguire and M. Spilsbury (1990) *Restructuring the Labour Market: The Implications for Youth*, London, Palgrave Macmillan.

Atkinson, J. and D. Gregory (1986) 'A flexible future: Britain's dual labour force', *Marxism Today*, April, pp. 12–17.

Bachrach, P. and M. Baratz (1963) 'Decisions and non-decisions', *American Political Science Review*, vol. 57.

Back, L. (1993) 'Race, identity and nation within an adolescent community in south London', *New Community*, vol. 19, no. 2.

Baggott, R. (2000) *Public Health: Policy and Politics*, Basingstoke, Palgrave Macmillan.

Bagguley, P. (1990) *Restructuring: Place, Class and Gender*, London, Sage.

Bakker, I. (1988) 'Women's employment in comparative perspective', in J. Jenson, E. Hagen and C. Reddy (eds), *Feminization of the Labour Force: Paradoxes and Promises*, Cambridge, Polity Press.

Bandura, A. (1965) 'Vicarious Processes: a case of no-trial learning', in L. Berkowitz (ed.), *Advances in experimental Psychology*, vol. 2, New York, Academic Press.

Banks, M., S. Beresford, D. Morrell, J. Waller and C. Watkins (1975) 'Factors influencing demand for primary medical care in women aged 20–44 years: a preliminary report', *International Journal of Epidemiology*, vol. 4, pp. 189–95.

Banton, M. (1988) *Racial Consciousness*, London, Longman.

Barakrishnan, P. (2000) 'Tigers in a Prize Fight', *Guardian, G2*, 22 May, p. 8.

Barker, C. (1997) *Global Television: An Introduction*, Oxford, Blackwell.

Barker, M. (1981) *The New Racism*, London, Junction Books.

Barnes, Colin (1996) 'What next? Disability, the 1995 Disability Discrimination Act and the Campaign for Disabled Peoples' Rights', text of the Walter Lessing Lecture (part 2), presented at the Skill (National Bureau for Disabled Students) Annual Conference, 2 March, http://www.leeds.ac.uk/disability-studies/

Barnet, C. (1986) *The Audit of War: the illusion and reality of Britain as a great nation*, London, Palgrave Macmillan.

Barrett, Michele (1981) *Women's Oppression Today: Problems in Marxist Feminist Analysis*, London, Verso.

Barrett, M. and M. McIntosh (1982) *The Anti-social Family*, London, Verso.

Bartky, S. (1990) *Femininity and Domination*, London, Routledge.

Barton, L. (1996) *Disability and Society*, London, Longman.

Baudrillard, J. (1988) *Selected Writings*, Cambridge, Polity Press.

Bauman, Z. (1989) *Modernity and the Holocaust*, Cambridge, Polity Press.

Bauman, Z. (1992) *Intimations of Postmodernity*, London, Routledge.

Bauman, Z. (1998) 'Postmodern Religion?', in P. Heelas, *Religion, Modernity and Postmodernity*, Oxford, Blackwell.

Beattie, J. (1964) *Other Cultures*, London, Cohen & West.

Beck, J. (1998) *Morality and Citizenship in Education*, London, Cassell.

Beck, U. (1992) *Risk Society*, London, Sage.

Beck, U., A. Giddens and S. Lash (1994) *Reflexive Modernization*, Cambridge, Polity Press.

Becker, D., et al. (1987) *Post Imperialism*, Boulder, CO, Lynne Rienner.

Becker, H. (1963) *Outsiders*, New York, Free Press.

Beechey, V. (1992) 'Women's employment in France and Britain: some problems of comparison', in L. McDowell and R. Pringle (eds), *Defining Women*, Cambridge, Polity Press.

Bell, D. (1973) *The Coming of Post-Industrial Society*, London, Heinemann.

Bell, E. (2000) 'The mother of all mergers', *Observer*, 16 January, p. 6.

Bell, S. G. and M. Yalom (eds) (1990) *Revealing Lives: Autobiography, Biography and Gender*, Albany, NY, State University of New York Press.

Bellah, R. (1967) 'Civil Religion in America', *Daedalus*, 96, pp. 1–21.

Benedict, R. (1983) *Race and Racism*, London, Routledge & Kegan Paul.

Benhabib, Seyla (1994) 'Feminism and the Question of Postmodernism', in *The Polity Reader in Gender Studies*, Cambridge, Polity Press, pp. 76–93.

Bennett, A. (1994) *Writing Home*, London, Faber & Faber.

Bennett, A. (2000) *Popular Music and Youth Culture: Music, Identity and Place*, Basingstoke, Palgrave Macmillan.

Benstock, S. (ed.) (1988) *The Private Self: Theory and Practice of Women's Autobiography*, London, Routledge.

Berger, P. (1973) *The Social Reality of Religion*, Harmondsworth, Penguin.

Berger, P. (1974) *The Homeless Mind*, Harmondsworth, Penguin.

Bergson, H. (1913) *Time and Free Will*, New York, Palgrave Macmillan.

Berman, M. (1983) *All That is Solid Melts into Air*, London, Verso.

Bernard, M. and J. Phillips (2000) 'The challenge of ageing in tomorrow's Britain', *Ageing and Society*, vol. 20, Part 1, pp. 33–54.

Bernstein, B. (1971) 'A critique of the concept of compensatory education', in B. Bernstein, *Class, Codes and Control*, vol. 1, London, Routledge & Kegan Paul.

Bernstein, B. (1973) *Class, Codes and Control*, St Albans, Paladin.

Bernstein, B. (1977) 'Class and pedagogies: visible and invisible', in J. Karabel and A. H. Halsey (eds), *Power and Ideology in Education*, New York, Oxford University Press.

Berrington, A. (1994) 'Marriage and Family Formation Among the White and Ethnic Minority Population in Britain', *Ethnic and Racial Studies*, 17, p. 517–46.

Beynon, H. (1973) *Working For Ford*, Harmondsworth, Allen Lane.

Beynon, H., R. Hudson and D. Sadler (1991) *A Tale of Two Industries*, Milton Keynes, Open University Press.

Bhavnani, Kum-Kum and Margaret Coulson (1986) 'Transforming Socialist Feminism: The Challenge of Racism', *Feminist Review*, vol. 20, pp. 81–92.

Biggs, S. (1997) 'Choosing not to be old? Masks, bodies and identity management in later life', *Ageing and Society*, vol. 17, pp. 553–70.

Biggs, S. (1999) (2nd edn) *Understanding Ageing*, Milton Keynes, Open University Press.

Bjorgo, T. and R. Witte (1993) *Racist Violence in Europe*, London, Palgrave Macmillan.

Blauner, R. (1964) *Alienation and Freedom*, Chicago, IL, University of Chicago Press.

Booth, C. (1903) *The Life and Labour of the People of London*, London, Williams & Northgate.

Bose, Christine E. (1987) 'Dual Spheres', in Beth B. Hess and Myra Marx Ferree (eds), *Analysing Gender*, London, Sage, pp. 267–86.

Bottomore, T. and R. J. Brym (1989) *The Capitalist Class: An International Study*, London, Harvester Wheatsheaf.

Bottrup, P. and B. Clematide (1992) *After Taylor and Braverman*, Brussels, CEC.

Boudon, R. (1974) *Education, Opportunity and Social Inequality*, New York, John Wiley.

Boudon, R. (1977) 'Education and social mobility: a structural model', in J. Karabel and A. H. Halsey, (eds), *Power and Ideology in Education*, New York, Oxford University Press.

Bourdieu, P. (1984) *Distinction*, London, Routledge & Kegan Paul.

Bourdieu, P. (1997) 'The Forms of Capital', in A. H. Halsey, H. Lauder, P. Brown and A. S. Wells (eds), *Education, Culture, Economy, Society*, Oxford, Oxford University Press.

Bourdieu, P. (1999) 'The Contradictions of Inheritance', in P. Bourdieu and P. P. Ferguson *The Weight of the World: Social Suffering in Contemporary Society*, Cambridge and Oxford, Polity Press in association with Blackwell.

Bourdieu, P. and J.-C. Passeron (1977) *Reproduction in Education, Society and Culture*, London, Sage.

Bowlby, J. (1965) *Child Care and the Growth of Love*, Harmondsworth, Penguin.

Bowlby, J. (1971) *Attachment and Loss*, vol. I, Harmondsworth, Penguin.

Bowlby, J. (1975) *Attachment and Loss*, vol. II, Harmondsworth, Penguin.

Bowlby, R. (1993) *Shopping With Freud*, London, Routledge.

Bowles, S. and H. Gintis (1976) *Schooling in Capitalist America*, London, Routledge & Kegan Paul.

Bowling, Ann (1998) *Research Methods in Health*, Buckingham, Open University Press.

Boyd-Barrett, O. (1997) 'Global News Wholesalers as Agents of Globalization', in A. Sreberny-Mohammadi, D. Winseck, J. McKenna and O. Boyd-Barrett (eds), *Media in Global Context*, London, Arnold.

Boyd-Barrett, O. and C. Newbold (eds) (1995) *Approaches to Media: A Reader*, London, Edward Arnold.

Bradley, Harriet (1989) *Men's Work, Women's Work*, Cambridge, Polity Press.

Brah, A. (1992) 'Women of South Asian origin in Britain', in P. Braham, A. Rattansi and R. Skellington (eds), *Racism and Antiracism: Inequalities, Opportunities and Policies*, London, Sage.

Brah, A. (1993) '"Race" and "culture" in the gendering of labour markets: South Asian young women and the labour market', *New Community*, April.

Brah, A. and R. Minhas (1988) 'Structural racism or cultural difference: schooling for Asian girls', in H. Woodhead and A. McGrath (eds), *Family, School and Society*, London, Hodder & Stoughton.

Braham, P., A. Rattansi and R. Skellington (eds) (1992) *Racism and Antiracism: Inequalities, Opportunities and Policies*, London, Sage.

Brantenberg, T. (1999) 'Sapmi (Sami Homeland) – the Making of a Nation: Building a new ethnopolitical exhibit at the University of Tromsø, Norway', Arctic Studies Center Newsletter, 7, pp. 15–18. Online: http://www.uit.no/ssweb/indexen.htm

Braverman, H. (1974) *Labour and Monopoly Capital*, New York, Monthly Review Press.

Brewer, J. (1994) 'The ethnographic critique of ethnography: sectarianism in the RUC', *Sociology*, vol. 28, no. 1, pp. 231–44.

Brown, C. (1984) *Black and White Britain*, London, PSI/Gower.

Brown, C. and P. Gay (1983) *Racial Discrimination: 17 Years After the Act*, London, PSI.

Brown, P. (1987) *Schooling Ordinary Kids*, London, Tavistock.

Brown, P. (1997) 'Cultural Capital and Social Exclusion: some observations on recent trends in education, employment, and the labour market', in A. H. Halsey, H. Lauder, P. Brown and A. S. Wells (eds), *Education, Culture, Economy, Society*, Oxford, Oxford University Press.

Brown, P. and L. Jordanova (1982) 'Oppressive dichotomies: the nature/culture debate', in E. Whitelegg and M. Arnot (eds), *The Changing Experience of Women*, Oxford, Martin Robertson.

Brown, P. and R. Scase (eds) (1991) *Poor Work: Disadvantage and the Division of Work*, Buckingham, Open University Press.

Brownmiller, Susan (1975) *Against Our Will: Men, Women and Rape*, Harmondsworth, Penguin.

Bruce, S. (2001) 'Religion, the Global and the Post-Modern', in M. Haralambos, *Developments in Sociology 17*, Ormskirk, Causeway Press.

Bruegel, I. (1994) 'Sex and race in the labour market', in M. Evans (ed.), *The Woman Question*, 2nd edn, London, Sage.

Bryan, B., S. Dadzie and S. Scafe (1985) *The Heart of the Race: Black Women's Lives in Britain*, London, Virago.

Buckingham. D. (1987) *Public Secrets – EastEnders and Its Audience*, London, British Film Institute.

Bull, H. (1977) *The Anarchical Society*, London, Palgrave Macmillan.

Burleigh, M. (2000) *The Third Reich: A New History*, London, Palgrave Macmillan.

Butler, D. and D. Kavanagh (1984) *The British General Election of 1983* London, Palgrave Macmillan.

Butler, Judith (1990) *Gender Trouble: Feminism and the Subversion of Identity*, London, Routledge.

Butler, Judith and Joan W. Scott (eds), (1992) *Feminists Theorize the Political*, London, Routledge.

Byrne, A. S. and B. E. L. Long (1976) *Doctors Talking to Patients*, London, HMSO.

Callinicos, A. (1989) *Against Postmodernism*, Cambridge, Polity Press.

Camilleri, J. M. (1999) 'Disability: a personal odyssey', *Disability and Society*, vol. 14, no. 4, p. 84.

Campbell, A. (1981) *Girl Delinquents*, Oxford, Blackwell.

Campbell, C. (1992) 'The desire for the new', in R. Silverstone and E. Hirsch (eds), *Consuming Technologies*, London, Routledge.

Cantril, H. (1997) 'The Invasion from Mars', in T. Sullivan and Y. Jewkes (eds), *The Media Studies Reader*, London, Edward Arnold.

Carby, H. (1982) 'White woman listen: black feminism and the boundaries of sisterhood', in Centre for Contemporary Cultural Studies Race and Politics Group, *The Empire Strikes Back: Race and Racism in 70s Britain*, London, Hutchinson.

Carmichael, S. and C. V. Hamilton (1968) *Black Power: The Politics of Liberation in America*, London, Jonathan Cape.

Carroll, W. K. and Lewis, S. (1991) 'Restructuring finance capital – changes in the Canadian corporate network 1976–1986' *Sociology*, vol. 25, no. 3, pp. 491–510.

Casey, B. and S. McRae (1990) 'A more polarised labour market', *Policy Studies*, vol. 11, pp. 31–9.

Cashmore, Ellis E. (1983) *Rastaman*, London, Allen & Unwin.

Cashmore, Ellis E. (1987) *The Logic of Racism*, London, Allen & Unwin.

Cashmore, Ellis E. (1991) 'Flying business class: Britain's new ethnic elite', *New Community*, April.

Castells, M. (1989) *The Informational City*, Oxford, Basil Blackwell.

Castells, M. (1996) *The Rise of the Network Society*, Oxford, Blackwell.

Castells, M. (1997) *The Power of Identity*, Oxford, Blackwell.

Castells, M. (1999) *End of Millennium*, Oxford, Blackwell.

Castles S., H. Booth and T. Wallace (1984) *Here for Good: Western Europe's New Ethnic Minorities*, London, Pluto Press.

Castles, S. and G. Kosack (1985) *Immigrant Workers and Class Structure in Western Europe*, London, Oxford University Press.

CEC, Commission of the European Communities (1994) *Human Resources in Europe*, Brussels, CEC.

Central Advisory Council for Education (England) (1967) *Children and their Primary Schools: A Report by Lady Plowden*, 2 vols, London, HMSO.

Centre for Contemporary Cultural Studies (CCCS) Race and Politics Group (1982) *The Empire Strikes Back: Race and Racism in 70s Britain*, London, Hutchinson.

Chadwick, E. (1842) *General Report on the Sanitary Conditions of the Labouring Classes of Great Britain*, Edinburgh, Edinburgh University Press.

Chambliss, W. (1976) 'The State and the Criminal Law', in W. Chambliss and M. Mankoff, *Whose Law? Whose Order?*, New York, Wiley.

Charlton, T. (2000) *Television Isn't Bad For Kids! Recent Findings from a Remote Community*, Promotions and Public Relations Office, Cheltenham and Gloucester College.

Cheal, D. (1991) *Family and the State of Theory*, Hemel Hempstead, Harvester Wheatsheaf.

Chodorow, N. (1978) *The Reproduction of Mothering*, Berkeley, CA, and London, University of California Press.

Clarke, J. and C. Critcher (1985) *The Devil Makes Work: Leisure in Capitalist Britain*, London, Palgrave Macmillan.

Clarke, S. (1998) 'The hard sell', *Guardian*, G2, p. 6.

Clarricoates, K. (1980) 'The importance of being Ernest . . . Emma . . . Tom . . . Jane', in R. Deem (ed.), *Schooling for Women's Work*, London, Routledge & Kegan Paul.

Clement, W. and J. Myles (1997) *Relations of Ruling: Class and Gender in Post-industrial Societies*, Montreal: McGill-Queen's University Press.

Clover, C. (1992) *Men, Women and Chainsaws*, London, BFI.

Cloward, R. and L. Ohlin (1960) *Delinquency and Opportunity*, New York, Collier-Macmillan.

Coates, D. (1984) *The Context of British Politics*, London, Hutchinson.

Cochrane, A. (1971) *Effectiveness and Efficiency: Random Reflections on the Health Service*, London, Nuffield Provincial Hospitals Trust.

Coffield, P., C. Borrill and S. Marshall (1989) 'On the dole', in B. Cosin, M. Plude and M. Hales (eds),

School Work and Equality, London, Hodder & Stoughton with the Open University.

Cohen, A. (1955) *Delinquent Boys*, Chicago, IL, Free Press.

Cohen, Louis and Lawrence Manion (1997) *Research Methods in Education*, 4th edn, London, Routledge.

Cohen, Nick and Rachel Borrill (1993) 'The new proletariat', *Independent on Sunday*, 16 May.

Cohen, P. (1992) '"It's racism what dunnit": hidden narratives in theories of racism', in J. Donald and A. Rattansi (eds), *'Race', Culture and Difference*, London, Sage.

Cole, M. (ed.) (1988) *Bowles and Gintis*, London, Palmer Press.

Collins, H. (1985) *Changing Order: Replication and Induction in Scientific Practice*, London, Sage.

Collins, H. and T. Pinch (1979) 'The construction of the paranormal', in R. Wallis (ed.), *On the Margins of Science*, Sociological Review Monograph No. 37, Keele, Keele University Press.

Collins, P. H. (1990) *Black Feminist Thought*, London, Unwin Hyman.

Collins, R. (1977) Functional and Conflict Theories of Educational Stratification, in J. Karabel and A. H. Halsey (eds), *Power and Ideology in Education*, New York, Oxford University Press.

Commission for Racial Equality (1997), http://www.cre.gov.uk/

Commission for Racial Equality (1998) *Education and Training in Britain*, London, CRE.

Connell, R. W. (1987) *Gender and Power*, Cambridge, Polity Press.

Connell, R. W. (2000) *The Men and the Boys*, Cambridge, Polity Press.

Cooley, C. (1922) *Social Organisation*, New York, Scribner.

Corn, J. (ed.) (1986) *Imagining Tomorrow*, London, MIT Press.

Coser, L. A. and B. Rosenberg (eds) (1969) *Sociological Theory: A Book of Readings*, 3rd edn, London, Collier-Macmillan.

Cosin, B., M. Plude and M. Hales (eds) (1989) *School, Work and Equality*, London, Hodder & Stoughton with the Open University.

Coward, R. (1989) *The Whole Truth: The Myth of Alternative Medicine*, London, Faber.

Crewe, I., B. Sarlvik and J. Alt (1977) 'Partisan De-alignment in Britain 1964–74', *British Journal of Political Science*, vol. 7, pp. 129–90.

Crick, F. (1994) *The Astonishing Hypothesis: The Scientific Search for the Soul*, London, Touchstone.

Croft, S. and P. Beresford (1998) 'Postmodernity and the Future of Welfare', in J. Carter (ed.), *Postmodernity and the Fragmentation of Welfare*, London, Routledge.

Crompton, R. (1993) *Class and Stratification*, Cambridge, Polity Press.

Crompton, R. (1998) *Class and Stratification: An Introduction to Current Debates*, 2nd edn, Cambridge, Polity Press.

Crompton, R. and K. Sanderson (1990) *Gendered Jobs and Social Change*, London, Unwin Hyman.

Crouch, D. (1994) *The Allotment: Its Landscape and Culture*, Nottingham, Mushroom Press.

Crow, G. and G. Allan (1990) 'Constructing the domestic sphere: the emergence of the modern home in post-war Britain', in H. Corr and L. Jamieson (eds), *The Politics of Everyday Life*, London, Palgrave Macmillan.

Crowley, H. (1992) 'Women and the Domestic Sphere', in R. Bocock and K. Thompson (eds), *Social and Cultural Forms of Modernity*, Oxford, Polity Press.

Cunningham, S. (1998) 'Global and Regional Dynamics of International Television Flows', in D. K. Thussu (ed.), *Electronic Empires*, London, Arnold.

Cunningham, S. and E. Jacka (1996) *Australian Television and International Mediascapes*, Melbourne, Oxford University Press.

Cunningham, S., E. Jacka and J. Sinclair (1998) 'Global and Regional Dynamics of International Television Flows', in D. K. Thussu (ed.) *Electronic Empires*, London, Edward Arnold.

Curran, J. (1991) 'Mass Media and Democracy: A Reappraisal', in J. Curran and M. Gurevitch (eds), *Mass Media and Society*, London, Edward Arnold.

Curran, J. and J. Seaton (1992) *Power without Responsibility*, London, Routledge.

Dahl, R. A. (1989) *Democracy and its Critics*, New Haven, CT, Yale University Press.

Dahl, R. A. and C. Lindblom (1976) *Politics, Economics and Welfare*, Chicago, IL, Chicago University Press.

Daly, Mary (1978) *Gyn/Ecology: the metaethics of radical feminism*, London, Women's Press.

Daniel, W. W. (1968) *Racial Discrimination in England*, Harmondsworth, Penguin.

Davis, A. (1981) *Women, Race and Class*, London, Women's Press.

Delphy, C. (1984) *Close to Home*, London, Hutchinson.

Deem, R. (1986) *All Work and No Play*, Milton Keynes, Open University Press.

Dennis, N. (1993a) *Rising Crime and Dismembered Families*, London, Institute of Economic Affairs.

Dennis, N. and G. Erdos (1993b) *Families Without Fatherhood*, London, Institute of Economic Affairs.

Dennis, N., F. Henriques and C. Slaughter (1956) *Coal is Our Life*, London, Eyre & Spottiswoode.

Denzin, N. (1984) *On understanding emotion*, San Francisco, CA, Jossey-Bass.

Department of Employment (1999) *New Earningss Survey 1999*, London, HMSO.

Department of Social Security (1999) *Family Resources Survey 1997–98*, London, HMSO.

Derrida, J. (1978) *Writing and Difference*, London, Routledge.

DETR (Department of the Environment, Transport and the Regions) (1999) Cm 4445 *Opportunity for all: tackling poverty and social exclusion: first annual report*, London, HMSO.

Deutscher, I. (1970) 'What we say what we do', *Sociological Focus*, vol. 3, pp. 19–30.

Devine, F. (1992) *Affluent Workers Revisited: Privatism and the Working Class*, Edinburgh, Edinburgh University Press.

Devine, F. (1997) *Social Class in America and Britain*, Edinburgh, Edinburgh University Press.

Devine, F. (1998) 'Class relations and the stability of class relations', *Sociology*, vol. 32, pp. 23–42.

Dey, I. (1996) *The Poverty of Feminisation*, Edinburgh, University of Edinburgh Press.

Dilnot, A. and P. Johnson (1992) 'What pension should the state provide?' *Fiscal Studies*, vol. 13, no. 4, pp. 1–20.

Dobash, R. and R. Dobash (1980) *Violence Against Wives*, London, Open Books.

Domestic Violence Data Source (2000) *The Day to Count*, London, Royal Holloway College.

Donald, J. (1992) 'Metropolis: the city as text', in R. Bocock and K. Thompson (eds), *Social and Cultural Forms of Modernity*, Cambridge, Polity Press.

Donald, J. and A. Rattansi (eds) (1992) *'Race', Culture and Difference*, London, Sage.

Douglas, J. W. B. (1967) *The Home and the School*, London, Panther.

Dorfman, A. and M. Mattelart (1975) *How to Read Donald Duck: Imperialist Ideology in the Disney Comic*, New York, International General.

DSS (Department of Social Security), (1993) *Households Below Average Income*, London, HMSO.

Duffin, J. (1999) *History of Medicine: A Scandalously Short Introduction*, Basingstoke, Palgrave Macmillan.

Duncan, S. and R. Edwards (eds) (1997) *Single Mothers in an International Context*, London, UCL Press.

Dunleavy, P. and C. Husbands (1985) *British Democracy at the Crossroads*, London, George Allen & Unwin.

Durkheim, É. (1915) *The Elementary Forms of Religious Life*, London, George Allen & Unwin.

Durkheim, É. (1933) *The Division of Labour in Society*, London, Collier-Macmillan.

Durkheim, É. (1952) *Suicide*, London, Routledge & Kegan Paul.

Durkheim, É. (1974) *Sociology and Philosophy*, New York, Free Press.

Durkheim, É. (1976) *The Elementary Forms of Religious Life*, London, Allen & Unwin.

Dworkin, Andrea (1981) *Pornography: men possessing women*, London, Women's Press.

Edgerton, D. (1996) *Science, Technology and the British Industrial 'Decline' 1870–1970*, Cambridge, Cambridge University Press.

Edholm, F. (1982) 'The unnatural family', in E. Whitelegg and M. Arnot (eds), *The Changing Experience of Women*, Oxford, Martin Robertson.

Edwards, P. (2000) 'Late Twentieth Century Workplace Relations', in R. Crompton, F. Devine, M. Savage and J. Scott, *Renewing Class Analysis*, Oxford, Blackwell.

Edwards, R. (1979) *Contested Terrain*, London, Heinemann.

Ehrenreich, B. (1979) *For Her Own Good*, London, Pluto Press.

Ehrenreich, B. (1983) *The Hearts of Men*, London, Pluto Press.

Eisenstein, Zillah R. (ed.) (1979) *Capitalist Patriarchy and the Case for Socialist Feminism*, London, Monthly Review Press, pp. 5–41.

Elder, G. H. Jr (1974) *Children of the Great Depression*, Chicago, IL, University of Chicago Press.

Elias, N. (1984) *The Civilising Process*, Oxford, Blackwell.

Engel, M. (1996) *Tickle the Public*, London, Indigo.

Equal Opportunities Commission (2000) *Women and Men in Britain 2000: Pay and Income*, http:// www. eoc.org.uk/

Esmail, A. and S. Everington (1993) 'Racial discrimination against doctors from ethnic minorities', *British Medical Journal*, vol. 306, March.

Estes, C. and E. Binney (1989) 'The biomedicine of ageing: dangers and dilemmas', *The Gerontologist*, vol. 29, no. 5, pp. 587–98.

Etzioni, A. (1993) 'The parental deficit', *Guardian*, 15 October.

Etzioni, A. (1995) *The Spirit of Community: Rights, Responsibilities and the Communitarian Agenda*, London, Fontana Press.

Etzioni, A. (1997) *The New Golden Rule: Community and Morality in a Democratic Society*, London, Profile.

Evans-Pritchard, E. E. (1937) *Witchcraft, Oracles and Magic Among the Azande*, Oxford, Clarendon Press.

Ewen, E. and E. Ewen (1982) *Channels of Desire*, New York, McGraw-Hill.

Fagot, B. I (1985) 'Differential reactions to assertive and communicative acts by toddler boys and girls', *Child Development*, vol. 56, pp. 1499–505.

Fanon, F. (1967) *The Wretched of the Earth*, Harmondsworth, Penguin.

Featherstone, M. (1991a) 'The body in consumer culture', in M. Featherstone, M. Hepworth and B. Turner (eds), *The Body: Social Process and Cultural Theory*, London, Sage.

Featherstone, M. (1991b) *Consumer Culture and Postmodernism*, London, Sage.

Felstead, H. and N. Jewson (eds) (1999) *Global Trends in Flexible Labour*, Basingstoke, Palgrave Macmillan.

Ferguson, M. (1983) *Forever Feminine*, London, Heinemann.

Fielding, N. (1993) 'Qualitative Interviewing', in G. N. Gilbert (ed.), *Researching Social Life*, London, Sage.

Finch, J. (1987) 'Family obligations and the life course', in A. Bryman, B. Blytheway, P. Allatt and T. Keil (eds), *Rethinking the Life Cycle*, London, Palgrave Macmillan.

Finch, J. and L. Hayes (1994) 'Inheritance, death and the concept of the home', *Sociology*, vol. 28, no. 2, pp. 417–34.

Fine, B. (1994) 'What we eat and why: a socio-economic study of standard items in food consumption', Economic and Social Research Council Research Programme, *The Nation's Diet*, Swindon.

Finlay, W. (1988) *Work on the Waterfront*, Philadelphia, Temple University Press.

Firestone, Shulamith (1979) *The Dialectic of Sex*, London, Women's Press.

Fiske, J. (1992) *Understanding Popular Culture*, London, Routledge.

Flax, Jane (1990) 'Postmodernism and Gender Relations in Feminist Theory', in Linda J. Nicholson (ed.), *Feminism/Postmodernism*, London, Routledge, pp. 39–63.

Flexner, A. (1910) *Report on Medical Education in the United States and Canada*, New York, Carnegie Foundation Bulletin.

Foucault, M. (1977a) *The Birth of the Clinic: an archaeology of medical perception*, London, Tavistock.

Foucault, M. (1977b) *The History of Sexuality: Volume 1, An Introduction*, London, Allen Lane.

Foucault, M. (1979) *Discipline and Punish: the birth of the prison*, New York, Vintage.

Foucault, M. (1980) *Power/Knowledge, Selected Interviews and Other Writings 1971–1977*, Brighton, Harvester.

Fox, R. (1967) *Kinship and Marriage*, Harmondsworth, Penguin.

Fox, S. (1990) 'The ethnography of humour and the problem of social reality', *Sociology*, vol. 24, no. 3, pp. 431–46.

Franklin, B. (1994) *Packaging Politics*, London, Edward Arnold.

Fraser, S. (1997) 'Introduction to the Bell Curve Wars', in A. H. Halsey, H. Lauder, P. Brown and A. S. Wells (eds), *Education, Culture, Economy, Society*, Oxford, Oxford University Press.

Freedman, Jane (2001) *Feminism*, Buckingham, Open University Press.

Freidson, E. (1988) *Profession of Medicine*, 2nd edn, Chicago, IL, Chicago University Press.

Friedan, Betty (1965) *The Feminine Mystique*, Harmondsworth, Penguin.

Friedman, A. L. (1977) *Industry and Labour*, London, Palgrave Macmillan.

Frissen, V. (1992) 'Trapped in electronic cages', *Media, Culture and Society*, vol. 14, pp. 31–49.

Frobel, F., J. Heinrichs and O. Kreye (1980) *The New International Division of Labour*, Cambridge, Cambridge University Press.

Fryer, P. (1984) *Staying Power: The History of Black People in Britain*, London, Pluto.

Fukuyama, F. (1989a) 'Forget Iraq – history is dead', *Guardian*, 7 September, p. 15.

Fukuyama, F. (1989b) 'The end of history?', *The National Interest*, no. 16.

Gagnon, J. and W. Simon (1973) *Sexual Conduct*, London, Hutchinson.

Gallie, D. (ed.) (1988) *Employment in Britain*, Oxford, Blackwell.

Gallie, D. (1991) 'Patterns of skill change', *Work, Employment and Society*, vol. 5, pp. 319–51.

Gamble, A. (1985) *Britain in Decline*, London, Palgrave Macmillan.

Garfinkel, H. (1967) *Studies of Ethnomethodology*, Cambridge, Polity Press.

Garnham, N. (1992) 'The Media and the Public Sphere', in C. Calhoun (ed.), *Habermas and the Public Sphere*, Cambridge, MA, MIT Press.

Geertz, C. (1984) 'Anti anti-relativism', *American Anthropologist*, pp. 263–78.

Gellner, E. (1974) *Legitimation of Belief*, Cambridge, Cambridge University Press.

Gellner, E. (1979) *Spectacles and Predicaments*, Cambridge, Cambridge University Press.

Gellner, E. (1992) *Postmodernism, Reason and Religion*, London, Routledge.

Geraghty, C. (1991) *Women and the Soap Opera*, Cambridge, Polity Press.

Gershuny, J. (1983) *Social Innovation and the Division of Labour*, Oxford, Oxford University Press.

Gerson, Kathleen (1985) *Hard Choices: How Women Decide about Work, Motherhood and Career*, Berkeley, CA, University of California Press.

Giddens, A. (1984) *The Constitution of Society*, Cambridge, Polity Press.

Giddens, A. (1985) *The Nation-State and Violence*, Cambridge, Polity Press.

Giddens, A. (1990a) *The Consequences of Modernity*, Cambridge, Polity Press.

Giddens, A. (1990b) 'Modernity and utopia', *New Statesman*, 2 November, pp. 20–22.

Giddens, A. (1991) *Modernity and Self-Identity: Self and Society in the Late Modern Age*, Cambridge, Polity Press.

Giddens, A. (1998) *The Third Way*, Cambridge, Polity Press.

Gilbert, G. N. and M. J. Mulkay (1984) *Opening Pandora's Box*, Cambridge, Cambridge University Press.

Gillespie, M. (1997) 'Local Uses of the Media: Negotiating culture and identity', in A. Sreberny-Mohammadi, D. Winseck, J. McKenna and O. Boyd-Barrett (eds), *Media in Global Context*, London, Edward Arnold.

Gilroy, P. (1987) *There Ain't No Black in the Union Jack*, London, Hutchinson.

Gilroy, P. (1993a) *The Black Atlantic*, London, Verso.

Gilroy, P. (1993b) *Small Acts*, London, Serpent's Tail.

Ginsburg, N. (1992) 'Racism and housing: concepts and reality', in P. Braham, A. Rattansi and R. Skellington (eds), *Racism and Antiracism: Inequalities, Opportunities and Policies*, London, Sage.

Gitlin, T. (1995) 'Media Sociology: the Dominant Paradigm', in O. Boyd-Barrett and C. Newbold, *Media: A Reader*, London, Edward Arnold.

Global Media Monitoring Project (GMMP) (2000) www.wacc.org.uk/womedia/mgm/mgm7/results.htm

Glyptis, S. (1989) *Leisure and Unemployment*, Milton Keynes, Open University Press.

Goffman, E. (1961) *Asylums*, Garden City, Doubleday.

Goffman, E. (1967) *Interaction Ritual*, Garden City, Doubleday.

Goffman, E. (1968) *Asylums*, Harmondsworth, Penguin.

Goffman, E. (1969) *The Presentation of Self in Everyday Life*, Harmondsworth, Penguin.

Goffman, E. (1974) *Frame Analysis*, Harmondsworth, Penguin.

Goldberg, D. T. (1993) *Racist Culture*, Oxford, Blackwell.

Golding, P. (1990) 'Political Communication and Citizenship', in M. Ferguson, *Public Communication: The New Imperatives*, London, Sage.

Golding, P. (1998) 'Worldwide Wedge', in D. K. Thussu (ed.), *Electronic Empires*, London, Edward Arnold.

Golding, P. and G. Murdock (1991) 'Culture, Communication and Political Economy', in J. Curran and M. Gurevitch (eds), *Mass Media and Society*, London, Edward Arnold.

Goldthorpe, J. (1973) 'A Revolution in Sociology?' *Sociology*, vol. 7, no. 3.

Goldthorpe, J. (1978) 'The Current Inflation: Towards a Sociological Account', in J. Goldthorpe and F. Hirsch (eds), *The Political Economy of Inflation*, London, Martin Robertson.

Goldthorpe, J. H. (1980) *Social Mobility and Class Structure in Modern Britain*, 1st edn, Oxford, Clarendon Press.

Goldthorpe, J. H. (1987) *Social Mobility and Class Structure in Modern Britain*, 2nd edn, Oxford, Clarendon Press.

Goldthorpe, J. (1988) 'Intellectuals and the Working Class in Modern Britain', in D. Rose (ed.), *Social Stratification and Economic Change*, London, Hutchinson.

Goldthorpe, J. (1996) 'Class Analysis and the Reorientation of Class Theory: the persistence of class differentials in educational attainment', *British Journal of Sociology*, vol. 49, pp. 481–505.

Goldthorpe, J. H. and G. Marshall (1992) 'The promising future of class analysis: a response to recent critiques', *Sociology*, vol. 26, pp. 381–400.

Goldthorpe, J. H., D. Lockwood, F. Bechhofer and J. Platt (1968) *The Affluent Worker: Industrial Attitudes and Behaviour*, Cambridge, Cambridge University Press.

Goldthorpe, J. H., D. Lockwood, F. Bechhofer and J. Platt (1969) *The Affluent Worker: Industrial Attitudes and Behaviour*, Cambridge, Cambridge University Press.

Goode, W. (1993) *World Changes in Divorce Patterns*, New Haven, Yale University Press.

Goodwin, A. (1994) 'Ideology and diversity in American television', in J. Mitchell and D. Maidment, *The United States in the Twentieth Century: Culture*, Milton Keynes, Open University Press.

Gordon, P. (1990) *Racial Violence and Harassment*, London, Runnymede Trust.

Gorz, A. (1982) *Farewell to the Working Class*, London, Pluto Press.

Gorz, A. (1989) *Critique of Economic Reason*, London, Verso.

Gould, S. J. (1984) *The Mismeasure of Man*, Harmondsworth, Pelican.

Gouldner, A. (1971) *The Coming Crisis of Western Sociology*, London, Heinemann.

Graefe, D. and D. Lichter (1999) 'Life-Course Transitions of American Children', *Demography*, 36, pp. 205–17.

Gramsci, A. (1971) *Selections from the Prison Notebooks*, ed. Q. Hoare and G. Nowell Smith, London, Lawrence & Wishart.

Granovetter, M. S. (1992) *Economic action and social structure – the problem of embeddedness*, Boulder, CO, Westview.

Granovetter, M. S. and R. Swedberg (eds) (1992) *The Sociology of Economic Life*, Boulder, CO, Westview.

Grauerholz, E. and B. Pescosolido (1989) 'Gender representation in children's literature', *Gender and Society*, March, pp. 113–25.

Green, A. (1990) *Education and state formation*, Basingstoke, Palgrave Macmillan.

Green, F. and D. Ashton (1992) 'Skill shortage and skill deficiency', *Work, Employment and Society*, vol. 6, no. 2, pp. 287–301.

Green, P. (1985) 'Multi-ethnic teaching and the pupils' self-concepts', Annexe B in *Swann Report, Report of Committee of Inquiry into the Education of Children from Ethnic Minority Groups*, Cmnd 9453, London, HMSO.

Greer, S. (1969) *The Logic of Social Inquiry*, Chicago, IL, Aldine.

Grey, C. (1994) 'Career as a project of the self and labour process discipline', *Sociology*, vol. 28, no. 2, pp. 479–98.

Grieco, M. (1987) *Keeping it in the Family*, London, Tavistock.

Grint, K. (1998) *The Sociology of Work*, 2nd edn, Cambridge, Polity Press.

Grundy, E., M. Murphy and N. Shelton (1999) 'Looking Beyond the Household: intergenerational perspectives on living kin and contacts with kin in Great Britain', *Population Trends*, vol. 97, pp. 19–27.

Gummett, P. (1991) *Future Relations Between Defence and Civil Science and Technology*, SPSG Review Paper No. 2, London, SPSG.

Habermas, J. (1972) *Knowledge and Human Interests*, London, Heinemann.

Habermas, J. (1976) *Legitimation Crisis*, London, Heinemann.

Habermas, J. (1981) 'Modernity versus Postmodernity', *New German Critique*, vol. 22.

Habermas, J. (1985) 'Modernity – an Incomplete Project', in H. Foster (ed.), *Postmodern Culture*, London, Pluto Press.

Habermas, J. (1987) *The Philosophical Discourse of Modernity*, Cambridge, Polity Press.

Habermas, J. (1991) *The Theory of Communicative Action Vol. 1*, Cambridge, Polity Press.

Hahn, H. (1989) 'Public support for rehabilitation programs: the analysis of US disability policy', *Disability, Handicap and Society*, vol. 1, no. 2, pp. 121–38.

Hall, L. (1991) *Hidden Anxieties: Male Sexuality, 1900–1950*, Cambridge, Polity Press.

Hall, S. (1983) 'The Great Moving Right Show', in S. Hall and M. Jacques (eds), *The Politics of Thatcherism*, London, Lawrence & Wishart.

Hall, S. (1988) *The Hard Road to Renewal*, London, Verso.

Hall, S. (1992a) 'The West and the Rest', in S. Hall and B. Gieben (eds), *Formations of Modernity*, Cambridge, Polity Press in association with Open University Press.

Hall, S. (1992b) 'The question of cultural identity', in S. Hall, D. Held and T. McGrew (eds), *Modernity and Its Futures*, Cambridge, Polity Press.

Hall, S. (1993) 'The television discourse – encoding and decoding', in A. Gray and J. McGuigan (eds), *Studying Culture*, London, Edward Arnold.

Hall, S. (2000) 'From Scarman to Lawrence', *Connections*, Spring, pp. 14–16, online: http://www.cre.gov.uk/index.html

Halliday, F. (2000) 'Global Governance: prospects and problems', in D. Held and A. McGrew, *The Global Transformations Reader*, Cambridge, Polity Press.

Halsey, A. H. (1977) 'Towards meritocracy? the case of Britain', in J. Karabel and A. H. Halsey (eds), *Power and Ideology in Education*, New York, Oxford University Press.

Halsey, A. H., A. Heath and J. Ridge (1980) *Origins and Destinations*, Oxford, Clarendon Press.

Halsey, A. H., H. Lauder, P. Brown and A. S. Wells (eds) (1997) *Education, Culture, Economy, Society*, Oxford, Oxford University Press.

Hamelink, C. (1995) 'Trends in World Communication', in *Mass Communications Handbook*, vol. 2, Leicester, University of Leicester.

Hamilton, M. (1995) *The Sociology of Religion: Theoretical and Comparative Perspectives*, London, Routledge.

Hammersley, M. (1992) 'On feminist methodology', *Sociology*, vol. 26, no. 2, pp. 187–206.

Handy, C. (1985) *The Future of Work*, Oxford, Blackwell.

Handy, C. (1991) *The Age of Unreason*, London, Century.

Hansard Society Commission (1990) *The Report of the Hansard Society Commission on Women at the Top*, London, Hansard Society for Parliamentary Government.

Hargreaves, D. (1967) *Social Relations in a Secondary School*, London, Routledge & Kegan Paul.

Hargreavbes, D., S. Hestor and P. Mellor (1975) *Deviance in Classrooms*, London, Routledge & Kegan Paul.

Hartley, D. (1997) *Re-Schooling Society*, London, Falmer.

Hartley, J. (1987) 'Invisible fictions: television audiences', *Textual Practice*, vol. 1, no. 2, pp. 121–38.

Hartmann, Heidi I. (1979) 'Capitalism, patriarchy and job segregation by sex', in Zillah R. Eisenstein (ed.), *Capitalist Patriarchy and the Case for Socialist Feminism*, London, Monthly Review Press, pp. 206–48.

Harvey, D. (1989) *The Condition of Postmodernity*, London, Blackwell.

Harvey, D. (1990) *The Condition of Postmodernity*, Oxford, Blackwell.

Haskey, J. (1995) 'Trends in Marriage and Cohabitation', *Population Trends*, no. 80, p. 5–15.

Haskey, J. (1996) 'Population Review (6): Families and Households in Britain', *Population Trends*, no. 85, pp. 7–24.

Heath, A. (1981) *Social Mobility*, Glasgow, Fontana.

Heath, A. and N. Britten (1984) 'Women's jobs do make a difference', *Sociology*, vol. 18, no. 4.

Heath, S. and A. Dale (1994) 'Household and Family Formation in Great Britain: An Ethnic Dimension, *Population Trends*, no. 84, pp. 5–13.

Hebdige, D. (1991) *Subculture: the Meaning of Style*, London, Routledge.

Heelas, P. (1998) *Religion, Modernity and Postmodernity*, Oxford, Blackwell.

Heffernan, Nick (2000) *Capital, Class and Technology in Contemporary American Culture*, London, Pluto.

Heidensohn, F. (1985) *Women and Crime*, London, Palgrave Macmillan.

Heidensohn, F. (1989) *Crime and Society*, London, Palgrave Macmillan.

Heidensohn, F. (2000) *Sexual Politics and Social Control*, Buckingham, Open University Press.

Held, D. (1980) *Introduction to Critical Theory*, London, Hutchinson.

Held, D. (1991) 'Democracy, the nation-state and the global system', in D. Held (ed.), *Political Theory Today*, Cambridge, Polity Press.

Held, D. (ed.) (1993a) *Prospects for Democracy*, Cambridge, Polity Press.

Held, D. (1993b) *Democracy and the New International Order*, London, Institute for Public Policy Research.

Held, D. (1995) *Democracy and the Global Order*, Cambridge, Polity Press.

Held, D., A. McGrew, D. Goldblatt and J. Perraton (1999) *Global Transformations: Politics, Economics and Culture*, Cambridge, Polity Press.

Henwood, M., L. Rimmer and M. Wicks (1987) *Inside the Family: Changing Roles of Women and Men*, London, Family Policy Study Centre.

Herman, E. and R. McChesney (1997) *The Global Media*, London, Cassell.

Herrnstein, R. and C. Murray (1997) *The Bell Curve: intelligence and class structure in American life*, London, Simon & Schuster.

Herzlich, C. (1973) *Health and Illness: A Social Psychological Analysis*, London, Academic Press.

Hessler, R. M. (1992) *Social Research Methods*, St Paul, Min.

Hewitt, R. (1986) *White Talk, Black Talk: Inter-racial Friendship and Communication Amongst Adolescents*, Cambridge, Cambridge University Press.

Higher Education Statistics Agency, http://www.hesa.ac.uk/

Hingel, A. J. (1993) 'A new model of European development: innovation, technological development and network-led integration', Brussels, CEC.

Hiro, D. (1991) *Black British, White British: A History of Race Relations in Britain*, London, Grafton.

Hirschi, T. (1969) *The Causes of Delinquency*, Berkeley, CA, University of California Press.

Hirst, P. and G. Thompson (1996) *Globalisation in Question*, Cambridge, Polity Press.

Hobsbawm, E. (1994) *Age of Extremes*, London, Michael Joseph.

Holmes, C. (1991) *A Tolerant Country? Immigrants, Refugees and Minorities in Britain*, London, Faber & Faber.

Home Office (1999) *Supporting Families*, London, HMSO.

Home Office Criminal Statistics for England and Wales, (1997), Cmnd 4162, London HMSO.

Honeyford, R. (1993) 'Why are we still fed the myth that Britain is a racist society', *Daily Mail*, 14 April.

Hood, R. (1992) *Race and Sentencing*, Oxford, Clarendon Press.

hooks, bell (1982) *Ain't I a Woman?*, London, Pluto Press.

hooks, bell (1984) *Feminist Theory, From Margin to Center*, Boston, MA, South End Press.

Horwitz, A. (1977) 'The pathways into psychiatric treatment', *Journal of Health and Social Behaviour*, vol. 18, pp. 169–78.

Hout, M. J. (1984) 'Status, autonomy and training in occupational mobility', *American Journal of Sociology*, vol. 89, pp. 1379–409.

Hughes, E. C. (1958) *Men and Their Work*, New York, Free Press.

Hughes, J. (1976) *Sociological Analysis: Methods of Discovery*, London, Nelson.

Hugman, R. (1994) *Ageing and the Care of Older People in Europe*, Basingstoke, Palgrave Macmillan.

Humphreys, L. (1970) *The Tea Room Trade*, London, Duckworth.

Husserl, E. (1931) *Ideas*, London, Allen & Unwin.

Hylland Eriksen, T. (ed.) (1997) *Flerkulturell forståelse*, Norway, Tano Aschehoug.

Illich, I. (1976) *Medical Nemesis*, New York, Pantheon.

ILO (International Labour Office) (1996) *Child Labour: What is to be done*, Geneva, ILO; see also, ILO (2001) *Child Labour in the Developing Economies*, available online at: http://www.ilo.org/public/english/standards/ipec/publ/policy/papers/

Inglehart, R. (1977) *The Silent Revolution: Changing Values and Political Styles among Western Publics*, Princeton, NJ, Princeton University Press.

Inglehart, R. (1990) *Culture Shift in Advanced Industrial Society*, Princeton, NJ, Princeton University Press.

Inkeles, A. (1993) 'Industrialisation, modernisation and the quality of life', *International Journal of Comparative Sociology*, vol. 34, no. 1, pp. 1–23.

Inland Revenue (1991) *British National Census Data*, OPCS, Cardiff.

Institute for Employment Studies, in conjunction with NOP Social and Political (1998) *Employment of Disabled People: Assessing the Extent of Participation*, http://www.employment-studies.co.uk/

Institute of Race Relations (2001a) 'Counting the cost: racial violence since Macpherson', http://www.irr.org.uk/

Institute of Race Relations (2001b) 'The Emergence of Xeno-Racism', http://www.irr.org.uk/

Irwin, S. (1999) 'Later life, inequality and sociological theory', *Ageing and Society*, vol. 19, pp. 691–715.

Jackson, Stevi and Sue Scott (1996) 'Sexual Skirmishes and Feminist Factions: Twenty-Five Years of Debate on Women and Sexuality', in Sue Scott and Stevi Jackson (eds), *Feminism and Sexuality*, Edinburgh, Edinburgh University Press.

Jagger, Alison M. (1983) *Feminist Politics and Human Nature*, Brighton, Harvester Press.

James, A. *et al.* (1998) *Theorising Childhood*, Cambridge, Polity Press.

Jay, M. (1973) *The Dialectical Imagination*, London, Heinemann.

Jenkins, A. (1994) 'Just-in-time regimes and reductionism', *Sociology*, vol. 28, pp. 21–30.

Jenkins, R. (1986) *Racism and Recruitment*, Cambridge, Cambridge University Press.

Jennings, H. (1985) *Pandaemonium*, London, André Deutsch.

Jensen, Arthur (1969) 'How much can we boost IQ and scholastic achievement?', *Harvard Educational Review*, vol. 39, pp. 2–51.

Jessop, B. (1982) *The Capitalist State*, Oxford, Martin Robertson.

Jessop, B., K. Bonnett, S. Bromley and T. Ling (1988) *Thatcherism*, Cambridge, Polity Press.

Johnson, T. (1972) *Professions and Power*, London, Palgrave Macmillan.

Johnson, R. and D. Robbins (1975) 'The development of specialities in industrialised science', *Sociological Review*, vol. 25, pp. 87–108.

Jones, L. and R. Moore (1996) 'Equal Opportunities, the Curriculum and the Subject', in J. Ahier, B. Cosin and M. Hales (eds), *Diversity and Change: education, policy and selection*, London, Routledge.

Jones, S. (1985) 'Depth interviewing', in R. Walker (ed.), *Applied Qualitative Research*, Aldershot, Gower.

Jones, S. (1988) *Black Culture, White Youth*, London, Palgrave Macmillan.

Jones, S. (1994) *The Language of Genes*, London, Flamingo.

Jones, T. (1993) *Britain's Ethnic Minorities*, London, PSI.

Jordanova, L. (1989) *Sexual Visions: Images of Gender in Science and Medicine Between the Eighteenth and Twentieth Centuries*, London, Harvester Wheatsheaf.

Joseph Rowntree Foundation (1998) *Income and Wealth: the Latest Evidence*, JRF, The Homestead, York.

Joseph Rowntree Foundation (1998) *Monitoring poverty and social exclusion*, ref. D48, http://www.jrf.org.uk/home.asp

Joseph Rowntree Foundation (1999) Young Caribbean men and the labour market: a comparison with other ethnic groups, ref. N69, http://www.jrf.org.uk/home.asp

Joseph Rowntree Foundation (2000) *Poverty and social exclusion in Britain*, ref. 930, http://www.jrf.org.uk/home.asp

Joseph Rowntree Foundation (2001) *Full-time work by parents of under-fives linked to risks of lower attainment for children*, http://www.jrf.org.uk/home.asp

Kaldor, M. (1991) *Europe From Below*, London, Verso.

Kamerman, S. and A. Kahn (eds) (1997) *Family Change and Family Policies in Britain, Canada, New Zealand and the United States*, Oxford, Clarendon Press.

Kamin, L. (1977) *The Science and Politics of IQ*, Harmondsworth, Penguin.

Karabel, J. and A. H. Halsey (eds) (1977) *Power and Ideology in Education*, New York, Oxford University Press.

Katz, E. and P. Lazarsfeld (1955) *Personal Influence*, New York, Free Press.

Kaufman, D. and B. L. Richardson (1982) *Achievement and Women*, New York, Free Press.

Keane, J. (1991) *The Media and Democracy*, Cambridge Polity Press.

Kessler, Suzanne J. and Wendy McKenna (1985) *Gender: An Ethnomethodological Approach*, Chicago, IL, and London, University of Chicago Press.

King, A. D. (1991) *Global Cities*, London, Routledge.

Kingdom, J. (1992) *No Such Thing As Society*, Buckingham, Open University Press.

Kirby, M. (1999) *Stratification and Differentiation*, Basingstoke, Palgrave Macmillan.

Kirk, G. (1991) 'The growth of central influence on the curriculum', in R. Moore and J. Ozga (eds) *Curriculum Policy*, Oxford, Pergamon.

Klein, R. (1995) *The New Politics of the NHS*, 3rd edn, London, Longman.

Kleineman, A. (1973) 'Towards a comparative study of medical systems', *Science, Medicine and Man*, vol. 1, pp. 55–65.

Knowles, C. and S. Mercer (1992) 'Feminism and antiracism', in J. Donald and A. Rattansi (eds), *'Race', Culture and Difference*, London, Sage.

Kohn, M. (1995) *The Race Gallery*, London, Jonathan Cape.

Kriesi, H., R. Koopmans, J. W. Dyvendak and M. G. Giugni (1995) *New Social Movements in Western Europe: Comparative Perspectives*, London, University College London Press.

Kuhn, T. (1970) *The Structure of Scientific Revolutions*, Chicago, IL, University of Chicago Press.

Kuhn, T. (1972) 'Scientific paradigms', in B. Barnes (ed.), *Sociology of Science*, Harmondsworth, Penguin.

Kumar, K. (1978) *Prophecy and Progress: The Sociology of Industrial and Post-Industrial Life*, Harmondsworth, Penguin.

Lacan, J. (1977) *Écrits; a selection*, London, Tavistock.

Laclau, E. and C. Mouffe (1987) 'Post-Marxism Without Apologies', *New Left Review*, vol. 166.

Lareau, A. (1997) 'Social-Class Differences in Family–School Relationships: the Importance of Cultural Capital', in A. H. Halsey, H. Lauder, P. Brown and A. S. Wells (eds), *Education, Culture, Economy, Society*, Oxford, Oxford University Press.

Lasch, C. (1979) *Haven in a Heartless World*, New York, Basic Books.

Lasch, C. (1980) *The Culture of Narcissism*, London, Abacus.

Lash, and J. Urry (1987) *The End of Organised Capitalism*, Cambridge, Polity Press.

Law, I. (2002) *Race in the News*, Basingstoke, Palgrave Macmillan.

Layder, D., D. Ashton and J. Sung (1991) 'The empirical correlates of action and structure: the transition from school to work', *Sociology*, vol. 25, pp. 447–64.

Layton-Henry, Z. (1992) *The Politics of Immigration*, Oxford, Blackwell.

Lea, J. and J. Young (1984) *What Is To Be Done About Law and Order?*, London, Penguin.

Lee, D. (1991) 'Class as a social fact', *Sociology*, vol. 28, no. 2, pp. 397–416.

Leadbeater, C. (1987) 'In the land of the dispossessed', *Marxism Today*, April, pp. 18–25.

Leadbeater, C. and G. Mulgan (1994) 'The end of unemployment: bringing work to life', *Demos*, vol. 2.

Lee, D. (1991) 'Poor work and poor institutions: training and the youth labour market', in P. Brown and R. Scase (eds), *Poor Work: Disadvantage and the Division of Work*, Buckingham, Open University Press.

Lees, Sue (1986) *Losing Out: Sexuality and Adolescent Girls*, London, Hutchinson.

Lemert, E. (1961) *Social Pathology*, New York, McGraw-Hill.

Lemert, E. (1974) *Human Deviance and Social Control*, Englewood Cliffs, NJ, Prentice-Hall.

Levi-Strauss, C. (1963) *Structural Anthropology*, New York, Basic Books.

Lewis, G. (1993) 'Black women's employment and the British economy', in W. James and C. Harris (eds), *Inside Babylon*, London, Verso.

Liebau, E. and L. Chisholm (1993) 'Youth, social change and education: issues and problems', *Journal of Education Policy*, vol. 8, no. 1, pp. 3–8.

Liebes, T. and E. Katz (1988) *The Export of Meaning*, Oxford, Oxford University Press.

Lipietz, A. (1987) *Mirages and Miracles*, London, Verso.

Lister, R. (1984) 'There is an alternative', in A. Walker and C. Walker (eds), *The Growing Divide*, London, CPAG.

Littlewood, R. and M. Lipsedge (1982) *Aliens and Alienists: Ethnic Minorities and Psychiatry*, Harmondsworth, Penguin.

Livingstone, S. and M. Bovill (1999) *Young People, New Media* (summary report of the research project 'Children, Young People and the Changing Media Environment', London School of Economics), London and Swindon: ONS and ESRC.

Loader, B. (1998) *Cyberspace divide: equality, agency and policy in the information society*, London, Routledge.

Luckman, T. (1983) *Life-World and Social Realities*, London, Heinemann.

Luhmann, N. (1982) *The Differentiation of Society*, New York, Columbia University Press.

Lukes, S. (1973) *Émile Durkheim*, London, Allen Lane.

Lukes, S. (1974) *Power: A Radical View*, London, Palgrave Macmillan.

Lyotard, J. F. (1984) *The Postmodern Condition: A Report on Knowledge*, Manchester, Manchester University Press.

MacDonald, R. (1997) *Youth, The Underclass and Social Exclusion*, London, Routledge.

MacDonald, R. and J. Marsh (2000) 'Employment, Unemployment and Social Polarization', in R. Crompton, F. Devine, M. Savage and J. Scott, *Renewing Class Analysis*, Oxford, Blackwell.

MacIntyre, S. and D. Oldham (1977) 'Coping with migraine', in A. Davies and G. Horobin (eds), *Medical Encounters*, London, Croom Helm.

MacKinnon, Catharine (1987) *Feminism Unmodified: Discourses on Life and Law*, London, Harvard University Press.

Madigan, R. and M. Munro (1991) 'Gender, House and "Home": Social Meanings and Domestic Architecture in Britain', *Journal of Architectural and Planning Research* vol. 8, no. 2, pp. 117–27.

Maguire, M., R. Morgan and R. Reiner (eds) *The Oxford Handbook of Criminology*, Oxford, Clarendon Press.

Malinowski, B. (1932) *The Sexual Life of Savages in North-Western Melanesia*, London, Routledge & Kegan Paul.

Mann, M. (1986) *The Sources of Social Power*, vol. 1, Cambridge, Cambridge University Press.

Marcuse, H. (1964) *One-Dimensional Man*, London, Routledge & Kegan Paul.

Marshall, Barbara L. (1994) *Engendering Modernity*, Cambridge, Polity Press.

Marshall, G., H. Newby, D. Rose and C. Vogler (1988) *Social Class in Modern Britain*, London, Hutchinson.

Marsland, D. (1996) 'From Cradle to Grave Mistake', *The Times, Higher Education Supplement*, 17 May.

Martin, B. (1981) *A Sociology of Contemporary Cultural Change*, Oxford, Basil Blackwell.

Martin, E. (1989) *The Woman in the Body: A Cultural Analysis of Reproduction*, Milton Keynes, Open University Press.

Martin, P. and D. L. Collinson (1999) 'Gender and sexuality in organisations', in M. M. Feree, J. Lorder and B. B. Hess (eds), *Revisioning Gender*, London, Sage.

Marx, K. (1859) *Preface to a Contribution to a Critique of Political Economy*, in K. Marx and F. Engels, *Selected Works*, London, Lawrence & Wishart.

Marx, K. (1875) *Critique of the Gotha Programme*, in K. Marx and F. Engels, *Selected Works*, London, Lawrence & Wishart.

Marx, K. (1954) *Capital*, vol. 1, Harmondsworth, Penguin.

Marx. K. and F. Engels (1848) *The Communist Manifesto*, in K. Marx and F. Engels, *Selected Works*, London, Lawrence & Wishart.

Marx, K. and F. Engels (1967) *The Communist Manifesto*, Harmondsworth, Penguin.

Marx, K. and F. Engels (1968) *Selected Works*, London, Lawrence & Wishart.

Mathieson M. and G. Bernbaum (1991) 'The British Disease: a British Tradition?', in R. Moore and J. Ozga (eds), *Curriculum Policy*, Oxford, Pergamon/ Open University.

Matoesian, Gregory (1993) *Reproducing Rape: Domination through Talk in the Courtroom*, Cambridge, Polity Press.

Matthews, J. and J. Young (eds) (1992) *Issues in Realist Criminology*, London, Sage.

Matza, D. (1964) *Delinquency and Drift*, New York, Wiley.

Maynard, M. (1990) 'The Re-Shaping of Sociology? Trends in the Study of Gender', *Sociology*, vol. 24, no. 2, pp. 269–90.

McChesney, R. (1998) 'Media Convergence and Globalisation', in D. K. Thussu (ed.), *Electronic Empires*, London, Edward Arnold.

McClone, F., A. Park and C. Roberts (1999) 'Kinship and Friendship: attitudes and behaviour in Britain 1986–1995', in S. McRae (ed.), *Changing Britain, Families and Households in the 1990s*, Oxford, Oxford University Press.

McDonald, K. and R. D. Parke (1986) 'Parent–child physical play', *Sex Roles*, vol. 15, pp. 367–78.

McDowell, L. (1992) 'Gender divisions in a post-Fordist era: new contradictions or the same old story?', in L. McDowell and R. Pringle (eds), *Defining Women*, Cambridge, Polity Press.

McGoldrick, M. and E. Carter (1982) 'The family life cycle', in F. Walsh (ed.), *Normal Family Processes*, New York, Guildford Press.

McGrew, A. (1992) 'A global society?', in S. Hall, D. Held and T. McGrew (eds), *Modernity and its Futures*, Cambridge, Polity Press.

McGuigan, J. (1992) *Cultural Populism*, London, Routledge.

McLellan, D. (ed.) (1997) *Karl Marx: Selected Writings*, London, Oxford University Press.

McLennan, G. (1992) 'The Enlightenment Project Revisited', in S. Hall, D. Held and T. McGrew (eds), *Modernity and its Futures*, Cambridge, Polity Press.

McLuhan, M. (1964) *Understanding Media: The Extensions of Man*, London, Routledge and Kegan Paul.

McPherson, A. and J. Willms (1989) 'Comprehensive schooling is better and fairer', in B. Cosin, H. Plude and M. Hales (eds), *School, Work and Equality*, London, Hodder & Stoughton with The Open University.

McRae, S. (1994) 'Labour supply after childbirth', *Sociology*, vol. 28, no. 1, pp. 99–122.

McRae, S. (1999) *Changing Britain, Families and Households in the 1990s*, Oxford, Oxford University Press.

Mead, G. H. (1934) *Mind, Self and Society*, Chicago, IL, Chicago University Press.

Meakin, D. (1976) *Man and Work*, London, Methuen.

Measor, L. and P. Woods (1988) 'Initial fronts', in M. Woodhead and A. McGrath (eds), *Family, School and Society*, London, Hodder & Stoughton.

Meethan, K. (2001) *Tourism in Global Society: Place, Culture, Consumption*, Basingstoke, Palgrave Macmillan.

Merton, R. (1949) *Social Theory and Social Structure*, Glencoe, IL, Free Press.

Meyrowitz, J. (1985) *No Sense of Place: The Impact of the Electronic Media on Social Behaviour*, New York, Oxford University Press.

Midwinter, E. (1997) *Pensioned Off: Retirement and Income Examined*, Milton Keynes, Open University Press.

Miles, R. (1989) *Racism*, London, Routledge.

Miles, R. (1993) *Racism After 'Race Relations'*, London, Routledge.

Miles, R. and A. Phizacklea (1984) *White Man's Country: Racism in British Politics*, London, Pluto.

Miles, R. and A. Phizacklea (1992) 'The British trade union movement and racism', in P. Braham, A. Rattansi and R. Skellington (eds), *Racism and Antiracism: Inequalities, Opportunities and Policies*, London, Sage.

Miles, S, (2000) *Youth Lifestyles in a Changing World*, Buckingham, Open University Press.

Miliband, R. (1968) *The State in Capitalist Society*, London, Weidenfeld & Nicolson.

Millar, J. (1993) 'The continuing trend in rising poverty', in A. Sinfield (ed.), *Poverty, Inequality and Justice*, Edinburgh, Edinburgh University Press.

Millar, J. (1999) 'State, Family and Personal Responsibility', in G. Allan, *The Sociology of the Family: a reader*, Oxford, Blackwell.

Miller, D. (1995) 'The Consumption of Soap Opera', in R. C. Allen (ed.), *To Be Continued: Soap Operas Around the World*, London, Routledge.

Miller, M. (1989) 'Prime time: deride and conquer', in T. Gitlin (ed.), *Watching Television*, New York, Pantheon.

Millett, Kate (1977) *Sexual Politics*, London, Virago.

Mills, C. W. (1970) *The Sociological Imagination*, Harmondsworth, Penguin.

Minde, H. (1992) 'The Development of Social Anthropological, Sociological and Historical Research into the Post-War Saami Society of Norway', paper presented at the first International Conference on

Arctic Social Sciences, Université Laval, Ste-Foy, Quebec, Canada. Available online from the Centre for Sami Studies, University of Tromsø, Norway: http://www.uit.no/ssweb/ indexen.htm

Mirrlees-Black, C., P. Mayhew and A. Percy (1996) *The 1996 British Crime Survey*, Home Office Statistical Bulletin 19/96, London, Home Office.

Mirrlees-Black, C., T. Budd, S. Partridge and P. Mayhew (1998) *The 1998 British Crime Survey*, Home Office Statistical Bulletin 21/98, London, Home Office.

Mirza, H. (1992) *Young, Female and Black*, London, Routledge.

Mitchell, Juliet (1975) *Psychoanalysis and Feminism*, Harmondsworth, Penguin.

Modood, T. (1992a) 'British Asian muslims and the Rushdie affair', in J. Donald and A. Rattansi (eds), *'Race', Culture and Difference*, London, Sage.

Modood, T. (1992b) *Not Easy Being British: Colour, Culture and Citizenship*, Stoke-on-Trent, Trentham.

Modood, T. (1994) 'Political blackness and British Asians', *Sociology*, November.

Money, J. and A. E. Ehrhardt (1972) *Man and Woman, Boy and Girl*, Baltimore, MD, Johns Hopkins University Press.

Mooney, J. (1994) *The Hidden Figure: Domestic Violence in North London*, London, Middlesex University.

Moore, B. (1967) *Social Origins of Dictatorship and Democracy*, London, Allen Lane.

Moore, H. (1994) *A Passion for Difference*, Cambridge, Polity Press.

Moore, R. (1988) 'The correspondence principle and the Marxist sociology of education', in M. Cole (ed.), *Bowles and Gintis*, London, Palmer Press.

Moore, R. (1996) 'Back to the Future: the problem of change and the possibilities of advance in the sociology of education', *British Journal of Sociology of Education*, vol. 17, no. 2, pp. 145–62.

Moores, S. (1993) *Interpreting Audiences*, London, Sage.

Morgan, D. H. J. (1985) *The Family, Politics and Social Theory*, London, Routledge & Kegan Paul.

Morgan, M. (1985) *Sociological Approaches to Health and Medicine*, London, Routledge.

Morley, D. (1986) *Family Television, cultural power and domestic leisure*, London, Comedia.

Morley, D. (1991) 'Changing Paradigms in Audience Studies', in E. Seiter, H. Borchers, G. Kreutzner and E. Warth, (eds), *Remore Control*, London, Routledge.

Morley, D. (1992) *Television Audiences and Cultural Studies*, London, Routledge.

Morris, L. (1994) *Dangerous Classes*, London, Routledge.

Morris, M. (1994) 'Economic inequality: new methods for new trends?', *American Sociological Review*, vol. 59, pp. 205–19.

Morrison, W. (1995) *Theoretical Criminology; from modernity to post-modernism*, London, Cavendish.

Mortimore, P. (1997) 'Can Effective Schools Compensate for Society?', in A. H. Halsey, H. Lauder, P. Brown and A. S. Wells (eds), *Education, Culture, Economy, Society*, Oxford, Oxford University Press.

Mumford, L. (1961) *The City in History: Its Origins, its Transformation and its Projects*, London, Secker and Warburg.

Murdock, G. (1989) 'Redrawing the map of the communications industries: concentration and ownership in the era of privatisation', in M. Ferguson, *Public Communication: The New Imperatives*, London, Sage.

Murdock, G. (2000) 'Digital Futures: European Television in the Age of Convergence', in J. Wieten, G. Murdock and P. Dahlgren (eds), *Television Across Europe: A Comparative Introduction*, London, Sage.

Murray, R. (2000) 'Bill to keep us in the dark', *Daily Telegraph*, 7 April, p. 23.

Navarro, V. (1986) *Crisis, Health and Medicine*, London, Tavistock.

Nettleton, S. and R. Burrows (1998) 'Individualisation Processes and Social Policy', in J. Carter, *Postmodernity and the Fragmentation of Welfare*, London, Routledge.

Nicholson, L. (1990) *Feminism/Postmodernism*, London, Routledge.

Noon, M. (1993) 'Racial discrimination in speculative applications: evidence from the UK's top one hundred firms', *Human Resources Management Journal*, vol. 3, no. 4.

Nordenstreng, K. and T. Varis, (1974) *Television Traffic: A One-way Street?*, Paris, Unesco.

Oakley, A. (1972) *Sex, Gender and Society*, London, Temple Smith.

Oakley, A. (1974) *The Sociology of Housework*, Oxford, Blackwell.

Oakley, A. (1979) *From Here to Maternity: Becoming a Mother*, Oxford, Martin Robertson.

Oakley, A. (1981) *Subject Women*, Oxford, Martin Robertson.

Oakley, A. (1984) *The Captured Womb: A History of Pregnant Women*, Oxford, Blackwell.

Oakley, A. (1987) 'From walking wombs to test-tube babies', in M. Stanworth (ed.), *Reproductive Technologies*, Cambridge, Polity Press.

Oakley, A. and L. Rajan (1991) 'Social class and social support: the same or different?', *Sociology*, vol. 25, pp. 31–60.

Offe, C. (1985) *Disorganised Capitalism*, Cambridge, Polity Press.

Office for National Statistics (1992) *Social Trends 22*, London, HMSO.

Office for National Statistics (1993) *Social Trends 23*, London, HMSO.

Office for National Statistics (1994) *Social Trends 24*, London, HMSO.

Office for National Statistics (1995) *Social Trends 25*, London, HMSO.

Office for National Statistics (1996) *Social Trends 26*, London, HMSO.

Office for National Statistics (1998) *Informal Carers*, London, HMSO.

Office for National Statistics (1998 and 1999) *Labour Force Survey*, no. 2–5, London, HMSO.

Office for National Statistics (ONS) (1999), *The ESRC Review of Government Social Classification*, Swindon, ONS/ESRC.

Office for National Statistics (1999) *Social Trends 29*, London, HMSO.

Office for National Statistics (2000a) *Social Trends 30*, London, HMSO.

Office for National Statistics (2000b) *Social Inequalities 2000*, London, HMSO.

Office for National Statistics (2001a) *Social Trends 31*, London, HMSO.

Office for National Statistics, (2001b) *New Social & Occupational Classifications*, http://www.statistics.gov.uk/

Office of Population Censuses and Surveys (OPCS) (1991) *1991 Census*, vol. 1, London, HMSO.

Office of Population Censuses and Surveys (OPCS) (1994) *Social Trends*, London, HMSO.

Ofsted (1999) *Raising the Attainment of Minority Ethnic Pupils: School and LEA Responses*, http://www.ofsted.gov.uk/pubs/minority/2.htm

Ohmae, K. (1990) *The Borderless World*, London, Collins.

Ohmae, K. (1995) *The End of the Nation State*, New York, Free Press.

Oliver, M. (1996) 'A sociology of disability or a disablist sociology?, in L. Barton (ed.) *Disability and Society*, London, Longman.

Packer, K. (1996) 'The context dependent nature of gendering of technical work: a case study of work in a scientific laboratory', *Work, Employment and Society*, vol. 10, no. 1.

Pahl, R. (1991) 'Debating social class', *The International Journal of Urban and Regional Research*, vol. 15, pp. 107–29.

Palmer, S. (1992) *Beyond the Cold War*, Cambridge, Cambridge University Press.

Parker, M. (1998) 'Nostalgia and Mass Culture: McDonalidization and Cultural Elitism', in M. Alfino, J. S. Caputo and R. Wynyard (eds), *McDonaldization Revisited: Critical Essays on Consumer Culture*, Westport, CT, Praeger.

Parker, R. (1995) *Mixed Signals: The Prospects for global television news*, New York, Twentieth Century Fund Press.

Parsons, T. (1939) *The Structure of Social Action*, New York, Free Press.

Parsons, T. (1951) *The Social System*, Glencoe, Illinois Free Press.

Parsons, T. (1954) *Essays in Sociological Theory*, New York, Free Press.

Parsons, T. (1961) 'An outline of the social system', in T. Parsons (ed.), *Theories of Society*, New York, Free Press.

Parsons, T. and R. Bales (1955) *Family, Socialization and Interaction Process*, New York, Free Press.

Pascal, G. (1995) 'Women on top? Women's careers in the 1990s', *Sociology Review*, vol. 4, no. 3, pp. 2–5.

Paterson, C. (1997) 'Global Television News Services', in A. Sreberny-Mohammadi, D. Winseck, J. McKenna and O. Boyd-Barrett (eds), *Media in Global Context*, London, Edward Arnold.

Payne, G. (ed.) (2000) *Social Divisions*, London, Palgrave Macmillan.

Pearce, F. (1976) *Crimes of the Powerful: Marxism, Crime and Deviance*, London, Pluto.

Penn, R. (1985) *Skilled Workers in the Class Structure*, Cambridge, Cambridge University Press.

Phillips, Ann and Barbara Taylor (1980) 'Sex and skill: notes towards a feminist economics', *Feminist Review*, no. 6.

Phillips, D. (1971) *Knowledge From What?*, Chicago, IL, Rand McNally.

Phillipson, C. (1998) *Reconstructing Old Age: New Agendas in Social Theory and Practice*, London, Sage.

Phizacklea, A. (1990) *Unpacking the Fashion Industry: Gender, Race and Class in Production*, London, Routledge.

Picot, G., M. Zyblock and W. Pyper (1999) 'Why do Children Move into and out of Low Income: Changing Labour Market Conditions or Marriage and Divorce?', Ottawa, Statistics Canada.

Piore, M. J. (1979) *Birds of Passage: Migrant Labour and Industrial Societies*, Cambridge, Cambridge University Press.

Platt, J. (1988) 'What can case studies do?', in R. G. Burgess, *Studies in Qualitative Methodology*, London, JAI Press.

Plummer, K. (1975) *Sexual Stigma: an Interactionist Account*, London, Routledge.

Plummer, K. (1979) 'Misunderstanding Labelling Perspectives', in D. Downes and P. Rock (eds), *Deviant Interpretations*, London, Martin Robertson.

Poggi, G. (1978) *The Development of the Modern State*, London, Hutchinson.

Polanyi, K. (1973) *The Great Transformation*, New York, Octagon.

Polanyi, M. (1958) *Personal Knowledge*, Chicago, IL, University of Chicago Press.

Policy Studies Institute (1997) 'Landmark Ethnic Minorities Survey Shows Mix of Poverty and Progress', press release, http://www.psi.org.uk/intro.htm

Pollock, K. (1988) 'On the nature of social stress: production of a modern mythology', *Social Science and Medicine*, vol. 26, pp. 381–92.

Porter, R. (1999) *A Medical History of Humanity from Antiquity to the Present*, London, Fontana.

Poulantzas, N. (1973) *Political Power and Social Classes*, London, New Left Books.

Poulantzas, N. (1978) *State, Power, Socialism*, London, Verso.

Price, C. (2000) 'Surfing on your sofa', *Guardian*, G2, 6 April, pp. 2–3.

Pringle, R. (1989) (*Secretaries Talk: Sexuality, Power and Work*, London, Verso.

Pryce, K. (1979) *Endless Pressure*, Harmondsworth, Penguin.

Quinney, R. (1980) *Class, State and Crime*, London, Longman.

Rabinow, P. (ed.) (1984) *The Foucault Reader*, Harmondsworth, Penguin.

Rabinow, P. (1986) 'Representations are Social Facts: Modernity and Postmodernity in Anthropology', in J. Clifford and G. E. Marcus (eds), *Writing Culture: The Poetics and Politics of Ethnography*, Berkeley, CA, University of California Press.

Radway, J. (1994) *Reading the Romance*, Chapel Hill, NC, University of North Carolina Press.

Raffe, D. (1987) 'Youth unemployment in the United Kingdom', in P. Brown and D. N. Ashton (eds), *Education, Unemployment and the Labour Market*, Lewes, Falmer.

Ram, M. (1992) 'Coping with racism: Asian employers in the inner city', *Work, Employment and Society*, vol. 6, no. 4.

Ramazanoglu, C. (1989) *Feminism and the Contradictions of Oppression*, London, Routledge.

Ramazanoglu, C. (1992) 'On feminist methodology: male reason versus female empowerment', *Sociology*, vol. 26, no. 2, pp. 207–12.

Reay, D. (1998) 'Engendering Social Reproduction', *British Journal of Sociology of Education*, vol. 19, no. 2.

Reeves, F. and M. Chevannes (1988) 'The Ideological Construction of Black Underachievement', in M. Woodhead and A. McGraph (eds), *Family, School and Society*, London, Hodder & Stoughton.

Reeves, G. (1993) *Communications and the Third World*, London, Routledge.

Reeves, G. (1995) (Comparative Media Histories in the Developing World', in *MA in Mass Communications Handbook*, vol. 2, Leicester, University of Leicester, pp. 73–114.

Reinharz, S. (1992) *Feminist Methods in Social Research*, Oxford, Oxford University Press.

Renzetti, C. and D. Curran (1989) *Women, Men and Society*, Needham Heights, MA, Allyn & Bacon.

Rex, J. and R. Moore (1967) *Race, Community and Conflict*, London, Oxford University Press.

Rex, J. and S. Tomlinson (1979) *Colonial Immigrants in a British City: A Class Analysis*, London, Routledge & Kegan Paul.

Rich, A. (1977) *Of Women Born: Motherhood as Experience and Institution*, London, Virago.

Rich, A. (1980) 'Compulsory Heterosexuality and Lesbian Experience', *Signs*, vol. 5, no. 4, pp. 631–60.

Rich, A. (1984) 'Compulsory heterosexuality and lesbian existence', in A. Snitow, C. Stansell and S. Thompson (eds), *Desire: The Politics of Sexuality*, London, Virago.

Rich, D. (1974) 'Private government and professional science', in A. Teich (ed.), *Scientists and Public Affairs*, London, MIT Press.

Richardson, J. and J. Lambert (1985) *The Sociology of Race*, Ormskirk, Causeway.

Richman, J. (1987) *Medicine and Health*, London, Routledge.

Riley, Denise (1988) *'Am I That Name?' Feminism and the Category of Women in History*, London, Palgrave Macmillan.

Riley, K. (1988) 'Black girls speak for themselves', in M. Woodhead and A. McGrath (eds), *Family, School and Society*, London, Hodder & Stoughton.

Ringer, F. (1979) 'Cultural Transmission in German Higher Education in the Nineteenth Century', in J. Karabel and A. H. Halsey (eds), *Power and Ideology in Education*, New York, Oxford University Press.

Ritzer, G. (1993) *The McDonaldization of Society*, Thousand Oaks, CA, Pine Forge Press.

Roberts, K. (2001) *Class in Modern Britain*, Basingstoke, Palgrave Macmillan.

Robertson, R. (1992) *Globalisation, Social Theory and Global Culture*, London, Sage.

Robins, K. (1994) 'Global local times', in J. Anderson and M. Ricci (eds), *Society and Social Science: A Reader*, Milton Keynes, Open University Press.

Robins, K. (1997) 'What is Globalisation?', *Sociology Review*, vol. 6, no. 3.

Robinson, C. C. and J. T. Morris (1986) 'The gender-stereotyped nature of Christmas toys', *Sex Roles*, vol. 15, nos 1/2, pp. 21–32.

Robinson, Peter (1999) 'Explaining the Relationship between Flexible Employment and Labour Market Regulation', in A. Felstead and N. Jewson (eds), *Global Trends in Flexible Labour*, Basingstoke, Palgrave Macmillan.

Rojek, C. (1995) *Decentring Leisure: Rethinking Leisure Theory*, London, Sage.

Roos, P. A. (1983) 'Marriage and women's occupational attainment in cross-cultural perspective" *American Sociological Review*, vol. 48, pp. 852–64.

Rorty, R. (1982) *The Consequences of Pragmatism*, Brighton, Harvester Press.

Rose, D. and K. O'Reilly (1998) *The ESRC Review of Government Social Classifications*, London and Swindon: ONS and ESRC.

Rose, S. and I. Frieze (1989) 'Young singles' scripts for a first date', *Gender and Society*, vol. 3, no. 2, pp. 258–68.

Rosenhan, D. (1973) 'On being sane in insane places', *Science*, vol. 179, pp. 260–8.

Rothman, B. K. (1987) 'Reproduction', in B. Hess and M. Ferree (eds), *Analyzing Gender*, London and Beverley Hills, CA, Sage.

Rubin, L. (1976) *Worlds of Pain: Life in the Working Class Family*, New York, Basic Books.

Rueschemeyer, D., E. H. Stephens and J. D. Stephens (1992) *Capitalist Development and Democracy*, Cambridge, Polity Press.

Rushdie, S. (1988) *Satanic Verses*, London, Viking.

Rustin, M. (1994) 'Incomplete Modernity: Ulrich Beck's Risk Society', *Radical Philosophy*, vol. 67.

6, P. (1998) *Escaping Poverty: From Safety Nets to Networks of Opportunity*, London, DEMOS.

Sadler, D. (1992) *The Global Region*, Oxford, Pergamon.

Saggar, S. (1992) *Race and Politics in Britain*, London, Harvester Wheatsheaf.

Saks, M. (1992) *Alternative Medicine*, Oxford, Clarendon Press.

Samad, Y. (1992) 'Book burning and race relations: political mobilization of Bradford muslims', *New Community*, July.

Sanderson, S. (1985) *The Americas in the New International Division of Labour*, New York, Holmes & Meier.

Sargent, Lydia (ed.) (1981) *Women and Revolution: The Unhappy Marriage of Marxism and Feminism*, London, Pluto.

Sassen, S. (1988) *The Mobility of Labour and Capital: A Study in International Investment and Labour Flow*, New York, Cambridge University Press.

Saunders, D. (1997) 'Voting and the Electorate', in P. Dunleavy (ed.), *Developments in British Politics 5*, London, Palgrave Macmillan.

Saunders, P. (1990) *Social Class and Stratification*, London, Unwin Hyman.

Saussure, F. de (1974) *Course in General Linguistics*, London, Fontana.

Savage, M., J. Barlow, P. Dickens and T. Fielding (1992) *Property, Bureaucracy and Culture: Middle-Class Formation in Contemporary Britain*, London, Routledge.

Scambler, G. (1991) *Sociology as Applied to Medicine*, 3rd edn, London, Balliere Tindall.

Scambler, G. (1997) *Sociology as Applied to Medicine*, 4th edn., London, W. B. Saunders.

Scambler, G. and P. Higgs (1999) 'Stratification, class and health', *Sociology*, vol. 33, pp. 275–96.

Scase, R. (1992) *Class*, Milton Keynes, Open University Press.

Schiller, H. (1976) *Communication and Cultural Domination*, White Plains, NY, International Arts and Sciences Press.

Schutz, A. (1976) *The Phenomenology of the Social World*, London, Heinemann.

Schwartz Cowan, R. (1983) *More Work for Mother*, New York, Basic Books.

Scott, J. (1982) *The Upper Class*, London, Palgrave Macmillan.

Scott, J. (1986) *Capitalist property and financial power: a comparative study of Britain, the United States and Japan*, Brighton, Wheatsheaf Books.

Scott, J. (1991) *Who Rules Britain?*, Cambridge, Polity Press.

Scott, J. (1994) *Citizenship, Deprivation and Privilege: Poverty and Wealth in Britain*, Harlow, Longman.

Scott, J. (1996) *Stratification and Power*, Cambridge, Polity Press.

Scott, J. (1997) *Corporate Business and Capitalist Classes*, OUP.

Scott, J. (2000) 'Class and Stratification', in G. Payne (ed.), *Social Divisions*, Basingstoke, Palgrave Macmillan.

Segal, L. (1994) *Straight Sex*, London, Virago.

Segal, Lynne (1999) *Why Feminism?* Cambridge, Polity Press.

Seidman, S. (1994) *Contested Knowledge: social theory in the postmodern era*, Cambridge, MA, Blackwell.

SEU (Social Exclusion Unit) (1999), *Poverty and Social Exclusion*, London, Cabinet Office.

Shakespeare, T., K. Gillespie-Sells and D. Davis (1996) *The Sexual Politics of Disability: Untold Desires*, London, Cassell.

Sharrock, W. and B. Anderson (1986) *The Ethnomethodologists*, London, Tavistock.

Shutt, J. and R. Whittington (1987) 'Fragmentation strategies and the rise of small unit cases from the North West', *Regional Studies*, vol. 21, pp. 13–23.

Signorelli, N. and M. Morgan (eds) (1990) *Cultivation Analysis*, London, Sage.

Silverstone, R. (1990) 'Television and Everyday Life', in M. Ferguson (ed.), *Public Communication: The New Imperatives*, London, Sage.

Sinclair, J., E. Jacka and S. Cunningham (1996) *New Patterns in Global Television*, Oxford, Oxford University Press.

Sivanandan, A. (1982) *A Different Hunger: Writings on Black Resistance*, London, Pluto Press.

Skeggs, B. (2000) 'Rethinking Class: class cultures and explanatory power', in M. Haralambos, *Developments in Sociology 16*, Ormskirk, Causeway.

Skellington, R. and P. Morris (1992) *Race in Britain Today*, London, Sage.

Sklair, L. (1991) *Sociology of the Global System*, London, Harvester Wheatsheaf.

Smart, B. (1983) *Foucault, Marxism and Critique*, London, Routledge.

Smart, B. (1993) *Postmodernity*, London, Routledge.

Smart, C. (1976) *Women, Crime and Criminology*, London, Routledge.

Smart, C. (1990) 'Feminist Approaches to Criminology, or Post-Modern Woman Meets Atavistic Man', in L. Gelsthorpe and A. Morris (eds), *Feminist Perspectives in Criminology*, Milton Keynes, Open University Press.

Smith, A. D. (1992) 'European unity', *International Affairs*, vol. 68, no. 1, pp. 55–76.

Smith, D. J. (1977) *Racial Disadvantage in Britain: The PEP Report*, Harmondsworth Penguin.

Smith, T. and M. Noble (1995) *Education Divides: Poverty and Schooling for the 1990s*, London, Child Poverty Action Group.

Smythe, D. (1987) 'Communications; blindspots of Western Marxism', *Canadian Journal of Political and Social Theory*, vol. 1, no. 3, pp. 1–27.

Snoddy, R. (2000) 'Why Television is so Insular', *The Times*, T2, 28 July.

Solomos, J. (1993) *Race and Racism in Contemporary Britain*, London, Palgrave Macmillan.

Solomos, J. and L. Back (1994) 'Conceptualizing racisms: social theory, politics and research', *Sociology*, February.

Sontag, S. (1979) *Illness as Metaphor*, New York, Random House.

Spelman, E. (1990) *Inessential Woman*, London, Women's Press.

Spender, D. (1985) *For the Record: The Meaning and Making of Feminist Knowledge*, London, Women's Press.

Spenner, K. I. (1990) 'Skill: meaning, methods and measures', *Work and Occupations*, vol. 17, pp. 399–421.

Sreberny-Mohammadi, A. (1991) 'The global and the local in international communications', in J. Curran and M. Gurevitch (eds), *Mass Media and Society*, London, Edward Arnold.

Stacey, M. (1989) *Sociology of Health and Healing*, London, Unwin Hyman.

Stanley, L. (1990a) 'Doing ethnography, writing ethnography', *Sociology*, vol. 24, no. 4, pp. 617–27.

Stanley, L. (1990b) *Feminist Praxis: Research, Theory and Epistemology in Feminist Sociology*, London, Routledge.

Stanway, A. (1982) *Alternative Medicine*, Harmondsworth, Penguin.

Stanworth, Michelle (ed.) (1987) *Reproductive Technologies: Gender, Motherhood and Medicine*, Cambridge, Polity Press.

Steedman, C. (1986) *Landscape for a Good Woman*, London: Virago.

Stehr, N. (1994) *Knowledge Societies*, New York, Sage.

Stevens, R. (1980) 'The future of the medical profession', in E. Ginsberg (ed.), *From Physician Shortage to Patient Shortage: The Uncertain Future of Medical Practice*, Boulder, CO, Westview Press.

Stewart, M. and D. Roter (1989) *Communicating With Medical Patients*, London, Sage.

Stone, J. (2000) *Losing Perspective: Global Affairs on British Terrestrial Television 1989–1999*, London, Stanhope Press.

Stone, M. (1981) *The Education of the Black Child in Britain*, London, Fontana.

Strange, P. (1990) *Rival States, Rival Firms*, Cambridge, Cambridge University Press.

Straubhaar, J. (1997) 'Distinguishing the Global Regional and National Levels of World Television', in A. Sreberny-Mohammadi, D. Winseck, J. McKenna and O. Boyd-Barret (eds), *Media in Global Context*, London, Edward Arnold.

Taylor, F. W. (1911) *Principles of Scientific Management*, New York, Harper & Row.

Taylor, I., P. Walton and J. Young (1975) 'Critical Criminology in Britain: Review and Prospects' in I. Taylor, P. Walton and J. Young (eds), *Critical Criminology*, London, Routledge & Kegan Paul.

Therborn, G. (1976) 'The rule of capital and the rise of democracy', *New Left Review*, no. 103.

Thomas, W. I. and D. S. Thomas (1928) *The Child in America*, New York, Alfred A. Knopf.

Thompson, E. P. (1967) 'Time, work discipline and industrial capitalism', *Past and Present*, vol. 38.

Thompson, E. P. (1978) *The Poverty of Theory*, London, Merlin.

Thompson, J. B. (1990) *Ideology and Modern Culture*, Cambridge, Polity Press.

Thompson, J. B. (1995) *Media and Modernity: A Social Theory of the Media*, Cambridge, Polity Press.

Thussu, D. K. (1998) 'Infotainment International', in D. K. Thussu (ed.), *Electronic Empires*, London, Edward Arnold.

Tizard, B. and A. Phoenix (1993) *Black, White or Mixed Race*, London, Routledge.

Tombs, S. (1990) 'Industrial injuries in Britian manufacturing industry', *Sociological Review*, May, pp. 324–43.

Tomlinson, J. (1999) *Globalization and Culture*, Cambridge, Polity Press.

Tong, Rosemarie (1989) *Feminist Thought: A Comprehensive Introduction*, London, Routledge.

Touraine, A. (1971) *The Post-Industrial Society*, New York, Random House.

Townsend, P. (1979) *Poverty in the United Kingdom*, Harmondsworth, Penguin.

Townsend, P. and N. Davidson (1982) *Inequalities in Health*, Harmondsworth, Penguin.

Toynbee, P. (1995) 'Happy families: a game of charades', *The Independent*, 22 February.

Trades Union Congress (1999) 'Black and excluded. News from the TUC Online', http://www.tuc.org.uk/vbuilding/tuc/browse/object.exe?18&0

Tuchman, G., A. Daniels and J. Benet (eds) (1978) *Hearth and Home: Images of Women in the Mass Media*, Oxford, Oxford University Press.

Tunstall, J. (1977) *The Media are American*, London, Constable.

Tunstall, J. (1996) *Newspaper Power*, Oxford, Clarendon Press.

Turner, B. (1987) *Medical Power and Social Knowledge*, London, Sage.

Turner, B. (1991) *Religion and Social Theory*, London, Sage.

Turner, B. (1992) *Regulating Bodies: Essays in Medical Sociology*, London, Routledge.

Turner, B. (1993) (ed.) *Citizenship and Social Theory*, Sage, London.

Turner, G. (1990) *British Cultural Studies*, London, Routledge.

Turner, R. (1961) 'Modes of Ascent Through Education: sponsored and contest mobility', in A. H. Halsey, J. Floud and C. A. Anderson (eds), *Education, Economy and Society*, London, Collier-MacMillan.

UNDP (United Nations Development Programme) (1999) *Annual Report*, Washington DC.

UNFPA (United Nations Population Fund) (2000) *The State of World Population 2000: Lives Together, Worlds Apart. Men and Women in a Time of Change*, www.unfpa.org/swp/2000/english

UNIFEM (United Nations Development Fund for Women) (2000) *Progress of the World's Women 2000*, www.unifem.undp.org/progressww/2000

United Nations Development Programme (UNDP) (1999) *Human Development Report*, New York, Oxford University Press.

Urry, J. (1990) *The Tourist Gaze*, London, Sage.

Urry, J. and S. Lash (1987) *The End of Organised Capitalism*, Cambridge, Polity Press.

Van den Haag, E. (1975) *Punishing Criminals*, New York, Simon & Schuster.

Van Dijk, T. A. (1991) *Racism and the Press*, London, Routledge.

Venturi, R., D. S. Brown and S. Izenour (1977) *Learning from Las Vegas*, Cambridge, MA, MIT Press.

Vernon, A. (1999) 'The dialectics of multiple identities and the disabled people's movement', *Disability and Society*, vol. 14, no. 3, pp. 385–98.

Vold, G. B., T. J. Bernard and J. B. Snipes (1998) *Theoretical Criminology*, 4th edn, Oxford, Oxford University Press.

Walby, S. (1989) 'Theorising patriarchy', *Sociology*, vol. 23, no. 2, pp. 213–34.

Walby, S. (1990) *Theorising Patriarchy*, Oxford, Basil Blackwell.

Walby, Sylvia (1992) 'Post-Post-Modernism? Theorizing Social Complexity', in Michele Barrett and Anne Phillips (eds), *Destabilizing Theory*, Cambridge, Polity Press, pp. 31–53.

Walker, A. (1988) *Living By the Word: Selected Writings 1973–1987*, London, Women's Press.

Walklate, S. (2001) *Gender, Crime and Criminal Justice*, Devon, Willan.

Wallace, M. (1990) *Black Macho and the Myth of Superwoman*, London, Verso.

Wallis, R. (ed.) (1979) *On the Margins of Science*, Sociological Review Monograph no. 37, Keele, Keele University Press.

Wallis, R. (1983) entry in M. Mann (ed.), *The Macmillan Student Encyclopaedia of Sociology*, London, Palgrave Macmillan.

Walvin, J. (1992) *Black Ivory: A History of British Slavery*, London, HarperCollins.

Ware, V. (1992) *Beyond the Pale: White Women, Racism and History*, London, Verso.

Warwick, D. and G. Littlejohn (1992) *Coal, Capital and Culture*, London, Routledge.

Watson, J. L. (ed.) (1977) *Between Two Cultures: Migrants and Minorities in Britain*, Oxford, Basil Blackwell.

Weber, M. (1964) *The Religion of China*, London, Collier-MacMillan.

Weber, M. (1970) 'Politics as a Vocation' and 'Science as a Vocation', in H. H. Gerth and C. W. Mills (eds), *From Max Weber*, London, Routledge & Kegan Paul.

Weber, M. (1978a) *Economy and Society*, Berkeley, CA, University of California Press.

Weber, M. (1978b) 'The Origins of Industrial Capitalism in Europe', in W. G. Runciman (ed.), *Weber: Selections in Translation*, Cambridge, Cambridge University Press.

Webster, A. (1979) 'Scientific controversy and socio-cognitive metonymy', in R. Wallis (ed.), *On the Margins of Science*, Sociological Review Monograph No. 37, Keele, Keele University Press.

Webster, F. and K. Robins (1993) 'I'll be watching you', *Sociology*, vol. 27, no. 2, pp. 243–52.

Weiner, G. (1994) *Feminisms in Education*, Buckingham, Open University Press.

Westergaard, J. and H. Resler (1976) *Class in a Capitalist Society*, Harmondsworth, Penguin.

Whale, J. (1977) *The Politics of the Media*, London, Fontana.

Whimster, S. and Lash, S. (eds) (1987) *Max Weber, Rationality and Modernity*, London, Allen & Unwin.

Wholey, D. R. (1990) 'The effects of formal and informal training on tenure and mobility in manufacturing firms', *Sociological Quarterly*, vol. 31, pp. 37–57.

Whyte, W. F. (1984) *Learning From the Field: A Guide From Experience*, London, Sage.

Wiener, M. (1981) *English Culture and the Decline of the Industrial Spirit 1850–1980*, Cambridge, Cambridge University Press.

Wild, P. (1979) 'Recreation in Rochdale, 1900–49', in J. Clarke, C. Critcher and R. Johnson (eds), *Working Class Culture*, London, Hutchinson.

Wilkinson, H. and G. Mulgan (1995) *Freedom's Children*, London, Demos.

Williams, R. (1974) *Television: Technology and Cultural Form*, London, Fontana.

Williams, R. (1976) *Communications*, 3rd edn, London, Penguin.

Williams, R. (1980) *Problems in Materialism and Culture*, London, New Left books.

Willis, P. (1977) *Learning to Labour*, Farnborough, Saxon House.

Willis, P. (1990) 'Symbolic work at play in everyday cultures of the young', in P. Willis, S. Jones, J. Canaan and G. Hurd (eds) *Common Culture*, Milton Keynes, Open University Press.

Wilson, B. (1982) *Religion in Sociological Perspective*, Oxford, Oxford University Press.

Wilson, E. (1977) *Women and the Welfare State*, London, Tavistock.

Wilson, J. (1975) *Thinking About Crime*, New York, Basic Books.

Winch, P. (1958) *The Idea of a Social Science*, London, Routledge.

Winship, J. (1987) *Inside Women's Magazines*, London, Pandora.

Wittgenstein, L. (1953) *Philosophical Investigations*, Oxford, Blackwell.

Wollstonecraft, Mary (1992) *A Vindication of the Rights of Women*, London, Everyman.

Wood, S. (1982) *The Degradation of Work? Skill, Deskilling and the Labour Process*, London, Hutchinson.

Woodhead, M. and A. McGraph (eds) *Family, School and Society*, London, Hodder & Stoughton.

Worsley, P. (1964) 'The distribution of power in industrial societies', in P. Halmos (ed.), *The Development of Industrial Societies*, Sociological Review Monograph 8, University of Keele Press.

Wright, C. (1994) 'A fallible safety system: institutionalised irrationality in the offshore oil and gas industry', *Sociological Review*, vol. 42, no. 1, pp. 79–103.

Wright, P. (1979) 'A study in the legitimisation of knowledge: the "success" of medicine and the "failure" of astrology', in R. Wallis (ed.), *On the Margins of Science*, Sociological Review Monograph, 27, University of Keele Press.

Wyn, J. and R. White (1997) *Rethinking Youth*, London, Sage.

Yates, A. and D. Pidgeon (1957) *Admission to Grammar Schools*, London, Newnes.

Yeatman, Anna (1986) 'Women, domestic life and sociology', in C. Pateman and E. Gross (eds), *Feminist Challenges: Social and Political Theory*, London, Allen & Unwin, pp. 157–72.

Yin, R. K. (1989) *Case Study Research: Design and Methods*, 2nd edn, London, Sage.

Young, Iris (1981) 'Beyond the unhappy marriage: a critique of dual systems theory', in Lydia Sargent (ed.), *Women and Revolution: The Unhappy Marriage of Marxism and Feminism*, London, Pluto, pp. 43–71.

Young, J. (1986) 'The Failure of Criminology: The Need for Radical Realism', in R. Matthews and J. Young (eds), *Confronting Crime*, London, Sage.

Young, J. (1992) 'Ten Points of Realism', in J. Young and R. Matthews (eds), *Rethinking Criminology: The Realist Debate*, London, Sage.

Young, M. and P. Willmott (1957) *Family and Kinship in East London*, Harmondsworth, Penguin.

Young, M. F. D. (1998) *The Curriculum of the Future: from the New Sociology of Education to a critical theory of learning*, London, Falmer.

Yuval-Davis, N. and G. Sehgal (eds) (1992) *Refusing Holy Orders: Women and Fundamentalism in Britain*, London, Virago.

Zeitlin, M. (1989) *The Large Corporation and Contemporary Classes*, Cambridge, Polity Press.

Zenith Media, (1998) *Television in Europe to 2007*, London, Zenith Media.

copyright acknowledgements

The authors and publishers wish to thank the following for permission to use copyright material:

The Century Foundation for a table from R. Parker, 'Mixed Signals: The Prospects for Global Television News' (1995).

The Commission for Racial Equality for data and text reproduced from their factsheet, 'Education and Training in Britain' (1998).

The Controller of Her Majesty's Stationary Office, for Crown Copyright material.

Susan Gellner for an extract from Ernest Gellner, *Legitimation of Belief* (third edition) (1974) pp. 191–207.

The Global Media Monitoring Project for Table 6.4, 'Predominance of men in the world's media, year 2000', based on material from G. Spears, K. Seydegart, M. Gallagher, *Who Makes the News? The Global Media Monitoring Project 2000* (2000) World Association for Christian Communication.

The *Guardian* for extracts from an article by Amitai Etzioni entitled 'The Parental Deficit', first published in the *Guardian*, 15 October 1993.

The *Independent* for extracts from an article by Polly Toynbee entitled 'Happy Families: a Game of Charades', first published in the *Independent*, 22 February 1995.

The International Labour Office for information taken from the ILO Labour Statistics database, LABORSTA, Table 6.1 Copyright © International Labour Organization 1998–2001.

Netsizer (part of Telcordia Technologies) for the chart appearing in Box 8.1, reproduced from www.netsizer.com

The *Observer* for figures in Table 8.1, first published in the *Observer*, 10 June 2001.

Oxford University Press for data extracted from Banks *et al.*, 'Factors influencing demand for primary care' in the *International Journal of Epidemiology*, Vol. 4, Issue 3 (1975).

Oxford University Press and the United Nations Development Programme for Table 12.8, reproduced from the *Human Development Report 1999*, pp. 53–6 (published by Oxford University Press).

Phillip Allan Publishers for Fig. 1 from Sanjiev Johal, 'Brimful of Brasia: British Asians and Issues of Culture and Identity', *Sociology Review*, September 1998.

Princeton University Press for Chart 8.2, reproduced from R. Inglehart, *Culture Shift in Advanced Industrial Society* (1990).

Routledge for extracts from A. D. King, *Global Cities* (1991), pp. 142–5, and S. Bartky, *Femininity and Diversity* (1990) pp. 69–71. Reproduction by permission of Routledge Inc., part of the Taylor & Francis Group.
Demos for Chart 8.3, reproduced from Wilkinson and Mulgan, *Freedom's Children* (1995).

Statewatch for data reproduced in Box 14.4, derived from *Statewatch Bulletin*, Vol. 6, No. 2, 1996.

D. C. Thomson & Co. Ltd for the cover of the 16 April 1955 edition of *Red Star Weekly* © D. C. Thomson & Co. Ltd.

The *Times Higher Education Supplement* for an extract from David W. Marsland, 'From Cradle to Grave', published in 17 May 1996 issue. David W. Marsland, M.D., is the A. Epes Harris M.D. and Fitzhugh Mayo M.D. Professor and Chairman in the Department of Family Practice at Virginia Commonwealth University.

The authors and publishers thank the following for permission to reproduce illustrative material:

AKG-Images, Berlin, for the portrait of Max Weber in Box 1.3 and Figure 8.2.

Allsport for the opening image for Chapter 5 (Phil Cole) and Figure 15.2 (Ross Kinnaird).

Corbis for the portrait of Émile Durkheim in Box 1.1.

Gamma for Figure 1.2 (Georges Merillon); the opening image for Chapter 3 (Bartholomew); Figure 7.3 (Frederic Reglain); Figure 8.1 (Viard); Figure 8.3 (Levy); Figure 9.3 (Elderfield); Fig 12.2 (B. Markel); the opening image for Chapter 15 (Benainous-Rey); Figure 16.3 (Julien Chatelin); Figure 17.1 (Nickelsberg).

Getty Images/Photodisc for Figure 5.4 and Getty Images/Tony Stone Images for the opening image for Chapter 7.

The Labour Movement Archives and Library for Figure 5.1.

The Public Record Office for Figure 2.1.

Rex for Figure 3.3 (Tamara Beckwith).

Anne Ronan for Karl Marx in Box 1.2 and Figure 17.2.

Patrick Salvadori for the opening images for Chapters 10, 16 and 17.

Trip for the opening images for Chapter 1 (H. Rogers), Chapter 2 (M. Lee), Chapter 4 (H. Rogers), Chapter 6 (H. Rogers), Chapter 8 (S. Grant), Chapter 9 (H. Rogers), Chapter 11 (H. Rogers), Chapter 12 (H. Rogers), Chapter 13 (J. Wender), Chapter 14 (J. Lister), Chapter 18 (H. Rogers), Chapter 19 (J. Ringland). Also for Figure 2.2 (T. Bognar); Figure 3.2 (S. Grant); Figure 4.1 (Ask Images); Figure 4.2 (H. Rogers); Figure 5.3 (H. Rogers); Figure 6.2 (B. Turner); Figure 7.2 (H. Rogers); Figure 9.1 (H. Rogers); Figure 10.2 (H. Rogers); Figure 11.1 (J. Greenberg); Figure 11.2 (H. Rogers); Figure 12.1 (H. Rogers); Figure 13.1 (S. Grant); Figure 13.2 (S. Grant); Figure 14.2 (H. Rogers); Figure 15.1 (Viesti Collection); Figure 16.1 (H. Rogers); Figure 16.2 (H. Rogers); Figure 18.1 (B. Vikander); Figure 19.1 (A. Tovy).

Twentieth Century Fox for Figure 6.3.

Photo research by Image Select International.

Every effort has been made to contact all the copyright holders, but if any have been inadvertently omitted the publishers will be pleased to make the necessary arrangement at the earliest opportunity.

subject index